ARCHITECTURE AND MATERIAL POLITICS IN THE FIFTEENTH-CENTURY OTTOMAN EMPIRE

In this book, Patricia Blessing explores the emergence of Ottoman architecture in the fifteenth century and its connection with broader geographical contexts. Analyzing how transregional exchange shaped building practices, she examines how workers from Anatolia, the Mediterranean, the Balkans, and Iran and Central Asia participated in key construction projects. She also demonstrates how drawn, scalable models on paper served as templates for architectural decorations and supplemented collaborations that involved the mobility of workers. Blessing reveals how the creation of centralized workshops led to the emergence of a clearly defined imperial Ottoman style by 1500, when the flexibility and experimentation of the preceding century was leveled. Her book radically transforms our understanding of Ottoman architecture by exposing the diverse and fluid nature of its formative period. It also provides the reader with an understanding of the design, planning, and construction processes of a major empire of the Islamic world.

Patricia Blessing is an assistant professor of art history at Princeton University. A scholar of Islamic architecture in the eastern Mediterranean, Iberian Peninsula, and Iran, she is the author of *Rebuilding Anatolia after the Mongol Conquest*.

ARCHITECTURE AND MATERIAL POLITICS IN THE FIFTEENTH-CENTURY OTTOMAN EMPIRE

PATRICIA BLESSING

Princeton University

CAMBRIDGE
UNIVERSITY PRESS

University Printing House, Cambridge CB2 8BS, United Kingdom

One Liberty Plaza, 20th Floor, New York, NY 10006, USA

477 Williamstown Road, Port Melbourne, VIC 3207, Australia

314–321, 3rd Floor, Plot 3, Splendor Forum, Jasola District Centre,
New Delhi – 110025, India

103 Penang Road, #05–06/07, Visioncrest Commercial, Singapore 238467

Cambridge University Press is part of the University of Cambridge.

It furthers the University's mission by disseminating knowledge in the pursuit of
education, learning, and research at the highest international levels of excellence.

www.cambridge.org
Information on this title: www.cambridge.org/9781316517604
DOI: 10.1017/9781009042727

© Cambridge University Press 2022

This publication is in copyright. Subject to statutory exception
and to the provisions of relevant collective licensing agreements,
no reproduction of any part may take place without the written
permission of Cambridge University Press.

First published 2022

Printed in the United Kingdom by TJ Books Limited, Padstow Cornwall

A catalogue record for this publication is available from the British Library.

ISBN 978-1-316-51760-4 Hardback

Cambridge University Press has no responsibility for the persistence or accuracy of
URLs for external or third-party internet websites referred to in this publication
and does not guarantee that any content on such websites is, or will remain,
accurate or appropriate.

Publication is made possible in part by a grant from the Barr Ferree Foundation Publication Fund,
Department of Art and Archaeology, Princeton University.

CONTENTS

Note on Transliteration, Spelling, and Dates	*page* vii
Acknowledgments	viii
Maps	x
INTRODUCTION: MATERIAL POLITICS OF ARCHITECTURE IN A FLUID EMPIRE	1
Pasts, Presents, Futures: Architecture and Sources	3
Shifting Architectures, Changing Actors	6
The Ottoman Empire and the Renaissance	9
Styles, International and Otherwise	10
Chapter Summaries	12
1 IMPERIAL AND LOCAL HORIZONS: LOOKING EAST AND WEST	15
Timurid Style in Ottoman Lands?	16
Moving toward Constantinople	19
The Çinili Köşk: Between Constantinople and Khurasan	21
Between Persianate and Byzantine Architecture	23
Epigraphic Artifice and Poetic Cosmology	26
The Tile Decoration of the Çinili Köşk	30
Istanbul beyond the Çinili Köşk	35
Mahmud Pasha's Patronage	39
Transfer to Skopje: Tile Work on the Move	48
Mid-Fifteenth-Century Aesthetics: Istanbul and Beyond	51
2 IMMERSIVE SPACE: EMPIRE BUILDING AND THE OTTOMAN FRONTIER	53
Shifting Styles: Constructing Past, Present, and Future	55
Mehmed I's Mosque-*Zāviye* Complex in Bursa	57
Dynastic Memory in Bursa	65
Tiles: Timurid, Saljuq, Aqqoyunlu?	68
Building Innovations: Creating Immersive Space	68
The Masters of Tabriz: Tiles and Origin	76
The Saljuq Past: Stone and Pre-Ottoman Anatolia	79
The Timurid Present: Bursa, Tabriz, and International Timurid Style	90
Entangled References	93
3 UNDER THE INFLUENCE: CREATING COSMOPOLITAN ARCHITECTURES	95
Mamluk Style in Ottoman Amasya: The Bayezid Pasha Mosque-*Zāviye*	99
Construction Sites: Workers and Designers	104
Paper and Architectural Design	107

v

Consolidating a Style: The Yörgüç Pasha Mosque-*Zāviye*	109
New Directions in Stone Carving: From Plasticity to Surface	116
Connecting the Mamluk and Ottoman Realms: Scholarship and Language	119
Mamluk Aesthetics on the Move in Western Anatolia and Thrace	121
Transmission and Design	134
Blue-and-White Tiles: A Shared Aesthetic?	135
The Masters of Tabriz beyond Bursa	140
The Virtual Kitabkhāna	142
Mobile Artists and Imperial Aspirations	144
4 BUILDING PARADISE: AFTERLIFE AND DYNASTIC POLITICS	145
Funerary Space and Dynastic Memory	145
The Sultan's Mausoleum	150
From the Written to the Built Space of Murad II's Death and Afterlife	157
Paradise in the Funerary Space	159
Ottoman Funerary Landscapes	166
Princely Burials in Bursa's Muradiye	168
Intertwined Spaces	173
5 AN OTTOMAN AESTHETIC: CONSOLIDATION CIRCA 1500	175
Centralizing Design on Paper	179
Design in the Age of Bayezid II: Amasya	188
Extending into the Balkans: Serres and Skopje circa 1490	194
Emerging Architects	199
Patronage for Sufi Communities in Contested Anatolia	205
Anatolia and Cilicia beyond the Ottoman Realm	207
An Ottoman Aesthetic	214
CONCLUSION	216
Notes	220
Bibliography	245
Index	270

NOTE ON TRANSLITERATION, SPELLING, AND DATES

Sources in Arabic and Persian appear in the original script when cited in footnotes. For terms and short quotations in the main text, I followed the transliteration system of the *International Journal of Middle East Studies* (*IJMES*). For Ottoman Turkish, the *IJMES* system is used throughout, except when directly quoting from a source that has been published in Latin script in a different transliteration. In personal names, special characters are omitted except for ʿayn, *hamza*, and the long ā in Ottoman Turkish names ending in –zāde – for example, ʿAşıkpaşazāde. Terms that have entered standard English usage, such as mihrab, muqarnas, and kadi, are not transliterated. Present-day place names (as of 2021) are used throughout, although some historical names are indicated on maps for reference. Dates are given according to the lunar *hijri* calendar as well as the Common Era when referring to specific, dated inscriptions or objects. Otherwise, Common Era dates are used. Unless otherwise noted, all translations into English are my own.

ACKNOWLEDGMENTS

This book grew out of the epilogue of my first monograph, *Rebuilding Anatolia after the Mongol Conquest* (Ashgate, 2014), where I reflected on the ways in which early Ottoman architecture was connected to the post-Mongol world. I conducted research for the new project as an H. Allen Brooks Travelling Fellow supported by the Society of Architectural Historians, as a Gerda Henkel Foundation postdoctoral fellow, and as an assistant professor first at Pomona College and now at Princeton University. All of these institutions provided indispensable research support, for which I am deeply grateful, as I am to the Barakat Trust for additional funding. A generous book subvention from the Barr Ferree Foundation Publication Fund, Department of Art & Archaeology, Princeton University enhanced the book's production.

For exceptional library access at Stanford University during the COVID-19 pandemic in 2020–21, I am deeply grateful to Debra Satz and R. Lanier Anderson in the Dean's Office of the School of Humanities and Sciences, Michael A. Keller at Stanford University Libraries, and Lisa Blaydes and Zack al-Witri at the Abbasi Program in Islamic Studies. Scanning services from the Princeton University Libraries and access to HathiTrust were also instrumental in completing the manuscript. For continued support, I thank Gülru Necipoğlu, who has been a role model in scholarly rigor, consistency, and mentorship; and Scott Redford, whose work has been an inspiration ever since I began studying medieval Anatolia. Avinoam Shalem has offered crucial support in cross-cultural studies of the medieval Islamic world and its neighbors, and inspiration to tackle questions of ornament and moveable objects.

I am deeply grateful to Alexander Key, who read the entire manuscript during the pandemic summer of 2020 and offered incisive, transformative suggestions. For timely comments and inspiring questions on elements of this project, I thank Sheila Canby, Moya Carey, John Curry, Walter B. Denny, Thomas Dittelbach, Antony Eastmond, Judson Emerick, Özer Ergenç, Fiona Griffiths, Lara Harb, Robert Hillenbrand, Jeremy Johns, Cemal Kafadar, Ahmed T. Karamustafa, Selim S. Kuru, Oya Pancaroğlu, Kathryn Starkey, Joel Walker, and Zeynep Yürekli.

Research would have been impossible without the help of curators, librarians, and archivists at the Bibliothèque d'études arabes, turques et islamiques at the Collège de France in Paris; the Museum für islamische Kunst in Berlin; the Metropolitan Museum of Art in New York; the Courtauld Institute, the School of Oriental and African Studies, and the Victoria & Albert Museum in London; the Ashmolean Museum in Oxford; ANAMED, Istanbul Archaeological Museum, İstanbul Üniversitesi Nadir Eserler Kütüphanesi, İstanbul Büyükşehir Belediyesi Atatürk Kitaplığı, Koç University Library, Türk ve İslam Eserleri Müzesi, and Türkiye Cumhuriyeti Cumhurbaşkanlığı Devlet Arşivleri Başkanlığı Osmanlı Arşivi Külliyesi (formerly Başbakanlık Osmanlı Arşivi) in Istanbul; Marquand and Firestone Libraries at Princeton University; Stanford University Libraries; and Honnold-Mudd Library at the Claremont Colleges. At Pomona College, Alexandra Dean, Cynthia Madrigal, and Susan K. Thalmann scanned my slides from Egypt, Turkey, and Syria so that I could include some of these images in this book. Jacob Wheeler in the Visual Resources Collection at Princeton greatly helped with securing image permissions. The staff of the Department of Art & Archaeology at Princeton, especially Maureen Killeen, have been a central source of support. Rachael Z. DeLue as department chair has offered crucial support in my early years at Princeton, for which I am deeply grateful. I also thank Michael Koortbojian who served the same role as I was about to start my position in summer 2020.

Participants at numerous conferences challenged me to refine aspects of this project. I especially thank Britta Dümpelmann and members of her Deutsche Forschungsgemeinschaft (DFG) research project for a series of fruitful meetings. I also thank Judith Pfeiffer and the 2017–18 members of the Alexander von Humboldt Kolleg "Islamicate Intellectual History" at the Rheinische Friedrich-Wilhelms-Universität in Bonn for their feedback. I presented aspects of this book at the "Ottoman Topologies" conference at Stanford University in 2014; at the Western Ottomanists' Workshop at the University of California, Davis in 2015; in the Eurasian Empires workshop at the Stanford Humanities Center, organized by Nancy Kollmann and Ali Yaycıoğlu, in 2017; at the Western Ottomanists' Workshop at the Claremont Colleges, and in the Near Eastern Languages and Civilization Department at the University of Washington, Seattle, both in 2019. Parts of Chapter 2 were published in *Gesta*, under the expert guidance of Linda Safran and Adam S. Cohen. An article published in *Muqarnas*, with detailed comments from Gülru Necipoğlu and Walter B. Denny and the editorial support of Maria Meister and Peri Bearman, laid the foundations of my engagement with Ottoman–Mamluk intersections.

Matt Gleeson's detailed work on the text pushed me to transform many aspects of the manuscript for the reader's benefit. Matilde Grimaldi produced architectural drawings and maps that transformed the final manuscript into a productive collaboration. At Cambridge University Press, I thank editor Beatrice Rehl, editorial assistant Edgar Mendez, the production team, Nigel Graves, and Mathi Mareesan. I thank Meridith Murray, who created a detailed index. I am also deeply grateful to the two anonymous reviewers whose comments transformed the first draft into the book that readers will encounter now.

For taking on the various roles of colleagues, mentors, neighbors, traveling companions, and fellow food enthusiasts, I offer heartfelt thanks to Ladan Akbarnia, Nilüfer Akpınar-Şahin, Tuna Artun, Nora E. Barakat, Charles E. Barber, the Başaran family, Deniz Beyazit, İ. Evrim Binbaş, Walter Borghini and Maria Cristina Carile, Ebru Çetin-Milci, Mary L. Coffey, Emre Can Dağlıoğlu and Tamar Nalcı, Lara Deeb, Rowan Dorin, Heather L. Ferguson, Mohammad Gharipour, Denise E. Gill, Dimitri Gondicas, George L. Gorse, Rachel Goshgarian, Christiane J. Gruber, Antonis Hadjikyriacou, Burcu Karahan, Burçak Keskin-Kozat, Arash Khazeni, Kıvanç Kılınç, Beatrice E. Kitzinger, Lorenz Korn, Juliet Koss, Francesca Leoni, Dunja Löbe, AnneMarie Luijendijk, Nina Macaraig, Katherine L. Marsengill, Yumna Masarwa, Richard P. McClary, Matthew Melvin-Koushki, Michelle Millard, Joanne R. Nucho, Tessa Paneth-Pollack, Pamela A. Patton, Bissera V. Pentcheva, Jennifer A. Pruitt, Aron Rodrigue, Eiren L. Shea, Amy Singer, Irene V. Small, Murat Somer, Laura P. Stokes, Hana Taragan, Fatih Tarhan, Baki Tezcan, Erik Thunø, Yektan Türkyılmaz, Nükhet Varlık, Kären Wigen, Elizabeth Dospěl Williams, Kenneth B. Wolf, Suzan Yalman, Anna Zadrożna, Adrien Zakar, and Nino Zchomelidse. Very special thanks to my community of academic mothers – you know who you are. For childcare in the middle of a pandemic, I thank Ayşenur Arıca, and Yina Morris and her team at the YWCA in Princeton.

As always, my family in Switzerland and Turkey bore the brunt of this project, tolerating strange travel schedules, joint treks to museums and sites, and suitcases and books piled on the floor. I thank everyone for their good spirits and support over many years of research. My husband, Ali Yaycıoğlu, has heard and read many iterations of this book, the failed ones and those realized. Our daughter, Aline Marianne Reyhan, was born as I was completing this book, and I dedicate it to her, her grandmother, and her great-grandmother, with whom she shares a middle name.

MAPS

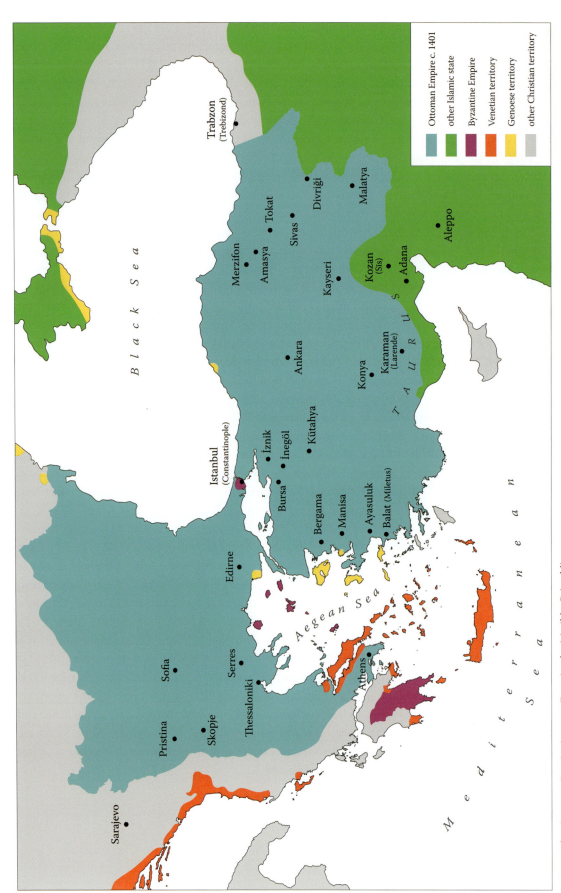

Map 1. The Ottoman Empire in 1401. Drawing by Matilde Grimaldi

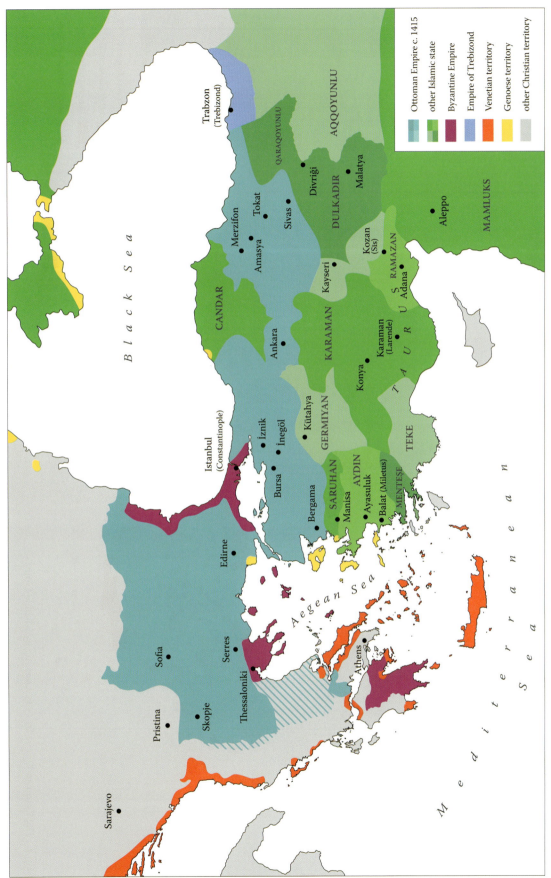

Map 2. The Ottoman Empire in 1415. Drawing by Matilde Grimaldi

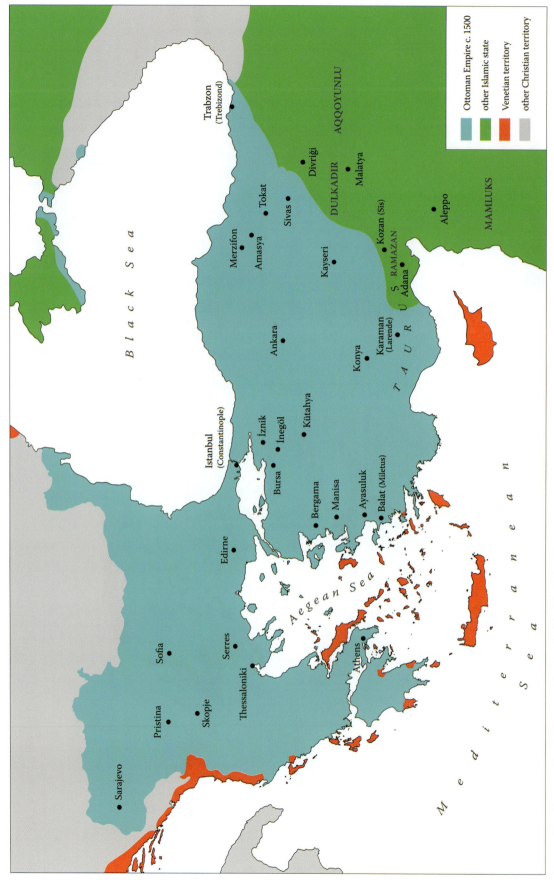

Map 3. The Ottoman Empire in 1500. Drawing by Matilde Grimaldi

INTRODUCTION

MATERIAL POLITICS OF ARCHITECTURE IN A FLUID EMPIRE

THE BUILDINGS DESIGNED AND BUILT BY THE ARCHITECT SINAN (D. 1588) IN THE IMPERIAL capital Istanbul, with their stripped-down aesthetic of impressive volumes and monumental domes, have become the epitome of Ottoman architecture. Active from the 1530s until the 1580s, Sinan designed monuments at both the large scale required by the sultans and the smaller one accorded to viziers, admirals, and princesses, as seen in the mosques built for Sultan Süleyman the Magnificent in 1550–77 and for one of his grand viziers, Rüstem Pasha, in 1563. Sinan's work and the work of the office of imperial architects (*hassa mimarları*) define our understanding of architecture in the Ottoman Empire from the sixteenth century onward, and they were integral parts of the functioning of a centralized empire that tightly regulated its administration and its aesthetic outlook.[1] But while these developments are well known, less understood is what happened in the first half of the fifteenth century, when what we now think of as classical Ottoman architecture began to coalesce. The transformation of Byzantine Constantinople into the Ottoman capital over the course of the second half of the fifteenth century under the patronage of Mehmed II has been examined in detail due to its crucial importance and the scale of the project, yet it has largely been analyzed in isolation from the broader context of architecture across the empire.[2] Moreover, equally important is the earlier part of the fifteenth century, when a visual identity was being actively shaped in a cultural and political context that was fluid and malleable enough to draw from an extremely varied array of sources and influences.

In this book, I analyze the fifteenth century on its own terms rather than looking backward from the vantage point of the unified imperial architecture of the mid-sixteenth century. As we shall see, Ottoman art and architecture of the fifteenth century stand at multiple crossroads: between Renaissance Italy and Timurid Central Asia, between Anatolia and the Balkans, and between Byzantine and Islamic architectural styles. In this fluctuating world, patrons, artists, and architects explored diverse modes of representation that eventually converged into a distinctly Ottoman aesthetic during the reign of Bayezid II (r. 1481–1512). The question is not one of origin – Eastern or Western, local or foreign – but one of how seemingly disparate elements of architecture were combined. Over time, an imperial Ottoman style came to be consolidated in connection to the larger epistemological project of the late fifteenth and early sixteenth centuries, when knowledge was methodically organized and cataloged. The study here

I

includes Ottoman monuments built both before and after the Ottoman conquest of Constantinople, to allow us to consider long-term developments that shed light on the wide range of architectural practice within the nascent empire. Such an approach also connects the dots back to studies that focus on Ottoman architecture built in the fourteenth century, and to the question of Ottoman emergence.[3] Chronologically, therefore, this book extends from the early fifteenth to the early sixteenth century, with forays into late fourteenth-century Ottoman and *beylik* (the Muslim-ruled principalities of Anatolia) architecture.

The choices made by the actors involved in these projects as they commissioned, designed, and built monuments form the core of the concept that I define as material politics. This concept includes, on the one hand, the politics of patronage – who commissions what, when, and where – that reflect the shifting power structures in the fifteenth-century Ottoman Empire. On the other hand, it also addresses the material preferences that are made on and for building sites – that is, the politics of stylistic choices, which come into play in the use of design models adapted from paper, and the hiring of workers with a wide variety of backgrounds, who then contributed to the formation of Ottoman identity through architecture.

Crucially, identity formation within the Ottoman Empire was closely intertwined with the multilingual and multireligious environment of the Balkans and Anatolia. The actors who were part of the fifteenth-century Ottoman landscape embodied the concept of Rūmī-ness coined by Cemal Kafadar. Seemingly disparate elements blended with ease in Rūmī-ness and Ottoman Turkish emerged as its literary expression, but without ethnic identity being fixed, in contrast to what twentieth-century nationalist historiographies state. The Rūmī identity was most fundamentally based on close ties to the geography of the Lands of Rūm.[4] In the Ottoman imaginary until the mid-eighteenth century, Rūm extended beyond the confines of the defunct eastern Roman Empire, from which the term derived, to include both the Ottoman Balkans (Rūm-ili, Rumelia) and Anatolia up to but not south of the Taurus Mountains.[5]

Definitions associating Anatolia with the territory of the Republic of Turkey and with Turkish ethnic identity emerged in the early twentieth century, in close parallel to the establishment of a nation-state in 1923. In history writing, M. Fuad Köprülü (1890–1966) was a central figure in the 1930s and 1940s for his work on the emergence of the Ottoman enterprise and on medieval Anatolia as a place where Turkish Islamic culture, including its literary and religious expressions, developed.[6] Köprülü pushed back against Western notions that presented the Ottoman Empire as a simple copy of the Byzantine Empire, which made no cultural contribution.[7] From the 1930s onward, cultural unity under the umbrella of *Anadoluculuk* (Anatolianism) was claimed as part of the Turkish nation-state's identity, with significant impact on the study of art history and archaeology, as Scott Redford explains.[8] Importantly, Anatolianism did not emphasize Islam as a unifying feature, but rather claimed that Anatolia had been a coherent political and cultural space since the Hittite period in the second millennium BCE. Beginning in the 1950s, historians of medieval Anatolia such as Osman Turan (1914–78) and İbrahim Kafesoğlu (1914–84) shifted to an approach that emphasized the emergence of a specifically Turkish and Muslim culture in Anatolia with the rule of the Saljuqs (*Türk-İslam sentezi*), starting in the late eleventh century.[9] Further, the notion of a Saljuq–*beylik*–Ottoman sequence was adopted for the study of the region, as Oya Pancaroğlu notes, erasing complex historical and cultural dynamics.[10] The Turkish Islamic culture proposed by Turan and others for the medieval period was correlated with the territories of the Turkish nation-state, especially Anatolia. National-territorial narratives of this sort emerged not only in Turkey but also in other nation-states – such as Armenia, Georgia, and Iran – that held territories in a wider region that was marked by close economic and cultural ties in the Middle Ages (and beyond).[11]

New scholarship over the past three decades has proposed to disentangle medieval and early modern Anatolia from nationalist historiographies; the concept of the Lands of Rūm is crucial in this body of work.[12] Within the context of architectural histories of the Lands of Rūm, attention to Rūmī identity is a way to escape the historiographical ballast of, on the one hand, nationalist designations of Ottoman, *beylik*, and Saljuq architecture as exclusively Turkish and, on the other hand, the blanket term "Islamic" with its attendant problems.[13] In this book, in line with my earlier work on the architecture of central and eastern Anatolia under Mongol rule, I view the region as one of cross-cultural interaction, multiethnic and multilingual populations, and complex political dynamics involving a wide range of actors.[14] Within this framework, architecture is strongly influenced not only by regional dynamics but also by transregional networks extending from the Mediterranean to Central Asia.

While these aspects of cultural formation can be traced in writing where literati and scholars in the Ottoman Empire and elsewhere in the Islamic world are concerned, they are also relevant for the makers (such as stonemasons, tile makers, calligraphers, and architects) who created buildings. Many of these makers remain anonymous, but their buildings give them voice. The "maker's share," a term that Svetlana Alpers established while studying the eighteenth-century Italian painter Tiepolo, is central to an understanding of works of art that moves beyond the roles of patron and viewer.[15] As Ethan Lasser explains in a study of nineteenth-century American decorative arts, the notion of the maker's share allows conceptual access to process.[16] Such an approach provides crucial insights into the emergence and consolidation of the Ottoman artistic milieu over the course of the fifteenth century, when written sources are much more attentive to scholar-bureaucrats and military and religious elites than to makers. The role of the architect – and indeed the very meaning of that term – and the roles of other building professionals are central points of discussion throughout this book, which covers a time period that saw changes to the ways in which construction sites were organized and run, from the design process to the completion of the building. These processes too constitute material politics.

Within the larger exploration of how the process of creating a monument functioned in the fifteenth-century Ottoman Empire, this book animates a number of central questions. How were architects trained? How did theory and practice intersect? What was the role of workshops? Who were the architects participating in the construction of Ottoman imperial commissions? How were building sites organized? Such questions are not exclusive to the study of Ottoman architecture: in fourteenth- and fifteenth-century Europe, the roles and education of architects, engineers, and designers similarly shifted.[17] In the Persianate world beginning in the fifteenth century, architects became increasingly visible in inscriptions on buildings that they created. Sussan Babaie notes that practices of architecture and the social standing of architects varied widely across the Islamic world, arguing that this fact has not been sufficiently taken into account in scholarship.[18] Thus the question of how architecture is conceived of and created has a global dimension in the fifteenth century that is not simply a matter of influence across regions.[19] By attending to the details of artistic production, then, we can gain an understanding of how architecture was shaped by those who worked on construction sites, from the planning and commissioning of a monument to its completion. Loose and shifting associations of makers connected the practice of architecture to networks of ulema, Sufis, scholar-bureaucrats, entrepreneurs, and poets, reaching beyond the text-based connections that have been traced in studies of such figures' writings.[20]

PASTS, PRESENTS, FUTURES: ARCHITECTURE AND SOURCES

With the foregoing in mind, I examine uses of past, present, and future in Ottoman architecture, frameworks that are closely tied to the ways in which the Ottomans wrote about and fashioned their own place in history. Since many of the first major Ottoman histories that have been preserved in full were written during the late fifteenth century, our perceptions of the earlier period are strongly influenced by those later historians' views. Titles of rulership, architectural patronage, and support for the arts and scholarship all tie into questions of Ottoman self-representation, as does history writing intended for the purpose of shaping a dynastic framework.[21] As Kafadar notes, however, the narratives that emerged during the reigns of Mehmed II and especially Bayezid II are by no means homogenous, and their authors' identities affect the ways in which they depict events and figures of the late thirteenth to the mid-fifteenth centuries, just as their affiliations determine how they judge their own present.[22] As these authors write about the past, they construct it according to the present's canon and establish narratives that make the present appear predestined.

In the early fifteenth century, crisis shook the Ottoman principality. Moving into Anatolia, Timur defeated Ottoman sultan Bayezid I (r. 1389–1402) at the Battle of Ankara in 1402. The sultan never returned from captivity and his sons became embroiled in a civil war as large swaths of territory in Anatolia were lost to the local rulers who had held them before the initial Ottoman expansion in that region.[23] The Ottomans' ways of writing their own history changed profoundly during and after the ensuing interregnum (1402–13). As Dimitri Kastritsis and Baki Tezcan have shown, the trauma of the Timurid conquest led to new narratives that asserted Ottoman legitimacy based on a claim that the Rūm Saljuq sultan (a constructed fictive version rather than a precise historical reality) had given authority to Osman.[24] Thus pre-Mongol Anatolia is strongly evoked in a period when the Timurids – Genghisid through Timur's marriage and subsequent claims – represented a threat equal to the one the Mongols had posed to the Rūm Saljuqs in the mid-thirteenth century.[25] Few histories written at this time have survived, but the ones that do exist provide unique views on this period in which the Ottoman principality was reshaped.[26] The long-lived ʿAşıkpaşazāde (1393–1502?), raised in the Wafāʾī zāviye of Elvan Çelebi in Mecidözü near Çorum, wrote a major history that includes eyewitness accounts beginning with the reign of Mehmed I.[27]

Mehmed I (r. 1413–21) emerged after the decade of interregnum and warfare as the new if contested ruler and set about rebuilding the realm. This effort went hand in hand with architectural patronage, particularly in the city of Bursa, closely associated with dynastic memory.[28] Buildings erected there between the 1410s and 1430s were essentially malleable monuments: the Byzantine architecture of the city, earlier and contemporary Islamic architectures of Anatolia, and contemporary monuments in Iran and Central Asia were all drawn upon in what was built in this Ottoman dynastic center. During the reign of Murad II (r. 1421–44, 1446–51), this engagement continued as architectural patronage expanded across the realm and cultural interests extended into the Mediterranean, while Edirne, the Ottomans' frontier capital, was a crucial site of patronage.[29]

In sources written during Mehmed II's reign (r. 1444–46, 1451–81), authors particularly praised the sultan for his role as conqueror of Constantinople and the corresponding rise in importance of the Ottomans and their empire, headed by a universal ruler.[30] Under Mehmed II, direct contact with artistic centers of the European Renaissance, as well as engagement with the Byzantine heritage and building fabric of the new capital Istanbul and the internal tradition of Ottoman architecture created since the early fourteenth century, led to numerous innovations.[31] During the reign of Bayezid II (r. 1481–1512), with which this book concludes, central workshops were established for most art forms produced for the Ottoman court. Simultaneously, new design practices brought architecture closely into the frame of an Ottoman project of knowledge gathering aimed at consolidating imperial ideology. These two practices led to the emergence of an Ottoman style that is easily recognizable in its plan schemes and volumes. This Ottoman imperial style offered a synthesis of the Ottoman architectures of the preceding century and firmly established the foundation of a new Ottoman future to be realized in the sixteenth century. Such specific engagements with past(s), present(s), and future, I argue, were a hallmark of the material politics of Ottoman architecture.

Such reflections are also relevant for the writing of history in that period. Murat Cem Mengüç argues that, rather than viewing history writing during Bayezid II's reign as a centralized, state-sponsored project, we should see the emergence of a range of histories as an expression of "emerging historical self-consciousness" among those who endeavored to write such texts and those who might read them.[32] According to Mengüç, historians acted on their own initiative; he notes that only Ruhi (d. 1522) states that he wrote at the sultan's behest.[33] This corresponds to Kafadar's observation that varying perspectives appear across different histories, so that, for instance, 'Aşıkpaşazāde's Sufi affiliation is clear throughout his work, including when he severely criticizes Mehmed II for taking away the lands of *gazi* families and Sufi communities, both instrumental actors in the rise of the Ottoman Empire throughout the fourteenth and fifteenth centuries.[34] Neşri (d. ca. 1520), on the other hand, works within the premises of his position as a member of the ulema.[35]

Diverse as these histories may be, in them and in the major biographical dictionary by Ahmed b. Mustafa Taşköprüzāde (d. 1561), *Shaqā'iq al-nu'māniyah fī 'ulāmā' al-dawlah al-'uthmānīyah*, which includes scholars whom the sixteenth-century compiler deemed important for the Ottoman context, narratives are shaped that conform to late fifteenth- and sixteenth-century Ottoman worldviews.[36] Since Taşköprüzāde himself was a *mudarris* and kadi trained in the Ottoman madrasa system, his choices are influenced by that specific background and his work is therefore also selective in that it includes and excludes individuals according to their place within the Ottoman system. The work's title, specifically evoking scholars tied to the Ottoman state (*dawlah*), is programmatic in that sense, tying into the centralized madrasa system that emerged with the construction of the Semaniye madrasas connected to Mehmed II's mosque complex in Istanbul.[37]

History writing and self-fashioning through sixteenth-century lenses, then, gloss over some of the complex social and material dynamics of architecture in the fifteenth century. Architectural history can offer certain correctives if we examine sources that record earlier views or stages of development. In his study of the Ottomans' emergence, Cemal Kafadar has demonstrated how effective sources such as hagiographies and epics can be in providing perspectives that were omitted in later history writing.[38] Architecture can offer similar insights. For example, inscriptions on monuments provide information about founders, dates, functions, and sometimes individuals involved in the construction. Many fifteenth-century buildings that today function as Friday mosques (Arabic *jāmi'*, Turkish *cami*) or smaller prayer spaces (Arabic *masjid*, Turkish *mescid*) were originally built as multifunctional structures that served the activities of dervish groups along with travelers, scholars, and other guests. Although such buildings lost their original functions as part of a larger transformation of imperial structures circa 1500, their foundation inscriptions retain the terms originally used. This allows us to recognize the overwhelming presence of such buildings, otherwise invisible in the current day due to later changes and modern naming.[39] These inscriptions are thus testimonies to those dervishes who, gathering converts to Islam in much larger numbers than many ulema, were crucial to the Ottomans' success, especially in formerly Christian-ruled lands.[40] In one particular case, that of the Alibey Camii in Manisa, a sixteenth-century inscription tells the story of the building's transformation into a Friday mosque.[41] Founded in 831 AH / 1427–28 CE by 'Ali Beğ b. Timurtaş, the building was not used for the Friday prayer. In 975 AH / 1567–68 CE, the founder's descendant, Haydar Çelebi, turned the building into a Friday mosque. Finally, in 978 AH / 1570–71 CE, Cafer Çelebi had the roof restored and added a *minbar* and minaret – elements visibly marking the building as a Friday mosque – as well as commissioning a new decorative program. While nothing survives of the Alibey Camii's fifteenth-century substance or sixteenth-century decorative program, the story of the monument's transformation can be read in the five lines of text that make up its inscription and in the building's minaret.

While I fully discuss the use of specific terms in foundation inscriptions when addressing specific examples, it is important to note here that *waqfīya*s, the endowment deeds connected to foundations, also provide information about buildings' functions, staff, and related financial arrangements. A substantial number of fifteenth-century Ottoman *waqfīya*s survive, in several cases jointly with the buildings for which they were established. Thus these documents offer glimpses of fifteenth-century worlds – albeit within the clearly delineated framework of endowments (*waqfs*) in Islamic law – that are not always available in other sources. This is, for instance, true for the lists of staff positions, where one or two posts often entail being responsible for the maintenance of a building's structure or of specific elements such as water features. Such mentions, along with the occasional appearance in inscriptions of the names of individuals who designed buildings or parts of their decoration (such as stonework or tiles) and furnishings (such as doors and *minbars*), provide insights into the building crafts of the fifteenth-century Ottoman Empire.

While Ottoman histories generally refer to the arts only in passing or as they relate to patronage, such inscriptions and mentions in *waqfīyas* allow for insights into the composition of the workforce at building sites, the kinds of roles available during and after construction, and at times the planning process. Together with close attention to architectural elements, then, such sources are helpful in making methodological inroads into a more comprehensive understanding of Ottoman architecture in the fifteenth century. This brings us to the question of architecture itself and of the monuments covered in this book.

The large number of extant monuments makes it crucial to select specific examples for in-depth treatment.[42] An interest in understanding interior spaces along with façades has led me to privilege examples in which original interior decorative programs are still extant or ones that, while restored, retain substantial parts of their original character.[43] The buildings discussed in this book are located in cities across Anatolia and the Balkans, in provincial centers as well as in the three imperial cities of Bursa, Edirne, and Istanbul. However, the survival of fifteenth-century monuments varies across different regions that were part of the Ottoman Empire, and this affects how we can study architecture – low survival rates of buildings can particularly be a factor in former Ottoman lands in southeastern Europe.[44]

SHIFTING ARCHITECTURES, CHANGING ACTORS

The formation of Ottoman architecture drew from two main strands at its outset in the fourteenth century. The Byzantine architecture present in the northwestern Anatolian lands the Ottomans conquered early on, along with monuments in Greece and the Balkans, was a crucial point of departure for Ottoman architecture. The transformation of churches into mosques in cities such as Thessaloniki was a crucial step in these conquests. The same construction techniques that could be observed in these Byzantine monuments continued to be used as the Ottomans had new buildings erected. Some of the makers of these pre-Ottoman architectures, remaining in the region under Ottoman rule, acted as building professionals, supplying knowledge of skills and locally available materials, and played a central role in establishing the technical and stylistic bases for the first Ottoman monuments.[45] Further, by the late fourteenth century, political and artistic connections beyond the Ottoman lands were reflected in architecture, with Mamluk and Italian elements appearing, for instance, in Murad I's and Bayezid I's foundations in Bursa.[46]

In the early fifteenth century, new aspects of architecture emerged. While earlier elements were still used, the Ottomans became increasingly aware of and interested in the Timurid cultural (rather than political) sphere, which extended from Samarqand to Tabriz. The prestige of Timurid court culture was such that the Ottomans moved to deploy its arts for their purposes. At the same time, a historical narrative was being constructed that erased the Mongol past that the Ottomans shared with the Timurids. Tile decoration in particular emerged as a central element of early fifteenth-century buildings in Bursa and Edirne, along with wall paintings. Gülru Necipoğlu has suggested viewing this set of references as a regional variant of the so-called international Timurid style – that is, the wide adaptation, within the eastern Islamic world throughout the fifteenth century, of stylistic choices that represented the Timurids' cultural clout.[47]

Throughout the fourteenth century and well into the fifteenth, the Ottoman Empire also operated within the post-Mongol context of Anatolia. When Bayezid I expanded his territories into Anatolia in the 1390s, reaching as far east as Malatya, the Ottomans came into close contact with the various political entities active there, from the *beyliks* of western Anatolia to Qadi Burhaneddin Ahmad (d. 1398), who reigned independently in the region between Sivas and Kayseri.[48] While these conquered Anatolian lands were lost following the Ottomans' defeat by Timur in 1402, Murad II and Mehmed II would again expand eastward, absorbing the *beyliks* of western Anatolia in the 1420s and the Karamanids and the Byzantine empire of Trebizond by 1470.[49] As I argue in my earlier work, the profound changes in patronage caused by the Mongol takeover of the Saljuq realm led to increasingly regionalized architectural styles beginning in the 1250s and continuing into the early fourteenth century.[50] Thus neither the imperial architecture of the Mongols in Iran nor the modes of Saljuq royal patronage of the early thirteenth century dominated monuments built by a wide range of Muslim patrons in central and eastern Anatolia between the mid-thirteenth century and the mid-fourteenth century, in large part parallel to the emergence of the Ottomans. Farther east in Anatolia, the Ottomans' rivalry with the Aqqoyunlu first came to a head in 1461, when Mehmed II's conquest of Trebizond led Uzun Hasan (r. 1453–78) to withdraw from the region.[51] After the Ottoman victory at the Battle of Otlukbeli (or Başkent) in 1473, the Aqqoyunlu ruler was forced to make peace.[52] Some territories in southeastern Anatolia and beyond the Taurus Mountains remained contested until the early sixteenth century.[53]

The references available in Anatolia for Ottoman builders were a mirror of this hybrid frontier region and their incorporation into Ottoman visual culture deserves careful analysis. This is not to say that Ottoman architecture should be construed as inherently Eastern and Islamic – a view that has been espoused in nationalist narratives to emphasize the Turkish Islamic aspects of Ottoman culture.[54] Rather, elements that can be traced back to Islamic architecture built by a range of patrons in Anatolia are one small part of the puzzle that is Ottoman architecture in the fourteenth and fifteenth centuries.

Throughout the fifteenth century, elements adapted from a wide range of styles were combined with remarkable ease, with different types of decoration flexibly used across media, demonstrating the cultural fluidity that would be expressed in Rūmī-ness by circa 1500. Regional powers within the Ottoman Empire remained in place until then and played a central part in architectural patronage. Families such as the Çandarlıs, the Mihailoğlus, and the Evrenosoğlus were major patrons of architecture and powerful political actors.[55] Figures such as Hajji ʿIvaz Pasha, Bayezid Pasha, and Yörgüç Pasha established pockets of local power, as Chapters 2 and 3 will show, and commissioned monuments in cities where they held influence. Only with Mehmed II's centralization policies were these regional powers dissolved and the powerful *gazi* families marginalized; land reforms affected them along with the Sufi communities who had been crucial in the expansion of the Ottoman Empire.[56] Criticism of this treatment by Mehmed II rose to such a point that Bayezid II reversed some of these policies, returning extensive landholdings and *waqf*s.[57]

The Ottoman Empire and its artistic landscape in this period cannot be understood in isolation: they were intimately bound up in a closely connected, transregional cultural and political scene. Circulation of knowledge is a central element in this context. In his study of the intellectual biography of Timurid scholar Sharaf al-Din ʿAli Yazdi (d. 1454), Evrim Binbaş investigates an informal network that scholar ʿAbd al-Rahman al-Hanafi al-Bistami (d. 1454), who settled in Ottoman Bursa, described as extending across the Ottoman Empire and into Mamluk Egypt.[58] Among the members of this network were figures such as Şeyh Bedreddin (d. 1416), who later rebelled against Mehmed I, and Şemseddin Muhammad b. Hamza al-Fenari al-Rumi, known as Molla Fenari (d. 1431 or 1434–35), who became the *müftü* of Bursa and was one of the most prominent Ottoman ulema of his time.[59] As Binbaş argues, Bistami reveals connections that were completely omitted in later Ottoman biographical dictionaries.[60] This later omission is unsurprising given the bloody suppression of Şeyh Bedreddin's uprising and the fact that its leader had been a classmate of both Molla Fenari and the poet Ahmedi in Cairo in the 1380s, associations that later Ottoman historians could have found improper.[61] Taken together, these scholars' endeavors are of encyclopedic proportion, addressing everything from astronomy to aesthetics.[62] These kinds of networks operated in addition to more formal ones – for instance, those established among scholars teaching in madrasas and their students, who could then move on to positions elsewhere. The kind of mobility that we see among scholars and intellectuals was also available to those I refer to as makers – that is, a wide range of people employed on building sites and in the creation of ceramics, books, and other objects. But how do we document their roles, if we often do not even know their names, let alone their biographies?

Due to the difficulties of reconstructing these looser, more diffuse networks, narratives that aim to explain the circulation of ideas and motifs within architectural contexts tend to assign an important role to traveling workshops. Yet such workshops, which tend to dominate scholarly narratives, often appear as abstract, nearly timeless entities that continue over decades, documented only in limited signed works and others attributed to them on stylistic grounds. While inscriptions containing the names of makers are generally designated as signatures, the term does need to be questioned. Thus Sheila Blair proposes a distinction between names included in formal building inscriptions – where they are part of carefully planned epigraphic programs – and informal signatures added in inconspicuous places on objects.[63] In what follows, I largely observe this distinction while arguing that some architectural inscriptions might also fall into the informal category. Questions of the workshop members' origin, the issue of possibly fictive labels conferring cultural prestige, and the idea that objects used in architecture could also move – again, either together with or independently of their makers – are rarely raised. In fact, as Jonathan Hay notes, the transfer of motifs does not necessarily require the movement even of objects; instead, a "mere two-dimensional notation, or even a memory, will do" in order to recreate a specific kind of decoration elsewhere.[64]

As an example of scholarly insistence on a workshop scheme, the Masters of Tabriz – tile workers who may or may not have actually come from that city – appear prominently in studies of fifteenth-century Ottoman tiles, and at times an argument has been made for the continuity of a single workshop over several generations from the 1420s to the 1470s. Builders from the Mamluk context seem to have arrived in late fourteenth-century western Anatolia. Thus there was clearly cross-pollination between the Ottoman Empire and other regions, but a central question to pursue is how much of it needs to be explained with the movement of people, and how much can be attributed to moving objects and works on paper. Art historian Michael Meinecke firmly stood on the side of moving workshops, an argument he pursued in focused studies of Mamluk architecture and of tiles in Anatolia from the Saljuq to the early Ottoman period, as well as in general study of patronage as a main motor for artists' movements.[65] In what follows, I argue that the movement of ideas, plans, drawings, and objects also played a central role.

Paper, which had become increasingly available since the fourteenth century, is an important presence – though often an invisible one – behind designs, calligraphies, and templates for architectural decoration.[66] Harder to trace is how building plans traveled, and the extent to which paper was relevant in those cases, at least before the late fifteenth century, when rare architectural drawings survive in the Ottoman context.[67] Design practices that include carefully aligned, custom-designed inscription panels, for instance, suggest that paper templates were used in some way by the late fourteenth century. It was especially likely that such templates would be useful as a means of communication in a process that required measurements of buildings to be provided to calligraphers, who would then create appropriate, proportional inscription designs that could be sent in small size to building sites and ceramic workshops to be scaled up when necessary for monumental use.

From these observations emerge three larger topics of discussion. First, the question of drawings in the process of architectural production needs to be examined in relationship to extant monuments and how they might have been planned, as well as in relationship to knowledge production. Second, the issue of how workshops were put together, how flexible they might have been, and how much we can read into their names is a central one. Third, the movement of objects – and this includes tiles, often silently assumed to be produced near the building site – appears as an important mode of transfer.[68] Such a collaborative environment, where relationships between teachers, students, and members of a workshop were crucial, also relates to the *kitabkhāna* setting – namely, workshops that produced books as well as designs for a wide range of objects. The notion of workshops, however, should not lead us to assume that the same members were always collaborating in a set formation: considering the changing nature of building sites in particular, we should imagine environments in which individuals could move around and changing sets of workers could collaborate on various projects.

THE OTTOMAN EMPIRE AND THE RENAISSANCE

The idea of the Renaissance, which scholars over the past three decades have reframed in global terms that extend beyond Italy, played a crucial role in the Ottoman context, particularly beginning in the second half of the fifteenth century.[69] As Lisa Jardine and Jerry Brotton note, with the recognition of these connections "comes the inevitable recognition that cultural histories apparently utterly distinct, and traditionally kept entirely separate, are ripe to be rewritten as shared East/West undertakings."[70] Within the Ottoman context, Gülru Necipoğlu and Julian Raby have conducted extensive research to uncover these shared undertakings and to highlight the crucial contribution of Ottoman patrons and artists to a pan-Mediterranean Renaissance.[71] In architectural history, such work allows for a study of the sixteenth-century Mediterranean that places the Ottoman Empire on equal footing with cultural and political centers of the Renaissance in Italy and generates an understanding of how ideas relating to building were received across this space in both directions – and such a study naturally poses many challenges.[72]

Working on Venice, Deborah Howard has examined the impact of Islamic art on the built environment of that city from the twelfth to the fifteenth century.[73] Exhibitions such as *Venice and the Islamic World* have examined connections between Venice and the Islamic world beyond the Ottoman context, from the ninth to the eighteenth centuries.[74] While objects, paintings, and drawings play a large role in these exchanges – being rife with imitation, copying, and catering to patrons' specific taste – the place of architecture in this dynamic of transfer is at times harder to trace.[75] And yet mutual influence is present in architecture: for instance, in the increasing symmetry of Ottoman mosque complexes starting with the mosque of Mehmed II in Istanbul (1463–70), which Necipoğlu argues was due to the influence of Italian models of urban planning.[76] The presence of artists such as Gentile Bellini (1429–1507), who stayed at the Ottoman court in 1479, contributed to exchanges governed by trade and diplomatic missions.[77] Mehmed II's efforts to invite artists and architects from Venice and Florence, his interest in classical Greek and Latin culture and history, and the translations from Greek and Latin into Arabic and Ottoman Turkish created at his court were part of the sultan's project of shaping Ottoman imperial identity – and his own claim to rule – as universal. Such invitations continued under Bayezid II, displaying persistent efforts to enhance artistic contacts with the cultural centers of Italy.[78] Thus, Bayezid II's unrealized project of building a bridge over the Golden Horn elicited correspondence in 1502 with Leonardo da Vinci, who got as far as making a sketch and writing a letter to the prospective patron, as well as with Michelangelo before 1506.[79]

In addition to these direct attempts at artistic exchange, trade between Europe and the Mamluk and Ottoman realms played a central role; major port cities such as Alexandria and Istanbul and trading centers such as Cairo and Bursa were of particular interest in these exchanges. Increased trade became possible after the lifting of a papal ban on trade with non-Christian lands that had been in effect from 1320 to 1344, and Beirut, Aleppo, and Damascus once more became major destinations for Venetian merchants.[80] Trade networks established in previous centuries, such as the caravan routes in Anatolia marked by many caravanserais created under Saljuq rule in the early thirteenth century, persisted. These trade routes connecting Anatolia and Iran were expanded by the Ilkhanids in the early fourteenth century in order to facilitate access to Tabriz, while Genoese trading colonies existed in Pera and the Black Sea.[81] Studies on trade demonstrate that cities such as Tabriz were major nodes in trade networks that extended from Genoa and Venice to China, with the Ottoman Empire as a crucial intermediary and point of passage in between.[82] Glass, soap, textiles, and paper were coveted goods taken from the Islamic world to Venice and Genoa.[83]

Of these goods, textiles in particular long played an important role in trade connections between the Islamic world and Europe. In the fifteenth century, the Ottoman Empire took on a role in this trade as increasing volumes of silk, mainly from Iran, passed through Bursa.[84] Onward trade to Europe consisted of both raw silk and finished textiles made in Bursa, although the raw material represented a larger part of the trade.[85] The manufacturing of textiles in Bursa increased in the sixteenth century, and at the same time fabrics were also made in Istanbul, where production of brocades and velvets peaked between 1550 and 1600.[86] In the other direction, the Ottoman Empire became the biggest export market for Italian textile producers due to demand created by the Ottoman court.[87] Producers of velvet in Italian centers – primarily Venice and Lucca – and in Bursa mutually influenced each other and similar motifs appeared on both sides of the Mediterranean as each market catered to the other while imitating imported products that appealed to local tastes.[88] At times, distinguishing between Italian and Ottoman productions is difficult or nearly impossible without close attention to minute technical details of weaving.[89] These connections are one manifestation of a mutual interest in similar types of objects that also extends to metalwork, ceramics, and glass, influencing production and consumption in multiple locations.[90]

STYLES, INTERNATIONAL AND OTHERWISE

While style is a concept ingrained in and derived from the framework of Western art history as an academic discipline, internal practices of connoisseurship and art appreciation can clearly be traced in Islamic art, especially beginning in the late fourteenth century.[91] In the Ottoman Empire, fifteenth-century ekphrastic poems exalting buildings demonstrate practices of aesthetic appraisal, as I examine in Chapter 1. In the seventeenth century, Evliya Çelebi uses the term *tarz* to designate style in a building that he admires during a visit to Bursa, to be examined in Chapter 2.[92] Within the fifteenth-century Ottoman Empire, we observe an epistemological project that involves art and architecture in the same way as history writing, science, philosophy, and poetry. While manuscripts and correspondence between scholars, scientists, and administrators provide a crucial base of sources that, when meticulously studied, provide access to the thinking behind this knowledge project, we often have to find ways to let objects and buildings speak for themselves as we work to appraise them within this same framework. Therefore style remains an indispensable tool in the analysis that follows. Furthermore, as transregional exchange and connections are crucial throughout the fifteenth century, the conceptual issue of international styles needs to be addressed at the outset.

Also crucially related to the aesthetic interpretation of objects and buildings, I trace the notion throughout the book that monuments built in this period reflect a complex engagement with sensory perception that reaches from the built environment onto the written page. In poetic inscriptions and poems, monuments were praised for their beauty using natural and cosmological metaphors. Poetry at times serves to guide sensory perception, highlighting ways in which a site should be experienced and providing points of comparison with natural, spiritual, and imaginary worlds. Within buildings, the visitor was immersed in spaces decorated with tiles, eliciting wonder at the artifice of their creation, and enveloped in the sounds of water features and prayers. In analyzing these aspects of architecture, approaches to aesthetics, poetics, and wonder are crucial.[93] Thus the engagement of the senses was pursued in the establishment of complex aesthetic frameworks that lay at the root of an imperial Ottoman architecture. With this in mind, the book engages with the sensory turn in medieval and Islamic art history, new approaches that strongly rely on attention to the intersection of poetic works, objects, and architecture, as well as on theoretical avenues connected to perception that extends to senses beyond vision: touch, smell, and sound.[94] These observations supplement those based on stylistic analysis.

An international Timurid style, spanning the late fourteenth to the early sixteenth centuries, has long been a central tool for understanding the arts of the eastern Islamic world. The concept was consolidated for art history with the 1989 exhibition *Timur and the Princely Vision*, which examined manuscripts and objects from Central Asia, Iran, and the Ottoman Empire within the framework of Timurid aesthetic hegemony derived from the central role of Timurid rulers such as Ulugh Beğ (d. 1449) and Sultan-Husayn Bayqara (r. 1469–1506) as patrons of the arts. As Binbaş explains, Russian historian Vasiliy V. Bartol'd (Wilhelm Barthold) first recognized the importance of Timurid courts in the intellectual and cultural life of the fifteenth century and of their rulers' outstanding patronage of scholars and artists alike.[95]

This historical premise was firmly established by the time *Timur and the Princely Vision* was displayed in the United States, the first major exhibition on Timurid art and its impact within the Islamic world. Transregional in scope and marked by post-Mongol ideals of kingship translated into a refined visual mode, a Timurid style is visible in miniature paintings and can also be traced in woodwork, in metalwork, and to some extent in architecture. The Timurid formulations of kingship were crucial for the Ottomans beginning in the fifteenth century and were adopted by the Safavids and Mughals in the sixteenth century.[96] Among these formulations, the title *ṣāhib-qirān*, lord of the auspicious conjunction, was a cosmological construct consolidated by occult philosophers in the service of the Aqqoyunlu and Timurids, closely tied to astronomy/astrology (*'ilm al-nujūm*).[97] The engagement with the Timurid cosmology of rulership came with an artistic side that was dominated by the works the Timurid *kitabkhāna* produced and put into circulation through its patrons' far-flung networks. The dissemination of this visual idiom throughout the eastern Islamic world, from the eastern Mediterranean to the Deccan, was the result of the association between style and rule that lay at the core of Timurid art, which persisted beyond the fall of the dynasty in the early sixteenth century and was seen as conferring prestige on the patrons who commissioned works in this international Timurid style.[98]

Focusing on the ancient Near East, Marian Feldman observes that "[t]he term international style has entered art historical parlance to describe the use of shared visual forms across multiple cultural regions."[99] As such, the concept of international style is used in contrast to national styles, which are defined in monolithic and culturally homogeneous terms. Feldman notes that two central examples of the use of the concept of international style are Gothic art in Central Europe in the fourteenth century (hence the term "international Gothic") and global modernist architecture beginning in the 1920s.[100]

In presenting the phenomenon of an "international Gothic style" – which included various media – two exhibition catalogues published in 1962 highlighted sculpture produced around 1400, when an elegant style commonly referred to as the "beautiful style" spread from Bohemia to Germany, France, and northern Italy.[101] In this respect, the 1960s iterations of the concept of international Gothic are in stark contrast to the first formulations of the international Gothic in nineteenth-century France, when it was stated that the Gothic was inherently French and its international spread was a sign of French cultural dominance.[102] However, Scott Nethersole notes that problematic notions emerge in these 1960s iterations through the positing of an internationalism rife with political undertones related to post–World War II ideas of Europe rather than medieval realities.[103] The exhibition catalogues reflect the historical moment of a reunified Europe in the 1960s, when the notion of an international style was based on the premise that artistic exchange and transfer, not political domination, form the core of an overarching yet not entirely unified stylistic mode.[104] Such issues of equating rule with style and imperial hold with nation, or of origin and reception, are inherent in any use of the concept of international style.[105] In the case of the eastern Mediterranean in the Late Bronze Age, Feldman notes that it is productive to consider international style as "the visual expression of a specific, intercultural, supraregional community of rulers that coalesced as a distinct socio-political entity."[106] Though caution is necessary if we apply a similar definition to a period several thousand years after the one Feldman studies, these ideas ring true for the international Timurid style. Timurid visual modes were used across the eastern Islamic world in the fifteenth century, and while studies have assumed a degree of homogeneity, regional variants are readily admitted – especially in the Ottoman context, where certain divergences are highlighted.[107] Thus, rather than a fixed style, international Timurid is perhaps best seen as a shared aesthetic framework that also had political dimensions.

In the early sixteenth century, the international Timurid style slowly faded, perhaps victim of the decline of Timurid power and prestige and the rising tensions between Ottomans and Safavids. With the Shaybanid Uzbeks' conquest of Herat in 1506, soon followed by a Safavid takeover in the city, Timurid rule ended and the *kitabkhāna* of Sultan-Husayn Bayqara, which for decades had produced many of the works admired elsewhere in the Islamic world, was dissolved.[108] Thus, as Necipoğlu notes, the shared culture of ornament of the fifteenth century, which included Ottoman, Turkman, and Timurid art from the Balkans to Central Asia, slowly disappeared.[109] Within the Ottoman context, this period brought with it the emerging creation of a unified visual idiom that stretched from tiles to silks, from ceramic vessels to carpets, promulgated by the court workshops responsible for creating designs – especially those with the stylized tulips, carnations, and peonies that were articulated in various media in the mid-sixteenth century.[110] While that particular period exceeds the scope of this book, the developments of the fifteenth century are nevertheless crucial for what would happen during Sultan Süleyman's long reign. Even if styles shifted with the formation of imperial identity, many of the structures of artistic production that were fully developed in the sixteenth century have their roots in the fifteenth century.

CHAPTER SUMMARIES

I open the book in the mid-fifteenth century, after the Ottoman conquest of Constantinople in 1453, in order to first reexamine the shifts in architecture brought about by this turning point in Ottoman history, focusing particularly on aesthetics and the question of styles. Chapter 1, "Imperial and Local Horizons: Looking East and West," connects the continuing Ottoman conquest of Anatolia in the second half of the fifteenth century to monuments in Istanbul. This chapter takes as its centerpiece the Çinili Köşk, built in 1472 on the premises of Topkapı Palace: this building was in part a direct reaction to the Ottoman defeat of the Karamanids in 1468 – a crucial step in expansion into Anatolia, allowing the Ottomans to secure a region that had been troublesome for centuries – and in part a complex negotiation between Islamic and Byzantine forms of architectural decoration. Poetry integrates the monument into a complex cosmological imaginary aimed at inciting wonder, and the building's tile mosaic, attributed to tile cutters from Iran, projects connections to the international Timurid style; the latter aspect, however, is ambiguous in that it has also been thought to evoke contemporaneous, no-longer-extant palatial structures in Karaman. I also examine the exterior use of tiles that appeared on the Mahmud Pasha Mausoleum in Istanbul and the Alaca Türbe in Skopje during this period, raising the question of how this technique traveled – with workers or on paper.

In the following chapter, I move back in time to the period after the interregnum, when Sultan Mehmed I (r. 1413–21) set about rebuilding the Ottoman realm. Thus Chapter 2, "Immersive Space: Empire Building and the Ottoman Frontier," discusses shifts in Ottoman architecture after Mehmed I established his base in Bursa. With the construction of his mosque-*zāviye* complex, beginning in 1419, Mehmed I consolidated Bursa's role as an Ottoman dynastic *lieu de mémoire*. This period shows the beginning of a new engagement with the Anatolian past and the Timurid present in Ottoman architecture, leading to deep transformations. Mehmed I's foundation in Bursa demonstrated an engagement with Timurid aesthetics and the Byzantine architecture of Bithynia, but also an interest in Anatolian architecture that was intentionally tied to claims to a connection to the Saljuq dynasty aimed at bolstering the Ottomans' legitimacy. The site's tile decoration, signed by the Masters of Tabriz, allows me to discuss the question of workshops' claims of origin. In the interior, this tile decoration plays a central role in creating an immersive space aimed at evoking wonder, while the foundation inscription raises complex questions about the building process.

Chapter 3, "Under the Influence: Creating Cosmopolitan Architectures," takes a discussion of how elements of Mamluk architecture were introduced into Ottoman architecture – quite likely along with the presence of traveling builders – and uses it as a departure point to explore the broader interconnections of intellectuals and makers in the fifteenth century. In particular, it addresses the ambiguous and flexible roles of workers and overseers on construction sites, including issues surrounding what are often assumed to be unified workshops and the potential use of paper for architectural design in a period before it is definitively documented. Mamluk architectural influence seems to have arrived in Ottoman lands partly by way of the *beyliks* of western Anatolia, briefly restored by Timur but largely reabsorbed into the Ottoman realm by circa 1430. In the early fifteenth century, Mamluk-style elements appear in Amasya, a city the Ottomans never lost to Timur and that was used as a base, along with Bursa, from which to reconsolidate the Ottoman Empire. A look at Amasya also lets us see how the establishment of Ottoman monumental presence played out in a central Anatolian city that was the site of important Saljuq and Ilkhanid monuments. Local power holders like Bayezid Pasha and Yörgüç Pasha reached beyond the region for inspiration in the buildings they constructed, with stylistic connections to Mamluk and local Saljuq and Ilkhanid architecture apparent in their stone carving. Such transregional connections, fostered by multilingual networks, also appear in monuments commissioned by Murad II in Edirne – the Üç Şerefeli Mosque and the Muradiye Mosque. The blue-and-white underglaze-painted tiles and wall paintings used in the latter raise the question of fifteenth-century convergences in taste between the Timurid, Mamluk, and Ottoman realms, as well as sites of production for ceramics.

Chapter 4, "Building Paradise: Afterlife and Dynastic Politics," focuses on the funerary complex of Murad II in Bursa, where concepts of immersive space already established in Mehmed I's mosque-*zāviye* are developed further. In its commemorative function, the Muradiye served to enhance dynastic prestige; tombs for members of the Ottoman family continued to be added until the mid-sixteenth century, creating an Ottoman necropolis that has both intriguing parallels to and crucial differences with the site of Eyüp in Istanbul. While Murad II's mosque-*zāviye* with its tile decoration offers elements similar to those in Mehmed I's earlier monument, the mausoleum of Murad II is a site of further experimentation with materials and immersive space. The marble cenotaph emerging from a marble floor, which emulates a body of water, and the open skylight that allows rainwater to reach the earth of the sultan's grave at once establish an architectural representation of paradise and foreground the element of artifice in the built space. Here and in other sites, representations of paradise are strengthened with the use of wall paintings showing landscapes and the cladding of large sections of walls to create immersive spaces.

Chapter 5, "An Ottoman Aesthetic: Consolidation circa 1500," turns to the centralization of design processes in the period around 1500, when architecture became integrated into the practices of the centralized workshops that were being established. As a discussion of the so-called Baba Nakkaş album shows, design intersected with collection practices that integrated the visual arts into the Ottoman epistemological project of gathering, sorting, and classifying that was fully underway at the time.

In artistic practice, this included designs on paper that were adapted in a wide range of media as well as the establishment of centralized production sites for objects, such as Iznik as the main site for ceramics. Focusing on buildings in Amasya, Edirne, Istanbul, Serres, and Skopje, I show that architecture increasingly took on a distinctly Ottoman shape in this period, imposing a distinct visual presence, especially in its exterior volumes and decorative elements, yet also retaining easily overlooked references to the architecture of previous decades. The chapter concludes with a study of monuments built in Adana in the sixteenth century, to show what was being built in a region that did not come under Ottoman rule until that period.

I conclude by returning to the question of how a reexamination of Ottoman architecture in the fifteenth century profoundly changes our understanding of the empire's architectural endeavor. This is true for the fifteenth century itself, when a wide range of elements drawn from the Mediterranean, Anatolia, and Iran and Central Asia were integrated into Ottoman architecture, both through the contributions of workers from these regions and through the wide-ranging networks of exchange of ideas in which the Ottomans actively participated. But our changed view also extends to the sixteenth century, in particular allowing us to better understand the extent to which the narratives created in the sixteenth century transformed the Ottomans' view of their own past and the monuments that remained from previous centuries.

ONE

IMPERIAL AND LOCAL HORIZONS
Looking East and West

IN HIS HISTORY OF MEHMED THE CONQUEROR, KRITOBOULOS OF IMBROS (D. AFTER 1467) sings the praises of the mosque of Ottoman grand vizier Mahmud Pasha Angelović (d. 1474), noting that it "was built with dressed stone and gleaming marbles, and with columns of outstanding beauty and size."[1] These words fit within the common practice of describing the luxurious materials and great financial expense that go into such buildings, a trope that readers encounter in a range of texts that mention architecture, beginning with medieval Islamic travel literature. Notions of wonder and astonishment are often expressed in such texts as well, in order to refer to the splendor of monuments whose means and materials of construction may not be apparent at first sight. This interest in process – or, rather, the fascination caused by the absence of knowledge about technical details – frequently appears as a cause of wonder (Arabic: *'ajab*), not just in Ottoman contexts but also more broadly in medieval and early modern Islamic sources. In poetry, artifice is considered a crucial device intended to evoke wonder and aesthetic pleasure in the recipient, a notion that medieval Arabic works on poetics examine in great detail.[2] In the fifteenth-century Ottoman context, where such poetry was well known, artifice as a device to evoke wonder appeared as well – including, I argue, in the creation of architecture. The Ottomans' close engagement with transregional intellectual and artistic networks has so far been examined overwhelmingly in the context of Istanbul and treated as a phenomenon rooted in Mehmed II's cosmopolitan patronage, but it had already begun in the first half of the century. Therefore, I begin this book with a chapter that reevaluates well-studied monuments in Istanbul, highlighting themes and connections that have not been previously explored. These themes and connections carry profound relevance for architecture in the first half of the fifteenth century, which I explore in subsequent chapters. I also turn to a late fifteenth-century structure in Skopje in order to explore how innovations were applied or created beyond the capital.

In this chapter, I investigate how the material politics of Ottoman architecture operated in Istanbul in the decades immediately following the Ottoman conquest of the city in 1453. Conscious choices about the materials to be used and the types of structures to be built were enacted, drawing on both earlier and contemporary ways of building within and beyond the Ottoman Empire, in a cultural universe that stretched from Venice to Central Asia. The monuments that Mehmed II (r. 1444–46 and 1451–81) and notables connected to his court built in this city offer a range of approaches to questions surrounding sensory perception, the meanings of different building materials, and the various layers of style and construction techniques.[3] These questions are combined with an investigation of the larger issue pursued throughout this book – namely, how Ottoman architects experimented over the course of the fifteenth century with a wide range of forms and references to past and present coming from cities near and far. If a clearly recognizable Ottoman dynastic architecture eventually emerged, as I argue in Chapter 5, beginning in the reign of Bayezid II (r. 1481–1512), this development was not predestined at the time the Mahmud Pasha mosque and its contemporaries were built. Instead, architecture was in flux, as malleable as the empire whose elites sponsored it.

The Ottoman conquest of Constantinople in 1453 and the resulting end of the Byzantine Empire marked a dramatic shift in the political and cultural setting of the eastern Mediterranean, with far-reaching effects on Europe and the eastern Islamic world from Anatolia to Central Asia. Yet this event was not a singular occurrence but rather part of a time of upheaval within the Islamic world as the Timurid dominance of the first half of the fifteenth century began to unravel. The transition from Qaraqoyunlu to Aqqoyunlu rule in Iran and parts of eastern Anatolia in the 1460s, the Ottoman conquest of most of Anatolia, and the conflict between Ottomans and Mamluks are only a few of the political developments that took place within a fragmented world where the post-Mongol political landscape of the late fourteenth and early fifteenth centuries slowly gave way. For the Ottomans, the conquest of Constantinople came in tandem with a larger project of establishing control over Anatolia – something that Mehmed I and Murad II had not fully achieved in the first half of the fifteenth century – which was reflected in major conquests such as that of Trebizond in 1461 and Karaman in 1468. These developments would peak during the reign of Bayezid II, when the Ottomans expanded into southeastern Anatolia, the rising Safavid enterprise was increasingly present, and a decisive campaign against the Mamluks began to brew, which would be completed by Selim I (r. 1512–20) in 1516–17. By the 1520s, a new age of early modern empires was in the making. And yet the architectures that those empires would build to reflect the identities they were consolidating are rooted in the cultural and artistic developments of the fifteenth century.

In the current chapter, I examine how after the Ottoman conquest of Constantinople, and in the course of the establishment of the imperial Ottoman capital, architecture was reshaped within parameters that balanced the Byzantine heritage of the city with the aesthetics of the greater post-Mongol Islamic world. While there was a larger imperial project at stake, as Çiğdem Kafescioğlu has examined in detail, there was also a continued engagement with Saljuq, Timurid, and Aqqoyunlu architecture that had begun earlier in the fifteenth century (more on this in Chapter 2). Focusing on the period after the Ottoman conquest of Constantinople allows me to highlight some of the major questions at stake throughout the book, such as the use of wide-ranging stylistic references, eventual shifts in patronage and workshop practices that would come around 1500, and the question of when Ottoman architecture became integrated into the process of the empire's political and cultural centralization. These questions are tied to the concept of material politics, in which the actions of makers and patrons intersect in the process of forming a distinct architectural style for the Ottoman Empire.

TIMURID STYLE IN OTTOMAN LANDS?

As we investigate Ottoman architecture in Istanbul, it is helpful to address the notion of an international Timurid style, a concept that has dominated much of the scholarly narrative about fifteenth-century Ottoman culture. Overarching questions that arise immediately are: How was an international Timurid mode adopted in the Ottoman context? Which motifs were adopted in art, and what was their relationship to the overall convergence between Ottoman and Timurid scholarly and courtly cultures in the second half of the fifteenth century?

Discussing a poem by Tacizāde Cafer Çelebi (d. 1515) that was composed in 1493–94 in praise of the mosque of Mehmed II in Istanbul, Gülru Necipoğlu notes that the text refers to the interplay of "'rūmī' (i.e., foliate arabesque of Rūm, known as islīmī or islāmī in the Timurid world) and ḫiṭāyī (chinoiserie motifs of Cathay) patterns."[4] Rūmī motifs are composed of vegetal scrolls, often stylized into spirals, with pointed palmette leaves attached to them (see Figures 62 and 63), while the ḫiṭāyī repertoire consists of flowers such as peonies and chrysanthemums (see Figures 143 and 144), both prevalent in Chinese art, along with cloud bands. Bernard O'Kane has examined these terms in Timurid sources, and noted that the motifs they refer to appear already in the art of Ilkhanid Iran in the fourteenth century.[5] Thus the scroll-and-leaf patterns that had frequently appeared in the Islamic architecture of medieval Anatolia under Saljuq and Ilkhanid rule since the twelfth century, both in stone carving and as part of tile mosaic, were integrated into a larger repertoire of Islamic ornament through the channels of the Mongol Empire that from the 1240s to the 1330s spanned from the Lands of Rūm to China. These types of ornaments were used in a wide range of materials, from tiles to stone to wood to metalwork, and would become firmly established within the repertoire of Islamic art – thus rūmī was not limited to Anatolia, and ḫiṭāyī spread across the Mongol Empire in the thirteenth century, persisting after this empire's breakdown in the fourteenth.

Overall, the combination of these types of motifs – the rūmī emerging from Saljuq Anatolia, and the ḫiṭāyī derived from Chinese art and transferred into Islamic art by way of Mongol patronage in Iran – is what came to be regarded as typical of the international Timurid style beginning in the late fourteenth century, with local variations stretching from Samarqand to Edirne. From that period onward, the arts of the Timurid courts of Samarqand and, later, Herat came to be regarded as the cutting edge of Islamic art in the eastern lands of Islam, from Anatolia to Central Asia. In part, the prestige associated with the art developed at these courts had to do with the world domination that Timur (r. ca. 1370–1405) had aspired to with the extensive campaigns he undertook within the Islamic world. (As we see in Chapter 2, the Ottomans were at the receiving end of one of these campaigns, resulting in upheaval in the first decade of the fifteenth century.) A further source of prestige was, however, the accomplishment of artists who were assembled in Timurid court ateliers. The members of the Timurid kitābkhānas (court workshops whose name means "house of the book" but that worked with a much wider range of materials than the name suggests) reached high levels of skill and had access to all necessary materials and tools for their work, sponsored by Timurid patrons who included rulers, scholar-administrators, and poets.[6] Many of these artists were prisoners taken during the campaigns of Timur and his successors, while others were workers who joined this artistic enterprise of their own free will. The high level of artistic skill in combination with extensive artistic patronage permitted the production of a wide range of sophisticated objects, including ceramics and metalwork, as well as works on paper. From artistic centers such as Samarqand, Herat, Tabriz, and Shiraz, these books were distributed widely and became important vehicles in the transfer of Timurid motifs across the eastern Islamic world. As we see in Chapter 2, contacts between the Timurid cultural sphere and the Ottomans developed in the early fifteenth century and had an impact on the material politics of Ottoman architecture at that time.

Within the Ottoman context, the taste for architectural decoration inspired by Timurid models persisted into the late fifteenth century, as reflected in the Çinili Köşk, built on the premises of Topkapı Palace in Istanbul in 1472 (Figure 1). As I discuss in what follows, craftsmen from Khurasan, possibly invited to the Ottoman capital to decorate this pavilion, were part of Mehmed II's project to advertise his goal of universal rule in the architecture of his palace and capital. Some fifty years later, a group of tile makers who were taken to Istanbul when Sultan Selim I (r. 1512–20) defeated the Safavids at the battle of Çaldıran in 1514 renewed Timurid stylistic impact in the Ottoman context.[7] This group

1. Lateral view of east and south façades, Çinili Köşk, 1472, Istanbul, Turkey. © Patricia Blessing 2014

"perpetuated a post-Timurid repertoire established earlier in the fifteenth century" in a time when Ottoman vocabularies were crystallizing – essentially, international Timurid style after Timurid rule had ended.[8]

With the emergence of so-called *saz*-leaf decoration in the 1540s (Figure 2), named after the dominant element of the design, an elongated leaf with serrated edges (though this appeared in combination with other vegetal motifs such as pomegranates, tulips, and carnations), the new preference for a specifically Ottoman style that turned away from the Timurid and post-Timurid motifs of the fifteenth century would become obvious. On tiles, these new motifs – initially developed on paper – were more easily executed in underglaze technique. Underglaze permitted more freedom in drawing than the black-line technique (explained in detail in Chapter 2) generally associated with Timurid and post-Timurid style, which required a design to be created with clear boundaries between colors. This lack of technical flexibility in black-line tile was most likely the reason for the technique's eventual disappearance from the Ottoman repertoire as expertise grew in creating complex underglaze designs requiring stencils and multiple colors (each with its own challenges in composition, application, and firing).[9]

As Necipoğlu notes, this turn from a largely Timurid to a fully developed Ottoman aesthetic in the sixteenth century was the result of a slow process of transformation rather than an abrupt shift. Earlier, cross-cultural interaction between Ottoman and Timurid courts was partly responsible for the pervasive Ottoman engagement with the culture of Timurid and post-Timurid Central Asia.[10] This is true for the movements of both objects and people, the latter including makers as well as scholars who moved between courts, establishing an international community of knowledge that connected the Ottoman, Mamluk, and Timurid realms (see Chapter 3).[11] This epistemological community included tile makers, painters, calligraphers, and architects who could move either along with their products or independently of them – or who could participate in this exchange without moving at all, simply by sending finished products and/or drawings to the place of destination. Although much of the architectural patronage in the fifteenth century is tied directly to the Ottoman sultan or to the inner circle of the Ottoman court, a clearly identifiable Ottoman style had not yet emerged, and building projects were sites of intense, focused experimentation.

2. *Saz*-leaf decoration on large tile, second quarter of the sixteenth century, now installed on the façade of the Sünnet Odası in Topkapı Palace, Istanbul, Turkey. © Patricia Blessing 2005

MOVING TOWARD CONSTANTINOPLE

The conquest of Constantinople and its subsequent transformation into the new Ottoman capital of Istanbul have been studied in detail, and some key elements of this process bear repeating here.[12] The demise of the Byzantine Empire in 1453 and the Ottoman takeover of its capital led to ideological changes for the Ottomans, who became more interested than ever in ideas of universal rule now that the long-standing goal of conquering Constantinople had been achieved. The Ottomans came into closer contact with the Adriatic world, already on their horizon through their Balkan possessions and through trade between Italy and the coastal regions of western Anatolia. With the presence of a Genoese colony in Pera, across the Golden Horn from the new Ottoman center, Renaissance Italy became an integral part of the Ottomans' cultural orbit, although Bayezid I had already fostered connections to Europe.[13] Venice was a major trade partner as well. As Julian Raby has shown, Mehmed II was an avid collector of art, interested in translations from Latin and Greek, and well read in classical literature. In the famous painting of the sultan by Gentile Bellini and in several bronze medals produced in Italy that depict him both in a detailed profile portrait and on horseback, Mehmed II is portrayed as an enlightened Renaissance patron and his empire is inserted into the world of early modern Europe.[14] In a study of patronage at Mehmed II's court, Gülru Necipoğlu argues that there was a conscious, complex set of negotiations in place that led to a "visual cosmopolitanism" attuned to both Renaissance Italian and Islamic art forms.[15]

This attitude of interest in other regions was not new to Mehmed II at the time of the conquest of Constantinople. When Mehmed II was again a prince following his brief, unsuccessful first reign as sultan in 1444–46, his marriage to the daughter of Sulayman b. Dulkadir, from the Dulkadir tribal confederation, had become a way to reach out to those powerful eastern Anatolian frontier lords. The Dulkadir tended to conclude alliances with the Mamluks, but Sulayman b. Dulkadir had been supporting the Ottomans in their protracted fight against the Karamanids, and the marriage consolidated these ties. As historians Neşri and ʿAşıkpaşazāde tell it, the unnamed wife of Hızır Ağa, governor of the province of Amasya, traveled from Amasya to Elbistan in order to select the bride, and again to fetch the young woman once Prince Mehmed's father, Sultan Murad II, had approved the choice.[16] The chosen princess, Sitti Shah Sultan, was taken to Edirne. The wedding took place in 1449 or 1450, before Murad II's death in February 1451 and the prince's second accession to the throne as Mehmed II.[17] A double frontispiece in a Byzantine manuscript held in the Biblioteca Marciana in Venice has long been identified as a double-portrait of the bride, seated in a litter on top of an elephant, and of her brother, Melik Arslan; the manuscript was thought to have been a wedding gift to the future sultan.[18] Recently, however, Merih Danalı has reexamined the manuscript and concluded that, first, it was never owned by the Ottoman court and, second, that the frontispiece is contemporaneous to the fourteenth-century manuscript produced in Thessaloniki. Thus Danalı lays to rest a long-standing art historical myth surrounding this double-portrait, which she identified as a representation of the philosopher and mathematician Hypatia of Alexandria (d. 415) and the geographer Ptolemy.[19]

Mehmed II also had close ties to his aristocratic Serbian stepmother, Mara Branković, who, along with Mahmud Pasha Angelović, was instrumental to connections to the Balkans.[20] Rum Mehmed Pasha (d. 1474?), another one of the notables of Mehmed II's court and grand vizier for a time after 1471, was married to a sister of Qilij Arslan, the Karamanid ruler of Alanya deposed by the Ottomans in 1471.[21] In the decades before, even Ottoman princesses had been married to Karamanids: a daughter of Murad I was married to ʿAla al-Din (r. 1357–98?) and commissioned a madrasa in Karaman in 1381–82.[22] In 1435, when Murad II campaigned against Taj al-Din Ibrahim (r. 1433–64), Murad's own sister was the Karamanid's wife, and she interceded on behalf of her husband, convincing her brother to cancel the deportation of the population of the city of Karaman (historical Larende) and to make peace.[23]

This interconnected courtly world thus abounded with family relationships between various dynasties in the Balkans and Anatolia; lengthy conflicts, movements of goods and artists, and complex modes of visual representation emerged. Necipoğlu points out that around 1400, Bayezid I was striving to include both Eastern and Western elements in his patronage, although these efforts were cut short by Timur's invasion of Anatolia in 1402 and the subsequent events.[24] As Raby notes, Mehmed II, who sponsored translation between Greek, Arabic, Persian, and Ottoman Turkish, showing interest in a wide range of works from Byzantine and Islamic cultures, also continued to engage in this kind of flexible and cosmopolitan patronage within the framework of his universal and imperial aspirations.[25]

The reshaping of Istanbul as an Ottoman capital was a central project in the fashioning of Mehmed II's royal identity. Nevertheless, as I argue, the focus on imperial projects in Istanbul provides only one, if central, side of the picture. Various conflicts notwithstanding, there was close cultural interaction between the Ottoman, Aqqoyunlu, Mamluk, and, beginning in the early sixteenth century, Safavid empires. Mehmed II's conquest of large parts of Anatolia and connections through scholarly and artistic networks to the Aqqoyunlu and Timurid realms were central to the political history of the time, together with the question of the Ottomans' engagement with the Byzantine imperial heritage. Influence from the eastern parts of the expanding empire reached Istanbul, where on several monuments there appears tile decoration that can be tied in various ways to the so-called international Timurid style. More than a simple adoption of style as a sign of triumph, these monuments may be seen as part of an ongoing conversation with an Eastern, post-Mongol world.

The varied and diverse character of Ottoman architecture had deep roots in earlier building campaigns, particularly in Bursa but also in Edirne, as we see in Chapters 2, 3, and 4, and so this transformation cannot solely be attributed to the material politics of Mehmed II's reign. These roots should be kept in mind as I move on to examine the architecture built in Istanbul. In this chapter, first I discuss the so-called Çinili Köşk, built in 1472 within the gardens of Topkapı Palace, and its combination of Persianate and Byzantine modes of construction. Then I analyze the mausoleum of Mahmud Pasha, built sometime before his execution in 1474, and investigate where it stands aesthetically between Persianate and Anatolian modes of construction. These two case studies will lead to a new understanding not only of these specific buildings but also of the aesthetic principles at hand as architecture engaged with Byzantine, Ottoman, and pre-Ottoman Islamic pasts, as well as Iranian and Central Asian presents, ideas that stemmed from the early fifteenth century.

THE ÇINILI KÖŞK: BETWEEN CONSTANTINOPLE AND KHURASAN

The Çinili Köşk (Tiled Pavilion), built in 1472 on the premises of Topkapı Palace, is a central example of the negotiation between various architectural modes, some current at the time and others drawn from the past of newly conquered lands. The Çinili Köşk (Figure 3; see Figure 1) today stands separated from Topkapı Palace by the massive complex of the Istanbul Archaeological Museum, built in the late nineteenth century. The original garden setting no longer exists.

The fact that the building was originally part of the palace gardens, though, is important to consider, as such man-made landscapes were crucial parts of aesthetic experience within Islamic architecture. As D. Fairchild Ruggles notes in her discussion of gardens in Islamic al-Andalus, the sounds of water and wind, the singing of birds, and the smells of vegetation and flowers would have thoroughly transformed perception of a given site.[26] Such was the case as well for the Çinili Köşk, known in Ottoman sources as *sırça sarāyı*: it was located in the palace's outer gardens, juxtaposed with two other pavilions built in Ottoman and Byzantine styles, as Tursun Beğ notes, in order to present within close proximity the stylistic variations available in the Ottoman realm.[27] In Tursun Beğ's text, the Çinili Köşk is specifically referred to as built "in the mode of the Persian kings."[28] In a study of water features within Topkapı

3. Frontal view from the steps of the Istanbul Archaeological Museum, Çinili Köşk, 1472, Istanbul, Turkey.
© Patricia Blessing 2015

Palace, Necipoğlu notes the extent to which these outer gardens were wooded and studded with water features, and argues based on several sources that the larger garden landscape around the Çinili Köşk contained wide-ranging references to the extent of Mehmed II's realm.[29] Further, water features included in this landscape also evoked paradisiacal motifs. In a late sixteenth-century painting in the *Hünernāme* of Seyyid Loqman, the Çinili Köşk and its neighbor, the "Ottoman Pavilion," are shown standing in front of a reflecting pool.[30] As Necipoğlu notes, the pool and "paradise garden" were praised in a fifteenth-century eulogistic poem.[31] Such elements are also evoked in the building's inscriptions, as we see later in this chapter, and the notion of reflections in water is relevant with regard to the extensive use of marble and tile on the structure, particularly given the strong water symbolism that marble carries in Roman and Byzantine contexts. The juxtaposition of this reflecting pool in the original garden setting with the marble facing used on the building would have created a doubling of meaning: actual water to reflect the symbolic water of the marble.[32] (I discuss this question further in Chapter 4.)

As Necipoğlu has argued, the Çinili Köşk may have specifically been commissioned in commemoration of the Ottomans' triumph over the Karamanids in 1468.[33] It features elements that evoked the architecture of the central Anatolian city of Karaman in the eyes of Giovanni Maria Angiolello (1451–ca. 1525) who spent time there in 1471–74, while he was living as an enslaved person at the Ottoman court.[34] Scholarship on the monument so far has focused on its connections to Timurid, Karamanid, and Aqqoyunlu architecture under the larger umbrella of the international Timurid style, which in the Ottoman context is thought to have been first adopted in the early fifteenth century under the patronage of Mehmed I in Bursa. (This context is discussed in Chapter 2.) I argue, however, that the Çinili Köşk's aesthetics cannot be entirely identified as either Persianate or Karamanid.

The Ottoman conquest of Karaman in 1468 to which the building is connected was the culmination of an extended conflict between the two dynasties that had begun in the early days of Ottoman emergence in the late thirteenth and early fourteenth centuries. Starting in the late thirteenth century, the Karamanids had made the city of Karaman their center; rivalry between them and the Ottomans began early on and was often entangled with the complex relationship between Ottomans and Mamluks. The latter had first tried to expand into Anatolia as part of their rivalry with the Ilkhanids in the second half of the thirteenth century, marked by Mamluk sultan Baybars I's incursion into southeastern and central Anatolia in 1277, an event that would take center stage in later Ottoman history writing because it boosted Karamanid power.[35] As noted before, in the late fourteenth century the Ottomans and Karamanids attempted to appease relations using dynastic marriage between a daughter of the Ottoman sultan Murad I and ʿAla al-Din I, the ruler of Karaman.[36] This is one of the earliest documented Ottoman dynastic marriages, a practice that would end in the early sixteenth century.[37] The attempt at reconciliation was hardly successful in the long term, and the Ottomans' struggle with the Karamanids would continue until the mid-fifteenth century.

After Timur defeated Bayezid I in 1402 and restored many of the *beyliks* that Bayezid had subdued, the Karamanids too reemerged as powerful lords in central Anatolia.[38] The Ottoman attack on the Karamanid realm in 1468 was triggered by the revolt of Pir Ahmed, who had ruled parts of the Karamanid lands under Ottoman suzerainty since 1466, the result of a war between brothers after his father, Taj al-Din Ibrahim, had died at the end of a long reign.[39] Yet the revolt did not come out of the blue; Sara Nur Yıldız argues that it was triggered by the Ottomans' increasing encroachment on the Karamanid hinterlands in previous years, and that after being touched off in this way, the rebellion may have served Mehmed II as an excuse to finally lead his armies toward Konya and Karaman.[40] In the city of Karaman, with the exception of military construction, the conquest was not marked with Ottoman construction projects and rebuilding – as happened in Constantinople – but rather with the destruction of Karamanid palaces. As the historian Şikari reports, these buildings were razed, a new citadel was built in their place, and inhabitants were forced to move to Istanbul to repopulate that city for the Ottomans' use.[41]

Between Persianate and Byzantine Architecture

The entrance façade of the Çinili Köşk features a tall marble porch that extends over two levels (see Figure 3). On the lower level, a central stone panel with a grilled window in the middle hides the stairs leading up to the entrance, which is located in a recess on the upper level. To the left and right of this central panel, five arches with the flattened profile of what is sometimes referred to as a Bursa arch (based on its frequent use in the early fifteenth-century architecture of that city) are supported by square pillars. On the upper level, a larger central arch is flanked by six narrower ones on each side. Fourteen octagonal columns with geometric capitals and square impost blocks support the roofline above.

One risk of analyzing the Çinili Köşk based on the presence of this monumental porch is the fact that it is not original to the building; in fact, a fire in 1737 destroyed what was likely a wooden porch and the current stone porch replaced it, although the exact date of the addition is unknown.[42] Similar wooden porches can still be seen in Iran and Central Asia – for instance, on the citadel of Bukhara – although extant examples date to the seventeenth and eighteenth centuries (Figure 4). In merely technical terms, a possible comparison also lies in the wood-column and wood-ceiling mosques of late thirteenth- and early fourteenth-century Anatolia, such as the Aslanhane Mosque in Ankara or the Eşrefoğlu Mosque in Beyşehir, although there is no continuity between these monuments and the Çinili Köşk.[43] Earlier pavilions from the Saljuq period survive only in fragments: the kiosk of Qilij Arslan II (r. 1156–92) in Konya, connected to the citadel walls, which collapsed in the early twentieth century, was built of brick with wooden beams and decorated with stucco and *minā'ī* tiles.[44] Larger Saljuq garden landscapes within central and eastern Anatolia extended to hunting preserves such as those in the region of Alanya in which small structures, generally built of stone, have survived as traces in the archaeological record.[45] As such, traces of gardens and pavilions predating the Çinili Köşk are rare.

The architecture of the Çinili Köşk as such is that of a garden pavilion of the type that was frequent across the eastern Islamic world, although few have been preserved that predate the seventeenth century; two central examples are the Chehel Sotun (1647; current porch 1708) and Hesht Behesht (1669–70) in Safavid Isfahan.[46] Overall, as Necipoğlu has noted, comparisons to garden pavilions in central Anatolia, Iran, and Central Asia are hampered by the fact that no fifteenth-century examples from those places have survived; still, her detailed analysis of the façade elevations and plan of the Çinili Köşk clearly

4. Reception hall, 1605–06, citadel, Bukhara, Uzbekistan. © Patricia Blessing 2007

5. Upper section of entrance *īwān* with tile mosaic decoration including foundation inscription, Çinili Köşk, 1472, Istanbul, Turkey. © Patricia Blessing 2015

supports such a comparison.[47] Once the visitor arrives on the upper level of the Çinili Köşk, in front of the entrance, however, the Persianate view is immediately, if not entirely, upset. It is true that large parts of the façade are decorated with tile mosaic and a long foundation inscription runs across the deep recess around the entrance (Figure 5). Yet the lower zone of the upper entrance level is composed of a dado of white-and-grey book-matched marble, and the door frame – probably spolia from a Byzantine building – is carved from two slightly different shades of white marble with purple veins (Figures 6 and 7). These reused architectural elements add another layer of visual cues and historical references.

Looking at the marble facing of the dado around the entrance, we can see that the slabs are cut and arranged so that the veins in the stone match. Examples of such book-matched marble cladding are prominent in the Byzantine monuments of Istanbul, including the nearby sixth-century church of Hagia Sophia, which was converted into a mosque immediately following Mehmed II's conquest of the city. The use of spolia for the door frame also introduces the past of the new Ottoman capital into the Çinili Köşk, breaking up an aesthetic that at first sight appears entirely Persianate. In fact, when the monument is seen from afar, this detail of the decoration remains obscured by the porch and does not emerge into view. It is only as one draws closer and finally enters the building that this other element, related to Istanbul's Byzantine (hence Roman imperial) past and Mehmed II's chosen role as *qayṣer-i rūm*, appears.[48] Thus the visual cosmopolitanism that Necipoğlu and Raby attribute to Mehmed II and his court is integrated into this building, which is constructed – figuratively and literally – as a microcosm of the meanings built into the garden's larger landscape. This observation points to the need to reassess the dynamics of past and present artistic forms and of engagements with Ottoman and non-Ottoman *lieux de mémoire* in this building.[49] Yet with regard to the tile mosaic (Figure 8) on the façade, the question remains whether it is a reference to Iran or Central Asia, fifteenth-century Karaman or thirteenth-century Konya, or a combination of all of these. This question is examined after a discussion of the cosmological concepts and notions of artifice involved in the Çinili Köşk's inscriptions, made of tile mosaic.

6. Partial view of the porch interior to the right of doorway, Çinili Köşk, 1472, Istanbul, Turkey. © Patricia Blessing 2014

7. Marble revetment to the right of doorway, Çinili Köşk, 1472, Istanbul, Turkey.
© Patricia Blessing 2014

Epigraphic Artifice and Poetic Cosmology

The inscription, composed in Persian, above the entrance to the Çinili Köşk spans all three sides of the portal recess. It is a particularly fine example of tile mosaic, and nothing similar has been preserved in Istanbul (or anywhere else in the fifteenth-century Ottoman world). The calligraphy is complex in that two texts overlap: the main inscription (Figures 9 and 10), which contains the date of construction, is the larger text set in white that runs in two lines. Another inscription in verse, further praising the beauty of the monument, is set in smaller script overlapping the top of the main inscription, with some words in yellow and others in white. Both inscriptions contain textual references that are crucial to an understanding of the cosmological aspects of the monument; more than this, they also provide insights into ways in which materiality operated in the fifteenth-century Ottoman context. Artifice was involved at multiple levels: in making the tiles needed for the tile mosaic, in putting together the tile mosaic itself, and in the poetic work of composing the text itself before it was inscribed on the building. Translated here into English, the text of the larger inscription reads:

> This pavilion, which is as lofty as the heavens, was so built that its great height would stretch up to Gemini. Its most worthless part would adorn the stars of Ursa Minor (*firq ferqdān*) and the highest sky of Saturn (*saqf-i keyvān*). Its emerald dome (*qubba-i zumurrudīn*) sparkles like the golden sky (*āsumān-i zerrīn*) and is adorned with inscription of stars (*kitābe-yi kewākeb*). Its courtyard floor of turquoise with multicolored flowers and designs (*nuqūsh*) of *būqalamūn* is a place of nature's beauty.[50] May it be everlasting – it was made to display the glory of the *khāqān*'s state and the good fortune of divine providence's assistance. By God's order – the building reflects the patron's importance[51] – it reached the honor of completion in the last days of the month of Rabīʿ ʾl-Ākhar in the time of the year eight hundred and seventy-seven.[52]

By mentioning the dome and the courtyard of the building, the larger inscription invites the reader to enter and admire the interior as well, with its splendid floor (which is either no longer extant or the subject of poetic hyperbole) and vault. In this inscription, as Necipoğlu has noted, the building is exalted

8. Detail of tile mosaic on entrance arch of Çinili Köşk, 1472, Istanbul, Turkey. © Patricia Blessing 2016

9. Detail of portal inscription, Çinili Köşk, 1472, Istanbul, Turkey. © Patricia Blessing 2014

10. Detail of portal inscription, Çinili Köşk, 1472, Istanbul, Turkey.
© Patricia Blessing 2014

with allusions to cosmic motifs: the emerald dome (*qubbat-i zumurrudīn*) and the heavenly mansion (*qaṣr-i falak*).[53] These motifs correspond to ones used in panegyric and ekphrastic poetry composed by Ottoman authors; such poems describe the Çinili Köşk using comparisons to the firmament and the sun and moon, and include allusions to activities such as feasts and receptions taking place there.[54] The motifs used certainly corresponded to ideas widely available among the poets and scholars of the Ottoman courts, and ones that were in line with the image of universal rule that was projected for Mehmed II. Open questions are who composed the inscription, who approved it for use on this royal building, and who read it. Would Mehmed II have been involved in the selection of these texts? Most likely so, considering that he was a keen patron, interested in art and architecture as much as literature.

The cosmological framework proposed in the inscription can be tied into notions of kingship such as the title *ṣāḥib-qirān* (lord of the auspicious conjunction, adapted from the Timurids), as well as the

Ottomans' interest in *'ilm al-nujūm* (astrology and astronomy combined), documented since the early fifteenth century.[55] The image of the emerald dome (*qubba-i zumurrudīn*) is not used to describe the building's actual dome but rather to metaphorically evoke *al-qubbat al-khaḍrā'* (lit. "the green dome") – the term denoting the heavens in the Islamic tradition, as Jonathan Bloom notes.[56] By the fifteenth century, the concept had become standard poetic imagery in both Arabic and Persian.[57]

In addition, the text contains references that are meaningful in the context of experiencing spaces in a multisensory way, addressing not only vision but also sound and touch. Specifically, the reference to designs of *būqalamūn* (*nuqūsh-i būqalamūn*) is relevant in this regard, since this polyvalent term can refer to a range of materials (both natural and man-made) that specifically appeal to notions of wonder (*'ajab*) and are often marked by shimmering color.[58] As Matthew Saba has shown in his insightful study of ninth-century Abbasid luster ceramics from the caliphal palace city of Samarra in Iraq, the term *būqalamūn* could refer to a range of objects with changing color effects, from peacock feathers to textiles.[59] In the inscription of the Çinili Köşk, the term is specifically used to describe the "courtyard floor"; currently, the floor inside the building is paved evenly with large rectangles of grey marble, a modern addition. What did the original floor look like? Was it a floor like the one preserved in the seventeenth-century Shaykh Lotfollah Mosque in Isfahan, made of rectangular turquoise tiles? Could the inscription refer to floor coverings? Carpets would certainly have been present in a palatial building like the Çinili Köşk, and they might have had the flower designs and changing colors to which the inscription refers. In the inscription, the floor is specifically connected to nature's beauty, an emphasis not on man-made aspects of the building but rather on allusions to natural things that elicit wonder and admiration. The cosmological motifs in the first part of the inscription tie into this kind of comparison as well: the beauty of the structure and its admirable features are compared to natural phenomena such as the firmament, the constellations, and the golden sky – a phrase that perhaps refers to dawn, which is invoked in the second inscription. Ultimately, by comparing the building's beauty to natural phenomena, the Çinili Köşk is equated with divine creation and, by extension, its patron is approached to God. (Although as we shall see, the text of the smaller inscription includes a reference to the ephemerality of worldly matters and humans.)

The smaller inscription in verse, which is woven into the larger one at the top edge of the inscription band, contains two separate *rubā'iyyāt* (a short, formulaic poem in Persian).[60] It contains further comparisons between the building and natural beauty within a cosmological framework:

> Oh, the portico holds abiding luxury
> [and] bears reference, as venerable as [it is] sacred.
> From the pleasantness of your building's air
> the bones are almost revived after having disintegrated[61]

> From the generosity of its portico: the qibla of the lords of kingship
> and from the felicity of its court: the site of the qibla for the people of religion
> The rising of the sun, [in] the east the desired dawn rises
> The beloved child of the sky and adornment on earth[62]

In this second inscription, the emphasis shifts slightly: a cosmological theme appears in the last verse, where the sun, dawn, and sky are evoked. The preceding verses praise the building's luxury as a setting for the court, although a reminder of the transitory nature of worldly and imperial glory appears in the use of the term *ramīm* (decayed), referring to a Qur'anic passage.[63] The verse obliquely evokes the famous lines that, according to Tursun Beğ, Mehmed II uttered when seeing the ruined nature of some of Constantinople's monuments: "The spider is holding the curtains in the palace of Khusraw. The owl is holding watch on the citadel of *Afrasiyab*."[64] Thus the inscription also contains a small hint at the fact that the world passes and that even the (here unnamed) royal patron's life is transitory. A related sentiment is expressed two centuries earlier in the Sırçalı Madrasa (1243) in Konya, where a medallion in the tile work, paired with another one containing the signature of Muhammad al-Tusi, praises the work and notes that the building will survive its maker, but that it too is ephemeral.[65]

As Paul Losensky notes, complex relationships can emerge between poetry and architecture in the sense that "verbal texts contribute an audible voice to mute buildings, while architectonic imagery lends material substantiality to the airy stuff of poetry."[66] Here the skillful material artifice of the two intertwined inscriptions in tile mosaic, which are easily legible despite the complex calligraphy translated into tile, mirrors the poetic artifice of the inscriptions.

The Tile Decoration of the Çinili Köşk

In addition to the double inscription above the entrance, the *īwān* frame around the entrance of the building is adorned with more tile mosaic: two interlocking floral scrolls that intersect with square kufic script alternately reading "*allāh*" and "*akbar*" (see Figure 8). These motifs – "part abstract, part mimetic"[67] – connect the design to Timurid tile work of the late fourteenth century onward. Altogether, the façade is the most intricate example of tile mosaic that has survived in Ottoman architecture. The tile mosaic also differs from earlier examples that survive in central Anatolia, especially Konya and Sivas, in that it includes such Timurid-style motifs, as well as tiles in yellow, expanding the earlier color palette.

It is important to note, as David J. Roxburgh emphasizes, that full-size paper models were needed for complex designs in tile mosaic. These models would be used to cut the tiles, assemble them, and prepare finished panels that could be installed on a monument.[68] In the case of the Çinili Köşk, such models, employed in assembly on the ground, would have been needed for the design just described on the frame around the *īwān*, and certainly for the two intertwined inscriptions above the doorway. The geometric patterns on the surfaces above and below the inscription, made out of square and rectangular tiles rather than cutouts, might have been assembled directly on the monument.

Certainly the Çinili Köşk's façade evokes the kinds of architectural decoration created in Timurid Samarqand beginning in the 1380s, when tile mosaic in flat panels began to dominate, and the earlier use of carved tiles, along with features such as non-load-bearing columns made of tiles, began to give way to sleek surfaces produced in mosaic.[69] The growth of the Timurid *kitabkhāna*, with its capacity to produce designs for use in a range of media, also fostered the use of tile mosaic in architecture and the creation of calligraphic models that could be either scaled up for architectural use or kept at a small scale in manuscripts and albums.[70] In technical terms, tile mosaic had the advantage that accidents of glazing and firing did not affect the finished product.[71] Financial loss was not so great if the monochrome pieces of tile from which the mosaic shapes would be cut were marred by misfiring. If this happened to a painted tile with several colors and a complex design, however, that was a different story, especially when colored glazes ran due to unsuitable firing temperatures. In that case, a decision needed to be made as to whether making a new tile should be attempted (again with the risk of misfiring) or whether a tile could be used anyway; a tile might still be usable, for instance, if the problem at hand was simply a color that had run because of inadequate firing temperature. In an Ottoman context, misfired underglaze-painted blue-and-white tiles can, for instance, be seen on the cenotaph of Sitti Hatun (ca. 1450), in the mausoleum of Mehmed I in Bursa; these misfired tiles might have been originally intended for the Muradiye Mosque (1435–36) in Edirne.[72]

The interior decoration of the Çinili Köşk has been only partially preserved, with blue and turquoise tiles, some with overlaid gold decoration (restored in places; Figures 11 and 12). Unlike the tile mosaic of the façade, which clearly belongs to an Iranian or Central Asian context, such monochrome tiles, both with and without gold overlay, can be found in earlier Ottoman buildings, including ones in Bursa (see Figure 48), as well as Saljuq monuments of the thirteenth century, such as the Karatay Madrasa in Konya (see Figure 69). To make matters more complex, representations of similar tiles also appear in Timurid

11. Interior view of room with blue and turquoise tiles with restored gold decoration, Çinili Köşk, 1472, Istanbul, Turkey. © Patricia Blessing 2018

12. Interior, detail of blue and turquoise tiles with unrestored gold decoration, Çinili Köşk, 1472, Istanbul, Turkey. © Patricia Blessing 2018

paintings – for instance, a depiction of "Bahram Gur and the Indian Princess in the Dark Palace," copied in Herat in the 1430s.[73] This is just one of many examples in the fifteenth-century Ottoman context where references can be polyvalent: thus the tiles with gold overlay can be a reference to three periods: the Saljuq past of Anatolia, a period that is evoked in the early fifteenth century to overcome the trauma of Timur's invasion; earlier Ottoman architecture in Bursa, the center of dynastic memory; and contemporary architectures in central Anatolia, Iran, and Central Asia. Simply based on stylistic analysis, it is impossible to decide which of these references prevailed in the mind of fifteenth-century Ottoman builders and patrons. Considering the complex material politics of the time, it is also possible that the multiple intersecting references were intended and consciously applied.

Although little has been preserved in Karaman itself, one example of Karamanid tile work, the mihrab of İbrahim Bey İmaret (1432), was removed from its original location and transferred to the Istanbul Archaeological Museum in the early twentieth century. While black-line tile covers most of its surface (this technique is discussed in the next chapter), it is noteworthy here that the muqarnas niche is filled with monochrome dark purple tiles. Such tiles, along with rare fourteenth- and fifteenth-century examples of tile mosaic in Konya, were the tail end of the kinds of tile work produced in central Anatolia under Saljuq and Ilkhanid rule, although the later programs are much less complex in their motifs and scale than the thirteenth-century ones.[74] In its design and style, the tile mosaic of Çinili Köşk is much closer to late fourteenth- and fifteenth-century examples in Iran and Central Asia than to thirteenth-century ones within Anatolia, pointing to a case of transregional exchange. With these issues in mind, the question of why Mehmed II and his architects chose exterior tile work that is much closer in style to Timurid examples to represent Karaman looms large. Was this a matter of opportunity, of a group of tile workers familiar with the techniques and motifs used in eastern Iran already being present in Istanbul? Was it a conscious choice inspired by the beauty of this kind of work and perhaps by an impulse to compete with the Aqqoyunlu at a moment when the conflict with Uzun Hasan was not yet settled?

A further challenge in expanding the discussion of possible references to the contemporaneous context of Anatolia beyond the realms of Karaman is the state of architectural evidence. In Chapter 3, I discuss the relationship between the architecture of the western Anatolian *beyliks* from the late fourteenth century onward and Ottoman building projects. I argue that close connections are present between these structures and Ottoman patronage in Iznik and Bursa, but that these happen at the level of stonework, rather than tile. (And indeed tile was rarely used in the western Anatolian *beyliks*). For central and eastern Anatolia, evidence is more limited. Thus nothing remains of the patronage of the powerful Qadi Burhaneddin Ahmad, who ruled from his center of Sivas from 1380 until the Ottomans defeated him in 1398.[75] The previous ruler of the region, Eretna (r. 1336–52), and his successors left behind buildings such as the Güdük Minare (1347–48), a monumental funerary structure built of brick with tile insets (a technique known as *bannā'ī*).[76] This technique had been used in Sivas since the early thirteenth century – for instance, on the minaret of the Great Mosque (1212–13), in the Şifaiye Madrasa (1216–17), and in the Çifte Minareli Madrasa and the Gök Madrasa (both 1270–71).[77] Another Eretnid monument, the so-called Köşk Madrasa (1339), originally located on the outskirts of Kayseri but now absorbed by the expanding city, is built of ashlar masonry like most thirteenth- and fourteenth-century buildings in the region.[78] While the entrance to the complex has drop-shaped stones forming its doorway and a frieze above, the muqarnas base of the mausoleum at its center is a direct reference to the Mahperi Hatun Mausoleum (ca. 1237–38) in the center of Kayseri.[79] Here too we are faced with the continuation of a local architectural idiom created in the twelfth and thirteenth centuries far into the post-Mongol period and up until the Ottoman conquest of the city in 1474. Tile work is not used in any of these buildings. For that, one has to look to the southeast, to the Zeynel Bey Türbe in Hasankeyf, built for a son of Uzun Hasan who fell at the battle of Otlukbeli between Ottomans and Aqqoyunlu in 1473. The building built of brick and tile survives today, but was moved to a new site in May 2017 to save it from the waters of the Ilısu Dam that have swallowed historic Hasankeyf.[80] *Bannā'ī* tile work, rather than tile mosaic, adorns this building.

Overall, tile mosaic is highly unusual both within Ottoman architecture and in fifteenth-century Anatolia more broadly. In Karaman, limited evidence from the late fourteenth century survived in the Hatuniye Madrasa (1381–82) until at least the 1960s.[81] The technique of tile mosaic was most widespread in the region of Konya in the mid-thirteenth century. Examples include the Sırçalı Madrasa, built in 1243

(Figure 13), and the Karatay Madrasa (Figure 14), built in 1251–52.[82] Beyond Konya, the Gök Madrasa in Tokat, an undated building that can be placed in the 1270 to 1280s, had extensive tile mosaic decoration in its courtyard, now fragmentary but better preserved on the *qibla īwān* (Figure 15).[83] In all of these examples, where breakage of tiles has occurred over the centuries, it is clear that the tiles were installed on top of the underlying walls (built of brick or stone, depending on the building) as premade mosaic panels, in the same manner as on the Çinili Köşk. Thus high levels of skill in producing tile mosaic had been achieved in Konya, but also in rarer examples in Tokat and Sivas. If the technique was no longer used on a large scale after the 1280s, this was due to the long-term effects on patronage of the Mongol conquest of Anatolia in 1243. Expensive and time-consuming techniques such as tile mosaic introduced at the height of Saljuq power in the 1220s and 1230s were still used in the first decades after the Mongol conquest, as notables who now filled in the role of intermediary between the largely powerless Saljuq sultans and the Mongol overlords became sufficiently wealthy to commission large complexes for themselves – including examples such as the Karatay Madrasa and the Sırçalı Madrasa, along with many more buildings constructed in central and eastern Anatolia between 1243 and circa 1280.[84] With the closer administrative integration of Anatolia into the Ilkhanid empire after 1277, however, patronage became increasingly local and small-scale, while larger construction projects were more likely to be completed in the Ilkhanid centers in Iran, especially Tabriz and Sultaniye.[85] In Ottoman architecture, large-scale tile programs first appear in Mehmed I's mosque-*zāviye* complex in Bursa, begun in 1419, and in the work connected to the Masters of Tabriz, a group of tile makers thought to have come from Tabriz in the existing scholarly literature. The work on which these makers' collective name appears – that is, the mihrab in Mehmed I's mosque-*zāviye* – refers to then-current fashions in tile decoration in Iran and parts of Central Asia.[86] Notably, though, tile mosaic was rarely used in the monuments connected to the Masters of Tabriz as Chapter 2 shows.

13. View of main *īwān* with tile mosaic, Sırçalı Madrasa, 1243, Konya, Turkey. © Richard P. McClary 2020

14. Interior view Karatay Madrasa, 1251–52, Konya, Turkey. © Richard P. McClary 2013

15. Detail of tile mosaic on the *qibla īwān*, Gök Madrasa, ca. 1270–90, Tokat, Turkey. © Patricia Blessing 2008

Ottoman architecture in the fifteenth century showed a conscious and sophisticated engagement with the past and present architectures of both its own realm and neighboring regions under Muslim rule. At the Çinili Köşk, the presence of complex references to a range of stylistic realms – Byzantine and Timurid first and foremost, but perhaps also Karamanid – is handled in two main ways. First, these stylistic references are embodied in the building's plan, elevation, and exterior decoration, where they seamlessly combine into a new whole, expressing the skill of Ottoman building workers in creating artifice and wonder as backdrops for the court's activities. Second, the poetry applied to the building's façade deploys some of the same ideas of rulership and cosmology as those expressed in Timurid contexts, but also notions of natural beauty embodied in the artifice of architecture. Originally, the garden landscape would have enhanced these effects with elements such as plants and reflections in pools. Thus architecture and poetry merge together in the creation of an aesthetic experience and its presentation to the court.

We can observe this close relationship between building and text in other monuments: in later chapters, I show how such dynamics worked in the first half of the fifteenth century, as the Ottomans reconsolidated their realm and later relaunched the expansion into Anatolia that Bayezid I had started. At the present moment, what matters is the fact that those responsible for Ottoman buildings (architects, tile makers, stone carvers, and also poets and calligraphers) in the fifteenth century engaged with complex references to multiple cultures and time periods. It is also important to point out that this sort of engagement began before Mehmed II's conquest of Constantinople in 1453, as Necipoğlu has argued.[87] Thus the Çinili Köşk with its multiple references also connects to that Ottoman past, and its architects did not reinvent the wheel in the name of commemorating Mehmed II's conquest of Karaman, although the renewed references to Byzantine architecture were an additional element peculiar to Istanbul's shaping as the Ottoman capital. Within the palace context, as Kafescioğlu argues, the Çinili Köşk and its no-longer-extant companion pavilions were part of a world where forms could be mixed freely within that consciously cosmopolitan aesthetic framework.[88]

The Çinili Köşk is the only example of tile mosaic that was produced in Istanbul in this period. A petition in the Topkapı Palace Archive suggests that tile cutters from Khurasan (*kāshī-tarāshān-e Khurasān*, as they refer to themselves) worked in Istanbul in the mid-fifteenth century and, as they fell on hard times, begged the sultan for more work. While the Çinili Köşk is not mentioned in the petition, Faik Kırımlı and Necipoğlu have both argued that it was after completing this very project that the tile cutters found themselves out of work.[89] Kırımlı even goes so far as to suggest that the same group also created the tile decoration of the Mahmud Pasha Mausoleum. However, we shall see that, from a technical standpoint, the tile decoration on that monument was made in a different and rarely used technique, suggesting that another workshop might have been responsible and that knowledge of the complexities of Timurid-style tile mosaic may not have been necessary. Expertise in creating complex geometrical patterns in stone, however, was a must.

ISTANBUL BEYOND THE ÇINILI KÖŞK

The Çinili Köşk was part of the larger project of turning Constantinople into an Ottoman city. In her analysis of the addition of mosque complexes under the patronage of Mehmed II's grand viziers, Kafescioğlu argued that these new construction projects operated as a way to structurally mark Istanbul with Ottoman presence and as a Muslim-ruled city.[90] In the architecture of these and other monuments of the time, which show close negotiation between Byzantine, earlier Ottoman, Anatolian, and Timurid models, one sees the same juxtaposition of stylistic modes that we just observed in the Çinili Köşk, and it is characteristic of Mehmed II's patronage. Thus the Rum Mehmed Pasha Mosque, built c. 1472 and towering on a hill on the Asian side of Istanbul, has the silhouette of a Byzantine church, with brick dominating its exterior (Figure 16). In the interior of the mosque, however, the surviving fragments of decoration (Figure 17) show that the dome was painted in scrolls and leaves that point to a use of Eastern motifs, the kinds of *rūmī* patterns associated with Saljuq architecture and its successors.[91]

In terms of fifteenth-century architectural decoration and the many stylistic references that are combined, it is worth considering Mehmed II's mosque in Istanbul, built in 1463–70. There, two tile

16. Üsküdar shoreline with Rum Mehmed Pasha Mosque, ca. 1472, Istanbul, Turkey. © Patricia Blessing 2015

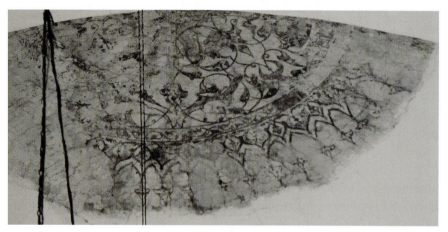

17. Detail of painted designs inside the dome, before restoration, Rum Mehmed Pasha Mosque, ca. 1472, Istanbul, Turkey. © Patricia Blessing 2014

lunettes survived the collapse of the mosque in an earthquake in 1766, after which much of the building was rebuilt.[92] These two panels are located over the windows in the bays of the courtyard portico where it joins the façade of the prayer hall (Figure 18). In an attempt to place these panels in context, Sandra Aube has suggested that the same workshop made both these tile panels and the ones produced for the Üç Şerefeli Mosque (1438–47) in Edirne, commissioned by Murad II, but this point implies the continuity of a single, unproven workshop tradition.[93] In fact, notable differences in types of decoration between the two panels on Mehmed II's mosque are revealed upon close observation, even though the overall effect when viewed from afar is similar.

In the panel located on the east side of the courtyard (Figure 19), the frame is divided into fields by interlinked white bands. The larger fields are filled with peonies from the *khiṭāyī* repertoire combined with leaves akin to the *saz* leaf that would appear in later decoration, although perhaps not quite as pointed.[94] In the central lunette, two overlapping inscriptions are placed on a *rūmī* scroll background; the larger, cursive text reads: "[and] the preservation of them both [Heaven and Earth] tires Him not, and He is the Most High, the Great" ("*lā yāʾduhu*

18. View along arcade on south side of courtyard, toward location of underglaze tile panel on west side of courtyard, Mosque of Mehmed II, 1463–70, Istanbul, Turkey. © Patricia Blessing 2014

19. Underglaze painted tile panel, east side of courtyard, Mosque of Mehmed II, 1463–70, Istanbul, Turkey. © Patricia Blessing 2016

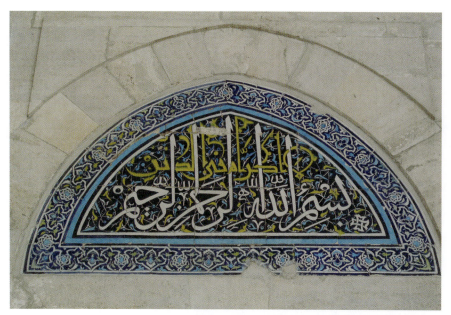

20. Underglaze painted tile panel, west side of courtyard, Mosque of Mehmed II, 1463–70, Istanbul, Turkey. © Patricia Blessing 2016

ḥifẓuhumā wa huwa l-ʿaālī l ʿaẓīm"; a passage from the Throne Verse, Qurʾan II:255).[95] While both the cursive and kufic inscriptions are in white on a blue-and-turquoise background, the frame has some yellow accents in addition to these colors.

In the tile panel located on the west side of the courtyard (Figure 20), a white band runs along the entire length of the frame, twisting itself into regular shapes that alternate between complex geometric knots and a motif whose form seems to be, for lack of a better term, a mix between a fleur-de-lys and a merlon; alongside it runs a thin scroll that carries cloud bands from the *khiṭāyī* repertoire and *saz* leaves. The inscription panel has a large *basmala* in white kufic script, and in yellow kufic the phrase "There is no compulsion in religion" (*lā ikrāh fī l-dīn*; Qurʾan II:256). As in the eastern panel, some yellow appears in the frame, but the color is even more prominent here because of its presence in the central field.

The central fields in both lunettes include the combination of *khiṭāyī* and *rūmī* forms noted by Tacizāde Cafer Çelebi, a madrasa-educated member of the Ottoman court, in the poem cited earlier in this chapter. In it, he describes windows in Mehmed II's mosque in these lines:

> *mülevven gūne gūne şīşelerden*
> *ḥaṭāyī rūmī yapraḳ cām-ı revzen*[96]

> colored using multi-colored blown glass
> *khiṭāyī* and *rūmī* leaf [of] window glass

Cafer Çelebi's poem, composed in 1493, is a panegyric about Istanbul, an example of the genre of *şehrengīz* or *masnavī-shahrāshūb*, which took hold first in Persian and then in Ottoman-Turkish poetry, becoming widespread in both literatures by the sixteenth century.[97] Titled *Vaṣf-ı ḥuṭṭa-i İslâmbol* – that is, "Description of the Region of İslâmbol," here designating Istanbul with the Ottoman expression that referred to the city's Islamization, as it literally means "full of Islam" – the poem begins with praise for Mehmed II as a conqueror. It then moves on to an engagement with the built environment of late fifteenth-century Ottoman Istanbul, including monuments such as the Hagia Sophia, the madrasas belonging to the mosque complex of Mehmed II, and Topkapı Palace.[98] The poetic description of parts of the city includes a wide range of cosmological motifs, including allusions to the Pleiades (*süreyyâ*) and the mythical spring of paradise (Arabic *kawthar*, Ottoman Turkish *kevser*).[99] Related to these are expressions of the astonishment and wonder the viewer experiences when contemplating the buildings (*temâşâ etmek*) from inside.[100] The poet expresses bewilderment (*ser-gerdânık*) as he visits the palace and is left amazed (*hayrân*) by the sight of the designs and images (*nakş u nigârı*).[101] In terms of materials mentioned, marble is central: it appears in descriptions of a hammam within the palace and of the mosque of Mehmed II.[102] Textiles make scarcer appearances, only in a reference to tent screens (*serâ-perde*) and curtains (*perde*) in the palace.[103] The Çinili Köşk is mentioned specifically, called *sırça-serâ* – another name with the same meaning, "tiled pavilion."[104] The building's beauty is exalted in the text with an emphasis on the pool of water lying in front of it and on its monumentality – a comparison is made to the dam that Alexander the Great built against the menace of Gog and Magog.[105]

The poem's description of the mosque of Mehmed II praises the building highly.[106] In addition to the verse emphasizing *khiṭāyī* and *rūmī* designs cited earlier, the beauty of the designs (again, the phrase *nakş u nigârı*) of the woodwork (*kündekârî*) on the doors is described, along with a range of architectural elements and decorative features within the building.[107] Materials are at times evoked – in the passage cited earlier, we see glass mentioned twice, once as colored glass in general and then specifically as window glass. The poem also describes the vast, marble-paved courtyard with its water features at the center, comparing the latter to *kevser*, the spring of paradise.[108] The praise lavished on the building is in tune with the building's importance in the Ottoman reshaping of Istanbul. The mosque of Mehmed II was part of a competition that Ottoman architects engaged in with the Hagia Sophia – its large central dome in particular. This competition would mark imperial architecture for centuries to come. The symmetrical arrangement of the mosque and subsidiary buildings, Necipoğlu argues, may be a nod to the principles of Renaissance architecture.[109] From this point of view, the mosque of Mehmed II presents a synthesis between the various aesthetic modes that late fifteenth-century Ottoman designers (and patrons) had at their disposal and is a built expression of the "visual cosmopolitanism" of Mehmed II's court.[110] Thus the Çinili Köşk was not unique in its combination of elements that evoke wide-ranging cultural references. That building, the palace, and Mehmed II's mosque were all part of a longer tradition of complex engagements with architectural pasts and presents within the Ottoman context that had already begun by the late fourteenth century. We now turn to another case from fifteenth-century Istanbul that features references that might be read as Timurid: the mausoleum of grand vizier Mahmud Pasha.

Mahmud Pasha's Patronage

Mahmud Pasha Angelović (d. 1474), a Serbian aristocrat turned Ottoman notable, served as grand vizier from 1456–68 and 1472–73, a career that ended in his execution after his second dismissal.[111] As a patron of architecture, he sponsored a mosque and related buildings in Istanbul beginning in 1463 (the date of the mosque[112]), two no-longer-extant *mescid*s in the same city, fountains, and a palace.[113] His patronage also extended to Thrace and the Balkans. In Edirne, Mahmud Pasha built the Taşluk Camii, demolished in 1939, and a hammam.[114] A mosque in Hasköy near Edirne and a palace in Skopje no longer survive, while a mosque in Sofia currently houses the city's archaeological museum.[115] The Fidan Han in Bursa, dated 866 AH / 1462 CE, has also been preserved.[116] Unlike some of his contemporaries, such as Zaganos Pasha, İshak Pasha, and Gedik Ahmed Pasha, who built mostly in the Anatolian cities that were their bases of power, Mahmud Pasha focused on Istanbul and the Balkans.[117]

The Mahmud Pasha Mosque (see Figure 21, center), built in 1463 near Istanbul's Grand Bazaar, is constructed on a variant of the inverse T-plan, a type of structure established in Ottoman architecture in the fourteenth century.[118] Small side domes and a porch enclose the larger domes of the prayer hall.[119] The mosque's exterior is covered with stone cladding devoid of decoration. Analyzing the mosque within the context of late fifteenth-century Ottoman architecture, Kafescioğlu points out

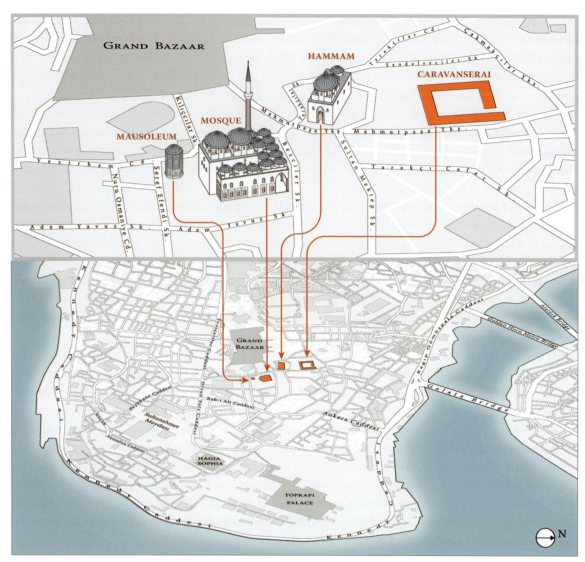

21. Inclined map of the Mahmud Pasha complex, 1461–74, Istanbul, Turkey. Drawing by Matilde Grimaldi

that the plan expands the notion of the mosque-*zāviye*, perhaps inspired by additions to existing churches that had been enlarged with subsidiary (often funerary) spaces, and thus clearly referred to the Byzantine architecture of Constantinople.[120] In adapting such a plan for an Ottoman mosque-*zāviye*, its builders used the areas wrapped around the main space as a way to "segregate the main prayer area (now functioning as a congregational mosque) from the later spaces of the convent."[121] This transformation also reflects changing attitudes toward such buildings and the dervish groups that traditionally used them, beginning in the late fifteenth century.[122] In Chapters 2 and 5, I discuss the role of mosque-*zāviye*s in the Ottoman context and their transformation into Friday mosques beginning in the second quarter of the sixteenth century. In Mahmud Pasha's complex, the mosque-*zāviye* served as the centerpiece of a larger intervention into the urban fabric of a busy commercial district, located between the grand bazaar and the shore of the Golden Horn (Figure 21). In addition to the mosque-*zāviye*, the complex consisted of the patron's mausoleum, a double hammam, khan, fountain, palace, public kitchen, and *mektep*. Of these, the mausoleum, khan, half of the hammam, and the fountain survive.[123]

A strong contrast to the sober, stone-clad exterior of the mosque is offered in the patron's mausoleum located behind the mosque. Its exterior decoration of turquoise tile inlaid into a marble covering, forming geometric patterns (see also Figures 27 to 29) lead us to examine techniques of stone carving and tile making. The difference in external appearance between the mosque and the mausoleum is striking and rare. The hammam belonging to the complex, which is located at some distance away from the mosque and mausoleum, is architecturally more akin to the mosque, with a sleek and monumental stone façade. As we shall see in Chapter 2, a similar mode of decorative variation between the exteriors of mosque, mausoleum, and madrasa is employed in Mehmed I's funerary complex in Bursa.

With the tile decoration of Mahmud Pasha's mausoleum, the question emerges whether the vizier was trying to emulate Mehmed II with it, perhaps emphasizing ambitions stoked by his participation in the conquest of Karaman in 1468. While this conquest took place after the construction of the mosque, the mausoleum was built in 1473–74, after the Ottomans conquered Karaman and a year after the construction of the Çinili Köşk. In effect, the two buildings are the only extant examples of exterior tile use in Istanbul – and rare examples within Ottoman architecture as a whole, together with Mehmed I's mausoleum (1421–24) in Bursa, the Alaca Türbe (1470s?) in Skopje, and the Yeşil Cami (1378–91) in Iznik.

Unlike his mausoleum, Mahmud Pasha's mosque and hammam do not stand out aesthetically among their fifteenth-century Ottoman counterparts. These buildings are in line with other monuments built by Mehmed II's viziers in Istanbul – for instance, those of Rum Mehmed Pasha, Has Murad Pasha, and Ishak Pasha, all part of the larger project of turning Constantinople into the new Ottoman capital.[124] This observation leads to the question of whether the "eastern" style of the mausoleum was an expression of the patron's taste. Was it a way to connect to Ottoman elite tastes as a Serbian prince? Could it have been one of the variants found in the repertoire of cosmopolitan Ottoman courtly aesthetics? And was the use of tile – a rare and somewhat exotic material in Istanbul at this time – a mark of status in and of itself? A closer look at the mausoleum's decoration and comparative examples will provide initial insights that also relate to other elements of the fifteenth-century Ottoman architectural project.

The Mahmud Pasha hammam (Figure 22), built in 1461, is partially preserved a short distance from the mosque and mausoleum. It was originally a double hammam, but the women's section fell into ruins by the late nineteenth century and the former men's section currently houses a number of small clothing stores.[125] Over the entrance, a poetic inscription (Figure 23) in Arabic praises the building's beauty, making a paradisiacal comparison: "It is a building filled with beauty and its marble [gleams] in the light like a lamp; the gardens of Eden: their rivers flow. Its date: it is the repose of spirits." This inscription includes a chronogram whose last phrase (*hiya rāḥat al-arwāḥ*) gives the date of construction: 871 AH / 1461 CE.[126] While no marble has been preserved in the interior of the monumental entry hall, this common material for the walls and floors of hammams appears in the caldarium.[127] The allusion to the interior space in the inscription over the entrance allows the reader to envision what one might have originally encountered upon entering the building. The references to paradise enhance the impression of beauty and the mention of the rivers of the gardens of Eden connects to the water that would certainly be present within the building, given its function. The chronogram furthermore emphasizes another sensory component of the monument: the relaxing environment of the hammam – "repose of spirits," as the inscription says – which would be enhanced by the sound of water flowing over marble within the building. At the same time, the hammam is built on a monumental, imposing scale, particularly visible from the outside. In the interior, although the original features of the hammam are no longer preserved, one would have had the sense of an intimate space where people gathered both for the cleansing rituals of bathing and to converse and share gossip as they lingered.[128]

22. Mahmud Pasha Hammam, 1464, Istanbul, Turkey. © Patricia Blessing 2016

23. Foundation inscription, Mahmud Pasha Hammam, 1464, Istanbul, Turkey. © Patricia Blessing 2018

24. Street view of Mahmud Pasha Mausoleum, 1474, Istanbul, Turkey. © Patricia Blessing 2016

25. View from parking lot, with lower part obstructed by railing, Mahmud Pasha Mausoleum, 1474, Istanbul, Turkey. © Patricia Blessing 2018

The mausoleum (Figures 24 and 25) is located in a cemetery behind Mahmud Pasha's mosque. Due to restoration of the mosque, ongoing since 2014, the cemetery is not currently accessible. The mausoleum, which was not included in the restoration project as of July 2019, the last time I was able to visit due to the COVID-19 pandemic that began in February 2020, is visible from a street running behind the eighteenth-century Nuruosmaniye Mosque down to the entrance of the Mahmud Pasha Mosque, and also from a parking lot behind two apartment buildings on Şeref Efendi Sokak in the vicinity of the Grand Bazaar. The octagonal building is decorated in a similar way on each of its sides: the bottom third of the wall is covered with grey marble paneling (Figure 26), while in the upper portion pieces of tile are set into geometrical strapwork composed of the same marble (Figure 27). Windows are set into the lower parts of the walls beneath carved stone lunettes on seven of the mausoleum's sides, while on the eighth – the north side pointing toward the mosque – the entrance is located.[129] Another higher set of windows appears in the upper section of the building among the tile work.

In her study of late fifteenth-century Istanbul, Kafescioğlu argues that the "Timurid style geometric patterns" were used as a way of carrying the Persianate visual idiom, otherwise restricted to the palace, where monument such as the Çinili Köşk stood, into the urban sphere beyond the royal precinct.[130] The visual connection between palace and city, extended by way of a patron closely associated with Mehmed II, is certainly an element that emerges in the mausoleum's tile decoration. Perhaps surprisingly, however, the mausoleum's façade does not simply repeat the tile mosaic of the Çinili Köşk. Rather, small pieces of tile are set into carved stone, a technique that does not have its roots within the Timurid context and that is indeed exceedingly rare among extant monuments within the Ottoman context and beyond.

The overall composition of the tile decoration follows the same model on each of the building's sides, with simple carved stone molding following the lateral and upper edges (Figures 28 and 29). The same

26. View from parking lot, Mahmud Pasha Mausoleum, 1474, Istanbul, Turkey. © Patricia Blessing 2018

27. Detail of stone and tile decoration, Mahmud Pasha Mausoleum, 1474, Istanbul, Turkey. © Patricia Blessing 2014

28. Detail of upper corner moldings, Mahmud Pasha Mausoleum, 1474, Istanbul, Turkey.
© Patricia Blessing 2018

29. Detail of pattern of *girih* tiles around window, Mahmud Pasha Mausoleum, 1474, Istanbul, Turkey.
© Patricia Blessing 2018

type of molding is used to form narrower rectangular frames that rise from the bottom of the structure, along the sides of the lower windows, up to about fifty centimeters below the roofline. The upper windows are placed above, within these same inner frames. The upper portion of the frame is filled with geometric tile patterns while stars and medallions are located in the spandrels of the upper windows, which form pointed arches. The space between the two sets of stone moldings is also filled with tile patterns, distinct from those surrounding the windows. In a rectangular frame surrounding each of the upper windows, *girih* (knot) motifs alternate in tile and stone.[131]

Such patterns based on *girih* designs were a long-standing tradition in Islamic art, reaching back to at least the so-called Sunni Revival in early twelfth-century Syria, when they emerged strongly.[132] Following the Mongol conquest of much of the eastern Islamic world in the second and third quarters of the thirteenth century, *girih* patterns continued to be used, often in combination with the new *khiṭāyī* patterns imported from East Asia via the Mongol channels of cultural exchange and trade. By the fifteenth century, such patterns had become fully integrated into the arts of the eastern Islamic world (and, to a lesser extent, the Mamluk realm), and geometric and floral patterns could be freely combined.[133] While this was not done in the tile work of the Mahmud Pasha Mausoleum, which sticks fully to geometric *girih* designs, the tile work of the Çinili Köşk to some extent shows this type of integration with the presence of square kufic medallions in the floral patterns and with the fully geometric designs underneath the roofline of the porch and in the fragments on interior arches (see Figures 5 and 6).

On each side of the mausoleum, patterns are repeated. One pattern is created with five-pointed stars arranged to form stacked polygons, with small kite-shaped quadrilaterals of dark-blue tile arranged in eight-pointed stars at their centers. In the rectangular panels beneath the windows, carved dodecagons are overlapped in such a manner as to form a stone grid of negative space that presents six-pointed stars, *girih* shapes, and badge-shaped hexagons that are filled in with tiles (see Figure 27). In the tile work, dark blue and turquoise alternate. Where tiles on the building have been broken, it is clear that they are made of red clay rather than fritware, which is off-white or white. (This will be relevant when discussing the possible sources of these tiles and their elusive makers.) In sections where tile elements have fallen out (see Figure 27), it becomes clear that the Mahmud Pasha Mausoleum is an achievement of stone carvers more than tile makers. The carefully arranged geometrical patterns are carved out of the stone with minute detail. The small pieces of tile would then have had to be cut to measure and inserted into the empty spaces. The workers who cut these tile insets were most likely familiar with the technique of tile mosaic, but only a limited number of simple geometric shapes were needed in this case, and their work would thus have been rather limited. Rather than creating a sleek surface, the technique highlights the materiality of both stone and tile, each appearing in sharp opposition to the other. Perhaps we are looking here at a one-off association between stone carvers and a group of tile cutters. The designs might have been drawn on paper, akin to the patterns found in the fifteenth-century Topkapı Scroll, which shows "a repertory of geometric designs for wall surfaces and vaults."[134] However, the actual types of templates that would presumably have been used have not been preserved.[135]

As Necipoğlu demonstrates in her extensive study of the Topkapi Scroll, the drawings contained in that source were not the actual designs used by architects on site, but rather "mnemotechnic devices that assured the preservation and transmission of architectural knowledge over the generations."[136] The same is perhaps true for earlier traces of architectural design, such as the famous Ilkhanid stone slab from Takht-i Sulayman and a carving from medieval Armenia bearing what appear to be patterns for muqarnas designs.[137] The actual paper templates themselves, however, do not survive precisely because they were designed to be cut up and used on site during the process of producing the tile work. Thus the materiality of the template – which, as anthropologist Tim Ingold notes, is an artifact that is made from specific materials, just like the object it serves to produce – is no longer accessible to us.[138] Initial, small-scale drawings and calligraphies that would eventually be used in architectural contexts may still exist in albums (which I discuss in Chapter 5), but they are most likely not recognizable as such, as preserved designs could have been used at a range of scales and in various media.

Since nothing comparable to the tile work on the Mahmud Pasha Mausoleum exists in Istanbul, the question is how this monument fits within the larger context of fifteenth-century Islamic architecture within and beyond the Ottoman realm. To what extent is this an Ottoman experiment? How did this monument's makers use architecture to express the Ottoman endeavor to carve out a place among the post-Mongol empires in the Islamic world? While Kafescioğlu is right to state that Timurid visual culture was a relevant reference in this context, the makers of the Mahmud Pasha Mausoleum also drew on a wider range of architectural practices in the Islamic world.

More than evoking Timurid architecture – in which stonework hardly played a role and tile mosaic had been the dominant form of decoration since the late 1380s – the patterns here draw from an aesthetic that harks back to the Saljuq monuments of central Anatolia. At first sight, the geometric motifs created with strapwork carved in stone and tile insets in the empty spaces evoke the geometric designs on the portals of thirteenth-century Saljuq monuments in central Anatolia or the tile work on certain other buildings of the same period. At the same time, the reference is one that does not find direct comparisons: thirteenth- and fourteenth-century examples are either carved solely in stone, such as on the Sultan Han (ca. 1230–34) near Kayseri, or created in tile mosaic, such as in the Gök Madrasa in Tokat (see Figure 15). The stone-and-tile combination is a new, creative solution, perhaps a case Jonathan Hay evokes in noting that at times, a memory will be enough for transmission of motifs.[139] In evoking these references, the Mahmud Pasha Mausoleum is unique within Istanbul, although examples in earlier Ottoman architecture are discussed in subsequent chapters.

TRANSFER TO SKOPJE: TILE WORK ON THE MOVE

Another example of the rare exterior use of tile in Ottoman architecture appears on the so-called Alaca Türbe (Figure 30) in Skopje. This mausoleum does not have an inscription, but Maximilian Hartmuth suggests that it was built in the 1470s, possibly for Paşa Beğ, one of the sons of İshak Beğ (d. 1445), the *ucbeyi* of Skopje.[140] It is located behind the *zāviye* that İshak Beğ built in 1438–39 as part of a larger complex; the madrasa and the hammam do not survive, but the Sulu Han, one of two *han*s (commercial buildings) connected to the

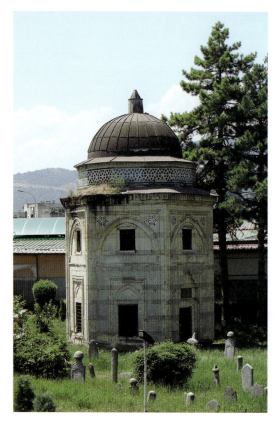

30. Alaca Türbe, 1470s, Skopje, North Macedonia. © Patricia Blessing 2016

foundation, still stands.¹⁴¹ On this building, blue and turquoise tile elements are placed around the drum of the dome (Figure 31), forming a geometric pattern set into the stone. Star- and flower-shaped medallions of tile are also set into the spandrels of the window arches (Figures 32 and 33).

Hartmuth argues that the tile decoration may have been created by workers sent from Edirne or Istanbul.¹⁴² This argument may have its merits, considering that there really are no other examples of

31. Detail of dome and tile decoration on drum, Alaca Türbe, 1470s, Skopje, North Macedonia. © Patricia Blessing 2016

32. Detail of upper-level window with tile medallion, Alaca Türbe, 1470s, Skopje, North Macedonia. © Patricia Blessing 2016

33. Detail of tile medallion, Alaca Türbe, 1470s, Skopje, North Macedonia. © Patricia Blessing 2016

fifteenth-century tile work in the Ottoman Balkans. At the same time, it also falls into the pattern of assuming movement from imperial centers – Istanbul and Edirne – to frontier peripheries. In the case of the Alaca Türbe, a further question emerges – namely, whether tile workers would have had to be present on site to create the decoration found on it. Would not pieces of tile, either precut or ready to be cut on site, have been enough? The geometric pattern around the drum of the dome is relatively simple, with irregular diamond shapes arranged to form hexagons. The spaces in between are filled with what looks to be copious amounts of modern mortar or concrete, so it is harder to understand how the tiles were originally installed in the stone structure. The medallions in the window spandrels are done differently, with the tile pieces set into spaces carved into the stone. The shapes are relatively simple here as well – namely, triangles of various sizes. Since none of the tiles are currently missing, perhaps thanks to restoration, it is impossible to tell how deep the cuts into the stone are; indeed, it seems that some of the tile triangles are not quite flush with the stone, perhaps an indication of unequal depth. Most importantly, however, this kind of decoration could easily have been completed by local stoneworkers who were provided with tile pieces that might have been shipped from anywhere – including Istanbul, where tiles were presumably produced at a relatively significant scale for the decoration of the Çinili Köşk as well as the no-longer-extant tile work on the Old Palace. That the stone carvers who were involved in building the Alaca Türbe were capable of precise work is clear from the carving of the moldings on the mausoleum and the muqarnas cornice just below the tile panel. Thus it is absolutely conceivable to imagine a scenario involving a design made in one place, tiles being requested from a place of production and shipped to Skopje, and the installation of the tiles there by the same workers who completed the stone carving. A moving workshop of tile makers – one of the big topics of debate in the context of much of fifteenth-century Ottoman production – is not necessary in this specific case.

From these observations emerge two larger topics of discussion. First, the question of drawings in the process of architectural production in the fifteenth-century Islamic world needs to be addressed. The most important starting point is Necipoğlu's discussion of the Topkapı Scroll, which raises the question of the relationship between the theoretical and practical elements of these and similar drawings. This also relates to a larger discussion in the history of sciences in the medieval Islamic world of the relationship between *ʿilm* (theoretical knowledge) and *ʿamal* (the practical expertise and skill in doing or making something). These are crucial in the realm of art and architecture, where we often see the results of *ʿamal* – namely, the buildings and objects created by its means – but know little how *ʿilm* feeds into it. The fifteenth-century manuscript *Fī tadākhul al-ashkāl al-mutashābiha aw al-mutawāfiqa* (Paris, Bibliothèque nationale de France, Ms. Persan 169, fols. 180r–199r) is a crucial text to advance our understanding of these issues with regard to architecture because it sits at the intersection of theoretical and practical applications of geometry.[143] A copy of a treatise probably compiled by Abu Bakr in the early fourteenth century in an Ilkhanid context, the manuscript presents "the unresolved implications concerning the intersection, or lack thereof, between mathematical knowledge and artisanal expertise."[144] With regard to the mathematical exactness or absence thereof of the geometrical figures, Jan P. Hogendijk notes that the manuscript may reflect some of the practical solutions used in the context of making art and architecture, rather than more complicated theoretical ones. Moreover, considering the fact that some figures are presented without textual explanations or only vague ones, the manuscript also assumes the presence of a teacher along with students, within an oral tradition of instruction rather than a written one of self-study.[145] Such a collaborative milieu, in which relationships between teachers and students or between members of a workshop were crucial, connects to the *kitabkhāna* environment.

The second question is the related issue of local traditions versus migrating artists, to use the terms from the subtitle of Michael Meinecke's book on that topic.[146] We should not necessarily assume stasis in these workshops and collaborations: considering the changing nature of building sites, in particular, we should imagine environments in which individuals could move around and changing sets of workers could collaborate. In the absence of detailed records about artists, their workshop genealogies, and often even their names, how can we understand if a building is the work of locals, a migrating group, or a combination of both? Is style always a trustworthy criterion? Which elements can deceive? To what extent are we to believe attributions that emerge from the recording of artists' names, particularly *nisbas* that seem to indicate place? These questions will reemerge along with some answers in the next two chapters.

MID-FIFTEENTH-CENTURY AESTHETICS: ISTANBUL AND BEYOND

In this chapter, I have examined how in Istanbul during the reign of Mehmed II, the aesthetic impact of the eastern Islamic world – the larger (post-)Timurid realms of Iran and Central Asia, but also contemporary Karamanid and thirteenth-century Saljuq Anatolia – became apparent in Ottoman-sponsored monuments, side by side with references to Renaissance Italy and the Byzantine Empire. Clearly these elements were consciously combined with ones that had been present in Ottoman architecture prior to the conquest of Constantinople.

In the case of the Çinili Köşk, the ideological intent behind the monument is to reflect and possibly surpass the monuments of the city of Karaman, as Necipoğlu has demonstrated. At the same time, the artistic means through which this is done are more varied than a simple copy of Karamanid architecture. Although the Ottomans destroyed the Karamanid palaces, what survives of the Karamanids' patronage in religious monuments suggests that the kind of extensive tile mosaic seen in the Çinili Köşk had largely fallen out of use by the mid-fifteenth century. In fact, as Meinecke shows, most extant examples of such rich tile mosaic in central Anatolia date to the thirteenth century, with the occasional example appearing in a fourteenth-century monument.[147] Thus the argument that the tile cutters from Khurasan with their desperate petition were indeed the makers of the Çinili Köşk's tile mosaic is quite convincing, particularly considering the specific expertise that would have been needed in order to complete a relatively large-scale project in this complex technique. The interwoven inscriptions of the portal would certainly have required the involvement of competent calligraphers, who were at hand in the *nakkaşhane* in Istanbul, an increasingly centralized workshop led during the reign of Mehmed II by the artist Baba Nakkaş, whom we encounter in Chapter 5. Meanwhile, the poetic content of these inscriptions, as well as poetic engagement with this and other buildings, displays the extent to which cosmological motifs and notions surrounding artistically produced beauty – hence the process of artifice – were appreciated and embedded in the architecture.

The case of the Mahmud Pasha Mausoleum is more complicated, for this is not a work of tile mosaic making as much as one of stone carving. While large-scale drawings could certainly have been made of the patterns, these would have been needed to serve the carving of the stone to create spaces for tile fill rather than to produce panels of tile mosaic for installation on the monument. The tile shapes used on this monument are limited to a few types, all fairly simple and all having straight edges, with none of the complicated curved shapes of the Çinili Köşk's inscriptions. In this case, tile cutters would not have been particularly challenged and could even have supplied the shapes while working off site from carefully measured templates. The stone carvers who completed the work on the Mahmud Pasha Mausoleum, on the other hand, would have needed to work meticulously to create the stone strapwork into which tiles were inserted and to make sure that it was uniform on all sides of the monument. Perhaps the fact that this technique did not catch on and was not repeated is a sign of how challenging this project proved. The Alaca Türbe in Skopje, as we have seen, has tile inserts on a much smaller scale and in far simpler designs, and it was not necessarily derived from the Çinili Köşk or made by the same group of tile cutters.

Finally, the tile lunettes in the mosque of Mehmed II in Istanbul point toward the future direction that Ottoman building ceramics would take – namely, increasingly complex underglaze-painted fritware that would culminate with the highly centralized production of Iznik in the mid-sixteenth century. In the second half of the fifteenth century, this was by no means determined as of yet: both vessels and tiles in a range of styles were produced at various sites including Istanbul and Iznik.[148] These developments would continue during the reign of Bayezid II, as the last chapter of this book shows, a period when designs created on paper may have taken precedence, leading to an increasing overlap in the decorations of manuscripts, tiles, pottery, textiles, and metalwork. At the same time, a dialogue with the pasts of lands now under Ottoman rule would increasingly be created in chronicles produced during Bayezid II's reign to present a carefully crafted Ottoman past that aligned with the empire's present.

The following chapters, however, explore how some of the features visible in the Çinili Köşk and the Mahmud Pasha Mausoleum have precedents in earlier fifteenth-century Ottoman architecture. I examine elements such as tile decoration with origins in the eastern Islamic (Timurid, but also Qaraqoyunlu and Aqqoyunlu) world and in the Saljuq architecture of Anatolia; dialogue in stonework with the Mamluk monuments of Greater Syria and Egypt; and the sensory experiences created by the combination of these elements. Chapter 2 focuses on the mosque complex of Mehmed I in Bursa, where such elements were introduced on a substantial scale, carrying meaning in a period of dynastic reconstruction that called for buildings that projected kingship as much as wonder.

TWO

IMMERSIVE SPACE
Empire Building and the Ottoman Frontier

ON A HILLTOP IN BURSA, A CITY IN THE WESTERN ANATOLIAN PROVINCE OF BITHYNIA, stands Sultan Mehmed I's funerary complex commonly known as the Yeşil İmaret.[1] Built between 1419 and 1424, this multifunctional complex consists of a mosque-*zāviye* (convent mosque), madrasa, bathhouse, and kitchen, as well as a posthumously built mausoleum for the sultan (Figure 34). The complex is testament to the rebuilding and reconsolidation of the Ottoman principality beginning with Mehmed I, once he became sultan in 1413 after a period of infighting and fragmentation. In this same period, new styles were developed in Ottoman architecture to express changing relationships with the past, present, and projected future of both the Ottoman realm and the territories the Ottomans hoped to conquer.

In 1402, after being defeated in the Battle of Ankara by the Central Asian conqueror Timur (r. 1370–1405), the Ottoman sultan Bayezid I (r. 1389–1402) was led into captivity together with two of his sons, Musa and Mustafa.[2] For the next eleven years, the sultan's remaining sons fought one another in a bloody civil war to regain fragments of the Ottoman principality and challenge Timurid domination. Over the course of the conflict, they came into contact with post-Mongol Anatolia, Iran, and Central Asia, and the resulting change in Ottoman outlook is evident in the arts of the period.

In 1413, Mehmed I emerged victorious from the civil war and rebuilt the Ottoman principality from his base in Bursa. The city became the site of the sultan's mosque-*zāviye* complex and, a few years later, his tomb. Mehmed I's son and successor, Murad II (r. 1421–44 and 1446–51), commissioned the mausoleum. The conflict with the Timurids, the rebuilding of the Ottoman *beylik*, and the emergence of a newly confident polity had far-reaching implications for the dynamics of artistic production, patronage, and style during the first half of the fifteenth century, as I show in this and the following chapter.

Recent studies that focus on early Ottoman architecture, from the emergence of Ottoman rule in the western Anatolian region of Bithynia in the late thirteenth century to the conquest of Constantinople in 1453, have begun to overturn long-held ways of viewing the subject. Oya Pancaroğlu, Robert Ousterhout, and Suna Çağaptay have pointed to the continuation of Byzantine building practices and their role in identity formation in the late thirteenth and early fourteenth centuries, when the Ottoman

34. Mausoleum (left) and mosque-*zāviye* (right), complex of Mehmed I, 1419–24, Bursa, Turkey. Sébah & Joaillier, ca. 1890–1910. Courtesy of Special Collections, Fine Arts Library, Harvard University

territories were consolidated,[3] a departure from the traditional view that ties these monuments to preconceived ethnic and religious categories such as Turkish, Greek, Armenian, Muslim, or Christian.[4] This scholarly reevaluation, however, has concentrated on the late thirteenth century and especially – because of the larger number of extant monuments – the fourteenth, when the Ottoman realm was first expanding and Ottoman identity was being formed. My focus here is on the transmission of style and techniques in Ottoman architecture during a somewhat later period when the dynamics of architecture and patronage had shifted. Scholars are slowly reconsidering the late fourteenth century and especially the early fifteenth century, a particularly complicated time in Ottoman history on the political and cultural levels. In the fifteenth century, Ottoman rulers and the administrators and scholar-bureaucrats connected to their court increasingly worked toward constructing a dynastic identity, as Linda Darling has shown.[5] The patronage of Mehmed I and in particular the buildings he commissioned in Bursa are part of this development, yet only recently has work on the historical context and primary sources made possible a new assessment of material culture in the fifteenth-century Ottoman Empire.

In this chapter, I argue that the elaborate tile and stone decoration of Mehmed I's mosque-*zāviye* and mausoleum creates a deliberate dialogue with earlier – mostly late twelfth-century to thirteenth-century – Islamic architecture in Anatolia and with the broader Persianate culture of Iran and Central Asia after the fall of the Mongol Empire. Among the elements of the architecture, it is the tiles most of all with their varied techniques, color schemes, and visual references that suggest how early fifteenth-century Ottoman visual culture reflected the constant renegotiation of power, rule, and representation among the sultan, historians, and builders.

My analysis of Mehmed I's funerary complex in Bursa addresses four central questions: How did the tile decoration on and in the buildings fit into the framework of a Timurid aesthetic? How did the engagement with Timurid art intersect with the reframing of Ottoman identity? How was the Saljuq and, more broadly, Islamic past of central and eastern Anatolia used as a point of historical and stylistic reference? How were notions of immersive space used in these buildings? During the period of political reconstruction and architectural rebranding of his realm, Mehmed I drew on the work of architects and craftsmen who may have had access to or at least knowledge of multiple stylistic, technical, and aesthetic models available in the Ottoman realm and neighboring regions. In the funerary complex, the tile decoration in particular notably engages the viewer with an array of local, global, historical, and contemporary points of comparison. Through these intersectional references an immersive space emerges in which the combination of media is directed at instilling wonder (ʿajab) at the building's beauty and astonishment at being unable to conceive its making. In the mosque-zāviye and mausoleum of Mehmed I, this goal is primarily achieved with extensive use of tiles, one of the main materials that effectively helped create tension between brilliant visual effect and unknown (to the nonexpert) material composition and fabrication.

SHIFTING STYLES: CONSTRUCTING PAST, PRESENT, AND FUTURE

When we look closely at Mehmed I's mosque-zāviye and mausoleum, we notice that they present stylistic connections to both Timurid Central Asia and pre-Ottoman Anatolia. While the term "pre-Ottoman" can be problematic in that it may imply a potentially teleological perspective focused on the rise of the Ottomans, I use it here as a way of moving beyond the specificity of such dynastic terms as "Saljuq" or "Ilkhanid," which have their own particular historiographies in the context of medieval Anatolia.[6] Moreover, "pre-Ottoman" should in this context not be understood as referring exclusively to Muslim rule, but also as including Christian realms such as the Byzantine Empire or, until the late fourteenth century, the Armenian kingdom of Cilicia. I use "Saljuq" here to refer to the architecture established in Konya and the surrounding region in the late twelfth and early thirteenth centuries, when the Anatolian Saljuqs were at the peak of their power. The patronage of Sultan ʿAla al-Din Kayqubad I (r. 1220–37) in particular led to the emergence of an architectural style associated with him and his capital city of Konya.[7] While some features of this style, such as monumental muqarnas portals with decorative frames, took hold elsewhere in Anatolia, a unified form of architecture did not fully emerge across the region and the beginnings of such a unified style remained confined to the central areas of the Rūm Saljuq realm. With the Mongol conquest of Anatolia in 1243, royal Saljuq patronage ceased and all standardizing efforts in architecture were abandoned. In the following decades and into the fourteenth century, regional styles – often centered on such major cities as Sivas, Erzurum, Kayseri, and Konya – were consolidated as local patrons took hold in the absence of centralized rule and patronage.[8] The breakdown of Mongol power in Anatolia in the 1330s only added to this political and cultural fragmentation and similar dynamics remained in place throughout the fourteenth century and well into the fifteenth.[9]

In the early fifteenth century, Ottoman recovery was centered on the Balkans and western Anatolia. Bursa in the province of Bithynia was the dynastic and cultural center of the realm under Mehmed I, but not the capital of the Ottoman Empire; Edirne served as a royal place of residence from the mid-1360s until the Ottoman conquest of Constantinople in 1453. While Bursa was at the cultural heart of Ottoman architectural innovation, it was also located on the edge of the post-Mongol eastern Islamic lands where a fragmented political situation still prevailed, especially after Timur's intervention. The Timurid invasion had effectively cut short Bayezid I's well-advanced attempt to unify Anatolia under Ottoman rule. Notably, the beyliks of Saruhan, Aydın, Menteşe, and Germiyan in western Anatolia, which Bayezid I had allied to the Ottomans or completely absorbed, were restored to their independent pre-Ottoman position in Timur's effort to rearrange the political landscape of Anatolia.[10] On the political level, due to Mehmed I's initial involvement in the civil war with his brothers, followed by the need to restore the empire to power from his base in Bursa and the attention to securing the Ottomans' Balkan possessions, new attempts to connect Anatolia to the Ottoman realm were largely left to Murad II and Mehmed II.[11] This did not, however, preclude a wider horizon when it came to gathering stylistic references – and workers – for Ottoman architecture.

Some of the actors emerging from the post-Mongol context came into direct conflict with Ottoman expansion; this was particularly the case for the Karamanids, as discussed in Chapter 1. Other dynasties established good if volatile relationships with the Ottomans. The Dulkadir in southeastern Anatolia and beyond the Taurus Mountains on the Ottoman–Mamluk frontier in the fourteenth and fifteenth centuries became close to Mehmed I before his accession. Nasireddin Mehmed (r. 1399–1442) gave the future sultan his daughter Emine Hatun in marriage and offered military support against Musa through his son, Süleyman. Throughout the fifteenth century, the Dulkadir served as the lords of the Ottoman–Mamluk frontier, at times extending as far west as Kayseri until the Ottomans conquered that city in 1474, siding with either power depending on the situation, and offering princesses in marriage to both Mamluks and Ottomans, such as Mehmed II, as described in Chapter 1.[12] This situation continued until Selim I forced the Dulkadir to come under Ottoman suzerainty in 1515 and expanded his empire to the southeast of the Taurus Mountains in the year before his conquest of Mamluk-held Aleppo. The Ottomans fully annexed these territories in 1522, when Ferhad Pasha had Dulkadir ruler ʿAli b. Şehsuvar (r. 1515–22) and his entourage killed with Süleyman the Magnificent's approval.[13] The Ramazanoğlu in Cilicia hung on to some lands until the early seventeenth century, perhaps making them the last of these dynasties to vanish; meanwhile, they slowly adjusted to Ottoman architecture and rule, as I discuss in Chapter 5.

Throughout the fourteenth century, central and eastern Anatolia were peripheral areas for Ottoman architecture; stylistic evidence suggests that Islamic monuments in these regions did not serve as references for Ottoman builders and patrons until the late fourteenth century, when elements such as monumental muqarnas portals began to appear – for instance, on the Great Mosque in Bursa (1396–1400).[14] In the same period, or even slightly earlier, references to Mamluk architecture found their way into Ottoman buildings based on closer diplomatic relations that developed in this period.[15] One example is the Great Mosque of Bergama, commissioned by Bayezid I in 1398–99, where a decorative band around the foundation inscription on the entrance evokes Mamluk marble inlay.[16] During the reign of Mehmed I, however, the architectural references expanded and were refined: the architecture of Konya, which harked back to a strong past under the Saljuqs before the advent of Mongol rule, became a more fundamental source of inspiration as Bursa was reshaped as a center of Ottoman dynastic memory. At the same time, the Byzantine architecture present in Bursa and the surrounding region remained relevant. My study here thus includes multiple peripheries as well as multiple centers, to the point that both notions nearly dissolve in the fluid environment of the fifteenth-century Ottoman Empire. The discourse of geography, history, and artistic production that Enrico Castelnuovo and Carlo Ginzburg present in their analysis of Italian art – in which they note that peripheries can be places of artistic innovation in their own right and that artistic mobility between "centers" and "peripheries" is not necessarily unidirectional – is nevertheless helpful when reflecting on these matters.[17] The dynamics I analyze also benefit from discussions of artistic geographies that span diverse regions and cultural spaces.[18]

During the time that Bursa emerged as the Ottoman cultural center with the establishment of the court, its attendant historians and poets, and the scholars and Sufis who were increasingly employed in royal foundations, Mehmed I and his court created a cultural horizon that looked east from his stable bases in the Balkans and the Anatolian region of Amasya and Merzifon. Considering the historical circumstances, including the need to seek both new allies and new cultural references after his father's defeat to Timur, this development was not at all a matter of chance. With the Timurid invasion of the Ottoman territories and the defeat of Bayezid I, the Ottoman territories became connected to the larger

Timurid realm. The exceedingly complex dynamics of center and periphery persisted after Mehmed I's reign and the influence of Timurid cultural production in the eastern Islamic world was at its peak throughout the fifteenth century.[19]

One vehicle through which Timurid cultural production may have entered the Ottoman realm is the movement of workshops and individual craftsmen.[20] This movement was crucial for disseminating styles and techniques across the Islamic world, supplemented by the use of templates on paper.[21] Considering that cultural concepts and artistic ideas (and perhaps workers) moved from the Timurid to the Ottoman realm, rather than in the opposite direction, Bursa and the Ottoman lands as a whole were one of the peripheries of the Timurid cultural orbit.

In early fifteenth-century Bursa, architectural evidence reveals a multilayered cultural environment invested in both local traditions and new trends imported from Iran and Central Asia. In order to assess the position Mehmed I's constructions occupy between the Timurid present and the Saljuq past, I first discuss the layout of Mehmed I's foundation, then analyze Bursa as a center of Ottoman patronage before turning to the buildings' tile decoration. This connects to the broader discussion of cultural and intellectual networks among the Ottoman, Mamluk, Timurid, and Qaraqoyunlu realms at the time.

MEHMED I'S MOSQUE-*ZĀVIYE* COMPLEX IN BURSA

The monumental groups of buildings Ottoman sultans commissioned in Bursa in the fourteenth and fifteenth centuries usually contained a mosque or mosque-*zāviye* and a mausoleum for the ruler, along with other buildings of various functions, including charitable services. Indeed it was in this city that the idea of such multifunctional complexes was established – an idea that would be further developed in Istanbul after 1453. The complex of Murad I, built in 1365–85, consists of a mosque with a madrasa on the upper floor, a bathhouse, and the sultan's mausoleum, which was destroyed in the 1855 earthquake and subsequently rebuilt.[22] The complex of Bayezid I (begun 1390, completed before 1395) originally comprised a mosque-*zāviye*, madrasa, bathhouse, kitchen, hospital, and palace, but only the first three of these buildings are extant; the sultan's mausoleum was added in 1406. Murad II's compound contains a mosque-*zāviye*, madrasa, and several mausolea, most added at later dates, as I discuss in Chapter 4.[23]

The components of the building complex Mehmed I commissioned in Bursa are arranged in close proximity to one another, but are not physically connected or contained within a unified enclosure (Figure 35).[24] It is unclear whether the mausoleum was included in the original project, but it is worth noting that the structure does not appear in the *waqfīya* dated 1419.[25] The mausoleum's portal inscription mentions that Mehmed I died in Jumadha I 824 AH / May 1421, but does not indicate when construction began or ended.[26] Considering that Ottoman sultans' mausolea were consistently built posthumously, commissioned by their sons and successors in order to affirm dynastic stability, succession, and loyalty, it is likely that the same happened here and that construction began in or after 1421.[27] Work on the interior of the mosque-*zāviye* continued for a few years after the patron's death, as an inscription dated 1424 suggests, noting that the decoration was completed in that year.[28] Ultimately the building's exterior was left unfinished. But clearly it was functional in 1419: the *waqfīya* mentions the mosque-*zāviye* as the central structure of Mehmed I's foundation, and the foundation inscription dated December 1419 suggests quite some degree of completion.[29] The mosque-*zāviye*'s porch was never built – although holes in the façade, just below the cornice, indicate where it would have connected to the walls – and some of the stone carving on the building's façade remains incomplete (see Figures 36 and 60).[30] It is not clear whether construction was abandoned because resources were required for the construction of Murad II's own mosque-*zāviye* in Bursa beginning in 1425, but this is certainly a possibility. As noted in the *waqfīya*, extensive properties were connected to Mehmed I's endowment to ensure the smooth functioning of the sultan's foundation.[31]

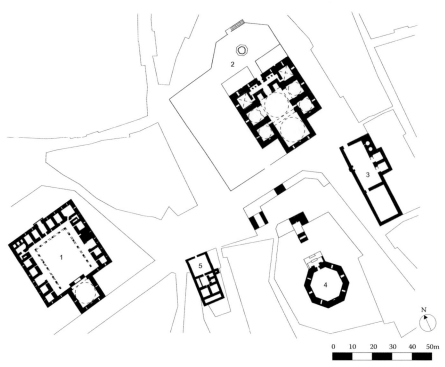

35. Plan, complex of Mehmed I: (1) madrasa, (2) mosque-*zāviye*, (3) kitchen, (4) mausoleum, (5) bathhouse. Drawing by Matilde Grimaldi

The document includes salaries for a shaykh, an imam, a muezzin, and Qur'an reciters, along with a *mudarris* for the madrasa, funding for thirty students, and other staff including bakers and two *miʿmār*s responsible for the buildings' upkeep.[32] The charitable distribution of food to the poor and to travelers is also stipulated.[33]

Further information about the conceptualization of the sultan's foundation can be gleaned from the mosque-*zāviye*'s foundation inscription, now painted and gilded, which runs in three lines around the recess in the portal façade, just over the entrance to the building (see Figure 59). It and the *waqfīya* are parallel written sources for reading and analyzing the building.[34] Rather than referring to the building as a *jāmiʿ* (Friday mosque), *masjid* (neighborhood mosque), *ʿimārat* (hospice), or *zāviye* (the term used in the *waqfīya*), the inscription employs the term *buqʿat*.[35] Franz Taeschner notes that the term *buqʿat* is used to mean a dervish convent ("Derwisch Kloster") in a late twelfth-century Ayyubid inscription, and that its use here might indicate that the structure Mehmed I commissioned was indeed a *zāviye*, yet he also cautions against unquestioningly accepting this translation.[36] In the early Ottoman context, *buqʿat* is one of several terms often used to refer to various multifunctional structures built with T-plans, along with other terms such as *zāviye*, *khānqāh*, *tekke*, or – the most commonly used term – *ʿimārat*.[37] Literally, the Arabic term *buqʿat* means "place" or "building" – here it may have been used for its ambiguity since it can encompass all of the functions of a mosque-*zāviye*.[38]

The full inscription, with its poetic metaphors given in rhymed prose, gives insight into some of the cosmological ideas behind the building's construction:

> (1) In the name of God, the Merciful, the Compassionate. Refuge is in His all-encompassing generosity. The product of the maker (*ṣāniʿ*) of creation, the work of the forger/goldsmith (*ṣāʾigh*), I mean[39] this noble building (*buqʿat*) [was] transcribed (*nusikhat*) as one of the copies (*nusakh*) of the garden of felicity [= paradise] and one of the meadows of the afterlife, and woven (*nusijat*[40]) from the splendor of life

(2) [The building] swaggered across the regions and diminished the cities [left] behind [it]. He has not granted anything like it to the ages (*adwār*) for as long as the whirling firmament (*al-falak al-dawwār*) has turned (*dāra*). The great sultan, the most generous *khāqān*, the sultan of East and West, and the *khāqān* of the non-Arabs/Persians and Arabs, the one supported by the support of the Lord of the World, Ghiyāth al-Dunyā wal-Dīn,

(3) the sultan son of the sultan Meḥemmed b. Bāyezīd b. Murād b. Orkhān founded it. May God perpetuate his rule in the caliphate on earth – and may He hurry his [the founder's] boat (*fulk*) across the sea of wishes in safety; He established its foundations, strengthened its pillars, and erected it in Dhū'l-ḥijja in the pilgrimage[41] of eight hundred and twenty-two [December 1419 to January 1420 CE].

The inscription thus compares the building to gardens and meadows in paradise, establishing a mimetic relationship through the verb *nasikha*, meaning to copy or transcribe. This also metaphorically connects the construction of the building to the craft of book making – one of multiple crafts invoked in the inscription. Implied in the following phrase – *nusijat bi-zahrati l-ḥayāt* – is a textile metaphor that compares the building to a precious fabric woven from life itself. As Margaret Graves has demonstrated in her study of medieval portable objects from the Islamic world, similar metaphors related to the making of textiles also appear in medieval Arabic and Persian works on poetics, where the poet is described as spinning a thread of words or weaving a poem.[42] Further, the term "goldsmith" (*ṣā'igh*) connects to crafts metaphors related to the creation of beauty, which compare the making of jewelry from precious metal to the "poet's craft,"[43] the use of the intricate workings of language to create poems.[44] Necipoğlu notes that in the Ottoman context, Muslih al-Din Mustafa Sururi (1491–1562) deployed crafts metaphors (tile making and wall painting) in works he wrote about the art of poetry, tying into earlier usage in Arabic and Persian.[45] Clearly whoever composed the foundation inscription for Mehmed I's mosque-*zāviye* was no stranger to these approaches to poetics. Together with the construction of a madrasa as part of the building complex, the erudite content of the inscription thus points to the larger intellectual milieu of early fifteenth-century Bursa, which, just like the contemporary building site, was marked by exchange and migration.

The comparison to the firmament, while relatively commonplace as we have seen in Chapter 1, is nevertheless notable because this is an early use of the trope in Ottoman epigraphy (here in Arabic) and establishes a precedent for the Persian poem on the face of the Çinili Köşk. The inscription also deploys a number of word games based on similar roots in Arabic – *nasikha* and *nasija* – and words derived from the same Arabic root like *fulk* (ship) and *falak* (firmament), displaying its author's erudition. Presenting Mehmed I as lord of East and West and as ruler of the non-Arabs and Arabs,[46] the inscription stakes a claim to rulership and universal aspirations that prefigure the (even more accentuated) claims made by the patron's grandson, Mehmed II, a few decades later.[47] Thus a cosmopolitanism that ties together references to a range of places within the known world is apparent in an age before Mehmed II's cosmopolitan court. Among the titles employed for Mehmed I, *al-sulṭān al-a'ẓam* is unsurprising, but the title *ghiyāth al-dunyā wal-dīn* was much more popular among the Saljuqs than among the Ottomans and does not appear after Murad II's reign. Further praise for the building is voiced on two inscriptions comprised of Persian poetry, which run along the walls of the two recesses located to the left and right of the entrance corridor in the same wall as the sultan's lodge.[48] The message praising the monument – and by implication the patron, who is not named except in the foundation inscription – is combined with a religious one that extends to inscriptions above the tiled dadoes of the two side *īwān*s (see Figure 48) and the qibla *īwān* to both sides of the mihrab. In these inscriptions, hadith passages are combined that emphasize charity, especially the dispensing of hospitality, food, and water, as one of the foremost duties of pious Muslims and a condition to be rewarded in the afterlife.[49] These functions are emphasized in the building's *waqfīya*, which lists when food should be distributed and what should be served for instance on religious holidays.[50] Another hadith passage mentions posthumous rewards that await a martyr (*shahīd*), as well as those Muslims who fight unbelievers.[51] The combined message of these hadith passages, together with the comparison of the building to paradise observed in the foundation inscription, might suggest that Mehmed I's mosque-*zāviye* was planned as part of a funerary complex from the start, even though the mausoleum was built after the patron's death.[52] We cannot be entirely sure whether this was indeed the case, however, since interior decoration continued after Mehmed I's death based on the inscription dated 1424, which could also mean that adjustments to the program were made as construction continued.

In its plan (Figure 35, no. 2), the mosque-*zāviye* belongs to a type of monument variously designated the *eyvan* mosque, Bursa type, reverse-T, multifunction mosque, mosque with side spaces (*yan mekânlı cami*), convent mosque, convent *masjid*, or cross-axial mosque (*çapraz-mihverli cami*).[53] The complicated historiography of these terms is related to the implications of their mixed use, and recent work has focused on the relationship between form and function in these buildings.[54] Architectural historian Semavi Eyice has suggested that mosque-*zāviye*s were intended for combined use: the *īwān* with the mihrab for prayer and the side chambers to accommodate travelers and Sufis, while the porch could serve for funerary prayers.[55] In Eyice's argument, the connection between form and function plays a major role.

Further, Eyice bases his argument on historian Ömer Lütfi Barkan's study of dervishes' role in Ottoman expansion, in which Barkan argues that *waqf* was a crucial tool to establish control over newly conquered territory.[56] The colonizing function attributed to *waqf* was relevant during Ottoman expansion into Christian territories in the Balkans, and also within Anatolia as Mehmed I and Murad II regained the lands lost to the Timurid invasion of 1402. *Waqf* documents do at times offer glimpses of the practice of jointly creating mosques and buildings designated for Sufis in close proximity; many structures that served both functions also existed. Thus in 1486, Ali Beğ, son of Yahşi Beğ, established an endowment for the *masjid* and *zāviye* that were located in his former mansion in Serres, northern Greece.[57] Additionally, Saygın Salgırlı posits that *zāviye*s offered ways of co-opting existing social and power structures, expanding on them and adapting them for Ottoman rule, rather than imposing a new top-down order.[58] Recently, scholars have emphasized the need to critically reassess earlier views that emphasize a *gazi* and frontier milieu for mosque-*zāviye*s; thus Çiğdem Kafescioğlu rightly notes that such buildings were built in well-established Ottoman cities such as Bursa and Amasya, as well as in frontier zones in the Balkans.[59] In her study of Bursa in the fourteenth century, Suna Çağaptay argues for the importance of the practical functions of these buildings in addition to religious ones, and notes that the latter have been overemphasized in much of the earlier scholarship.[60]

The extensive properties tied to the imperial *waqf*s established in the fifteenth century by the sultans and their notables were a further tool for spatial and imperial consolidation as the lands and villages connected to these endowments became part of the Ottoman system of rule, property, and taxation. The endowments of Hajji ʿIvaz Pasha and Bayezid Pasha in the period of Mehmed I, of Yörgüç Pasha in the period of Murad II, and of Mahmud Pasha in the period of Mehmed II are just a few examples of extensive *waqf* property established under the patronage of Ottoman officials who held significant local power.[61] (Mehmed II's seizing of *waqf* properties in the hands of notables such as the disgraced Çandarlı Halil Pasha, executed in 1453, was part of this establishment of control over lands and real estate along with revenues, although Bayezid II's return of some of the confiscated properties complicates the matter.[62])

Many of these endowments were centered around mosque-*zāviye*s precisely to enhance the role of dervish groups in consolidating Ottoman rule. As imperial expansion and centralization advanced, however, the training of a home-grown Ottoman scholarly elite educated in the madrasas founded by the sultans became a priority, especially after the opening of the prestigious Sahn-Madrasas in connection to Mehmed II's mosque in Istanbul.[63] These changes affected the relationships between ulema and Sufis (especially antinomian dervishes) in the Ottoman Empire, as well as the political roles each group took on.[64] As a result, beginning in the 1520s, most mosque-*zāviye*s were transformed into mosques, particularly congregational/Friday mosques, turning away from flexible use and toward the orthopraxy of Hanefi Islam, which emphasized observance of and regular attendance at the five daily prayers, in particular the Friday prayer.[65]

Within Aptullah Kuran's detailed classification of early Ottoman mosques, Mehmed I's mosque-*zāviye* is called a "cross-axial *eyvan* mosque," a variant of the T-shaped plan in which the basic form is expanded with additional side rooms. The central domed courtyard and the use of *īwān*s (*eyvan*s in Turkish) – rectangular vaulted spaces framed by large arches opening on the central courtyard – are thought to be based on the layouts of thirteenth-century Saljuq madrasas.[66] Indeed the madrasas commissioned by Saljuq and other Muslim patrons in Anatolia beginning in the late twelfth century are variations on two- or four-*īwān* designs in which vaulted spaces face each other across open or covered courtyards. Examples include the Karatay Madrasa in Konya (1251–52; see Figure 14) with its domed courtyard and the Gök Madrasa in Sivas (1271–72), which is open at the center. Given the large number of medieval two- and four-*īwān* madrasas in Anatolia, it is reasonable to assume that the Ottoman reverse-T plan refers in part to earlier Islamic monuments in the region.[67] Changes in function and spatial additions during the Ottoman transformation of these earlier architectural forms, however, turned the two- or four-*īwān* structure into an entirely new building type. The integration of different functions into one structure without these multiple purposes being apparent on the building's exterior was a new feature in Ottoman architecture in the late fourteenth century. Earlier multifunctional monuments in central Anatolia, such as the Mahperi Hatun Complex in Kayseri (1237–38) and the Sahib Ata Complex in Konya (1258–84), read as composites on the outside even when the different parts of the structure are directly connected in the interior: in both of these examples, the mausoleum can be accessed through a madrasa or *khānqāh*, while the mosque retains a separate entrance.[68]

The plan of Mehmed I's mosque-*zāviye*, in contrast with those two earlier monuments, continues a line of development that began in Bursa at the end of the fourteenth century. The interior space departs from the expectations that viewers familiar with thirteenth-century monuments in central and eastern Anatolia would have had based on the façade with its muqarnas portal (Figure 36). This portal leads to a vestibule that is connected by a hallway to the central courtyard, which is covered by a dome and has a fountain in the middle. At the end of the central axis is the largest *īwān*, its floor level raised four steps above the courtyard. This *īwān* served as the prayer room, underscored by the large tiled mihrab on its southeastern wall. Two smaller *īwān*s to the east and west are also raised above the level of the courtyard; these served as rooms for Sufi teaching and also as lodgings for guests. Two square rooms, accessible by doors located on the left and right before the steps leading up to the prayer room, and two rectangular rooms that can be entered from the vestibule complete the ensemble. The three *īwān*s and the two subsidiary spaces near the mosque *īwān* are domed; these rooms could serve, for instance, as guest or assembly rooms and were thus flexible in their ritual and social uses.[69] Above the vestibule, a second floor contains the sultan's loggia (*hünkār mahfili*), which includes several small rooms and a balcony overlooking the monument's central space, all likely reserved for the sultan and his entourage.[70] The domes are visible from the exterior (Figure 37). The walls, built of stone (and in some parts brick[71]), are clad in marble and intricate carving decorates the portal, two rows of windows on the portal façade, and the windows on the lateral walls. Small inserts of turquoise tile emphasize the location of the *qibla* on the building's exterior, forming thin bands around the window frames of its western wall and the single window on the south wall.

To the south of the mosque-*zāviye*, Mehmed I's mausoleum, an octagonal domed structure, is situated in an elevated location (Figure 38). The mausoleum's exterior walls are covered in turquoise tiles and

36. Elevation, Mehmed I's mosque-*zāviye*, 1419–21, Bursa, Turkey. Drawing by Matilde Grimaldi

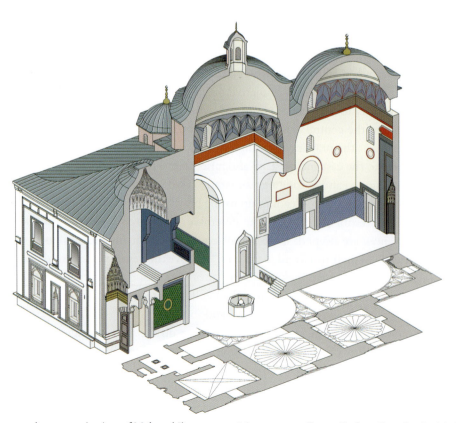

37. Axonometric view of Mehmed I's mosque-*zāviye*, 1419–21, Bursa, Turkey. Drawing by Matilde Grimaldi

38. Mehmed I's mausoleum in 1936, 1421–24, Bursa, Turkey. The Myron Bement Smith Collection, FSA_A.04, Freer Gallery of Art and Arthur M. Sackler Gallery Archives, Gift of Katharine Dennis Smith, Nicholas V. Artamonoff, FSA_A.04_2.06.55.060

inscription panels are placed above each window. Slabs of grey marble cover the corners of the building and form blind arches on the sides of the structure. An architectural cross-section indicates that a crypt lies beneath the mausoleum; this is where bodies were buried.[72] It is the only surviving Ottoman mausoleum built with a crypt.[73]

The kitchen (Figure 35, no. 3) has been rebuilt in modern times, and only fragments of the hammam (Figure 35, no. 5) remain. Farther away, the madrasa built of stone and brick adheres to Bursa's Byzantine architectural tradition (Figure 25, no. 1; Figure 39). The portal on its north face leads to an open courtyard with arcades on three sides that are interrupted by *īwān*s on either extreme of the east–west axis. The monument's central axis terminates in a large domed chamber. Steep steps lead to its entrance

39. Mehmed I's madrasa, 1419–21, Bursa, Turkey. © Patricia Blessing 2016

several meters above the courtyard level; this is where lessons would have been held for the madrasa's students, who were lodged in the series of rooms located on two sides of the courtyard.

Known in the fifteenth century as the Sultaniye Madrasa, this was one of the most prestigious madrasas of its time, at least until the construction of Mehmed II's mosque complex in Istanbul.[74] Its first *mudarris* was Mehmed Şah Fenari (d. 1435?), son of Molla Fenari.[75] Among the subsequent holders of the post was ʿAla al-Din ʿAli Tusi (d. 1482), who came to the Ottoman Empire from Iran during the reign of Murad II; later, Mehmed II would appoint him as a *mudarris* in a former church in Istanbul newly converted into an Islamic religious building, although he eventually left the Ottoman realm following a scholarly conflict.[76] For scholars like Molla Fenari, who had a close interest in Sufism, Bursa, with its multiple building complexes where mosque-*zāviye*s stood side by side with madrasas, would have been an ideal environment in which ulema and dervishes could mingle. This is not unlike what happened, for instance, in thirteenth-century Konya, where Sufis such as Jalal al-Din Rumi interacted with ulema.[77] This larger context of multifunctional buildings and the presence of intellectuals who had a strong interest in both Sufism and Islamic law (although these should not be seen as diametric opposites, especially not in the period discussed here) points to the larger issue of the relationship between dervishes and ulema in the early Ottoman Empire and ultimately to how this relationship transformed in the late fifteenth and early sixteenth centuries.[78]

The structures of Mehmed I's complex are distributed unevenly over a hilly site that affords maximum visibility for the buildings and offers views (now partially obscured by trees and modern construction) of the city center, the complex of Bayezid I, and the fertile alluvial plain to the north, the Yeşilova (visible in the background of Figure 34).[79] Mehmed I's mausoleum, with its elevated location and turquoise tile cladding, stands at the center of attention. Because of the spatial arrangement of the site, which lacks symmetry and is devoid of enclosing walls, the building complex does not have the appearance of a single structural unit. This lack of emphasis on spatial unity contrasts with the later mosque ensembles of the Ottoman sultans in Istanbul, beginning with that of Mehmed II (built 1463–70).[80] In Mehmed I's complex, the buildings are instead linked by visual connections and by inscriptions that mention their patron. A key element in the creation of these visual ties is the tile decoration. Before exploring this decoration in detail, however, it will be useful to consider the issue of dynastic memory in early Ottoman architecture and the role of Bursa as former capital and necropolis of the Ottoman sultans, considerations that lie behind Mehmed I's motives in founding the mosque-*zāviye* and related buildings.

DYNASTIC MEMORY IN BURSA

The interregnum after Bayezid I's death had strong repercussions for Ottoman geopolitics, and Bursa was a contested location throughout the conflict. Three sons of Bayezid I – the princes Mehmed Çelebi, İsa, and Emir Süleyman – were initially the main actors. The victorious conqueror Timur appointed Emir Süleyman ruler of Rumelia and installed a nephew of Bayezid I in Bursa; the latter was soon ousted by İsa when Timur confirmed him as ruler of Bithynia. In 1403, Bayezid I's son Musa was released from Timurid captivity into Mehmed Çelebi's custody, but he later rebelled and was defeated in battle in 1413.[81]

Once Mehmed Çelebi became sultan as Mehmed I, his rule remained contested; his last surviving brother, Mustafa, led a revolt in 1416 after he had been released from Timurid captivity.[82] He appeared in Bulgaria in October 1416, only to flee to Thessaloniki, which had been returned to Byzantine rule at the time, with Mehmed I in pursuit.[83] Having taken refuge in the city, Mustafa survived in Byzantine captivity and was released in 1421.[84] He immediately started another rebellion against the new sultan, his nephew Murad II, which continued until 1423. Murad II presented his uncle as an impostor, applying the epithet *düzme* (false) to him.[85] The first of Mustafa's revolts was closely followed by the rebellion of Şeyh Bedreddin, who had been Musa's *kazasker* in Rumelia and was exiled to Iznik by Mehmed I in 1413. Şeyh Bedreddin's background played a crucial role in his ability to gather diverse followers: he was the son of a *gazi* and a Byzantine fortress commander's daughter, as well as a scholar and Sufi; he claimed Saljuq ancestry to boot.[86] He mounted the revolt with his associate Börklüce Mustafa, who was centered in the region of Aydın and thus responsible for the Anatolian side of the uprising, while Şeyh Bedreddin acted in Rumelia, where he had fled from his exile in Iznik in summer 1416.[87] Şeyh Bedreddin's great success while advancing toward Edirne pushed Mehmed I to suppress the revolt: accused of heresy, Şeyh Bedreddin was captured and executed in Serres in December 1416.[88]

Amid this tumultuous power contest, the Ottoman realm was reconsolidated during Mehmed I's rule, paving the way for later conquests. Bursa was a central site in this process of conflict and reconsolidation: it changed hands multiple times during the civil war among Bayezid I's sons and was threatened by a Karamanid siege in 1415.[89] Possessing Bursa was an important sign of power and prestige for Ottoman sultans and pretenders to the throne. Thus Mehmed I's decision to commission his mosque-*zāviye* complex in this city was both an affirmation of dynastic memory and a mark of his success in consolidating his rule. Mehmed I connected his patronage to the fact that Bursa represented an established site of Ottoman memory with the burials of Ottoman sultans, Osman (r. 1302–24) and Orhan (r. 1324–62), and stood at the intersection of the dynastic past and the projected future.[90]

In the fourteenth century, Ottoman interventions in Bursa had adapted Byzantine urban space to a new reality and preexisting architectural elements were translated into a new style specifically tied to the formation of an Ottoman identity.[91] At the same time, the Ottomans appropriated Bursa's landscape for their own construction projects, establishing a pattern of organization centered on the monumental complexes of the sultans. Scholars have argued that the construction of multifunctional building complexes at the behest of several Ottoman sultans between the mid-fourteenth and the mid-fifteenth centuries created a specific topography suited to notions of imperial domination and helped establish additional urban cores in different sections of the city.[92] Construction projects in new suburbs and the established city center around the citadel and market area marked the patronage of the early Ottoman sultans; the mosque ensembles of Bayezid I and Murad I in particular formed landmarks in new sections of the city.[93] Pancaroğlu emphasizes the need to study Bursa as an integral cityscape rather than as a series of individual monuments and to avoid viewing the city as a mere prelude to Edirne and Istanbul.[94]

Bursa's importance is testified to by the mausoleum of Bayezid I (Figure 40), which was built near his mosque-*zāviye* and its surrounding structures in 1406, probably on the orders of Emir Süleyman, whose name appears on the foundation inscription. It cites 1 Muharram 809 AH / 18 June 1406 CE as the date

40. Mausoleum of Bayezid I, 1406, Bursa, Turkey. © Patricia Blessing 2014

on which construction began.[95] Sources describe how Mehmed Çelebi, after conquering Bursa in 1404, obtained his father's body from the Germiyan ruler Yakub II (r. 1388–90 and 1402–29), whom Timur had conveniently restored to power and ordered to bury the sultan.[96] Yet though it was Mehmed Çelebi who recovered his father's body, Emir Süleyman conquered Bursa only a few months later and it was he who oversaw the completion of the mausoleum.[97]

Mehmed Çelebi's efforts to recover Bayezid I's body for reburial in Bursa show his desire to honor his father's memory and enhance the city's status as a site of dynastic memory. A source from the time of the brothers' civil war, *Aḥvāl-i Sulṭān Meḥemmmed bin Bāyezīd Ḫān* (*Tales of Sultan Mehmed, Son of Bayezid Han*), describes the recovery of the body and its reburial in Bursa.[98] Bayezid I's mausoleum continued the line established with the burials of Osman, Orhan, and Murad I, affirming Bursa's role as a dynastic *lieu de mémoire*.[99] Mehmed Çelebi's efforts and Emir Süleyman's patronage show that both brothers used the notion of dynastic memory tied to specific sites as part of their competition with each other for the throne. Once Mehmed Çelebi emerged victorious, his patronage in Bursa can be seen as a maintenance of this effort. Notably, the *waqfīya* of the foundation, dated 822 AH / 1419 CE, refers to the city of Bursa as *dār al-mulk*, emphasizing its persistent status as capital at the time the document was written, during a period when Edirne had also taken on this role to an extent – at least as one of the royal residences and as a staging ground for campaigns in the Balkans.[100] In the thirteenth century, the term *dār al-mulk* was used in the Saljuq context to refer to Konya – the capital but also the place of dynastic burial and hence commemoration of the Saljuq rulers of Rūm.[101]

The concept of Bursa as the *dār al-mulk* connects to a renegotiation of Anatolia's history and the Ottoman place within it that was entailed by Mehmed I's ascension after the chaotic period of the interregnum. The Mongol conquest of Anatolia in the 1240s had brought about the gradual end of Saljuq rule in the region. Although members of the dynasty can be identified as late as 1307, the Saljuqs lost political power when they became vassals of the Mongol khan and were embroiled in decades-long internal succession struggles.[102] The dynasty slipped further into obscurity after the Mamluk invasion of Anatolia in 1277, when the sultan of Egypt and Syria, Baybars I (r. 1260–77), held the region for six months before retreating to Syria. As a consequence of this invasion, the Mongol Ilkhanids of Iran, the main rivals of the Mamluks and overlords of much of central and eastern

Anatolia, tightened control over the region, levying taxes and appointing governors.[103] Beginning in the second quarter of the fourteenth century, the Mongols' hold over the region slowly dissolved. This was part of a process that began after the death of the Ilkhanid sultan Abu Saʿid (r. 1316–35) and eventually led to the collapse of the Ilkhanid realm in the 1350s. Former Mongol vassals and governors formed independent realms in central and eastern Anatolia as Ilkhanid power waned and similar regional dynasties emerged in Iran and Iraq.[104] Thus central and eastern Anatolia from the mid-thirteenth century on were closely connected to the Mongol Empire and rooted in a post-Mongol world, even after the fall of the Ilkhanid dynasty in Iran.[105] The region's fluid power dynamics, in the frontier zone between Islam and Christianity, marked the context in which the Ottoman principality was formed and expanded in its initial stages. During the reign of Osman, the Mongols remained the dominant force in much of central and eastern Anatolia and were effectively overlords of several *beylik*s in western Anatolia.

Baki Tezcan has argued that the Ottomans' attitude toward Anatolia's Mongol past shifted over time, a change reflected in early Ottoman chronicles.[106] In texts written in the late fifteenth century during the reign of Bayezid II, late thirteenth-century Anatolia was transformed into something distinctly more Saljuq than the Mongol-dominated historical reality. The past became an elaborate fiction in which the Ottomans were connected to local Saljuq rather than invading Mongol overlords, and legitimacy was based on Islamic power relations. A Saljuq sultan named ʿAla al-Din – not a specific historical figure, but rather a conflation of ʿAla al-Din Kayqubad I (r. 1220–37) and ʿAla al-Din Kayqubad III b. Faramarz (r. 1297–1302) – was said to have conferred ruling authority on Osman, although historical timelines do not match up.[107] Despite this shift toward a Saljuq-centered narrative of legitimacy, dervish-historian ʿAşıkpaşazāde also drew on earlier sources harking back to the late thirteenth and fourteenth centuries that referred to the Mongols rather than the Saljuqs, as Tezcan shows. This demonstrates that such texts did exist and were known in the fifteenth century, but they were reinterpreted to suit the needs of Ottoman dynastic politics in a period when Ottoman consolidation was advancing in the wake of Mehmed II's conquests of Konya, Karaman, and Trebizond. At the time of the earlier sources used by ʿAşıkpaşazāde, the Ottomans had seen a close connection between their rule and that of the Mongols. After 1402, the traumatic defeat of Bayezid I by Timur turned the post-Mongol world into enemy territory for the Ottomans, bringing about the shift away from the Mongols and toward the Saljuqs.[108] ʿAşıkpaşazāde's writings reveal the extent to which Ottoman perception of the Mongol past had changed since 1300.

The fifteenth-century shift in the writing of history raises many questions, including to what extent the Ottomans' changing attitude toward the Anatolian past might have been reflected in architecture after Mehmed I's victory over his brothers in the succession war of 1402–13. Architecture helps us understand the complexities of this historical context, reflecting realities that were obscured or erased in later histories. Whereas architectural regionalism was pronounced in early Ottoman Bithynia, in Bursa in the early fifteenth century, and to a lesser extent in Edirne, we can detect an emerging interest in the thirteenth- and fourteenth-century architecture of central and eastern Anatolia, regions that were not yet under Ottoman rule but that fit into the narrative of legitimacy purportedly conveyed by the Saljuqs. Even though late fourteenth- to early fifteenth-century monuments in central and eastern Anatolia show marked regional differences, the references the Ottomans chose were more consistent with the style associated with a brief period of Saljuq dominance in the first half of the thirteenth century than with the local styles that emerged after the Mongol conquest in the 1240s.[109] In reality, though, these regionally ingrained architectural styles persisted well beyond the end of Saljuq and even Mongol control over Anatolia, as discussed in Chapter 1. Mehmed I's foundation in Bursa, built at an important juncture in the history of the Ottoman realm, exemplifies the volatile dynamics of memory and identity formation that were at stake. In what follows, I examine how the tile decoration and stonework of Mehmed I's mosque-*zāviye* complex reflect the pre-Ottoman Islamic past of central and eastern Anatolia, but also the present of Iran and Central Asia under Timurid cultural influence.

TILES: TIMURID, SALJUQ, AQQOYUNLU?

Within Mehmed I's complex in Bursa, the mosque-*zāviye*, mausoleum, and madrasa are decorated with various types of tile work combined with stone and brick architecture, together carrying multiple historical and cultural references. The use of tiles on such an extensive scale was new to Ottoman architecture, as were the kinds of tiles that were introduced. The Timurid present and the Saljuq past are especially prevalent in the complex's variegated tile decoration, though the historical and stylistic references implied in the complex as a whole can at times be ambiguous. Both a central Anatolian past and a Bithynian and Byzantine one are evoked. While this section focuses specifically on the tile decoration as a rich visual device used to guide perceptions of past, present, and future, it is important to note that Mehmed I's entire complex is just such an exercise in manipulating the past for the benefit of a new Ottoman future. Far from creating a dichotomy between past and future, the ornament may have been used to tie the architecture of the present – reflecting Ottoman recovery – to both a new future that lay ahead in the patron's hopes and the past in which Bursa had been the main dynastic center.

Building Innovations: Creating Immersive Space

The madrasa is the least elaborately decorated of the extant monuments. Only small pieces of tile are used on the exterior, in lunettes over the windows, inserted into brick to form checkerboard and similar patterns (Figure 41). Inside, tile mosaic forms geometric patterns in the vaults of the lateral *īwāns*.[110] Tile decoration is much more extensive inside the mosque-*zāviye* and on the mausoleum's interior and exterior.

The mausoleum's exterior is entirely clad in turquoise-glazed tiles interrupted by calligraphic lunettes over the windows (Figure 42), while on the portal (Figure 43), black-line tiles are framed by carved,

41. Entrance, Mehmed I's madrasa, 1419–21, Bursa, Turkey. © Patricia Blessing 2014

42. Calligraphic lunette over window, Mehmed I's mausoleum, 1421–24, Bursa, Turkey. © Patricia Blessing 2014

43. Detail of portal, Mehmed I's mausoleum, 1421–24, Bursa, Turkey. © Patricia Blessing 2014

glazed terra-cotta around the inscription panels. The tiles were restored in 1863 following the earthquake of 1855, and the ceramic facing was also removed (and reinstalled) during a restoration project in 1941–43, leaving some questions as to the amount of original tile still preserved on site.[111] The use of tile on the exterior of Mehmed I's mausoleum is unique in medieval Anatolia. The climate does not lend itself to the type of tile decoration prevalent in Timurid Iran and Central Asia, where large sections of monuments are clad in tile mosaic or *bannāʾī* (glazed tiles alternating with brick). The wet winters of Anatolia, with abundant snow and rainfall and strong frosts, are particularly hard on tile decoration, which often suffers water damage and cracks when subjected to humidity and cold temperatures. Outdoor tile use in Anatolia is generally limited to the open courtyards of madrasas, including the Sırçalı Madrasa in Konya (1243; see Figure 13) and the late thirteenth-century Gök Madrasa in Tokat (see Figure 15).

In both of these monuments, the courtyard walls are covered with damaged tile mosaic while their exterior façades are built of stone and devoid of tile decoration.

In the mausoleum's interior, turquoise tiles covering the lower half of the walls are interrupted by medallions in black-line technique (Figure 44), and the mausoleum's mihrab is composed entirely of black-line tile (Figure 45).[112] The tiles made with this method are often called *cuerda seca* (dry cord) tiles. Due to technical differences, however, *cuerda seca* is a misnomer here, and "black-line" is the more appropriate term in the eastern Islamic context.[113] In black-line tiles from Central Asia, Iran, and Anatolia, the tile is first covered with a slip to create a uniform background and then fired. Black (and sometimes red) outlines are then drawn on the tile and filled with different pigments. During a second firing, these outlines remain visible and the colored sections assume their brilliant glaze.[114] Black-line tiles compose a large part of the decoration in the mausoleum, but other tile-work techniques, including monochrome underglaze tiles, tile mosaic, and painted terra-cotta relief, were used as well. Even though such tiles appear in Timurid Central Asia beginning in the late fourteenth century, here they are not necessarily directly associated with Timurid dominance, as we shall see.

In the center of the mausoleum, a low platform is covered in monochrome turquoise tiles. This platform is the base for several cenotaphs, most prominently that of Mehmed I, which is placed at the center and richly decorated with black-line tiles bearing inscriptions and floral ornament; some of these tiles are molded to bear decoration in relief. Other figures buried in the mausoleum, marked by smaller cenotaphs clustered around the sultan's monumental one, include Mehmed I's sons Mustafa (d. 1423), Mahmud (d. 1428), and Yusuf (d. 1428); his daughters Selçuk Hatun (d. 1485), Hafsa Sultan, Ayşe Hatun, and Sitti Hatun; and the sultan's wet nurse.[115]

Tile mosaic is used for the soffits of deep window niches inside the mausoleum (Figure 46). This technique is found in both Timurid and Saljuq architecture, but the color palette of the panels here, limited to blues, white, and purple, is closer to the latter. Tile mosaic – the prevalent technique for tile decoration in Anatolia from the mid-thirteenth to the mid-fourteenth centuries – is only rarely found in the fifteenth century. The few examples include the Hasbey Darülhuffaz in Konya (1421) and the Pir Hüseyin Bey Mosque in Sarayönü, near Konya (1408–09).[116]

In Mehmed I's mosque-*zāviye*, tile decoration extends over large parts of the structure's interior: the lower parts of walls in the entrance hallway and the *īwān*s around the courtyard are covered in tiles glazed in dark blue and turquoise. In the hall, large roundels in black-line tile interrupt fields of monochrome

44. Interior, Mehmed I's mausoleum, 1421–24, Bursa, Turkey. © Patricia Blessing 2014

45. Detail of mihrab, Mehmed I's mausoleum, 1421–24, Bursa, Turkey. © Patricia Blessing 2014

tile (Figure 47). On the hexagonal dark-green tiles in the two side *īwān*s, gold decoration has been preserved (Figure 48) beneath inscriptions in black-line tile. The mihrab is richly decorated with black-line tiles in blue, purple, and yellow (Figure 49). Even in this central part of the monument, the patterns on neighboring tiles do not quite match, suggesting a degree of experimentation.[117] The lower parts of the walls in all three *īwān*s are covered in dark blue tiles without gold overlay, and inscription bands in black-line tile run above them. Black-line tiles also appear in the sultan's lodge on the building's upper level, above the vestibule and entrance corridor, where tiles are combined with stucco and wood carving. Black-line tiles with geometric motifs cover the lateral walls and ceiling of the central room of the sultan's lodge. Viewed from the building's central space, the opening of the lodge, which allowed the sultan to look out over this space, is framed with inscription bands in black-line tiles (Figure 50).

The sultan's lodge is a strongly immersive space, an effect created by both its visual impact and its haptic potential. The space is completely lined with tiles: walls and ceiling are covered with black-line tiles with geometric motifs composed of hexagons, octagons, and stars (Figure 51). Along the meeting point between walls and ceiling, a row of muqarnas is formed of tiles decorated with floral motifs. The railing of the lodge, a lattice screen of hexagons, is also covered with tiles on both the interior and exterior faces. The floor of the lodge is tiled as well, and so are the steps leading up to it. Within the lodge, the geometric motifs are not flatly painted on the tiles' surface but rather molded and then painted in black-line technique, adding additional projecting relief. This presents a strong contrast to the slick surfaces of the *īwān*s below, where monochrome gilded tiles dominate. Thus the architecture here engages not only vision but also touch, bridging a sensory divide that is often present in twentieth- and twenty-first-century modes of perception, which tend to focus on vision at the expense of the other senses, touch in particular.[118] As Mark Paterson notes, however, vision and touch are not mutually

46. Tile mosaic in window niche, Mehmed I's mausoleum, 1421–24, Bursa, Turkey. © Patricia Blessing 2014

47. Monochrome tile with black-tile medallion, hallway between vestibule and prayer hall, Mehmed I's mosque-*zāviye*, 1419–21, Bursa, Turkey. © Patricia Blessing 2016

48. Hadith inscription in black-line tile and dado tiles with gold overlay in west *īwān*, Mehmed I's mosque-*zāviye*, 1419–21, Bursa, Turkey. © Patricia Blessing 2016

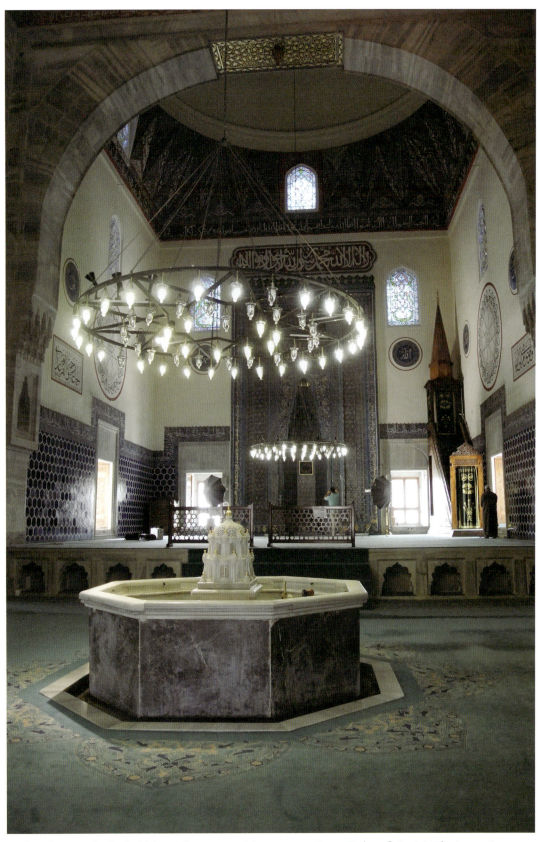

49. Interior toward mihrab, Mehmed I's mosque-*zāviye*, 1419–21, Bursa, Turkey. © Patricia Blessing 2016

50. Sultan's lodge, Mehmed I's mosque-*zāviye*, 1419–21, Bursa, Turkey. © Patricia Blessing 2016

51. Detail, sultan's lodge, Mehmed I's mosque-*zāviye*, 1419–21, Bursa, Turkey. © Patricia Blessing 2016

exclusive, but can rather be explained as part of the same system of perception once a multisensory approach is recognized: "[T]he haptic is not in opposition to the optic. It does not oppose the eyes with the hands, but acknowledges the sensory interdependence of the whole haptic (hand-eye-motion) system."[119]

Once the supremacy of vision is no longer taken for granted, it is indeed possible to understand monuments through different, multisensory lenses that include the activation of touch. Similarly, Juhani Pallasmaa has argued that touch should be taken seriously as a way to understand architecture.[120] Touch can mean not only tactility but also the haptic sense, which can be defined as *potential* touch, the evocation of desire to access out-of-reach objects and surfaces with touch. Laura Marks has addressed haptic space and abstract line within the context of Islamic art and suggested that both concepts are useful in order to "avoid the figurative prejudice of art-historical discourse" when discussing aniconic art – such as the geometric decoration of the lodge here, but also the overall decorative program of the buildings.[121]

The space of the sultan's lodge is both tactile space for its occupants and haptic space for those who are in the mosque below and gaze up at its eye-catching colors and textures, perhaps hoping to catch a glimpse of the sultan. The multisensory effects of the lodge potentially would have been heightened by the presence of objects such as carpets to cover the floors, lamps and candles, and incense burners.[122] Thus the senses of vision, touch, and smell would all have been addressed as would hearing with the sound of recitations and prayers in the mosque-*zāviye*.[123] In the current space, another source of sound is water running in the fountain in the covered courtyard; as Kafescioğlu notes, a court record dated 1552 includes a request for the fountain to be removed from the building since overflow threatened to pollute what was now part of the prayer hall following the building's transformation into a Friday mosque.[124] The request for a change (eventually not completed) proves that the fountain is an original feature. Most likely the courtyard would have been paved and free of carpets, whereas the *īwān* containing the mihrab would have been carpeted because of its function as a prayer room.[125] A plate in Léon Parvillée's book about his restoration work in Bursa in the 1860s shows the interior of the building with a paved floor underneath the first dome; carpets only appear in the *qibla īwān*.[126] Thus the current state of the building with carpeting throughout distorts its image and obscures its original multifunctional nature and flexible use.[127]

The multisensory appeal of the space is clear, and it was not lost on Ottoman viewers like seventeenth-century traveler Evliya Çelebi, who noted the outstanding splendor of the mosque-*zāviye*'s tile work and carved marble with the pair of terms "*tarz-i acîb ve tavr-i garîb*."[128] By using these terms, "wondrous" and "astonishing," Evliya Çelebi links his description of the building to the literary tradition of *ʿajīb* and *gharīb* (*ʿajāʾib* and *gharāʾib* in the plural). These notions of wonder and astonishment are essential to poetic traditions in Arabic and Persian, where they appear early on and are used to designate natural phenomena as wonders of creation, as well as to describe man-made objects that impress either because of their sensory properties or because the process of their making is not obvious to the beholder.[129] This mode of expression is used not only in poems but also in descriptions of art objects, as Matthew Saba demonstrates in his study of Abbasid luster ceramics, which are specifically made to produce effects of color that change depending on lighting.[130] Thus wonder was a highly sought-after effect when producing objects and it could be elicited through a wide range of sensory appeals, from the iridescent effects of luster ceramics to the rustling of silk. While the reception of these terms in the Ottoman context needs to be studied further, it is notable that the vocabulary connected to them was known, as Evliya Çelebi's use of the paired words *acîb* and *garîb* shows, and as the use of the related word *būqalamūn* in the foundation inscription of the Çinili Köşk, discussed in Chapter 1, further establishes. The high praise Evliya Çelebi also has for the mosque-*zāviye*'s mihrab, comparing it to the artistry of painter Bihzad (d. ca. 1535), active at the Timurid and Safavid courts, speaks to the impression the tile work made even two hundred years after its creation.[131]

In line with the effort to create an immersive, wonder-inducing space, diverse tile techniques were used in the mosque and mausoleum, displaying the full array of skills in which craftsmen were proficient at the time of construction: black line, mosaic, inlays in stone, monochrome with gold overlay, and carved terra-cotta. Tiles were also combined with decorative elements in stucco, carved wood, painting, and carved stone. This diverse set of techniques and styles and the creative combination of these elements to create a wholly distinct architecture in many ways prefigure what was done in Istanbul in the late fifteenth century. There, as noted in Chapter 1, the patronage of Sultan Mehmed II and his grand viziers drew on a wide range of materials, styles, and techniques – Byzantine, Timurid, early Ottoman, Renaissance Italian – to present aspirations to universal rule.[132] Even though such ambitions were not yet central in Mehmed I's Bursa, a desire to display knowledge of a wide range of past and present styles, along with the related prestige of being able to hire craftsmen capable of working on them, was certainly part of the material politics of the time.

When Murad II commissioned the addition of the mausoleum, the Persianate aesthetic promulgated by the Timurid courts would have been more desirable than it had been previously, and the Ottoman sultan may have been keen to embrace the prevalent Islamic elite culture. This may explain, at least in part, why Mehmed I's mausoleum looks more Persianate and Timurid, especially on the inside, while the mosque-*zāviye* works with a different aesthetic dominated by stone and supplemented with tile. Viewing these buildings today also poses the question of their effect on a fifteenth-century inhabitant of Bursa. Would the tiles have registered as Timurid? Would other references have come to mind for a local? To Bursalıs who had never ventured far from their hometown, the tiles on the sultan's mausoleum would certainly have appeared vastly different from anything they had ever seen, as the contrast with earlier and contemporary Ottoman buildings in the city is marked. Thus, even if the Persianate aesthetic the patron

76 IMMERSIVE SPACE

and his advisors may have had in mind did not register with the population, the effect of creating a visible mark of Ottoman presence in a new style would have.

The Masters of Tabriz: Tiles and Origin

The tile decoration of Mehmed I's mosque-*zāviye* and mausoleum was new not only in Bursa but also in Anatolia, for the color palette included yellow and light purple in addition to the range of blue, turquoise, white, and nearly black purple generally used in thirteenth- and fourteenth-century tile decoration in central Anatolia. This new type of decoration would become common, if intermittent, in Ottoman architecture: it was used in the mosque-*zāviye* of Murad II in Bursa (1425–26), the Şah Melek Pasha Mosque (1429) and the Muradiye Mosque in Edirne (1435–36), and the mosque of Mehmed II in Istanbul (1463–70).[133] Elsewhere in Anatolia beyond the Ottoman realm, however, such tiles were rare. In the mausoleum of the Germiyan ruler Yakub II (d. 1429) in Kütahya, black-line tile borders were used alongside hexagonal turquoise and triangular purple tiles on the cenotaph. Considering that Yakub II visited Bursa and Edirne in 1428, it is possible that he saw the mosque-*zāviye* and mausoleum of Mehmed I and the mosque-*zāviye* of Murad II and was influenced in his choice of style when he commissioned his own mausoleum.[134] As Mustafa Çağhan Keskin suggests, it is possible that the tiles were commissioned from a production site in the Ottoman realm or that workers traveled to Kütahya to complete the decoration of the mausoleum.[135] Considering that Yakub II's mausoleum is the only extant example of tile use in fifteenth-century Kütahya, the first option is more likely and may provide an early example of the shipping of tiles, as opposed to a traveling workshop. Incidentally, this artistic exchange is another instance of the close connections between the *beylik* of Germiyan and the Ottomans – because of their previous alliance through the marriage between Yakub II's sister and Bayezid I in 1381, the Ottomans acquired Yakub's territories by treaty in 1428, a year before his death, as he had no male heir.[136]

Farther east in Anatolia, the mihrab of the İbrahim Bey İmaret in Karaman (1432) offers one example of black-line technique. Meinecke suggests a close connection between the black-line tiles in Karaman and those in Bursa based on the use of both red and black lines to separate fields of colored glaze, a rather unusual combination of the two types of dividing lines.[137] Rare examples of black-line tile in southeastern Anatolia, in the region between Mardin, Hasankeyf, and Diyarbakır, are located in the same geographic zone as Tabriz and hence are more likely to stem from a direct connection to workshops active in that city.[138]

The tiles in the mosque-*zāviye* and mausoleum of Mehmed I are assumed to have been produced locally, although kilns have not been found in Bursa.[139] The makers of the tiles left a collective mark on the monument: on the mosque's mihrab is written in Persian the phrase " *'amal-i ustādhān-i Tabrīz*" (work of the Masters of Tabriz).[140] While this inscription is often described as a signature, it actually occupies a liminal place within the distinction Sheila Blair proposes between formal building inscriptions (such as the one mentioning Hajji 'Ivaz Pasha; see Figure 53) and informal signatures on objects.[141] While the inscription is part of an architectural element – namely the mihrab – it is also rather small and inconspicuous, requiring a viewer to approach closely in order to see and read it. Later in this chapter and in Chapter 3, we will see that the phrase "work of the Masters of Tabriz" has become the foundation of a complex knot of art historians' speculations related to who these workers were, where they came from, and what region and style the tiles they made were representative of. Several other makers' names in the complex include "Muhammad the Mad" (Muhammad al-majnūn) on an arch in the sultan's lodge, and "'Ali ibn Hajji Ahmad of Tabriz" on the mausoleum's wooden doors.[142]

Another signature in particular has been at the center of a debate about the attribution of the tile decoration, though it is not found on the tiles: painted onto the wall above the sultan's lodge is the name

'Ali ibn Ilyas 'Ali, in an inscription dated 827 AH / 1424 CE (see Figure 50 at top).[143] An elaborate biographical narrative has been developed for this figure: according to it, 'Ali ibn Ilyas 'Ali, also known as *naqqāsh* 'Ali, was taken captive as a young man during the Timurid conquest of Bursa and deported to Samarqand, where he was trained as a craftsman.[144] Twenty years later, *naqqāsh* 'Ali miraculously reappeared in his hometown and became a leading figure in the construction of Mehmed I's mosque-*zāviye*. As Marthe Bernus-Taylor notes, this account is often repeated without evidence.[145]

The narrative is based on Taeschner's study of the building, published in 1932, in which the German historian refers to an account by the Ottoman historian and biographer Ahmad b. Mustafa Taşköprüzāde (d. 1561), who, in his *Shaqā'iq al-nu'mānīyat*, a biographical dictionary of learned men active in the Ottoman Empire, names 'Ali al-Naqqash as the grandfather of the poet Lami'i Çelebi (d. 1532).[146] In his youth, 'Ali al-Naqqash, according to Taşköprüzāde, was taken from Bursa to Transoxiana as Timur's captive, trained as a *naqqāsh* (which can be translated as carver of either stone or wood, or more generally as decorator or designer), and, on returning to Bursa, became one of the foremost representatives of his craft in Anatolia.[147] Taşköprüzāde's account does not, however, offer a date for 'Ali al-Naqqash's return to Bursa, nor does it connect him to Mehmed I's mosque-*zāviye*. Moreover, it remains unclear whether the 'Ali al-Naqqash of Taşköprüzāde's account and 'Ali ibn Ilyas 'Ali, whose name appears in Mehmed I's mosque-*zāviye*, are one and the same person. The fact that Lami'i Çelebi, the purported grandson of the celebrated *naqqāsh*, wrote a poetic elegy for his hometown, Bursa, may have contributed to the link established in Taeschner's and later publications.

'Ali al-Naqqash's presumed stay in Samarqand, taken together with the signature of the Masters of Tabriz, has led to broader speculations about the place of origin of these workers. Thus, because of 'Ali al-Naqqash's Samarqand connection, literary scholar Michele Bernardini suggests that the Tabriz of the signatures is really Samarqand, albeit without elaborating why he thinks this is the case.[148] Why use the placeholder Tabriz to refer to the ultimate center of Timurid artistic production at the time, Samarqand? In his argument, Bernardini follows Lisa Golombek, who rightly emphasized that the largest body of Timurid black-line tile is found in the Shah-i Zinda complex in Samarqand beginning in the 1380s, and that Tabriz did not emerge as a major center of tile production until the last quarter of the fifteenth century. Golombek concluded that a direct connection between the tiles produced in Bursa and workshops in Timurid Samarqand should be considered, in part because no early fifteenth-century black-line tiles have survived in Tabriz.[149]

Meanwhile, the roots of origin stories based on Tabriz are twofold. In addition to the story of 'Ali al-Naqqash, it is known that the Timurid prince Ulugh Beğ released master craftsmen from their forced residence in Samarqand in 1411; these individuals, whose names are largely unknown, were captured during Timur's campaigns in Iran, Syria, and Anatolia, and it is thus possible that workers originally from Tabriz were among them. Perhaps the Masters of Tabriz spent time in Khurasan before making their way to Bursa. In addition, O'Kane, though agreeing with Golombek about the dates of the earliest Timurid black-line tiles, convincingly suggests that the high quality of tiles made in Tabriz in the second half of the fifteenth century would not have been possible without previous production.[150] The geographic proximity between Bursa and Tabriz (about 1,800 km along well-established trade routes that had functioned since at least the thirteenth century) makes a tie between these two cities more probable than one with the more distant Samarqand, although we should not underestimate mobility within the medieval Islamic world. The claim to Tabriz in the signature – whether the tile makers came from there or elsewhere – demonstrates how important the city was as a cultural center at the time.

If these workers indeed came from Tabriz, who hired them? Were they already in Anatolia and did they come to Bursa hoping for work? Were they specifically invited for this project? Who coordinated collaborations between tile workers, stonemasons, and architects? Who organized the delivery of materials to the building sites? In short, who served as a general contractor mediating between patron and workers? Such specific questions about the planning of imperial Ottoman construction projects are central when examining a period in which little such information is available, unlike in the sixteenth century and later. On Mehmed I's mosque-*zāviye*, an inscription gives crucial clues: the name "Ḥājjī Iwāḍ bin Akhī Bāyazīd" is carved onto the second of two rectangular cartouches (Figures 52 and 53) in the sides of the building's portal recess, to the right and left of the entrance (see Figure 59).[151]

This inscription refers to an important figure at the court of Mehmed I, better known as Hajji 'Ivaz Pasha, who became a vizier, possibly in 1415 after he had successfully fended off the Karamanids' attack

52. First part of inscription with Hajji 'Ivaz Pasha's name, portal of Mehmed I's mosque-*zāviye*, 1419–21, Bursa, Turkey. © Patricia Blessing 2014

53. Second part of inscription with Hajji 'Ivaz Pasha's name, portal of Mehmed I's mosque-*zāviye*, 1419–21, Bursa, Turkey. © Patricia Blessing 2014

on Bursa during his tenure as *subaşı*.[152] Originally from the region of Tokat, Hajji 'Ivaz Pasha used the power he gained at the Ottoman court to establish foundations in Tokat, Beyoba, and Bursa.[153] He died in 1428, fallen from favor and possibly blinded.[154] Facing Hajji 'Ivaz Pasha's name, another inscribed cartouche states that he was involved in the construction of the mosque-*zāviye* with phrases that in loose translation refer to "numbering, organizing, and determining basic rules" for the building (see Figure 52).[155] The terms suggest that Hajji 'Ivaz Pasha served as an overseer of sorts, perhaps similar to the Mamluk office of *shād al-'amā'ir*, responsible for supervising workers on royal building sites.[156] Such a function could include a wide range of tasks related to the planning and execution of a project.

Further, Hajji 'Ivaz Pasha's name appears in an inscription on the southern portal of the mosque founded by Mehmed I in Didymoteichon (Dimetoka). In this inscription, which commemorates the completion of the building in 848 AH / 1421 CE, he is mentioned together with the local kadi, Sayyid 'Ali, and a builder, Toghan b. 'Abdallah. The latter may also have been active in Amasya, and again appears in the next chapter. In the Didymoteichon inscription, Hajji 'Ivaz Pasha is described as "the pride of the engineers, and the choice of the builders, the skilled master of his craft."[157] The term *muhandis* (mathematician or engineer) with which Hajji 'Ivaz Pasha is referred to here points to skills with calculations and numbers, just as the description of calculating measurements and proportions in the Bursa inscription suggests.

Ottoman historians of the late fifteenth century credit Hajji 'Ivaz Pasha with bringing foreign craftsmen to the Ottoman court in addition to his active role in building. While these historians do not refer to specific projects, he could indeed have hired the Masters of Tabriz and others.[158] A project of the scale and complexity of Mehmed I's complex would have required the collaboration of a number of highly qualified workers – not only the Masters of Tabriz but also stone carvers to create the monumental muqarnas and intricately carved decoration of the mosque-*zāviye*'s portal, wood carvers for the doors and shutters, those who made the stucco decoration in the mosque-*zāviye*, and those who made carpets and other furnishings such as the candlesticks, Qur'an stands, and incense burners necessary to properly furnish a sultan's funerary complex. To focus on the Masters of Tabriz as singular makers of a work of genius is therefore not helpful.

Thus, while the tile makers' signatures point to Tabriz, other workers – for instance, those responsible for the stone carving – must have come from different contexts within or beyond the Ottoman realm, even though they did not sign their work. The dominance of Tabriz in narratives about Mehmed I's patronage therefore only accounts for part of what happened on a building site that would have been impossible to complete without collaboration between a diverse cast of workers, perhaps under Hajji 'Ivaz Pasha's expert supervision. Moving beyond the tiles, I now engage with the other elements of the building complex, particularly the stone carving, since it presents further insights into the dynamics of making and patronage that are at play. Later I return to the implications of Timurid style for the larger significance of the buildings.

THE SALJUQ PAST: STONE AND PRE-OTTOMAN ANATOLIA

In Mehmed I's mosque-*zāviye*, there is a tension between interior and exterior that is articulated in the façade, with a muqarnas portal of the type often associated with thirteenth-century Saljuq architecture (see Figure 59). The same type of portal is, in fact, used beyond the central territories of Saljuq rule in central and eastern Anatolia and even found in the post-Mongol period, but its history is fraught with overly simplified correlations to Saljuq central power and patronage.[159] Such portals first appeared in Anatolia on caravanserais sponsored by the Saljuq sultans in the second quarter of the thirteenth century; later they appeared in mosques, madrasas, and mausolea across central and eastern Anatolia built by Saljuq and other patrons, while other types of portals also remained in use. Carved in marble, the portal of

Mehmed I's mosque-*zāviye* is one of the first portals of this type to appear in an Ottoman monument; the few earlier examples include the Timurtaş *zāviye* in Bursa (1389–1402) and the Eski Cami in Edirne (1404–13).[160] In the Great Mosque in Bursa (1399–1402), a large-scale muqarnas portal was used on the building's north side; while this portal has some of the features typical of thirteenth-century central Anatolia, the ornamental frames on it are much less elaborate than those on the portal of Mehmed I's mosque-*zāviye*.[161]

The two-story façade of Mehmed I's mosque-*zāviye* also recalls the immediate Ottoman past, in particular the mosque-*zāviye* of Bayezid I and the mosque-madrasa of Murad I in Bursa, both of which have two-story façades, but without the prominent muqarnas niche over the entrance found on Mehmed I's building. While the façade of Bayezid I's mosque-*zāviye* (built in 1390) does feature muqarnas, this is limited to decorative niches in the lateral walls of the portal recess (Figures 54 and 55) and underneath the porch (Figure 56). Over the entrance, an empty panel sits where the foundation inscription would have been placed, and above it a niche with a stilted arch is whitewashed (Figure 57). Since the building was damaged in the 1855 earthquake, it is unclear what it would have looked like originally.[162] Thus, while stone carving was certainly available for Bayezid I's mosque and the portal, the façade, and the exterior of the porch were clad with marble panels, the choice to include a full-scale muqarnas portal was not made here and the carving remains limited to the frames of niches, engaged capitals on the entrance, and moldings around doors and windows. On the mosque-madrasa of Murad I (1365–85), the façade (Figure 58), which has two clearly articulated stories, is built with courses of brick and stone and features brick ornament in lunettes over the arches. It demonstrates both Byzantine elements and Italian influence, perhaps by way of Dalmatia, as Çağaptay argues.[163] Anatolia's pre-Ottoman Islamic past is conspicuously absent.

The portal of Mehmed I's mosque-*zāviye* (Figure 59) differs from most thirteenth- and fourteenth-century examples by being flush with the façade rather than set into a salient block, but it has ornamental frames that highlight the central muqarnas niche and doorway. As noted before, the intended porch was never built, and thus the muqarnas portal with its extensive carved decoration is in full view. The fact that the monument was not completed is also evident in the unfinished carved decoration on some of the windows (Figure 60) – an indication, incidentally, that at least some of the decoration was carved directly on the building after the marble cladding had been installed. In addition to the muqarnas niche over the entrance, stone carving is found in the spandrels to both sides of the muqarnas niche just above the foundation inscription, in the recesses of the portal, and around the exterior window frames on the north, east, and south façades. Thus, even if it was not built to jut out from the façade, the portal evokes the Saljuq model of a series of rectangular frames. What is more, the ornamental frames were carved into a cavetto, further emphasizing the recess toward the entrance (Figure 61).

While the frames in Saljuq monuments feature predominantly geometric decoration, Mehmed I's mosque-*zāviye* introduces greater variety. From the outermost frame going inward, they feature: floral ornament inserted into a geometric structure; a large inscription in *thuluth* script; floral ornament that is symmetrically structured and closely evokes some of the tile borders inside; a plan molding; an inscription in floral kufic script; and floral ornament with stylized chrysanthemums and leafy scrolls that belong in the realm of *khitāyī* ornament. This last frame, rather than leading all the way around the portal like the others, ends in the corners of the spandrels around the muqarnas niche and wraps around the engaged columns with muqarnas capitals and bases that form the front corners of the entrance recess.

In the spandrels (Figure 62), large-scale *rūmī* leaves and scroll patterns dominate the portal.[164] While it is unusual to see them carved in stone, a nearly matching set of large leaves is found in a late fifteenth-century Ottoman velvet (Figure 63). Woven in gold thread on a dark red background, the leaves on the velvet illustrate how motifs could move back and forth between architecture and textiles and back – a phenomenon that would become more common in the sixteenth century but that is visible here at an earlier stage. The relief carving and the weave of the velvet both have the

54. First muqarnas niche in portal recess, right side, mosque of Bayezid I, 1390–95, Bursa, Turkey. © Patricia Blessing 2014

55. Second muqarnas niche in portal recess, right side, mosque of Bayezid I, 1390–95, Bursa, Turkey. © Patricia Blessing 2014

56. Muqarnas niche on porch to left of entrance, mosque of Bayezid I, 1390–95, Bursa, Turkey. © Patricia Blessing 2014

57. Portal, mosque of Bayezid I, 1390–95, Bursa, Turkey. © Patricia Blessing 2014

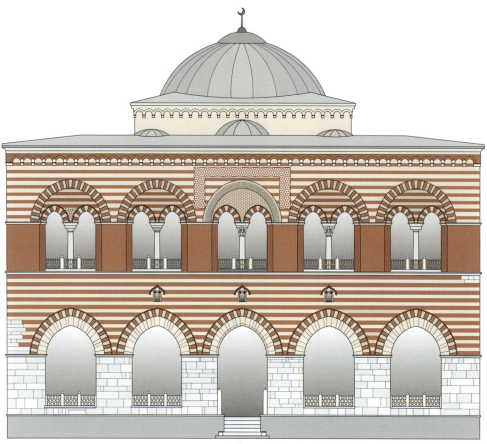

58. Elevation, mosque-madrasa of Murad I, 1365–85, Bursa, Turkey. Drawing by Matilde Grimaldi

potential to activate haptic space: their textures invite touch, and the carving on Mehmed I's mosque-*zāviye* provides a visual tie to textile patterns that connects to a desire to touch fabric. Even though the scrolls and leaves of the top of the façade are out of reach, other parts of the carving are not. The motifs found on these frames are repeated in other places on the façade: in the spandrels and recesses of the niches on its lower level – one such niche is located at the center of each wing of the façade – and in the niches in the sides of the portal recess. These carvings display the many possible variations on these motifs, introducing a wide range of leaves, scrolls, and tendrils – in some cases arranged symmetrically along an axis, in others not. The portal decoration also establishes a dialogue with the tile decoration to come in the interior. This connection is subtle and involves the use of similar epigraphy and scroll motifs in both stone and tile. The portal thus prepares the viewer for the mihrab, which is located on the same axis (although elevated by the platform of the qibla *īwān*) and makes use of the same motifs and structural devices such as the frames and the muqarnas niche.

We can see that while the structure of the portal is ultimately derived from Saljuq architecture (albeit its later forms built under Mongol rule), details of the carving expand beyond that repertoire and include new motifs. The *rūmī* motifs are certainly part of the Saljuq vocabulary, but they are here used on a more monumental scale. The rows of muqarnas around window frames appear in buildings completed for the *beylik* rulers of western Anatolia in the late fourteenth and early fifteenth centuries. On the window grilles of Mehmed I's mosque-*zāviye*, silver inlay – the first occurrence in architecture of such a feature in Anatolia – points directly to Mamluk work.[165] Thus, while Saljuq architecture provides a basis for the Bursa façade, the net of stylistic references is cast more widely. As noted, this wide range of designs used on the façade includes *khiṭāyī* motifs even though they are not as conspicuous as they are in early

59. Portal, Mehmed I's mosque-*zāviye,* 1419–21, Bursa, Turkey. © Patricia Blessing 2016

60. Unfinished carving on window frame, portal façade, Mehmed I's mosque-*zāviye,* 1419–21, Bursa, Turkey. © Patricia Blessing 2014

61. Detail of frames, portal of Mehmed I's mosque-*zāviye,* 1419–21, Bursa, Turkey. © Patricia Blessing 2014

62. Detail of large-scale *rūmī* designs, portal of Mehmed I's mosque-*zāviye,* 1419–21, Bursa, Turkey. © Patricia Blessing 2016

63. Brocaded velvet, silk and metal thread, 114 x 156cm, Ottoman Turkey, ca. 1500–40, Victoria & Albert Museum, London, inv. no. 326-1895. V&A Images, London/Art Resource, NY

sixteenth-century examples such as the border tiles in the mausolea of princes Mahmud (d. 1503) and Ahmed (d. 1513) in the Muradiye cemetery in Bursa.[166]

On the monument's exterior, further decoration in carved stone appears around the frames of windows. On the lower level of the portal façade, two windows are placed to either side of the portal, with the previously mentioned muqarnas niches between them (Figure 64). The windows are framed in simple moldings that follow their rectangular outlines. Around each window opening proper, a frame consisting of small muqarnas cells is applied. Above is a lunette filled with different patterns in each of the four windows. The lunette of the first window from the left (Figure 65) contains a pattern that at first looks geometric, but up close reveals itself to be kufic script with the letters running upside down along the rounded side of the lunette with their lengths intertwined to form a medallion at the center of the lower, straight edge. The second window from the left has *rūmī* motifs in the lunette, as does the third (Figure 66). The fourth window again has the knotted kufic script in its lunette, but it looks different because details of the carving are unfinished. In all four windows, a further frame runs around the outside of the muqarnas frame and encompasses the lunette, running in parallel with its rounded side. This frame consists of alternating inscribed cartouches and empty roundels. The carving is incomplete to varying degrees in all four windows. The spaces between this last frame and the outer molding are filled with *rūmī* motifs in all four windows. On the upper level of the façade, four openings in the shape of so-called Bursa arches appear. The stone railings are composed of carved geometric patterns.

Further carving appears on the windows in the south and west façades of the monument. These windows are all uniformly rectangular, and a thin border of turquoise tile – the only color on the façade,

64. Niche and window in the lower half of the façade toward north-eastern corner, Mehmed I's mosque-*zāviye*, 1419–21, Bursa, Turkey. © Patricia Blessing 2014

65. Lunette of the first window from the left, façade, Mehmed I's mosque-*zāviye*, 1419–21, Bursa, Turkey. © Patricia Blessing 2014

66. Second window from the left, façade, Mehmed I's mosque-*zāviye*, 1419–21, Bursa, Turkey. © Patricia Blessing 2014

67. Detail of window on west façade, Mehmed I's mosque-*zāviye*, 1419–21, Bursa, Turkey. © Patricia Blessing 2014

apart from the (re)painted foundation inscription – forms their outer perimeter (Figure 67). Otherwise, like the windows on the portal façade, they have muqarnas frames around the window openings and lunettes with *rūmī* motifs above them – some with the addition of a half-medallion of Arabic script with the letters upside down, although now in *thuluth* rather than kufic script, and others without. A similar use of small tile elements on the façade and related calligraphic compositions – although in the interior rather than on the exterior of the building – appear on the İlyas Bey Mosque in Balat-Miletus, begun in 1404, discussed in Chapter 3.

Meanwhile, the immediate Ottoman past of Bithynia was not forgotten, though it was reshaped. Targeted use of spolia in Ottoman monuments often highlighted specific stylistic connections. Such spolia generally come from Byzantine and Roman monuments rather than Saljuq ones. In the madrasa of Mehmed I, spolia were used for the columns and capitals that surround the courtyard (Figure 68), and walls were built of courses of stone and brick, borrowing from local Byzantine architecture. In contrast, very little spolia was used in the mausoleum and mosque-*zāviye*, a difference of approach that is consistent with the fact that there is no stylistic unity among the three extant buildings of the complex. The niches (see Figure 64) in the lower half of the mosque-*zāviye*'s façade display the only obvious use of spolia on that building's exterior: the engaged colonettes of each niche are made of green granite. (Of course, it is possible that the marble used for cladding exterior and some interior walls was not newly

68. Reused capital, Mehmed I's madrasa, 1419–21, Bursa, Turkey. © Patricia Blessing 2014

69. Tiled dado, Karatay Madrasa, 1251–52, Konya, Turkey. © Patricia Blessing 2010

quarried, but if so, this reuse is not deployed in any visible way.) In the vestibule, two pairs of Byzantine columns with Corinthian capitals are displayed, the only spolia used in the interior of the building.[167]

Among the tiles in Mehmed I's mosque-*zāviye*, the ones most closely reflective of Saljuq models as opposed to Timurid ones are those covering the lower zones of walls in the vestibule, the hallway linking the vestibule to the courtyard, the side *īwān*s, and the prayer-room *īwān*. In the lateral *īwān*s, the addition of gold-leaf decoration on the monochrome turquoise tiles is closely related to techniques prevalent in Islamic monuments in central and eastern Anatolia built in the mid- to late thirteenth century. One of the most striking parallels is at the Karatay Madrasa (see Figure 14) in Konya, founded in 1251–52 by Jalal al-Din Qaratay (d. 1254).[168] There the lower zone of the walls around the central space is decorated with hexagonal turquoise tiles adorned with gold ornament (mostly inscriptions), which balance the dome's rich tile mosaic (Figure 69). This monument was built after the Mongol conquest of Anatolia and therefore is not, strictly speaking, Saljuq. Yet such categories are problematic, for we do not know what distinction if any a fifteenth-century Ottoman viewer would have made between monuments built in Konya (and central Anatolia more broadly) in the first third of the thirteenth century and others built after the Mongol conquest in 1243, including later Karamanid rule. This historiographic observation does not in any case undermine my argument that Anatolia's Saljuq past was evoked. Rather, Konya, in its role as the former Saljuq *dār al-mulk*, could represent the idealized image of Islamic monuments built in Anatolia before Ottoman expansion, despite the fact that the *beylik* of Karaman, a long-standing rival of the Ottomans whose lands Timur restored, held the city during Mehmed I's reign.

In Mehmed I's mosque-*zāviye*, then, a strong link to central Anatolia's Islamic past is established with the muqarnas portal, moving away from the Byzantine architecture of Bithynia and toward a more diverse Ottoman style that was open to a wide range of influences, including Saljuq and *beylik* architectures. These connections are strongest on the building's exterior, while the Timurid-style mode of decoration dominates inside, with the prevailing use of black-line tiles (though this mode is perhaps hinted at on the exterior too with the *khiṭāyī* chrysanthemums in the portal's frame). Yet Anatolia's architectural past is present inside too, in the turquoise tiles with gold leaf, similar to those found in Konya. Such references to Saljuq architecture were a visual manifestation of the textual narratives the Ottomans created to tie their legitimacy to the Saljuqs.

THE TIMURID PRESENT: BURSA, TABRIZ, AND INTERNATIONAL TIMURID STYLE

The fact that the tiles of Mehmed I's complex have been stylistically placed in the context of Timurid visual culture is crucial to the relationship between early fifteenth-century Ottoman architecture and the so-called international Timurid style. Bernus-Taylor has argued that, despite differences in decorative details, these tiles evoke Timurid tile work, such as that on the mausolea of Qutluq Aqa (1361), Shad-e Mulk Aqa (1371–83), Amir Husayn ibn Tughluq Tekin (1376), and Shirin Bika Aqa (1385–86) in the cemetery of the shrine complex of Shah-i Zinda in Samarqand.[169] The portal of Qutluq Aqa's mausoleum features several techniques: in the muqarnas niche over the entrance, black-line tiles alternate with cut terra-cotta (Figure 70). On the frames around it, a rich play emerges between tiles in relief

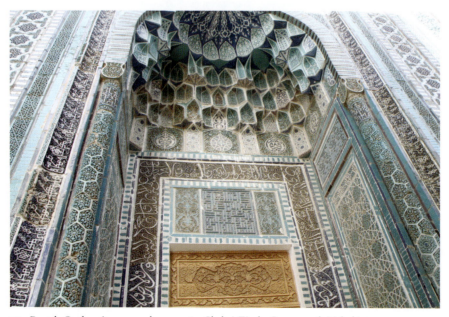

70. Portal, Qutluq Aqa mausoleum, 1361, Shah-i Zinda, Samarqand, Uzbekistan.
© Patricia Blessing 2007

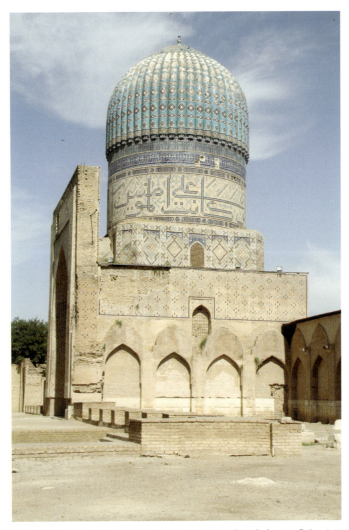

71. Bibi Khanum Mosque, 1398–1405, Samarqand, Uzbekistan. © Patricia Blessing 2007

with varying depths and bands of simple tile mosaic.[170] At the Bibi Khanum Mosque in Samarqand (1398–1405), black-line tiles were used on a large scale on the drum of the dome, above the section decorated in *bannāʾī* technique (Figure 71), and in the *qibla īwān*.[171]

In these Timurid monuments, as in Bursa, combined tile techniques meet the eye. The tile on the Ottoman architecture in Bursa, however, departs from the aesthetic of Timurid buildings where large sections of *bannāʾī* tile work dominate the exterior. The intimate funerary structures in the Shah-i Zinda cemetery resemble the interior decoration of Mehmed I's mosque-*zāviye* and mausoleum in their jeweled and fragmented aesthetic of varied tile motifs and techniques. Still the overall effect is different. In Mehmed I's mausoleum, the central section of the portal looks entirely Timurid, but the rest of the exterior establishes a different aesthetic – one that is Ottoman by virtue of its stylistic position at the intersection of the Timurid present and Saljuq past.

Here the questions about attribution and tile production discussed earlier in relation to the reference to Tabriz in two of the four artists' signatures in Mehmed I's foundation in Bursa become germane to the larger Timurid cultural context. The western Iranian city had emerged as an important commercial center under Ilkhanid rule, connecting Iran to major trade routes to Anatolia; later it was a site of Turkmen patronage, as the Qaraqoyunlu and Aqqoyunlu dynasties consolidated their rule and competed against each other and the Timurids.[172] While the cultural and political importance of Tabriz is uncontested, the state of monument preservation raises a central problem. Earthquakes in 1641 and 1780 destroyed many buildings and the Ottoman–Safavid wars of the sixteenth and seventeenth centuries damaged the city.[173] Hence the vestiges of fourteenth- and fifteenth-century Tabriz are few.[174] Monuments likely suffered in the aftermath of the fall of the Ilkhanids in the 1350s, when Tabriz repeatedly changed hands between local successor dynasties for more than a century.[175] From the fifteenth century, only the Masjid-i Muzaffariya, also known as the Blue Mosque or the Masjid-i Kabud, has survived. Khatun Jan Begum founded the building in 1465 as a funerary complex for her husband, the Qaraqoyunlu ruler Abu Muzaffar Jahanshah (r. 1436–67).[176] The tile decoration of the Masjid-i Muzaffariya presents a wide range of techniques, mostly tile mosaic, but also two types of blue-and-white tiles, *bannāʾī*, hexagonal dark blue tiles with fragments of gold decoration, and a few underglaze-painted and luster tiles.[177]

As a major cultural center in the fourteenth and fifteenth centuries, Tabriz may have been the ideal point of reference for high-quality production in a specific style by artists or patrons subscribing to a particular aesthetic. Tabriz was an admired artistic center whose works spoke to a periphery that included the Ottoman realm. Examples of such ideal artistic centers abound in art history. Prague, for instance, was the source of stylistic points of reference for international Gothic in fourteenth-century Central Europe. Regional differences remained in place, though, and local artists could interpret given forms with or without the impetus of a traveling workshop.[178] This observation is crucial with regard to Bursa, where, as we have seen, the presence of a workshop from Tabriz is likely, but is not sufficiently well documented to be taken for granted. Moreover, considering the geographical spaces at stake, it is important to note that the international Gothic style operated within a much smaller area – Prague to Paris, roughly – than the one that has been subsumed under the international Timurid label, which stretches from Samarqand to Edirne. Eventually, this Timurid cultural space expanded further, developing into a transregional Islamic space that Shahab Ahmed has designated the "Balkans-to-Bengal complex," which continued to exist long after the end of Timurid rule in the early sixteenth century and was not associated with any dynasty in particular.[179]

Combining different tile techniques to accentuate specific parts of a monument was not exclusive to Bursa; the practice can also be observed in Iran. In the Friday Mosque in Yazd, a tiled dado was added to the prayer hall in the early fifteenth century (Figure 72). The tile work closely resembles the interior wall decoration of Mehmed I's mausoleum, although in Yazd, the medallions were completed in tile mosaic rather than black-line tile.[180] In her study of medieval monuments in Yazd, Renata Holod argues that the tiled dado was completed after 1423.[181] This would mean that the tile programs in the two sites – Mehmed I's mosque-*zāviye* and mausoleum in Bursa and the Friday Mosque in Yazd – were completed in close chronological proximity. Further, in their discussion of the Masjid-i Shah in Mashhad (1452) and the Masjid-i Muzaffariya in Tabriz (1465), Donald Wilber and Golombek cite Mehmed I's mosque-*zāviye* in Bursa as a related example of a tiled dado and T-shaped plan.[182] While their observation is limited to stylistic connections, it suggests that Mehmed I's mosque-*zāviye* may have become a model for monuments built in western Iran. The plan of the Masjid-i Muzaffariya has been viewed as a variant of the Ottoman T-shaped plans, and Bursa may have been the node between Ottoman architecture and craftsmen from Tabriz, who could have carried knowledge of Ottoman building practices back to Iran.[183] Thus it is possible to argue that Bursa became the model for Yazd, suggesting that the Ottoman city formerly peripheral to the Timurid cultural realm had successfully been turned into a new center, thanks to the efforts of Hajji ʿIvaz Pasha and the makers he hired.

In their adaptation of the style, aesthetic, and name belonging to Tabriz, Ottoman patrons and builders in Bursa asserted their own city's status as a dynastic node of Ottoman rule by associating it with a major cultural center. The choice did not fall on Samarqand, which was eclipsed as an artistic center by Herat during the rule of Timur's successor Shah Rukh (r. 1405–47). Instead, Tabriz – geographically closer to

72. Detail of dado in prayer hall, 1420s?, Great Mosque, Yazd, Iran. © Patricia Blessing 2019

Bursa and less closely associated with Timurid rule – became the point of stylistic reference. I speculate but cannot prove that this choice came from an effort to eschew direct imitation of the art related to a dynasty that defeated an Ottoman sultan. Thanks to Mehmed I's patronage, Bursa was relieved of its peripheral status in the cultural world of the post-Mongol eastern Islamic lands and gained leverage as a center for the arts in its own right. The reference to a present that has been referred to as Timurid, but that might more specifically tie to Tabriz as a cultural center within a larger Timurid cultural sphere that outlasted political domination, was therefore one of the major elements in the tile decoration.

Thus the complex of Mehmed I makes two claims at once: one to the Saljuq past of Anatolia and to dominion over all of Anatolia, tying into fifteenth-century Ottoman modes of legitimizing rule, as we saw in the previous section; and another to the Timurid cultural sphere of the contemporaneous eastern Islamic world, signaling that Bursa was an up-and-coming cultural center to be reckoned with. Effectively, in creating this complex system of references within Mehmed I's mosque-*zāviye* and later his mausoleum, the buildings' makers amply prove their ability to turn Bursa into such a cultural center.

ENTANGLED REFERENCES

The buildings of Mehmed I's foundation in Bursa contain a multilayered set of references to the architecture of Bithynia, central Anatolia, Iran, and Central Asia. Depending on which building is being looked at, one allusion or another is prevalent, but the overall message points to the revived aspirations of the Ottoman realm under Mehmed I, when rebuilding of the realm went hand in hand with patronage. The construction of the mosque-*zāviye* and adjacent buildings marked Mehmed I's power in Bursa, a city that changed hands multiple times during the war that followed Bayezid I's death. With the commission of a mosque complex there, Mehmed I continued the tradition of sultanic patronage and funerary complexes in the city, enhancing its status as an Ottoman dynastic *lieu de mémoire.* The details of the architecture and decoration bore important implications as the sultan renegotiated the Ottomans' position between the Timurid present, Saljuq past, and Ottoman future.

There is no straightforward way to attribute each element to a point of origin; instead, it seems that various visual models were used with the goal of both presenting current artistic production (and displaying the wealth necessary for it) and emphasizing ties to local and regional pasts. The madrasa is closely connected to early Ottoman architecture in Bursa, with the exception of the tile mosaic in its *īwān*s, which points to central Anatolia. The interior of the mosque-*zāviye* refers to both Saljuq Anatolia and Timurid Central Asia by way of Tabriz, whereas the portal points to Iran and Central Asia in its shape and decoration, and the overall shape of the structure has local roots. The interplay between past and present through visual cues continues in the mausoleum, yet it strikes a somewhat different balance from that seen in the mosque-*zāviye*, where interior and exterior carry different associations (Timurid interior and Saljuq exterior): inside and out, the emphasis in the mausoleum is on tile decoration and a Persianate aesthetic, although the building's plan and elevation are typical of Islamic funerary architecture in Anatolia. The dynamic of center and periphery is less a dichotomy between Tabriz as center and Bursa as periphery than one in which Bursa, as a center of Ottoman memory, became a new point of reference and slowly moved out of its peripheral role. Peripheries took on new prominence when former centers lost their importance.

Stone carving takes the place of the arabesque, but multiple allusions to Anatolia, Iran, and Central Asia and to Konya, Tabriz, and Samarqand appear in the tile decoration. In fifteenth-century Bursa, Anatolia's Saljuq past, particularly in its pre-Mongol form, became a point of visual reference that helped complicate the use of Timurid style in Ottoman architecture. It is true that the Timurid invasion of the Ottoman realm was both traumatic and fruitful. It was traumatic in that the Ottomans were nearly wiped from the map and had to struggle fiercely for nearly a century to regain the full extent of territory they had held toward the end of Bayezid I's rule. In history writing, the result of this trauma was a shift toward narratives of legitimacy that emphasized the Saljuqs as sole rulers of Anatolia and glossed over the complex historical and political context of the region in Mongol and post-Mongol times.

Culturally, however, the process of recreating an imperial Ottoman identity was twofold. On the one hand, elements derived from Saljuq architecture were integrated into Ottoman monuments, connecting to the new way of writing history. On the other hand, the Timurid cultural realm was now within reach. Traveling workers became available once they had been released from Timurid captivity, while the rising Ottoman court of Mehmed I was able to provide patronage and an expert like Hajji ʿIvaz Pasha knew how and where to hire talent. Thus Timurid-trained artists from a range of centers, including artists who were either from Tabriz or claimed that city as their own, were available to work for the Ottomans in building a new Ottoman future. In Chapter 3, we explore how practices of planning and construction can be traced and reimagined and how ties to Mamluk architecture in Egypt and Syria created a complex triangle of exchange and transfer.

THREE

UNDER THE INFLUENCE

Creating Cosmopolitan Architectures

WHILE UP UNTIL NOW I HAVE EXAMINED OTTOMAN ARCHITECTURE IN RELATION TO contemporaneous events and developments in Anatolia, the Balkans, Iran, and Central Asia, this chapter turns to connections between the Ottomans and the Mamluk sultanate of Egypt and Greater Syria. Gift exchange was a central aspect of Mamluk–Ottoman relations, and a similar interchange also appears in architecture.[1] This is the case in one of the earliest Ottoman monuments to have survived in Amasya: the Bayezid Pasha mosque-*zāviye* (Figure 73), which is located on the banks of the Yeşilırmak and was completed in 1414, early in Mehmed I's rule. An examination of this building will serve as the starting point to discuss the possible presence of Mamluk workers in Anatolia and the ways in which their stylistic approaches were integrated into Ottoman architecture in the late fourteenth and fifteenth centuries.

While these Mamluk–Ottoman connections have been noted, much remains to be done in terms of analyzing the ways in which they were established, and in particular the question of how transfer occurred remains to be examined in detail.[2] Answering the latter question is one of my tasks in what follows. In his study of Mamluk architecture in Syria and Egypt, Michael Meinecke insistently argued that workers migrated in the second half of the fourteenth century from Cairo to other parts of the Mamluk realm such as Syria and from there on to Anatolia, where more work was available than in Egypt, which was shaken by fiscal and political crises.[3] While his argument relies on a careful study of late fourteenth-century *beylik* and Ottoman monuments, Meinecke is also adamant about the mobile nature of workshops within a framework of style transfer largely driven by fashion and economic resources.[4] Moving away from such frameworks, in a study of a restoration begun in 1392 at the early fourteenth-century mosque and mausoleum of Tankiz al-Nasiri in Damascus, Ellen Kenney argues that stylistic choice could also be tied to particularly historical and political moments, providing a more expansive view on the dynamics of stylistic change.[5] This raises the question of whether we need to exclusively rely on the movement of craftsmen as the only explanation for stylistic connections, without considering other modes of exchange such as trade and the transfer of drawings. Might paper models and drawings have been other avenues in this case, the way they were in the Ottoman exchange with Iran and Central Asia, as documented in the Topkapı Scroll? In the absence of extant drawings, is it possible to understand

95

73. Bayezid Pasha mosque-*zāviye*, 1414, Amasya, *Turkey*. © Patricia Blessing 2018

the role paper might have played as a source for new designs? What is the stylistic impact of historical and political aspirations on the part of patrons?

The Mamluks emerged in the mid-thirteenth century out of a succession crisis among the Ayyubids, who had ruled Egypt and Greater Syria since Salah al-Din Ayyub (d. 1193, known in the West as Saladin) rose to power in the context of Sunni resistance against the Shiʿi caliphate of the Fatimids on the one hand, and Crusaders from Europe who had established themselves in the Levant since the late 1090s on the other. The Mamluks, former military elites under the Ayyubids, were rough contemporaries of the Ottomans in their emergence, and they would continue to rule until Ottoman sultan Selim I (r. 1512–20) conquered their capital, Cairo, in 1517. Despite their long-term rule, the Mamluks did not (with few exceptions) establish dynastic succession. Rather, they continued to recruit enslaved soldiers, mostly from the Caucasus and the region north of the Black Sea, who were able to rise in the ranks, with some eventually becoming sultan – often amid considerable strife and rebellion. Major cities under Mamluk rule – Cairo, Damascus, Aleppo – were centers of scholarship and cultural innovation, as they had been for centuries before.

The Mamluks and the Ottomans were both relative newcomers on the political scene in the medieval Islamic world, and as such strove to gain legitimacy. As noted in Chapter 2, the Ottomans created elaborate narratives in which they were appointed by a fictive Saljuq sultan who in turn (in this Ottoman fiction) had received credentials from the Abbasid caliph in Baghdad, the ultimate source of legitimacy. The Mamluks went a step further: after the Abbasid caliph was killed in the Mongol conquest of Baghdad in 1258, they found another pretender and promptly installed him in Cairo, where the office would continue until 1517.

Throughout the fourteenth century, the Ottomans and Mamluks competed for status while at the same time exchanging embassies. Before 1350, the Mamluks had higher status considering that they controlled important urban centers such as Cairo and Damascus, as well as the Abbasid caliphate, while the Ottomans were busy expanding their rule in the Balkans and western Anatolia.[6] Ottoman–Mamluk–Aqqoyunlu borderlands extended from Cilicia across the Taurus Mountains as far west as the region of Kayseri and Divriği near Sivas.[7] Eventually, with the Ottomans' first eastward expansion beginning in the 1380s, these regions would become a frontier zone between Mamluks, Ottomans, and, until 1468, Karamanids. Mamluk chroniclers continued to describe the Ottomans as minor rulers, but Bayezid I's conquest of Malatya in 1399 significantly upset this dismissive attitude.[8] The consequences of Bayezid's action soon became clear when the Mamluks – concerned about the breach of trust it entailed, as the attack on Malatya happened in a period of turmoil after the death of Mamluk sultan Barquq – refused to support the Ottomans against Timur. We saw in Chapter 2 what this led to.

Ties between the Mamluks and Ottomans shifted in the fifteenth century after the Ottoman interregnum of 1402–13. Embassies traveled back and forth between the two realms while the Timurids loomed as a military threat to both sides. The epigraph previously cited, describing the gifts Murad II sent with an embassy to Barsbay in Cairo in 1428, reflects a high point in Ottoman–Mamluk connections before conflict between the two powers emerged during Mehmed II's reign.

The frontier between the Ottoman and Mamluk realms in eastern and central Anatolia was complicated by the presence of Turkmen tribal confederations such as the Qaraqoyunlu and Aqqoyunlu.[9] Throughout the fifteenth century, parts of central and eastern Anatolia were under Mamluk authority – if not directly, then through local governors and proxy rulers who included affiliates of the Aqqoyunlu and the Dulkadir, among others. Mamluk power in these borderlands had increased after the Armenian kingdom of Cilicia was defeated in 1375 with the fall of its last capital of Sīs (today Kozan) to Sultan al-Ashraf Shaʿban (r. 1363–77).[10] Architectural evidence of Mamluk presence in Anatolia during the fourteenth and fifteenth centuries survives in sites such as Kozan, Divriği, Hasankeyf, and Mardin, often the result of the patronage of Mamluk governors or affiliates.[11] Further, stylistic influences from Mamluk architecture appear in buildings throughout Anatolia, including ones built for Ottoman patrons.

Monuments in the city of Amasya – a crucial location, as it was one of the sites where Ottoman princes were appointed to office in their childhood and youth – play a central role in this chapter. Amasya came under Ottoman rule in 1398, when Bayezid I captured the city.[12] Unlike many cities in western Anatolia, where Timur restored *beylik* rule after his victory over Bayezid I in 1402, Amasya stayed in Ottoman hands, albeit with a brief challenge by Kara Devletşah, who had been affiliated with Kadı Burhaneddin.[13] Mehmed Çelebi created his base there while he was engaged in civil war with his brothers and at the same time striving to regain lost Ottoman territories.[14] Soon after he became sultan as Mehmed I, he commissioned a madrasa in Merzifon in 1414, and Bayezid Pasha (d. 1421) founded his mosque-*zāviye* in Amasya in the same year.

Incidentally, the same individual's name appears prominently in the inscription programs of both monuments: Abu Bakr b. Muhammad, known as Ibn Mushaymish al-Dimashqi.[15] Though we must take proper caution regarding *nisba*s such as "al-Dimashqi" – that is, components of names that imply origin though it might sometimes be several generations back – the signature is nevertheless a fruitful inroad in pursuit of the question of Mamluk connections, particularly because a possible ancestor of this architect, ʿAli b. al-Mushaymish al-Dimashqi, signed the İsa Bey Mosque in Ayasuluk (Selçuk) near Ephesus in 1375.[16] That building, discussed later in this chapter, shows stonework with clear connections to Mamluk architecture in Aleppo. Someone who was possibly from a later generation of the same clan, Sinan al-Din Ahmad b. Abi Bakr al-Mushaymish, signed the Karaca Bey Mosque in Ankara in 1427–28.[17]

In the late fifteenth century, Amasya saw strong patronage tied to the court of Bayezid II, who was appointed to this city while he was a prince. Amasya would thus once more become a site of prolific building activity beginning in the 1480s, and its architecture would shape the building practices of the late fifteenth and early sixteenth centuries more broadly – a question examined further in Chapter 5. For the moment, I address the following questions in the present chapter: How did patrons affiliated with Mehmed I and Murad II shape Amasya in the first half of the fifteenth century? What was the impact of Mamluk architecture in fifteenth-century Anatolia? How were ideas related to design and architecture transmitted between the Ottoman and Mamluk realms? How did artists and patrons in both contexts react to Timurid art? How did Mamluk-style elements transform and evolve in the Ottoman context?

Connected to the last three questions are the blue-and-white underglaze-painted tiles used in the second quarter of the fifteenth century at almost the same time in Cairo, Damascus, and Edirne. While I have addressed the technical details involved in the production of these tiles elsewhere, here I analyze the ways in which they elucidate questions of traveling workers, moveable ideas, and portable objects.[18] These observations about movements of makers and objects tie in with the growing interactions between the Mamluk and Ottoman courts as the latter increasingly became an actor to be reckoned with on the international scene, including the embassies that carried gifts between their respective rulers.[19] Further, Mamluk–Ottoman contacts were enhanced through networks of scholars who traveled from the Ottoman realm to Cairo and Damascus to study, later returning to appointments in the Ottoman madrasa system, which was being consolidated but as of the 1420s was not yet training sufficient numbers of scholars at home to fill available positions.[20]

An underlying question in this chapter, relevant to the entire conquest of central and eastern Anatolia between the late fourteenth and early sixteenth centuries, is what happened to Ottoman architecture when it entered a geographical space that had been under Muslim rule for several centuries. Unlike Bursa and Edirne, both of which were Ottoman conquests taken from Byzantine rule as Istanbul would be in 1453, Amasya had been part of Danishmendid and later Saljuq, Ilkhanid, and Eretnid realms since the late eleventh century.[21] Thus the main monuments needed in a Muslim-ruled city – first and foremost a Friday mosque, but also neighborhood *masjid*s, madrasas, shrines, and hammams – already existed when the Ottomans conquered Amasya. In the dynamics of urban change observed with the Ottoman conquests of cities in the Balkans such as Serres (1383), Thessaloniki (first conquered in 1387, lost in 1402, conquered again in 1430), and Skopje (1392), a first act of patronage was generally the creation of a Friday mosque, either by converting an existing church or through new construction.[22] Such steps were not necessary in Amasya. While nothing remains of twelfth-century Danishmendid patronage, a number of monuments built in the thirteenth and fourteenth centuries survive, which became part of the architectural references integrated into the emerging Ottoman architecture of the city.[23] In this manner, Amasya was arguably a prototype for later developments in central and eastern Anatolia, as Ottoman rule expanded to cities such as Konya, Kayseri, and Karaman in the late fifteenth century. The integration of architecture that was already present in conquered sites had been achieved with the adaptation of Byzantine forms in Bursa in the fourteenth century. The presence of Saljuq and Ilkhanid monuments in Amasya, then, allowed for a direct encounter with the kinds of forms that had been current in the Islamic architecture of Anatolia since at least the twelfth century. Here, perhaps, lies another explanation for the connections observed in Chapter 2, in which an ideal Saljuq and pre-Mongol Anatolian past was posited as one of the models for the architecture of Mehmed I's realm as it was being rebuilt, combined with the Byzantine tradition of Bursa as well as multiple references to the architectures of the present.

MAMLUK STYLE IN OTTOMAN AMASYA: THE BAYEZID PASHA MOSQUE-*ZĀVIYE*

Like many similar structures built in the late fourteenth and early fifteenth centuries in the Ottoman realm, the Bayezid Pasha mosque-*zāviye* in Amasya, built in 1414 (see Figure 73), has a T-shaped plan. In this particular version of the plan, the building comprises a vestibule, a domed central hall, a domed prayer area, four large side rooms, and a five-bay porch. The prayer *īwān* on the south side of the building is raised to a height of one step above the rest of the monument's central section, which would perhaps not have been carpeted in the building's original function as a mosque-*zāviye*. Four rooms intended for other purposes – teaching, housing guests, serving meals – are accessible from the central hall.[24] It is worth noting, however, that in a city like Amasya, under Muslim rule since the late eleventh century, the colonizing and Islamizing function of the type of buildings described by Barkan and Eyice in their discussion of dervish groups and the construction of mosque-*zāviye*s as part of Ottoman expansion in previously non-Muslim territories did not apply.

The five-bay porch, with its massive masonry pillars and domes over each bay, forms the street façade of the monument. On its exterior, a range of inscriptions appear that indicate some of the building's creators and comprise an extract from the *waqfīya*. On the building's portal (Figure 74), built into a recess in the central axis of the building past the porch, the foundation inscription appears along with a builder's signature. The original wooden doors are still in place (Figure 75); inscriptions name Mustafa al-Najjar as their maker and contain hadith passages on scroll backgrounds in addition to geometric patterns that extend over the central parts of both wings.[25] The type of bowknot shape with a circle at its center seen in the stonework of the portal, just above the doorway, is an unmistakable reference to Mamluk architecture, where this element is frequently used – for instance, on the portal of the madrasa of Mithqal al-Anuki in Cairo (1361–63; Figure 76), although there the motif is flush with the façade rather than raised.[26]

On the portal of the Bayezid Pasha mosque-*zāviye*, inscriptions are arranged in a complex manner. The foundation inscription is placed on three panels, beginning on the right side of the portal recess, continuing on a central panel over the doorway, and finishing on the left side of the portal recess (Figure 77). The central panel is enclosed in a frame of thick carved molding, which goes on to form the bowknot shape beneath the inscription described earlier. This inscription names the patron, Bayezid Pasha, and the date of the building, Muharram 817 AH / March–April 1414 CE.[27] Bayezid Pasha had been part of Mehmed I's circle ever since the prince's youth, sticking with him during the war among brothers, and he became grand vizier, remaining in this role at the beginning of Murad II's reign, until he was killed in the rebellion of the "false Mustafa" in 1421.[28] While at first sight it appears as if the foundation inscription continues on either side, wrapping around the front corners of the portal recess, these bits of text in fact constitute a different inscription: they name *muʿallim* Abu Bakr b. Muhammad, known as Ibn Mushaymish al-Dimashqi (which literally means "the little apricot from Damascus"), split between the two panels.[29] (I discuss possible interpretations of terms such as *muʿallim* shortly.)

The *waqf* inscription (Figure 78) is located at the top of the porch façade, carved into reddish stone, flecked with grey, that offers a contrast with the whitish façade (part limestone, part marble). It is integrated into the decorative program to such an extent that, when viewed from afar, it is not obvious where the geometric decoration above the arches of the porch ends and the inscription, running straight across the width of the porch, begins. The text of the inscription has deteriorated. Recently, Ali Yardım meticulously studied this text and managed to decipher nearly the entire inscription, which lists the names of villages in the region of Amasya, Merzifon, and Tokat, as well as vineyards, fields, mills, and houses; most of these properties are located outside of Amasya.[30]

A longer *waqf* inscription carved on a stone is located across the river, first identified by Ayverdi.[31] In a detailed study of this inscription, Yardım was able to reconstruct it in large part and provide a

100   UNDER THE INFLUENCE

74. Portal, Bayezid Pasha mosque-*zāviye*, 1414, Amasya, Turkey. © Patricia Blessing 2018

75. Wooden door, Bayezid Pasha mosque-*zāviye*, 1414, Amasya, Turkey. © Patricia Blessing 2018

76. Portal, madrasa of Mithqal al-Anuki, 1361–63, Cairo, Egypt. © Patricia Blessing 2006

77. Foundation inscription, Bayezid Pasha mosque-*zāviye*, 1414, Amasya, Turkey. © Patricia Blessing 2018

78. *Waqf* inscription, Bayezid Pasha mosque-*zāviye*, 1414, Amasya, Turkey. © Patricia Blessing 2018

transcription and Turkish translation.[32] In eight lines, the inscription on the rock face provides a summary of major properties belonging to the endowment, such as several villages, vineyards, a bathhouse in an unspecified location, arable land, and shares in a mill; the text is dated Dhū'l-Hijjat 820 AH / January 1418 CE.[33] This *waqf* inscription, as with the one on the building's façade, is similar to others often applied to buildings, such as the one in the interior of the Yakutiye Madrasa, built in Erzurum in 1310.[34] These inscriptions do not replace the full *waqfīya* on paper, which describes the locations of the properties in detail, lists the number and salaries of staff appointed to specific roles within the building, and notes the chain of transmission for the role of *mutawallī* (overseer).[35] As I have argued elsewhere, *waqf* inscriptions functioned as a publicly visible (if not necessarily legible to the general public) reminder of the endowment, while the *waqfīya* on paper constituted the legal document complete with witnesses' signatures and a kadi's endorsement.[36] The Bayezid Pasha mosque-*zāviye* is a rare case in which both inscriptions and the *waqfīya* on paper have survived, allowing for comparative analysis, as Yardım proposes. He argues that the three texts complement each other and are not just repetitive versions of the same type of information.[37] According to this view, then, the three texts are all needed in order to ensure a full understanding of the endowment, and neither the inscriptions nor the paper *waqfīya* function as stand-alone documents – even if the latter is still the version that would have been relevant for legal transactions. Clearly, those responsible for establishing the Bayezid Pasha *waqfīya* in its multiple forms had a complex understanding of the ways in which written documentation functioned and of how to ensure that a record of main elements existed in multiple locations, two of them publicly visible.

Such visibility is especially prominent on the building's façade, where the same stone used for the *waqf* inscription also appears in two short building inscriptions integrated into two of the porch pillars. The pillar on the right of the central axis (Figure 79) has an inscription in two lines naming "Yaʿqub b. ʿAbdallah, one of the enslaved people of Bayezid Pasha," as the *miʿmār* of the gate (*bāb*), dated 822 AH / 1419–20 CE.[38] The one-line inscription on the pillar to the left of the central bay (Figure 80)

79. Building inscription 1, Bayezid Pasha mosque-*zāviye*, 1414, Amasya, Turkey.
© Patricia Blessing 2018

80. Building inscription 2, Bayezid Pasha mosque-*zāviye*, 1414, Amasya, Turkey.
© Patricia Blessing 2018

81. Western side of porch with building inscription 3 at the top, Bayezid Pasha mosque-*zāviye*, 1414, Amasya, Turkey. © Patricia Blessing 2018

contains the name of *muʿallim* Zayn al-Din b. Zakariya and is undated.[39] Since the date on the right-hand pillar is later than that of the foundation inscription above the building's entrance (1414), Ayverdi has argued that these inscriptions refer to a repair campaign, perhaps following an earthquake that occurred in 1418.[40] Another inscription appears toward the top of the porch (Figure 81), on its western face, also in the same red-brown stone; it contains the name of another individual referred to as *miʿmār*, and Uzunçarşılı's, Ayverdi's, and Keskin's studies each give different readings of one of his names.[41] Yardım, however, reads the inscription as containing a professional title followed by a name, deciphering the text as "*miʿmāruhā Toghān b. ʿAbdallāh ʿatīq Bāyezīd Bāshā*," referring to the *miʿmār* in question, Toghan b. ʿAbdallah, as a formerly enslaved person in the household of Bayezid Pasha.[42] Making allowances for a rather awkwardly written *hā*, this reading is, in my opinion, plausible. This inscription is not dated and so does not give us any further clues about the progress of construction.

Construction Sites: Workers and Designers

Even with the new reading of the inscription with Toghan b. ʿAbdallah's name, roles on the construction site are far from clear. Yardım argues that *miʿmār* Toghan b. ʿAbdallah was the architect of the entire monument because the feminine ending -*hā* in Arabic would necessarily refer to *ʿimārat*, the term used in the foundation inscription. It cannot refer to the masculine noun *bāb* (door, gate, portal) used in the inscription on the porch that names Yaʿqub b. ʿAbdallah. Yardım therefore suggests that Toghan b. ʿAbdallah built the monument with the assistance of *muʿallim* Zayn al-Din b. Zakariya, while the portal was built by *miʿmār* Yaʿqub b. ʿAbdallah with the assistance of *muʿallim* Abu Bakr b. Muhammad, known as Ibn Mushaymish al-Dimashqi.[43] This argument implies, however, that the *miʿmār* has a more elevated role than the *muʿallim*, who, in Yardım's assessment, appears as a subordinate assistant. Yet the attested use of such terms in the fifteenth century and the fact that the name of Ibn Mushaymish al-Dimashqi appears prominently on the building's portal at the same height as the foundation inscription call such assumptions into question.

Revisiting the role of architects in the Timurid and Safavid contexts, Sussan Babaie argues that the specific terms used are not central; rather, "the named architect/builder/engineer, regardless of his *nisbat* (professional epithet) as a *bannā'* or a *mi'mār*, assumes a role in insinuating a space within his own socially and culturally determined concept of subjectivity."[44] For example, in Gawhar Shad's Great Mosque in Mashhad, completed in 1418, the inscriptions on the façade of the *qibla īwān* mention Qavam al-Din Shirazi in separate panels using the epithet "*al-tayyān*" (plasterer), while the foundation inscription exalts the patron Gawhar Shad (d. 1457) – the spouse of Timurid ruler Shah Rukh (r. 1409–47) – and mentions the calligrapher who designed the epigraphic program, her son Baysunghur.[45] In a study of this same Qavam al-Din Shirazi (active 1410–38), who is documented in a number of monuments built for Gawhar Shad, Donald Wilber assumes that Qavam-al-Din was responsible for both structural matters and the overall design of decorative programs, largely tile work.[46] The use of "*al-tayyān*" in his signature, then, is not just a mark of humility in the face of his royal patron, but may also point to his role in the design process (in which plaster was involved), and it puts forward the architect's own subjectivity.[47] Such readings allow for reflections on the social status of those active on building sites beyond the question of who did what.

Certainly, assessing the exact role certain individuals played in a construction project and the meaning of specific terms that designate them is challenging, as Doris Behrens-Abouseif notes in the case of Mamluk architecture, focusing on three specific terms: *muhandis*, *shād*, and *mu'allim*.[48] Behrens-Abouseif argues that the role of the *muhandis* was technical, relating to tasks such as the construction of aqueducts but not to creative aspects of design, a point Nasser Rabbat also supports.[49] In examining an early thirteenth-century text by 'Abd al-Latif al-Baghdadi, Rabbat argues that in medieval Egypt, the *muhandis*'s task of "design" included both conceptual aspects and practical ones such as laying out the foundations of a building, but, it appears, without resorting to drawings.[50] According to Rabbat, 'Abd al-Latif's implication may have been that such a technique was specific to Egypt, while in other regions that he was familiar with, drawings were more likely to be used, and perhaps by a *muhandis*.[51] Behrens-Abouseif notes that the roles of *shād* and *mu'allim* are difficult to precisely distinguish based on available sources, for they overlap in tasks related to overseeing construction, ranging from the creation of cost estimates to the hiring of workers.[52] The *shād* was also responsible for "the general design and scheme of the building."[53] Tasks like these, related to the design and planning of a building, are implied in the inscriptions that mention Hajji 'Ivaz Pasha, discussed in Chapter 2; it appears that in the early fifteenth-century Ottoman context, there was no specific term for this role and that it might have been a temporary office rather than a permanent career. Certainly, Hajji 'Ivaz Pasha also held other offices in the Ottoman administration.

On the Bayezid Pasha mosque-*zāviye*, Zayn al-Din b. Zakariya and Abu Bakr b. Muhammad, known as Ibn Mushaymish al-Dimashqi, are both designated as *mu'allim*. If the Mamluk definition of the word applies, were these two individuals perhaps responsible for running the construction site and supplying materials as general contractors of some sort? While the terms *muhandis* and *shād* do not appear on the Bayezid Pasha mosque-*zāviye*, similar issues arise for the term *mi'mār*, commonly translated as architect based on the word's modern meaning in Arabic and Turkish. The term *mi'mār* appears twice on this building, specifying Ya'qub b. 'Abdallah's work on the *bāb* and Toghan b. 'Abdallah's work, probably on the *'imārat* – that is, the entire mosque-*zāviye*. On the Eski Cami (1404–13) in Edirne, an undated inscription (Figure 82) on the western side portal names "the pride of viziers (*iftikhār al-ṣudūr*) 'Alā al-Dīn" as the *mi'mār* and 'Umar b. Ibrahim as the *'āmil*.[54] While the reference to a vizierial role for 'Ala al-Din may suggest that he was – like Hajji 'Ivaz Pasha – deployed to the project in a temporary, supervising role, 'Umar b. Ibrahim is also documented on two hammams built in Bolu and Mudurnu in the 1380s and would have been a seasoned professional by the 1410s when he appears in Edirne.[55] Whether *'āmil* could be a role similar to that of *mu'allim* as it appears on the Bayezid Pasha mosque-*zāviye* in Amasya is difficult to determine.

82. Inscription, western portal Eski Cami, 1403–14, Edirne, Turkey. © Patricia Blessing 2019

Crucially, Behrens-Abouseif emphasizes that in the Mamluk context *miʿmār* did not mean architect; rather, the term was reserved for "a specialist for repair and restoration works."[56] In the Ottoman context, this use of *miʿmār* also exists in the early fifteenth century: two *miʿmār*s are stipulated in the *waqfīya* of Mehmed I's foundation in Bursa; each of them was to receive one dirham per day and one *mudd*[57] of wheat each month.[58] In the *waqfīya* of Murad II's foundation in Bursa, two *miʿmār*s were specifically employed to take care of the fountains and water features as well as repairs to the *zāviye* and *madrasa*.[59] To see to upkeep in the foundation of Hajji ʿIvaz Pasha, one *miʿmār* was paid one dirham per day.[60] By the late fifteenth century, however, the term did mean architect in the Ottoman context, as seen with the establishment of the *hassa mimarları* in Istanbul – although here too maintenance was part of a *miʿmār*'s job in addition to design and construction.[61]

In the case of the Bayezid Pasha mosque-*zāviye*, then, roles are far from clear: Ibn Mushaymish al-Dimashqi's name is highly visible on the entrance, so was he the main contractor who supervised construction and reported to the patron? (In the Mamluk context, this would have been the *shād*, but I have yet to encounter the term in Ottoman sources.[62]) The participation in the construction project of two individuals connected to Bayezid Pasha's entourage is also striking: were Toghan b. ʿAbdallah and Yaʿqub b. ʿAbdallah responsible for ensuring that the patron's wishes were applied and for reporting back to him? Considering that both of these names appear on the porch, the division of labor suggested by Yardım between individuals responsible for building the portal and others responsible for the rest of the mosque-*zāviye* seems difficult to uphold, and the fact that no restoration is mentioned also makes Ayverdi's argument of a repair campaign somewhat unlikely. Did Ibn Mushaymish al-Dimashqi indeed have a more important role than other individuals mentioned in the inscriptions based on the placement of his name? Or was he perhaps specifically responsible for the stonework on the portal, where his name appears? This type of specific placement is found with the wood-carvers' names on the door in this monument and in the mausoleum of Mehmed I in Bursa. As we saw in Chapter 2, strategic placement of such inscriptions is also applied with the inscription referring to the Masters of Tabriz on the mihrab and the name of Muhammad al-Majnun on the sultan's lodge in Mehmed I's mosque-*zāviye* in Bursa, so it might be the case in Amasya.

Just as we are not sure if the Masters of Tabriz were really from Tabriz, Abu Bakr b. Muhammad, who claims the name of a Mamluk ancestor, Ibn Mushaymish al-Dimashqi, poses a similar problem. Clearly the unusual name referring to Damascus carried some prestige if Abu Bakr b. Muhammad chose it, yet we don't know if the family connection so prominently displayed was real or whether it was a form of branding for Abu Bakr Muhammad and perhaps his team, a selling point to attract patronage and convince Bayezid Pasha's agents to hire them. Tracing individuals beyond inscriptions on single buildings is often difficult. As Ekrem Hakkı Ayverdi has noted, the name Toghan b. ʿAbdallah also appears on Mehmed I's mosque in Didymoteichon (Dimetoka) in Greece, dated 1420–21, together with kadi Sayyid ʿAli and, tantalizingly, Hajji ʿIvaz Pasha.[63] In her analysis of early Ottoman modes of patronage, Zeynep Yürekli argues that individuals like Toghan b. ʿAbdallah, who worked successfully on construction projects commissioned by pashas, could then be hired again to work on projects built for the Ottoman sultan.[64] In this view, the Bayezid Pasha mosque-*zāviye* becomes a testing ground from which Toghan b. ʿAbdallah moved on to Didymoteichon and Ibn Mushaymish al-Dimashqi moved on to nearby Merzifon.

In some ways, such an approach might have been a form of risk management when hiring workers who had recently come to the Ottoman realm – perhaps at the explicit invitation of individuals such as Hajji ʿIvaz Pasha, as discussed in the previous chapter – and a way to limit technical risks on building sites for royal projects. If such a process of vetting workers existed, as Yürekli argues, it may not have been consistently applied: the "Masters of Tabriz," for instance, do not appear to have worked on another project before undertaking Mehmed I's mosque-*zāviye* in Bursa. Was there such a project that did not survive? Or did these workers come with flawless references? Or were Mehmed I and Hajji ʿIvaz Pasha willing to take the risk, perhaps after being shown samples of tiles?

PAPER AND ARCHITECTURAL DESIGN

Related to the question of the roles of architects and other builders who might have worked on monuments like the Bayezid Pasha mosque-*zāviye* is the question of architectural drawings and models. While no ground plans from the early fifteenth century have survived in the Ottoman context, Gülru Necipoğlu has identified such drawings in the Topkapı Palace Archive that she dates to the second half of the fifteenth century based on watermarks. In these drawings, two of which show hammams, one of which shows a partial layout of a mosque (likely a rejected design for Mehmed II's Istanbul mosque), and one of which shows four versions of a Sufi mausoleum, several consistent conventions emerge. These ground plans were based on blind, incised grids and labeled with details that describe parts of the structure.[65] In the case of the mosque plan especially, Necipoğlu notes, the drawing conventions used were closely related to those of Renaissance Italy, ensuring that "portable ground plans would have been easily legible whichever direction they traveled."[66] The drawing of the mausoleum is designated as *kārnāme*, a term Necipoğlu interprets as a type of drawing that involved a ground plan with instructions, and at times might also include sketches of elevations as well, but drawn at different scales.[67] Notably, Necipoğlu shows, no measured elevation drawings or models clearly intended for architectural use have survived. Therefore, she argues that ground plans were the crucial element in transmitting architectural concepts from the site of design in Istanbul, once this work had been centralized there, to the sites of construction throughout the Ottoman Empire. This emphasis on ground plans also goes a long way in explaining differences in elevations between buildings that have similar, often nearly identical ground plans.[68] The centralization of construction planning within the Ottoman Empire, beginning with the creation of an office in Istanbul in the second half of the fifteenth century, would increase the practice of sending ground plans from the capital to the provinces.[69]

While drawings of this type have not been documented for the early fifteenth century, paper could still have played a role in these earlier construction projects, used for sketches or stonework designs. As noted in Chapter 1, drawings were needed to transmit calligraphic designs to building sites and to scale them up for use on monuments. The argument for the central role of paper in the transmission of architecture is strengthened by the fact that, in fifteenth-century imperial Ottoman projects, it is rare to find inscriptions squeezed awkwardly into stone panels with too little space for the text; rather, they appear as generally balanced calligraphic designs carefully adapted to the available surface. Consistent design of architectural decorations could also have been improved with the help of patterns created on paper to be applied to various parts of buildings' interiors and exteriors.

In the case of the Bayezid Pasha mosque-*zāviye*, design elements are repeated across the monument, on both the façade and in the interior, in an attempt to tie together the decoration, and these designs are of the type that could have been aided by paper patterns. The decoration of the porch is comprised of carefully planned and executed stone carving, with a wide band of geometric ornament running outside of the inscriptions and vegetal ornament carved into the reddish-brown stone. A muqarnas corniche forms the top edge of the porch. The mosque-*zāviye*'s interior decoration (Figure 83) is limited to simple terms (if one disregards the recently painted voussoirs), but the overall design logic is compelling. Elements of the façade's geometric decoration are picked up again on the mihrab: in the lower section of the niche, a portion of a geometric design appears, cut off at the edges so as to suggest indefinite repetition (Figure 84). Inside each of the central twelve-pointed stars of this design, a swirl pattern is used that recalls the decorative inner structure of a one of the porch domes. The alternating red and white on this niche's corner colonnettes refers to the *ablaq* (the use of alternating pieces of stone in different colors, often black and white or red and white) on the porch, although the red on the colonnettes may be paint while the white segments show the natural color of the stone. The muqarnas of the mihrab niche also mirrors the muqarnas of the portal, although this is a principle applied far more widely, beginning with many Saljuq monuments, and is not unique to the Bayezid Pasha mosque-*zāviye*. The principle of repeating exterior decoration in the interior, or vice versa, is, however, expanded here with the use of the geometric patterns, swirls, and *ablaq*. This use of architectural decoration stands in strong contrast to

83. Interior, Bayezid Pasha mosque-*zāviye*, 1414, Amasya, Turkey. © Patricia Blessing 2018

84. Lower section of mihrab, Bayezid Pasha mosque-*zāviye*, 1414, Amasya, Turkey. © Patricia Blessing 2018

the mosque-*zāviye* of Mehmed I in Bursa, where the stone carving of the exterior leaves the visitor largely unprepared for the tile decoration of the interior, and where the façade functions more as a screen than as an extension of the building's interior. At the Bayezid Pasha mosque-*zāviye*, a different solution is put to work, with interior and exterior decorations responding to each other in terms of motifs and color schemes.

The most obvious influence of Mamluk architecture on the Bayezid Pasha mosque-*zāviye* is visible in the *ablaq* on the porch arches, with alternating white and red stone. At the same time, the strong tradition of stonework in Amasya may also have had an impact on the building, at least in the fact that trained stonemasons could easily have been available to hire for the project, in addition to those who belonged to Bayezid Pasha's entourage, as well as Abu Bakr b. Muhammad. Not present on this monument, unlike in Bursa and Edirne, is tile work that connects to the Saljuq monuments of central Anatolia, to Tabriz, and to the larger question of the "Masters of Tabriz" discussed in the previous chapters. Indeed, the Bayezid Pasha mosque-*zāviye* shows no sign of any stylistic choices related to the wider discussion of an international Timurid aesthetic in the fifteenth century.

CONSOLIDATING A STYLE: THE YÖRGÜÇ PASHA MOSQUE-*ZĀVIYE*

A similar style to that established at the Bayezid Pasha mosque-*zāviye* is continued and elaborated in Amasya in the following decade. Located close to the bank of the river, the Yörgüç Pasha mosque-*zāviye*, built in 1430, is another small T-shaped building, and one that is particularly impressive for the stonework on its portal and porch (Figures 85 and 86). Unlike

85. Yörgüç Pasha mosque-*zāviye*, 1430, Amasya, Turkey. © Patricia Blessing 2018

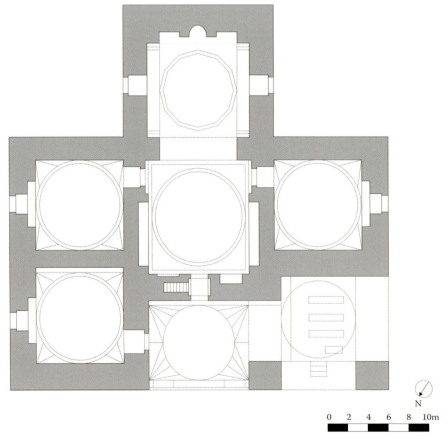

86. Plan, Yörgüç Pasha mosque-*zāviye*, 1430, Amasya, Turkey. Drawing by Matilde Grimaldi

the Bayezid Pasha mosque-*zāviye*, where much of the stonework is based on geometric designs, here vegetal motifs prevail, except for a panel of geometric decoration over the entrance. The building's patron, Yörgüç Pasha, was closely connected to the courts of Mehmed I and Murad II; he possibly served as the latter's *lala* while the prince was appointed to Amasya from 1414 until his accession in 1421, at which point Yörgüç Pasha became governor of Amasya.[70] In this last role especially, Yörgüç Pasha held a significant level of local power that allowed him to contribute to the consolidation of Ottoman rule in the region. In the 1420s, Yörgüç Pasha helped to suppress Turkmen tribes during the revolt of the false (*düzme*) prince Mustafa who attempted to dethrone Murad II.[71] He actively engaged in expanding Ottoman control in the region between Amasya, Tokat, and Ordu on the Black Sea coast.[72] He is next mentioned in historical sources in 1430, fighting back against Qaraqoyunlu Iskandar Mirza's incursion into Anatolia alongside the *beylerbeyi* of Anatolia, Umur Beğ b. Timurtaş.[73] Yörgüç Pasha died in May 1442 and was buried in Amasya, within his foundation, where his tombstone survives.[74] His origins are somewhat unclear; this was noted as early as Halil Edhem's 1911 publication about inscriptions relating to Yörgüç Pasha's patronage, where the author points out unsolved problems in the Ottoman notable's life story.[75] The inscriptions on the mosque-*zāviye* and on Yörgüç Pasha's tombstone both note his name as Yörgüç Pasha b. 'Abdullah; two different, complex genealogies that have been proposed for him may well be fictive.[76]

The foundation inscription (Figure 87) of Yörgüç Pasha's mosque-*zāviye* in Amasya, located over the portal, names the patron, his overlord Sultan Murad II, and the date of construction:

> He is eternal. [It] built this blessed '*imārat* destined for the poor and the miserable during the days of the reign of the greatest sultan and the great *khāqān* Ghiyāth al-Dunyā wal-Dīn, the Father of Conquest, Murad Khan son of the late Meḥemmed known as son of 'Uthmān, may God preserve his rule, the great *amīr* and the significant *wazīr* Yūrkūj [Yörgüç] Pasha son of 'Abdallāh, al-Atābakī in the beginning of the month of Muharram in the year 834 [September 1430].[77]

This inscription is placed on a single panel above the entrance, connected to a larger decorative panel, keel-shaped, in which a Qur'anic inscription forms the top parts of the frame and the foundation inscription the lower part, while the central field is filled with geometric patterns composed of intersecting polygons.[78] As on the mihrab of the Bayezid Pasha mosque-*zāviye*, an illusion of infinity is created by running the geometric pattern to the edge of the frame in a way that suggests its continuation, although here the use of different types of polygons makes for a more irregular pattern than in the earlier monument. These are the same kinds of patterns that we observed in Chapter 1 on the façade of the Mahmud Pasha Mausoleum in Istanbul, carved into stone and set with tiles.

At the historical level, the geometric panel of the Yörgüç Pasha mosque-*zāviye* also evokes, in its inscribed frame, the foundation inscription of the Burmalı Minare Mosque in the same city (Figure 88), built during the reign of Saljuq sultan Ghiyath al-Din Kaykhusraw II (r. 1237–46). The earlier inscription is smaller in size than the later panel, runs along a much flatter arch, and does not have interior fill, but it employs a similar arrangement of text, one that is quite unusual in both Saljuq and Ottoman architecture, and so this may well be a case of a local cross-reference.[79] To bolster this claim, the titles *ghiyāth al-dunyā wa'l-dīn abū l-fatḥ* are used for Murad II in the

87. Foundation inscription and carved panel above entrance, Yörgüç Pasha mosque-*zāviye*, 1430, Amasya, Turkey. © Patricia Blessing 2018

88. Foundation inscription, Burmalı Minare Mosque, circa 1237–46, Amasya, Turkey. © Patricia Blessing 2018

foundation inscription of the Yörgüç Pasha mosque-*zāviye*, and while this is not a unique case of these titles being applied in praise to that sultan, it is nevertheless a possible connection to the Ottomans' claiming of a pre-Mongol Saljuq past, as discussed in Chapter 2. Mehmed I used the same title in the foundation inscription of his mosque-*zāviye* in Bursa. The inscription on the Yörgüç Pasha mosque-*zāviye* effectively mirrors the one on the Burmalı Minare Mosque in certain details of its wording: in both, the overlord is introduced in a certain way (*fī ayyām al-dawlat*, followed by the name) and the patron is inserted at the end. (The Yörgüç Pasha mosque-*zāviye*'s inscription is, however, dated.)

Just as the foundation inscription presents the building as an *'imārat*, pointing to its role as a mosque-*zāviye*, the *waqfīya* confirms this function. Two identical copies of the document have survived, both dated 3 Rabi' I 840 AH / 15 September 1436 CE.[80] A *dhayl* (addition) is in each case dated 21 Dhū'l-Qa'dat 840 AH / 27 May 1437 CE. In the following lines, I base my study on my reading of BOA EV.VKF. 19/7, a document in scroll form with 171 lines of main text in addition to extensive witness signatures and the *dhayl*.[81] The document notes that the *waqfīya* was recorded in Amasya by kadi 'Abd al-Rahim b. Muhammad al-Muslih.[82] Following an introduction composed of pious formulations, both Murad II (as the Ottoman sultan at the time the endowment was established) and Yörgüç Pasha (as the founder) are named with extensive titles.[83] The endowment deed notes the construction of a building (*dār*) within an enclosing wall, domed rooms, a space containing a spring to be equipped with drinking glasses, a treasury, and a kitchen, all located in the vicinity of (literally opposite) a building identified as the Torumtay Madrasa (*madrasa Ṭurumṭāyīat*).[84] The latter building is likely the so-called Gök Madrasa, standing right next to the Torumtay Mausoleum.[85] This entire complex is referred to as an *'imārat*.[86] A bathhouse belonging to the endowment is listed separately farther below in the document.[87] Charitable provisions for Muslim travelers are also included, with the formulation "[. . .] for the poor and destitute, arriving in or leaving [Amasya], among the community of the imam of the prophets and those who are sent out."[88] No mention of a madrasa is made in the *waqfīya*.[89] Extensive landed properties in the surroundings of Amasya are attached, including vineyards and orchards, as well as bathhouses in Tokat and İskilip near Çorum and a *khān* in Tokat.[90] The buildings in Amasya are staffed with a shaykh, an imam, a headman, a doorkeeper, a servant to take care of the lamps and carpets, a cook with one apprentice, a baker with one apprentice, a scribe charged with record keeping, and a treasurer.[91]

While these elements of the endowment are straightforward for a mosque-*zāviye*, the building has some features that diverge from the standard plan. Unlike the regular façade of the Bayezid Pasha mosque-*zāviye* with its symmetrical porch, the frontal view of the Yörgüç Pasha mosque-*zāviye* offers a more complicated picture. Although the type of ground plan employed in the building would normally lead one to expect a three- or five-bay porch, such a structure does not exist. The central bay of the porch is deeply recessed (see Figure 85) with the portal at the back, devoid of the muqarnas niche that often appears on contemporaneous Ottoman portals. This central bay is also taller and wider than the ones to the left and right, with the arch and recess forming an *īwān*, albeit covered with a dome. The tall arch framing this bay shows red-and-white *ablaq* in a frontal view, and when seen from underneath, it has a panel carved with vegetal patterns at its apex (Figure 89). The façade surrounding the arch is clad with white marble with faint grey veins. The same stone is also used around the entrance and for the mihrab. (A different type of stone was used for the side and back walls, which are interspersed with spolia.)

The northern bay of the porch is enclosed, forming a side room.[92] On the exterior façade, stones appear irregularly cut and assembled, and this raises the question of whether this section might have been closed off at a later stage. One point against this argument is the entrance to this side room,

89. Underside of arch on central porch bay, Yörgüç Pasha mosque-*zāviye*, 1430, Amasya, Turkey. © Patricia Blessing 2018

90. Entrance to side room within porch, Yörgüç Pasha mosque-*zāviye*, 1430, Amasya, Turkey. © Patricia Blessing 2018

ocated within the entrance *īwān*, above which a carved panel with vegetal motifs appears (Figure 90). These motifs for the most part belong to the category of *rūmī* ornament, although a case could perhaps be made that the flowers in the frame are peonies belonging to the *khiṭāyī* repertoire. Similar *rūmī*-inspired forms appear above the doorway that leads into the building's main room, although they are obscured by the thick plastic curtain covering the door opening.

The western bay is occupied by an elevated platform with steep steps leading up to it, on which four coffin-shaped tombstones are placed (Figures 91 and 92).[93] Three of these belong to the patron Yörgüç Pasha, his son Yunus Beğ (d. Rabiʿ I 844 AH / July–August 1440 CE), and his daughter Khundi Khatun (d. Jumadha II 846 AH / October–November 1442 CE).[94] This unusual way of creating a funerary section within a building raises the question of whether the current placement of the tombstones is indeed original, or if the tombstones were moved to their current location at a later date. When Halil Edhem wrote in 1911 about the inscriptions on the Yörgüç Pasha mosque-*zāviye* and other monuments sponsored by the same patron, he described this same arrangement.[95] A tiny opening in the west side of the enclosure allows viewing and access for prayers.

91. Corner of porch with platform for tombstones, from West, Yörgüç Pasha mosque-*zāviye*, 1430, Amasya, Turkey. © Patricia Blessing 2018

92. Tombstones, Yörgüç Pasha mosque-*zāviye*, 1430, Amasya, Turkey. © Patricia Blessing 2018

New Directions in Stone Carving: From Plasticity to Surface

With regard to the *rūmī* motifs on the Yörgüç Pasha mosque-*zāviye*'s façade, one observation to be made is that these were not newly introduced to Amasya by the projects of Ottoman builders, but rather had been present in the city's architectural past, reaching back to the thirteenth and fourteenth centuries. Most notably, such motifs appear on the Torumtay Mausoleum (Figure 93), built in 1278 and located only about a hundred yards north of the Yörgüç Pasha mosque-*zāviye*.[96] There they appear prominently on a square panel placed on the mausoleum's façade. But there is one main difference between these motifs and the ones on the Ottoman monument, namely that the forms on the Torumtay Mausoleum are carved in a much more sculptural manner with fleshy forms that jut out from the plane of the wall. A similar deployment of these forms in Amasya appears on the Bimarhane, built in 1308, where they are part of a portal decoration that also includes geometric motifs, muqarnas, and capitals shaped with those same *rūmī* forms (Figure 94).[97]

93. Detail of carved panel, Torumtay Mausoleum, 1278, Amasya, Turkey.
© Patricia Blessing 2008

94. Detail of right side of portal, Bimarhane, 1308, Amasya, Turkey.
© Patricia Blessing 2018

While these forms appear prominently in Amasya, they are not inherently local: rather, they are part of a broader use of vegetal motifs in thirteenth- and fourteenth-century Anatolia. As I have shown elsewhere, the Great Mosque and Hospital of Divriği (1228–29), where such motifs appear on a monumental scale as part of a larger repertoire of vegetal forms, is of crucial importance for the later proliferation of such forms, which hinges on construction projects in Sivas in the late thirteenth century.[98] Similarly, Oya Pancaroğlu has demonstrated how the forms in Divriği are related to both stonework connected to Ahlat in southeastern Anatolia and carved wood connected to Tbilisi, and has argued for the inherent flexibility with which these motifs move across media.[99] In addition to their adaptability to a range of materials such as stucco, stone, and wood, these motifs are also highly scalable: the monumental shapes of Divriği are scaled down in Sivas and Amasya. They appear at even smaller scales in the woodwork that Pancaroğlu describes, as well as in carved stone *khach 'k 'ar*s in medieval Armenia, where these motifs intersect with crosses on "multiple surface planes" in carvings highly evocative of architectural decoration.[100]

While these thirteenth- and fourteenth-century examples provide precedent for the motifs still used in fifteenth-century Ottoman architecture, they are also different precisely in their sculptural quality and layering. In contrast, Ottoman examples such as the carvings on the Yörgüç Pasha mosque-*zāviye* stick much more closely to the surface. Rather than intersecting in different layers and jutting out from the façades they are inserted in, the forms on the Yörgüç Pasha mosque-*zāviye* are carved in one plane without the fleshy substance of the earlier examples. The panel over the entrance to the side chamber on the Yörgüç Pasha mosque-*zāviye* in particular works much more with surface than with plasticity and space in its design.

At the level of design, this raises once more – as in the tile mosaic discussed in Chapter 1 – the question of paper and its relationship to other media. If in the thirteenth- and fourteenth-century examples the multiple layers and plastic forms have a strongly tactile and sculptural quality that is hard to evoke in a drawing, other aspects come to the fore in the Yörgüç Pasha mosque-*zāviye*. Here the panels – both the geometric one over the main entrance and the one featuring *rūmī* motifs over the entrance to the side chamber – are designed in a way that could be done on paper, either on a smaller scale meant for enlargement or at actual size. This shift from volume to surface and line can be observed elsewhere in fifteenth-century Ottoman architecture: a similar strategy was used on the portal of Mehmed I's mosque-*zāviye* in Bursa, where *rūmī* motifs are enlarged to monumental scale but plasticity is reduced to a minimum (see Figure 62).

There is indeed something about fifteenth-century Ottoman architectural decoration that makes it an art of surface: volume is granted to the building, and decoration is given the role of breaking up surfaces into different planes, on which a relationship between smooth and striated surfaces is constructed, to use the terms deployed by Gilles Deleuze and Félix Guattari to define not only spaces but also surfaces such as textiles and water. In assigning the labels *smooth* and *striated*, Deleuze and Guattari note that the first type of surface (for instance, a quilt) can be extended indefinitely, while the latter (for instance, a woven fabric) has a sense of directionality and clear boundaries – defined, in the case of textile, by weft, warp, and selvedge.[101]

This model is not easily applied to architectural wall decoration, and yet the engagement with surface Deleuze and Guattari propose is fruitful in order to understand the shift I note in the stone carvings of Amasya from the thirteenth and fourteenth centuries to the fifteenth. The earlier examples such as the Torumtay Mausoleum and the Bimarhane have stone carving in which layers of decoration with lower or higher levels of relief intersect and overlap. The fields of stone are clearly bordered, either by frames as on the Torumtay Mausoleum or by the outer bounds of the structure overall as on the portal of the Bimarhane. Hence decoration is not designed in a way that suggests a desire on the part of the maker for the viewer to imagine its indefinite extension. In part, this is possible because the decoration on the

Torumtay Mausoleum and the Bimarhane is vegetal rather than geometric. The kind of polyhedral isometric geometry that we observe on the mihrab of the Bayezid Pasha mosque-*zāviye* or on the façades of the Mahmud Pasha Mausoleum discussed in Chapter 1 can be extended indefinitely and is designed with that idea in mind. As Wendy M. K. Shaw notes, such geometries create rhythm and movement, pointing to proportional relationships that are crucial for an understanding of aesthetics in the medieval Islamic world.[102] These types of geometries are already present in the twelfth- and thirteenth-century architecture of Anatolia and continued to be crucial elements in design in the fourteenth and fifteenth centuries, as in the treatise on the construction of geometrical figures discussed in Chapter 1.

By and large, the geometric decoration of the Yörgüç Pasha mosque-*zāviye* and the Bayezid Pasha mosque-*zāviye* maps onto the idea of a smooth surface, as the framing in these cases suggests continuity rather than finite ornament. The geometric panel above the main doorway in the former (see Figure 89) and the decoration on the mihrab of the latter (see Figure 84) are both bordered in ways that suggest the potentially infinite continuation of the pattern. Yet the prevalent use of smooth surfaces in these buildings does not exclude the use of striated ones: in the Yörgüç Pasha mosque-*zāviye*, the panel of vegetal motifs over the lateral doorway (see Figure 90) is carefully fitted into the surrounding border with leaf scrolls squeezing into corners and brushing up against the frame in a striated surface with a clearly defined end. Indefinite extension is not part of this design, which is instead a carefully drawn composition that could just as easily appear on paper. Like on the portal of the mosque-*zāviye* of Mehmed I in Bursa, the motifs are for the most part *rūmī* leaves and scrolls, and yet the occasional flower appears that hints at the *khiṭāyī* repertoire. These multiple elements reach out beyond Amasya to an aesthetic that is forming in the early fifteenth century Ottoman Empire, drawn from different sources, appearing in a structure that at first sight is dominated by a typical Ottoman plan and shows some Mamluk-style elements in the *ablaq* of its voussoirs. Thus the malleable style of the period is at play here as well as in Bursa.

Unfortunately, we do not know whether this aesthetic continued in the interior of the building, as none of the original decoration has been preserved (Figure 95). Ayverdi notes frequent flooding due to

95. Interior, Yörgüç Pasha mosque-*zāviye*, 1430, Amasya, Turkey. © Patricia Blessing 2018

the proximity of the river; this would indeed have been a problem before the banks of the river were consolidated and raised in order to prevent floods in the city.[103] These earlier inundations may explain the elevated placement of the tombs and some of the damage to the stone in the lower sections of the building's outer walls. Considering that the painted decoration now adorning the upper sections of the walls and the interior of the dome does not appear in Ayverdi's photographs, these elements were likely added after the 1960s, along with the painted scroll patterns in the interior of the dome's drum. Thus, in the case of this building, an assessment of the original interior decoration and its effect on the viewer is impossible.

The careful treatment of carved surfaces on the exterior, however, suggests that the unknown architects of the Yörgüç Pasha mosque-*zāviye* had learned their lessons from earlier buildings in the city, both Ottoman and pre-Ottoman, and integrated the elements used there into a minutely designed program of stone carving. The stone carving here shows engagement with some of the Mamluk-style forms present in the earlier Bayezid Pasha mosque-*zāviye*, elements drawn from pre-Ottoman monuments in Amasya, and skill at designing and carving stonework that would prove useful for later construction sites – though late fifteenth- and early sixteenth-century Ottoman monuments show less of the kind of vegetal and geometric ornament we have seen here, the transmission of this skill in stone carving is apparent in the minute work executed on the mosque complex of Bayezid II in Amasya sixty years later (more on this in Chapter 5). Before I begin to examine the ways in which such stylistic and technical features along with how workers moved between regions – with all the necessary caveats explored earlier in this chapter and in Chapter 2 – a look at Ottoman–Mamluk cultural and scholarly ties is helpful in establishing the ground on which artistic exchange could happen.

CONNECTING THE MAMLUK AND OTTOMAN REALMS: SCHOLARSHIP AND LANGUAGE

As Cihan Yüksel Muslu demonstrates, and as laid out in the beginning of this chapter, Ottoman–Mamluk relations in the fourteenth and fifteenth centuries were not consistently smooth; indeed, they were volatile and complex. Conflict and negotiation alternated over the course of these two centuries, culminating in the Ottoman–Mamluk war of 1485–91 and the Ottomans' conquest of the Mamluk lands in 1516–17. Trouble, however, began much earlier, when Bayezid I attacked Mamluk lands in southeastern Anatolia in 1399.[104] As noted in the beginning of this chapter, a direct consequence was that the Mamluks did not support Bayezid I against Timur in 1402.[105] While political relations faltered, though, scholars with Mamluk backgrounds continued to be present at the Ottoman court. For example, Shams al-Din Muhammad ibn al-Jazari (1350–1429), kadi in his native Damascus from 1391 to 1396, moved to the court of Bayezid I after falling out of favor with the Mamluks.[106] Switching allegiances once again, he followed Timur to Samarqand and was later appointed by Pir Muhammad b. ʿUmar-Shaykh as kadi in Shiraz, where he died in 1429; the Timurids even attempted to recover his property, which the Mamluks had confiscated.[107] Quite possibly, al-Jazari had met Timurid intellectual Sharaf al-Din ʿAli Yazdi (d. 1454) during the latter's stay in Cairo in the late fourteenth century, when both scholars were in training there; this encounter points to the larger context of intellectuals' interactions spanning across the Islamic world.[108] One of al-Jazari's sons, Shaykh Abu al-Khayr, moved to Edirne to become a *munshī* (administrative clerk) at the Ottoman court.[109]

Scholars at the Mamluk, Ottoman, and Timurid courts were generally versed in range of languages. During Mehmed I's reign, Ahmed-i Daʿi (d. after 1421), probably a native of Kütahya in western Anatolia, tutored the future Murad II in Persian and created one of the earliest beginners' manuals of this language within an Ottoman context, adding Persian–Turkish glossaries.[110] A Mamluk scholar at Mehmed I's court in Edirne, Ibn ʿArabshah, was responsible for writing correspondence to Mamluk sultan al-Muʾayyad Shaykh (r. 1412–21) in Arabic, but his career involved complications far beyond a simple move from the Mamluk to the Ottoman court.[111] Born in Damascus in 1389, he was only a child when he, along with his mother, sister, and perhaps a nephew, was taken to Samarqand in 1401 in the wake of Timur's attack on their hometown.[112] In Samarqand until about 1409, Ibn ʿArabshah studied with scholars including al-Jazari and al-Jurjani, who both left Samarqand after Timur's death in 1405.[113] Between 1409 and around 1413, he led a peripatetic life, traveling first to an unknown destination east of Samarqand, then back west to Khwarazm, Saray in the Crimea, and Astrakhan before moving into the Ottoman realm.[114] His childhood friend from Samarqand, al-Jazari's son Shaykh Abu al-Khayr, likely provided the required introductions to secure Ibn ʿArabshah a post as *munshī*.[115] After spending roughly a decade at the Ottoman court in Edirne, he moved back to the Mamluk realm, possibly after Mehmed I's death, arriving in Aleppo at the end of 1421 and settling eventually in Damascus.[116] He died during a stay in Cairo in 1450.[117]

A few decades later, Molla Gürani (d. 1488), likely from Guran in Iraq, studied in the Mamluk realm; dismissed from a teaching position at the madrasa of Sultan Barquq in Cairo and exiled to Syria in 1440, he left that region after a few years in favor of better opportunities in Ottoman lands.[118] There, he served as a *mudarris* in Bursa and as a tutor for the future Mehmed II in Manisa.[119] After Mehmed II's conquest of Constantinople in 1453, Molla Gürani wrote the victory proclamation sent to the Mamluk court, which was taken to Cairo by an Ottoman embassy that arrived in October of the same year.[120] Later, he intermittently served as kadi of Bursa and then of Istanbul; from 1480 until his death in 1488, he was *shaykh al-islām*.[121]

Just as these scholars moved between the Ottoman, Mamluk, Karamanid, and Timurid realms, embassies traveled back and forth between the courts, carrying gifts and negotiating agreements.[122] On the Mamluk side, Badr al-Din al-ʿAyni (d. 1451) is a compelling case in point with regard to the impact that such exchange could have on architecture and stylistic changes. Intermittently appointed as the *muḥtasib* (market overseer) of Cairo from 1398 to 1426, and thereafter as chief kadi for the Hanafi school of law of the same city until his death, Badr al-Din al-ʿAyni traveled to Karaman in 1424 as part of a delegation to receive the Karamanids' pledge of allegiance to the Mamluk ruler, a journey in which his knowledge of Turkish would have been of use.[123] In his funerary madrasa in Cairo, a now-destroyed mihrab made of tile mosaic may have been a direct result of the trip to Karaman, as Leila Ali Ibrahim and O'Kane suggest – a rare example that directly connects a patron moving between languages and regions to a possible product of mobile makers. The monument was built in 1411, yet a restoration inscription is dated 831 AH / 1428 CE, making it possible that the mihrab was the work of craftsmen who traveled to Cairo from Karaman at the patron's behest.[124] It is also conceivable that only the design itself traveled and the mihrab was built by local workers in Cairo, since no other connected works were created in the city in the early fifteenth century. Because the mihrab can no longer be examined, observations about technique are impossible. Such exchange at the architectural level between the Mamluk and Karamanid realms was mutual, appearing, for instance, in the restoration of the Great Mosque of Aksaray (1409–30; building first founded in the mid-twelfth century), a building that, as Evgenii Kononenko argues, combines Mamluk and Karamanid elements with Ottoman and Saljuq ones, particularly in the plan scheme.[125]

The example of Badr al-Din al-ʿAyni also allows for an observation about language at the intersection of the Mamluk, Ottoman, and Timurid realms. As a scholar and judge, Badr al-Din al-ʿAyni was able to use Arabic with ease, yet he also spoke Turkic languages, being a native of ʿAyntab (modern Gaziantep) and a member of the largely Turkic-speaking Mamluk elite. Such multilingual actors and contexts were also present within the fifteenth-century Ottoman Empire, including the scholars discussed earlier, although flawless command of several languages was not a given. The *waqfīya* of Mehmed I's mosque-*zāviye* in Bursa, for instance, was written in Arabic, but the scribe resorted to Turkish place-names such as

İnegöl, at times used words mixing Turkic and Arabic elements, and made occasional spelling mistakes.[126] A few decades later, as discussed in Chapter 1, disgruntled tile workers sent a petition in Persian to the Ottoman court, hoping to receive more work. At the time, Persian was one of the major languages of exchange in the eastern Islamic world, from the Ottoman Empire to India, and was particularly used for bureaucratic and literary exchanges such as the ones between scholars discussed earlier.[127]

Translations were crucial in this environment: a wide range of texts were translated into Ottoman Turkish for the use of the Ottoman elites, and Arabic and Persian played a crucial role in Ottoman language formation and the development of a distinct Rūmī identity.[128] It is within such environments that the buildings studied in this chapter were built and that the people using them often communicated – speaking different languages at varying levels of proficiency, surely, but nevertheless within a context that was not culturally or linguistically monolithic. Nor should the focus on Islamic architecture gloss over the fact that fifteenth-century Anatolia and neighboring regions had large Christian communities of various denominations and linguistic backgrounds.[129] Such polyglot identities, closely connected to the concept of Rūmī-ness, were crucial for the formation of Ottoman architecture. Building sites where workers of various origins collaborated and had to communicate with each other and with project supervisors were laboratories for such identities in a day-to-day context, closely tied to the material politics of architecture, unlike the learned environment of madrasas or the Ottoman chancellery.

MAMLUK AESTHETICS ON THE MOVE IN WESTERN ANATOLIA AND THRACE

The signature of Abu Bakr b. Muhammad, known as Ibn Mushaymish al-Dimashqi, on the portal of the Bayezid Pasha mosque-*zāviye* poses the larger question of connections between Mamluk architecture (and architects, with all the caution that needs to be applied in using that term, as discussed earlier) and Ottoman building sites in fifteenth-century Anatolia. A central question to address is through which avenues Mamluk style – and the builders who brought it – reached the Ottoman Empire. The main methodological difficulty is the need to avoid making formalistic comparisons between buildings simply based on the assumption of Mamluk origin or ancestry for an individual such as Ibn Mushaymish al-Dimashqi. In the following discussion, I introduce comparisons between fifteenth-century Ottoman buildings and Mamluk monuments with methodological care in order to consider geographical and chronological distance. I also explore possible connections to earlier buildings within Anatolia that were or could have been the work of Mamluk-trained builders, such as the İsa Bey Mosque in Ayasuluk (1375) and the İlyas Bey Mosque in Balat-Miletus (1404).

The name of Ibn Mushaymish al-Dimashqi connects the Bayezid Pasha mosque-*zāviye* to the earlier İsa Bey Mosque in Ayasuluk (1375), which carries the name of ʿAli ibn Mushaymish al-Dimashqi, the purported or real ancestor of the *muʿallim* active in Amasya and Merzifon in 1414.[130] This earlier monument's patron, İsa Beğ (r. 1365–90), was the ruler of Aydın; after his death, the *beylik* fell under the rule of the Ottoman sultan Bayezid I, who was married to Hafsa, one of İsa's daughters.[131] More so than any of the other monuments under discussion in this chapter, the İsa Bey Mosque presents as a Mamluk building within fourteenth-century Anatolia rather than one that integrates the occasional element pointing toward Bilad al-Sham or Egypt. The marble work over the mihrab (Figure 96) shows a particularly strong connection to the Mamluk monuments of Aleppo and Damascus, where this type of meticulously carved and assembled stonework had been firmly established.[132] In addition to the mihrab, the building also carries exterior stonework decoration that can be more easily connected to Mamluk architecture than to contemporaneous monuments in Anatolia. Thus the upper section of the courtyard portal (Figure 97) shows Syrian-style stonework akin to that on the mihrab. The most famous work to which it can be compared within the Syrian context is likely the mihrab of the Madrasa Firdaws in

96. Mihrab, İsa Bey mosque, 1375, Ayasuluk/Selçuk, Turkey.
© Patricia Blessing 2016

97. Courtyard portal, İsa Bey Mosque, 1375, Ayasuluk/Selçuk, Turkey. © Patricia Blessing 2016

Aleppo, founded in 1235 by Dayfa Khatun, who would soon be regent of the Ayyubid polity of Aleppo in her grandson's name.[133]

Many Ayyubid and Mamluk examples of such stonework with intersecting forms and knotted designs in different colors of stone appear in the interior of monuments, but a direct parallel used on an exterior appears on the façade of the mausoleum of Araq al-Silahdar in Damascus (1349–50; Figure 98), although with the addition of tile in the spaces left between the intersecting bands of stone.[134] To complicate matters, though, a closed-off portal in the Alaeddin Mosque in Konya, founded in the late eleventh century and rebuilt by ʿIzz al-Din Kayqawus (r. 1211–19) and ʿAla al-Din Kayqubad (r. 1220–37), also uses this type of stereotomic stone pattern, perhaps allowing the argument that it arrived in Anatolia earlier, as part of the close relationship between Ayyubids and Saljuqs that both Redford and Suzan Yalman have examined.[135] Thus, though the maker's name on the mihrab of the İsa Bey Mosque provides evidence that it is the work of a Mamluk architect, the monument that was produced was perhaps not as unfamiliar to viewers in late fourteenth-century Anatolia as we might presume at first sight: a similar portal could be found in Konya, at least.

Yet the stylistic message is mixed: on the courtyard portal of the İsa Bey Mosque, the inscription (Figure 99) wraps around an exterior corner in a way that recalls Mamluk architecture more than it does other monuments in Anatolia. The portal of the Hamam Bishtak in Cairo (1341) is one such example of a wraparound inscription, even though the overall decoration of the hammam's portal is entirely different (Figure 100), reproducing the rays carved into stone that first appeared in Cairo with Fatimid architecture. The *khiṭāyī* chrysanthemums that adorn the İsa Bey Mosque's inscription panel before the text begin to tie back into the same repertoire of chinoiserie that J. Michael Rogers observed on the Sultan Hasan Madrasa in Cairo (1356–60).[136] The tile patterns on the pendentives of the dome in front of the İsa Bey Mosque's mihrab, however, are again evocative of mid-thirteenth-century monuments such as the small burial chamber in the Buruciye Madrasa in Sivas (1271–72), where similar patterns appear, although without the rows of what looks like mini-muqarnas made of tile.[137] It's worth noting that many of the Mamluk parallels to this building date to the mid-fourteenth century, leaving enough time for the forms to potentially have been transmitted by way of the movement of architects and stoneworkers. To what extent the appearance of such designs on the İsa Bey Mosque, and in western Anatolia more broadly, might indeed be connected to the dissolution of the workshop employed at the Sultan Hasan Madrasa once construction was stopped in 1360 is difficult to ascertain.[138] There is, however, a clear case to be made for strong architectural ties between Anatolia, Bilad al-Sham, and Egypt throughout the fourteenth century, even reaching back as far as the second quarter of the thirteenth century.

A family connection between ʿAli ibn Mushaymish al-Dimashqi, who signed the İsa Bey Mosque, and Abu Bakr b. Muhammad, known as Ibn Mushaymish al-Dimashqi, whose name appears on the Bayezid Pasha mosque-*zāviye*, cannot be firmly established. Meinecke suggests such a connection, while also noting that by the first quarter of the fifteenth century, Abu Bakr b. Muhammad, the architect with Mamluk ancestry, had become completely Ottoman in his work.[139] Based on stylistic comparison, Meinecke also suggests that the muqarnas window frames of the mosque of Bayezid I in Bursa (1394–95) may be based on Mamluk architecture by way of Ayasuluk and the Yeşil Cami (1378–91) in Iznik.[140] As shown in Chapter 2, muqarnas window frames were firmly integrated into Ottoman architecture and continued to be used in Mehmed I's mosque-*zāviye* in Bursa (1419–21). In addition to these observations, Sema Gündüz Küskü argues for the strong formal connections between early Ottoman architecture and Saljuq architecture, including the monumental muqarnas portals that first appear in buildings under the patronage of Bayezid I – such as his mosque-*zāviye* and the Great Mosque in Bursa – but also admits the Mamluk connection.[141]

The *beyliks* of western Anatolia were crucial conduits of connection to the Mamluk cultural sphere. This is true for the fourteenth century, before Murad I and Bayezid I absorbed many of the *beyliks* into the Ottoman realm, and for the few decades of revival after 1402, when Timur returned

98. Mausoleum of Araq al-Silahdar, 1349–50, Damascus, Syria. © Patricia Blessing 2005

99. Inscription on courtyard portal, İsa Bey Mosque, 1375, Ayasuluk/Selçuk, Turkey. © Patricia Blessing 2016

lands to several former *beylik* rulers, as noted in Chapter 2. In both periods, the *beylik* rulers – like the Ottomans – were patrons of architecture, but also of scholars who came to Anatolia from other regions within the Islamic world. This role of *beylik* rulers as patrons for Mamluk-trained scholars is one of the main points that Sara Nur Yıldız raises in her study of Hacı Pasha (d. ca. 1425). He was a physician and scholar who was trained in Mamluk Cairo and was appointed to the court of the same İsa Beğ who commissioned the mosque in Ayasuluk, although it is unknown where Hacı Pasha

100. Hamam Bishtak, 1341, Cairo, Egypt. © Patricia Blessing 2006

finished his career after his Aydinid patron passed away in 1391.[142] The connection established between the intellectual circles of Cairo and the Aydinid court was paralleled by architectural connections such as those we have observed in the İsa Bey Mosque. Thus, just as in the context of Timurid intellectual networks and their artistic counterparts, court contexts connected both scholars and artists between the Mamluk realm and western Anatolian *beylik*s.

That such connections to the Mamluks were not unique to the Aydinids is apparent when we look at the İlyas Bey Mosque near the town of Balat, commissioned by the ruler of Menteşe, İlyas (r. 1402–21) and completed in 806 AH / 1404 CE.[143] İlyas was among the rulers appointed by Timur to lands taken from the Ottomans. Previously, in 1389–90, the *beylik* of Menteşe had submitted to the Ottomans.[144] Newly restored to rule in 1402, İlyas seized the opportunity to build the mosque complex in Balat two years later.[145] The complex also contained a madrasa, placed so as to form a courtyard in front of the mosque, as well as two hammams (one newly built, the other a reuse and restoration of a preexisting Byzantine structure).[146] The building complex is located adjacent to the ancient city of Miletus, and thus it shares with the İsa Bey Mosque at Ayasuluk a location close to a major, though abandoned, urban center, which could also easily serve as a source of stone for new construction. Moreover, both cities had ports in antiquity. Although both ports were partially abandoned in the late Byzantine period due to changes in urban settlement and because of silting, they were revived under *beylik* rule in the fourteenth century, as Çağla Caner Yüksel shows.[147] This access facilitated trade and Venetian and Genoese merchants used western Anatolian ports in order to access caravan routes through Anatolia to Iran, bypassing Constantinople.[148] Further, trans-Mediterranean connections to Italy and Egypt also left their mark on architecture; as Ayda Arel notes, Gothic arches appear in the architecture of the *beylik* of Menteşe by the mid-fourteenth century.[149]

The İlyas Bey Mosque both serves the further exploration of connections between Mamluk and Anatolian architectures and contains elements that are similar to those in the mosque-*zāviye* of Mehmed I in Bursa, examined in Chapter 2. In its layout, however, the İlyas Bey Mosque is entirely different from Mehmed I's mosque-*zāviye*: the building is based on a single, square room covered with a single dome. The approach to the building leads through a gateway that is slightly off-center and located on the opposite side of a courtyard that is formed by what might be the remains of a madrasa.[150] The courtyard is paved with spolia, presumably taken from Miletus. All four façades of the mosque are clad with slabs of

126   UNDER THE INFLUENCE

grey and grey-white marble in various shades and sizes; these too are likely reused pieces, considering the significant variation they show in size and coloring.

A wide, pointed arch takes up most of the mosque's entrance façade (Figure 101); underneath the arch, three bays of equal width are placed. The central one is the entrance to the mosque, elevated three steps above the level of the courtyard, with the foundation inscription placed above it. Between the lintel of the entrance and the foundation inscription, a flat arch in *ablaq* spans a panel broken up by three small, polylobed windows; muqarnas in stone forms a frame on the left, bottom, and right sides of these windows. On both sides of the entrance, large columns with muqarnas capitals carry the *ablaq* arch, and there are similar arches over the left and right bays. In each of these bays, an opening beneath the arch allows light to enter the mosque; above each arch, a roughly semicircular panel contains geometric patterns outlined in marble carving. In the right-side bay, this semicircular panel is filled with carefully cut pieces of reddish stone and turquoise glazed tile (Figure 102). In the left-side bay, the semicircular panel contains a slightly different geometric pattern, and only reddish and grey stones are used for its fill. On the underside of the arch over each of these upper panels, a polygon pattern carved deeply into dark grey stone has been inlaid with tile. On the lateral sections of the façade, outside the large arch, a band of *rūmī* patterns is carved into the stone at a height of 1.8 meters above the ground.

In the interior of the mosque, all of the walls are clad in marble, just like the exterior. The mihrab (Figure 103) at the center of the southern hall is placed between two rows of rectangular windows stacked one above the other. Like the rest of the wall decoration, the mihrab is carved in marble; the central niche is framed by two colonnettes, one on either side, and topped with muqarnas. The spandrels are carved with monumental *rūmī* motifs, and a band of alternating round and oblong medallions forms a frame that connects to the colonnettes. Muqarnas niches flank the central niche, with rectangular panels above them that contain geometric motifs similar to those on the façade, but without inlay. High above each of these panels appears a carved lamp within a niche, with an inscription panel between them placed within a muqarnas frame. An outer frame that encompasses the entire composition on three sides is also composed of muqarnas. Flower-shaped crenellations carved of stone are arranged along the top of the mihrab. An inscription on this mihrab, on the cubic blocks above the muqarnas capitals on the corner colonnettes, is now mostly destroyed, but it was read in the early twentieth century as "'amal-i Naṣīr al-dīn Altana."[151] Based on the Turkic name Altana, M. Baha Tanman suggests that the individual mentioned here came from a context where Turkic language had a central role – possibly the Mamluk realm.[152] Further, since the inscription is placed on the mihrab rather than the portal, Tanman suggests that Nasir al-Din Altana was not the building's architect but rather a master stonemason.[153]

In the carvings of this mihrab, parallels appear with the mosque-*zāviye* of Mehmed I in Bursa, discussed in Chapter 2, which was begun in 1419. In the İlyas Bey Mosque, we see the crucial link through which Mamluk influence filtered into Mehmed I's complex. The connections to Mamluk architecture are stronger in the İlyas Bey Mosque – for instance, in the use of *ablaq* on the façade – and less evident in the mosque-*zāviye* of Mehmed I, where, as we have seen, motifs stemming from Saljuq and post-Saljuq architecture of central Anatolia were heavily used, especially on the façade, and where any Mamluk influence had transformed enough to make it almost impossible to trace directly. Yet when we look at *beylik* architecture, the possible line of transmission becomes clear, along with the material politics behind this transfer that eventually extended to Ottoman architecture. We do not know who the stonemasons were who worked on either the İlyas Bey Mosque or Mehmed I's complex, but striking parallels exist that force us to consider whether workers – or designs – could have moved from Balat to Bursa in the decade between the completion of the former and the beginning of construction of the latter. The alternating round and elongated medallions with inscriptions that are used on the mihrab of the İlyas Bey Mosque, for instance, also appear around some of the windows of Mehmed I's

MAMLUK AESTHETICS ON THE MOVE 127

101. İlyas Bey Mosque, 1404, Balat-Miletus, Turkey. © Patricia Blessing 2019

102. Detail of geometric panel on entrance façade, İlyas Bey Mosque, 1404, Balat-Miletus, Turkey. © Patricia Blessing 2019

mosque-*zāviye* (see Figure 65) appear as well in the interior of the İlyas Bey Mosque, again above the windows (Figure 104), although the frame is not structured the same way it is in Bursa. The *rūmī* motifs of the İlyas Bey Mosque's mihrab are used on some window lunettes in Bursa, and at a much larger scale on the portal of Mehmed I's mosque-*zāviye* (see Figures 59 and 62).

Thus many of the motifs that appear for the first time in Bursa on Mehmed I's building are present fifteen years earlier on the İlyas Bey Mosque – though in the latter they largely appear in the interior,

103. Mihrab, İlyas Bey Mosque, 1404, Balat–Miletus, Turkey. © Patricia Blessing 2019

104. Lunette above window, interior of İlyas Bey Mosque, 1404, Balat-Miletus, Turkey. © Patricia Blessing 2019

while on Mehmed I's foundation they are found on the exterior. This difference is, of course, due in part to the fact that the Bursa monument's interior is predominantly decorated with tiles. Did Hajji ʿIvaz Pasha's cosmopolitan hiring practices extend to western Anatolia? While the Mamluk elements in Ottoman buildings often appear in a form that has been filtered through the architecture of the western Anatolian principalities, they are nevertheless present; in Mehmed I's foundation in Bursa in particular, they offer a sharp contrast with the Saljuq-style muqarnas portal and the Persianate tiles. At the same time, the attribution of such stylistic elements to either *beylik* or Ottoman production is complicated by other examples, in particular the Firuz Bey Mosque in Milas, built in 1394 for the Ottoman governor of Menteşe while the region was first under Ottoman rule. Elements perhaps closely connected to Mamluk architecture, such as muqarnas corniches, appear on that building, while the T-shaped plan is once more a mark of Ottoman presence.[154] Arel argues that because there is no contemporary parallel to the Firuz Bey Mosque within western Anatolia, the monument must have been built by "a group of qualified craftsmen from the Ottoman region [who] migrated to the Menteşe Emirate."[155] She suggests that the Firuz Bey Mosque and the İlyas Bey Mosque were built by the same workers and, later in her argument, proposes Ottoman parallels for stonework in constructions commissioned by Bayezid I in Amasya and Mudurnu, in addition to the Yeşil Cami (1378–92) in Iznik.[156] Once more, a narrative of unified workshops and migrating workers is employed in the scholarship.

By the early fifteenth century, the presence of builders who had migrated from the Mamluk realm to Ottoman lands, most likely via the *beylik*s of western Anatolia, had visible effects on Ottoman architecture. In Meinecke's view, this appears most notably in the layout of the Üç Şerefeli Mosque in Edirne (1437–48), where a large dome is placed over the space in front of the mihrab, extending across the entire depth and more than half the width of the prayer hall (Figures 105 and 106).[157] In Anatolia, an earlier variation on this type of layout is the Great Mosque of Manisa, built in 768 AH / 1366–67 CE for the ruler of Saruhan, İshak (r. 1362–88).[158] The *beylik* of Saruhan was established in the early fourteenth century with its center in Manisa; in 1390, it was absorbed by the Ottomans under Bayezid I. Restored by Timur in 1402, the *beylik* again came under Ottoman rule in 1412.[159] Meinecke argues that the Great Mosque of Manisa may have been the model for the Üç Şerefeli Mosque, and that it points to a relationship between Ottoman architecture and the building practices of the western Anatolian *beylik*s.[160]

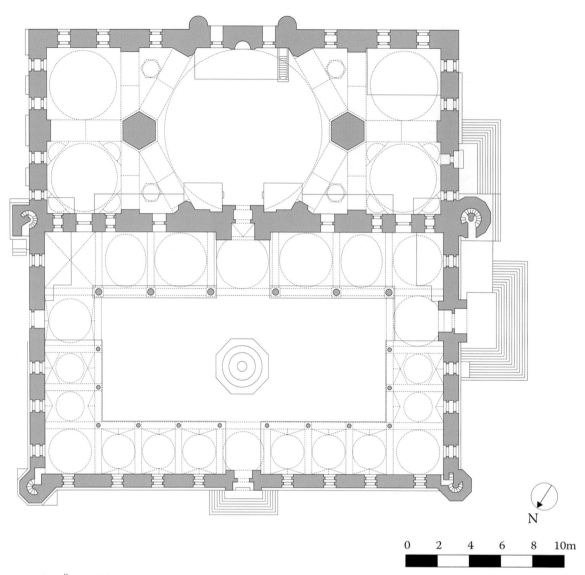

105. Plan, Üç Şerefeli Mosque, 1437–48, Edirne, Turkey. Drawing by Matilde Grimaldi

Here, as in the example of connections between the İlyas Bey Mosque and the mosque-*zāviye* of Mehmed I, a chain of transmission that filters Mamluk forms – likely with the presence of building professionals emigrating from Egypt and the Levant to western Anatolia – through *beylik* and eventually into Ottoman architecture is extremely likely. Mamluk precedents for this layout include the mosque of al-Nasir Muhammad in the citadel of Cairo (built in 1318 and expanded in 1335) and the mosque of Yalbugha al-Yahyawi in Damascus (1346); the type did not survive into the fifteenth century in the same form.[161] Yet the Mamluk genealogy is contested: Necipoğlu argues that the buildings in Edirne, Manisa, and Ayasuluk are ultimately variations on the plan of the much earlier Umayyad Great Mosque of Damascus (715), which has a forecourt and a small dome in front of the mihrab.[162] In terms of their plans, the greatest difference between the Great Mosque in Manisa and the Üç Şerefeli Mosque in Edirne is that in the latter building four small domes cover the sections of the prayer hall beyond the large central dome, while in Manisa these sections are vaulted.[163] In terms of other ties to Mamluk architecture, the Great Mosque in Manisa (Figure 107) has a few alternating red and white stones inserted into the sides of its

MAMLUK AESTHETICS ON THE MOVE 131

106. Interior, Üç Şerefeli Mosque, 1437–48, Edirne, Turkey. © Patricia Blessing 2016

107. Portal, Great Mosque, 1366–67, Manisa, Turkey. © Patricia Blessing 2019

108. Western entrance of courtyard, Üç Şerefeli Mosque, 1437–48, Edirne, Turkey. © Patricia Blessing 2016

portal recess, combined with flower-shaped medallions, one of which (to the left of the entrance) retains a turquoise-glazed tile boss at its center, and pieces of tile inlay among the stonework that are reminiscent of rare fourteenth-century Mamluk examples of exterior tile use in Cairo.[164]

Beyond its plan, the Üç Şerefeli Mosque has stonework on its exterior that ties to a broader Mamluk context, with voussoirs colored in alternating red and white on windows and doorframes (Figure 108) as well as *ablaq* on its minarets: these are elements that cannot be tied to the stoneworking traditions of Byzantine, Armenian, Saljuq, and Ilkhanid Anatolia, but they do appear on the Ottoman monuments in Amasya discussed in the first half of this chapter. Therefore, the transmission into Ottoman architecture took place a few decades before the Üç Şerefeli Mosque was built, rather than during its construction. The entrance to the prayer hall (Figure 109) is a particularly complex combination of a range of architectures: the tall portal with the broad muqarnas cells above the entrance, all carved in grey-white marble, with a stilted arch framing the portal, is close to the scheme used earlier at the Ulu Cami in Bursa and, also in Edirne, on the entrance to the prayer hall of the Eski Cami, founded in 1402 by Emir Süleyman and completed in 1414 by Mehmed I.[165] The Üç Şerefeli Mosque's foundation inscription (Figure 110) is written in *naskhī* over a scroll background, with a kufic overlay in the upper section. A similar combination of scripts and background appears on two tile panels over windows in the

109. Entrance to prayer hall, Üç Şerefeli Mosque, 1437–48, Edirne, Turkey. © Patricia Blessing 2016

110. Foundation inscription, Üç Şerefeli Mosque, 1437–48, Edirne, Turkey. © Patricia Blessing 2016

111. Tile panel in courtyard, Üç Şerefeli Mosque, 1437–48, Edirne, Turkey.
© Patricia Blessing 2016

courtyard, where similar calligraphies were created in underglaze painting in blue, turquoise, and purple on white (Figure 111).

Elsewhere I have discussed in detail how these panels may have been reassembled from fragments of a greater number of tile panels after an earthquake in the eighteenth century, and considered what scholars have suggested about their connection to the Masters of Tabriz.[166] In the present context, what concerns us is the way in which similar calligraphic models were executed in both tile and stone, adapted to a different material in each case, but part of an overarching aesthetic that allows for consistent themes to emerge across the monument, working toward a visual unity that is present in several places. We see this unity in the calligraphy that spans both tiles and stone carving (and interior painting, if the few fragments of inscriptions not touched by a recent restoration project are any indication), as well as in the small elements of *ablaq* stonework that appear on the courtyard portals, on the minarets, and on the window frames on the exterior of the *qibla* wall.

In stylistic terms, the Üç Şerefeli Mosque is a prime example of the ways in which Timurid, Mamluk, and the forming Ottoman style overlap and become in this period part of a new style in which it is no longer easy – or necessary – to distinguish them clearly. If the mosque's calligraphies appear more Timurid, the red-and-white stonework is more closely tied to Mamluk architecture. The muqarnas cells running along the corner columns are a stylistic connection to the mosque-*zāviye* of Mehmed I in Bursa, where they adorn window frames in an example of Mamluk style filtered through the *beylik*s of western Anatolia, as noted earlier – so here the question is perhaps not so much how the Mamluk element arrived, but when and how it became Ottomanized.

TRANSMISSION AND DESIGN

In order to understand how those styles that we term Ottoman, Mamluk, and Timurid overlapped and intersected in the fifteenth century, we need to turn to further elements of architectural decoration, including tiles and calligraphies. In the following section, rather than examining the minutiae of stylistic elements and spending time on formalist analysis and attribution, I focus on ways and means of transmission. Further, we need to note that the Ottomans were not necessarily just at the receiving end of Mamluk and Timurid influence, but that some innovations happened simultaneously in different regions. Blue-and-white tiles are one such case.

Blue-and-White Tiles: A Shared Aesthetic?

Blue-and-white tiles appear in significant number in both the Ottoman and Mamluk contexts in the first half of the fifteenth century. Here I examine to what extent such tiles are part of a shared aesthetic that reflected a widespread interest in porcelain imported into the Islamic world from China. A crucial point is that there is overlap in the general blue-and-white aesthetic but also a wide range of motifs and drawing styles across Ottoman, Mamluk, and rarer Timurid and Aqqoyunlu examples, the latter from the second half of the fifteenth century.[167] Further, in addition to blue and white, a larger color palette appears in some of the Mamluk examples, including black, turquoise, and purple.

It is worth noting that little clear evidence for the continuous production of underglaze-painted tiles across the fifteenth century has survived. Chronologically, after examples in the Muradiye and Üç Şerefeli Mosques in Edirne, the next extant tiles are two panels in the mosque of Mehmed II (1463–70) in Istanbul (see Figures 19 and 20); these are likely the remains of a larger program damaged in the eighteenth-century earthquake that destroyed large parts of the mosque. A few tiles that may date to the 1470s or 1490s have survived in the Cem Sultan Mausoleum (1479, renovated 1499; see Figures 132 and 134) in Bursa's Muradiye complex, but it is unclear when and where they were produced.[168]

In the Ottoman context, the largest number of such blue-and-white tiles in a single building appears in the Muradiye Mosque (1435–36) in Edirne.[169] Hexagonal tiles with a range of floral and geometric blue-and-white motifs cover three walls of the *qibla īwān*, interspersed with triangular turquoise tiles. The mihrab (Figure 112) is made of both black-line tile – identical to that in the mosque-*zāviye* of Mehmed I in Bursa – and segments in blue and white; some parts of the muqarnas have black-line and blue-and-white on the same tile, making it clear that both types of tiles were produced jointly.[170] While the exact motifs on the individual hexagonal tiles vary, they fall into three larger categories. The first (Figure 113, top row) comprises floral motifs that revolve around a central point, with identical flowers or leaves placed in each of the tile's six corners and at its center. Such tiles are fully symmetrical in all directions. The second category (Figure 113, lower row) has a similar arrangement of six flowers or leaves in the corners, but with a different, larger central motif and bilateral symmetry. A variant of this second category has a different, often almond-shaped motif in the bottom corner, creating the effect of a sprig of flowers

112. Detail of mihrab, Muradiye Mosque, 1435–36, Edirne, Turkey. © Patricia Blessing 2016

113. Blue-and-white tiles, east wall of *qibla īwān*, Muradiye Mosque, 1435–36, Edirne, Turkey. © Patricia Blessing 2016

114. Blue-and-white tiles, east wall of *qibla īwān*, Muradiye Mosque, 1435–36, Edirne, Turkey. © Patricia Blessing 2016

emerging from that point (four variants are visible in Figure 114). In all of these tiles with floral-based motifs, the blue motifs stand out against the dominating white background. This color balance is slightly different in the third category: on these tiles, a geometric shape, generally with a six-pointed star or hexagon as its basis, is drawn as a grid, with the gaps filled with vegetal or geometric patterns painted in a range of blues, from very light, nearly transparent blue to opaque dark blue. In several instances, these tiles reveal much less white background than those with floral motifs. Seen from afar, the differences in shades are evident, as the color of the tiling does not appear uniform.

The tiles with floral motifs are examples of decoration classified in Ottoman terms as *khiṭāyī*. *Rūmī* motifs, however, are prominently employed in the black-line tiles of the mosque, and it is possible that the blue-and-white border seen on the left in Figure 114 might also fall into this category. In other words, both categories of motifs are used concurrently, but in specific locations and clearly separate from each other, with specific purposes, rather than conjointly. We must also note that tiles are not the sole decoration that appears in the building's interior: above the tiled dado and surrounding the mihrab are fragments of wall paintings that include monumental trees – painted in a naturalistic fashion from the Timurid repertoire of landscape painting – floral and geometric ornament, and inscriptions (Figures 115 and 116).[171] The oldest layer of these paintings has been dated to the same period as the tiles,[172] and so it is also relevant to consider how the floral motifs on the tiles may have been combined with the much larger motifs in the wall paintings to create an entire landscape within the building, producing an immersive space akin to that of Mehmed I's mosque-*zāviye* in Bursa, but with different artistic means. While a full discussion of extant examples of fifteenth-century wall paintings will need to be the subject of a separate study, we will see in Chapter 4 how in the Muradiye mausolea in Bursa, tiles and paintings were combined to create evocations of paradise in funerary contexts.[173]

These various types of blue-and-white tiles are part of a larger Ottoman–Mamluk aesthetic network; blue-and-white tiles and vessels were most likely produced, bought, and used in both realms simultaneously. In the Ottoman context, such tiles were used in Edirne and (to a lesser extent) Bursa, while in the Mamluk realm, tiles and vessels have been found in Damascus and Cairo. (We also must consider that in the Ottoman context, almost nothing remains of the palace in Edirne and the Old Palace in Istanbul, so that we are missing a large portion of architectural decoration.) Some tiles are still installed in the buildings where they originally belonged. However, many tiles – probably hundreds – are no longer in situ, but held in museum collections where a large proportion of them is attributed to Damascus, often without clear provenance information. Some of the known vessels have been found in archaeological excavations, while others are of unknown provenance. Analyzing such tiles in the Mamluk and Ottoman contexts, Golombek notes that the motifs are closely connected to Timurid landscape paintings, but that Chinese porcelains also played a role as sources for these motifs, although this influence most likely was indirect, by way of other types of ceramics and book paintings, rather than through the copying of objects imported from China.[174]

Places of production for tiles are a matter of discussion, just as in the case of black-line tiles and the Masters of Tabriz, in which Tabriz and Bursa emerge as central sites. For the blue-and-white tiles in the Mamluk context, narratives hinge on the name of "Ghaybi," which was signed on blue-and-white underglaze-painted vessels (on which black was often also used) in Cairo in the second quarter of the fifteenth century, as well as on one tile in Damascus. Over time, the name may have become a workshop's brand, as Yui Kanda has argued.[175] Thus the "Ghaybi" signatures raise questions about moving workshops and signatures as brands rather than marks of artistic individuality in the context of tile and vessel production.

In Damascus, the name "Ghaybi Tawrizi" appears in the prayer hall of the mosque of Ghars al-Din Khalil al-Tawrizi (d. 1423), built in 1420–23, signed on a panel that depicts a mihrab.[176] This site, together with the same patron's mausoleum, contains perhaps the largest documented number of blue-and-white underglaze-painted tiles preserved in situ in either a Mamluk or early Ottoman context: John Carswell counted a total of 1,362 tiles in the mosque and mausoleum.[177] The tiles were not installed in a uniform manner: some are interspersed with triangular turquoise tiles, while others are applied without monochrome tiles in between, creating a dense pattern of blue and white with the occasional glimpse of purple and black. It appears that the tiles in this mosque were not all from the same batch, considering the wide range of motifs.[178] Since both the mosque's patron and the maker of the mihrab tile (although not necessarily the entire collection of tiles) use the *nisba*

115. Stone carving, blue-and-white tiles and wall paintings, east wall of *qibla īwān*, Muradiye Mosque, 1435–36, Edirne, Turkey. © Patricia Blessing 2019

116. Blue-and-white tiles and wall paintings, east wall of *qibla īwān*, Muradiye Mosque, 1435–36, Edirne, Turkey. © Patricia Blessing 2019

Tawrīzī in their names, a connection to Tabriz emerges. Effectively, we do not know if any of the tiles were specifically produced for this building or whether all of them were reused tiles or overstock from other monuments.[179] Certainly, the presence of a single tile panel with a maker's name should not lead to the assumption that a workshop produced these tiles locally. While that is certainly possible, other scenarios ranging from tiles imported from elsewhere to multiple workshops in Damascus and other cities in the Mamluk realm producing similar types of tiles are equally plausible.

Since this mosque and mausoleum contain the largest corpus of such tiles in situ in a Mamluk monument, tiles in museum collections that do not come with a clear provenance have often been attributed to Damascus. These attributions are not necessarily wrong, but it is important to note that a wide range of motifs and styles can be found in such tiles. A panel of tiles attributed to Syria in the Ashmolean Museum, for instance, includes tiles with vegetal motifs – trees and flowers growing in bunches out of one corner of the tile – and six-pointed stars with various fills.[180] In all of these tiles, the blue glaze is dark, nearly black, and applied in a fluid, sketch-like manner. Unlike the tiles in the Muradiye Mosque, which are so precise as to likely have been painted with the help of stencils, these examples appear to have been drawn freely. A group of fourteen tiles in the

Victoria and Albert Museum have in common that many of the outlines are drawn in black, fills are added in dark blue, and relatively little of the white background appears.[181] Motifs range from the type of rotating floral compositions found in Edirne – but here not entirely symmetrical, suggesting an absence of stencils – to star motifs, a hanging lamp, and two peacocks standing to either side of a lute. Again, it is unknown whether these tiles came from the same site, although they are attributed to Damascus.[182] Hundreds of single tiles of all these types exist in these and other collections and await fuller study, not just of their motifs but also their technical composition.

The name Ghaybi also appears in Cairo, and with this material there is clearer evidence of its provenance. We find the name on a range of pottery fragments found in archaeological contexts in Fustat, which confirms that production indeed took place there. On some of these objects, the name (at times added in inconspicuous places, such as the bottom of vessels) reads "Ghaybi al-Shami" (Ghaybi the Damascene), leading Marilyn Jenkins-Madina to argue that Ghaybi al-Tawrizi moved from Damascus to Cairo, changing his *nisbat* – and brand – in the process.[183] Other pieces carry the related name "Ibn Ghaybī," and a tile fragment from the mosque of Sayyida Nafisa in Cairo, now in that city's Museum of Islamic Art, is signed "Ibn Ghaybī al-Tawrīzī."[184] The two names presumably belong to father and son, and a direct connection appears on the fragment of a plate: it is signed "Ibn Ghaybī" on the bottom of the bowl and "Ghaybī" on the underside of the foot.[185] Yui Kanda notes that the "Ghaybī" signature is found written by several distinct hands, and that signatures belonging to other potters have also been found on underglaze blue-and-white pottery from Fustat. Thus Kanda clarifies that a larger production of blue-and-white underglaze pottery existed in fifteenth-century Cairo that was not solely dependent on a presumed migrant or migrants from Tabriz by way of Damascus.[186] Hence "Ghaybi" – like the Masters of Tabriz and perhaps (Ibn) Mushaymish al-Dimashqi – was a brand that carried prestige in the fifteenth-century Ottoman–Mamluk (and perhaps Aqqoyunlu–Qaraqoyunlu) context.

The Masters of Tabriz beyond Bursa

A further look at the question of black-line tiles and the Masters of Tabriz beyond Bursa elucidates these points about how designs and techniques moved in the fifteenth century – specifically, returning to the mihrab of the Muradiye Mosque in Edirne (see Figure 112), with its mix of black-line and blue-and-white tiles. If the mihrab were made of black-line tile only, one might argue that the blue-and-white underglaze-painted tiles on the *qibla īwān*'s walls had been installed earlier or later. Yet since the mihrab has both types of tiles combined in such a way that suggests a single phase of production and installation, it appears that the two types of tiles were produced at the same time. This use of tiles produced in different techniques is not unique. In the case of the Uzun Hasan Mosque (ca. 1477–84) in Tabriz, Sandra Aube has shown that blue-and-white tiles, tile mosaic, gilded cobalt tiles, and tiles painted with black motifs under dark green or yellow glazes were used together.[187] Despite the focus on black-line tiles in many studies of the mosque-*zāviye* and mausoleum of Mehmed I in Bursa, other techniques such as tile mosaic, carved terra-cotta, and gilded turquoise and dark blue tiles were used there too.

Therefore the combined use of tiles in different techniques in the Muradiye Mosque in Edirne was not just a rare coincidence. What does this mean with regard to the production of these tiles? There are three main possibilities. First, the workshop responsible for producing the black-line tiles generally attributed to the Masters of Tabriz may have acquired new expertise (or a new member who already knew how to make blue-and-white tiles). Second, the blue-and-white tiles could have been ordered from another production site, based on drawings, and transported to Edirne to be installed. Third, the entire tile program could have been produced elsewhere (perhaps in Bursa) and moved to Edirne.

A closer look at the narrative surrounding the Masters of Tabriz is in order. The theory has been proposed that the Masters of Tabriz moved from city to city, and scholars have long argued that the T-plan İbrahim Bey İmaret in Karaman, completed in 1432, might be the chronological hinge between the work completed in Bursa between 1419 (the beginning of construction at the mosque-*zāviye* of Mehmed I) and 1425 (the construction of Murad II's mosque-*zāviye*) and the Muradiye Mosque (1435–36) in Edirne.[188] As discussed in Chapter 2, the mihrab from the İbrahim Bey İmaret is an example of black-line tile,[189] with a range of colors comparable to that found in the Muradiye Mosque in Edirne and the mihrabs in the mosque-*zāviye* and mausoleum of Mehmed I, as well as in the small amount of (heavily restored) black-line tile that has been preserved along the cornice above the entrance to the mosque-*zāviye* of Murad II in Bursa (see Figure 123).

Examining the timeline of the introduction of black-line tiles to Anatolia, Aneta Samkoff notes that two black-line tiles in the collection of the Metropolitan Museum of Art, attributed to the mausoleum of Jalal al-Din Rumi in Konya based on their curved shape, are a further piece of evidence for the production of such tiles in the Karamanid realm. While the museum dates these tiles to the late fourteenth century, Samkoff suggests that a fifteenth-century date is more likely.[190] The existence of fragments of similar black-line tiles from Anatolia in Berlin and New York suggests that the mihrab of the İbrahim Bey İmaret was not a one-off use of black-line tile in Karamanid territory.

The Ottomans' destructive acts in the city of Karaman after they conquered it in 1468 do mean that little was preserved, as discussed in Chapter 1. But Karaman and Konya are indeed possible sites of tile production – regardless of whether the Masters of Tabriz ever made their way into Karamanid territory. Further, a neat chronology of the Masters of Tabriz moving sequentially from Bursa to Karaman and then Edirne is upset by the fact that black-line tiles were used in the Şah Melek Pasha Mosque in Edirne, built in 1429.[191] Of course, it is possible that these tiles were installed later and had been overstock from another site in Bursa or Edirne. These potential scenarios certainly emphasize the fact that, in addition to the possibility of workshops traveling widely, we do need to take seriously the question of whether tiles could be sent from production sites to building sites (and not necessarily just within one city) or rerouted to another monument.

Why the need to highlight this argument? In the case of tiles in general and the Masters of Tabriz in particular, scholarship has strongly emphasized traveling tile makers, a narrative that certainly ties into the ʿAli al-Naqqash narrative discussed in Chapter 2. Yet tiles could indeed be packed and transported, just as ceramic vessels could. Considering archaeological finds of ceramics that were transported over great distances, such as from China to Siraf in the ninth and tenth centuries, or even the importation of Ming blue-and-white wares to the fifteenth-century Ottoman Empire, there is no reason that tiles could not have been packed and transported in the same way.[192] The most well-known case is perhaps that of the Great Mosque of Kairouan in Tunisia, where, in the ninth century, luster tiles imported from Iraq were installed – possibly in conjunction with local imitations.[193] Further, luster tiles produced in Kashan (Iran) from the late twelfth to the early fourteenth centuries were transported overland to sites as far as 1,000 kilometers away.[194] In the Ottoman context, larger numbers of tiles produced in Iznik were taken to imperial foundations in Istanbul in the sixteenth century. Further afield, as Walter Denny has shown, Iznik-style tiles were added to the Ramazanoğlu Mosque and Mausoleum in Adana in several phases of restoration in the 1540s to 1570s. As we will see in Chapter 5, these tiles included ones that might have been made either locally or in Damascus in the 1540s, alongside ones most likely produced in Iznik in the late 1550s and 1560s. Denny raises two crucial issues: first, that artisans in Iznik were able to work with drawings and measurements to produce custom-made tiles, which could then be transported, and second, that tiles could easily be reused and moved within or between monuments.[195] Thus long-distance transportation of tiles, reuse of tiles from destroyed buildings, and use of overstock from completed construction projects are plausible options that we need to take seriously when considering the monuments in Edirne and Bursa.

Given that tiles could be made to measure and then installed in a location removed from the site of production, what if it was not the members of the Masters of Tabriz workshop who moved, but rather its products? This is not to say that tiles would have had to be transported from Tabriz all the way to Bursa and Edirne. Equally possible is a workshop established in Bursa in the 1420s, which could have continued to produce tiles until the 1430s, also for use in other cities. There were times when a ruler of Karaman could have ordered tiles from a workshop operating within the Ottoman realm, but, given the volatile relationship between the Ottomans and the rulers of Karaman, this would not always have been possible. A further possibility, if we consider that workshops were not static entities and individual members could leave and move on, is that parallel productions might have emerged if workshops broke up and members moved individually. A fundamental economic question would have been relevant: Was the cost of moving a production site, establishing new kilns, and acquiring all the necessary materials higher than the cost of shipping tiles, accounting for breakage, and factoring in the fact that one of the tile makers perhaps had to travel with the tiles to supervise installation?

In the existing literature, the Masters of Tabriz are evoked whenever black-line tiles appear, and they are assumed to be a group of workers who travels between all these sites and produces the tiles at each site, but we do not actually know whether either of these assumptions is true. As a matter of fact, we do not know for certain that the Masters of Tabriz constituted a workshop with a set cast of members (although some scholars argue that such a workshop may have continued over several generations, with new members being trained as older ones retired or passed away). Therefore, we need to consider that tile production could have taken place in one location and tiles could have been transported to various construction sites. The comfort of easy attribution to the label Masters of Tabriz is illusory, as we need to think more deeply about the ways in which designs and objects traveled, in parallel with but also in lieu of workers' mobility.

The Virtual Kitabkhāna

Glimpses of makers' stories at times emerge, providing insight into trans-imperial, if not always successful careers: for instance, Ahmad b. Abdallah al-Hijazi, a book artist who, in a petition written in Edirne in 1441–42, traces the beginnings of his career back to Shiraz in the 1420s (while also lamenting that he has been unable to find work in his new Ottoman home).[196] The range of skills (painting, calligraphy, poetry) the hapless artist mentions in his petition shows Ahmad previously worked in a *kitabkhāna*, a place where sensibilities that appreciate literature, education, and poetry were closely connected to artistic practice.[197] Such convergences were central to Timurid aesthetics.[198] This broader context also ties back to our exploration in Chapter 1 of the relationship between calligraphy and tile mosaic by way of full-size paper templates that were scaled up from calligraphic works. Beyond the relationship between paper and tile, we encounter relationships between calligrapher, tile worker, painter, and architect. Some of these relationships could be indirect, mediated by paper. In this regard, building sites in the fifteenth-century Ottoman Empire required a virtual *kitabkhāna* of sorts, except that the complex results of their work were buildings, not intricately illustrated and bound manuscripts. In a building like the Üç Şerefeli Mosque, architects, stoneworkers, painters, calligraphers, and tile workers had to closely collaborate – whether at the actual building site or indirectly by way of letters and calligraphic pages sent back and forth – in order to create this multimedia monument.

Such connections did not have to be limited to different cities within the Ottoman Empire, as we can see from the moment in the early fifteenth century when blue-and-white ceramics – in different local interpretations that showed quite some variation – were popular in both the Mamluk and Ottoman realms. Perhaps this period constituted one of shared aesthetic interests that emerged in a period of increased contact between the two powers, who were both opposed to the Timurids but still fascinated by the arts of that rival empire and its cultural centers of Samarqand, Herat, and Shiraz, along with Tabriz with its changing rulers. During the reigns of Murad II and Barsbay (r. 1422–38), Ottoman–Mamluk relations were increasingly friendly, as discussed in the beginning of this chapter.[199] Those who traveled with embassies going back and forth between the two realms could easily have visited monuments during their trips and taken an interest in the types of architecture built in the other of the two realms.

Rather than a straightforward relation of influence and imitation, though, I wish to posit a context in which aesthetic interest could shift based on experience, including the receipt and subsequent use of gifts, as well as on the opportunity to acquire objects – including tiles – to transport back home. All of these aspects played into the material politics operating on building sites, which were likely quite a bit more flexible than one may imagine based on the workshop narratives that have dominated and structured our ways of thinking about these things. Overall, a building site did not have to be a workshop in which all workers involved in the project were physically present. Instead, we can imagine a context in which designs could be sent from one point to another – just the way that, in the sixteenth century, the *hassa mimarları* in Istanbul would prepare architectural drawings, mostly of ground plans, to be sent across the empire. Within the context of Timurid–Mamluk–Ottoman connections, we face not only extensive intellectual and artistic networks, but also an expansive, transregional market on which products such as blue-and-white tiles and vessels could be traded. At the building site, someone competent to direct workers would be needed to begin and carry out the project: for the Bayezid Pasha Mosque, this may have been any of the four individuals mentioned in the inscriptions, and for the mosque-*zāviye* of Mehmed I in Bursa, Hajji ʿIvaz Pasha appears to have had this role, perhaps with assistance.

Paper surely played a central role in the transmission of motifs, although this aspect is much harder to trace. Turning to designs such as calligraphies that could be used to decorate small-scale objects and large-scale buildings alike, paper looms large – if invisibly – behind their transmission. Calligraphies certainly traveled on paper and could be adapted for use in a range of materials including stone and tile. The important point here is that calligraphy is not medium-specific: a detailed template can, in the hands of a skilled artist, be adapted in any number of materials. This is similar to what Roxburgh notes in the Timurid context.[200] Contained in full manuscripts as well as on single pages to be pasted into albums, calligraphies could travel easily and move through a range of scales – a Timurid epigraphic design possibly created in Herat before 1447, with intersecting kufic and cursive inscriptions, for instance, is contained in one of the Topkapı Palace albums.[201] (I return to the subject of albums in Chapter 5.)

Design templates and drawings (such as landscapes) on paper could be copied, and scaled up (or down) using grid paper, for use on tiles, in painting, or on stone carving. They could easily have been made in a *kitabkhāna* anywhere within the Islamic world, within or beyond the Ottoman realm, and adapted to style, wall painting, stone carving and woodwork in equal measure, always taking on the characteristics of the specific material. The design itself, however, would be made with the utmost material flexibility in mind. Such large-scale templates were used for the creation of tile mosaic, as discussed in Chapter 1; in those cases, the template would need to be cut up to create the individual tile shapes, which explains why these paper models have not been preserved.[202] As Bloom notes, pricked drawings became common in the eastern Islamic world beginning in the fourteenth century and could be transferred to tiles as well as the pages of books.[203] The use of stencils is documented in the production of Iznik tiles in the sixteenth century.[204] And looking back to the precisely painted tiles at the Muradiye Mosque in Edirne, we can perhaps surmise that they were used there as well. Edirne did have a book workshop and chancellery in the first half of the fifteenth century, and so the necessary talent was available to produce the templates for such stencils, and perhaps even small-scale sketches that could be enlarged for wall paintings.

Paper also quite likely facilitated the production and movement of tiles. Measurements of monuments written down during the planning process or taken as the building neared completion, along with sketches of specific elements, could have been sent to workshops producing tiles, where commissions could have been completed before being transported to the construction site. While we do not have any of these paper templates, plans, and sketches prior to the last quarter of the fifteenth century, the architecture and tile programs carry in them the proof for their existence. Within such a context, Cairo and Tabriz, as archaeologically documented centers of ceramic production, can become crucial purveyors of tile and the movement of workers in these cases becomes much less crucial. A signature on an object, after all, signifies a maker's claim, not their physical presence at the site where it appears.

MOBILE ARTISTS AND IMPERIAL ASPIRATIONS

If we follow Meinecke's argument, the mobile Mamluk workshops of the fourteenth century had, by the start of the fifteenth century, become fully integrated into the fabric of construction work in Anatolia, both in the Ottoman and the (shrinking) *beylik* realms. Thus the presence of elements that may appear "Mamluk" when read with a formalist eye had perhaps become part of a more internationalized practice of architecture within the Ottoman realm. Seen this way, Ottoman architecture becomes a product of the fusion of a range of architectures: Saljuq, Aqqoyunlu, and Timurid, as discussed in Chapter 2; Central Asian and Renaissance Italian, as noted in Chapter 1; Byzantine, as noted in both those chapters; and Mamluk, as described here.[205] Thus the idea of Ottoman exceptionalism in architectural development on the one hand, and the notion of an overwhelming international Timurid style that dominated much of the cultural production of the eastern Islamic world in the late fourteenth and fifteenth centuries on the other, make for a schema that is too simple to explain the wide range of phenomena taking place within this larger chronological and geographical context. In this period, the Ottoman Empire was uniquely positioned to engage with a range of cultural worlds as it rose – Renaissance Europe, Timurid Iran and Central Asia, Mamluk Egypt and Syria – and its patrons and architects formed a new aesthetic by participating in these varied realms of art and architecture. Tiles, one of the main vehicles of engagement with Saljuq, Timurid, and Aqqoyunlu architecture, remained ingrained in Bursa, Edirne, and later Istanbul. Within the context of a global Renaissance, Bayezid I, for instance, was actively involved in negotiating a ransom of Arras tapestries depicting the life of Alexander the Great in exchange for John, the son of Philip the Bold, Duke of Burgundy, who had been captured at the Battle of Nicopolis in 1396.[206]

These examples reflect the larger scope of transregional networks that included Europe, the Ottoman Empire, Mamluk Egypt, and Iran and Central Asia. We have seen in this chapter that these networks crucially involved not only the movement of workers – documented in some cases, not in others – but also the potential transportation of objects such as tiles and the use of paper as a crucial element for transmission. The close connections between Ottoman and Mamluk architecture did not persist into the period of Bayezid II.[207] The conflict between Ottomans and Mamluks once more broke out in the late fifteenth century, with a full-on war from 1485 to 1491 that mostly involved Cilicia.[208] In Mamluk hands since the late fourteenth century when the Armenian kings of the region were defeated, the region was crucial for the Ottomans as they extended their rule to the southeast of the Taurus Mountains. In the second half of Bayezid II's reign, the Ottomans also needed to secure their new eastern frontiers as the Safavids began to rise in Iran and caused problems with Turkmen nomads living in the areas between the two realms where rule was far from clear.

Ottoman and Mamluk architecture diverged more and more for these reasons, and also because Ottoman builders in the second half of the fifteenth century increasingly developed a clearly recognizable and unified style that drew less and less on elements taken from other stylistic contexts. Further, the centralization of the design and planning process meant that traveling workers became less relevant in the Ottoman context and that designs became increasingly consistent across imperial commissions. These matters are discussed in Chapter 5. Before that, however, Chapter 4 further examines Ottoman dynastic architecture in Bursa within the specific context of the Muradiye complex.

FOUR

BUILDING PARADISE
Afterlife and Dynastic Politics

Mausolea were built for sultans, male and female members of the Ottoman dynasty and the sultan's larger household, Sufi *shaykhs*, and military leaders. In each case, carefully planned endowments recorded in detailed *waqf* deeds determine the nature of the charity dispensed, maintenance offered, prayers said, and Qur'an passages recited for the benefit of the soul of the deceased in the mausoleum and often in connected monuments such as mosques or madrasas. In Bursa, the Ottoman capital for a few decades in the fourteenth century and the center of dynastic memory for much longer, funerary complexes for several Ottoman sultans have been preserved, and these provide insights into these afterlife politics, a subject broached in Chapter 2 with the case of Mehmed I and his role in the revival of the Ottoman dynasty. In this chapter, the focus is placed on the Muradiye, a dynastic cemetery centered around the mausoleum of Sultan Murad II (d. 1451), whose testament prescribed aspects of the site's architecture, establishing the spatial relationship between burials and the connection between the deceased sultan, nature, and the afterlife. After first discussing the setting of the Muradiye cemetery, this chapter examines the complex issues involved in identifying the burials and places the mausolea within the larger context of Ottoman funerary practices. The interiors of the mausolea, with their varied decorations that employed tiles, marbles, and wall paintings to create spaces that connected visitors to the afterlife, are another central aspect of this chapter. I argue paradise is brought into the present moment – that of the visitor, who may have come to pray at a grave – through the landscapes depicted in wall paintings and the presence of water, real and symbolic. Thus the tombs also serve as a memento mori, immersing visitors in spaces that are both monuments of memory in the here and now and a prefiguration of what awaits after death. In this aspect, the Muradiye site doubly ties into medieval and early modern notions of sacred landscapes – on the one hand, in its location within the Ottoman dynastic landscape of Bursa, and on the other hand, as a representation of the invisible landscape of paradise.

FUNERARY SPACE AND DYNASTIC MEMORY

The Muradiye is located on a plateau in Çekirge, an otherwise hilly section of eastern Bursa (Figure 117). At the time of construction beginning in 1424, the buildings were specifically placed to become the

145

117. The Muradiye Quarter in Bursa, Abdullah Frères, ca. 1880–93. Library of Congress, Prints & Photographs Division, Abdul Hamid II Collection, LC-USZ62-81544

center of a new neighborhood, a feature it has in common with other early Ottoman funerary complexes in the city, such as those of Murad I and Mehmed I.[1] Thus the Muradiye was one of multiple expansions of the Ottoman dynastic landscape of Bursa, which had been established with the city's conquest in 1326, as discussed in Chapter 2. The Muradiye consisted of a mosque-*zāviye*, madrasa, *mektep*, soup kitchen, hammam, and a series of mausolea for members of the Ottoman family (Figure 118).[2] A later copy of a *waqfīya* that retains the original date of 22 Shawwal 833 AH / 14 July 1430 CE lists the mosque-*zāviye*, the madrasa, and a soup kitchen destined for orphans and the poor, along with the staff affiliated with the complex.[3]

The dynastic cemetery developed over time. While the mosque-*zāviye*, madrasa, *mektep*, soup kitchen, and hammam were built between 1424 and 1428, Murad II's mausoleum was likely added after his death in 1451, based on its inscription and Ottoman royal practice.[4] Most of the other funerary structures within the gardens of the complex were added at later dates from the 1440s to the late sixteenth century. With its many mausolea reserved for members of the Ottoman family – Sultan Murad II and his immediate relatives, but also his male and female descendants – the Muradiye came to be a dynastic necropolis. Most of the mausolea on the site contain several burials, although not all of these burials have been identified with certainty.

In its role as a dynastic burial site extending over several generations, the Muradiye cemetery is unique within the early Ottoman context. The Muradiye's spatial structure and its location within Bursa are part of the creation of an Ottoman dynastic memory closely tied to topography and place – a dynastic space connected to and rooted in this city. This memorial, dynastic function was allowed to continue even as the commemoration of sultans was transferred to Istanbul beginning with the burial of Mehmed II in 1481 in a mausoleum behind the Friday mosque he had commissioned in 1463.

Murad II's foundation seamlessly continued the construction of a dynastic landscape in Bursa, although the cemetery developed unique features soon after the sultan's death, and particularly in the early sixteenth century, when dynastic politics became visible in the addition of the burials of several of

FUNERARY SPACE AND DYNASTIC MEMORY 147

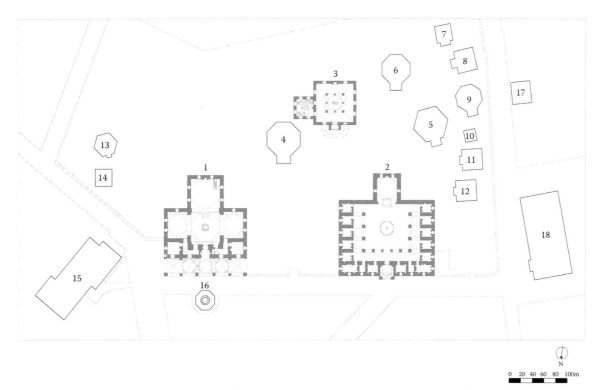

118. Site plan, Muradiye Complex, Bursa, Turkey. 1) mosque-*zāviye* 2) madrasa 3) mausoleum of Murad II 4) Prince Ahmed mausoleum, also known as Mustafa-yi Atik mausoleum 5) Cem Sultan mausoleum 6) Prince Mustafa mausoleum 7) Gülşah Hatun mausoleum 8) Mükrime Hatun mausoleum 9) Prince Mahmud mausoleum 10) Ebe Hatun mausoleum 11) Gülruh Hatun mausoleum 12) Şirin Hatun mausoleum 13) Hatuniye Türbesi 14) Cariyeler Türbesi 15) imaret 16) ablution fountain 17) Karışdıran Süleyman mausoleum 18) hammam. Drawing by Matilde Grimaldi

Selim I's brothers and nephews, victims of dynastic fratricide. From then on, it seems, the Muradiye became a place where difficult members of the dynasty could be honored while at the same time being safely tucked away in a site that was neither close to the central marketplace of Bursa nor, more importantly, located in the capital, Istanbul. Thus the large necropolis of Eyüp was not chosen for the burials of executed princes. Rather, the Muradiye was used in several such cases discussed in what follows.

As noted in Chapter 2, the model of burial complexes containing a mosque and other monuments was established in Bursa. This model continued to be used in Istanbul up through the burial of Süleyman the Magnificent in 1566, whose mausoleum, together with that of his wife Hürrem Sultan (d. 1558), is located behind the sultan's Friday mosque. Süleyman's son and successor Selim II (r. 1566–74) diverged from this tradition. He chose to build his mosque complex in Edirne in 1569–75 and was buried in the garden of the Hagia Sophia in Istanbul along with five of his sons in a mausoleum built after his death by Murad III.[5] As Gülru Necipoğlu has noted, not a single Ottoman sultan was buried in Edirne, a fact that points to the lasting frontier character of that city even during its tenure as capital from circa 1362 to 1453, when Bursa was still at times referred to as *dār al-mulk*.[6] To this one might add that by the early fifteenth century, Edirne was the military capital and center of diplomatic meetings, while Bursa maintained its role as the dynastic center until the conquest of Constantinople.[7] Notably, burials of sultans consistently took place in Bursa; when Mehmed I died in Edirne in 1421, his death was concealed for more than a month until Murad II was able to get to Bursa in order to take the throne.[8] Thus, as Amy Singer notes, several "mobile capital spaces" coexisted and the assumption of a linear progression of the Ottoman capital from Bursa to Edirne to Istanbul does not hold up, especially considering the importance of other cities such as Amasya, Manisa, Iznik, or Didymoteicho.[9]

The various monuments connected to Murad II's foundation served the population with charitable functions such as the distribution of food to the poor, education in the Qur'an school for children, and access to water at the fountain and in the hammam. The site of Çekirge is significant for its natural features, particularly thermal springs that would be used for hammams and fountains. Murad II's complex integrates this topography of water into Ottoman Bursa, tying it into the dynastic city. As Ömür Harmanşah notes in his work on nature and landscape in Hittite Anatolia, such natural features became part of sacred and dynastic landscapes both through "the situated activities of daily users of space, on the one hand, [and] the grandiose interventions of the political elite, on the other."[10] At the Muradiye, such use is shaped through the designing of buildings for daily, public use as the city expanded, especially involving fountains where residents could fetch drinking water and hammams that served as public bathhouses. Further, even though the Muradiye is today part of the dense urban fabric of Bursa, in the fifteenth century, it was located *extra muros*, at quite a distance from the dense urban core surrounding the late fourteenth-century Great Mosque, the marketplace, and the citadel. Thus the Muradiye was also the center of a new neighborhood as the city expanded – the same was true for other Ottoman foundations in Bursa, as noted in Chapter 2.[11] Within this new urban space, the mosque-*zāviye* and mausolea were sites for prayer and commemoration. Even if it is unclear whether the mausolea were publicly accessible, the fact that they have windows suggests ways for interacting with the royal dead, as passersby could offer prayers. Thus, rather than being remote, closed-off royal sites, the Muradiye and other foundations in Ottoman Bursa were sites of dynastic memory, commemoration, and charity all at once – visible to the population, but also useful in daily life.[12] These monuments fulfilled a double function of imposing imperial presence visually and spatially on the one hand, and providing services that were not otherwise widely accessible on the other.

Most of these services have now ceased, but the mosque-*zāviye* is still in use (as a Friday mosque) and the mausolea remain standing and open to the public. Another site of commemoration would have been the non-dynastic cemetery that grew around it over time and was still used in the nineteenth century, although its tombstones have now largely been removed. While some of the burials and attendant tombstones in this graveyard are still in their original positions between mosque and madrasa, and nineteenth-century photographs show an extensive cemetery at the site, it is unclear how many of these burials dated back to the fifteenth and sixteenth centuries. The Muradiye cemetery became a collection point for tombstones from other cemeteries in the Çekirge neighborhood as these were removed in the 1930s.[13] Thus the fate of tombstones seen in early photographs of the Muradiye complex is unclear, as large numbers of them are placed behind the mosque but do not appear to be in their original locations given the close and orderly rows.

The mosque-*zāviye* and madrasa are aligned with each other, their façades forming a straight line; a gap between them serves as the entrance to the funerary garden located behind the two main buildings (Figure 119). The mosque-*zāviye*, dated 828–30 AH / 1425–26 CE in its foundation inscription, is built on an inverted T-plan (Figure 120) with a five-bay porch.[14] In Chapter 2, I discussed another important example of this plan type in Bursa, the mosque-*zāviye* built by Murad II's father and predecessor Mehmed I (r. 1413–21). That building's porch remained unfinished after its patron's death, but otherwise the ground plans of the two monuments are similar, other than the fact that the mosque-*zāviye* of Murad II only has two – rather than four – domed side chambers.[15] Rather than being fully covered with marble facing, the façade of Murad II's mosque-*zāviye* shows a combination of brickwork on the exterior of the porch, marble columns, and marble facing on the corner pillars, while just under the roofline of the porch, brick is used to create geometric strapwork into which pieces of turquoise tile are inserted (Figure 121). With its masonry, the mosque-*zāviye* of the Muradiye is inserted into the Ottoman spatial tradition that had been created in Bursa over the course of the previous century since the city's conquest in 1326, while the tile work picks up newly introduced elements first seen in Mehmed I's mosque-*zāviye* and mausoleum.

FUNERARY SPACE AND DYNASTIC MEMORY   149

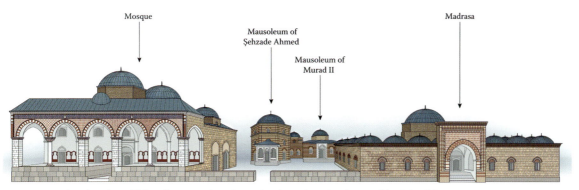

119. Perspective drawing of Muradiye complex, Bursa, Turkey. Drawing by Matilde Grimaldi

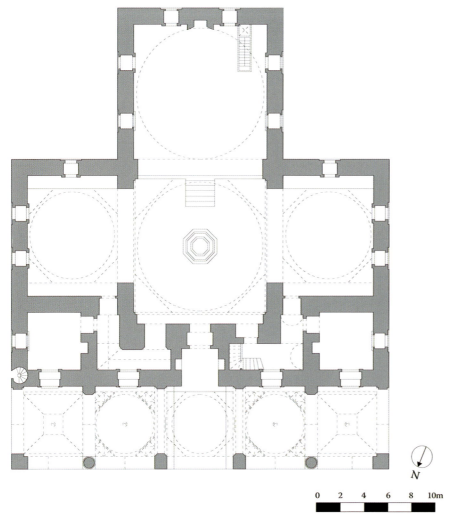

120. Plan, mosque-*zāviye* of Murad II, 1425–26, Bursa, Turkey. Drawing by Matilde Grimaldi

As I have discussed elsewhere, the remaining tile decoration of the mosque-*zāviye*, particularly black-line tiles on the upper section of the porch, is connected to the complex story of the Masters of Tabriz, as well as the larger question of the role of traveling workshops and the relationship between moving workers and moving objects in the fifteenth-century Ottoman Empire.[16] Unfortunately, only parts of the mosque-*zāviye*'s interior decoration have been preserved; the building was heavily damaged in the

121. Detail of upper central section of porch façade, mosque-*zāviye* of Murad II, 1425–26, Bursa, Turkey. © Patricia Blessing 2016

1855 earthquake. As in Mehmed I's mosque-*zāviye* and mausoleum, the remaining tile decoration throughout the Muradiye was restored under the direction of French architect Léon Parvillée beginning in 1863. Parvillée did not shy away from using new tiles produced in Kütahya to replace what had been damaged or from removing original tiles from the sites he worked on.[17] The interior decoration that remains extant today – with the caveat that much of it is likely the result of Parvillée's work – is as follows: monochrome blue, green, and turquoise tiles are arranged in patterns on the lower walls of the *qibla īwān*; the borders are made of black-line tiles (Figure 122). The mihrab is painted, which was most likely done in the mid-nineteenth century, perhaps to replace a tiled mihrab (akin to the one in the Muradiye Mosque in Edirne or the one in Mehmed I's mosque-*zāviye* in Bursa). Under the portico of the mosque, in front of the entrance, tile mosaic with borders and a muqarnas frieze in black-line technique have been preserved (Figure 123).

Given that construction of Murad II's mosque-*zāviye* began in 1425, the year after Mehmed I's mausoleum was completed, it is plausible that some of the same workers stayed on in Bursa for the new sultan's construction project. Since the question of workshops and the Masters of Tabriz was discussed in great detail in Chapters 1, 2, and especially 3, I do not delve into these questions here, but rather move on to new concerns, namely the funerary aspects of the Muradiye as a carefully orchestrated site of dynastic memory that presents notions of wonder and artifice connected to the presence of nature.

THE SULTAN'S MAUSOLEUM

The Muradiye in Bursa follows the principle in Ottoman architecture of giving each part of a larger architectural complex its own foundation inscription, with distinct dates, and usually without referencing other parts of the foundation. The foundation inscription over the entrance to the main space of the mosque-*zāviye* (Figure 124) reads:

> The sultan of the Arabs and the non-Arabs, the shadow of God in the world, sultan son of the sultan, sultan Murad son of Mehemmed, son of Bayezid khān, may God make eternal his reign, ordered the construction of this noble *ʿimārat* in the month of Rajab 828 (May–June 1425). The completion took place in the month of Muharram, the holy, 830 (November 1426).[18]

122. Interior, mosque-*zāviye* of Murad II, 1425–26, Bursa, Turkey.
© Patricia Blessing 2016

123. Tile decoration under porch, mosque-*zāviye* of Murad II, 1425–26, Bursa, Turkey. © Patricia Blessing 2016.

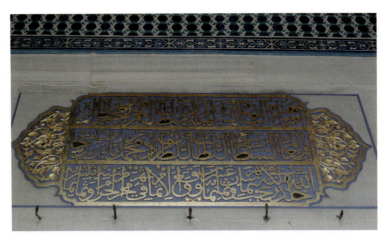

124. Foundation inscription, mosque-*zāviye* of Murad II, 1425–26, Bursa, Turkey. © Patricia Blessing 2016

125. View of Murad II's mausoleum, after 1451, Bursa, Turkey. © Patricia Blessing 2016

While the foundation inscription does not refer to the mausoleum, this is not unusual, especially considering that the latter building was built after Murad II's death in 1451, twenty-five years after the mosque. The posthumous construction of sultans' mausolea, according to Necipoğlu, was rooted in the Ottomans' focus on dynastic commemoration and continuity, as opposed to the glorification of a ruler during his lifetime; the latter emerges in the funerary constructions of, for instance, Mamluk or Mughal rulers, who often commissioned their own mausolea to be completed during their lifetime.[19]

Murad II's mausoleum was thus built during the early part of Mehmed II's second reign, once he had regained the throne following his father's death. The mausoleum was built based on Murad II's *vasiyetnāme*, a text akin to a testament that also describes in quite some detail how the ruler should be buried.[20] This mausoleum (Figures 125 and 126) is composed of two connected square chambers. The larger room contains only the sultan's burial at its center (Figure 127). The cenotaph is plainer than the

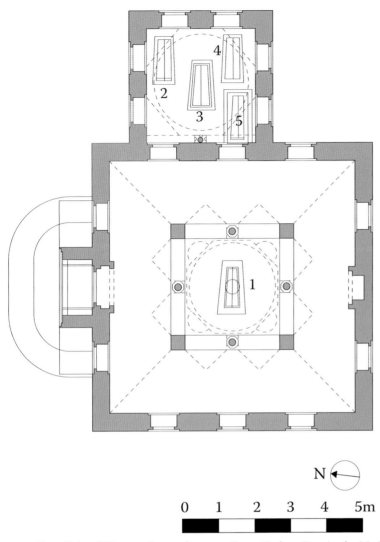

126. Plan of Murad II's mausoleum, after 1451, Bursa, Turkey. Drawing by Matilde Grimaldi

elaborately tiled one of Mehmed I (see Figure 44), which was placed on a stepped platform in the center of the mausoleum above the underground crypt where the burial was located. In Murad II's case, a coffin-shaped enclosure, open on top, was built of marble, with the long sides composed of slightly irregular quadrilateral slabs and the head- and foot-ends reminiscent of tombstones. At other sites, cenotaphs were generally closed and were often covered with textiles, including kaftans that had belonged to the deceased and fragments cut from textiles used to cover the Kaʿba in Mecca and the Prophet Muhammad's tomb in Medina, which were renewed on a regular basis. But in Murad II's mausoleum, the earth that covers the grave is visible, piled up in the center of the coffin-shaped enclosure, just as it would be over a body buried outdoors in a cemetery.[21]

Indeed the notions of interior and exterior are further subverted in the building's architecture: the dome of the mausoleum was originally open at its apex (although the opening is now covered with glass) so that rainwater could fall onto the grave. While this opening in some ways adheres to the hadith that prescribes open tombs, the building nevertheless violates another set of Islamic traditions that entirely prohibit the building of permanent structures on graves.[22] Of course, by the time Murad II's mausoleum

127. Interior of Murad II's mausoleum, after 1451, Bursa, Turkey. © Patricia Blessing 2016

was built, such structures were exceedingly common for elites in the Muslim world, from rulers to ulema and Sufi *shaykhs*, and extensive legal decisions existed to justify or condemn such buildings.[23]

The smaller chamber contains the burials of Murad II's sons Ahmed (d. 1441[24]) and ʿAlaeddin ʿAli (d. 1443), who both died before their father, marked by simple cenotaphs, now covered with textiles that do not date to the fifteenth century (Figure 128).[25] Yet the bare looks deceive: a porphyry column with a basket capital on top and a Corinthian capital serving as its base is placed against the wall between the two chambers (Figure 129). This feature mirrors the marble columns supporting the dome of Murad II's mausoleum, some of which contain one type of reused capital at their apex and another type as a base. In each case, the pieces used are spolia. These architectural details also suggest that there may have originally been further decoration added to the mausolea that has not survived. Certainly these were not plain structures, as shown by the attention paid to details such as the spolia and the marble floor of the main chamber. We cannot exclude the possibility that tile decoration was once present in this space but was damaged to such an extent that even Parvillée didn't try his hand at recreating it.

Considering that the sultan's mausoleum was built after his death in 1451, its location relative to the mosque-*zāviye* and madrasa may have been defined by the princes' burials. Perhaps the mausoleum was planned around these preexisting burials, or, conversely, the two princes were buried in the location the sultan had already chosen for his own funerary monument. It is certain that ʿAlaeddin ʿAli was moved to Bursa for burial: the prince was executed in Amasya in 1443.[26] The Ottomans occasionally moved burials, so we cannot completely exclude this being the case here; the example of Prince Mustafa, who

128. Cenotaphs in the second burial chamber attached to Murad II's mausoleum, ca. 1440–51, Bursa, Turkey. © Patricia Blessing 2016

was buried in Konya for twenty years before being moved here to the Muradiye, is a case in point, as we shall see in what follows. Since the mosque was built in 1425–26, only a few years after Murad II's accession, it is reasonable to assume that the sultan chose this location to be a funerary complex, following the tradition established in Bursa by his three immediate predecessors. It is also possible that the multiple mausolea behind the mosque and Murad II's burial may have been implied in the original scheme, even if they were not fully planned out, considering the substantial number of later additions.

The text of the foundation inscription on the portal of Murad II's mausoleum provides further insights into the spatial terms in which life and death were conceived:

> In the name of God, the Merciful, the Compassionate. Praise to God the Unique for his persistence, exempt from decline and void. May God's blessing be on him whom he instructed in sincere religion, [on] him and his family and his noble companions. And concerning him [Murad II], he moved from the ephemeral and vain world to the eternal and joyful world, from the place of pain and chagrin to the place of abundance and joy, the sultan of sultans of the age, the sovereign of the kingdoms of land and sea, the leader of the warriors and promoters of holy war, the pride of the sultans of the line of Osman, the one who benefits from God's care, the sultan son of the sultan, sultan Murad, son of sultan Mehmed, son of sultan Bayezid Khan, may the All-High guide him towards the fresh place of Paradise, and spread on him the [illegible] of forgiveness! At the hour of sunrise on Wednesday of the new moon in the holy month of Muharram 855 [February 3, 1451].[27]

The exact date and time of the sultan's death are given, confirming that this inscription was completed after Murad II had died. Such specificity is rare: more often only the day or, sometimes, the month and year of death are given. The spatial vocabulary used in the inscription is crucial: it refers to the sultan's journey from life to afterlife, depicting death as a transition that takes the soul from this world to paradise. The phrase "he set out [*intaqala*] from the ephemeral and vain world to the eternal and joyful world, from the place [Arabic: *manzil*, lit. 'way station'] of pain and chagrin to the place [Arabic: *mahfil*, lit. 'gathering place for collecting water'] of abundance and joy" contains spatial references imbued with meaning. Similar but much shorter phrases appear in earlier funerary inscriptions, such as that on the cenotaph of Sahib ʿAta Fakhr al-Din ʿAli (d. 1285), who was a notable at the strategic junction between Saljuq and

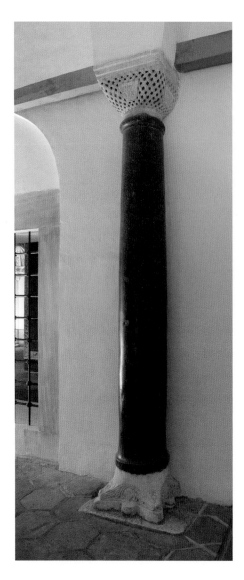

129. Porphyry column in the second burial chamber attached to Murad II's mausoleum, ca. 1440–51, Bursa, Turkey. © Patricia Blessing 2016

Ilkhanid rule in Anatolia, in his mausoleum in Konya.[28] Unlike that earlier text, in the inscription on Murad II's mausoleum, the sites of movement – the world and the afterlife – are described in spatial terms as a rest stop / way station (*manzil*), a term suggesting that life is only an intermediary step on a journey to the afterlife, and as a gathering place with abundant water (*mahfil*), which corresponds to paradise, the soul's eventual destination (or so the person preparing for the afterlife would hope). Not only are both this world and the next described as places, but the sultan is also depicted as traveling from one to the other, from a vain, worldly place to a joyful paradise.

Importantly, paradise is not an imaginary landscape, but rather one that will become accessible – after resurrection – to the friends of God, while those deemed unworthy will be consigned to hell. This fate is decided in the grave, when the angels Nakir and Munkar interrogate the dead about their lives and beliefs; afterward, previews of the afterlife in either paradise or hell are presented twice daily to the spirits of the dead, who were generally believed to remain in their tombs until the day of resurrection, with a few exceptions for particularly pious individuals.[29] While death and the torments of the grave are not mentioned in the inscription, the description of the passage from life to afterlife as a journey may perhaps imply these intermediary steps as well – steps that no Muslim, however pious, could escape unless they had died as a martyr (shahīd).[30] Further, even though the word is not used in the inscription, the emphasis on movement between separate spaces may also imply an awareness of the concept of barzakh, a term that appears in the Qur'an and is often interpreted as a liminal, transitional space that serves as a barrier between the living and the dead, between the world (dunyā) and the afterlife (ākhira).[31] Rituals at the funeral, the prayers of those visiting the tomb, and readings of the Qur'an could alleviate the pains of the deceased soul's waiting period, although over the centuries, Muslim scholars' opinions varied greatly when it came to judging how effective such practices were in changing the dead's fate in the afterlife.[32] This painful part of the journey is omitted in the inscription on Murad II's mausoleum, as only the space of this world and the final one that is doubtlessly expected to await the pious sultan matter.

FROM THE WRITTEN TO THE BUILT SPACE OF MURAD II'S DEATH AND AFTERLIFE

The vasiyetnāme (testament) of Murad II implies that a discussion of burial practices was ongoing in the fifteenth-century Ottoman Empire, and that the ruler and his (spiritual and legal) advisers were concerned with the intersection of traditions that had persisted in Anatolia since the late eleventh-century Saljuq conquest of the region and the rules surrounding burials and mausolea as written out in the Islamic legal tradition. Sources for the latter range from hadith to later treatises concerned with the widespread construction of mausolea and the veneration of the dead as saints, with the practice of ziyārat – that is, the visiting of tombs – a matter of particular concern, although more so for the Hanbali school of law than the Hanafi, which had been prevalent in Anatolia since Saljuq times.[33] These texts were clearly known to ulema within the orbit of Murad II's court and must have informed the writing of his vasiyetnāme, even though no specific references to texts other than the sunna – that is, traditions of the Prophet Muhammad – are made.

The vasiyetnāme states specific conditions for the sultan's burial and the form of his mausoleum, and many of these features indeed appear in the mausoleum, suggesting that the instructions were taken seriously. The text exists in three versions, one in Arabic and two in Ottoman Turkish.[34] The Arabic version of the document, which is the basis for the following discussion, is dated to the middle of Jumadha II 850 AH / September 1446 CE.[35] While the document goes into detail discussing endowments to be made in the sultan's memory at various sites, including in Mecca and Medina, I concentrate here on the section that describes the burial and mausoleum, which reads:

> [The sultan] requested in his will that he shall be buried in the city of Bursa next to his son prince ʿAlā al-Dīn[36] [at a distance of] three [to] four cubits ... and he shall be hastened to the grave as the inherited Sunna [dictates]; further, there shall be no sardab [perhaps meaning crypt here] made for him – the greatest of sultans – and he dictated that around their noble tomb four walls shall be built and be covered with a roof above. Its four sides should be [built in such a manner] that the reciters [of the Qur'an] may sit on them and the center of the roof should be open so that rain may fall on the grave; it [the rain] is one of the testimonies of God's mercy ... 5,000 florins should be spent of this money, and he dictated that none of his children and relatives shall be buried next to him. If he [Murad II] – may God the All-High lengthen his life in good fortune – should not die in the city of Bursa, he shall be brought there so that he arrives on Thursday and is buried in the soil before Friday begins at nightfall.[37]

There are clear indications here about the funerary practices that should be applied to the sultan, and many of the injunctions are specifically intended to follow basic rules for an Islamic burial according to sharīʿa, with the basic aspects being that the body should be washed, wrapped in a shroud, and buried facing Mecca very soon after death.[38] Thus the condition that the sultan should be buried quickly and that burial should take place in the ground are part of this set of conditions. At the same time, another injunction almost immediately follows that seems to contradict the rule that burial should take place as soon as possible.[39] Namely, the document states that, no matter where Murad II died, his body should be taken to Bursa for burial (*wa-awṣā annahu inna lam yatawaffa ṭūla allāhu taʿāla ʿumrahu bil-taqfīqi fī l-madīnati Burūsa yuʾatī ilayhā*), which posed the problem of delaying the burial for the number of days it would take to get the sultan's body to Bursa if he did not die there. The importance of the dynastic site of Bursa therefore superseded attempts to adhere to *sharīʿa*, which the ruler had otherwise established for his burial. Perhaps this tension between *sharīʿa* and concerns of dynastic memory was rooted in the ruler's religious life: Murad II had retired from rule in 1444 in order to pursue spiritual goals. Soon he was forced to return to the throne when a Crusader army threatened the Ottoman realm in 1445, and again in 1446, when his son Mehmed II was unable to quell a rebellion.[40] After this last event, Murad II remained on the throne until his death. The sultan died in Edirne in early Muharram 855 AH / early February 1451 CE, after a dervish he encountered predicted his fatal illness.[41] Writing in the early sixteenth century, historian Neşri notes that Murad II's death was hidden for thirteen days until Mehmed II, who took the throne again as his successor, had reached Edirne. Only then was the sultan's body sent to Bursa for burial.[42] How the body was preserved in the meantime, and how the sultan's entourage reconciled the wait with Islamic practice, is not recorded.

We can assume, though, that the transportation of Murad II's body would surely have called for embalming techniques, considering the nearly two-week delay in announcing the sultan's death to ensure succession and the time it would have taken to travel the roughly 400 kilometers from Edirne to Bursa. Such techniques for preserving bodies – either in the long term or in the shorter term, until burial could take place – were known and discussed in medical treatises. Camphor (Arabic: *kāfūr* or *qāfūr*) was used to wash bodies and to mask the smell of decay.[43] Its properties were useful when a corpse needed to be transported over long distances. In the Ottoman context, such techniques were needed whenever the bodies of sultans were transported from their place of death back to one of the capitals for burial, which was not the case only for Murad II. Murad I, murdered in 1389 after the battle of Kosovo, was first buried on the battlefield, but his body was exhumed soon after Bayezid I's accession and taken to Bursa to be buried in a mausoleum next to his mosque-madrasa.[44] After his death in Hungary in 1566, Süleyman the Magnificent's heart was buried near Szigetvar, where he had passed away, while his body was taken back to Istanbul and buried behind the mosque he had founded there.[45] His close entourage took careful precautions to avoid discovery of the sultan's death before his body reached the capital.[46] These cases demonstrate clearly that the practices of embalming described in medical treatises and in manuals on the use of plants such as camphor were more than just theoretical musings; they were useful tools. In the mid-nineteenth century, Armin Vambery described caravans carrying the bodies of Shiʿa Muslims who had passed away in Iran to places of burial in the Shiʿi holy cities of Najaf and Karbala in Iraq, underlining the unpleasant aspects of the practice of *naql al-janāʾiz* (transfer of corpses).[47] Hence, even though burial soon after death was desirable, the location of burial could be more important than observing these rules; this was true for those who wanted to be buried near the Shiʿi shrines as well as for the Ottoman sultans, who were buried without fail in Bursa or Istanbul, no matter where they had died.

In addition to the conditions of burial, the *vasiyetnāme* had an impact on the construction of Murad II's mausoleum in several ways. First, the mausoleum was built without a crypt and the sultan's body was placed in the ground below the mausoleum.[48] In this respect, Murad II's mausoleum would set the tone for the site, as the other mausolea in the Muradiye are equally devoid of crypts. The placement of the sultan's grave shows a marked shift from the practice observed in many thirteenth- and fourteenth-century mausolea in Anatolia, of placing bodies in wooden coffins in a crypt, with burials marked by cenotaphs placed on the floor above.[49] This practice could lead to natural mummification, perhaps aided by embalming: several such cases were documented into the early twentieth century, with mummified bodies preserved until that time.[50] The explicit demand in Murad II's *vasiyetnāme* to build no crypt and to

130. Dome in Murad II's mausoleum, after 1451, Bursa, Turkey. © Patricia Blessing 2016

adhere to Islamic funerary ritual – which requires that the naked body be wrapped in a simple white shroud and buried directly in the ground without a coffin – suggests that in the early fifteenth century, the practice of placing bodies in crypts was known and perhaps still observed. Even Mehmed I's mausoleum has a crypt, although it is unclear whether the bodies were laid in coffins and placed on the floor inside it or whether they were buried in the ground beneath.[51] The funerary practices North African traveler Ibn Battuta (d. 1368–69) observed in the 1330s in Manisa, where a deceased prince's embalmed body was visible in a suspended coffin, may still have been present in the region during the lifetime of Murad II a century later.[52] These practices would shift over the course of the fifteenth century and crypts would disappear from Ottoman funerary architecture.[53]

Further, Murad II's statement that rain should be allowed to fall onto his grave had a direct effect on the design of the mausoleum. The center of the mausoleum's dome was originally open to the sky (Figure 130), and, as described earlier, rather than having a closed cenotaph, the sultan's grave is covered with earth held within a marble enclosure that is open on top. Finally, no other burials were added to the mausoleum at later dates – something that was common practice and that can be observed in Mehmed I's mausoleum, where a number of burials were added in the mid-to-late fifteenth century. As noted in the description of the space, the graves of Murad II's sons 'Alaeddin 'Ali (d. 1443) and Ahmed (d. 1441) are located in the adjacent, connected mausoleum, along with two unidentified tombs.[54] Only 'Alaeddin 'Ali is mentioned in the *vasiyetnāme*; the requested distance between the burials of father and son, coming to about four meters, was observed. At the Muradiye complex, the sultan's desire to prevent the addition of new burials to his mausoleum was adhered to. This did not, however, preclude the construction of further mausolea in the complex, on the one hand, and the addition over time of new burials in several of these mausolea, on the other hand.

PARADISE IN THE FUNERARY SPACE

In Murad II's mausoleum, the open dome of the main chamber is a striking aspect of the architecture, and so is the open cenotaph that allows the earth on the grave to show. Both of these details are unusual when compared to other Ottoman mausolea (although the open cenotaphs also appear in other burials in the Muradiye, suggesting that a site-specific tradition emerged). These two unique elements are also crucial to cosmological references to paradise evoked in the mausoleum. Unlike in the Çinili Köşk, discussed in Chapter 1, where the cosmological aspects of the building are spelled out in poetic inscriptions for those who care to read them (and are able to), here the architecture itself is primarily left to do the work of establishing references to nature and artifice. However, one reference is indeed spelled out with the mention of paradise in the foundation inscription; the mausoleum becomes a liminal space between the world of the visitor – Bursa, the Ottoman Empire, the here and now – and the afterlife. And while Victor and Edith Turner coined the concept of liminal space with regard to pilgrimage, the notion is also apt here.[55] As noted earlier in this chapter, *ziyārat* (effectively a kind of pilgrimage) was accepted in the Hanafi school of law to which the Ottomans adhered, and the mausoleum, where the visiting of tombs occurred, could itself be such a liminal space.

Similar to what we saw in Chapter 1, this space is imbued with meaning that reaches into imaginaries of nature, afterlife, and paradise. While Murad II's *vasiyetnāme* describes the general setup of the space – the open dome (described as a roof), walls, benches for reciters of the Qur'an to sit on – it does not name specific materials for any of these components, and so it does not allow us to either understand the choices in materials or reconstruct aspects of the interior decoration that have not been preserved (for instance, the mihrab or wall claddings). But the monument speaks for itself even if these elements have not been preserved. The expanse of the marble floor (Figure 131) quite possibly ties into a Roman and late antique imaginary that connects marble with water.[56] As Marcus Milwright has shown, such connections were carried over into Islamic contexts, and close ties to late antique practices in the Mediterranean can be found in sources from the Islamic world that involve cladding walls and floors with marble of various colors.[57] And while Milwright does not extend his survey of sources into the Ottoman period, such ideas of marble and water were still relevant, for instance, after the Ottoman conquest of Constantinople.[58] While we do not know the exact reasons for choosing this floor for the mausoleum, such associations, as well as a wish to evoke water and thus al-Kawthar, the famed waters of paradise, are plausible.

With the open dome, the divide between interior and exterior is, if not dissolved, then certainly softened. This dome can be seen as symbolizing the cosmos – but this simple connection is deepened with the oculus at the apex: the sky is visible, and the bounty of rain (and snow, in Bursa's climate) coming from above is allowed to enter. Perhaps this might even permit seeds from trees and plants in the

131. Detail of cenotaph and floor in Murad II's mausoleum after 1451, Bursa, Turkey.
© Patricia Blessing 2016

PARADISE IN THE FUNERARY SPACE   161

132. Interior of the Cem Sultan mausoleum, ca. 1479–99, Bursa, Turkey. Sébah & Joallier, 1894, Pierre de Gigord Album, 96.R.14(A28), Getty Research Institute and Library, Los Angeles

surrounding area to be blown in. The *vasiyetnāme* of Murad II, specific as it is in its description of the grave, refers only to rain and not plants, but the earth within the sultan's cenotaph was ready to receive both, and perhaps plants were indeed able to grow naturally on the grave. This is what George Goodwin suggests when he notes that the earth on Murad II's grave was left exposed so that rain could fall on flowers planted below.[59] In relation to the possibility of flowers growing on this grave, a late nineteenth-century photograph (Figure 132) of the interior of the Cem Sultan Mausoleum shows dried-out plants growing on three cenotaphs of the same type as Murad II's. This mausoleum's dome is closed at the top, so any plants or seeds on the graves would have needed to be introduced by visitors or caretakers, or at the very least watered in the case of seeds that might have blown in through an open door. While we risk distortion if we conclude that a nineteenth-century practice applied three centuries earlier, the suggestion that plants might be added to the funerary space is nevertheless tantalizing. In Murad II's mausoleum in particular, the interior is not sealed off, connected to the outside only through a single entrance: rather, the exterior world is invited in.

In Islam, the concept of paradise is one of an otherworldly realm, heavily reliant on notions of lush vegetation and abundant water. Crucially, the elements that constitute this larger context of the present world and the afterlife are all part of God's creation; hence both vegetation and water are equally central to fifteenth-century cosmology. In the Qur'an, paradise is evoked with references to gardens and abundant water in several instances, and the Arabic term for paradise, *jannat*, translates as garden, although other terms such as *firdaws* (derived, like the English word *paradise*, from Greek) are also used.[60] Moreover, as Carole Hillenbrand notes, in hadith rain is often associated with God, and particularly with the angels; Egyptian jurist al-Suyuti (d. 1505), for instance, states: "Every day Gabriel is immersed in al-Kawthar, and then he shakes himself; every raindrop is created from an angel."[61] Thus the open dome in the mausoleum of Murad II gains additional significance: the rain that is admitted is not just a part of nature but a potentially sacred element as well. An explicit connection between a water feature, Qur'an passages alluding to water and paradise, and a funerary space exists in the complex of Saljuq-Ilkhanid official Sahib ʿAta Fakhr al-Din ʿAli in Konya, built between 1258 and 1285. There, a fountain on the mosque façade is framed with Qur'an passages (XXV: 48–51; LXXVIII: 14–16; XXXIX: 21–22; LXXVI: 5–6, 10, 17) that refer to water and springs, while an inscription in the mausoleum explicitly evokes paradise.[62] Also in thirteenth-century Konya, the madrasa founded by Jalal al-Din Qaratay in 1251–52 had an oculus at the apex of its dome with a water basin located below.[63]

Water is, of course, further present in the water features connected to the Muradiye complex. It is noteworthy that the *waqfīya* mentions two *miʿmār*s whose duties, in addition to the upkeep of the buildings, include maintenance of the fountains and water conduits, clearly pointing to the importance of these features, which also have charitable functions in providing water to the neighborhood.[64] Thus the *vasiyetnāme*, the structure of the mausoleum, and its foundation inscription are closely connected in the creation of a carefully planned funerary space in which the artifice ties into natural elements, particularly water, which in turn tie into notions of paradise.

The concept of regarding mausolea as symbolic representations of paradise, or of the afterlife more broadly, appears in funerary contexts beyond the Islamic world as well. In a study of seventh- and eighth-century royal Tang tombs in China, Jonathan Hay argues that new insights into the construction and meaning of such funerary structures emerge when the perspective of the deceased who are buried in them is considered.[65] That is, he suggests that the designers' and builders' conceptions of how the deceased would experience the afterlife were integrated into the tombs and their decoration, affecting both painted and stone elements, such as funerary couches and sarcophagi.[66] An important distinction, apart from thoroughly different conceptions of the afterlife in early medieval Buddhism and fifteenth-century Islam, lies in the visibility and accessibility of these tombs after the occupant was buried. In the case of the Tang tombs, the decoration Hay addresses was located in underground sections that were sealed during the funeral and thereafter no longer accessible to the living.[67] Thus any kind of commemoration had to take place above ground while the tomb remained the realm of the dead. This allows for the argument that these spaces were first and foremost created and decorated according to the needs of the deceased as they entered the afterlife and were poised to remain there eternally.

In contrast, medieval Islamic mausolea, once the form of a domed structure – either freestanding, as in the case of most Ottoman mausolea, or part of a larger building complex, as in many Mamluk examples – had been firmly established, were highly ornate spaces that catered to the living visiting the dead while also projecting the deceased elite individual's prestige.[68] Crypts, particularly in twelfth- and thirteenth-century Saljuq mausolea, complicate this notion slightly, in that there were two separate spaces, one of which was generally inaccessible to the living (although not completely sealed off) and the other of which was above it, with the cenotaph that marked the burial being the first place of encounter for those coming to visit. In the Yörgüç Pasha mosque-*zāviye* in Amasya, discussed in Chapter 3, stairs allow access to the tombstones located on a platform, suggesting that proximity was crucial – both in order to view and to touch!

As noted previously, however, crypts were no longer used in Ottoman mausolea at the time the Muradiye cemetery was established, and thus the visible and accessible space needs to be reckoned with. This space allows for commemoration in the form of prayers, readings of the Qur'an, and lighting of lamps – activities noted in endowment deeds relating to funerary structures. The decoration in these spaces can take on various forms, and at the Muradiye, it mostly relies on painting and tile, at least where these have been preserved. Like the allusions to water we saw in the marble floor of Murad II's mausoleum, the use of blue tiles in several other structures creates a visual effect of an environment filled with water, evoking images of paradise in the viewer.

References to paradise are also present in garden motifs used in mosque decoration, as Goodwin notes.[69] Such motifs appear in wall paintings in Timurid, Mamluk, and Ottoman monuments, and their funerary associations are important to discuss.[70] Within the Ottoman context, a few examples have survived, including two in Edirne and the Yahşi Bey Mosque in Tire (building undated, *waqfīya* 845 AH / 1441 CE).[71] Although it is now heavily restored and repainted, the interior of the Üç Şerefeli Mosque in Edirne featured wall paintings that connect to a Timurid mode of decoration, featuring trees and other vegetal motifs.[72] O'Kane notes that these paintings of trees, which he was able to observe during an ongoing restoration in 1994, had unfortunately been painted over by the time he visited again in 2001, while other parts of the decoration were repainted in colors far removed from the original.[73] Currently, only small sections of inscription bands remain in an unrestored state. Motifs of trees and flowers in a Timurid mode also appear in wall paintings in the Muradiye Mosque in Edirne (1435–36). Fragments of paintings have been preserved on the walls of the *qibla īwān*; on its east wall (see Figures 115 and 116), for instance, a large cypress-tree shape was created of flowers, and the fragments of two twisted tree trunks are still visible.

The idea of integrating landscapes into the wall decoration of buildings appears in the early fifteenth-century Timurid context, often but not exclusively in funerary buildings. Similar landscape paintings also appear in the late fourteenth-century Bihbihani anthology, separating the poetic texts that make up the manuscript.[74] The eleven landscape paintings within this manuscript can convincingly be dated to 1398, the same time as the text, and attributed to Shiraz.[75] Moreover, O'Kane connects the paintings of the Bihbihani anthology to similar landscapes that appear in the shrine of Pir-i Bakran in Linjan near Isfahan, where they may have been created in the early fourteenth century, and in the Masjid-i Gunbad in Azadan (1364–66) in the same region.[76] Thus such paintings existed both in books and on monuments before the first Timurid examples emerged.

In analyzing the scarce paintings that have survived in Timurid contexts, Golombek notes the funerary connotations of landscapes.[77] This is the use that also emerges in the Muradiye complex, although the Ottoman examples of landscape paintings in mosques show that a broader set of meanings could be attributed to them, beyond the funerary and commemorative realm. The evocation of nature in the paintings, in the Muradiye complex and elsewhere, is in tune with what Oleg Grabar noted about the use of vegetal ornament, namely that vegetation "suggests or evokes life. Without representing life, it provides a sense of growth and movement."[78]

While some of the painted decoration in the mausolea of the Muradiye complex remained visible in the early twentieth century and can be seen in Albert Gabriel's photographs of the site, much of what was likely an extensive use of landscape paintings at the site no longer survives.[79] Meanwhile, when we examine mausolea added to the Muradiye in later years, we see that the naturalism of earlier examples of landscape painting in the Timurid mode becomes more stylized by the beginning of the sixteenth century. By the mid-sixteenth century, it disappears from the Ottoman repertoire along with the international Timurid style. Nevertheless, despite this stylistic change, decoration in the interiors of sixteenth-century mausolea at the Muradiye continues to bear relation to funerary concerns and hold allusions to paradise.

The walls of the Gülruh Hatun Mausoleum and the Prince Mahmud Mausoleum were whitewashed in the mid-nineteenth century, and the painted decoration in these mausolea was not uncovered until the most recent restoration, completed under the auspices of the Bursa municipality in 2013–15. In both of them, the decoration of the dome was uncovered while only fragments of the inscriptions above the tiled dadoes were visible in earlier images taken during the restoration.[80] During the restoration, the inscriptions in the Gülruh Hatun Mausoleum, which dates to circa 1520, were recreated to run around the base of the

133. Interior of dome, Gülruh Hatun mausoleum, ca. 1520, Bursa, Turkey. © Patricia Blessing 2016

dome, with representations of lamps formed of calligraphy shown to be hanging from the lower border. No tiles were used in this building. The color scheme is dominated by red and grey, and the "Ottomanized *khiṭāyī*" of circa 1500 appears prominently in the paintings inside the dome (Figure 133). Thus the shift in taste of the late fifteenth and early sixteenth centuries, which Necipoğlu analyses in tiles, is also present in the wall paintings of the Muradiye mausolea.[81] Moving away from the Ottoman interpretation of the international Timurid style, in which wall paintings contained naturalistic trees and flowers, more stylized forms are now deployed; Ottomanized *khiṭāyī* motifs can be seen in several of the complex's buildings.

Both tiles and paintings were used in the Cem Sultan Mausoleum (Figure 134), which was originally built around 1479 for the burial of Mehmed II's son Mustafa (d. 1474) but was redecorated around 1499, when the brother of Bayezid II, Prince Cem (d. 1495), was buried there. The painted decoration includes floral motifs and strongly stylized, monumental bouquets of flowers emerging from vases. The tiled blue dado appears rather like water basins placed next to the abundant vegetation in a garden setting.[82] The blue tiles on the dado (Figure 135) are enhanced with gold leaf and are similar to tiles in the interior of the Çinili Köşk (see Figures 11 and 12). The frames around these tiled fields are composed of black-line tiles, a technique also used in Mehmed I's complex in Bursa and on the mihrab of the Muradiye Mosque in Edirne.[83]

In the Prince Mahmud Mausoleum, built after 1507, the decorative program is closely related to that of the Cem Sultan Mausoleum: turquoise and dark blue hexagonal tiles with gold overlay form the dado. In a departure from the Cem Sultan Mausoleum, however, the borders of the tile fields are composed of blue-and-white underglaze-painted tiles with Baba Nakkaş motifs, one of the first architectural uses of this type of ceramic produced in Iznik (more on that production in Chapter 5).[84] On the walls, the same type of stylized flowers sprouting from vases are painted as in the Cem Sultan Mausoleum; the dome (Figure 136), like in the Gülruh Hatun Mausoleum, shows *rūmī* and *khiṭāyī* motifs fused into an increasingly recognizable Ottoman idiom. Both tiles and paintings are deployed with this aim.

The prevalence of vegetal decoration continues in the interior of the Prince Mustafa Mausoleum, a product of the late sixteenth century. There, painted decoration is combined with mid-to-late

134. Interior, Cem Sultan mausoleum, ca. 1479–99, Bursa, Turkey. © Patricia Blessing 2016

135. Blue-and-gold and black-line tile, Cem Sultan mausoleum, ca. 1479–99, Bursa, Turkey. © Patricia Blessing 2016

136. Interior of dome, Prince Mahmud mausoleum, after 1507, Bursa, Turkey. © Patricia Blessing 2016

137. Interior, Prince Mustafa mausoleum, 1573, Bursa, Turkey. © Patricia Blessing 2016

sixteenth-century Iznik tiles, with the painted work repeating the motifs that appear in the tiles (Figure 137). Even the inscription that runs around the interior of the mausoleum – painted above a tiled dado in the earlier examples mentioned – is made of tiles containing Qur'an passages, a quotation from the hadith, and a poem in Ottoman Turkish. On the exterior, above the door, a foundation inscription is wrapped into an Ottoman Turkish poem, with a chronogram indicating the date 981 AH / 1573–74 CE.[85]

What these decorative programs have in common is the evocation of garden spaces with trees and flowers as prominent motifs, all of them possible references to paradise. In the Muradiye complex, the presence of the garden behind the mosque and surrounding the mausolea adds to these references. In the examples examined in this section, tiles and painting were used to create spaces that would evoke such lush places, and ultimately the afterlife. Further, these examples also allow us to follow the development of Ottoman style at a single site over the course of a century.

OTTOMAN FUNERARY LANDSCAPES

The discussion thus far has pointed to the close relationship between conceptions of paradise, gardens, landscape, and funerary contexts, themes D. Fairchild Ruggles addresses in her study of gardens within medieval and early modern Islamic contexts. Some examples, particularly in Mughal India, use the *chahār bāgh* model of a quadripartite garden divided by watercourses. Ruggles notes that in this particular type of garden, frequently encountered in Timurid, Safavid, and Mughal contexts, paradisiacal associations are inherent.[86] One of the earliest well-preserved examples of a *chahār bāgh*, complete with the original water supply, although it is not a funerary garden, is the Bagh-e Fin in Kashan (Figure 138), built circa 1587 and restored in 1797–1834.[87] In Mughal adaptations of the *chahār bāgh* for funerary purposes, a mausoleum could be the garden's center point, as with the mausoleum of Iʿtimad al-Dawlat in Agra (1622–28), or it might be one of several structures within a larger garden complex, as with the Taj Mahal (1632–43), which is not located at the intersection of the water axis.[88]

In the Ottoman Empire, despite close engagement with Timurid art forms in other contexts, gardens did not conform to the quadripartite form but rather proposed a more flexible engagement with landscapes, both natural and carefully orchestrated.[89] The gardens of Topkapı Palace, for instance, were structured with pools and pavilions such as the Çinili Köşk discussed in Chapter 1, and terraces within the palace offered dramatic views over the Bosphorus and the Golden Horn, allowing visual access to the natural environment, particularly the sea. As a funerary garden, the Muradiye in Bursa offers a planned but not geometrically structured landscape, delimited by the aligned façades of mosque-*zāviye* and madrasa, which served as a visual gateway into the funerary garden.

Considering that the Muradiye was the nucleus of a new suburb of Bursa when it was built, we also need to consider that its surroundings would not yet have been built up and hence they could have served as an extension of the landscape created around the mausolea. Such a natural landscape would have prepared visitors for the experience of the mausolea, where ideas of landscape more broadly, and paradise more specifically, are reflected in the marble floors, the tiled and painted walls, and perhaps even the open cenotaphs that might – tantalizingly – be planted. The emphasis in the *waqfīya* on maintaining water features shows that a reliable water supply was crucial to both the public fountain and the larger complex. Landscape at the Muradiye is thus put to work in three steps: the suburb of Çekirge, the garden around the mausolea, and the interior of the funerary structures. The space available for sensory

138. Water axis in *chahār bāgh*, Bagh-e Fin, 1630s to nineteenth century, Kashan, Iran. © Patricia Blessing 2019

experience contracts as the visitor is directed first from the wooded suburb into the garden – perhaps containing fountains and certainly full of the smells of plants and the sound of birds – and then into the mausolea, where a landscape of painted and tiled artifice awaits, wrapped in the sound of Qur'an recitation and the smell of incense. Wonder is evoked step by step.

In the number of mausolea and additional gravestones placed in the Muradiye, and the site's location in an Ottoman capital, a striking parallel emerges with the Eyüp Sultan Mosque in Istanbul and its surrounding funerary landscape consisting of mausolea and graves, although sultanic burials are absent from the latter site. Just like the Muradiye complex when it was founded, Eyüp was originally located *extra muros*; the site, built after the conquest of Istanbul, took shape around an initial shrine. This is not to suggest, however, that the shrine at Eyüp was created in parallel to the Muradiye complex – it certainly was not a dynastic burial site, despite its close association with the Ottoman dynasty and succession. Eyüp was the supposed location of the grave of Abu Ayyub al-Ansari, a companion of the Prophet Muhammad who was martyred during a siege of Constantinople in the early 670s. The fifteenth-century tomb and mosque complex centered on Abu Ayyub al-Ansari's burial do not survive. The site was co-opted into dynastic use soon after the Ottoman conquest of the city in 1453, but not for the burials of sultans.[90] Although Sultan Bayezid II (r. 1482–1512) wished to be buried in Eyüp, his son and successor, Selim I (r. 1512–20), had him buried in a mausoleum in the garden of the mosque complex in Istanbul instead.[91]

Similarities between Eyüp and the Muradiye lie, rather, in the way in which, over decades and centuries, burials were added to both sites, creating veritable cities of the dead – in Eyüp this occurred on a much larger scale than at the Muradiye, and such use continues today, with burials being added on the slopes of the hill to the west of the shrine complex. (Yet if the Muradiye and Eyüp both appear exceptional today, and historically were so in their large scale, one must note that extensive cemeteries existed near most mosques, mausolea, and shrines until the mid-1920s. At that point some, though by no means all, mosque-cemeteries were dissolved as part of the secularist push of the newly founded Turkish republic and tombstones were removed to museums or, as in the case of the Muradiye in Bursa, grouped together in one site in each neighborhood.[92])

Despite their differences, the two sites share the entanglement of dynastic memory and funerary sites in a location *extra muros*, within prominent landscape settings. The presence of water in the Golden Horn is crucial to Eyüp, as are the vistas toward the city and Topkapı Palace. Burial *ad sanctos*, as in Eyüp, and *ad sultanem*, as in the Muradiye, were perhaps related concepts. But while Eyüp was a crucial site for Ottoman dynastic ceremonies, particularly at the accession of a new sultan, it did not hold the tombs of any family members. By contrast, the Muradiye cemetery in Bursa, centered on Murad II's tomb, became a dynastic necropolis for both male and female members of the Ottoman family and household.

PRINCELY BURIALS IN BURSA'S MURADIYE

A discussion of the Muradiye's other mausolea is useful not only in assessing the detailed chronology of the site but also first and foremost in establishing the particular ways in which the site functioned as a tool of dynastic memory. There is a difficulty in the fact that several mausolea do not have foundation inscriptions providing names and dates, and most of the cenotaphs are not inscribed either.[93] The information panels placed on site during the most recent restoration, completed in fall 2015, are the basis of the discussion that follows when inscriptions are absent. When we compare the information about the burials noted on these panels with publications about the site, we can see that it is likely that the source for these texts was the *Bursa Kütüğü*, a detailed collection of information about local notables and sites based on Ottoman sources, published in 2009.[94] Discrepancies with French archaeologist Albert

Gabriel's identification of certain mausolea are also discussed, since his book on Bursa remains a reference work for Ottoman architecture in the city.[95] Various sources that identify burials, although sometimes they contain conflicting information, include Evliya Çelebi's seventeenth-century *Seyahatnāme* and Gazzizāde ʿAbdüllatif Efendi's *Hulāṣatü'l-vefāyāt*, completed in 1815.[96]

The continued establishment of endowments for the upkeep of the cemetery's mausolea remained an important feature in commemoration. Thus in 909/1503–04, Bayezid II established an endowment for the burials of his brother Mustafa (d. 1474) and sons ʿAbdullah (d. 1485) and ʿAlemşah (d. 1503).[97] Alemşah's death earlier that year may have been the incentive for establishing this endowment, and the fact that all three burials are located in the structure now known as the Cem Sultan Mausoleum, but initially built for Mustafa, explains the joint endowment. The extensive endowment deed, for instance, allocates income from thirteen villages (*qariyat*) connected to the town (*qaṣabat*) of Michailich in the province of Bursa in order to finance the reciting of the Qur'an at the three princes' tombs.[98] The document clearly states that all three princes are buried in the same mausoleum in the garden of Murad II's foundation in Bursa.[99] In particular, separate sections of the endowment deed address separate recitations of the Qur'an for each of the three princes, Mustafa, ʿAlemşah, and ʿAbdullah.[100] Lamp oil is similarly provided for the three burials.[101] No mention, however, is made of the fact that Bayezid II's brother and rival Cem (d. 1495) had also been buried in the same mausoleum in 1499, four years before the endowment was made. To state so would have been to inappropriately honor the defeated rival of the ruling sultan who established the *waqf*. Nor are Qur'an recitations included for Cem in the endowment.

Any understanding of the placement of burials is tied to the complex genealogy of the Ottoman family in the fifteenth and sixteenth centuries. In assessing the creation and use of the cemetery, the presence of the burials of both male and female members of the dynasty should also be considered. In addition to sources related specifically to women and children of the Ottoman dynasty, Çağatay Uluçay's work on Ottoman genealogies, which gives particular attention to women, is crucial for what follows.[102] The burials of female members (consorts and daughters of sultans and princes) or associates (such as wet nurses and midwives) of the Ottoman dynasty in the mausolea of the Muradiye cemetery are attested, although identification is unfortunately rather difficult given the bias of the sources toward describing princes' burials in more detail. Thus, while he provides more information about the mausolea of princes, Evliya Çelebi simply states, with significant exaggeration when it comes to numbers: "several hundred princes and daughters and women and mothers of sultans are buried [there]."[103]

As stated earlier in this chapter, Murad II's mausoleum is most likely the oldest structure within the cemetery, and the first burials on the site were those of his two sons, ʿAlaeddin ʿAli and Ahmed, now located in the annex of the sultan's mausoleum. According to Gabriel, one mausoleum was possibly older, namely a structure locally known as the Prince Mustafa-yi ʿAtik Mausoleum (see no. 4 in Figure 118).[104] (This structure is now known as the Prince Ahmed Mausoleum.) The designation "Mustafa-yi ʿAtik" (Mustafa the Elder) was used to distinguish the structure from the Mustafa-yi Cedid (Mustafa the Younger) Mausoleum, built in 1573 by Selim II for his brother Mustafa, who had been executed at the order of their father, sultan Süleyman the Magnificent, in 1553.[105] Rejecting the attribution to Mustafa-yi ʿAtik, Gabriel suggests that the mausoleum had instead been built for Ahmed, a son of Mehmed I who died of the plague in 1429.[106] This is likely a misattribution since this piece of information does not appear elsewhere. Gabriel also identified two of the other burials in this mausoleum as those of ʿAbdullah and ʿAlemşah, sons of Bayezid II.[107] These two princes are, however, buried in the Cem Sultan Mausoleum.[108]

Gazzizāde noted that Prince Mustafa (d. 1474), son of Mehmed II, was buried "close to the burial of prince ʿAlaeddin."[109] As we have seen, ʿAlaeddin ʿAli's burial is located in the annex of Sultan Murad II's mausoleum. Unlike what Gazzizāde suggests, however, Mehmed II's son was buried in 1479 in the structure today known as the Cem Sultan Mausoleum (see no. 5 in Figure 118). Gazzizāde's reference suggests that the attribution of the Prince Ahmed Mausoleum to Mustafa "the Elder" may have existed by the early nineteenth century. Clearly, it was still locally known under that name when Gabriel conducted his research in the early twentieth century. However, while Gabriel suggested that Ahmed, son of Mehmed I, was buried in this mausoleum, it is much more likely that the burial belongs to a different Ahmed: a son of Sultan Bayezid II with that name who died in 1514, defeated in the race for succession by his half-brother, Selim I (r. 1512–20).[110] Selim I built the mausoleum for his late brother, and the decoration clearly marks it as an early sixteenth-century structure.[111]

Relatives of Sultan Bayezid II (r. 1481–1512) are particularly well represented in the mausolea.[112] Between 1474 and 1517, based on those burials that have been identified, two of this sultan's brothers (Cem, d. 1495, and Mustafa, d. 1474), three of his consorts, eight of his children, and seven of his grandchildren were buried at the Muradiye complex (Table 1). After 1513, three more burials were added: that of Sultan Süleyman's executed son, Mustafa (d. 1553), in 1573;[113] that of Mustafa's mother, Mahidevran, after her death in 1580–81;[114] and possibly (although there are conflicting accounts in various sources) that of Sultan Süleyman's grandson Osman, executed along with his father, Prince Bayezid, and his brothers in 1561.[115] Thus the 1480s to 1510s were the most active period in terms of expanding the dynastic burials, even though a number of undated and/or unidentified tombs leave some uncertainty. Overall, however, there is a clear use of the Muradiye as a dynastic cemetery for several decades, before burials of members of the Ottoman household began to be placed in Istanbul for the most part, in sites such as the garden around Selim II's mausoleum behind the Hagia Sophia, where other burials and mausolea were added in the late sixteenth and seventeenth centuries.[116]

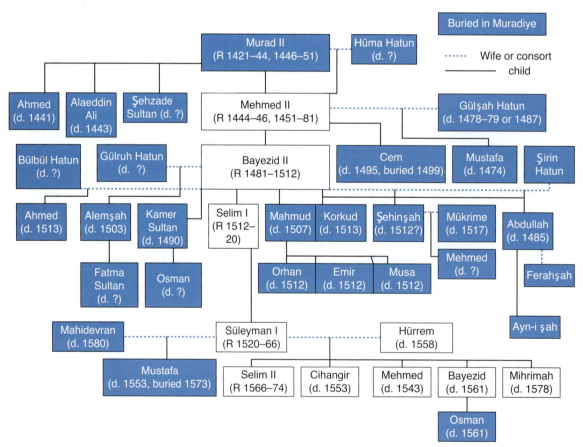

Table 1: Family tree of individuals buried at the Muradiye cemetery (indicated in blue) Patricia Blessing.

As noted earlier, the identification of several burials is disputed, and in two cases in particular conflicting accounts emerge from primary sources. The first is that of Prince Korkud (d. 1512), killed after the accession of his brother Selim I. According to Evliya Çelebi, Korkud was buried in a mausoleum close to that of Sultan Murad II.[117] According to Gazzizāde's account, however, the prince was buried in the mausoleum of Sultan Orhan, which is located close to the citadel in the market area of Bursa.[118] The second discrepancy concerns the burials of the brothers Orhan, Emir, and Musa, sons of Prince Mahmud and grandsons of Sultan Bayezid II, executed at the behest of their uncle Selim I in 1512.[119] Evliya Çelebi places their burials in the mausoleum of Sultan Orhan, near the citadel, while Gazzizāde locates them in the Muradiye cemetery.[120] Secondary sources generally prefer the latter identification, placing the burials of the three princes in the mausoleum of their father, Prince Mahmud (d. 1507).[121]

A simple solution to these conflicting accounts is not in sight, as no inscriptions have been preserved on the cenotaphs that might belong to Korkud, Orhan, Emir, and Musa. The shape of the cenotaphs, many of which are modeled on that of Murad II – marble enclosures devoid of decoration or inscriptions, with earth exposed inside – is part of the issue, making them impossible to date on stylistic grounds. All of the cenotaphs in both the mausoleum of Prince Ahmed and the mausoleum of Prince Mahmud, the two structures that have been suggested as containing the burials of Korkud and the three brothers, correspond to this model.

During Bayezid II's reign, and shortly after his death in 1512, numerous burials were added. This period probably saw the most clearly concerted effort to establish a family cemetery on site. (The large number of princes killed in the two years after Selim I's accession also sparked a need for additional funerary spaces – many of these burials were added to the Muradiye.[122]) The fact that the mothers of several princes were also buried in the Muradiye mausolea suggests dynastic intent. Certainly the ample enclosed garden behind the mosque-*zāviye* and madrasa was available for such an expansion of burial space. At the same time, a given expansion did not necessarily involve the construction of a new mausoleum: many tombs were added to existing mausolea.

Apart from Murad II's mausoleum, two buildings at the site contain single burials. The first is the Hatuniye Mausoleum, built by Mehmed II for his mother and completed in Rajab 853 AH / August–September 1449 CE, according to the foundation inscription over the entrance.[123] Though it is clearly stated in the inscription that the mausoleum was built for Mehmed II's mother before he became sultan (for the second time) in 1451, her name does not appear. This is not a unique instance of hidden identity, and it points to the larger problem of gender in the Ottoman dynastic context. Several possibilities have been suggested for her missing name, such as Hatice (by Gabriel) and Hüma (by Önkal).[124] The second single burial is that in the Gülbahar Hatun Mausoleum, a simple dome open on all four sides. This structure is associated with the wet nurse (*ebe hatun*) of Mehmed II.[125] All other mausolea contain multiple burials, visible in the number of cenotaphs. To the extent known, the additional burials in existing mausolea are as follows.

The Cem Sultan Mausoleum, discussed earlier, was originally built in 1479 for the burial of Mustafa, a son of Mehmed II who had died in 1474. Cem Sultan, the brother and unsuccessful rival of Bayezid II (we learn more about Cem in Chapter 5), died in Naples in 1495 and was buried in this already existing mausoleum in 1499, and the structure eventually took on his name.[126] Two more burials were subsequently added to it: those of 'Abdullah (d. 1485 or 1509) and 'Alemşah (d. 1503), both sons of Sultan Bayezid II.[127] The Prince Ahmed Mausoleum, built in 1513, contains the burials of Ahmed (d. 1513), his mother Bülbül Hatun (d.?), his brother Şehinşah (d. 1511), Şehinşah's son Mehmed (d. 1512), and possibly Selim I's brother Korkud (d. 1512).[128] The Prince Mahmud Mausoleum was built in 1507 for a son of Bayezid II.[129] His sons Orhan, Emir, and Musa are possibly buried there, as discussed previously; the three princes were executed after their uncle Selim I's accession in 1512.[130] The Mükrime Hatun Mausoleum was built in 1517 for a concubine of Bayezid II's son Şehinşah; the other burials in the structure are unidentified.[131] The Gülruh Hatun Mausoleum was built, probably after 1527 for a consort of Bayezid II; additional burials are those of Bayezid II's daughter Kamer

Sultan (d. after 1491) and her son Osman, and Bayezid II's granddaughter Fatma Sultan.[132] The Gülşah Hatun Mausoleum was built for a concubine of Mehmed II who was the mother of Prince Mustafa (d. 1474). The second cenotaph within it is at times identified as that of 'Ali, son of Bayezid II, but this prince does not appear in sources from the period.[133] The undated Şirin Hatun Mausoleum was built for the mother of Prince 'Abdullah b. Bayezid, and also contains the burials of her granddaughter 'Ayn-ı Şah and her daughter-in-law Ferahşah.[134] The Prince Mustafa Mausoleum was built in 1573 over the grave of Sultan Süleyman's eldest son, who had been executed near Konya in 1553 following his father's suspicions that the prince was planning to rebel.[135] Mustafa's mother Mahidevran was buried next to her son in 1580–81, and a son of Mustafa's half-brother Bayezid was possibly buried in this same mausoleum in 1561.[136] The young prince shared with his uncle Mustafa the fate of having been executed after his father, Prince Bayezid (d. 1561), planned to rebel against Süleyman the Magnificent.[137] All of these mausolea reflect the practice of adding the graves of relatives to existing structures over time when space permitted.

Overall, information about the burials of women at the Muradiye is difficult to gather: of the twenty-six identified burials, only eight are those of women. Of these, five are mothers of princes, one is a daughter of Sultan Bayezid II, one the granddaughter of the same sultan, and one purportedly the wet nurse (*ebe hatun*) of Mehmed II. In three cases, mothers and their sons are buried in the same mausoleum: Kamer Sultan (d. after 1491) and her son Osman (d. ?) in the Gülruh Hatun Mausoleum; Ahmed (d. 1513) and his mother Bülbül Hatun (d. ?) in the Prince Ahmed Mausoleum; Mustafa (d. 1553) and his mother Mahidevran (d. 1580–81) in the Prince Mustafa Mausoleum. This leaves unidentified burials, some of which may also have belonged to women – for instance, those in the so-called Cariyeler Mausoleum.[138] While women are included in the dynastic space of Bursa, they occupy a less prominent place than princes do. Of the eight identified women, four are buried in the main grave in a mausoleum named after them, while the others are buried in structures initially constructed to hold the graves of relatives (male in three cases, and female in one case); the practice of establishing mausolea and then adding the burials of relatives was carried out for both men and women. The presence of these numerous Ottoman dynastic burials in Bursa once again raises the question of transporting bodies over distances from the place of death to the place of burial, and suggests that the practices discussed earlier in this chapter were quite common for high-status individuals, not just the sultans.

The construction of the Muradiye in the suburb of Çekirge, at the time a little-developed area, allowed for this larger dynastic cemetery to be created and expanded over time. The area behind the mosque and madrasa, where the sultan's mausoleum was built, offered the space needed for the addition of mausolea. Similarly, the flat terrain of the site would have been convenient for construction compared to the hills found in other parts of the city. The other three sultanic funerary complexes in Bursa (those of Murad I, Bayezid I, and Mehmed I) are all built on slopes with their components stacked on terraces. None of them have room for extensive cemeteries, and burials were added within the sultan's mausoleum (in Mehmed I's case) rather than in a surrounding garden. The fact that the mausolea in the Muradiye cemetery were for the most part added during the reign of Bayezid II may point to a conscious decision by this ruler to expand the presence of dynastic burials on the site, an argument supported by the endowment he provided for at least one of the mausolea. Hence the question emerges of to what extent the site of the Muradiye complex was planned as a dynastic cemetery from the start.

As noted, Murad II's *vasiyetnāme* mentions his sons' burials, which were to be connected to his own mausoleum but not placed within the same structure. After Selim I's accession in 1512, a number of his brothers and nephews were killed in the name of dynastic fratricide. At least five of these individuals were buried in the Muradiye cemetery, where they joined Prince Cem. With these six burials, the Muradiye cemetery took on the role of a burial site for Ottoman princes who remained in exile even in death, at a safe distance from Istanbul, but were still given the honor of being buried in the vicinity of a ruling ancestor. In fact, Murad II's son 'Alaeddin 'Ali (d. 1443) was the first executed prince to be buried in the Muradiye cemetery, even before his father (d. 1451), and so perhaps he created the precedent that was then followed.

Once Ottoman sultans began to be buried in Istanbul beginning with Mehmed II, the new capital clearly was not the site of choice for those princes who were unsuccessful in the quest for the throne or who, like Süleyman's son Mustafa (d. 1553), were suspected of rebellion. The Muradiye cemetery in Bursa became a site to safely contain the burials of figures who may have caused trouble in life and might do so again in death. By placing these burials in the cemetery of an imperial foundation, control became possible: the overseers of the waqf could ensure that *ziyārat* did not take on the trappings of a cult of saintly figures. Thus any potential for rebellion centered on the site of an executed Ottoman prince was contained. A tomb for Mustafa in Konya – where he was executed, and where nearly eighty years earlier Cem had held a strong power base – could have become a center of unrest. Was this perhaps on Selim II's mind when he built a mausoleum for his brother decorated with the most recent fashion in Iznik tiles – but also safely corralled off? Bursa, as the dynastic city, was a place of memory and honor for the Ottoman family, but also a site under tight control, part of the empire since 1326, never lost except for very brief periods during the interregnum in the early fifteenth century, and its space closely regulated by imperial *waqf*s and their administrators.

INTERTWINED SPACES

We have observed a set of different spaces and types of space that overlap in the Muradiye complex. In terms of built space, the Muradiye has the appearance and features of a typical Ottoman sultanic complex, composed, at the time of building in the early to mid-fifteenth century, of mosque-*zāviye*, madrasa, subsidiary buildings, and mausoleum. If anything is different, it is the number of mausolea: twelve such structures crowd the site, where normally just one mausoleum is present. This observation leads to the second important notion, that of dynastic space. Within the Muradiye complex, a considerable number of members of the Ottoman dynasty – including individuals who met their ends because they were perceived as problematic in the succession process – are buried in proximity to one of the sultans. These burials were placed there over a period of about 150 years, after which priorities seem to have shifted and the site was no longer used to bury members of the Ottoman household. Space was certainly still available; thus the decision was likely for other reasons, perhaps related to the increased focus on Istanbul. The conquest of the latter city opened the way for the consolidation of a new capital away from Bursa, to an extent that Edirne had never served because of that city's inherent frontier character, due to both its location and its role as a staging ground for campaigns into the Balkans. With this, the funerary landscape of the Ottoman dynasty shifted, with Istanbul becoming the privileged site beginning with Mehmed II.

Within Bursa, the Muradiye complex is the last of four sultanic funerary complexes built between the late fourteenth and the mid-fifteenth centuries. The dynastic space of Bursa was maintained to an extent, though, with burials added to this complex well into the sixteenth century. This continuity may reflect the importance that was still given to the dynastic memory embedded in Bursa, the city where the earliest Ottoman sultans were buried and also the place from which Mehmed I consolidated the empire after its near demise following defeat at the hands of Timur in the early fifteenth century. From this point of view, Bursa remained a crucial point in the Ottoman imperial network of memory and commemoration, together with the sites of different battles and conquests, perhaps with Eyüp at its very center.

This spatial landscape is closely related to the dynamics of past and present, present-day and afterlife, across the Ottoman Empire. By including narratives of the afterlife, the site of the Muradiye also pushes beyond the dynastic space into a cosmological and spiritual one. Thus the dynastic space of Bursa becomes closely intertwined with a spiritual imaginary in which commemoration through architecture, prayer at graves, and endowments asking for Qur'an recitation and the lighting of candles at tombs are practices intended to affect the deceased's fate in the afterlife. In this sense, the dynastic space of Bursa also becomes imbued with the Ottomans' religious identity. Its endowments benefited a wide range of actors – ulema, dervishes, and the local population alike – in ways that could harness prayer for the dynasty's benefit as these varied actors performed their religious life on these sites, and used them in their daily goings about, actively commemorating the founders.

FIVE

AN OTTOMAN AESTHETIC

Consolidation circa 1500

WITH THIS CHAPTER, I RETURN TO THE LATE FIFTEENTH CENTURY – NAMELY TO A TIME period that includes the end of Mehmed II's reign and the succeeding reign of Bayezid II (r. 1481–1512). While at the outset of the book I worked to highlight the extent to which a wide range of sources of inspiration from across the Islamic world and the Mediterranean were drawn from in Mehmed II's project of reshaping Istanbul as a capital, the main question of this chapter is how a consistent, specifically Ottoman style progressively emerged in the following period, between circa 1470 and 1510. Artists at the Ottoman court in the period discussed here made and selected pieces to include in albums and designs that could be reproduced in a range of materials used for objects and buildings.

The late fifteenth century was a period of increasingly centralized organization in the creation of art for the Ottoman court, and during Bayezid II's reign in particular, projects that aimed at cataloguing and classifying knowledge – including books in the palace library, but also various visual templates to be used as the basis for new art – abounded. As previous chapters have shown, especially when discussing the possible presence of migrating workers from Iran and the Mamluk lands and their interactions with local patrons and workers, for much of the fifteenth century we can only make inferences based on style, construction techniques, and rare signatures as to who may have participated in a certain construction site and how elements of decoration may have been designed. This design process, as discussed in Chapters 1 and 3, probably involved the use of paper, with calligraphic templates scaled up for use on site by stone carvers or used at production sites for ceramics such as tiles (as the Üç Şerefeli Mosque in Edirne showed). In the late fifteenth century, paper itself appears in the form of album pages that allow for reflection on the relationship between paper templates and other materials (such as metalwork, wood, and textiles).

At Mehmed II's court, a leading artist takes palpable shape in the figure of Baba Nakkaş (literally "Father Designer" – his name was Mehmed b. Shaykh Bayezid), who is documented in a *waqfīya* dated 1475.[1] As early as 1466, Baba Nakkaş had been granted property in the village of Kutlubey near Çatalca on the outskirts of Istanbul.[2] Baba Nakkaş's work is primarily known from a series of drawings included in a compilation, *Mecma'u'l-'acâ'ib* (İstanbul Üniversitesi Kütüphanesi, Nadir Eserleri, F.1423), known as the Baba Nakkaş Album, which A. Süheyl Ünver has discussed in detail.[3] One particularly striking page, folio 13a, holds three designs attributed to Baba Nakkaş and his circle that are pasted in on separate pieces of paper (see Figure 139).

175

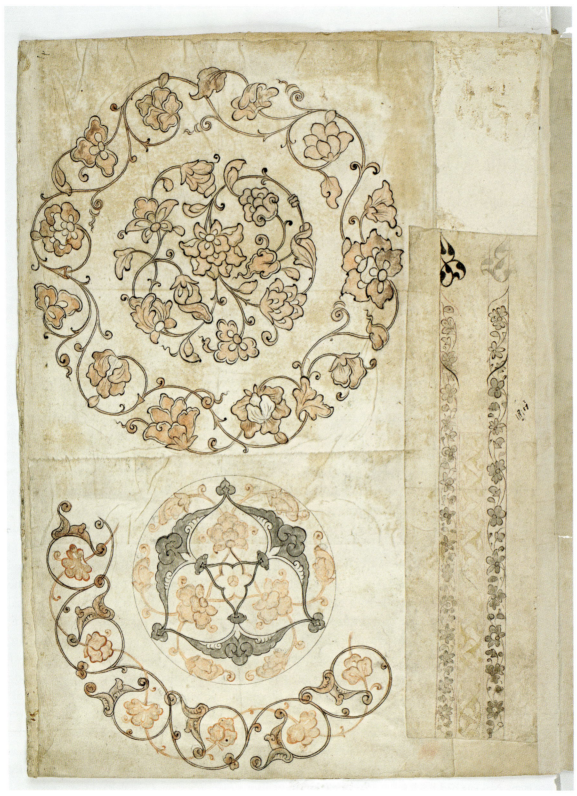

139. *Rūmī* and *khiṭāyī* designs, ca. 1470–1500. Ink and pencil on paper, pasted on paper, support page 38.5 x 28 cm. Baba Nakkaş Album, Nadir Eserler Kütüphanesi, Istanbul University Library, F.1423, fol. 13a. © Istanbul University

These designs, drawn in black ink and red chalk and shaded lightly in reddish pigment or charcoal, show the traces of their making: in the central medallion of the drawing at the bottom of the page, we can see the circle marked in pencil that was the basis for its design. The largest design, in the top left corner of the page, is pure *khiṭāyī*: a medallion of flowers at the center, with a band of the same flowers encircling it. A similar design pasted below it is composed of both *rūmī* and *khiṭāyī* elements: in the central medallion, the same flowers as above intersect with *rūmī* leaves, and the half-drawn circular band around it similarly intertwines *khiṭāyī* flowers and a scroll of *rūmī* leaves. These drawings serve as an example of the ways in which designs made on paper could become a driving force of stylistic formation – and part of a larger Ottoman epistemological project that focused on classification, cataloguing, and fixing categories of knowledge as integral parts of central administration.

This is the period before the architect Sinan redefined Ottoman architecture during the reigns of Süleyman the Magnificent (r. 1520–66) and Selim II (r. 1566–74). As Gülru Necipoğlu has demonstrated, Sinan's work and that of the *hassa mimarları* (in full: *cemāʿat-i miʿmārān-i ḫāṣṣa*, the office of imperial architects) are crucial for our understanding of architecture in the Ottoman Empire from the sixteenth century onward and the functioning of a centralized empire that imposed tight control in both administrative and aesthetic domains, or at least claimed to do so in its official rhetoric.[4] However, the architectural developments of this period would have been impossible without the lessons learned from the malleable settings in construction sites of previous centuries: by the time Sinan designed his mosques, there were more than two centuries of Ottoman building practice to look back on, and crucial innovations, particularly of the fifteenth century, that could be developed further. The large dome of the Süleymaniye Mosque, for instance, would not have been possible without the earlier projects of the mosques of Mehmed II and Bayezid II in Istanbul (more on the latter farther along in this chapter), both of which in turn looked back to the Üç Şerefeli Mosque in Edirne, as well as the Hagia Sophia.

In the late fifteenth and early sixteenth centuries, earlier lessons were fully integrated, together with other lessons taken from the Renaissance architectures of the Mediterranean and from a range of objects transmitted through trade in both directions. A big surge in Ottoman textile production led to shifts that included renewed, deep-seated contacts with Italy, to the point that certain types of velvet produced in Bursa, Venice, and Lucca became hard to distinguish as each side imitated the other. This chapter examines how what at first sight seems to be a paradoxical development – the "Ottomanization" of architecture, at a time when textiles became more international – reflected the dynasty's global interests, which were fully developed at Mehmed II's cosmopolitan court and expanded during Bayezid II's reign.

Developments such as the establishing of the *hassa mimarları* and a central *nakkaşhane* in Istanbul, and the increasing production of ceramics in Iznik, were crucial steps in this period, leading to the close intertwining of Ottoman artistic production with the simultaneous formation of Ottoman cultural and imperial identities at the time. A strong tendency circa 1500 was the more and more clearly defined expression of Rūmī identities – which included individuals of various ethnic and social backgrounds, but increasingly involved the use of Ottoman Turkish as the main language of administration and cultural expression. Importantly, as Cemal Kafadar notes, Rūmī-ness was not an imperially imposed concept, but rather one that emerged organically.[5] Within the context of empire formation, architecture was part of a larger epistemological project in the hands of the Ottomans – not the sultans so much as the scholars, administrators, and makers associated with the court. Those involved in creating monuments were full participants in this knowledge, although we know the names of only a few Ottoman architects in the time before Sinan and have little firm documentation related to their projects and biographies.

The prolonged accession conflict between the brothers Bayezid II, who claimed the throne in 1481, and Cem (d. 1495) was a central historical condition of the period, resolved only with the latter's death in exile.[6] Defeated, Cem first retreated to Cairo and then, after a second failed attempt at gaining power in Anatolia, moved to Rhodes in 1482. Far from helping Cem in his quest to gain the Ottoman sultanate, however, the resident Knights Hospitallers made an agreement with Bayezid II. A letter that the sultan sent in 1484 to Pierre d'Aubusson, Grand Master of the Knights Hospitallers of Rhodes, mentions an arm relic of John the Baptist offered as a gift to the knights in order to ensure Cem's prolonged stay on the island, in addition to an annual payment of 40,000 ducats that Bayezid had agreed to in 1483.[7] Cem, however, did not remain on Rhodes but was sent to France, where he lived until 1489.[8] At that point he was taken to Rome at the behest of Pope Innocent VIII, after an agreement to that effect concluded by Bayezid II.[9] In 1495, Cem was moved to Naples, where he died the same year. As we saw in Chapter 4, his body was returned to the Ottoman Empire in 1499, and ultimately, he was given the posthumous honor of burial in the Muradiye cemetery, in an existing mausoleum refurbished for the occasion.

By not having Cem killed immediately after gaining the throne in 1481, Bayezid II created a new problem for himself: the continued existence of a living rival who had a power base in Konya and Karaman, where Cem had served as a prince.[10] This situation would also affect Bayezid II's choices in architectural patronage. In the succession conflict, Bayezid II was supported by factions connected to Amasya, the city where he had spent much of his life before gaining the throne.[11] Therefore, after his accession, he first concentrated his patronage there. Later he would expand his patronage to include Konya, to consolidate his reign in Cem's former power base.

A large number of monuments were added in Amasya, including a mosque complex that Bayezid II himself commissioned in 1485, before his mosque complexes in Edirne and Istanbul.[12] In 1485–86, for instance, Bayezid II endowed villages in the region of Merzifon for the mausoleum of Pir İlyas in Amasya.[13] Pir İlyas (d. ca. 1412), a native of Amasya who was trained in the Halveti line of Sufism during exile in Shirvan following Timur's incursion into Anatolia in 1402, introduced this Sufi tradition when he returned to his hometown.[14] The descendants of Pir İlyas and his disciples had played a central role in Bayezid II's succession.[15] Early in the new sultan's reign, these Halvetis, led by Çelebi Halife (d. 1494), were invited to Istanbul, where Bayezid II had them accommodated in a complex built by Koca Mustafa Pasha in 1486, one of several buildings created or adapted for their use.[16] While the Pir İlyas mausoleum in its current form is the result of rebuilding in the nineteenth century, a foundation inscription dated 887 AH / 1482–83 CE is integrated into the structure above the entrance. No patron is named, but Uzunçarşılı has suggested, based on Hüseyin Hüsameddin's *Amasya Tarihi*, that Gümüşlüzāde Ahmed Pasha, a descendant of Pir İlyas, commissioned the rebuilding while Bayezid II provided the endowment.[17] Thus the sultan's patronage of the Halvetiye was closely tied to both Amasya and its local elites, who played a central role in his accession.

The Ottoman–Mamluk war of 1485–91, in which the Dulkadir – an important power in eastern Anatolia – were embroiled and switched sides, created new uncertainty as to the fate of the eastern limits of the Ottoman realm, after Mehmed II had consolidated this territory to some extent by conquering Trebizond and Karaman.[18] Southeastern Anatolia remained contested, particularly the zone east of the Taurus Mountains, where local patrons powerfully emerged, as I show in the last section of this chapter. Contemporaneously, the rise of the Shi'i Safavids in Iran loomed large on the political horizon, with Kızılbaş Turkmen tribes loyal to the Safavid Sufi order and its leader, Shah Isma'il (r. 1501–24), causing unrest in northeastern Anatolia in particular.[19] Both conflicts would come to a head under Selim I (r. 1512–20): a crucial victory against the Safavids in 1514 was closely followed by the Ottomans' defeat of the Mamluks in 1517. The conflict with the Safavids would lead to the increasing Sunnitization of the Ottoman territories and its architecture, as described earlier in the discussion of the later fate of mosque-*zāviye*s turned into Friday mosques. The subsequent conquest of Syria and Egypt would extend Ottoman territory far beyond Anatolia and place the Ottoman sultan in a new position of prestige, that of the guardian of the two holiest sanctuaries of Islam: the Ka'ba in Mecca, and the tomb of the Prophet Muhammad in Medina. Gaining these positions would support the Ottoman claim to universal rule and the taking on of the title of caliphate for their realm.[20] Our story in this chapter will not extend that far, however.

At the artistic level, these political conflicts also meant that the earlier, nearly universal prestige of the Timurid arts lessened, a factor compounded with the fall of the last Timurid artistic center – Herat under Sultan Husayn Bayqara (r. 1470–1506) – to the Safavids in 1506. Many of the Herat workshops were moved to Safavid Tabriz, including that of the famous painter Bihzad (d. 1535), who was central to the development of Safavid book painting. Like Sinan, Bihzad is a figure central to the emerging myth of individual artists forming a canon, facilitated by increasing self-reflection among artists themselves within their work.[21] In the Mamluk context, the architecture of the late fifteenth century, particularly the large number of monuments built during the long reign of Qaytbay (r. 1468–96), focuses on virtuoso stonework, especially geometric and floral patterns that make domes appear to have textiles draped over them, and multicolored marble inlay used both on façades and in interiors.[22] Thus artists across the three empires nimbly worked to establish separate aesthetic identities while history writing reshaped views of the past. Gülru Necipoğlu argues that floral ornament as it developed beginning in the 1520s was created within an artistic dialogue that spanned the rival Ottoman and Safavid empires.[23] Within the Ottoman context, the move toward centralization of artistic production beginning in the 1470s, and increasing after 1500 in particular, would lead to a more and more clearly defined Ottoman aesthetic, not only in monuments and their decoration but also in objects such as ceramic vessels and metalwork.

In this chapter, I first analyze how we can understand the role paper played in this centralization of artistic processes and aesthetic understanding, focusing on the so-called Baba Nakkaş album. Then I examine how the style of ornament that emerges from certain drawings in the Baba Nakkaş album was adapted for ceramics – increasingly produced in Iznik – and other types of objects such as metal candlesticks and textiles.[24] Next I move on to the city of Amasya, a center of patronage and building activity by Bayezid II and members of his court, where we can see certain traits that will appear elsewhere in the Ottoman realm. Examining the wide spread of the new architecture of Bayezid II's reign, as patronage expanded throughout the empire after a period of near-exclusive focus on Istanbul under Mehmed II, I examine examples in Serres and Skopje to demonstrate the impact of this developing Ottoman aesthetic in the Balkans, before turning to Bayezid II's mosque complexes in Edirne and Istanbul. The chapter then returns to Anatolia, addressing Ottoman patronage of Sufi shrines in central Anatolia – activity closely tied both to the succession conflict between Cem and Bayezid and to attempts at controlling Safavid influence in the region. Finally, I discuss the patronage of the Ramazanoğlu in Adana, located in a region that would not be fully absorbed into the Ottoman Empire until the second quarter of the sixteenth century.

CENTRALIZING DESIGN ON PAPER

We have seen that designs on paper quite likely played a crucial role in Ottoman architecture since at least the first half of the fifteenth century. Yet how were these designs on paper made? How did they reach building sites? From the biographies of some of the traveling scholars discussed in Chapter 3, we know that Edirne did have an office of scribes in the early fifteenth century. The case of the hapless artist from Timurid Shiraz who tried and failed to find work in Ottoman Edirne in the 1420s suggests that there was a place where the individual in question may have hoped to be employed and that indeed represented an attractive prospect.[25] In the late fifteenth century the *nakkaşhane* in Istanbul was reorganized, while the one in Edirne was mostly likely closed down at the same time, bringing the production of manuscripts and other products on paper into a new, centralized order.[26] The central *nakkaşhane* in Istanbul was located, along with other imperial workshops, in the first court of Topkapı Palace, although little has survived of these structures.[27]

It is likely that by the late fifteenth century, much of the Ottoman production of works on paper took place in that setting. The drawings in the Baba Nakkaş album (F.1423) introduced at the start of this chapter, Ünver argues, were the product of such a collaborative workshop environment, although individual artists like Baba Nakkaş certainly rose to prominent roles, as the assignment of imperial property suggests. Most likely the designs in this album were created in Mehmed II's court workshop and assembled into a collection in the time of Bayezid II.[28] Designs similar to those in the album – "Ottomanised *ḫaṭāyī*"[29] – were adapted in a wide range of media between circa 1480 and 1520, from ceramics (both vessels and tiles) to metalwork.[30] As Necipoğlu emphasizes, the work of Baba Nakkaş and his collaborators "indigenized the so-called international Timurid–Turkmen style" as a crucial part of Ottoman art.[31] Under Mehmed II's patronage, these elements came together with ones drawn from Italian Renaissance and Byzantine art to form a cosmopolitan style on par with the sultan's ambitions for universal rule.[32]

In F.1423, the designs associated with Baba Nakkaş appear on 11 of 134 pages and so constitute only a small part of the album's content, but they have taken on outsized proportion in its reputation, largely because of their attribution to Baba Nakkaş. This attribution is based on his important role in Mehmed II's *nakkaşhane* rather than on any signature – signed works have not been found so far. A much larger contingent in the album is made up of various calligraphies, which appear in a range of forms including Qur'an pages pasted in, at times several to an album page (e.g., fols. 28a, 28b, and 29a); full pages of calligraphy completed with frames (fol. 17a); long poems praising Mehmed II (fols. 37a to 54a); and a page that contains a piece of Uyghur script, duly labeled as such and accompanied by fanciful writing described as Chinese (fol. 60a). Even the phrase that appears on the album's title page (fol. 1a) and gives it its name in the catalog, *Mecma'u'l-'acā'ib*, is a pasted-in fragment of calligraphy in Arabic that reads *majmā' al-'ajā'ib* (compilation of wonders), and which has a somewhat jagged outline due to less-than-careful cutting.

As Ünver notes, the diverse nature of the Baba Nakkaş designs suggests that they were made in a workshop environment, perhaps over time (none of them are dated). These designs could certainly have been used as templates in a range of media, an argument that is supported by the fact that most of them are not fully colored but rather combine pencil, ink, and light blushes in a range of color. Returning to folio 13a (see Figure 139), described at the opening of this chapter, the smaller design on the right margin of the page gives insight into workshop practices and the practical use of such pieces before they were collected in albums. Drawn very lightly, almost appearing to be a sketch, this design is composed of two narrow bands of flowers on a thin scroll; at the top, each culminates in a finial composed of *rūmī* leaves, filled in with black. In the bottom half of the design, a slightly wider band of *rūmī* leaves is nestled between the two flower bands.

More important than the design itself, though, are the tiny prick marks that appear on all three bands (Figure 140): evidence that this small piece of paper was indeed a template meant to be copied in a workshop setting by placing it on top of another sheet of paper and sprinkling coal dust that would fall through the perforations to create a fine outline below (a technique that could also be used in the production of ceramics).[33] Here we have tangible proof that pieces of paper with designs such as those in the F.1423 album were indeed scraps from an active *nakkaşhane*. While none of the other designs in F.1423 have these marks, many appear to be sketches that could have been used as templates in a workshop setting: a piece of paper with torn edges pasted onto folio 61a contains three variations of a poly-lobed medallion of *rūmī* leaves and a quickly sketched single leaf. Other designs (fols. 15a, 60b, 61a top) are encased in squares and rectangles made of thin lines in black and gold ink that not only give them a more finished appearance but also provide options for infinite repeat, while light shading only hints at fully colored illuminations (Figure 141). Others (fol. 25a, top) have similar frames and contain color accents in addition to ink and pencil shading in the technique known as *qalamsiyāhī* (black pen), which was developed in Ilkhanid Iran in the early fourteenth century.[34]

Yet another design drawn in black ink is filled with pastel pink and green (fol. 30b top). These colors, which let the paper shine through, are nothing like the opaque, brilliant colors that appear on fully painted pages within the album, including samples of calligraphy, a carpet page of *rūmī-khiṭāyī*

140. Detail of Figure 139, showing design with pricking marks. Ink and pencil on paper, pasted on paper, full support page 38.5 x 28 cm. Baba Nakkaş Album, Nadir Eserler Kütüphanesi, Istanbul University Library, F.1423, fol. 13a. © Istanbul University

(fol. 25a bottom), and a full-page medallion (fol. 13b). Taken together, the pencil sketches, exercises in shading, extendable designs, suggestions for color combination, and fully painted designs provide a repertoire of what a workshop might have had lying around – and the torn edges and corners and the fold marks on several of the designs in F.1423 suggest that they had indeed served as templates. The selection, however, was not made by the artists who used the designs, but rather was part of a practice of album making that pursued different goals – documentation of knowledge rather than the direct practice of art.

As with many albums, dating F.1423 is complicated by the fact that the materials collected in it range widely both in date and origin. Raby notes that two poems praising Bayezid II suggest that the album was assembled during that sultan's reign.[35] For two albums in the Topkapı Palace Library, H.2153 and H.2160, the probable date of assembly is after Selim I's invasion of Tabriz in 1514, since H.2153 contains a substantial amount of material that is likely to stem from that city, along with pieces that likely belonged to Mehmed II's collection.[36] Raby suggests that F.1423 as well as the two albums in the Topkapı Palace Library could have been created at either Bayezid II's or Selim I's court, but either way the notion emerges that much of the material from Mehmed II's court was kept in a loose state, and inventoried and organized in albums at a later stage.[37] Such a project also aligns with Bayezid II's project of establishing a catalog of the palace library and a more systematic approach to classification – which also involved the emergence of art historical thinking, as documented in the albums.[38]

141. *Rūmī* and *khitāyī* designs, leaf, and calligraphies, ca. 1450–1500. Ink, pencil, watercolor and gold on paper, pasted on paper, support pages 38.5 x 56 cm. Baba Nakkaş Album, Nadir Eserler Kütüphanesi, Istanbul University Library, F.1423, fol. 60b–61a. © Istanbul University

That project of cataloging the palace library is now much better understood, with the recent editing and publication of a catalog that Bayezid II commissioned librarian Hayrüddin Hızır ʿAtufi (d. 1541) to assemble and write in 1502–03.[39] ʿAtufi was from Merzifon in the region of Amasya, and was possibly educated in Bursa before moving to Istanbul at an unknown date to complete his education and begin his career. He entered palace service sometime after the death of his first patron Çandarlı Ibrahim Pasha in 1499, and first served as a tutor to the palace's servants, an appointment he perhaps owed to an acquaintance with Bayezid II through shared ties to Amasya.[40] The catalog presents "hierarchies of knowledge and the beginning of textual canon formation" as they took place in the early sixteenth-century Ottoman Empire.[41] As Cornell Fleischer notes, the catalog is "a snapshot *in medias res*" of the project of forming a distinct Ottoman imperial identity that was in progress at the time of its writing.[42] Within the catalog, the universalist aspirations of both Mehmed II and Bayezid II are visibly reflected in the project of collecting books and commissioning new manuscripts from scholars living within the Ottoman realm.[43] With this in mind, we need to overcome the position taken by some scholarship that claims that Mehmed II engaged with the Renaissance and expanded the Ottomans' horizon, while Bayezid II was not capable of doing so.[44] Knowledge from across the Islamic world as well as Europe was taken in and absorbed in the project of building the palace library's collection.[45] At this point in the process of Ottomanization, the fifteenth century began to recede, becoming a distant and hard-to-understand past, a phenomenon that would increase over the course of the sixteenth century as the empire further consolidated its imperial ideology and administration.[46]

In both the assembling of albums and the cataloging of the palace library, we see a push toward classifying knowledge. In the case of the albums, elements such as the Baba Nakkaş designs reflect a choice to focus on motifs that were commonly used in the Ottoman context at that point – the Ottomanized *khiṭāyī*, for instance – and that reflected the aesthetic convergence that was ongoing within the art production of the Ottoman court. Thus these motifs could be disseminated to workshops producing metalwork and tiles, to be included in designs in these media. They could also be used for new *tezhib* (gilding, illumination) and calligraphy in manuscripts commissioned by members of the Ottoman court.

Yet there is also the question of absences. If materials from Mehmed II's collection and workshops were transmitted in a loose state, how can we gain a sense of how much of this material was indeed included in the albums? Do the albums really reflect the taste of Mehmed II's court, or do they rather reflect the aesthetics preferred under Bayezid II or Selim I? That is to say, are the albums a reflection of Mehmed II's cosmopolitan tastes or of the aesthetic convergence and consolidation that took place under his two successors, with the help of the centralized workshop system that Mehmed II had begun to establish? Perhaps both – but we should remember that absences are possible, that fragments of paper among the bits and pieces that emerged from the *nakkaşhane* may have been discarded. The small size of some of the fragments in F.1423, such as a single leaf that only covers about one-eighth of folio 61a, or a bit of a floral design measuring about 128 by 56 millimeters on folio 25b, suggests that even tiny pieces were valued if the design was considered beautiful or relevant.[47] But what were the parameters for judging this beauty or relevance? As I argue in what follows, these parameters were tied to the aesthetic convergence of Ottoman art that would lead to the full consolidation of imperial style that we see after 1520.

Further, it is also relevant to note that those individuals at the Ottoman court who were responsible for putting together these albums were engaging in an internal practice of art history. Similar to the scholars and historians who assembled knowledge for the Ottoman court with reference to the broader intellectual past and trends of the Islamic world, the collectors assembling these albums were engaged in a knowledge project that connected the Ottoman Empire to an aesthetic world beyond its boundaries. Therefore, album making was part of a larger epistemic endeavor, just like ʿAtufi's library catalog. It was no longer enough to gather information, whether in the form of books, documents, or drawings; this information had to be organized and classified so that it might be put to use in shaping the Ottomans' imperial project in manifold ways. This does not imply monolithic thinking at this stage in the late fifteenth and early sixteenth centuries: rather, just as the shaping of ideologies of rulership in this period left room for "variegated ideological subcultures,"[48] as Christopher Markiewicz notes in his telling of Idris-i Bidlisi's contribution to the project of Ottoman history writing, the aesthetic endeavor allowed for a range of currents that eventually became part of the sixteenth-century repertoire. Within this endeavor, over time we note the increasing emergence of individual artists, about whom more and more information is recorded: witness not only Baba Nakkaş but also, more prominently a few decades later, Sinan, whose life is recorded in autobiographical account, which exists in five versions.[49]

Similar developments took place elsewhere in the Islamic world. As Roxburgh has argued, the creation of the first albums in Timurid Herat in the early fifteenth century was a form of collecting performed for and by a small number of elite patrons, in a format that was convenient for viewing in small groups.[50] While the first albums were collections of existing materials, by the sixteenth century custom-made elements were produced for them, which could be combined with historical, collected materials.[51] As such, Roxburgh argues, albums can be analyzed "as sites of art historical and aesthetic formation."[52] In Safavid Iran, the album preface composed by Dost-Muhammad in 1544 presents a historical account of both calligraphers and painters, providing a narrative with which to stylistically and historically contextualize the samples pasted into the album, without, however, explaining the reasons for selecting certain materials over others.[53] Yet Roxburgh cautions against using album prefaces as texts to be unquestioningly mined for historical information, when they were complex literary products.[54] The Baba Nakkaş album does not contain a preface, and its original binding was replaced in the late nineteenth century with a red leather one in preparation for its move to the Yıldız Palace library.[55] Thus we do not have an introduction that was created for this album – if one ever existed – but we can firmly state that, first, it was part of the Ottoman epistemic project circa 1500, and, second, that design developments in other media were closely tied to said project. I elaborate on the second point in the following section.

CENTRALIZING DESIGN BEYOND PAPER

Artists working in a wide range of media were fundamental participants in the Ottoman imperial and epistemic project. In the movement of motifs from paper to objects, ceramics are a case in point. The rising popularity of the types of motifs attributed to the circle of Baba Nakkaş was contemporaneous with the accelerating development of the ceramic industry in Iznik, and the predominant use of these motifs on late fifteenth- and early sixteenth-century Iznik ceramics was likely the central vector for the style's spread. Iznik had been a center of production since at least the early fifteenth century, when so-called Miletus ware, blue-and-white underglaze-painted vessels with an earthenware body, was produced there. The term "Miletus ware," a misnomer, emerged following excavations in Miletus in the 1930s, where large numbers of these ceramics were found and attributed to local production in the late fourteenth century, during the tenure of the *beylik* of Menteşe.[56] Not until Oktay Aslanapa excavated kiln sites in Iznik in the 1960s was this city revealed as a major production site for the so-called Miletus wares.[57]

A crucial point in understanding where ceramics were produced concerns the use of fritware: the alkaline-lead fritware characteristic of Iznik ceramics, both vessels and tiles, was used consistently beginning in the early sixteenth century, while earlier production showed wider ranges of variation in chemical composition.[58] No fritware vessels with blue-and-white glazes are known to have been produced in the early fifteenth-century Ottoman Empire, a noteworthy gap considering the widespread taste for Chinese porcelain, which inspired the tiles installed in the Muradiye Mosque in Edirne. In order to address the question of continuity in tile production, Henderson and Raby analyzed tiles from a range of sites located in present-day Turkey, dating from the late thirteenth to the early sixteenth centuries.[59] Since many of the tiles included in the analysis are attributed to the Masters of Tabriz, Henderson and Raby attribute both black-line and blue-and-white underglaze-painted tiles to a unified workshop, active from the 1420s to the 1470s.[60] Strikingly, Henderson and Raby note that within this supposedly unified production, the composition of the tiles' bodies was not consistent: the color and chemical composition changed.[61] This observation would seem to run counter to the assumption that a single workshop (such as the Masters of Tabriz) created all of these tiles, and raises the point that as-yet-unidentified sites of ceramic production may have existed in the Ottoman Empire, at least until the early sixteenth-century Iznik production emerged as dominant. Further, we must seriously consider the possibility of tile imports from production sites beyond the Ottoman realm, such as Cairo or Tabriz.

Between the 1480s and the first decade of the sixteenth century, Iznik fritware pottery emerged in full force, with the production of a range of vessels as well as tiles with blue-and-white décor. Though few architectural tile revetments were created in the Ottoman Empire at the time, rare examples of Iznik tiles with Baba Nakkaş motifs appear in the mausolea of Prince Mahmud (after 1507) and Prince Ahmed (after 1513) in the Muradiye cemetery in Bursa, where they form borders around fields of monochrome turquoise and purple tiles.[62] On ceramic vessels, motifs from within the expanding Ottoman repertoire that built upon the Baba Nakkaş designs were combined with nearly direct copies of Chinese blue-and-white painted porcelain. Lead frit was introduced in the early sixteenth century; the so-called Abraham of Kütahya Ewer (Figure 142), signed with that name in Armenian inscription on the underside and

142. Abraham of Kütahya, ewer, dated 1510 CE. Fritware, diameter: 7.3 cm (foot), diameter: 7 cm (rim), height: 17.1 cm. London, British Museum, inv. no. G.1. © The Trustees of the British Museum/Art Resource, NY

dated 1510 CE (959 in the Armenian calendar), provides a chronological point of reference that fits that of the mausolea in Bursa.[63] Yet the sixteenth-century date, the presumed production site of Kütahya in western Anatolia due to the potter's name, and the association with a Christian maker define these ceramics too narrowly: similar fragments were also found in Iznik in substantial numbers, and a range of similar objects exist that can be dated between the 1470s and 1520s.[64] In terms of their decoration, Atasoy and Raby observe, the earlier examples contain a greater number of *rūmī* designs mixed with *khiṭāyī* motifs, while later ones more strongly rely on the latter.[65]

Another shift took place in the color scheme: in the earlier examples, from the period of Mehmed II, blue dominates, with the backgrounds almost completely filled with that color, while motifs are left unfilled so that the white color of the slip with which the ceramic was covered remains.[66] For instance, on a plate (Figure 143) that can be dated to circa 1480, four thin white rings separate a central medallion and three broader concentric bands in which blue dominates.[67] The central medallion is filled with a complex combination of *rūmī* leaves and *khiṭāyī* cloud bands that are interwoven in a shape based on geometric interlace springing from an eight-pointed star at the center. Baba Nakkaş–style flower motifs fill the circular band that immediately surrounds it. In the next band, the same kinds of motifs, this time placed on spirals rather than a waving line, form the background to a kufic inscription that stands out in white. The outermost band is identical to the inner one, with the Baba Nakkaş flowers connected to a waving line that undulates round the circle. The motifs are all painted in reverse with blue as the dominating color. The underside of the same piece, however, has larger Baba Nakkaş–style flowers on a white background. It is this latter color balance, with blue motifs on white, that would come to dominate in Baba Nakkaş–style ceramics that are usually dated to the first quarter of the sixteenth century, sometimes with a cutoff of circa 1520.[68]

A deep bowl with the latter color scheme (Figure 144), dating to the first quarter of the sixteenth century, has blue Baba Nakkaş–style flowers against a white background on the outside, while the inside is decorated with alternating cypress trees and oval medallions containing Baba Nakkaş flowers on a blue background.[69] Thus, while white backgrounds appear more prominently overall on this and similar pieces,

143. Plate. Fritware, diameter 40 cm, height 7.4 cm, Iznik, last quarter of fifteenth century. Paris, Musée du Louvre, inv. no. OA6321. © RMN-Grand Palais/Art Resource, NY

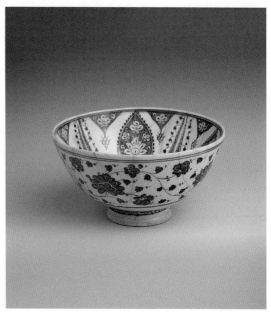

144. Bowl. Fritware, diameter 25.4 cm, height 13.1 cm, Iznik, first quarter of sixteenth century. New York, Metropolitan Museum of Art, Rogers Fund, 1932, Accession Number: 32.34. Public Domain/CC0

there are still elements like these oval medallions in which the difficult and labor-intensive technique of painting in reverse is used. What these ceramics all have in common is the transfer of designs that were initially developed on paper and mostly likely distributed from a central source onto a different medium – painted onto ceramics, they took on a life of their own as they moved from the page to the vessel. The same is true for tile revetments created early in the reign of Sultan Süleyman the Magnificent, such as those in the Şehzadeler Mausoleum and the mausoleum of Selim I (both 1522) in Istanbul, and the Çoban Mustafa Pasha Mosque in Gebze (1528). In these monuments, motifs similar to Baba Nakkaş designs appear, but they are combined with an emerging new repertoire tied to the *saz* style and, in the case of the two Istanbul mausolea, black-line tile as well, here likely reintroduced by artists whom Selim I took from Tabriz.[70]

For early fifteenth-century designs such as the ones on the tiles of the Muradiye and Üç Şerefeli Mosques in Edirne, I could only speculate on the potential relationship between paper and tile, and between designer and tile maker. But in the case of the figure of Baba Nakkaş and the style named after him, we can more definitely show this relationship. Clearly the designs attributed to Baba Nakkaş were successfully adapted in ceramics and, more rarely, metalwork and wood carving as well.[71] The link between paper and other media is clearly documented, and the same is true as we move forward into the sixteenth century with, for instance, the development of the *saz* style, which was used on paper (Figure 145) and tiles (see Figure 2), as well as on textiles in the second half of the sixteenth century.[72] A similar case of coexistence of designs on both paper and tile is the so-called *tuğrakeş* style (previously known as Golden Horn wares[73]), in which the background is populated with the spiral designs that appear in sultans' *tuğra*s (calligraphic imperial monograms) beginning in the 1520s. A mosque lamp from circa 1525–40 (Figure 146), modeled on the shape commonly used in glass, shows this type of decoration, overlaid with a kufic inscription in blue that cuts across it.[74] Such spirals were also integrated into the *tuğra* of Süleyman (r. 1520–66) and later sultans, although they disappeared from ceramics and were never used on tiles.[75]

The examples of work on paper and ceramic show an increasing centralization in the design process across media: motifs created on paper in the imperial *nakkaşhane* were adopted in ceramics over the course of the late fifteenth and early sixteenth centuries. The ceramics were more and more centrally produced in Iznik, quite likely exclusively so in the case of the fritware with Baba Nakkaş designs. While the specific motifs examined here rarely appear in architectural decoration, aside from the few tiles with

145. Dragon in foliage with lion and phoenix heads, Istanbul, mid-1500s, attributed to Şahkulu. Ink, gold, opaque watercolors on paper, 17.3 x 40.2 cm. Cleveland, The Cleveland Museum of Art, Purchase from the J. H. Wade Fund 1944.492. Public Domain/CC0

146. Ceramic vessel in shape of a mosque lamp. Fritware, height 17 cm, Iznik, ca. 1525–40. New York, Metropolitan Museum of Art, Harris Brisbane Dick Fund, 1959, Accession Number: 59.69.3. Public Domain/CC0

Baba Nakkaş motifs mentioned earlier, changes to the design process also profoundly affected the creation of architecture beginning in the last quarter of the fifteenth century. In the following sections, I focus on examples of buildings created during the reign of Bayezid II in order to demonstrate how the emergence of the *hassa mimarları* led to more and more consistent aesthetics in Ottoman architecture, particularly at the level of volumes and structure – for instance, the consistent use of central domes on squinches, and squares as basic units of plans.

DESIGN IN THE AGE OF BAYEZID II: AMASYA

During the reign of Bayezid II, Amasya experienced a veritable construction boom: Ayverdi records a total of fifty-one monuments built during this period.[76] Clearly the city benefited from the rise of Bayezid II, who had lived in Amasya as a prince from 1454 until his ascent to the throne in 1481.[77] He was just one of many junior Ottomans appointed to the city between the late fourteenth century and the mid-fifteenth century.[78] Once Bayezid II became sultan, he transferred many in his entourage to Istanbul, including the calligrapher Şeyh Hamdullah (d. 1520), who was part of the larger Halveti network that moved from Amasya to the capital.[79] In light of Hasan Karataş's argument that Amasya was relatively neglected in the 1460s and 1470s, the extensive construction there during Bayezid II's reign can perhaps be seen as a way of reclaiming the city, particularly after the crucial role its elites played in Bayezid II's accession.[80] Amasya already had a substantial number of Ottoman and pre-Ottoman buildings, as discussed in Chapter 3. In this section, I focus on a few examples in order to examine

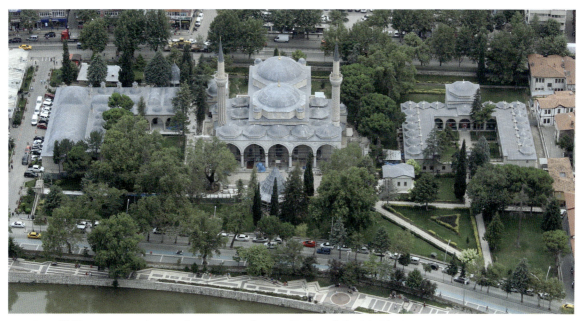

147. Bayezid II's mosque-*zāviye* complex, 1485–86, Amasya, Turkey. © Patricia Blessing 2018

broader trends in architecture at this time and then move on to discuss these trends in other cities within the Ottoman Empire.[81]

In 1485, Bayezid II commissioned a complex in Amasya consisting of a mosque-*zāviye*, madrasa, and hospice (Figure 147), as well as a *mektep* and a bridge that have not been preserved.[82] It is located on the bank of the Yeşil Irmak, with the entrances of the mosque-*zāviye* and madrasa facing the river, as can easily be seen when viewed from the city's citadel. The mausoleum located behind the mosque was built for Prince Osman (d. 1513), one of Bayezid II's grandsons, who was killed after Selim II's accession along with his father Prince Ahmed.[83] As Ayverdi, Yüksel, and Dündar note, the buildings were badly damaged in earthquakes in 1939 and 1943 and subsequently rebuilt in a major restoration campaign of the entire complex between 1952 and 1971.[84] The foundation inscription of the mosque-*zāviye* is dated 891 AH / 1486 CE, placed in three panels above the doorway.[85] The ground plan of the mosque is a variation on the T-plan, with two large domed chambers one behind the other, a five-bay porch, and three side rooms on each side of the building. In the foundation inscription, it is called "*'imāratan li-qulūbi l-fuqarā' wa-l-ahālī*" (building for the hearts of the poor and the people), designating it for Sufi use.[86] Once more, we see that the building was originally not just a mosque, although the concept of the mosque-*zāviye*, so central for much of the fourteenth and fifteenth centuries, would soon disappear.[87] As a result of the restoration campaign between 1952 and 1971, the painted interior decoration described in the late fifteenth-century document is no longer preserved, having been replaced with new designs.[88]

The site of Bayezid II's complex in Amasya is now cut off from the river by a road and a tall embankment, but originally, the complex would have been integrated with the city's topography – a topography dominated by the river, in a valley rising steeply on both sides. The side-by-side placement of mosque and madrasa recalls the funerary complex of Murad II in Bursa, where the alignment of the mosque-*zāviye*'s and madrasa's façades frames the entrance to the funerary complex (see Figure 119). It is also noteworthy that several of the fifteenth-century Ottoman monuments in Amasya, including the Bayezid Pasha Mosque and the Yörgüç Pasha mosque-*zāviye* (discussed in Chapter 3), the Mehmed Pasha Mosque (1486), the Hatuniye Mosque (1486), and the Büyük Ağa Madrasa (1488), are located along the river. These particular projects represented a specific topographic intervention, separate from monuments that were added elsewhere in Amasya, such as the *bedesten* (1485) and the Kilari Süleyman Aga *masjid* (1489) in the market area, and the Sofular Mosque (1485) and the Pir İlyas Mausoleum (1497, rebuilt in the nineteenth century) on the slopes facing the citadel.

Following the course of the river eastward, the Mehmed Pasha Mosque is located next to the early fourteenth-century Bimarhane. The patron of this structure, Mehmed Pasha (d. 1494 or 1498–99) – a nephew of Yörgüç Pasha, whom we met in Chapter 3 – was appointed as *lālā* to Bayezid II's son Prince Ahmed in 1486.[89] The foundation inscription dates the monument to 891 AH / 1486 CE and uses the term ʿ*imārat* – as noted before, one of the terms that frequently appear in the inscriptions on mosque-*zāviyes*.[90] Two restoration inscriptions are dated 1236 AH / 1820 CE and 1280 AH / 1863–64 CE, respectively.[91] The mausoleum is undated, and Ayverdi notes that it may not be contemporaneous with the mosque.[92] A madrasa and other subsidiary buildings do not survive.[93] The plan of the Mehmed Pasha Mosque is an irregular variant on the T-shaped plan; it has one domed chamber flanked by two rooms on either side, but these are not precisely symmetrical.[94] On the east side, the mausoleum shares a wall with the second side room, but this side room can only be accessed from the exterior. A six-bay porch is attached to the mosque's façade; like the side rooms, the porch is not symmetrical: two bays are placed to the east of the central bay, and three to the west.

The building is built of irregular masonry, somewhat at odds with the carefully cut ashlars of Bayezid II's mosque, although in Amasya earthquake damage is always a potential factor to take into account. In the interior, no original decoration has survived except for a relatively simple marble mihrab. The *minbar* (Figure 148), made of the same material, was likely not part of the original construction, since Friday

148. Minbar of Mehmed Pasha mosque-*zāviye*, early sixteenth century, Amasya, Turkey. © Patricia Blessing 2018

DESIGN IN THE AGE OF BAYEZID II 191

sermons were not held at mosque-*zāviye*s and hence a pulpit for the imam was not needed. Its decoration does, however, suggest that it was added by the early sixteenth century, when the building, at an unknown date, was transformed into a Friday mosque, as happened with most mosque-*zāviye*s.[95] Set against the *qibla* wall, the *minbar* is a veritable showcase of early sixteenth-century Ottoman ornament carved in stone. On the doors that close off the stairs leading to the *minbar*'s top, the decoration, identical on each of the two door panels, is carved in low relief in four sections, and partially highlighted with reddish-brown paint. From bottom to top, the motifs are the following: a square with a geometrical pattern, a rectangular panel containing the polygon and star motifs common on wooden *minbar*s, a square kufic calligraphy, and a panel fit into the curvature of the arch, which evokes *kündekārī* woodwork despite the fact that the *minbar* is made of stone. Above these doors, a horizontally laid block contains a panel carved with letters that seem to float in the air because their background is entirely broken through. A row of tiny muqarnas connects this calligraphic panel to the *minbar*'s lower section. On the *minbar*'s sides, *rūmī* and *khiṭāyī* patterns are arranged in a complex composition that corrals them into separate fields: they do not mix within the same panel or band. At the base of the *minbar*, below the stairs, extends a row of three panels – two solid, one broken through – containing ogee arches; past these panels and adjacent to the wall, a much taller panel contains a trefoil arch that is left open. Each of the three lateral panels is enclosed in molding in the shape of a pointed arch, which is set into a square. The rightmost of these panels is filled with *khiṭāyī* motifs and the left-side one with *rūmī* leaves intersecting with *khiṭāyī* knots – motifs that are highly reminiscent of those on near-contemporaneous textiles (see Figure 63). Above this row of panels, a large right triangle, its hypotenuse running parallel to the railing of the stairs, is filled with swirling *rūmī* leaves enclosed in a frame of polygons and five-pointed stars. *Rūmī* leaves also appear on the railings that enclose the stairs, here carved with a background fully broken through to the other side and arranged in symmetrical compositions within two elongated medallions that end in ogees on each side.

The top of the railing, solid, is decorated with a band of *khiṭāyī* flowers that continues, filling in the space around and between the panel with the elongated medallions, the large triangular fields, and the row of small panels at the bottom, thus tying the entire composition together. To the right, the side of the *minbar*'s gate is carved with geometric interlace. To the left, on the taller side adjacent to the wall, the trefoil arch connecting to the wall has *rūmī* leaves in its spandrels. Above it, a broken-through rectangular panel of *rūmī* and *khiṭāyī* motifs – *khiṭāyī* flowers and *rūmī* leaves arranged in such a way that they evoke *khiṭāyī* cloud bands – appears beneath a square panel on the side of the *minbar*'s upper section in which small stars and polygons are cut into the stone. In the *minbar*'s upper section, four thick, dark grey pillars form the supports of the pavilion with a row of reddish crenellations along its top. A bulbous finial in grey stone tops off the piece.

Across the *minbar*, the full repertoire of early sixteenth-century Ottoman ornament appears, with *rūmī* and *khiṭāyī* motifs used both separately and in combination, along with geometric interlace and square kufic and cursive calligraphies. These motifs are introduced into the architectural space by way of the placement of objects within it: while none of them appear elsewhere on the building, they take center stage on the *minbar* and allow for the richness of ornament to be displayed. A viewer today can imagine the original presence of additional objects such as candlesticks or carpets.[96] We see closely related motifs integrated into the architectural decoration of Bayezid II's mosque in Istanbul (1501–05), where they appear on corner colonettes on the portal (Figure 149). These motifs further support an early sixteenth-century date for the *minbar* in Amasya. This repetition of motifs in different contexts and media demonstrates that designs produced on paper were inherently scalable and for the most part not produced for medium-specific use but rather meant to be usable in a wide range of materials. We can find, for instance, a close analogue to the *rūmī-khiṭāyī* design that appears on the side panel of the *minbar* toward the wall in an early-sixteenth-century silk brocade (*kemha*) tent-hanging, containing inscriptions praising

149. Corner colonette with *rūmī-khiṭāyī* design, Bayezid II Mosque, 1501–05, Istanbul. K.A.C. Creswell Photographs, Biblioteca Berenson, Fototeca, I Tatti – The Harvard University Center for Italian Renaissance Studies

the tent's beauty.[97] Similar motifs also appear in sixteenth-century Uşak medallion carpets.[98] Vast differences in scale, color, and material do not diminish the visual effectiveness of these motifs, which worked across the empire to create an increasingly unified Ottoman aesthetic.

Within Amasya, relatively large buildings such as Bayezid II's mosque-*zāviye* and the Mehmed Pasha mosque-*zāviye* were joined by smaller structures such as the Kilari Süleyman Ağa *masjid* (1484), a single-room structure with a two-bay porch,[99] and the Sofular Mosque (1485).[100] These buildings, as well as the Mehmed Pasha Mosque – aside from the irregularities likely caused by later earthquake damage – are variants on a type of ground plan that became dominant in the construction of Ottoman mosques: a square, domed prayer room, prefaced by a porch with two, three, or five domed bays, depending on the building's size. These layouts could easily be built at various scales and distributed as easily legible plan drawings. Similar schemes also existed for commercial buildings: the *bedesten*, a covered market building (Figure 150), was built in 1483 under the patronage of *kapu ağası* Hüseyin Ağa. The same patron also commissioned the so-called Büyük Ağa Madrasa in 1488.[101]

The Amasya *bedesten* is located north of the river and south of the Kilari Süleyman Ağa *masjid* and the thirteenth-century Burmalı Minare Mosque. Built of courses of roughly hewn stone and brick, the *bedesten* now has four domes, all of equal size, but originally would have had six: the southernmost bays are missing, and it is clearly visible on the building where those sections were attached; the current shape of the building dates back to restorations in the 1970s.[102] The foundation inscription on the building's eastern façade would thus have originally been at its center. The text mentions the patron, his overlord Bayezid II, and the date of 888 AH / 1483 CE.[103] Amasya was located on trade routes connecting Anatolia to Tabriz in Iran, and it would have been a way station for the silk trade, in which raw materials were imported from Iran to Bursa, a major center of weaving.[104] During Bayezid II's reign in particular, Amasya surpassed Tokat as a major node of exchange in the silk trade between Iran and the Ottoman

DESIGN IN THE AGE OF BAYEZID II 193

150. Bedesten, 1483, Amasya, Turkey. © Patricia Blessing 2018

Empire.[105] The *bedesten*'s construction falls within a period when this trade in silk was on the rise, before the Ottoman–Safavid wars of the early sixteenth century. With these wars, Selim I would ban imports of silk from Iran and Iranian merchants would have to leave the Ottoman Empire.[106] These disruptions would lead to the development of sericulture within the Ottoman Empire, and particularly in Bursa, although it would not reach its peak until the seventeenth century, after trade with Iran had been restored.[107] In this prior period, however, *bedesten*s to promote trade were built in cities across the empire into both Anatolia and the Balkans.[108] Like the mosques that were built on the "squared dome chamber plus porch" scheme, these commercial structures created both visual unity and an imperial style that was easily recognizable.

EXTENDING INTO THE BALKANS: SERRES AND SKOPJE CIRCA 1490

Basic and easily reproduced design schemes enabled a visual consistency in structure and volume that came to dominate cityscapes across the Ottoman-ruled lands. This was the case as well in monuments built during Bayezid II's reign in the Balkans, where Ottoman rule had been consolidated by the end of Mehmed II's reign – although in many parts of that region, the Ottomans had held sway since the fourteenth century. In the last decades of the fifteenth century, monuments continued to be added in cities in the Balkans where the Ottomans had long asserted their rule – for instance, Serres (conquered in 1383) and Skopje (conquered in 1392). The ideas developed in Istanbul and used in locations across Anatolia and in the former capitals of Bursa and Edirne were implemented in these locations as well: Ottoman architecture became more and more consistent in its visual presence, with prominent central domes, domed porches (often surrounding courtyards), and pencil minarets. Aptullah Kuran notes that Ottoman architecture of this period throughout the empire vacillates between the developing "classical Ottoman style" and elements that were part of the style of previous decades.[109]

In Serres, the Mehmed Beğ Mosque was built in 1492–93 (Figures 151 and 152).[110] The patron it is named after was a descendant of grand vizier Gedik Ahmed Pasha (d. 1482) and served as the *sancakbeyi*, appointed by Bayezid II; Bayezid's daughter Selçuk Sultan was Mehmed's wife.[111] The structure, now out of use and in a ruinous state, has a single large dome, with a mihrab that takes the shape of a small chamber attached to the *qibla* wall. Two side rooms are connected to either side of the dome chamber and also have openings onto the five-bay porch, whose domes have collapsed.[112] Three windows in each of the lateral sides admit light into the building, though the inside is not currently accessible due to the building's fragile structural state. The porch columns have finely carved muqarnas capitals, akin to the ones on Bayezid II's mosque-*zāviye* in Amasya. The minaret is no longer extant. Overall, the walls of the monument are built of carefully cut stone, which gives it a sleek and monumental appearance even though the dome's lead covering is long gone and the brick underneath is exposed.

151. Mehmed Beğ Mosque, 1492–93, Serres, Greece. © Patricia Blessing 2009

152. Detail of porch, Mehmed Beğ Mosque, 1492–93, Serres, Greece. © Patricia Blessing 2009

A closely related structure in terms of both its ground plan and elevation is the Mustafa Pasha Mosque (Figure 153) in Skopje, built in 1492, with a domed chamber that measures 20 meters by 20 meters and a dome diameter of 16 meters.[113] Its patron has not been successfully identified with any specific Ottoman grandee: the date of death on the mausoleum behind the mosque, 1519, excludes Koca Mustafa Pasha (d. 1512, and buried in Bursa).[114] Located prominently on a hill to the west of the historical city center, the building faces the mosque of Murad II, founded in 840 AH / 1436–37 CE but rebuilt in the sixteenth century and restored in the eighteenth and twentieth centuries.[115] In plan, the Mustafa Pasha Mosque is a simple domed chamber with a three-bay porch. While much of the building is built of stone courses with bricks between them, the porch is built of ashlar masonry in marble. Maximilian Hartmuth notes that the traditional construction technique of cloisonné masonry that was resorted to may have been a cost-saving method that permitted the use of marble on the porch and portal.[116] The interior of the Mustafa Pasha Mosque contains more recent painted decoration. The marble mihrab and *minbar* have relatively little decoration and do not display elements of the *rūmī* and *khiṭāyī* decoration that was prominent in Anatolia, Istanbul, and Edirne at the same time. Like the Mehmed Beğ Mosque, the Mustafa Pasha Mosque is a variant of the single-domed mosque, which could be built in various sizes and with varying numbers of small domed bays in their porches (generally two to five).[117] As a standardized, scalable design, this type of mosque was ideally suited for a more centralized design process in which standard ground plans could be produced and adapted to different sites, terrains, and local circumstances such as the size of the Muslim community in a specific city or neighborhood.

While neither of the two mosques described earlier retains its original decoration, two hammams in Skopje preserve remnants of stucco decoration that play into the Ottoman repertoire of motifs at the time, tying back to some of the designs in the Baba Nakkaş album. *Rūmī* decoration is present in the Çifte Hamam (Figure 154), a double bathhouse with separate sections for men and women that was built by İsa Beğ (d. 1476?), son of İshak Beğ and brother of Paşa Beğ who is likely buried in the Alaca Türbe in Skopje, discussed in Chapter 1.[118]

196 AN OTTOMAN AESTHETIC

153. Mustafa Pasha Mosque, 1492, Skopje, North Macedonia. © Patricia Blessing 2016

In the stucco decoration that has been preserved in this building, we see *rūmī* leaves that branch out from scrolls – patterns that will by now be familiar from stonework, tiles, metalwork, and textiles discussed in previous sections. In this case, these motifs, rooted in the Islamic art of pre-Ottoman Anatolia, fully integrated into the Ottoman repertoire by the early fifteenth century, and developed further in a range of materials, have spread to the Balkans. Skopje, a former frontier city – it was less so by the mid-fifteenth century after additional conquests, including that of Bosnia, in which İsa Beğ played an important role – received a layer of Rūmī identity in the form of these architectural elements that are representative of the new, increasingly unified Ottoman vocabulary. At first sight, other marks of Ottoman presence in the urban space appear more obvious: for instance, the addition of Murad II's Friday mosque and of several mosque-*zāviye*s, including that of İsa Beğ's father İshak Beğ, built in 1438–39, and the one that İsa Beğ himself commissioned in 1475–76.[119] At the same time, the use of specific types of ornament also indicates that the addition of new buildings connected to Islamic religious practice was not the only way in which the Ottoman cultural sphere expanded itself in the realm of architecture. These stucco motifs offer a glimpse of

154. Detail of stucco decoration, Çifte Hamam, third quarter of fifteenth century? Skopje, North Macedonia. © Patricia Blessing 2016

Ottoman aesthetics in a time when they were becoming more and more consolidated, spanning increasingly large sections of the empire, appearing beyond its current and former capitals and beyond the sultans' own personal patronage.

The monumentality of the Çifte Hamam is exceeded by that of the Davud Pasha Hamam (Figure 155), built toward the end of the fifteenth century under the patronage of grand vizier Davud Pasha (d. 1498).[120] In 1485, the same patron also built a mosque complex in Istanbul, including a mausoleum where he is buried.[121] While only very small sections of motifs like those in the Çifte Hamam have been preserved here, extensive muqarnas decoration made of brick with plaster layered over it appears in the pendentives of the domes in several rooms, as well as along the monumental arches supporting the domes.[122]

Returning to the Mustafa Pasha Mosque, both *rūmī* and *khiṭāyī* motifs appear on the long sides of a stone cenotaph located behind the mosque (Figure 156), placed around cartouches containing Persian poetry that evokes paradise. The short sides of the cenotaph, where intersecting *rūmī* and *khiṭāyī* motifs are also visible on the weathered stone, have patterns that particularly evoke the kinds of textile produced both in the Ottoman Empire and Italy starting in the late fifteenth century. The cenotaph is undated, and its popular attribution to "Ümmi," a purported daughter of Mustafa Pasha, does not appear to have any roots in historical fact.[123] On stylistic grounds, however, a date between circa 1480 and 1510 is probable. The inscriptions in Persian verse on the two long sides of the cenotaph contain neither date nor name.[124]

The patterns bring to mind the practice of using textiles to drape cenotaphs in mausolea. While most such textiles have long been moved to museums, a mid-nineteenth-century watercolor of Mehmed I's mausoleum in Bursa shows the sultan's cenotaph fully covered in various fabrics, with only the lowest tile border visible (Figure 157). While it would not have been practical to place textiles on the outdoor cenotaph in Skopje, the patterns carved into the stone are close enough to ones that appear on this sort of luxury textiles to potentially create such an association. In an example in the Victoria and Albert Museum (see Figure 63) *rūmī* and *khiṭāyī* motifs are combined.

Thus we see that the *rūmī* and *khiṭāyī* motifs on the cenotaph tie it to larger aesthetic trends of the late fifteenth- and early sixteenth-century Ottoman Empire, just as the Mustafa Pasha Mosque is tied to

155. Interior, Davud Pasha Hamam, last quarter of fifteenth century, Skopje, North Macedonia. © Patricia Blessing 2016

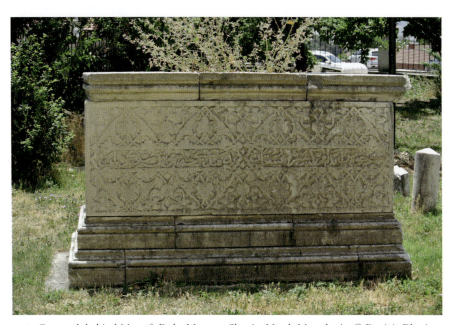

156. Cenotaph behind Mustafa Pasha Mosque, Skopje, North Macedonia. © Patricia Blessing 2016

157. Interior of Mehmed I's mausoleum in Bursa, with textiles covering the sultan's cenotaph. John Frederick Lewis, ca. 1840. Pencil and watercolor on paper, 32.4 x 70cm. London, Victoria and Albert Museum, inv. no. 718–1877. V&A Images, London/Art Resource, NY

architectural trends, being a Friday mosque commissioned by a figure other than the sultan, and a single-dome structure without traces of an integrated *zāviye*. The difficulty in attributing the roughly contemporaneous textiles to either Italy or the Ottoman Empire (likely Bursa, if the latter is the case) also highlights the close aesthetic entanglement between the Ottoman Empire and Renaissance Italy, particularly when it came to such textiles.[125] The cosmopolitan scope of Ottoman art that emerges here is implied as well in the architectural decoration that evokes such fabrics. Thus, the visual unification of the Ottoman Empire appears in Skopje and in Serres in the examples just analyzed, as well as in Anatolia with the buildings discussed in Amasya and in further structures in Tokat, Manisa, and elsewhere.[126]

EMERGING ARCHITECTS

The fact that Bayezid II commissioned three mosque complexes – the one in Amasya, discussed earlier, one in Edirne (1484–88), and one in Istanbul (1501–07) – allows us to understand the consequences of centralized design processes in architecture across these three major cities of the Ottoman realm in Rumeli and Anatolia. The building complex in Edirne was the first to be commissioned, when Bayezid visited the city on the way to his campaign in Akkirman and Kilis.[127] While the complex now is located in a less densely built-up part of the city, this would not have been the case in the late fifteenth century.[128] Like the same sultan's mosque complex in Amasya, the construction project in Edirne was intended to revive a city that had been neglected during Mehmed II's reign, when imperial patronage largely focused on Istanbul, to the point of causing resentment.[129] This also explains why Bayezid II did not commission a mosque complex in Istanbul until 1501.[130]

The Edirne complex originally consisted of a mosque with two integrated *tabhane*s, a madrasa, a kitchen complex, a hospital, and a hammam (Figure 158).[131] With the exception of the hammam,

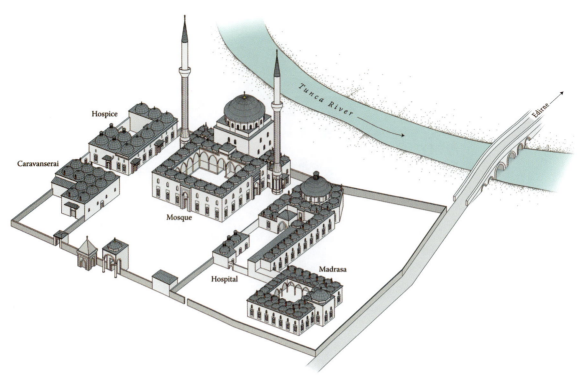

158. Axonometric drawing, Bayezid II mosque complex, 1484-88, Edirne, Turkey. Drawing by Matilde Grimaldi

the complex has survived, and a museum dedicated to the history of medicine in the medieval and early modern Islamic world is now housed in what was formerly the hospital.[132] The buildings' architect is unknown, and nineteenth-century attributions to Hayrüddin, which also present him as the architect of Bayezid II's complexes in Amasya and Istanbul, can be considered apocryphal.[133]

In its foundation inscription, the mosque of the Edirne complex is designated as a *masjid*, thus moving away from the mosque-*zāviye* model that we observed in the first half of the fifteenth century. Placed to either side of the prayer hall, the two *tabhane*s, which were used for a range of functions previously performed by the mosque-*zāviye*, are physically connected to the mosque but are not accessible from within the prayer hall. Rather, they have separate entrances from the mosque's courtyard. In Bayezid II's mosque in Istanbul (Figure 159), a similar spatial strategy of attached *tabhane*s with separate entrances is implemented, with the *tabhane*s attached to the main prayer hall as two wings extending from its east and west sides.[134] Since the courtyard and prayer hall in the Istanbul mosque are of the same width, the *tabhane*s stick out noticeably beyond the outlines of the central structure, thus having a more independent appearance than the ones in Edirne. There, the *tabhane*s project only slightly beyond the width of the courtyard, which is substantially wider than the prayer hall. Adding a global dimension to the mosque's design is a dialogue with contemporary architecture in Italy which was ongoing at the particular time when the monument was built. Necipoğlu notes that Bayezid II's attempts to commission first Leonardo da Vinci and then Michelangelo to design a bridge over the Golden Horn in those same years makes such a dialogue more likely – indeed, it supports the argument regarding exchange between the Ottoman Empire and Italy in a more direct way than do observations about the shared use of architectural structures such as central domes.[135]

In fact, the way in which the *tabhane*s are integrated into the Istanbul mosque is a direct consequence of the fact that its plan closely follows that of the mosque of Mehmed II, which used the Hagia Sophia's domed structure as its point of reference.[136] As Kafescioğlu notes, the integrated *tabhane*s of Bayezid II's mosque in Istanbul had ideological underpinnings: in Mehmed II's mosque complex in the same city, the

159. Bayezid II Mosque, 1501–05, Istanbul, Turkey. K.A.C. Creswell Photographs, Biblioteca Berenson, Fototeca, I Tatti – The Harvard University Center for Italian Renaissance Studies

hospice was built separately from the mosque.[137] The distance Mehmed II put between himself and major Sufi groups who had played a crucial role in the formation of the Ottoman polity and now found themselves sidelined along with the *gazi* families likely played a role in this structural move.[138] The addition of *tabhane*s in Bayezid II's mosque in Istanbul thus may also symbolize the reversal of some of Mehmed II's policies of confiscating the property of *gazi* families, as well as Bayezid's generally closer relationship to Sufi communities, particularly the Halvetis, who had been instrumental in his accession to the throne.[139] The design, however, was not new; rather, it had a precedent in Bayezid II's mosque in Edirne, where structures designated for Sufis were first integrated in an innovative way – the building is designated a *masjid* in its foundation inscription but in de facto terms functions as a mosque-*zāviye* due to the inclusion of *tabhane*s. Thus the Sufi contribution to Bayezid II's accession was already recognized in 1484, only three years after he gained the throne. The inclusion of *tabhane*s in the body of the mosque was repeated in the Selimiye Mosque (1520–22) in Istanbul. The inclusion of these rooms, an acknowledgment of the presence of dervishes, made clear that the *gazi* ethos dervish groups were central to was once more recognized as an important part of the imperial order. These groups had been crucial to the expansion of the Ottoman empire, especially into Christian-ruled territories, in conquests led by the *gazi* families. The settlement of dervish groups in mosque-*zāviye*s sponsored by these same families, as well as the Ottomans, was an essential tool for converting local populations to Islam.[140]

On the aesthetic level, Bayezid II's mosque complex in Edirne proposes a unified design across all of the structures that make it up. We observed several instances from the first and second quarter of the fifteenth century in which a range of construction techniques were employed within the same building complex. Thus, in Mehmed I's foundation in Bursa, all four façades of the mosque-*zāviye* are clad in marble, the mausoleum is clad in tile and stone, and the madrasa is built with visible layers of brick and stone. The Üç Şerefeli Mosque in Edirne is built of ashlar masonry made of limestone, with marble used to accentuate important areas such as the entrance to the prayer hall; in the adjacent madrasa, however, brick is interspersed with the limestone. In Bayezid II's foundation, such differences in materials are no longer applied: stone masonry is used for all buildings, from the mosque to the hospital. Further, all structures are marked by a monumentality that in part springs from clean lines and stripped-down decoration. Careful stone carving is the main mode of decoration – on the muqarnas capitals in the mosque's courtyard, for instance, or the carved frames around the three panels composing its foundation inscription.

The mosque's architecture also successfully offers an approach to the mosque in which the prayer hall's entrance is framed within the courtyard portal and the dome emerges slowly into view as the visitor enters the courtyard and approaches its center (Figure 160). The same structure already appears in the Üç Şerefeli Mosque, where one of the three courtyard portals allows a similar approach to the prayer hall (Figure 161). The flatter profile of the Üç Şerefeli Mosque's dome, however, makes it barely visible above the prayer hall's main façade; thus, Bayezid II's mosque with its taller single dome is more successful in creating a staggered approach that emphasizes the building's monumentality, culminating upon entry into the building. This strategy, of course, would be perfected in the Süleymaniye Mosque in Istanbul, but it is important to emphasize that aspects of this architectural strategy go back to the first half of the fifteenth century, and thus they are not exclusively the result of Ottoman reactions to the Hagia Sophia but also of the engagement with Mamluk and *beylik* architecture.

The monumentality of dome construction is also particularly visible in the hospital of Bayezid II's complex, where a sequence of a larger rectangular courtyard and a smaller square one lead into a domed space surrounded by smaller rooms, each with its own dome. The entire structure is built on a hexagonal plan, something that is not readily apparent in the building's interior. There the dome dominates,

160. View through courtyard portal, Bayezid II mosque, 1484–88, Edirne, Turkey. © Patricia Blessing 2019

161. View through courtyard portal Üç Şerefeli Mosque, 1437–48, Edirne, Turkey. Adobe Stock Photo

supported on muqarnas squinches over a central space with a fountain basin in its middle (Figure 162). Here too the emphasis is placed on carefully executed stone carving in the profiles of the arches that separate the side rooms from the central space, in the muqarnas of the squinches, and in the fountain basin. This kind of architecture, which demonstrates a synthesis of forms developed over the course of the fifteenth century, would be further developed in the sixteenth century.

In part, the progressive development of this synthesis of forms can be attributed to a continuous architectural culture, with architectural training often passing from father to son in a period when the *hassa mimarları* were not yet as firmly established as an institution as they would be during Sinan's tenure as chief architect.[141] As a formal imperial office, the *hassa mimarları* began during Bayezid II's reign, although it is likely that formal structures for imperial architectural production emerged in the mid-fifteenth century.[142] In the sixteenth century, when the training of those involved in building design was centralized, the *hassa mimarları* were consolidated as a hierarchical organization with a head architect (*hassa mimarbaşı* or *ser-miʿmaran-i hassa*) at the top.[143] While these developments were not fully formalized in the period we are discussing here, the process of establishing them had begun. Organizational structures at construction sites, however, were becoming clearer, as reflected in a gift register that covers the years 909–33 AH / 1503–27 CE.[144] Among those rewarded on 16 Jumādha II 909 AH / December 6, 1503 CE for their participation in the construction of Bayezid II's Istanbul mosque complex are *nāẓir-i binā* Mustafa Beğ *mīrlivā* of Çankırı; *emīn-i binā* Husam Beğ *kātib-i binā* Husam; *miʿmar* Yaʿqubshah; Aydın Beğ the agha of the Istanbul janissaries; *khalīfe-hāyi binā* Ali and Yusuf; a group of 30 stewards

162. interior, hospital of Bayezid II, 1484–88, Edirne, Turkey. © Patricia Blessing, 2019

(*mu'temedān*); and a group of janissaries presumably employed in the construction.[145] Palace librarian 'Atufi is mentioned in the same section for having donated a book to the library of the complex.[146] Meriç argues that *mi'mar* Ya'qub Shah b. Sultan Shah was the main architect of the complex and that he was of Iranian origin.[147] On the latter point, Necipoğlu notes that an Armenian architect named Ya'qub Shah, documented as making repairs at the castle of Kilis in 1485–90, is the same person and, further, that the high value of the rewards he received for this work on Bayezid II's mosque complex (3,000 *akçe* and a robe of honor) is compatible with his having held a role similar to that of chief architect.[148] On 23 Sha'ban 909 AH / February 11, 1504 CE, Ya'qub Shah received another gift of a robe of honor with otter-fur trim.[149] On 17 Dhū l-Hijja 909 AH / June 1, 1504 CE, he was again highly rewarded with 3,000 *akçe* and a robe of honor, along with several of the same individuals listed in December 1503 when he received his first gift.[150] The June 1504 entry in the gift register is the last mention we have of Ya'qub Shah, who may have passed away soon after that.[151]

This register is one of the earliest sources about Ottoman *mi'mar*s, with much greater documentary value than the semi-legendary accounts about, for instance, 'Atik Sinan and the construction of Mehmed II's mosque in Istanbul.[152] In two of these accounts, Mehmed II is dissatisfied with the dome's span and height, as they fail to surpass the Hagia Sophia. Questioned about the reasons for this failure, the architect defends his choice with structural justifications: a taller dome with a larger diameter would not withstand the next earthquake.[153] What comes next differs in each version. In the late fifteenth-century anonymous account, which claims eyewitness status for the author, the architect is beaten to death. In Evliya Çelebi's seventeenth-century version, he is punished by having his hands amputated, not because the dome's span was too small but because he dared to lower its height by shortening valuable columns brought from Egypt to be used in the construction; however, he successfully applies for damages.[154] While these accounts appear extreme, Barkan notes that the fifteenth-century source also contains criticism of Mehmed II for what are described as overreaching inspections of building sites intended to root out corruption among those directing them.[155] This comment not only aligns with broader criticism of Mehmed II's centralizing policies but also points to increasing administrative control over imperial construction projects, something that would continue under Bayezid II.

The gift register allows for observations about the organization of an early sixteenth-century construction site and the relationship between the imperial administration and the building professions. As Meriç observed, the *nāzir-i binā* Mustafa Beğ is first listed (on December 6, 1503) as *mīrlivā* of Çankırı[156]; then as *mīrlivā-yi piyādegān-i Karahiṣār-i ṣāhib* (on 7 Sha'ban 909 AH / January 25, 1504)[157]; in a later instance, on May 27, 1504, he appears as *mīrlivā* of Afyon Karahisar[158], again in his role of building overseer.[159] Mustafa Beğ was thus clearly a member of the Ottoman military-administrative elite, with changing appointments, who was put in charge of certain oversight duties at the construction site of Bayezid II's Istanbul mosque complex. During the period covered by Sinan's work as chief architect, Necipoğlu notes, it was usual for building overseers to be chosen from among high-ranking imperial officials.[160] The structure including a building overseer (*nāzir-i binā*; *bina nazırı*), a building supervisor (*emīn-i binā*; *bina emini*), and a secretary (*kātib-i binā*; *bina katibi*) that emerges in the gift register is an early document of the standardized practice of financial management on imperial construction sites.[161] In this system, a building supervisor ideally had both financial expertise and knowledge of construction practices, while the secretary was responsible for record keeping.[162] The overseer perhaps took care of higher-level administrative matters and reported back to the sultan on progress, while leaving the nitty-gritty of the construction site and communications with workers to supervisor and architects. An example from the record books of the Süleymaniye Mosque in Istanbul (1550–57) recounts how the *beylerbeyi* of the province of Şam went to Baalbek accompanied by a local *mi'mar*, who participated as an expert with knowledge of building materials, in order to select columns to be shipped to the construction site in Istanbul. When transportation arrangements failed and the *mi'mar* passed away in his home base of

Damascus during the winter, a member of the *hassa mimarları* was sent instead to make sure everything went smoothly.[163] Thus, when local arrangements failed, the centralized system could take over to fix any shortcomings, effectively superseding what had been previously set into motion at the provincial level.

Such logistical challenges certainly emerged with all kinds of building materials, including ones sourced closer to Istanbul.[164] As we have seen in Chapter 2, a similar although perhaps less formal arrangement for the acquisition of building materials, as well as hierarchies on construction sites, may already have existed in the early fifteenth century, with Hajji ʿIvaz Pasha taking on a role that appears to have combined the later positions of overseer and supervisor into one. What we see in the case of Mustafa Beğ is that by the early sixteenth century oversight over construction projects had become a matter of state that was entrusted to the empire's administrative-military elite; this system served as the hinge between the larger imperial administration and the artistic offices, such as the *hassa mimarları*, that were consolidated during that same period to the point of becoming hierarchically organized units that provided training in a specific field. Thus, when we read this gift register, we see the integration of architecture and its practice into the imperial classification and knowledge project taking place before our eyes.

At the structural level, mosque plans in particular converge on a relatively small range of types. The Mustafa Pasha Mosque in Skopje and the Mehmed Beğ Mosque in Serres, discussed previously, are two examples of a late fifteenth-century Ottoman architecture focused on single-dome mosques with carefully carved decoration: structures that could be built based on designs that were perhaps indeed transported on paper. These spaces have a composition that certainly allows for being drawn on the blind grids Necipoğlu observed in the rare extant drawings, as addressed in Chapter 3. Skilled stonemasons and a supervising *miʿmar* would certainly have been needed to successfully execute such construction, and the central office of the *hassa mimarları* was a logical consequence of an imperial building program that, while it left room for a range of elite patrons beyond the ranks of sultans and grand viziers, nevertheless took on an aesthetic unity that created clearly Ottoman marks on cityscapes. As discussed earlier, this effect may perhaps have been less striking in the Balkans, where the construction of the first Ottoman mosques and mosque-*zāviye*s upon conquest would have already changed the cityscape more dramatically. In cities like Skopje and Serres, all Islamic monuments were the result of Ottoman patronage, and thus the Islamic built environment was relatively uniform from the start, as a certain level of coherence emerged with building types such as T-plan mosque-*zāviye*s build by the *gazi* leaders. (The idea of stylistic coherence is complicated, though, when we look at what occurred in cities such as Thessaloniki, where the conversion of churches into mosques was a central development.[165]) In Anatolia, however, buildings built by Muslim patrons could range from the late eleventh to the late fifteenth century, depending on when a specific city was conquered. This made for a checkered built environment where Ottoman presence was not immediately a clear visual factor, also because monuments built by previous Muslim rulers came in a range of styles.

PATRONAGE FOR SUFI COMMUNITIES IN CONTESTED ANATOLIA

While Istanbul was transformed into the center of the Ottoman realm, both at the architectural level and in terms of its place within the administrative and cultural structure of the Ottoman Empire, other regions remained out of reach for the Ottomans. This is was especially true for parts of Anatolia that would remain contested into the sixteenth century. The second Ottoman conquest of Anatolia (working to recapture the lands lost after Bayezid I's defeat to Timur in 1402) advanced under Mehmed II, with Trebizond and Karaman being the main territorial acquisitions in the 1460s. The crucial central Anatolian city of Kayseri came under Ottoman rule in 1474, after changing hands between the Karamanids and the Dulkadir several times in the previous decades.[166] While the Karamanids were completely defeated, the Dulkadir remained present as a major actor in eastern Anatolia for several decades to come, and the influence of the Safaviyya Sufi order centered in Ardabil in western Iran rose, which eventually led to the demise of the Aqqoyunlu.[167] Thus, while Ottoman control over Anatolia was increasingly consolidated over the course of the last quarter of the fifteenth century, rule over the region remained in flux, and the immediately post-Mongol political landscape had not disappeared completely. By and large, the architectural consequences of the Ottomans' attention to central and eastern Anatolia would not emerge until the reign of Bayezid II, in large part due to Mehmed II's Istanbul-centric patronage, which left little room for construction projects elsewhere, especially ones that were not sponsored directly by the sultan.

In addition to the sites created for Halvetis in Istanbul and Amasya, Bayezid II's patronage of Sufi groups – in contrast to his father, Mehmed II, who had not supported them – changed the architectural landscape of several long-standing shrine complexes in central Anatolia. This was the case for the Mevlevi shrine in Konya, centered on the dynastic mausoleum of Jalal al-Din Rumi (d. 1273) and his descendants; the shrine of Hacı Bektaş (d. 1271?) in the town of Hacıbektaş, about 100 kilometers to the west of Kayseri; and the Seyyid Battal Gazi Shrine in Seyyitgazi, 35 kilometers south of Eskişehir. In her study of Ottoman patronage of the latter two shrines, Zeynep Yürekli notes that Bayezid II's policy of returning private lands that had been turned into imperial fiefs by Mehmed II to their original owners (or those owners' descendants) was intended to keep two potential sources of unrest – the powerful *gazi* families who had shared the Ottomans' success since early times, and Sufi groups – in check and aligned with Ottoman imperial goals in the face of the mounting threat that the Safavids posed on the empire's eastern borders.[168] This was especially crucial in the province of Karaman, where Cem had garnered substantial support during the succession conflict, particularly from the Zeyniyye Sufi order.[169] Once Bayezid II's succession was secure, support for the Mevlevis in Konya was a way to create imperial ties to another Sufi group and thus gain closer control in a city where this group was extremely powerful.

The Mevlevi shrine in Konya had been founded during Jalal al-Din Rumi's lifetime, receiving patronage from elites who negotiated a relatively comfortable position under the Ilkhanid overlords who had brought the Saljuqs under their dominance beginning in 1243.[170] In the fourteenth and early fifteenth centuries, the Karamanids were major patrons.[171] The first Ottoman intervention in the shrine did not happen until Bayezid II's reign, when the mausoleum was redecorated.[172] Indeed, the patronage of the shrine established by Bayezid II led to a long and close relationship between the Mevleviye and the Ottoman dynasties: future sultans throughout the sixteenth century would continue their patronage, with Sultan Süleyman the Magnificent commissioning a *masjid* and *semahane* in 1559–60.[173] Further, in a renewed alliance of Sufi and *gazi* forces, the remodeling of Seyyitgazi, beginning circa 1493–94, was done with the patronage of the Mihaloğlu *gazi* family, who had ancestral ties to the region.[174] In the fifteenth century, they held two townships of Harmankaya as *mülk* but lost them because of Mehmed II's centralization policy. Bayezid II returned the lands to them, now on a hereditary basis, and work on the shrine eventually began.[175] Farther east, in the case of the shrine of Hacı Bektaş, the late thirteenth- and fourteenth-century structures were first remodeled between 1494 and 1520, and around 1501 Balım Sultan (d. ca. 1516) moved to the shrine at Bayezid II's request to exert influence on the Anatolian followers of the Safavid Sufi order centered in Ardabil, who would be designated as *kızılbaş* beginning in the 1510s.[176] In 1519, Dulkadir ruler ʿAli b. Şehsuvar (r. 1515–22), who ruled the region where the shrine is located as a vassal of the Ottomans, built a mausoleum for Balım Sultan, adding a mosque in 1520.[177] As Cemal Kafadar notes, such Ottoman-steered patronage was also an attempt "to tame cults that had not yet become fully anti-Ottoman" as the conflict between Ottomans and Safavid-affiliated *kızılbaş* was rising.[178]

In all three cases, interventions during Bayezid II's and Selim I's reigns transformed shrines that had been present since the thirteenth century, founded under Saljuq patronage and later expanded by a range of rulers during the political fragmentation of large parts of Anatolia in the fourteenth and fifteenth centuries. Ottoman-connected patronage of these sites could thus be seen not only as a political move to tie Sufi groups to the Ottoman dynasty but also as part of an Ottoman project of gaining tighter control over Anatolia. Such a move was crucial at a time when, on the one hand, Mehmed II's conquest had brought central Anatolia and the Black Sea coast under Ottoman rule but, on the other hand, Mamluks and Safavids were causing trouble on the eastern and southeastern frontiers. During Bayezid II's reign, patronage extended to cities such as Manisa (like Amasya, a major princely residence), where Husn-i Shah, the mother of Prince Shahinshah, founded the Hatuniye Mosque and its complex in 896 AH / 1490– 91 CE.[179] In Tokat, Bayezid II built the Hatuniye Mosque in honor of his mother, Gülbahar Hatun, in 898 AH / 1493 CE, thus expanding his own patronage beyond Amasya, Edirne, and Istanbul.[180]

ANATOLIA AND CILICIA BEYOND THE OTTOMAN REALM

Despite the Ottomans' efforts to expand toward the east, a fully Ottoman Anatolia was not yet realized at the start of the sixteenth century: both the northeast – including the region around Erzurum, a troublesome borderland between the Dulkadir, the Aqqoyunlu, and the emerging Safavids – and the southeast were their own worlds, politically and architecturally. Regions southeast of the Taurus Mountains – a physical obstacle that had long influenced the history of Anatolia – were under the rule of the Dulkadir (since 1337) and the Ramazanoğlu (since 1352), the latter centered in Adana. Architecture in these principalities followed a different trajectory from that of central Anatolia, and Ottoman influence was slow to take hold – not really becoming established until the mid-sixteenth century in the case of Adana.[181] Cilicia was also for a long time a frontier territory between Ottomans and Mamluks, finding itself embroiled in dispute particularly while the Karamanids were still present in central Anatolia, but afterward too, as the Dulkadir and Ramazanoğlu took on similar roles as allies who could switch sides at any time or enter into simultaneous alliances.

Mamluk presence in the region translated into architecture in monuments such as the Hoşkadem Camii in Kozan (historical Sīs), built in 1448 by Amir Aqbay, during the reign of al-Zahir Chaqmaq (r. 1438–53).[182] This monument does not have the characteristics of fifteenth-century architecture from the Mamluk heartlands of Syria and Cairo; rather, it is a relatively plain building built of stone, with little decoration beyond the foundation inscription, which is awkwardly squeezed into and spilling over the borders of a panel above the doorway, and a fragmentary, damaged inscription on the mihrab.[183] The latter is in Mamluk-style *thuluth*, the only extant stylistic sign of the patron's origin.[184]

In the city of Adana, the Ramazanoğlu emerged as patrons of architecture, with the Great Mosque being the old city center's main religious monument, close to the river and market area.[185] Founded by Halil Beğ (d. 1510), the mosque was expanded several times during the reign of his son Piri Mehmed (r. 1510–68), who became a vassal of the Ottomans early in his reign. An inscription on the mosque's east portal (Figure 163), which has a minaret (Figure 164) strongly reminiscent of Mamluk architecture in northern Syria, records the building's foundation date as 913 AH / 1507–08 CE, included in a chronogram that praises Halil Beğ's charity.[186] This chronogram appears in the first part of the inscription on the right face of the portal recess. On the west portal, the building's expansion or completion is mentioned with the date 948 AH / 1541 CE; in this inscription, the Ramazanoğlu prince pledges allegiance to Ottoman sultan Süleyman.[187] While Max van Berchem notes that "Mustafa b. Piri" is a possibility for the patron mentioned in the inscription, he also acknowledges that he was working from a copy and that the wording differed from that in another copy available to him.[188] A close look at the inscription, however, reveals that the words used are "Pīrī Pāshā."[189] Thus, in addition to acknowledging Ottoman rule with the mention of Sultan Süleyman, the Ramazanoğlu prince also uses his Ottoman title, Pasha, which he likely acquired the same year the construction project was created – that is, 1541.[190]

Piri Mehmed also left a foundation inscription on the madrasa that faces the mosque, and another on the mosque's *minbar*, respectively dated 947 AH / 1540 CE and 926 AH / 1520 CE.[191] Attached to the mosque, the family's mausoleum provides further clues to the building's date: it contains the cenotaphs of

163. East portal, Great Mosque, 1507–08, Adana, Turkey. © Patricia Blessing 2018

164. Minaret, Great Mosque, 1507–08, Adana, Turkey.
© Patricia Blessing 2018

Halil (d. 1510), Mehmed Shah (d. 1524), and Mustafa (d. 1552).[192] All three are clad in Iznik tiles (Figure 165), with end panels that were clearly custom made for the site, fitting the cenotaphs exactly and displaying inscriptions that identify the burials, while the dadoes are covered in fragments that were removed from the prayer hall.[193] The walls of the mausoleum and the prayer hall are also covered in tiles, whose chronology is complex. According to Walter B. Denny, a first program of tile decoration in the prayer hall was probably installed in the 1540s, possibly in conjunction with the building campaign during Piri Mehmed Pasha's reign, documented in the inscriptions on the west portal and on the *minbar*. At this time, hexagonal tiles were added to the walls of the prayer hall and the chamber to the west of it; these might have been produced locally or in Syria, although a firm conclusion on the matter is not possible.[194] The next step probably occurred in the 1560s, based on the quality of the tiles (and with a possible *terminus ante quem* of Piri Mehmed Pasha's death in 1568): new tiles were added to the *sanduka*s, and a carefully fitted tympanum was installed above the mihrab (Figure 166).[195] The fact that the tympanum's blue-and-red border with *rūmī* motifs and the *saz*-style central field with a white background have some tiles in common further supports Denny's argument that this panel was made to measure. Most likely, the tiles for the cenotaphs and the mihrab were made to order in Iznik, and they could have been shipped from there to Adana on a coastal route.[196] Finally, the tiles within the mihrab niche likely date to the 1570s, on stylistic grounds.[197] The tiles – in part imported from Iznik, in part produced locally or in Syria – are entirely within the stylistic range of mid-to-late sixteenth-century Iznik tiles, and thus part of the Ottoman court style of the period.

165. Mausoleum, tiles 1540s, Great Mosque, Adana, Turkey. © Patricia Blessing 2018

As Denny notes, their use in Adana is an example of elites in the provinces – and in this case, non-imperial ones – adopting Ottoman taste and style.[198] Yet the visual Ottomanization of the Great Mosque of Adana was gradual and incomplete. The exterior, built between the 1500s and the 1540s, is fully in line with a local architectural tradition closely connected to late Mamluk architecture in Syria, particularly the closest major Mamluk center of Aleppo. On the portal, built in 1508, *ablaq* in white, yellow, and black appears. A heavy lintel of grey marble closes off the rectangular doorway, and between it and the foundation inscription, black, white, and reddish stone in joggled, interlocking shapes forms a decorative band (see Figure 163). Above this, after a narrow band of grey marble, is the foundation inscription, wrapping around the three sides of the portal recess. A muqarnas niche fitted into a blunt pointed arch follows, framed by *ablaq*, and the top of the portal ends in a muqarnas cornice.

Close comparisons to both the minaret and the portal are found on the Madrasa of Qadi Ahmad b. al-Saffah (821–28 AH / 1418–25 CE) in Aleppo (Figure 167), where the polygonal shape of the minaret's shaft and the *ablaq* on the portal appear in a very similar manner.[199] As Meinecke notes, this example is nearly a century older than the mosque in Adana, but later examples in Aleppo such as the Khan Khayrbek (1515) preserve similar *ablaq* stripes.[200] The façade of the hammam of Yalbugha al-Nasiri (ca. 1382–89) was most likely restored after the Ottoman conquest of Aleppo in 1516, and it also has a nearly identical pattern of *ablaq* (Figure 168).[201] Thus, while the closest comparison to the portal in Adana is indeed older, similar examples that are near contemporaries also exist, supporting the argument that Aleppo's Mamluk architecture is the source for the forms in Adana.

In commissioning this monument, the Ramazanoğlu chose a range of paths: on the exterior, starting in the early sixteenth century, they took Mamluk architecture as the model, and perhaps workers indeed came to Adana from Aleppo. It is noteworthy that in 1507, when the mosque was founded, the Mamluks were still ruling in Egypt and Syria. Only a decade later, in 1517, the Ottomans would integrate these lands into their own realm.[202] This period of change would also be crucial for the Ramazanoğlu family as the region around Adana became a *sancak* in 1517, though it retained some independence until 1608. Piri

166. Tiles on mihrab, 1560s, Great Mosque, Adana, Turkey. © Patricia Blessing 2018

167. Madrasa of Qadi Ahmad b. al-Saffah, 1418–25, Aleppo, Syria. © Patricia Blessing 2005

168. Hammam of Yalbugha al-Nasiri, late fourteenth century with façade restoration ca. 1520, Aleppo, Syria. © Patricia Blessing 2005

ANATOLIA AND CILICIA BEYOND THE OTTOMAN REALM 213

Mehmed was at its helm from 1520 onward.²⁰³ Entering the Ottoman elite, he was *beylerbeyi* of Karaman in 1541 and 1548, and of Damascus around 1545 and in 1549, all while still exerting some level of control in Adana, where he returned permanently in 1559 until his death in 1568.²⁰⁴ The additions to the Great Mosque of Adana fall mostly within this period. In the 1540s Piri Mehmed's son Mustafa built the west portal of the mosque, and perhaps other sections of it as well, considering that the inscription on the west portal refers to construction rather than restoration.²⁰⁵ The northern section of the building, which contains a row of small domes over courtyard arcades that continue around the northwestern corner and beyond the west portal, is a likely candidate, considering the distinctly Ottoman flavor of these details. And if the east portal is Mamluk in style, the west portal is Ottoman (Figure 169): the stilted arch over the muqarnas hood, the hanging elements of stone within the muqarnas, and the corner colonettes are all elements that were fully ingrained in Ottoman architecture at this time. In fact, similar examples can be found as early as the late fourteenth century in the Great Mosque (1399–1400) and the mosque of Bayezid I (ca. 1390–95) in Bursa. The muqarnas niches on either side of the Adana mosque's west portal also find parallels in late fourteenth- and early fifteenth-century Ottoman buildings, several of which were discussed in earlier chapters, including the mosque-*zāviye* of Mehmed I in Bursa. Ultimately, this approach to a portal derives from Saljuq versions of the thirteenth century, although most of these comprised portal blocks jutting out from the façade, a solution that is rare in the Ottoman context.²⁰⁶ The flowery crenellations at the top of the portal are also an element found in contemporaneous or

169. West portal, added in 1541, Great Mosque, Adana, Turkey.
© Patricia Blessing 2018

somewhat earlier Ottoman architecture, including the central courtyard portal of the mosque complex of Bayezid II in Istanbul.

Despite these concessions to Ottoman ideas about architecture, other elements of the Adana Great Mosque are more difficult to place, including the steep muqarnas dome that emerges behind the west portal. Again, this is a nod toward Syria, although the form is rare there, and extant examples such as the Maristan Nuri in Damascus date to the twelfth century. Nevertheless, it is certain that Piri Mehmed Pasha undertook a construction project that introduced Ottoman elements (the portal, the courtyard domes, and the first phase of the tile decoration) to his family's major mosque foundation in Adana. Were these elements he had seen on a visit to Istanbul in the late 1520s?[207] Did his connections to the imperial center provide him with access to the designs of imperial architects and tile makers? The first steps taken in the 1540s were not enough to integrate the family's mosque into the realm of Ottoman imperial taste, as the custom-made, high-quality Iznik tiles added in the 1560s confirm. One can only speculate what the effect of these changes in sixteenth-century Adana would have been. Perhaps the new architecture would have appeared just as new and strange to local residents (at least those who had never traveled to more thoroughly Ottomanized cities) as the tiles on Mehmed I's mosque-*zāviye* and mausoleum would have looked to residents of Bursa more than a century earlier. Clearly, an patron who had become part of the Ottoman cultural and political orbit brought Ottoman architecture to Adana, and it was there to stay, though mixed with local elements.[208] A further example of this process in Adana is the Hasan Kethüda Mosque, built in 1558, a perfect example of a small Ottoman mosque: a dome covering the sanctuary, a square courtyard with arcades covered with little domes, and a pointed (if slightly squat) minaret with a muqarnas balcony. Is Ottomanization complete here? In fact, even this building retains local elements in the form of the intersecting stones that compose the arch of the entrance into the prayer hall. Here, as in other sites that formerly lay on the fringes of the Ottoman realm and were only integrated in the 1510s, architecture is tenaciously local, and constant negotiation with local forms appears.

AN OTTOMAN AESTHETIC

In this chapter, I have explored several central questions relating to the centralization of the arts in the Ottoman realm. First, examining the Baba Nakkaş album and the style combining *rūmī* and *khiṭāyī* designs that emerges from specific drawings within it, I observed that designs produced in the *nakka-şhane* – by circa 1500 a centralized workshop in Istanbul – were adapted into a range of media. The practices established for the *nakkaşhane* and for the transfer of such designs to production sites for metalwork and, most importantly, ceramics – for which Iznik emerged as the main site of production after 1480 – were part of the larger Ottoman epistemic project of the period, in which skills and knowledge were harnessed for imperial consolidation. This included administration, imperial ideology, scholarship, science, and increasingly the artistic production tied to the Ottoman court.

Within this context, the formation of the *hassa mimarları*, the imperial office of architects, during this same period provided a platform for the creation of designs that could be adopted across the empire at various scales, in the foundations of both sultans and other members of the Ottoman courts, from the mothers of princes to grand viziers and governors. The increasingly consistent aesthetic created with the façades and domed profiles of mosques, mausolea, and even commercial buildings led to a distinct visual appearance, associated with the Ottomans rather than the previous Christian and Muslim rulers of the various territories that were now part of the Ottoman Empire, in cities stretching from the Balkans to central Anatolia. To this end, new monuments were added to cities that had been under Ottoman rule for longer periods of time, such as Serres, Skopje, Thessaloniki, Amasya, and Manisa. Similar programs were pursued in more recently conquered locations such as Konya and Kayseri, which did not come under Ottoman rule until the 1470s. Along with this visual unification went the integration of Sufi communities – particularly the Halvetis, Mevlevis, and Bektashis – under the imperial umbrella in a way that moved beyond the earlier patronage of various Sufi affiliates with the building of mosque-*zāviye*s for their use across the empire, especially in western Anatolia and the Balkans. Imperial patronage of major shrines and their leaders under Bayezid II consolidated the position of more close-knit Sufi communities within the imperial structure.

These processes of consolidation, from design to production, from imperial patronage to its execution on the ground, would continue during the reigns of Selim I and Süleyman I. At the larger, global scale, the architectural developments in design and the emergence of clearer information about architects was similar to developments in northern and southern Europe from the late Middle Ages into the Renaissance, with contacts between these regions and the Ottoman Empire increasing from Mehmed II's reign onward, particularly supported by trade in textiles. Within the Islamic world, the changing situation created by the emergence of the Safavids and the Ottoman conquest of the former Mamluk territories would shift aesthetic concerns toward the formulation of distinct dynastic vocabularies in the Ottoman, Safavid, Mughal, and Uzbek Empires, even though movements of makers between these empires would continue.

CONCLUSION

It has become clear that in the sixteenth century, architecture was made more uniform in imperial projects as a result of the Ottoman Empire's performance as a centralized state. Eventually, the fifteenth century receded into a distant past that was hard to comprehend from the point of view of the empire's so-called Classical Age. This is true for history, reshaped by sixteenth-century historians in ways that made sense in their own present, and it is also true for the built environment, which was transformed by later uses and perceived in new ways. This aspect of the long-term development of the Ottoman Empire with its closely intertwined administrative, imperial, and artistic interventions emerges in the material politics of the architecture analyzed in this book.

I have followed the trajectory of Ottoman architecture as it unfolded from the late fourteenth to the early sixteenth centuries. Analyzing buildings in Anatolia, Cilicia, Istanbul, and the Balkans, built between circa 1390 and circa 1510, I have shown how Ottoman architecture was transformed as the empire took shape. Memory and dynastic commemoration were central aspects of this architectural endeavor. First, as shown in Chapter 2, Bursa was shaped in ways intended to closely reflect dynastic memory across the cityscape, with funerary monuments built to every sultan from Osman to Murad II. This commemorative function was maintained into the second half of the sixteenth century in the mausolea of the Muradiye, where princesses and princes were buried to continue the dynastic *lieu de mémoire*, as discussed in Chapter 4. Bursa was also the site where Mehmed I's rebuilding of the Ottoman principality was embodied in his mosque-*zāviye* complex, which combined elements drawn from Byzantine, Saljuq, Ilkhanid, Timurid, *beylik*, Aqqoyunlu, and Mamluk architecture, examined in Chapter 2. The cosmopolitan nature of this monument – a precursor of what Mehmed II's patronage would establish in Istanbul less than a half century later – was also due to the presence of a diverse cast of makers on the construction site who worked on masonry, stone carving, tiles, and woodwork. The vizier Hajji ʿIvaz Pasha, who emerges as one of the Ottomans' early building supervisors, was reputed for hiring artists from faraway lands. While the sources are not specific on the origins of these makers, the fact that this aspect is noted in late fifteenth- and early sixteenth-century sources shows that an emphasis on the manifold contributions to Ottoman architecture continued to be appreciated for decades to come. In this, the material politics of the period of Mehmed I were successfully perpetuated, at least until the second quarter of the sixteenth century. Thereafter, different views emerged that materialize in the architecture of the Classical Age.

While the mobility of workers was central to the material politics of Ottoman architecture, moving objects and design templates on paper are likely to have been sources for Ottoman construction practices throughout the fifteenth century. In the case of the Masters of Tabriz, the established narrative assumes a multigenerational, mobile enterprise that worked in Bursa, Edirne, Karaman, and perhaps even Istanbul from the 1410s to the 1480s. It is, however, equally possible that tiles were transported to the various construction sites from a single as-yet-unknown production site. This might have been Tabriz, but in the absence of concrete archaeological evidence predating the 1460s in that city, the question of the Masters of Tabriz as a brand of high cultural capital versus an actual, functioning workshop remains wide open. Considering that it is clearly established how many thousands of tiles were transported from Iznik in western Anatolia to imperial construction sites in the sixteenth and seventeenth centuries, we cannot exclude the possibility of something similar taking place in the fifteenth century.

With the Ottoman conquest of Constantinople in 1453, the center of Ottoman patronage and royal commemoration shifted to that city. New solutions were established that combined Byzantine, Italian, and Timurid modes of royal representation and construction, while the rich repertoire established in the first half of the fifteenth century continued to be deployed. In examining the Çinili Köşk and the mosque complex of Mahmud Pasha in Chapter 1, I showed how poetry both in building inscriptions and on the written page established aesthetic experiences – in the physical space of the building and in the imagined space in the reader's mind – that were based on likening monuments to natural and cosmological phenomena such as the shimmering effect of peacock feathers or constellations in the firmament. In Bursa, similar dynamics of inscribed poetic space intertwined with complex uses of materials can be observed in both Mehmed I's mosque-*zāviye* complex and the mausolea of the Muradiye. A particularly striking case is Murad II's own mausoleum, where the wide marble expanse of the floor and the open dome, combined with the building's inscription, engage with nature and paradise, with the earthly present and the afterworld. Complex sensory landscapes of this sort exist across fifteenth-century Ottoman architecture, even though often they are not easy to trace and are made more difficult to comprehend by the absence of original furnishings that were either lost to time or removed to museums for safekeeping beginning in the early twentieth century.

A further element important to the understanding of the interiors of buildings is wall decoration: tiles, but also the more rarely preserved wall paintings, which could present landscapes that turned wall into nature. Such is the case in the Muradiye Mosque in Edirne, studied in Chapter 3, where some such paintings have survived along with tile decoration that requires thinking about the complex relationship between the Masters of Tabriz narrative and the beginnings of ceramic production in Iznik, which coincides with the rapid expansion of the Ottoman Empire beginning in the 1430s. Workshops (*kitabkhāna* in Persian, *nakkaşhane* in Ottoman Turkish) that engaged in creating designs on paper were crucial for such monuments where the mobility of makers was not the sole driving factor. Edirne had such a *nakkaşhane* in the first half of the fifteenth century. It is likely that *nakkaşhane* designs (made locally or elsewhere within or beyond the Ottoman Empire) were used to produce the blue-and-white underglaze painted tiles of the Muradiye Mosque, as well as the calligraphic panels of the Üç Şerefeli Mosque. Thus the question of designs made on paper as it applied to the production of architectural decoration – tiles, wall paintings, stonework – is central. Within the complexity of such architectural decoration lies the evidence for close collaboration between those working on building sites and those working on paper. Here too a wide field of possibility emerges for mobile participation, both through presence on site and through the exchange of paper templates, even though most of the makers involved in these processes remain anonymous.

Only with the example of Baba Nakkaş in the late fifteenth century, examined in Chapter 5, are we able to observe a case of designs on paper that we have on hand and that appear in ceramics, wood, metalwork, and stone carvings. In formalistic terms, it is clear that drawings in this style must have been used as templates in a range of media. Like the Masters of Tabriz, over time "Baba Nakkaş" became an artistic brand and, in the context of twentieth-century art history, a stylistic label. Around 1500, with the emergence of internal, Ottoman practices for documenting artists and preserving their works in the practice of album making, adapted from Timurid examples, the previously elusive paper trail of the *nakkaşhane* finally emerges. The same is true for architects, who, as the imperial institution of the *hassa mimarları* was formed, take shape in administrative records. With Sinan, such documentation branched out into the additional form of autobiographical narratives. The transformation of the role and formation of the *mi'mar* that occurred in the first quarter of the sixteenth century ties back to the discussion in Chapter 3 of what this term and others used in connection to the building crafts meant in the fifteenth-century Ottoman, Mamluk, and Timurid contexts. Inscriptions on buildings that point to the contributions of various individuals in the construction process are often the only sources on these questions for much of the fifteenth century. What we find in these inscriptions forces us to rethink the functioning of a building site from design to the sourcing of materials and on through construction and completion – effectively the physical and logistical aspects of the material politics of architecture.

The idea of the maker's share took central stage in my discussion of the creation of Ottoman monuments and reflections on the ways in which collaborations at building sites could have happened. In several chapters, I argued that the fifteenth century was a period of shifting associations of makers who worked in a flexible system that allowed for new combinations of experts – tile makers, masons, and calligraphers, among others – in each new project. These associations of makers are crucial to the material politics of Ottoman architecture in the fifteenth century, a project that combined skills, materials, and forms in a wide range of possible combinations. The stakes were double: on the one hand, they were aesthetic and cultural in that these projects demonstrated the Ottomans' knowledge of a wide range of styles from within their own expanding territories and beyond. On the other hand, the stakes were political and economic, in that these projects served to display the Ottomans' financial and logistical power in assembling the associations of makers, finding the materials needed, and bringing projects to completion. Thus the terms "experimental" and "eclectic," often used in connection to fifteenth-century Ottoman architecture, do not do justice to the sophisticated milieu of experts who were active on construction sites and provided designs for elements such as inscriptions and tiles, nor to the intentionality of the design decisions made. The resulting buildings were representative not only of Ottoman presence, rule, and power but also of a cultural and visual literacy that involved local and transregional sets of expertise – hence the term "material politics" that governs these multiple aspects of Ottoman architectural patronage and making.

I arrived at this view of the fifteenth century in part through questions that remained at the end of my first book project, in which, although I focused on central and eastern Anatolia in the thirteenth and fourteenth centuries, the question of Ottoman architecture was always present. Just how did Ottoman architectural patronage develop from the late thirteenth century, when the Ottomans are first recorded, through the fourteenth and fifteenth centuries? While the fourteenth century has been examined in detailed studies, work on the fifteenth century has so far concentrated on the period after the Ottoman conquest of Constantinople in 1453 and on the resulting project of establishing a new Ottoman capital. The question of competition with and respect for the architectural achievement of the Hagia Sophia is central in that narrative, which leads in a straight line to the focus on Sinan and his engineering feats centered on building the expanding domes now marking the skyline of Istanbul. The same aesthetic, by way of the *hassa mimarları*, was exported across the Ottoman lands beginning in the sixteenth century, eventually creating an element of visual unity within regions under Ottoman rule.

Yet the type of architecture Sinan eventually designed was not what builders, masons, and designers had in mind while they were creating buildings throughout the fifteenth century as the material politics of architecture were not yet tied to a centralizing imperial vision that would not emerge until the late fifteenth century. Instead, architecture was malleable in that multiple sources of materials and motifs were of interest and could be flexibly combined. While certain plan types, particularly those used for mosque-*zāviye*s, were developed and used fairly consistently in the fifteenth century, engineering was not directed at one single dome-centric outcome. The ways in which monuments were adorned were equally diverse and open to the influx of new ideas and workers.

The centralization of production in the sixteenth century brought about a marked shift that resulted in the standardized architectures – inside and out – that were created by the imperial workshops for architectural designs, tiles, and textiles in Istanbul, Iznik, and Bursa. Architecture became an integral part of the Ottomans' push to set themselves apart from other polities – the rivaling Safavids centered in Iran in particular – an impulse that also had effects on archival practices, administrative structures, and religious life. The material politics of architecture became a crucial vector in this centralizing endeavor. It affected new and existing buildings alike. As part of this project, buildings like Mehmed I's mosque-*zāviye* in Bursa were turned into Friday mosques, brought in line with more recent religious and functional developments within the Ottoman imperial project. For the sixteenth-century Ottomans, the artistic dynamics that were crucial for their fifteenth-century ancestors became expressions of a foreign universe that did not align with the imperial Ottoman present. Thus the roots of the narrative I dismantled in this book indeed lie within the sixteenth-century Ottoman Empire itself, and not purely in historiographies created in post-Ottoman Turkey and in twentieth-century art history.

NOTES

INTRODUCTION MATERIAL POLITICS OF ARCHITECTURE IN A FLUID EMPIRE

1. Necipoğlu, *Age of Sinan*.
2. Necipoğlu, "From Byzantine Constantinople to Ottoman Kostantiniyye"; Necipoğlu, "Visual Cosmopolitanism"; Kafescioğlu, *Constantinopolis/Istanbul*.
3. Pancaroğlu, "Architecture, Landscape, and Patronage"; Çağaptay "Prousa/Bursa, a City within the City"; Çağaptay, "Frontierscape"; Ousterhout, "The East, the West, and the Appropriation of the Past"; Ousterhout, "Ethnic Identity and Cultural Appropriation"; Yürekli, "Architectural Patronage"; historical background in Fleet, "The Rise of the Ottomans."
4. Kafadar, *Between Two Worlds*, 1–2; Kafadar, "A Rome of One's Own," 12–15. On language formation in literature: Kuru, "Literature of Rum," 558–59.
5. Kafadar, "A Rome of One's Own," 17–18.
6. On early Ottoman history: Köprülü, *Bizans Müesseselerinin Osmanlı Müesseselerine Te'siri Hakkında Bazı Mülâhazalar* and Köprülü, *Les origines de l'empire ottoman*. On literature, religion, and Sufism: Köprülü "Anadolu'da İslâmiyet," Köprülü, *Türk Edebiyatında İlk Mutasavvıflar*; On sources for Saljuq history: Köprülü, "Anadolu Selçuklu Tarihinin Yerel Kaynakları."
7. Kafadar, *Between Two Worlds*, 29–44 (including discussion of Paul Wittek's work on early Ottoman and *beylik* history, especially Wittek, *The Rise of the Ottoman Empire*).
8. Redford, "What Have You Done for Anatolia Today?"
9. Strohmeier, *Seldschukische Geschichte*, 76–90; Osman Turan, *Selçuklular Zamanında Türkiye*; Kafesoğlu, *A History of the Seljuks*.
10. Pancaroğlu, "Formalism."
11. Blessing and Goshgarian, "Introduction: Space and Place," 3, 6–12, with further literature. On the Caucasus, see Foletti and Thunø, "The Artistic Cultures of the South Caucasus," and further chapters in the same volume, including specifically on Islamic architecture in Armenia: Blessing, "Medieval Monuments from Empire to Nation-State." On Iran, see Grigor, *Building Iran*, 21–27, and Rizvi, "Art History and the Nation."
12. Kafadar, "A Rome of One's Own," 19; Bozdoğan and Necipoğlu, "Entangled Discourses," 3.
13. Bozdoğan and Necipoğlu, "Entangled Discourses," 1–4, with crucial questions to pursue in future research posed on page 4.
14. Blessing, *Rebuilding Anatolia*, 1–18; Blessing, "All Quiet on the Eastern Frontier?" 202–03; Blessing and Goshgarian, "Introduction: Space and Place."
15. Alpers, "No Telling, with Tiepolo," 340.

16. Lasser, "Maker's Share." I thank Frances K. Pohl for suggesting this article.
17. On Italy, see Huppert, "Material Matters"; on the Netherlands, see Hurx, *Architecture as Profession*. For the problem of the term "architect" in medieval European sources, see Pevsner, "The Term 'Architect.'"
18. Babaie, "Chasing after the Muhandis," 23–25. On the rising social status of craftsmen in fifteenth-century Mamluk Egypt, see Behrens-Abouseif, "Craftsmen."
19. In addition to the literature on the Islamic world and Europe, see also Campbell, *What the Emperor Built*, 29–35, for Ming China.
20. Binbaş, *Intellectual Networks*; Markiewicz, *Crisis of Kingship*; Genç, "Rethinking Idris-i Bidlisi"; Grenier, Carlos, *The Spiritual Vernacular of the Early Ottoman Frontier*.
21. On the role of mosque construction in this development: Crane, "The Ottoman Sultan's Mosques."
22. Kafadar, *Between Two Worlds*, 99–103.
23. Kastritsis, *The Sons of Bayezid*.
24. Kastritsis, "The Historical Epic *Ahvāl-i Sultān Mehemmed*"; Tezcan, "The Memory of the Mongols."
25. Peacock, "Seljuq Legitimacy," 86–88.
26. Kastritsis, ed. and trans., *The Tales of Sultan Mehmed*; Kastritsis, ed. and trans., *An Early Ottoman History*. See also Darling, "Political Literature."
27. İnalcık, "How to Read 'Āshık Pasha-Zāde's History?" 140; Kafadar, *Between Two Worlds*, 100–102; Anderson, "The Complex of Elvan Çelebi."
28. Kuran, "Spatial Study of Three Ottoman Capitals"; Pancaroğlu, "Architecture, Landscape, and Patronage"; Blessing, "Seljuk Past and Timurid Present."
29. Kafadar, *Between Two Worlds*, 148; Gökbilgin, "Edirne"; İnalcık, "Conquest of Edirne (1361)." For the city's architecture, see Aslanapa, *Edirnede Osmanlı Devri Âbideleri*; Tanman, "Edirne'de Erken Dönem Osmanlı Camileri"; Boykov, "T-shaped Zaviye/İmarets of Edirne"; Boykov, "Reshaping Urban Space"; Blessing, "Blue-and-White Tiles"; Singer, "Enter, Riding on an Elephant."
30. Tursun Beğ, *Târîh-i Ebü'l-Feth*, ed. Tulum, partial English translation in Tursun Beğ, *The History of Mehmed the Conqueror*, ed. and trans. İnalcık and Murphey; Kritovoulos, *History of Mehmed the Conqueror*, trans. Riggs.
31. Kafescioğlu, *Constantinopolis/Istanbul*; Necipoğlu, *Architecture, Ceremonial, and Power*; Necipoğlu, "Visual Cosmopolitanism"; Necipoğlu, "From Byzantine Constantinople to Ottoman Kostantiniyye"; Rodini, *Gentile Bellini's Portrait*, 17–31.
32. Mengüç, "Histories of Bayezid," 373.
33. Ibid., 379–80.

34. İnalcık, "How to Read ʿĀshık Pasha-Zāde's History?" 144–46; Kafadar, *Between Two Worlds*, 100–103. On the reflection of such conflicts in early sources, see Kastritis, "Tales of Viziers and Wine."

35. Kafadar, *Between Two Worlds*, 100–103.

36. Yavuz, "Taşköprizade Ahmed Efendi."

37. Atçıl, *Scholars and Sultans*, 59–82.

38. Kafadar, *Between Two Worlds*, 60–117.

39. Necipoğlu, *Age of Sinan*, 55–57; Kafescioğlu, "Lives and Afterlives of an Urban Institution," 256, 275–76, 287–97; Eyice, "İlk Osmanlı Devrinin Dini İçtimai Bir Müessesesi," 4, 53.

40. Kafadar, *Between Two Worlds*, 73.

41. Arabic text in Uzunçarşılı, *Afyon Karahisar*, 77. The inscription is now embedded in the wall to the right of the entrance. With the exception of the minaret, much of the current building consists of later construction. Author's observation on site, August 2019.

42. The most complete survey of Ottoman architecture from the late thirteenth century to the period of Mehmed II remains the monumental work of Ekrem Hakkı Ayverdi (1899–1984): Ayverdi, *Osmanlı Mimârîsinin İlk Devri*; Ayverdi, *Osmanlı Mimârîsinde Çelebi ve II. Sultan Murad Devri*; Ayverdi, *Fatih Devri Mimarî Eserleri*. Monuments in the Balkans are covered in greater detail in Ayverdi, *Avrupa'da Osmanlı Mimârî Eserleri*. The reigns of Bayezid II and Selim I are covered in the work of Ayverdi's collaborator İ. Aydın Yüksel: *Osmanlı Mimârîsinde II. Bâyezid ve Yavuz Selim Devri*. For Ayverdi's life and work, see Tanman, ed. *Ekrem Hakkı Ayverdi*.

43. The issue of restored interior spaces is particularly fraught in Bursa, with Léon Parvillée's work after the 1855 earthquake: St. Laurent, "Léon Parvillée."

44. On issues of conservation, see Kiel, "Incorporation of the Balkans," 156–58; Lewis, "Ottoman Architectural Patrimony of Bulgaria Revisited"; Petersen, "'Under the Yoke': The Archaeology of the Ottoman Period in Bulgaria." For the impact of the wars following the breakdown of Yugoslavia in the 1990s, which greatly affected Ottoman monuments in Bosnia and Kosovo, see Riedlmayr, "Foundations of the Ottoman Period in the Balkan Wars of the 1990s." For archaeological work, see Gerelyes et al., "Ottoman Europe." See also Survey of Ottoman architecture in Greece in Androudis, *Hē prōimē Othōmanikē technē kai architektonikēs*.

45. Ousterhout, "The East, the West, and the Appropriation of the Past"; Çağaptay, "Prousa/Bursa."

46. Necipoğlu, *Age of Sinan*, 50, 78–79; Çağaptay, "Prousa/Bursa"; Çağaptay, "Frontierscape"; Salgırlı, "Radicalizing Premodern Space"; Çağaptay, *The First Capital*.

47. Necipoğlu, "International Timurid," 136–37.

48. Uzunçarşılı, *Anadolu Beylikleri*; Yıldız, "Post-Mongol Pastoral Polities"; Paul, "Mongol Aristocrats and Beyliks."

49. For the period of Mehmed I and Murad II, see Lindner, "Anatolia, 1300–1451," 131–37. On Mehmed II's expansion in Anatolia, see Boyar, "Ottoman Expansion in the East," 75–91.

50. Blessing, *Rebuilding Anatolia*; Blessing, "All Quiet on the Eastern Frontier?"

51. Quiring Zoche, "Āq Qoyunlū."

52. Kastritsis, *An Early Ottoman History*, 205–06; Woods, *The Aqquyunlu*, 87 and 118–21; Yüksel Muslu, *The Ottomans and the Mamluks*, 130–31; Necipoğlu, "Visual Cosmopolitanism," 19.

53. Yüksel Muslu, *The Ottomans and the Mamluks*, 156–71; Har-El, *Struggle for Domination in the Middle East*.

54. Bozdoğan and Necipoğlu, "Entangled Discourses."

55. On patronage of the main *gazi* families, see Çağaptay, "The Road from Bithynia to Thrace"; Lowry, *The Shaping of the Ottoman Balkans*; Lowry, *Fourteenth Century Ottoman Realities*; Kiel, "Incorporation of the Balkans," 164–67, 174–75, 178; Boykov, "Borders of the Cities"; Uzunçarşılı, *Çandarlı Vezir Ailesi*, 23–27 and 84–86.

56. Kafadar, *Between Two Worlds*, 96–97; İnalcık, "How to Read ʿĀshık Pasha-zāde's History?" 144–46.

57. İnalcık, "How to Read ʿĀshık Pasha-zāde's History?" 146.

58. Bistami describes this network as the *ikhwān al-ṣafā wa-khillān al-wafā* (Brethren of Purity and Friends of Loyalty), alluding to the eponymous tenth-century group active in Basra: Binbaş, *Intellectual Networks*, 8 and 105–07; Fazlıoğlu, "İlk Dönem Osmanlı İlim ve Kültür Hayatında İhvânu's-safâ," 235, 239–40; Necipoğlu, "The Spatial Organization of Knowledge," 43.

59. Binbaş, *Intellectual Networks*, 106. Molla Fenari is sometimes considered the first *şeyhülislam*. For his biography, see Aydın, "Molla Fenârî."

60. Binbaş, *Intellectual Networks*, 106.

61. Balivet, *Islam mystique et révolution armée*, 43–44.

62. Ikhwān al-Ṣafā, *Epistles of the Brethren of Purity*, ed. and trans. el-Bizri and de Callataÿ. For the *Epistles of the Brethren of Purity* as a source for art history, see Graves, *Arts of Allusion*.

63. Blair, "Place, Space and Style."

64. Hay, "The Passage of the Other," 68.

65. Meinecke, *Patterns of Stylistic Changes*; Meinecke, *Die mamlukische Architektur*; Meinecke, *Fayencedekorationen seldschukischer Sakralbauten*.

66. Bloom, *Paper before Print*; Roxburgh, "Timurid Architectural Revetment," 127–29.

67. Necipoğlu, "Plans and Models." For the use of architectural drawings in early fifteenth-century Ming China, see Campbell, *What the Emperor Built*, 24.

68. Redford, "Portable Palaces"; Hoffman and Redford, "Transculturation in the Eastern Mediterranean."

69. In a review essay published in 2010, Francesca Trivellato notes an expansion of scholarship that considers the Renaissance in a larger Mediterranean context, in which the relationships between the art market and trade as whole are central topics: Trivellato, "Renaissance Italy and the Muslim Mediterranean," 132–40. Further reframing of the Renaissance with perspectives that take into account the Islamic world appear in Darling, "Renaissance and the Middle East" and MacLean, "Introduction: Re-Orienting the Renaissance."

70. Jardine and Brotton, *Global Interests*, 8.

71. Necipoğlu, *Architecture, Ceremonial, and Power*; Necipoğlu, "Visual Cosmopolitanism"; Necipoğlu, "From Byzantine Constantinople to Ottoman Kostantiniyye"; Raby, "Mehmed the Conqueror's Greek Scriptorium"; Raby, "A Sultan of Paradox"; Raby, "Mehmed II Fatih and the Fatih Albums"; Raby, "Cyriacus of Ancona."

72. Necipoğlu, "Architectural Dialogues," 594–97.

73. Howard, *Venice & the East*.

74. On view at the Institut du Monde Arabe, Paris in 2006, and the Metropolitan Museum of Art, New York, in 2007: Carboni, ed., *Venice and the Islamic World*.

75. Necipoğlu, "Architectural Dialogues," 600; Naser Eslami, "Emulazione."

76. Necipoğlu, *Age of Sinan*, 84–88.

77. Jardine and Brotton, *Global Interests*, 8–9; Rodini, *Gentile Bellini's Portrait*.

78. Naser Eslami, "Emulazione," 155–59.

79. Necipoğlu, "Architectural Dialogues," 600; Naser Eslami, "Emulazione," 164–70, with Leonardo da Vinci's project shown in figure 12 and the Ottoman Turkish translation of his letter to Bayezid II in figure 13.

80. Howard, *Venice & the East*, 16.

81. Blessing, *Rebuilding Anatolia*, 173–79; Sinclair, "Venetian Merchants."

82. Pfeiffer, ed., *Politics, Patronage*.

83. Howard, *Venice & the East*, 15; Mack, *Bazaar to Piazza*.

84. Çizakça, "A Short History of the Bursa Silk Industry," 142.

85. Faroqhi, "Ottoman Textiles," 231, 235; Contadini, "Sharing a Taste?" 45; Mackie, *Symbols of Power*, 282–85. Raw silk was not produced locally until the late sixteenth century, and not in large quantity until the late seventeenth century: Contadini, "Sharing a Taste?" 45; Mackie, *Symbols of Power*, 282; Atasoy, Denny, and Mackie, *İpek*, 155–75; İnalcık, *Studies on the History of Textiles*.

86. Mackie, *Symbols of Power*, 284–85; Phillips, *Sea Change*, 112–19.

87. Mackie, *Symbols of Power*, 323; Contadini, "L'ornamento," 61–66.

88. Contadini, "Sharing a Taste?" 47.

89. Faroqhi, "Ottoman Textiles," 237; Contadini, "Sharing a Taste?" 47–48; Mackie, *Symbols of Power*, 324–27; comparative technical analysis in Sardjono, "Ottoman or Italian Velvets?"

90. Norton, "Blurring the Boundaries"; Contadini, "Sharing a Taste?"

91. Roxburgh, *The Persian Album*, chapter 1, section Perspectives on the Persian Album as Collection, Yale AAE e-book without page numbers.

92. Evliya Çelebi, *Seyahatnâme*, 2:13.

93. Key, *Language between God and the Poets*; Saba, "Abbasid Lusterwares"; Harb, *Arabic Poetics*; Rabbat, "ʿAjīb and Gharīb"; Mottahedeh, "ʿAjāʾib in *The Thousand and One Nights*"; Puerta Vílchez, *Historia del pensamiento estético árabe*, translated as Puerta Vílchez, *Aesthetics in Arabic Thought*.

94. Shaw, *What Is "Islamic" Art?*; Graves, *Arts of Allusion*; Rizvi, ed. *Affect, Emotion, and Subjectivity*; Ergin, "A Sound Status among the Ottoman Elite"; Ergin, "The Fragrance of the Divine"; Ergin, "The Soundscape of Sixteenth-Century Istanbul Mosques"; Ruggles, "Listening to Islamic Gardens and Landscapes"; Blessing, "The Vessel as Garden."

95. Binbaş, *Intellectual Networks*, 3–4. This vein of thinking is particularly visible in Bartol'd, *Ulugh Beg*.

96. Melvin-Koushki, "Early Modern Islamicate Empire," 354–56.

97. Markiewicz, *Crisis of Kingship*, 166–91; Melvin-Koushki, "Early Modern Islamicate Empire," 357–59, where the close connection to lettrism (ʿilm al-ḥurūf) is also discussed.

98. Lentz and Lowry, *Timur and the Princely Vision*, 303–04. For the extension into the Deccan, see Overton, "Introduction to Iranian Mobilities," 16–28. For architecture specifically, see Mondini, "Vague Traits"; and Blair and Bloom, "From Iran to the Deccan."

99. Feldman, *Diplomacy by Design*, 1.

100. Ibid., 2.

101. Schmidt, "Beautiful Style"; *The International Style*; Pächt, "Die Gotik der Zeit um 1400." Discussed in Feldman, *Diplomacy by Design*, 1–2.

102. Nethersole, "Review of Exhibition," 760–62.

103. Ibid., 763–64.

104. Pächt, "Die Gotik der Zeit um 1400," 53; Schmidt, "Beautiful Style," 105 and 111n1.

105. Feldman, *Diplomacy by Design*, 1–4.

106. Ibid., 8.

107. Necipoğlu, "From International Timurid to Ottoman"; Lentz and Lowry, *Timur and the Princely Vision*, 313–19.

108. Balafrej, *The Making of the Artist*, Roxburgh, "Kamal al-Din Bihzad."

109. Necipoğlu, "Early Modern Floral," 133.

110. Ibid., 143 and 149.

1 IMPERIAL AND LOCAL HORIZONS

1. Kritoboulos, *A History of Mehmed the Conqueror*, 141. On Mahmud Pasha see the comprehensive study in Stavrides, *Sultan of Vezirs*.

2. Mottahedeh, "ʿAjāʾib in *The Thousand and One Nights*"; Rabbat, "ʿAjīb and Gharīb"; Saba, "Abbasid Lusterware"; Harb, "Poetic Marvels"; Harb, *Arabic Poetics*.

3. Avcıoğlu, "Istanbul: The Palimpsest City," 189–93.

4. Necipoğlu, "International Timurid," 138; Ottoman Turkish text in Tacizâde Cafer Çelebi, *Heves-nâme*, ed. Sungur, 181, verse 248. On the author see Erünsal, "Tâcî-zâde Câfer Çelebi,"; Woodhead, "Cafer Çelebi, Tacizade," *EI3*; Erünsal, *Life and Works of Tâcî-zâde Caʿfer Çelebi*, XVII–XLVI.

5. O'Kane, "Poetry, Geometry and the Arabesque," 76–78; Kadoi, *Islamic Chinoiserie*, 43–49, 58–65; Akbarnia, "Khitâʾī: Cultural Memory," 10–11; Necipoğlu, "Early Modern Floral," 135.

6. On the development of the Timurid *kitabkhāna* see Lentz and Lowry, *Timur and the Princely Vision*, 159–236; Roxburgh, "Persianate Arts of the Book," 668–69, 682–85. The Ottomans used the term *nakkaşhane* for a similar type of workshop.

7. Necipoğlu, "International Timurid," 137–39; Necipoğlu, *Architecture, Ceremonial, and Power*, 216.

8. Necipoğlu, "International Timurid," 140–41. Black-line tiles were still used in the second quarter of the sixteenth century: see pages 141–43 and Figures 6–7, 9–15.

9. Necipoğlu, "International Timurid," 143, 148–52. On the emergence of these motifs see Denny, "Dating Ottoman Turkish Works in the *Saz* Style."

10. Necipoğlu, "International Timurid," 155–58; Lentz and Lowry, *Timur and the Princely Vision*, 315–18.

11. Binbaş, *Intellectual Networks*; on Idris-i Bidlisi, who moved from the Aqqoyunlu to the Ottoman court in the late fifteenth century, see Markiewicz, *Crisis of Kingship*. For the Ottoman context see Atçil, *Scholars and Sultans*.

12. The most comprehensive study of this transition with regard to architecture and urbanism is Kafescioğlu, *Constantinopolis/Istanbul*.

13. Necipoğlu, "Visual Cosmopolitanism," 3; Contadini and Norton, eds., *The Renaissance and the Ottoman World*; Brotton and Jardine, *Global Interests*, 76.

14. Raby, "A Sultan of Paradox"; Necipoğlu, "Visual Cosmopolitanism," 36. For the portrait (The National Gallery, London, inv. no. 3099) see Roxburgh, ed. *Turks*, cat. no. 226, pp. 273 and 434. On portrait medals of Mehmed II see Necipoğlu, "From Byzantine Constantinople to Ottoman Kostatiniyye," 271–73; Naser Eslami, "Emulazione," 146–47; Rodini, *Gentile Bellini's Portrait*, 29–31.

15. Necipoğlu, "Visual Cosmopolitanism," 1.

16. Neşri, *Cihânnümâ*, ed. Öztürk 278–79; ʿAşıkpaşazāde, *Âşıkpaşazâde Tarihi*, ed. Öztürk, 184–85, 184–85; Kastritsis, *An Early Ottoman History*, 173; Singer, "Enter, Riding on an Elephant," 100–03. As Amy Singer notes, the round trip would have taken about eighty-three days on horseback: Singer, "Enter, Riding on an Elephant," 102n48.

17. İnalcık, "Meḥemmed II," *EI2*; Ventzke, "Dulkadir," *EI3*; on the debate regarding the date see Singer, "Enter, Riding on an Elephant," 102. Babinger argued for 1449; see Babinger, "Mehmed's II. Heirat," 224–26.

18. Biblioteca Nazionale Marciana, Venice, Gr. 516, fols. 2v–3r: Redford, "Byzantium and the Islamic World," 388 and 394–95; Singer, "Enter, Riding on an Elephant," 89–90 and 100–101.

19. Danalı Cantarella, "Art, Science, and Neoplatonic Cosmology," 30–79. I thank Merih Danalı for sharing her unpublished work with me.

20. Necipoğlu, "Visual Cosmopolitanism," 2.

21. Ibid., 2; Reindl-Kiel, "Rum Mehmed Paşa."

22. Blessing, "All Quiet on the Eastern Frontier?" 211–14.

23. Kastritsis, *An Early Ottoman History*, 162–63.

24. Necipoğlu, "Visual Cosmopolitanism," 3. For Murad I's court and Italy, see Saygın Salgırlı, "Alternative Narratives of Medieval Mediterranean Architecture: The Play of the Local and the Global in Fourteenth-Century Ottoman Bursa," unpublished paper presented at the College Art Association Annual Conference, New York, February 12, 2015.

25. Raby, "A Sultan of Paradox"; Raby, "Mehmed the Conqueror's Greek Scriptorium."

26. Ruggles, "Listening to Islamic Gardens."

27. Necipoğlu, "Virtual Archaeology," 333–34.

28. Ibid., 334. In Ottoman Turkish: "ve bu bağçe içinde, tavr-ı ekâsir üzre bir sırça sarây-ı." Tursun Beğ, *Târîh-i Ebü'l-Feth*, ed. Tulum, 74.

29. Necipoğlu, "Virtual Archaeology," 334–36.

30. Ibid., 334, and Figure 11. The pavilions are shown in the lower left corner of the painting.

31. Ibid., 325; Necipoğlu, *Architecture, Ceremonial, and Power*, 217. The poem is published in *Ahmed Paşa Divanı*, ed. Tarlan, 23–32.

32. On water in Roman, late antique, and Byzantine contexts, see Barry, "Walking on Water"; for a similar concept in Islamic architecture, see Milwright, "Waves of the Sea."

33. Necipoğlu, *Architecture, Ceremonial, and Power*, 213, notes that Franz Babinger mentions a now-lost inscription that recorded the start of construction in 870 AH / 1465–66 CE; see Babinger, *Mehmed the Conqueror*, 246, 467. Miller, *Beyond the Sublime Porte*, 33, mentions the inscription without citing it.

34. Necipoğlu, *Architecture, Ceremonial, and Power*, 213. On Angiolello, see Piemontese, "Angiolello, Giovanni Maria."

35. Yüksel Muslu, *The Ottomans and the Mamluks*, 7; Amitai, *Mongols and Mamluks*, 157–78.

36. This Ottoman princess, named Nefise Hatun or Melike Hatun, commissioned the Hatuniye Madrasa in Karaman in 1381–82; see Blessing, "All Quiet on the Eastern Frontier?" 211–14. On the marriage, see also Yüksel Muslu, *The Ottomans and the Mamluks*, 70–71; Meinecke, *Fayencedekorationen*, 2:166. One of the last dynastic marriages was likely that of Bayezid II's daughter ʿAyn-ı Şah to Ahmad b. Ughurlu Muhammad, a prince of the Aqqoyunlu Bayandur clan. Crucially, the prince was the son of Mehmed II's daughter Gevher, and hence Bayezid II's nephew, and had been raised at the Ottoman court, so perhaps the marriage between cousins served to affirm the family bond: Markiewicz, *Crisis of Kingship*, 62 and Uluçay, *Padişahların Kadınları ve Kızları*, 48.

37. Peirce, *Imperial Harem*, 28–39.

38. Yıldız, "Razing Gevele," 308.

39. ibid., 309–11; Kramers, "Ḳaramān-Oghlu," 749 and 751; Uzunçarşılı, *Anadolu Beylikleri*, 30–33. A brother, Ishaq, held the remaining lands with the support of the Aqqoyulu; see Yıldız, "Razing Gevele," 317; and Yüksel Muslu, *The Ottomans and the Mamluks*, 122–24; Uzunçarşılı, *Anadolu Beylikleri*, 33–34.

40. Yıldız, "Razing Gevele," 311.

41. Şikari, *Şikâri'nin Karaman Oğulları Tarihi*, 196–97.

42. Ayverdi, *Fatih Devri*, 4:737–39; Necipoğlu, *Architecture, Ceremonial, and Power*, 216.

43. Surveys of these monuments in Otto-Dorn, "Seldschukische Holzsäulenmoscheen" and Hayes, "The Wooden Hypostyle Mosques"; on the Aslanhane in Ankara, see Blessing, "All Quiet on the Eastern Frontier?" 205–07, and Blessing, *Rebuilding Anatolia*, 192–97.

44. Redford, *Landscape and the State*, 56–58; McClary, *Rum Seljuq Architecture*, 28–32; Kuniholm, "Dendrochronologically Dated Ottoman Monuments," 132–33. For recent archaeological evidence for additional pavilions along the same citadel wall, see Çelebi, "Konya İç Kalesi ve Anadolu Selçuklu Sarayı." I thank Richard P. McClary for sharing his observations from a visit to the site in September 2020 with me.

45. Redford, *Landscape and the State*, 30–52, catalog of sites in the hinterland of Alanya, 139–293.

46. On the importance of garden settings for medieval and early modern Persianate palaces, see Wilber, "The Timurid Court" and O'Kane, "From Tents to Pavilions." On the buildings in Isfahan, see Babaie, *Isfahan and Its Palaces*, 186–206.

47. Necipoğlu, *Architecture, Ceremonial and Power*, 213–15.

48. Necipoğlu, "Visual Cosmopolitanism," 19.

49. Nora, "Between Memory and History."

50. A partial translation in O'Kane, *The Appearance of Persian*, 145, ends here.

51. تحكي همة البناني المباني An almost identical phrase in Arabic appears in the foundation inscription of the Muradiye mosque in Edirne: (إنَّ المباني تحكي همةَ البناني) see Blessing, "Blue-and-White Tiles," 104). While تحكي also means "speaks," here it is best translated as "reflects." I thank Lara Harb for this suggestion.

52. بنيان معلاى پايهِ اين قصر فلك كه از فرط علو دست در كمر جوزا زند خضيض ساحتش بروج فرق فرقدان و سقف كيوان أعلى شرف بخشد مانند قبهِ زمرّدين از آسمان زرين كه بكتابهِ كواكب تزيين يابد وصحن پيروزهِ زمين كه بازهار گوناگون ونقوش بوقلمون نزهت جاى خلد بزين كردد بفر عز دولت خاقانى و يمن همم سايه يزدانى و بحكم آن المباني تحكي همة البناني شرف إتمام يافت در أواخر ماه ربيع الآخر در تاريخ سنة سبع و سبعين ثمانمائة

Author's translation, based on photographs of the inscription, on the printed Persian text in Ayverdi, *Fatih Devri*, 4:754, and on the partial English translation in O'Kane, *The Appearance of Persian*, 145. An alternate English translation that I was not able to consult until the final stages of this project is in Kolsuk, "Turkish Tiles," 58.

53. Necipoğlu, *Architecture, Ceremonial and Power*, 216.

54. Ibid., 217. On ekphrastic poetry praising palaces in Persian, see Meisami, "Palaces and Paradises."

55. Şen, "Reading the Stars," 572–73. For new framing of how to address these and other sciences deemed occult, see Melvin-Koushki, "Toward a Neopythagorean History."

56. Bloom, "The 'Qubbat al-Khaḍrā.'"

57. Ibid., 138–39.

58. Huisman, "Abū Kalamūn."

59. Saba, "Abbasid Lusterwares."

60. Fouchecour, Doerfer, and Stoetzer "Rubāʿī (pl. Rubāʿiyyāt)."

61. This hemistich alludes to Qur'an 36:78 (من يحيي العظام وهي رميم); in English translation: Who will quicken the bones when they have decayed?). I thank Lara Harb for spotting a mistake in my earlier reading and for identifying this passage. Ayverdi, *Fatih Devri*, 4:755, mistakenly reads الغظام

62. أي درت پيشگاه خلد نعيم حرمت كشته محترم چو حريم أز لطافت هواي بقعهِ تو كاد يحيي العظام و هي رميم

أز كرامت پيشكاهش قبلهِ أرباب ملك وآز سعادت آستانش قبله كاهي أهل دين مطلع خرشيد رفعت مشرق صبح مراد نور چشم آسمان و زينت روى زمين

Author's reading based on own photographs of the inscription and the printed Persian text in Ayverdi, *Fatih Devri*, 4:755. I thank Lara Harb for important corrections to my translation.

63. See note 62.

64. "Perde-dâri mî-küned der tâq-ı kisrâ ankebût; bûm nevbet mî-zened der kalʿa-i Efrâsiyâb," Tursun Beğ, *Târîh-i Ebü'l-Feth*, ed. Tulum, 64. The verse is skipped in the abbreviated English translation, Tursun Beğ, *The History of Mehmed the Conqueror*, ed.

and trans. İnalcık and Murphey, 37. The poem is often attributed to Saʿdi Shirazi in a variant in Persian: پرده داری می کند در قصر قیصر عنکبوت بوم نوبت ی زند بر گنبد افراسیاب The term "tāq-ı kisrā" can also refer to the Sasanian palace of Ctesiphon in present-day Iraq, a monument much admired in Islamic poetry as early as the ninth century: Ali, *Arabic Literary Salons*, 153–70; Sperl, "Crossing Enemy Boundaries."

65. O'Kane, *The Appearance of Persian*, 41. The medallion with the verses is now in the Museum of Islamic Art in Berlin, object record at www.smb-digital.de/eMuseumPlus?service=ExternalInterface&module=collection&objectId=1525426&viewType=detailView (accessed November 22, 2019).

66. Losensky, "Square as a Bubble," 44.

67. Roxburgh, "Timurid Architectural Revetment," 129.

68. Ibid., 122–23. Jonathan Bloom notes that the earliest evidence for the use of paper models dates to the fourteenth century and that this practice was consolidated by the fifteenth century: Bloom, *Paper before Print*, 191–92. The cutting of tile shapes is mentioned in a report from the Timurid workshop found in the album TSMK, H.2153, fol. 98a, translation and Persian text in Thackston, *Album Prefaces*, 43–46, at 45.

69. Roxburgh, "Timurid Architectural Revetment," 120–22; Necipoğlu, *Architecture, Ceremonial, and Power*, 214.

70. Roxburgh, "Timurid Architectural Revetment," 127–28, and fig. 10.8 for an epigraphic design with two intersecting inscriptions on a floral background, TSMK, H.2125, fol. 22a, Herat before 1447 (?). For the impact of increasingly centralized workshops on the development of modes of ornament in the early sixteenth-century Ottoman and Safavid realms, see Necipoğlu, "Early Modern Floral," 133–34.

71. Roxburgh, "Timurid Architectural Revetment," 127.

72. Blessing, "Seljuk Past and Timurid Present," fig. 14.

73. *Bahram Gur and the Indian Princess in the Dark Palace on Saturday*, fol. 23v from a Haft Paykar (Seven Portraits) of the *Khamsa* of Nizami, copied circa 1430 in Herat. Ink, opaque watercolor, and gold on paper, painting dimensions H. 8 1/2 in. (21.6 cm), Metropolitan Museum of Art, New York, Gift of Alexander Smith Cochran, 1913, inv. no. 13.228.13.4, object record at www.metmuseum.org/art/collection/search/455057 (accessed February 17, 2021). I thank Meghan Montgomery for bringing this painting to my attention.

74. Meinecke, *Fayencedekorationen*, 1:93–96.

75. Blessing, "All Quiet on the Eastern Frontier?" 202. On the historical context, see Zachariadou, "Manuel II Palaeologos."

76. Blessing, "All Quiet on the Eastern Frontier?" 207–09.

77. Blessing, *Rebuilding Anatolia*, 77–89, 104–15; McClary, *Rum Seljuq Architecture*, 91–178.

78. Gabriel, *Monuments turcs*, 1:67–70 and plate XIX; Blessing, "All Quiet on the Eastern Frontier?" 209–11; Durukan, "Köşkmedrese."

79. Blessing, "Buildings of Commemoration," 230–38; Yalman, "The 'Dual Identity' of Mahperi Khatun," 237–40.

80. Gabriel, *Voyages archéologiques*, plate XLVIII; Meinecke, *Fayencedekorationen*, 1:96–97, and 2:cat. 43.

81. Diez, Aslanapa, and Koman, *Karaman Devri Sanatı*, 82–84; Meinecke, *Fayencedekorationen*, 2:166; Blessing, "All Quiet on the Eastern Frontier?" 211–14.

82. Blessing, *Rebuilding Anatolia*, 39–47.

83. Ibid., 63, 93–94.

84. Ibid., 30–121.

85. Ibid., 71–73, 165–203. On patronage in Ilkhanid Iran, see Pfeiffer, ed. *Politics, Patronage, and the Transmission of Knowledge*; Wilber, *The Architecture of Islamic Iran*; Blair, "The Mongol Capital of Sulṭāniyya."

86. Aube, *La céramique dans l'architecture en Iran au XVe siècle*, 195–201; Mahi, "Les 'Maîtres de Tabriz,'" 39–40.

87. Necipoğlu, *Age of Sinan*, 79; Necipoğlu, "Virtual Cosmopolitanism," 3–4.

88. Kafescioğlu, *Constantinopolis/Istanbul*, 62.

89. Kırımlı, "İstanbul Çiniciliği," 96–97, and facsimile of the document, TSMA, E. 3152, ibid., 106; Necipoğlu, "International Timurid," 137–38. Printed Persian text and French translation in Mahi, "Les 'Maîtres de Tabriz,'" 64.

90. Kafescioğlu, *Constantinopolis/Istanbul*.

91. Restoration was ongoing in summer 2019. I was unable to travel to Turkey in spring and summer 2020 due to the COVID-19 pandemic.

92. Ayverdi, *Osmanlı Mi'mârisinde Fâtih Devri*, 3:363–68; Kafescioğlu, *Constantinopolis/Istanbul*, 75–82. On restorations in the aftermath of the 1766 Istanbul earthquake, see Mazlum, *1766 İstanbul Depremi*.

93. Aube, *La céramique dans l'architecture en Iran au XVᵉ siècle*, 203; Blessing, "Blue-and-White Tiles," 110–11, noting that these panels too are probably the result of reassembling fragments after earthquake damage.

94. Denny, "Dating Ottoman Works in the Saz Style."

95. Identified as the Throne Verse without specifying the exact section of the text in Ayverdi, *Fâtih Devri*, 3:379 and caption to unnumbered color plate, ibid., 368–69.

96. Tacizāde Cafer Çelebi, *Heves-nâme*, ed. Sungur, 181, verse 248.

97. For a discussion of ekphrasis in the medieval Islamic world, see Graves, *Arts of Allusion*, 204–10. On şehrengīz, see Bernardini, "The *masnavī-shahrāshūb*s as Town Panegyrics"; Bernardini, "Lo *Şehrengīz-i Borūsā* di Lāmi'ī Çelebī"; specifically in Ottoman literature, see Tacizāde Cafer Çelebi, *Heves-nâme*, ed. Sungur, 5–25.

98. Tacizāde Cafer Çelebi, *Heves-nâme*, ed. Sungur, 165–97, verses 104–417. The Hagia Sophia is also praised as a model for Mehmed II's mosque in Istanbul in Tursun Beğ, *Târīh-i Ebü'l-Feth*, ed. Tulum, 70.

99. Tacizāde Cafer Çelebi, *Heves-nâme*, ed. Sungur, 170, verses 150–51; 171, verse 159; 172, verse 168; 173, verse 172.

100. Ibid., 172, verse 165.

101. Ibid., 171, verses 152–53.

102. Ibid., 172, verse 171; 182, verse 263; 184, verse 285.

103. Ibid., 17, verses 160–61.

104. Ibid., 174, verse 204.

105. Ibid., 174–75, verses 204–12.

106. Ibid., 180, verse 239.

107. For the doors, see ibid., 181, verses 250–51.

108. Ibid., 184–85, verses 284–91.

109. Necipoğlu, *The Age of Sinan*, 82, 87–88.

110. Necipoğlu, "Visual Cosmopolitanism."

111. Stavrides, *Sultan of Vezirs*, 181–84; Kafescioğlu, *Constantinopolis/Istanbul*, 110.

112. Stavrides, *Sultan of Vezirs*, 271; Kafescioğlu, *Constantinopolis/Istanbul*, 110.

113. Stavrides, *Sultan of Vezirs*, 267–77; Kafescioğlu, *Constantinopolis/Istanbul*, 109–10.

114. Stavrides, *Sultan of Vezirs*, 277.

115. On the museum, see http://naim.bg/en/content/category/300/54, accessed November 27, 2018; Stavrides, *Sultan of Vezirs*, 279. On the Mahmud Pasha mosque in Sofia and its relationship to Renaissance architecture, see Hartmuth, "Architecture, Change, and Discontent."

116. Stavrides, *Sultan of Vezirs*, 279–80.

117. Ibid., 283–84. For later copies of Mahmud Pasha's endowments, see Ünver, "Mahmud Paşa Vakıfları ve Ekleri." Kafescioğlu, *Constantinopolis/Istanbul*, 110n160, notes that the original fifteenth-century documents have not been found.

118. See Chapter 2 for a discussion of the term *T-plan* and its historiography.

119. See plan in Kafescioğlu, *Constantinopolis/Istanbul*, 111, no. 1. Restorations in the Mahmud Pasha Mosque begun in 2012 and ongoing as of summer 2019 prevented me from studying the building in detail. Due to the COVID-19 pandemic, I was unable to complete a planned site visit in summer 2020.

120. Kafescioğlu, *Constantinopolis/Istanbul*, 110–13; Kafescioğlu, "Lives and Afterlives of an Urban Institution," 275–79.

121. Kafescioğlu, *Constantinopolis/Istanbul*, 113.

122. Kafescioğlu, "Lives and Afterlives of an Urban Institution," 273–80.

123. Kafescioğlu, *Constantinopolis/Istanbul*, 110.

124. All three grandees' projects are examined in Kafescioğlu, *Constantinopolis/Istanbul*, 109–29.

125. Ayverdi, *Fatih Devri Mimarisi*, 4:602.

126. Author's translation after the inscription itself. Turkish translation, with a possible mistake, in Delibaş, *Kitabelerin Kitabı*, 307; printed Arabic text in Ayverdi, *Fatih Devri Mimarisi*, 4:606.

127. Kafescioğlu, *Constantinopolis/Istanbul*, 107, fig. 75.

128. Macaraig, *Çemberlitaş Hamami*, chapter 4, on social functions of hammams.

129. Plan, section, and elevation drawings in Ayaşlıoğlu, "İstanbul'da Mahmud Paşa Türbesi," 152–54.

130. Kafescioğlu, *Constantinopolis/Istanbul*, 114.

131. Lu and Steinhard, "Decagonal and Quasicrystalline Tilings," fig. 1.

132. Necipoğlu, *The Topkapı Scroll*, 97–100; Tabbaa, *The Transformation of Islamic Art during the Sunni Revival*, 73–192; Necipoğlu, "Ornamental Geometries," 24–31.

133. Necipoğlu, *The Topkapı Scroll*, 111–12.

134. Ibid., 9. Rather than being a single scroll, the Topkapı Scroll was pieced together from fragments of various scrolls at an unknown date, totaling a length of 29.5 m: ibid., 31.

135. On nineteenth-century examples from Iran and their use, see Carey, "In the Absence of Originals," and Necipoğlu, *The Topkapı Scroll*, 14 and 43–48.

136. Necipoğlu, *The Topkapı Scroll*, 12 and 171–73, for adaptation of designs over time.

137. Dold-Samplonius and Harmsen, "The Muqarnas Plate found at Takht-i Sulayman"; Ghazarian and Ousterhout, "A Muqarnas Drawing."

138. Ingold, *Making*, 43.

139. Hay, "The Passage of the Other," 68.

140. Hartmuth, "Ottoman Architecture in the Republic of Macedonia," 4.

141. On İshak Beğ and the role of *zāviye*s in fifteenth-century Skopje, see Hartmuth, "Late Fifteenth-Century Change," 4–6; Hartmuth, "Ottoman Architecture in the Republic of Macedonia," 2–3.

142. Hartmuth, "Building the Ottoman City," 4–5.

143. Necipoğlu, ed., *The Arts of Ornamental Geometry*.

144. Necipoğlu, "Ornamental Geometries," 6–7.

145. Hogendijk, "A Mathematical Classification of Contents," 152.

146. Meinecke, *Patterns of Stylistic Changes*.

147. Meinecke, *Fayencedekorationen*, 1:93–96 and 2:165–75, 374–82.

148. Atasoy and Raby, *Iznik*, 82–83; Aslanapa, "Pottery and Kilns"; Demirsar Arlı, "İznik Çini Fırınları."

2   IMMERSIVE SPACE

1. While two of the main buildings are known today as Yeşil Cami (Green Mosque) and Yeşil Türbe (Green Mausoleum), I refer to them as the mosque-*zāviye* and mausoleum of Mehmed I. The name Yeşil İmâret appears in Evliya Çelebi's seventeenth-century account: Evliya Çelebi, *Seyahatnâme*, 2:13.

2. Kastritsis, *The Sons of Bayezid*, 41. On the historical myths surrounding the sultan's time as Timur's prisoner, see Milwright and Baboula, "Bayezid's Cage."

3. Pancaroğlu, "Architecture, Landscape, and Patronage"; Ousterhout, "The East, the West, and the Appropriation of the Past"; Ousterhout, "Ethnic Identity"; Çağaptay, "Frontierscape"; Çağaptay, *The First Capital*.

4. Historiographical overview in Çağaptay, "Frontierscape," 158–62; Çağaptay, *The First Capital*, 69–77; Kafescioğlu, "Lives and Afterlives of an Urban Institution," 255–60. On the problem of nationalist narratives for the study of medieval Anatolia, see Pancaroğlu, "Formalism."

5. Darling, "Introduction: Ottoman Identity"; Darling, "Political Literature."

6. Pancaroğlu, "Formalism"; Redford, "What Have You Done for Anatolia Today?"; Blessing, *Rebuilding Anatolia*, 1–7.

7. Redford, "The Alaeddin Mosque"; Yalman, "Ala al-Din Kayqubad Illuminated"; Yalman, "Building the Sultanate of Rum."

8. Rogers, "Patronage in Seljuk Anatolia"; Crane, "Notes on Saldjūq Architectural Patronage"; Blessing, *Rebuilding Anatolia*, esp. 21–25, 73–74, 77–98, 104–15.

9. Blessing, "All Quiet on the Eastern Frontier?" 200–202; Yıldız, "Post-Mongol Pastoral Polities."

10. Kastritsis, *The Sons of Bayezid*, 2.

11. For the complex context of Anatolian *beyliks*' absorption into the Ottoman Empire, see Uzunçarşılı, *Anadolu Beylikleri*, 1–179.

12. Venzke, "Dulkadir"; Wing, "Submission, Defiance, and the Rules of Politics." On the architectural patronage of the Dulkadir, see Gündoğdu, *Dulkadırlı Beyliği Mimarisi*.

13. Venzke, "Dulkadir." For the extent of the Ottoman territory at Mehmed II's death in 1481, see Kafescioğlu, *Constantinopolis/Istanbul*, fig. 1.

14. Çağaptay, *The First Capital*, 62–65; Gündüz Küskü, *Osmanlı Beyliği*, 202–03.

15. Necipoğlu, *Age of Sinan*, 78; Yüksel Muslu, *The Ottomans and the Mamluks*, 68–85; Çağaptay, *The First Capital*, 53–59.

16. Ersoy, "Bergama Ulu Camii"; Kiel, "Cross-Cultural Contacts," 72–73.

17. Castelnuovo and Ginzburg, "Symbolic Domination."

18. Kaufmann, *Toward a Geography of Art*, 1–13; Campbell, "Artistic Geographies."

19. Lentz and Lowry, *Timur and the Princely Vision*.

20. Castelnuovo and Ginzburg, "Symbolic Domination," 11; Meinecke, *Patterns of Stylistic Changes*, 1–3, 89–91.

21. For a rare late fifteenth-century pattern scroll, probably from Central Asia, see Necipoğlu, *The Topkapı Scroll*.

22. Çağaptay, "Frontierscape," 172–79; Çağaptay, *The First Capital*, 54–58; Kuran, *Mosque in Early Ottoman Architecture*, 98 and 102–04; Ayverdi, *Osmanlı Mimârîsinin İlk Devri*, 231–64. On the 1855 earthquake, see Çağaptay, "Depremler, Arkeoloji ve Bursa'nın Erken Osmanlı Dönemin Arkeolojisi"; and Çağaptay, "Results of the Tophane Area GPR Surveys."

23. Kuran, *Mosque in Early Ottoman Architecture*, 102–04, 111–13, 120–23.

24. Overview in Yavaş, "Yeşilcami Külliyesi." The *waqfīya*, dating to 822 AH / 1419 CE, is preserved as İ.B.B. Atatürk Kitaplığı (hereafter İ.B.B.AK.), MC_Fr_000005, and accessible at http://ataturkkitapligi.ibb.gov.tr/kutuphane3/Fermanlar/MC_Fr_000005.pdf (last accessed May 22, 2020); a facsimile and a brief summary of contents are published in Öcalan, Sevim, and Yavaş, *Bursa Vakfiyeleri I*, 300–27.

25. İ.B.B.AK., MC_Fr_000005.

26. Taeschner, "Die Ješil Ǧami," 145; Mantran, "Les inscriptions arabes de Brousse," 105, no. 31.

27. Necipoğlu, "Dynastic Imprint," 27, 33–34.

28. Taeschner, "Die Ješil Ǧami," 143–44, see also note 143 of this chapter.

29. İ.B.B.AK., MC_Fr_000005, lines 38–40.

30. Bernus-Taylor, "Le décor du 'Complexe Vert' à Bursa," 252; Gabriel, *Une capitale turque*, 1:81; Kafescioğlu, *Constantinopolis/Istanbul*, 240n49.

31. İ.B.B.AK., MC_Fr_000005, lines 43–195. The *waqfīya* extends over 260 lines on a scroll measuring 32 cm x 740 cm.

32. İ.B.B.AK., MC_Fr_000005, lines 208–34. In the early fifteenth-century context, *mi'mār* should not be translated as architect but rather as someone responsible for repairs and maintenance, as is further discussed in Chapter 3.

33. İ.B.B.AK., MC_Fr_000005, lines 202–05.

34. I thank Alexander Key for suggesting this formulation.

35. Mantran, "Les inscriptions arabes de Brousse," 92, no. 6; Taeschner, "Die Ješil Ǧami," 140–42; Kunter, "Kitâbelerimiz," 439; İ.B.B.AK., MC_Fr_000005, line 38.

36. Taeschner, "Die Ješil Ǧami," 141n4. Pancaroğlu, "Bursa Yeşil Cami İnşa Kitabesinde Hiyerarşik İmgeleme," 178, notes that the inscription's scope is exceptional for its time.

37. Necipoğlu, *The Age of Sinan*, 49; Kafescioğlu, "Lives and Afterlives of an Urban Institution," 257.

38. In the Ilkhanid Yakutiye Madrasa (dated 710 AH / 1310 CE) in Erzurum, the term *buq'at* is used in the *waqf* inscription in the interior, while the foundation inscription on the portal contains the term *madfan* (place of burial), pointing to the attached mausoleum: Blessing, *Rebuilding Anatolia*, 142–58.

39. "I" here is a lyric device rather than being indicative of a specific speaker.

40. A play on words with *nusikhat*, although both words are written so similarly that one is inclined to read *nusikhat* in both instances.

41. In this place, the term *sanat* (year) would be more usual. Taeschner notes that the use of the word might be an error, but nevertheless uses the translation "Pilgerfahrt" (pilgrimage) for *hijjat*: Taeschner, "Die Ješil Ǧami," 141–42; Kunter translates it as year: Kunter, "Kitâbelerimiz," 439.

42. Graves, *Arts of Allusion*, 144–45. For a detailed analysis of eleventh-century Arabic poetics, see Key, *Language between God and the Poets*.

43. Graves, *Arts of Allusion*, 144.

44. Ibid., 42–50, 144–50. For such metaphors in Persian poetry, see Clinton, "Esthetics by Implication."

45. Necipoğlu, *The Topkapı Scroll*, 185; Güleç, "Sürûrî."

46. The phrase "of the Arabs and non-Arabs" is more common.

47. Pancaroğlu notes aspects of political competition manifested in the inscription: Pancaroğlu, "Bursa Yeşil Cami İnşa Kitabesinde Hiyerarşik İmgeleme," 179–80.

48. Ayverdi, *Osmanlı Mimârîsinde Çelebi ve II. Sultan Murad Devri*, 74–75.

49. Full Arabic text with identification of hadith and Qur'an passages in Ayverdi, *Osmanlı Mimârîsinde Çelebi ve II. Sultan Murad Devri*, 71–74.

50. İ.B.B.A.K., MC_Fr_000005, lines 202–05.

51. Ayverdi, *Osmanlı Mimârîsinde Çelebi ve II. Sultan Murad Devri*, 74.

52. I thank one of the anonymous reviewers for Cambridge University Press for suggesting this line of argument.

53. Aptullah Kuran coins the term "*eyvan* mosque" and provides an overview of such structures in *Mosque in Early Ottoman Architecture*, 71–72. Critical discussion of the various terms is found in Çağaptay, "Frontierscape," 158; Kafescioğlu, "Lives and Afterlives of an Urban Institution," 255–60; Pancaroğlu, "Bursa Yeşil Cami İnşa Kitabesinde Hiyerarşik İmgeleme," 183; Necipoğlu, *The Age of Sinan*, 49–50.

54. For discussion of the available literature and introduction of the term "multipurpose mosque," see Salgırlı, "Architectural Anatomy," 318n27.

55. Eyice, "İlk Osmanlı Devrinin Dini İçtimai Bir Müessesesi," 4–9, 22–25.

56. Barkan, "Osmanlı İmparatorluğunda."

57. VGMA defter no. 989, sayfa 116–17, sıra 82, summary and printed Arabic text in Eren, Oğuz, and Mete, eds., *Balkanlar'da Osmanlı Vakıfları: Vakfiyeler, Yunanistan*, 3:440–42, facsimile of the document in 5:510.

58. Salgırlı, "Radicalizing Premodern Space," 54–56.

59. Kafescioğlu, "Lives and Afterlives of an Urban Institution," 262–63.

60. Çağaptay, *The First Capital*, 71–72.

61. See Chapter 1 for Mahmud Pasha and Chapter 3 for Bayezid Pasha and Yörgüç Pasha. Hajji 'Ivaz Pasha is discussed later in this chapter.

62. Uzunçarşılı, *Çandarlı Vezir Ailesi*, 78–84; Necipoğlu, *The Age of Sinan*, 50.

63. On the development of madrasa education in the Ottoman Empire, see Atçıl, *Scholars and Sultans* and Atçıl, "Mobility of Scholars."

64. For the development of Sufism in the fifteenth-century Ottoman Empire, see Yürekli, *Architecture and Hagiography*; Karamustafa, *God's Unruly Friends*, 65–84; Karamustafa, "Origins of Anatolian Sufism." The fundamental study of Sufis' role in Ottoman expansion remains Barkan, "Osmanlı İmparatorluğunda."

65. Necipoğlu, *The Age of Sinan*, 55–57; Eyice, "İlk Osmanlı Devrinin Dini İçtimai Bir Müessesesi," 4, 53; Kafescioğlu, "Lives and Afterlives of an Urban Institution," 287–91.

66. Eyice, "İlk Osmanlı Devrinin Dini İçtimai Bir Müessesesi," 12–14; Kuran, *Mosque in Early Ottoman Architecture*, 72, 114–19.

67. Eyice, "İlk Osmanlı Devrinin Dini İçtimai Bir Müessesesi," 19–22; Çağaptay, *The First Capital*, 72–73.

68. Blessing, "Buildings of Commemoration."

69. Çağaptay, "Frontierscape," 158.

70. Yürekli, "Architectural Patronage," 746.

71. Gabriel, *Une capitale turque*, 1:86.

72. Ayverdi, *Osmanlı Mimârîsinde Çelebi ve II. Sultan Murad Devri*, fig. 169; Gabriel, *Une capitale turque*, 1:94 and fig. 29.

73. The mausolea of Osman, Orhan, Murad I, and Bayezid I were destroyed in the 1855 earthquake and rebuilt afterward: Gabriel, *Une capitale turque*, 1:43, 61–62, 75; Eyice, "Bursa'da Osman ve Orhan Gazi Türbeleri." As I show in Chapter 4, the absence of this feature in other mausolea is closely tied to changes in funerary practices in the second quarter of the fifteenth century.

74. Atçıl, *Scholars and Sultans*, 36 and 150–51; Bilge, *İlk Osmanlı Medreseleri*, 117. The *waqfīya* does not designate the building with this name.

75. Bilge, *İlk Osmanlı Medreseleri*, 120; Deliçay, "Mehmed Şah Fenârî."

76. Bilge, *İlk Osmanlı Medreseleri*, 121; Atçıl, *Scholars and Sultans*, 60n5 and 81. Some of these madrasas, including the Zeyrek Madrasa, lost their functions as imperial places of education after the construction of the Sahn Madrasas in the 1470s: Kafescioğlu, *Constantinopolis/Istanbul*, 22.

77. Aşkar, "Osmanlı Devletinde Alim-Mutasavvıf Prototipi." For scholars and Sufis in thirteenth-century Konya, see Blessing, *Rebuilding Anatolia*, 30–53. For the presence of dervishes in fifteenth-century mosque-*zâviyes*, see Eyice, "İlk Osmanlı Devrinin Dini İçtimai Bir Müessesesi," 22–25.

78. Yılmaz, *Caliphate Redefined*, 238–49.

79. Pancaroğlu, "Architecture, Landscape, and Patronage," 42, 45.

80. Necipoğlu, "Visual Cosmopolitanism," 23–25; Pancaroğlu, "Architecture, Landscape, and Patronage," 45; Kafescioğlu, *Constantinopolis/Istanbul*, 68–70.

81. Kastritsis, *The Sons of Bayezid*, 2, 41–50; see 129–94 for Musa's military actions once he became a major actor in the conflict.

82. Kastritsis, *The Sons of Bayezid*, 2–3, 41.

83. Kiel, "Selânik."

84. Balivet, *Islam mystique et révolution armée*, 84–85, 90.

85. Kastritsis, *The Sons of Bayezid*, 2–3, 82. Balivet, *Islam mystique et révolution armée*, 90. In a case of "*gazi*–dervish networking," 'Aşıkpaşazāde joined Murad II's campaign in the retinue of Mihailoğlu Mehmed Beğ: Kafadar, *Between Two Worlds*, 102.

86. Melvin-Koushki, "Early Modern Islamicate Empire," 360; Kastritsis, *The Sons of Bayezid*, 2–3, 9, 160–64; Kafadar, *Between Two Worlds*, 143; Balivet, *Islam mystique et révolution armée*, 38–41; *Islam mystique et révolution armée*, 38–41; Kastritsis, "The Şeyh Bedreddin Uprising." On Şeyh Bedreddin's education, including a long stay in Cairo from circa 1382 to 1405 (with a brief interruption), where he morphed from '*ālim* to Sufi, see Balivet, *Islam mystique et révolution armée*, 41–53.

87. Kastritsis, *The Sons of Bayezid*, 38; Balivet, *Islam mystique et révolution armée*, 57, 80–82. On Börklüce Mustafa, see Balivet, *Islam mystique et révolution armée*, 74–79.

88. Balivet, *Islam mystique et révolution armée*, 82–87. See Salgırlı, "Architectural Anatomy," for a spatial analysis of Şeyh Bedreddin's execution, albeit with a problematic focus on the "lord–tenant relationship" as a cause for the rebellion, which does not do justice to the complexity of the event.

89. Kastritsis, *The Sons of Bayezid*, 26–27, 45–50, 77–81, 84.

90. Pancaroğlu, "Architecture, Landscape, and Patronage," 41; Eyice, "Bursa'da Osman ve Orhan Gazi Türbeleri"; Çağaptay, "Prousa/Bursa," 52–62.

91. Çağaptay, "Frontierscape," 62–65, 157–58, 164; Çağaptay, *The First Capital*, 1–46; Pancaroğlu, "Architecture, Landscape, and Patronage," 47.

92. Kuran, "A Spatial Study of Three Ottoman Capitals," 114–18; Pancaroğlu, "Architecture, Landscape, and Patronage"; Çağaptay, "Prousa/Bursa."

93. Kuran, "Spatial Study of Three Ottoman Capitals," 117–18; Pancaroğlu, "Architecture, Landscape, and Patronage," 41–46; Kafescioğlu, *Constantinopolis/Istanbul*, 70; Çağaptay, *The First Capital*, 79–95. Similarly, funerary complexes for the sultans became landmarks in Istanbul: Necipoğlu, "Dynastic Imprints."

94. Pancaroğlu, "Architecture, Landscape, and Patronage," 40–41.

95. Ayverdi, *Osmanlı Mi'mârîsinin İlk Devri*, 464–69; Kastritsis, *The Sons of Bayezid*, 99; Mantran, "Les inscriptions arabes de Brousse," 104, no. 29.

96. The *beylik* of Germiyan, with its capital at Kütahya, existed from the late thirteenth century until its absorption by the Ottomans in 1427–28, during Murad II's expansion in western Anatolia. Kastritsis, *The Sons of Bayezid*, 84, 97–100; Kastritsis, ed., *The Tales of Sultan Mehmed*, 15–16; 'Aşıkpaşazāde, *Âşıkpaşazâde Tarihi*, ed. Öztürk, 153.

97. Kuran, *Mosque in Early Ottoman Architecture*, 112.

98. Kastritsis, *Tales of Sultan Mehmed*, 18. This text is part of the Oxford Anonymous Chronicle, Bodleian Library, The University of Oxford, Ms Marsh 313; full English translation in Kastritsis, *An Early Ottoman History*.

99. Nora, "Between Memory and History."

100. İ.B.B.A.K., MC_Fr_000005, line 42.

101. For thirteenth-century Konya as the Saljuq *dār al-mulk*, see Yalman, "Building the Sultanate of Rum," 229–322.

102. Cahen, *The Formation of Turkey*, 179–95; Turan, *Selçuklular Zamanında Türkiye*, 485–97; Yıldız, *Mongol Rule in Thirteenth-Century Seljuk Anatolia*, 160–254.

103. Cahen, *Formation of Turkey*, 196–226; Amitai-Preiss, *Mongols and Mamluks*, 168–77.

104. On the architectural landscape of Anatolia in this period, see Blessing, "All Quiet on the Eastern Frontier?" For Iran, see O'Kane, "Architecture of the Interregnum."

105. Yıldız, "Post-Mongol Pastoral Polities."

106. Tezcan, "The Memory of the Mongols."

107. Peacock, "Seljuq Legitimacy," 86–88; Kastritsis, *An Early Ottoman History*, 19.

108. Tezcan, "The Memory of the Mongols," 23–25.

109. Gabriel, *Monuments turcs*, 1:67–70, 79–82, and 2:162–64; Diez, Aslanapa, and Koman, *Karaman Devri Sanatı*; Schneider, "Research on the Rizk Mosque of Hasankeyf"; Gündoğdu, *Dulkadırlı Beyliği Mimarisi*; Göde, *Eratnalılar*, 157–73.

110. Blessing, "Seljuk Past," figure 9.

111. Parvillée, *Architecture et décoration turques*, 4, 14–15; Ayverdi, *Osmanlı Mimârîsinde Çelebi ve II. Sultan Murad Devri*, figs. 170, 171, 173; Kural, "Çelebi Mehmed'in Yeşil Türbesi." On the nineteenth-century restoration, see also St. Laurent, "Léon Parvillée." Pieces of tiles possibly belonging to the mausoleum are also held in the TİEM collection, inv. no. 3404A/B.

112. Degeorge and Porter, *L'art de la céramique*, 24, 196.

113. In *cuerda seca* tiles produced in Spain, waxed cords are used to separate the different colors. The cords burn during firing, resulting in an unglazed line between fields of different color. O'Kane ("Tiles of Many Hues," 182) notes that the term *cuerda seca* is better translated as "colorless line." Bernus-Taylor, "Le décor du 'Complexe Vert' à Bursa," mentions the technical differences but continues to use the term *cuerda seca* for the sake of convenience. Meinecke, *Fayencedekorationen*, 1:103, refers to these tiles as "Glasurfarbenfliesen mit 'toten Rändern'" (underglaze tile with dead – i.e., unpainted – edges); see also O'Kane, "Tiles of Many Hues," 191.

114. Samkoff, "From Central Asia to Anatolia," 200–201. For the chemical analysis of examples from Bursa and Samarqand, see O'Kane, "Tiles of Many Hues," 200–203.

115. Selçuk Hatun, a daughter of Mehmed I, is mentioned in the foundation inscription of her mosque in Bursa, built in 1450: Mantran, "Les inscriptions arabes de Brousse," 98, no. 18. For the inscription on her cenotaph in Mehmed I's mausoleum, see ibid., 107, no. 35; Ayverdi, *Osmanlı Mimârîsinde Çelebi ve II. Sultan Murad Devri*, 113–17; Taeschner, "Die Ješil Ğami," 149.

116. Meinecke, *Fayencedekorationen*, 1:93–95; pl. 41, figs. 1–2, and pl. 42, fig. 3; 2:cat. nos. 91–94.

117. O'Kane, "Tiles of Many Hues," 191.

118. Paterson, *Senses of Touch*, 66–67 and 75–79. Wendy M. K. Shaw argues for a "perceptual culture" in Islamic art that does not primarily rely on vision to produce meaning: Shaw, *What Is "Islamic Art"?*, 20–32.

119. Paterson, *Senses of Touch*, 87.

120. Pallasmaa, *The Eyes of the Skin*, 11–13, 30–41.

121. Marks, "The Taming of the Haptic Space," 258.

122. For incense burners in sixteenth-century and later endowment deeds, see Ergin, "The Fragrance of the Divine."

123. See Ergin, "Soundscape," for a discussion of this issue in sixteenth-century Istanbul.

124. Kafescioğlu, "Lives and Afterlives of an Urban Institution," 292 and 296.

125. Goodwin, *Ottoman Architecture*, 62; Eyice, "İlk Osmanlı Devrinin Dini İçtimai Bir Müessesesi," 6. The niches inserted into the step leading up to the mosque-*īwān* from the central space, known as *pabuçluk* (shoe racks) in modern Turkish, may also suggest that the central space was not carpeted. I thank one of the anonymous reviewers for Cambridge University Press for this suggestion.

126. Parvillée, *Architecture et décoration turques*, plate 8.

127. Albert Gabriel's undated watercolor of the interior of Mehmed I's mosque-*zāviye* shows carpets in the courtyard, although of course this does not allow for conclusions as to when these would first have been added: Gabriel, *Une capitale turque*, vol. 2, plate XCVIII. The current wall-to-wall carpeting does not allow for a view of the floor underneath. Eyice suggests that transformations in the sixteenth century, when *zāviye*s became irrelevant and were turned into neighborhood mosques, are responsible for current usage: Eyice, "İlk Osmanlı Devrinin Dini İçtimai Bir Müessesesi," 4, 53. For a more recent discussion of this transformation, which also critically discusses the earlier literature, see Kafescioğlu, "Lives and Afterlives of an Urban Institution."

128. Evliya Çelebi, *Seyahatnâme*, 2:13.

129. Mottahedeh, "ʿAjāʾib in The Thousand and One Nights"; Rabbat, "ʿAjīb and Gharīb; Harb, "Poetic Marvels," 1–11.

130. Saba, "Abbasid Lusterware."

131. Evliya Çelebi, *Seyahatnâme*, 2:13. On Bihzad, see Balafrej, *The Making of the Artist in Late Timurid Painting*.

132. Necipoğlu, "Visual Cosmopolitanism," 1–5, 22–45; Kafescioğlu, *Constantinopolis/Istanbul*, 2–5, 22–28, 66–84, 109–30.

133. Riefstahl, "Early Turkish Tile Revetments"; Bernus-Taylor, "Le décor du 'Complexe Vert' à Bursa," 256; Degeorge and Porter, *L'art de la céramique*, 196–97. For later examples, see Necipoğlu, "International Timurid," 140–48.

134. On the visit, see ʿAşıkpaşazāde, *Âşıkpaşazâde Tarihi*, ed. Öztürk, 152–53.

135. Keskin, "II. Yakub Bey Türbesi," 158–63. Keskin overall supports the Masters of Tabriz narrative and thus suggests that tiles could have been taken to Kütahya from Edirne, where the Şah Melek Pasha Mosque was built in 1429 with similar black-line tiles.

136. Ibid., 161; Uzunçarşılı, *Anadolu Beylikleri*, 47–52.

137. Meinecke, *Fayencedekorationen*, 1:98, 2:172–75; Blessing, "Seljuk Past," 238.

138. Mahi, "Tile Revetments"; Mahi, "Les 'Maîtres de Tabriz'"; Aube, *La céramique dans l'architecture en Iran au XVᵉ siècle*, 181–94. More broadly on Hasankeyf in this period, see Çeken, "Anadolu'da bir Seramik Üretim Merkezi" and Schneider, "Research on the Rizk Mosque of Hasankeyf."

139. On some of the earliest excavated Ottoman kilns, see Aslanapa, "Pottery and Kilns."

140. Ayverdi, *Osmanlı Mimârîsinde Çelebi ve II. Sultan Murad Devri*, 68 and fig. 100d. The signature is paired with a verse from Saʿdi's *Gulistan*: ibid., 68 and fig. 100e.

141. Blair, "Place, Space and Style."

142. Bernus-Taylor, "Le décor du 'Complexe Vert' à Bursa," 257; Mantran, "Les inscriptions arabes de Brousse," 105–06, no. 32; Ayverdi, *Osmanlı Mimârîsinde Çelebi ve II. Sultan Murad Devri*, 79, 109, and figs. 120, 178. Hajji ʿIvaz Pasha is also mentioned as the driving force behind the commission of the doors in the same inscription panel that contains ʿAli ibn Hajji Ahmad of Tabriz's signature: Ayverdi, *Osmanlı Mimârîsinde Çelebi ve II. Sultan Murad Devri*, 109; and Yürekli, "Architectural Patronage," 744. As Yürekli notes, this inscription also suggests Hajji ʿIvaz Pasha's continued role in the construction project after Mehmed I's death in 1421.

143. Taeschner, "Die Ješil Ǧami," 143–44, noting that the inscription was most likely repainted during repairs following the 1855 earthquake.

144. Bernus-Taylor, "Le décor du 'Complexe Vert' à Bursa," 257; and Gabriel, *Une capitale turque*, 1:91. Ayverdi (*Osmanlı Mimârîsinde Çelebi ve II. Sultan Murad Devri*, 94, 327) mentions Naqqash ʿAli's signature and identifies him as the grandfather of Lami'i Çelebi.

145. Bernus-Taylor, "Le décor du 'Complexe Vert' à Bursa," 257; See also discussion in Necipoğlu, "International Timurid," 136, with reference to Ayverdi, *Osmanlı Mimârîsinde Çelebi ve II. Sultan Murad Devri*; and Taeschner, "Die Ješil Ǧami," 166–67.

146. Taeschner, "Die Ješil Ǧami," 166–67.

147. Taşköprüzāde, *al-Shaqāʾiq al-nuʿmānīyat*, 262.

148. Bernardini, "Lo Şehrengīz-i Borūsā," 55.

149. Golombek, "Timurid Potters Abroad," 580–82.

150. O'Kane, "Tiles of Many Hues," 189.

151. Bernus-Taylor, "Le décor du 'Complexe Vert' à Bursa," 256–57; Mantran, "Les inscriptions arabes de Brousse," 93, no. 7; Uzunçarşılı, "Hacı İvaz Paşa'ya Dâir," 35; Taeschner, "Die Ješil Ǧami," 143; Mayer, *Islamic Architects*, 75; Pancaroğlu, "Bursa Yeşil Cami İnşa Kitabesinde Hiyerarşik İmgeleme," 182.

152. Âşıkpaşazâde, *Âşıkpaşazâde Tarihi*, ed. Öztürk, 115–16; Uzunçarşili, "Hacı İvaz Paşa'ya Dâir," 26–27.

153. Uzunçarşılı, "Hacı İvaz Paşa'ya Dâir"; Pay, *Bursa İvaz Paşa Külliyesi*. On the *waqfīya* of his foundation in Bursa, see Öcalan, Sevim, and Yavaş, *Bursa Vakfiyeleri I*, 359–73, with a facsimile of VGMA defter 591, sayfa 191–96, sıra 188. For the foundation in Tokat, see BOA EV.VKF. 19/19, dated 827 AH.

154. Pay, *Bursa İvaz Paşa Külliyesi*, 40.

155. My translation of "rāqimuhu wa nāẓimuhu wa muqanninu qawānīnihi." Full Arabic text in Mantran, "Les inscriptions arabes de Brousse," 93, no. 7.

156. Behrens-Abouseif, "Muhandis, Shād, Muʿallim," 295. Pancaroğlu, "Bursa Yeşil Cami İnşa Kitabesinde Hiyerarşik İmgeleme," 182, argues that Hajji ʿIvaz Pasha may have been more broadly responsible for design.

157. Modified translation after Yürekli, "Architectural Patronage," 745. Ayverdi, "Dimetoka," 15, and Ayverdi, *Avrupa'da Osmanlı Mimârî Eserleri*, 4:194, reads "al-muʿāmirīn," which doesn't mean anything. Yürekli, "Architectural Patronage

NOTES TO PAGES 79–97

and the Rise of the Ottomans," 745, suggests the unusual term "*muʿammirūn*" and translates it as "architects/builders," but in my opinion, this reading misses a letter in the inscription. From this point of view, Ayverdi's *muʿāmirūn* seems more correct in that it includes an *ālif* after the *ʿayn*, but there is the matter of its translation. Another possibility might be *muʿallimīn*, although this option must presume a spelling mistake in that the plural ending *-īn* is not tied to the final *mīm* of *muʿallim*. The translation "builders" is valid even if the inscription indeed reads "*muʿallimīn*": see the discussion of terms to designate the building crafts in fourteenth- and fifteenth-century Ottoman and Mamluk contexts in Chapter 3. Due to the COVID-19 pandemic, I had to cancel a planned visit to Didymoteicho in July 2020 that would have allowed me to view the inscription. On the building, see Androudis, *Hē prōimē Othōmanikē technē kai architektonikē* 99–102 and figures 30–75.

158. "Ve hem gayrı iklimden ehl-i hünerleri ve dahi üstâdları Rum'a ol [Hacı İvaz Paşa] getirtmişti." Neşri *Cihânnümâ*, ed. Öztürk, 350. Öztürk's edition is based on Franz Taeschner's facsimile of a manuscript owned by Theodor Menzel, believed to have been lost during the battle for Berlin in 1945 at the end of World War II. Taeschner had to work based on a photocopy: Neşri *Ǧihānnümā*, ed. Taeschner, 1:14–16. Taeschner also describes this manuscript in his list of known copies of the work: Neşrî, *Ǧihānnümā*, ed. Taeschner, 1:20. This account is noted in Necipoğlu, "International Timurid," 136. Necipoğlu cites a manuscript of Neşrî's *Cihânnümâ*, Millet Kütüphanesi, Istanbul, Ali Emiri, no. 220, fol. 209b; and ʿĀşıkpaşazāde, *Die altomanische Chronik des ʿAšikpašazāde* ed. Giese, 197 (see Necipoğlu, "International Timurid," 166n5). For the same passage in a recent edition of Âşıkpaşazâde's work, see ʿĀşıkpaşazāde *Âşıkpaşazâde Tarihi*, ed. Öztürk, 296: "Ve hem gayrı iklimden ehl-i hünerler ve üstadlar Rum'a o getürmişdür."

159. Pyle, "Seljuk Portals of Anatolia"; Wolper, "Portal Patterns."

160. Gündüz Küskü, *Osmanlı Beyliği*, 202–03.

161. Çağaptay, *The First Capital*, 62–65.

162. Gabriel, *Une capitale turque*, 1:65–67.

163. Çağaptay, "Frontierscape," 170–75; Çağaptay, *The First Capital*, 54–58.

164. Necipoğlu, "International Timurid," 138. On the use of these terms in Timurid sources, see O'Kane, "Poetry, Geometry and the Arabesque," 76–78.

165. Yürekli, "Architectural Patronage," 746.

166. Necipoğlu, "International Timurid," 138; Blessing, "Blue-and-White Tiles," 116.

167. Ermiş, "The Reuse of Byzantine Spolia."

168. Redford, "Intercession and Succession"; Blessing, *Rebuilding Anatolia*, 41–47.

169. Bernus-Taylor, "Le décor du 'Complexe Vert' à Bursa," 258–60 and fig. 10; Golombek and Wilber, *The Timurid Architecture*, 1:cat. nos. 14, 15, 17. For overall parallels in the tile decoration of fifteenth-century Ottoman and Central Asian monuments, see Necipoğlu, "International Timurid," 137.

170. Roxburgh, "Timurid Architectural Revetment," 127–29.

171. O'Kane, "Tiles of Many Hues," 188.

172. Pfeiffer, "Introduction: From Baghdad to Marāgha"; and Minorsky, "Tabrīz," 583.

173. Minorsky, "Tabrīz," 583; Ökten, "Imperial Aqquyunlu Construction," 373; Melville, "Historical Monuments and Earthquakes."

174. Wilber, *The Architecture of Islamic Iran*, 129–31 and 146–49; Blair, "Tabriz," 333–37.

175. Blair, "Tabriz," 345; Minorsky, "Tabrīz," 586–88; Woods, *The Aqquyunlu*, 96–101.

176. Blair, "Tabriz," 346–48; Aube, "La mosquée bleue de Tabriz," 241–43; Aube, "Tabriz x. monuments (1): The Blue Mosque"; Aube, "The Uzun Hasan Mosque in Tabriz," 45–50; Ökten, "Imperial Aqquyunlu Construction," 375–77.

177. For a detailed study of the different tile techniques and their placement in the mosque, see Aube, "La mosquée bleue de Tabriz," 250–68.

178. Schmidt, "Beautiful Style," 105; Ramírez-Weaver, "Reading the Heavens," 75–76.

179. Ahmed, *What Is Islam?*, 32, 73–75, 514–15, 525–27, 540–41.

180. Golombek and Wilber, *Timurid Architecture*, 1:cat. no. 221 and 2:pl. XVI. For the use of monochrome tiles in Timurid dadoes, see O'Kane, *Timurid Architecture in Khurasan*, 67; and Holod, "The Monuments of Yazd," 95–122.

181. Holod, "The Monuments of Yazd," 92–93.

182. Golombek and Wilber, *Timurid Architecture*, 1:36, 409; O'Kane, *Timurid Architecture in Khurasan*, 67 and pl. 26.3.

183. Aube, "La mosquée bleue de Tabriz," 245–47.

3 UNDER THE INFLUENCE

1. Muhanna, "The Sultan's New Clothes."

2. Necipoğlu, *The Age of Sinan*, 78–79; Meinecke, *Die mamlukische Architektur*, 1:126, 131–43; Tanman, "Mamluk Influences"; Kiel, "Cross-Cultural Contacts."

3. Meinecke, *Die mamlukische Architektur*, 1:126, 131–43.

4. This applies throughout the two volumes of Meinecke, *Die mamlukische Architektur*, as well as in Meinecke, *Patterns of Stylistic Changes*.

5. Kenney, "A Mamluk Monument Reconstructed," 154–57.

6. Yüksel Muslu, *The Ottomans and the Mamluks*, 1.

7. Ibid., 7; Wing, "Submission, Defiance, and the Rules of Politics."

8. Yüksel Muslu, *The Ottomans and the Mamluks*, 71–82.

9. Wing, "Submission, Defiance, and the Rules of Politics."

10. Büchner, "Sīs."

11. Sourdel-Thomine, "Diwrīǧī"; Pancaroğlu, "The Mosque-Hospital Complex at Divriği," 171n9. On the Hoşkadem Mosque in Kozan (Sīs), see Meinecke, *Die mamlukische Architektur*, 2:368, cat. 35/46. Also see *Vakıf Abideleri*, 1:35–37. On Mardin and Hasankeyf, see Meinecke, *Die mamlukische Architektur*, 1:143–50; Venzke, "Dulkadir."

12. Şahin and Emecen, "Amasya," 1.

13. Kastritis, *The Sons of Bayezid*, 71–72.

14. Şahin and Emecen, "Amasya," 1; Taeschner, "Amasya"; Kastritis, *The Sons of Bayezid*, 65–73.

15. Meinecke, *Die mamlukische Architektur*, 1:141; Mayer, *Islamic Architects*, 37; Çerkez, "Merzifon'da Türk Devri Mimari Eserleri," 322 and 495; Tanman, "Mehmed I Medresesi"; Akok, "Merzifonda Çelebi Mehmet Medresesi."

16. Meinecke, *Die mamlukische Architektur*, 1:137–38; Meinecke, *Patterns of Stylistic Changes*, 93.

17. Konyalı, *Karacabey Mamuresi*, 6–7; Meinecke, *Die mamlukische Architektur*, 1:141; Ayverdi and Yüksel, *Osmanlı Mimârisi*, 1:372; Meinecke, *Patterns of Stylistic Changes*, 98.

18. Blessing, "Blue-and-White Tiles."

19. Yüksel Muslu, *The Ottomans and the Mamluks*, 86–102; Muhanna, "The Sultan's New Clothes"; Behrens-Abouseif, *Practising Diplomacy*, 84–94.

20. Atçıl, *Scholars and Sultans*, 28–45.

21. Şahin and Emecen, "Amasya," 1. While Balıkesir, formerly ruled by the Karesioğulları, came under Ottoman rule as early as the 1350s, that city had only come under Muslim rule in 1304 and thus did not have the same historical urban fabric containing Islamic monuments that Amasya had: İskit and Orgun, *Mufassal Osmanlı Tarihi*, 10:20–21; İlgürel, "Balıkesir."

22. Boykov, "The Borders of the Cities," 249–56.

23. On thirteenth- and fourteenth-century architecture in Amasya, see Gabriel, *Monuments turcs*, 2:20–61; Blessing, *Rebuilding Anatolia*, 198–202; Yinanç, "Selçuklu Medreselerinden Amasya Halifet Gazi Medresesi ve Vakıfları." For a detailed map and list of monuments in Amasya from the Danishmendid to the Ottoman period, see Gündüz Küskü, *Osmanlı Beyliği*, 494–95.

24. Kuran, *Mosque in Early Ottoman Architecture*, 82–85.

25. Yardım, *Amasya Kaya Kitâbesi*, 53–61.

26. Meinecke and Flemming, *Die Restaurierung der Madrasa des Amīrs Sābiq ad-Dīn Miṯqāl al-Ānūkī*, 29–78; Meinecke, *Die mamlukische Architektur*, 2:234–35, cat. 21/4.

27. Gabriel, *Monuments turcs*, 2:29; Ayverdi, *Osmanlı Mimârisinde Çelebi ve II. Sultan Murad Devri*, 22.

28. Taneri, "Bayezid Paşa"; Karataş, "The City as Historical Actor," 37; ʿAşıkpaşazâde, *ʿAşıkpaşazâde Tarihi*, ed. Öztürk, 128–29.

29. عمل العبد الفقير المحتاج إلى رحمة الله تعالى المعلِّم أبو بكر بن محمّد المعروف بابن مُشيمِش الدمشقي

Ayverdi, *Osmanlı Mimârisinde Çelebi ve II. Sultan Murad Devri*, 22; Uzunçarşılı, *Kitâbeler*, 113; Yardım, *Amasya Kaya Kitâbesi*, 69–71. French translation in Gabriel, *Monuments turcs*, 2:30.

30. Transcription of the Arabic text along with detailed photographs of the inscription and a Turkish translation in Yardım, *Amasya Kaya Kitâbesi*, 98–126. The results are summarized in English in Peacock, "Waqf Inscriptions," 189–90.

31. Ayverdi, *Osmanlı Mimârisinde Çelebi ve II. Sultan Murad Devri*, 24. On *waqf* inscriptions, see also Cantay, "Türklerde Vakıf ve Taş Vakfiyeler"; Blessing, *Rebuilding Anatolia*, 153–58. Eyice, "Bayezid Paşa Camii," 243, notes that two versions of the *waqfīya* on paper survive. The document held at BOA is reproduced in Yardım, *Amasya Kaya Kitâbesi*, 137–45; description in ibid., 4–5. Catalogued as BOA A.E.SMMD.I 1/2, the document has not been digitized and the original document is not available for viewing. This problem applies to the entire Ali Emiri *tasnifi* of early Ottoman documents. The *waqfīya* is also discussed in Karataş, "The City as Historical Actor," 36–37.

32. Yardım, *Amasya Kaya Kitâbesi*. 9–25; Keskin, "Bayezid Paşa," 18 and figs. 5 and 6.

33. Yardım, *Amasya Kaya Kitâbesi*, 23–25.

34. Blessing, *Rebuilding Anatolia*, 153–58.

35. For a comparison of the content of the inscription with that of the paper *waqfīya*, see Yardım, *Amasya Kaya Kitâbesi*, 27–38.

36. Blessing, *Rebuilding Anatolia*, 156–57.

37. Yardım, *Amasya Kaya Kitâbesi*, 97.

38. معمار هاذ الباب يعقوب ابن عبد الله من ممالك بايزيد پاشا أعظم الله جلال قدره ونفذ أحكام أمره لسنة إثنين وعشرين وثمانمائة
Transcription and line drawing in Yardım, *Amasya Kaya Kitabesi*, 78. As Yardım notes, Ayverdi, *Osmanlı Mimârîsinde Çelebi ve II. Sultan Murad Devri*, 22, and Uzunçarşılı, *Kitâbeler*, 112–33, read "*binā*" instead of "*bāb*."

39. عمل العبد الفقير المعلِّم زين الدين ابن زكريا
Ayverdi, *Osmanlı Mimârîsinde Çelebi ve II. Sultan Murad Devri*, 23; Uzunçarşılı, *Kitâbeler*, 112–13; transcription and line drawing in Yardım, *Amasya Kaya Kitabesi*, 79.

40. Ayverdi, *Osmanlı Mimârîsinde Çelebi ve II. Sultan Murad Devri*, 22.

41. "Faghān (?) Ṭoghān b. ʿAbdallāh": Uzunçarşılı, *Kitâbeler*, 113. "Kanan Tughan b. ʿAbdallah": Ayverdi, *Osmanlı Mimârîsinde Çelebi ve II. Sultan Murad Devri*, 22. "Fuqa Togan b. Abdallah": Keskin, "Bayezid Paşa," 21–22. Unfortunately, the placement of inscriptions is mixed up in figure 6 of the same article, as well as in Keskin, "Syrian-origin Architects," fig. 2.

42. Yardım, *Amasya Kaya Kitâbesi*, 85–86.

43. Ibid., 86–87; Mayer, *Islamic Architects*, 37, 126, 132, 135.

44. Babaie, "Chasing after the Muhandis," 27.

45. Ibid., 40–41.

46. Mayer, *Islamic Architects*, 115–16; Wilber, "Qavam al-Din ibn Zayn al-Din Shirazi"; Babaie, "Qavam al-Din Shirazi." Qavam al-Din Shirazi's name appears in inscriptions at the Great Mosque of Gawhar Shad in Mashhad and posthumously at Ghiyath al-Din's madrasa in Khargird (1438–44). Three further monuments are described as his work in Timurid chronicles: Wilber, "Qavam al-Din ibn Zayn al-Din Shirazi," 31–36; Babaie, "Chasing after the Muhandis," 21–22 and 42. For Gawhar Shad's complex in Herat, see Aube, Lorain, and Bendezu-Sarmiento, "The Complex of Gawhar Shad," 64, 74, 77–82, where the authors argue for a consistent style in tile decoration across the buildings attributed to Qavam al-Din Shirazi. This begs the question whether Qavam al-Din Shirazi was indeed an architect, or perhaps rather the designer of large-scale tile programs. The two functions need not be mutually exclusive considering how little we know about the exact roles of Timurid building professionals. Dawlatshah Samarqandi refers to Qavam al-Din Shirazi's skills in "*muhandisi* (engineering), *tarhi* (design or drawing) and *miʿmari* (architecture)," pointing to a central role in design: Wilber, "Qavam al-Din ibn Zayn al-Din Shirazi," 31; Babaie, "Chasing after the Muhandis," 21–22, 38–42; Aube, Lorain, and Bendezu-Sarmiento, "The Complex of Gawhar Shad," 79.

47. Babaie, "Chasing after the Muhandis," 27–28 and 41–42.

48. Behrens-Abouseif, "*Muhandis, Shād, Muʿallim*," 293.

49. Ibid., 294–95; Rabbat, "Design without Representation," 148. For terms used in the Persianate context, see Babaie, "Chasing after the Muhandis," 26–27.

NOTES TO PAGES 105–113

50. Rabbat, "Design without Representation," 148–49.

51. Ibid., 150.

52. Behrens-Abouseif, "*Muhandis, Shād, Mu'allim*," 295–97, 306.

53. Ibid., 295.

54. Yürekli, "Architectural Patronage," 741 (noting a date of 1414 CE, which date actually appears on the inscription over the main portal: Ayverdi, *Osmanlı Mimârîsinde Çelebi ve II. Sultan Murad Devri*, 159).

55. Yürekli, "Architectural Patronage," 741; Ayverdi, *Osmanlı Mimârîsinin İlk Devri*, 353–54 and 384.

56. Behrens-Abouseif, "*Muhandis, Shād, Mu'allim*," 296.

57. A measure of volume, about 1.05 liters in Iraq, 3.673 liters in Syria, and 2.5 liters in Egypt: "mudd," *EI2*, Glossary and Index of Terms, http://dx.doi.org/10.1163/1573-3912_ei2glos_SIM_gi_03189 (accessed May 22, 2019). The *mudd* in medieval and early modern Anatolia could vary widely, from 69.5 kg (90 liters) of wheat in Kastamonume, Konya, Iznik, Manisa, and Antalya to 2.05 (2.66 liters) in Mardin. The Ottoman imperial *mudd* as recorded in 1474 corresponded to 513.12 kg (666.45 liters) of wheat, while in Kütahya and Bursa, one *mudd* corresponded to 112.5 liters: Hinz, *Islamische Masse und Gewichte*, 46–47.

58. İ.B.B.A.K., MC_Fr_000005, lines 220–21.

59. Öcalan, Sevim, and Yavaş, *Bursa Vakfiyeleri*, 1:415.

60. Ibid., 1:362; Pay, *Bursa İvaz Paşa Külliyesi*, 177. The original *waqfiya* has not survived, but two sixteenth-century copies and one nineteenth-century copy exist: ibid., 19–21. A facsimile of VGMA, defter 591, sayfa 191–96, sıra 188, is reproduced in Öcalan, Sevim, and Yavaş, *Bursa Vakfiyeleri*, 1:368–73; Yardım, *Amasya Kaya Kitâbesi*, 32–35.

61. Turan, "Osmanlı Teşkilâtında Hassa Mimarları"; Necipoğlu, *The Age of Sinan*, 153–55.

62. Behrens-Abouseif, "*Muhandis, Shād, Mu'allim*," 295.

63. Ayverdi, "Dimetoka," 15; Yürekli, "Architectural Patronage," 743; Androudis, *Hē prōimē Othōmanikē technē kai architektonikē*, 101–02.

64. Yürekli, "Architectural Patronage," 742–43.

65. Necipoğlu, "Plans and Models," 225–31; Necipoğlu, *The Age of Sinan*, 168–73; Necipoğlu, "Architectural Dialogues," 598. In the Mamluk context, Behrens-Abouseif notes that construction methods appear to have been based on practice, and extensive "safety margins," used, for instance, in the thickness of walls, were often somewhat excessive to ensure stability: Behrens-Abouseif, "*Muhandis, Shād, Mu'allim*," 305.

66. Necipoğlu, "Architectural Dialogues," 599.

67. Necipoğlu, "Plans and Models," 230–31 and 241–42; Necipoğlu, *The Age of Sinan*, 171–74.

68. Necipoğlu, "Plans and Models," 243.

69. Necipoğlu, *The Age of Sinan*, 153–60; Turan, "Osmanlı Teşkilâtında Hassa Mimarları"; Şerafettin Turan, "Mimarbaşı."

70. Başar, "Yörgüç Paşa." Halil Edhem, "Yörgüç Paşa," 533, takes these accounts with a grain of salt, noting that they do not appear in sources of the period, but rather in later works such as Hoca Sadeddin Efendi's (d. 1599) *Tacü't-Tevarih*.

71. Başar, "Yörgüç Paşa"; Halil Edhem, "Yörgüç Paşa," 534 and 536; 'Aşıkpaşazade, *Âşıkpaşazâde Tarihi*, ed. Öztürk, 147–49.

72. Başar, "Yörgüç Paşa"; Halil Edhem, "Yörgüç Paşa," 536.

73. Halil Edhem, "Yörgüç Paşa," 536–37. The family of Umur Beğ b. Timurtaş is another case of locally established power. In Bursa, Umur and his father, Timurtaş, created foundations that are recorded in extant *waqfiyas*. Umur's endowment included an extensive list of books, reflecting the growing involvement of the Ottoman elites with learning as part of an overall expansion of intellectual worlds: Yüksel, "Kara Timurtaş-Oğlu Umur Bey'in Bursa'da Vakfettiği Kitaplar"; Stanley, "The Books of Umur Bey." For the document, see İ.B.B.A.K. Yazma Eserler, MC_Fr_000038. Umur's brother, 'Ali, founded a mosque-*zāviye* in Manisa in 1427: introduction, p. 5.

74. Halil Edhem, "Yörgüç Paşa," 531, no. 2, and 537.

75. Ibid., 533.

76. Başar, "Yörgüç Paşa."

77. هو الباقي أنشاء هذه العمارةَ المباركةَ المنسوبة إلى الفقراء والمساكين في أيام دولة السلطان الأعظم والخاقان المعظّم غياث الدنيا والدين أبو الفتح السلطان مراد خان بن المرحوم محمّد المشتهر بابن عثمان خلّد الله سلطانهُ الأميرُ الكبيرُ والوزيرُ الخطيرُ جلال الدولة والدين يوركوج باشا بن عبد الله الأتابكي في غرّة محرّم سنة أربع وثلثين وثمانمائة

The inscription has been published in Halil Edhem, "Yörgüç Paşa," 530–31; Uzunçarşılı, *Kitâbeler*, 116–17; Ayverdi, *Osmanlı Mimârîsinde Çelebi ve II. Sultan Murad Devri*, 222. For a French translation, see Gabriel, *Monuments turcs*, 2:31–33, albeit with a mistaken reading of the date as 832 AH / 1428 CE.

78. *Basmala* at the top, IX:18 on the left side of the panel, and IX:19 on the right side of the panel: Ayverdi, *Osmanlı Mimârîsinde Çelebi ve II. Sultan Murad Devri*, 221.

79. Uzunçarşılı, *Kitâbeler*, 99–100.

80. BOA EV.VKF. 19/7 and VGMA 747/245. For a detailed study and Turkish summary of the VGMA version, see Toruk, "Yörgüç Paşa Vakfiyesi"; the BOA version has not, to my knowledge, been published previously except for a brief mention in Ayverdi, *Osmanlı Mimârîsinde Çelebi ve II. Sultan Murad Devri*, 215–16. Karataş, "The City as Historical Actor," appears to work with the Turkish summary available at VGMA (mentioned in Toruk, "Yörgüç Paşa Vakfiyesi," 17).

81. The Ottoman archive in Istanbul does not provide measurements in the catalog or with digital copies of documents. For comparison, the *waqfiya* of the mosque-*zāviye* of Mehmed I in Bursa has 260 lines and measures 740 centimeters in length (İ.B.B.A.K., MC_Fr_000005).

82. BOA EV.VKF. 19/7, lines 5–6.

83. Ibid., lines 27–36.

84. Ibid., lines 40–48.

85. Blessing, *Rebuilding Anatolia*, 201.

86. BOA EV.VKF. 19/7, line 47. A few lines later, the term *buq'at* is used: BOA EV.VKF. 19/7, line 49.

87. BOA EV.VKF. 19/7, line 61.

88. على الفقراء والمساكين الصادرين مين أمّة إمام الأنبياء والمرسلين BOA EV.VKF. 19/7, lines 52, 59, 114.

89. The assumption that a madrasa was part of Yörgüç Pasha's foundation in Amasya appears to be based on Hüseyin Hüsameddin [Yaşar]'s *Amasya Tarihi*, first published in 1911–15, where the author notes that a madrasa took the form of "some cells (*hücre*) located within and in front of the mosque"

and claims that this madrasa was listed in a (unspecified) *waqfiya*. Hüseyin Hüsameddin further gives a list of scholars appointed as *mudarris* to this madrasa in the eighteenth and nineteenth centuries: Hüseyin Hüsameddin, *Amasya Tarihi*, 1:312–13; Hüseyin Hüsameddin, *Amasya Tarihi*, ed. Yılmaz and Akkuş, 1:253–54. Ayverdi, *Osmanlı Mimârîsinde Çelebi ve II. Sultan Murad Devri*, 215, refers to this source in his mention of a madrasa.

90. BOA EV.VKF. 19/7, lines 63–107; for the buildings in Tokat and İskilip, see lines 80–83.

91. BOA EV.VKF. 19/7, lines 108–22.

92. Dönmez suggests that this section may have been a room of a madrasa that does not survive: Dönmez, "Yörgüç Paşa Camii." Apart from this possibility of a potential awkward physical connection between mosque-*zâviye* and madrasa in a period when Ottoman builders generally built separate structures for each function within a building complex, evidence for the existence of a madrasa is limited (see n. 89).

93. Uzunçarşılı, *Kitâbeler*, 117, only notes three tombstones. All four are illustrated in Ayverdi, *Osmanlı Mimârîsinde Çelebi ve II. Sultan Murad Devri*, 224–26.

94. Uzunçarşılı, *Kitâbeler*, 117–18.

95. Halil Edhem, "Yörgüç Paşa," 531.

96. Blessing, *Rebuilding Anatolia*, 201. The monument was undergoing restoration in 2018, so I was unable to take new photographs without scaffolding obscuring the stonework.

97. Ibid., 199–202.

98. Ibid., 98–104.

99. Pancaroğlu, "The Mosque-Hospital Complex at Divriği," 184–88.

100. Maranci, *The Art of Armenia*, 145.

101. Deleuze and Guattari, "The Smooth and the Striated," 475–77.

102. Shaw, *What Is "Islamic" Art?*, 268–69, 274–87.

103. Ayverdi, *Osmanlı Mimârîsinde Çelebi ve II. Sultan Murad Devri*, 222.

104. Yüksel Muslu, "Ottoman–Mamluk Relations," 52; Yüksel Muslu, *The Ottomans and the Mamluks*, 82.

105. Yüksel Muslu, *The Ottomans and the Mamluks*, 83–84.

106. Ibid., 35; Binbaş, *Intellectual Networks*, 92; Ben Cheneb, "Ibn al-Djazarī"; Atçıl, *Scholars and Sultans*, 42; McChesney, "A Note on the Life and Works of Ibn ʿArabshāh," 216.

107. Binbaş, *Intellectual Networks*, 92 and 134; McChesney, "A Note on the Life and Works of Ibn ʿArabshāh," 217.

108. Binbaş, *Intellectual Networks*, 92.

109. Some confusion about this figure's name appears. He is named as Muhammad al-Ashgar in Yüksel Muslu, *The Ottomans and the Mamluks*, 35 (based on Taşköprüzāde). The name Shaykh Abu al-Khayr appears in McChesney, "A Note on the Life and Works of Ibn ʿArabshāh," 216, as a son of al-Jazari who moved to the Ottoman court. Binbaş, *Intellectual Networks*, mentions al-Jazari's son Muhibb al-Din Abi al-Khayr as a vizier of Timurid Ibrahim Sultan (92n42); on that figure, with the name variant Shaykh Muhibb al-Din Abu'l-Khayr, a political actor in Fars in the 1430s and 1440s, see Manz, *Power, Politics, and Religion*, 249–51.

110. Inan, "Imperial Ambitions," 80–82; Yazıcı, "Dāʿī." On Persian identities at the late Mamluk court, see Mauder,

"Being Persian"; on long-term interactions, see Heidarzadeh, "Patronage, Networks, Migration."

111. Yüksel Muslu, *The Ottomans and the Mamluks*, 35, 90–91; Pedersen, "Ibn ʿArabshāh." The letters are discussed in Veselý, "Ein Kapitel aus den osmanisch-mamlukischen Beziehungen," 242–50.

112. Pedersen, "Ibn ʿArabshāh"; Binbaş, *Intellectual Networks*, 181; McChesney, "A Note on the Life and Works of Ibn ʿArabshāh," 209–15.

113. McChesney, "A Note on the Life and Works on Ibn ʿArabshāh," 215–21.

114. Ibid., 221–27.

115. Ibid., 227–28.

116. Ibid., 226–33.

117. Pedersen, "Ibn ʿArabshāh"; McChesney, "A Note on the Life and Works on Ibn ʿArabshāh," 209, 243.

118. Walsh, "Gūrānī."

119. Ibid.

120. Yüksel Muslu, *The Ottomans and the Mamluks*, 35–36 and 111–13; Walsh, "Gūrānī."

121. Walsh, "Gūrānī"; Atçıl, *Scholars and Sultans*, 80.

122. Yüksel Muslu, *The Ottomans and the Mamluks*, 50–51, 74–75, 79–80, 97–98, 109–14, 119–21; Muhanna, "The Sultan's New Clothes."

123. Ibrahim and O'Kane, "The Madrasa of Badr al-Dīn al-ʿAynī," 254–56.

124. Meinecke, *Mamlukische Architektur*, vol. 2: 349, cat. 33/66; Ibrahim and O'Kane, "The Madrasa of Badr al-Dīn al-ʿAynī," 257.

125. Kononenko, "Ulu-dzhami Aksaraia," 154–60. For additional perspectives on Karamanid–Mamluk exchange, see Şaman Doğan, "Kültürel Etkileşim Üzerine."

126. İ.B.B.A.K., MC_Fr_000005. For the use of Turkish placenames in the *waqfiya* of Bayezid Pasha, see Yardım, *Amasya Kaya Kitâbesi*, 45–46.

127. Green, "Introduction: The Frontiers of the Persianate World," 17–29; Hagen, "Translations and Translators," 130–34. On the increasing use of Persian in the Ottoman Empire beginning in Mehmed II's reign, see Inan, "Imperial Ambitions."

128. Hagen, "Translations and Translators," 100–134.

129. See, for instance, Carlson, *Christianity in Fifteenth-Century Iraq*; Goshgarian, "Social Graces and Urban Spaces."

130. Meinecke, *Die mamlukische Architektur*, 1:137–38; Meinecke, *Fayencedekorationen seldschukischer Sakralbauten*, vol. 2: 414–17, cat. no. 103; Otto-Dorn, "Die İsa Bey Moschee," 122. Ogan, "Aydın Oğullarından İsa Bey Cami'i," 79, omits "Mushaymish."

131. Uzunçarşılı, *Anadolu Beylikleri*, 112–13; Otto-Dorn, "Die İsa Bey Moschee," 115–17.

132. Otto-Dorn, "Die İsa Bey Moschee," 117–18 and 128, notes that when she conducted her research, the lower section of the mihrab was missing and replaced with rough masonry, while the upper section had been damaged. See also Ogan, "Aydın Oğullarından İsa Bey Cami'i," 78–79.

133. Tabbaa, "Dayfa Khātūn."

134. Meinecke, *Die mamlukische Architektur*, vol. 1: 111, 117, vol. 2: 213–14, cat. 19A/20. In a separate article, Meinecke discusses the monument in the context of a study of a workshop of tile

makers, possibly from Tabriz, active in the 1330s to 1350s: Meinecke, "Die mamlukischen Fayencemosaikdekorationen," 130, where the author notes that the Mausoleum of Araq al-Silahdar is one of the first examples of tile inserted into a stone façade.

135. Redford, "Paper, Stone, Scissors"; Yalman, "'Ala al-Din Kayqubad Illuminated"; Yalman, "Building the Sultanate of Rum."

136. Rogers, "Evidence for Mamluk–Mongol Relations."

137. Blessing, "Allegiance, Praise, and Space," 437.

138. Meinecke, *Die mamlukische Architektur*, 1:126–35.

139. Ibid., 1:141.

140. Ibid., 1:141.

141. Gündüz Küskü, *Osmanlı Beyliği*, 196–205.

142. Yıldız, "From Cairo to Ayasuluk," 263–64. While in Cairo, Hacı Pasha frequented the same circles as Ahmedi, Molla Fenari, and Şeyh Bedreddin: Balivet, *Islam mystique et révolution armée*, 43.

143. Meinecke, *Patterns of Stylistic Changes*, 98.

144. Emecen, "Western Anatolia in the Period of the Emirates," 34–37; Arel, "The Architecture of the Menteşe Emirate," 56–58; Wulzinger, Wittek, and Sarre, *Das islamische Milet*, 5.

145. The date 806 AH / 1404 CE appears on the mosque's foundation inscription above the entrance: Wulzinger, Wittek, and Sarre, *Das islamische Milet*, 89–90.

146. Overview in Durukan, "İlyas Bey Külliyesi."

147. Caner Yüksel, "A Tale of Two Port Cities." On Balat, see also Baykara, "Balat" and Türkantoz, "The Urban Fabric."

148. Caner Yüksel, "A Tale of Two Port Cities," 348–50 and 355–56; Yılmaz, "Kazı Buluntuları"; Fleet, *European and Islamic Trade*.

149. Arel, "The Architecture of the Menteşe Emirate," 65.

150. Ibid., 78–81.

151. Wulzinger, Wittek, and Sarre, *Das islamische Milet*, 31, figs. 20–21, and 93; Tanman, "Some Reflections," 87–88.

152. Tanman, "Some Reflections," 88 and 90.

153. Ibid., 88–89.

154. Arel, "The Architecture of the Menteşe Emirate," 73–75.

155. Ibid., 73.

156. Ibid., 75 and 81, referring to Cantay, "Amasya Mesud Türbesi'nin İnşa Yılı."

157. Necipoğlu also notes these connections to Mamluk architecture: Necipoğlu, *The Age of Sinan*, 78–79.

158. Riefstahl, *Turkish Architecture in Southwestern Anatolia*, 5–14; Otto-Dorn, "Die İsa Bey Moschee," 130, for the connection between the plans in Manisa and Ayasuluk. While the mosque is not signed, the adjoining madrasa (780 AH / 1378 CE) has, on its portal below the foundation inscription, the text (after Uzunçarşılı, *Afyon Karahisar*, 76): عمل الفقير إلى الله الغني الحاج أحمت ابن عثمان عفى الله عنه While Amat b. ʿUthmān is generally assumed to be the madrasa's architect, the general term "work of" used to introduce him poses the same problem noted for the Masters of Tabriz in Chapter 2.

159. Uzunçarşılı, *Anadolu Beylikleri*, 84–91.

160. Meinecke, *Die mamlukische Architektur*, 1:136–37; Meinecke, *Patterns of Stylistic Changes*, 98–99.

161. Meinecke, *Die mamlukische Architektur*, 1:136–40; Meinecke, *Patterns of Stylistic Changes*, 92. On the mosque of al-Nasir

Muhammad on Cairo's citadel, see Rabbat, *The Citadel of Cairo*, 263–74.

162. Necipoğlu, *The Age of Sinan*, 79; Goodwin, *Ottoman Architecture*, 93–99.

163. Plans in Meinecke, *Die mamlukische Architektur*, 1:138–39, figs. 89–91.

164. Meinecke, *Die mamlukische Architektur*, 1:136–37; Meinecke, *Fayencedekorationen seldschukischer Sakralbauten*, vol. 2: 400–104, cat. no. 97.

165. Ayverdi, *Osmanlı Mimârîsinde Çelebi ve II. Sultan Murad Devri*, 150, 159; Gündüz Küskü, *Osmanlı Beyliği* 158–59, 230–32.

166. Blessing, "Blue-and-White Tiles," 109–12.

167. On the issue of Timurid blue-and-white tiles, see ibid., 121–22. For late fifteenth-century Aqqoyunlu Tabriz, see Aube, *La céramique dans l'architecture de l'Iran*, 84–89. For tile fragments from fifteenth-century Herat, see Aube, Lorain, and Bendezu-Sarmiento, "The Complex of Gawhar Shad," 69–72. For the shared interest in Chinese porcelain in the Persianate world, see Kadoi, "From Acquisition to Display."

168. Blessing, "Blue-and-White Tiles," 116–18.

169. Four hundred and seventy-nine tiles used to be in place before several were stolen in 2001, and others were broken in the process of removal: Muradiye Camii Çinileri Onarılıyor," NTV-CSNBC Turkey, November 30, 2003, http://arsiv.ntv.com.tr/news/245838.asp (accessed 30 March 2020); Akçıl and Özer, "Murâdiye Külliyesi." Original count of tiles in Carswell, "Six Tiles," 99. For photographs showing the same wall in 1967 and 2016, see Blessing, "Blue-and-White Tiles," 107, figures 10a and 10b.

170. Blessing, "Blue-and-White Tiles," 104–08.

171. On the relationship between Ottoman, Timurid, and Mamluk landscape painting, see O'Kane, "The Arboreal Aesthetic." For Timurid landscape paintings in manuscripts and buildings, see Golombek, "Paysage," 245–46; O'Kane, "The Bihbihani Anthology"; Aga-Oglu and Hall, "Landscape Miniatures."

172. Gasparini, *Le pitture murali della Muradiye di Edirne*.

173. For the Yahşi Bey Mosque in Tire (building undated, *waqfiya* 845 AH / 1441 CE), see Kalfazade, "Yeşilimaret Camii"; and O'Kane, "The Arboreal Aesthetic," 230. In the Üç Şerefeli Mosque in Edirne, O'Kane observed paintings similar to those of the Muradiye in 1994, but notes that by the time of his next visit in 2001, the landscape elements had been painted over: O'Kane, "The Arboreal Aesthetic," 227 and 229, and pl. 26–27. O'Kane also mentions heavily restored paintings in the Eski Cami in Edirne: O'Kane, "The Arboreal Aesthetic," 230 and fig. 14.6.

174. Golombek, "Paysage," 241–42. On the global reach of Chinese porcelain in the fourteenth and fifteenth centuries, see Gerritsen, *The City of Blue and White*, 114–33.

175. Kanda, "Revisiting the So-Called Ghaybī Workshop," 40–47.

176. Millner, *Damascus Tiles*, 77 and figure 3.20; Meinecke, *Die mamlukische Architektur*, vol. 2: 328, cat. 29/53.

177. Carswell, "Six Tiles," 99–100.

178. Millner, *Damascus Tiles*, figs. 3.11 to 3.15.

179. Meinecke argues that the tiles of the al-Tawrizi Mosque may have been overstock from a restoration of the Umayyad Great Mosque of Damascus in 1416, which is recorded in an

179. inscription on stucco decoration on the northern interior wall: Meinecke, "Syrian Blue-and-White Tiles," 210.

180. Ashmolean Museum, Oxford, inv. no. EA1981.48; Blessing, "Blue-and-White Tiles," 119, fig. 29. It is unclear whether the current assemblage of tiles reflects an original group or simply the modern art market.

181. Victoria and Albert Museum, London, inv. no. 418-1898; Blessing, "Blue-and-White Tiles," 119, fig. 30.

182. https://collections.vam.ac.uk/item/O179375/tile-unknown (accessed March 30, 2020). A total of 106 tiles purchased for the V&A's collections between 1881 and 1900 have been attributed to Damascus, although Carswell notes that the group bought in 1898 was acquired in Cairo and the tiles in 1900 were bought from London dealers: Carswell, "Six Tiles," 104.

183. Jenkins, "Mamluk Underglaze-Painted Pottery," 104 and 111.

184. Ibid., 111–12; illustrated in Riefstahl, "Early Turkish Tile Revetments," fig. 28, and Millner, *Damascus Tiles*, fig. 3.34; Kanda, "Revisiting the So-Called Ghaybī Workshop," 42–43.

185. Jenkins, "Mamluk Underglaze-Painted Pottery," 112 and plate 15a and b; New York, Metropolitan Museum of Art, inv. no. 1973.79.20.

186. Kanda, "Revisiting the So-Called Ghaybī Workshop," 40–47.

187. Aube, "La mosquée bleue de Tabriz," 250–68; Aube, *La céramique dans l'architecture en Iran au XVᵉ siècle*, 85 ff.; Aube, "Uzun Hasan Mosque," 36–44.

188. Riefstahl, "Early Turkish Tile Revetments," 268–69; Meinecke, *Fayencedekorationen seldschukischer Sakralbauten*, 1:98; 2:172–75; Aube, *La céramique dans l'architecture en Iran au XVᵉ siècle*, 199–200; Mahi, "Les 'Maîtres de Tabriz,'" 45–46; Keskin, "Siyasi-kültürel İlişkiler," 457–58.

189. Konyalı, *Âbideleri ve Kitâbeleri ile Karaman Tarihi*, 408–10; Diez, Aslanapa, and Koman, *Karaman Devri Sanatı*, 67–84; Blessing, "All Quiet on the Eastern Frontier?" 214–18.

190. Samkoff, "From Central Asia to Anatolia," 199–202. The tiles are in the Metropolitan Museum of Art, New York, inv. no. 08.185 a, b. As Samkoff notes, Meinecke examined not these tiles, but a similar fragment in the Museum of Islamic Art in Berlin (inv. no. I. 1309, see www.smb-digital.de/eMuseumPlus?service=ExternalInterface&module=collection&objectId=1520949&viewType=detailView [accessed May 23, 2019]) to make his case for late-fourteenth-century Karamanid production: Meinecke, *Fayencedekorationen seldschukischer Sakralbauten*, vol. 2: 346–49, cat. no. 84.

191. Ersoy, "Edirne Şah Melek Camii'nin Tanıtımı"; Ünver, "Edirne Şah Melek Paşa Cami'i"; Aslanapa, *Edirnede Osmanlı Devri Âbideleri*, 100–103; Ayverdi, *Osmanlı Mimârîsinde Çelebi ve II. Sultan Murad Devri*, 417–20. This monument is mentioned in the chronology of the Masters of Tabriz, but not discussed further, in Atasoy, Raby, and Petsopoulos, *Iznik*, 88. Broken fragments of tiles from the Şah Melek Pasha Mosque in the Museum of Islamic Art in Edirne clearly show a red body and exclusively black lines: author's observation, August 2019.

192. Whitehouse, "Siraf."

193. Marçais, *Les faïences à reflets métalliques de la Grande Mosquée de Kairouan*.

194. Map in Watson, *Persian Lustre Ware*, 16–17.

195. Denny, *Iznik*, 64. On the Ramazanoğulları, see Uzunçarşılı, *Anadolu Beylikleri*, 176–79.

196. Thackston, *A Century of Princes*, 332; Necipoğlu, *The Topkapı Scroll*, 213.

197. Necipoğlu, *The Topkapı Scroll*, 212–13; Lentz and Lowry, *Timur and the Princely Vision*, 159–236.

198. O'Kane, "Poetry, Geometry and the Arabesque."

199. Yüksel Muslu, *The Ottomans and the Mamluks*, 94–101.

200. Roxburgh, "Timurid Architectural Revetment," 127.

201. TKSM H.2152, fol. 22a: Roxburgh, "Timurid Architectural Revetment," 127–28 and fig. 10.8.

202. Bloom, *Paper before Print*, 192.

203. Ibid., 189–90.

204. Atasoy, Raby, and Petsopoulos, *Iznik*, 59–60.

205. Necipoğlu, *The Age of Sinan*, 77–103.

206. Phillips, *Tapestry*, 32. Jardine and Brotton, *Global Interests*, 76; Necipoğlu, "Diez Albums," 537 with sources; Necipoğlu, "Visual Cosmopolitanism," 3–4, arguing that one of the tapestries may have ended up in Samarqand as part of Timur's booty following his defeat of Bayezid I.

207. Yüksel Muslu, *The Ottomans and the Mamluks*, 134–52.

208. Har-El, *Struggle for Domination*, 133–214.

4   BUILDING PARADISE

1. Ergenç, *XVI. Yüzyılın Sonlarında Bursa*, maps 3 and 5.

2. Goodwin, *Ottoman Architecture*, 70–73; Kuran, *Mosque in Early Ottoman Architecture*, 120–23; Gabriel, *Une capitale turque*, 1:105–29; Ayverdi, *Osmanlı Mimârîsinde Çelebi ve II. Sultan Murad Devri*, 298–327. The madrasa has been used as a community health clinic, and during my most recent visit in March 2016 it was undergoing restoration.

3. VGMA, defter 741, sayfa 225–28, sıra 126. Facsimile in Öcalan, Sevim, and Yavaş, *Bursa Vakfiyeleri*, 430–35; Turkish summary ibid., 414–16.

4. The Oxford Anonymous Chronicle mentions the mausoleum as part of the sultan's foundations, but since this work was not compiled until the 1490s, this does not necessarily have to be taken at face value. For the passage, see Kastritsis, *An Early Ottoman History*, 170.

5. Necipoğlu, "Dynastic Imprint," 27–29. On the Selimiye Mosque in Edirne, see Necipoğlu, *The Age of Sinan*, 238–56.

6. Necipoğlu, "Dynastic Imprint," 26.

7. Singer, "Enter, Riding on an Elephant," 91–92, 97.

8. Ibid., 94.

9. Ibid., 108.

10. Harmanşah, "Introduction: Towards an Archaeology of Place," 1.

11. Kuran, "Spatial Study of Three Ottoman Capitals," 117–18; Pancaroğlu, "Architecture, Landscape, and Patronage," 41–46.

12. Singer, *Charity in Islamic Societies*, 67–145.

13. Mermutlu and Öcalan, *Bursa Hazireleri*, 526. I thank Özer Ergenç for providing me with a copy of this book.

14. Kuran, *Mosque in Early Ottoman Architecture*, 71–72; Salgırlı, "Architectural Anatomy of an Ottoman Execution," 318n27; Necipoğlu, *The Age of Sinan*, 49–50; Çağaptay, "Frontierscape," 158. On Murad II's mosque-*zāviye*, see Emir, "Reconstructing an Early Ottoman Building."

15. Blessing, "Seljuk Past," 228.

16. Blessing, "Blue-and-White Tiles," 114.

17. St. Laurent, "Léon Parvillée," 252–53 and 259–63; Turnbull, "The Muradiye," 224–25; Eroğlu and Güleç, "Victoria & Albert Müzesi"; Walter B. Denny, email communication to the author, July 2018.

18. Gabriel, *Une capital turque*, 1:111; Mantran, "Les inscriptions arabes de Brousse," 94, no. 11.

أمر ببناء هذه العمارة الشريفة المباركة سلطانُ العربِ والعجم ظلُّ الله في العالم السلطانُ بنِ السلطانِ السلطانُ مراد بن محمّد ابن بايزيد خان خلّد الله ملكَهُ في شهر رجب سنة ثمن وعشرين وثمانمائة ووقع الاتمام في شهر محرّم الحرام ثمن وثلاثين ثمانمائة

19. Necipoğlu, "Dynastic Imprint," 33.

20. Ibid., 27; Vatin and Veinstein, *Le sérail ébranlé*, 21. The *vasiyet-nāme*, further discussed later in this chapter, is published in Sertoğlu, "İkinci Murad'ın Vasiyetnamesi"; Uzunçarşılı, "Sultan II. Murad'ın Vasiyetnamesi"; İnalcık, *Fatih Devri Üzerinde Tetkikler ve Vesikalar*, 204–14.

21. Mackie, *Symbols of Power*, 22–26. Generally, the renewal of textiles at both sites was the privilege of the ruler who claimed sovereignty over them – that is, the Mamluks from 1258 until 1517 and the Ottomans from 1517 to 1918.

22. Leisten, "Between Orthodoxy and Exegesis," 12–14.

23. Ibid., 18–19; Leisten, *Architektur für Tote*, 5–23. On early examples, see Grabar, "The Earliest Islamic Commemorative Structures"; Michailidis, "Landmarks of the Persian Renaissance."

24. In contradiction to this identification, Neşri notes that Ahmed was buried in the mausoleum of Mehmed I: Neşri, *Cihânnümâ*, ed. Öztürk, 281.

25. Gabriel, *Une capitale turque*, 1:118. Two further sons of Murad II, Orhan (d. 1451) and Hüseyin (d. 1450), are buried in a mausoleum behind the Darü'l-Hadis Mosque in Edirne: Ayverdi, *Osmanlı Mimârîsinde Çelebi ve II. Sultan Murad Devri*, 384–85.

26. İnalcık, *Fatih Devri Üzerinde Tetkikler ve Vesikalar*, 57; Karataş, "The City as Historical Actor," 48.

27. Author's translation with modifications after the readings in Gabriel, *Une capitale turque*, 116–18; Mantran, "Les inscriptions arabes de Brousse," 109, no. 39; and Ayverdi, *Osmanlı Mimârîsinde Çelebi ve II. Sultan Murad Devri*, 321.

بسم الله الرحمن الرحيم الحمدُ لله المتوحّد بالبقاء المنزّه عن الزوّال والفضاء و صلّى الله على من أرسلَهُ بالحنفية البيضاء و آلِهِ و أصحابِه الكرام أمّا بعد فقد إنتقل من دار الفَنَاء وغرور الى دار البقاء والسرور ومن منزل العناء والترح الى محفل الغناء والفرح سلطانُ سلاطين الدهر مالِك ممالِك البرّ والبحر سلطانُ الغزاة والمجاهدين ملجأ الضعفاءِ والمساكين فخرُ السلاطين آل عثمان مخصوص بعناية المَلِك المنان السلطانُ بن السلطان مراد ابن السلطان مِحمّد بن السلطان بايزيد خان نواءُهُ اللهُ تعالى على غرف الجنان و افاض عليه … الغفران ضحوةَ الأربعاء غرّة محرّم الحرام سنةِ خمس وخمسين وثمانمائة

28. إنتقل من دار الفناء إلى دار البقاء الصاحب المعظّم فخر الدين علي بن الحسين نوّر الله مثواهُ في أوج من شوال سنة أربع وثمانين وستمائة *RCEA*, No. 4863; *Thésaurus d'épigraphie islamique*, no. 3563, 2b. Analysis in Blessing, "Commemoration," 247.

29. Halevi, *Muhammad's Grave*, 198–200 and 213–15. Smith and Haddad, *Islamic Understanding*, 33 and 41–46.

30. Halevi, *Muhammad's Grave*, 208.

31. Carra de Vaux, "Barzakh"; Zaki, "Barzakh"; Smith and Haddad, *Islamic Understanding*, 9; Halevi, *Muhammad's Grave*, 201–05.

32. Halevi, *Muhammad's Grave*, 226–33.

33. Meri, *Cult of Saints*, 126–38; Heffening and Schacht, "Ḥanafiyya," *EI2*; Beránek and Ťupek, *The Temptation of Graves*, 40–48.

34. All three documents are published in printed Arabic script and discussed in İnalcık, *Fatih Devri Üzerinde Tetkikler ve Vesikalar*, 204–15. Turkish translation and facsimile of the Arabic document in Sertoğlu, "İkinci Murad'ın Vasiyetnamesi"; Turkish translation of the same document in Uzunçarşılı, "Sultan II. Murad'ın Vasiyetnamesi." The Arabic document is cataloged as a *waqfiya* in BOA Maliye'den Müdevver Vakfiyeler 162/14: Sertoğlu, "İkinci Murad'ın Vasiyetnamesi," 67; and İnalcık, *Fatih Devri Üzerinde Tetkikler ve Vesikalar*, 209.

35. *Vasiyetnāme* of Murad II, after unpaginated facsimile in Sertoğlu, "İkinci Murad'ın Vasiyetnamesi," l. 62–63. Sertoğlu, "İkinci Murad'ın Vasiyetnamesi," 67, gives the date as the middle of Jumadha I 850 AH / July 1446 CE. On page 69, however, the same author correctly reads the date as the "middle of Jumadha II 850," so the first mention is most likely the result of an editing mistake. Sertoğlu and Uzunçarşılı ostensibly refer to the same document since Sertoğlu indicates BOA Maliye'den Müdevver Vakfiyeler 162/14 (p. 67) while Uzunçarşılı indicates BOA Maliye'den Müdevver, A kismi, no. 162/14, cataloged as *waqfiya* for Murad II's mosque in Bursa ("Sultan II. Murad'ın Vasiyetnamesi," 1, note 1). While Uzunçarşılı gives a facsimile of the Arabic document, the text he renders is that of a fifteenth-century Turkish version of the document: Uzunçarşılı, "Sultan II. Murad'ın Vasiyetnamesi," 1. Uzunçarşılı does not give the archival catalog reference, but this probably corresponds to the current catalog number BOA AE.SMRD.II 1/6, dated Rajab 850 AH / September 22 to October 19, 1446 CE.

36. ʿAlā al-Dīn ʿAlī: Uzunçarşılı, "Sultan II. Murad'ın Vasiyetnamesi," 3n8.

37. وأوصى أَن يُدفنَ في مدينة بُروسا يأتي جَنَبَ ولدِهِ السلطان على الدين بعيد منهُ مقدارٌ ثلاثةَ أذرع أو أربعة ويُضعُ على التراب كم هو؟ … السنّةُ المتوارثة ولا يجعل له سرداباً أكابِر السلاطين وأوصى أَن يُبنى حولَ مرقدِهما الشريف جدرانٌ اربعةٌ و يسقّفُ فوقها من الجوانب الأربعة ليجلس تحتَها القِراء ويكون وسطُ سقف مكشوفاً … لِيُنزل عن المرقد غيبْ هو مين آثار رحمة الله ويُصرفُ إلى بنايهِ خمسة آلاف افلوري من ذلك المالِ و أوصى أَن لا يُوضعَ فيها بعدَهُ احدْ من أولاده و اقربائه و أوصى أنه إن لم يتوفَ طولَ الله تعالى عمره بالتوفيق في مدينة بُروسا يؤتي به الى اليها بحيث يصل اليها في يوم الخميس ليكون اوّل ما يبيت تحت الأرض ليلة الجمعة

Vasiyetnāme of Murad II, l. 45–53. Arabic text after unpaginated facsimile in Sertoğlu, "İkinci Murad'ın Vasiyetnamesi," and İnalcık, *Fatih Devri Üzerinde Tetkikler ve Vesikalar*, 211–12.

38. Campo, "Burial." None of these rules regarding the handling of corpses are contained in the Qur'an; rather, they are based on hadith: Halevi, *Muhammad's Grave*, 206–07.

39. Halevi, *Muhammad's Grave*, 158–59.
40. Kramers, "Murād II"; İnalcık, "Murad II."
41. Neşri, *Cihânnümâ*, ed. Öztürk, 280–81; ʿAşıkpaşazâde, *Âşıkpaşazâde Tarihi*, ed. Öztürk 188–89; Vatin and Veinstein, *Le sérail ébranlé*, 21.
42. Neşri, *Cihânnümâ*, ed. Öztürk, 280–81. The thirteen-day delay is also noted in ʿAşıkpaşazâde, *Âşıkpaşazâde Tarihi* ed. Öztürk, 188–89; Kastritsis, *An Early Ottoman History*, 174; Ahmed Tevhid, "İlk Altı Padişahımızın Bursa'da Kāʾin Türbelerinden Hüdavendigar Murad Han Türbesi ve Sultan Murad Han Sani Türbesi," 1056.
43. Schönig, "Camphor"; Dietrich, "Kāfūr."
44. İnalcık, "Murad I"; Vatin and Veinstein, *Le sérail ébranlé*, 38–39; Oğuz Kursar, "Sultans as Saintly Figures," 82–86. On the memorial structure built on the battlefield, see Eren, "Kosova'da I. Murad Hüdavendigar Türbesine Ait Tarihî Bir Belge"; and Samsakçı, ed., *Kosova Kitâberleri*, 46–53. On Murad I's death and burial in Bursa, see Neşri, *Cihânnümâ*, ed. Öztürk, 127–29; and Oruç Beğ, *Oruç Beğ Tarihi*, ed. Öztürk, 29–30.
45. Kovács and Rabb, "On the Preservation of Ottoman Monuments in Hungary," 178 and 189n43.
46. Eldem, *İstanbul'da Ölüm*, 90–95.
47. Goodwin, "Gardens of the Dead," 61. The account is found in Vámbéry, *Arminius Vámbéry*, 89–91. On the development of these corpse transfers from Iran to Ottoman Iraq from the sixteenth to the nineteenth centuries, see Ateş, "Bones of Contention"; and Nakash, *The Shi'is of Iraq*, 184–201.
48. For a section and plan of the mausoleum, see Gabriel, *Une capitale turque*, vol. 1: fig. 57.
49. On the construction of crypts where bodies could sometimes be kept on the floor, perhaps in shrouds or coffins, rather than buried in the ground, see Önkal, "Türk Türbe Mimarisinde Cenaze Katının Gelişimi."
50. On the practice of mummification in medieval Anatolia, see Konyalı, "Türklerde Mumya ve Mumyacılık"; Sümer, "The Seljuk Turbehs and the Tradition of Embalming." The bodies Konyalı describes have since disappeared, and since no medical studies were performed, it is unclear if embalming techniques involving medicinal plants were used. One such plant is discussed in Schönig, "Camphor."
51. Gabriel, *Une capitale turque*, vol. 1: fig. 39.
52. Ibn Baṭṭūta, Rihlat, ed. al-Mahidi, 1:195. This reference needs to be taken with caution since the suspended coffin may be a reference to the apocryphal story about the Gunbad-i Kabus, built for the Ziyarid ruler Qabus b. Vushmgir in Gurgan, Iran, in 1006–07, a structure medieval chroniclers describe as containing a suspended crystal coffin: Michailidis, "Landmarks of the Persian Renaissance," 280–81.
53. While Mehmed I's mausoleum has a crypt, the mausolea of Osman, Orhan, and Murad I were completely rebuilt after the 1855 earthquake. Osman and Orhan were originally buried in adapted Byzantine ecclesiastical or monastic buildings: Eyice, "Bursa'da Osman ve Orhan Gazi Türbeleri; Çağaptay, "Prousa/Bursa," 53–62; Çağaptay, *The First Capital*, 39–46. Remains of an opus sectile floor in Orhan's current mausoleum are a central piece of evidence: Çağaptay, "Prousa/Bursa," 57–59.

54. A third burial is labeled as that of Şehzade Sultan, daughter of Murad II, in the site label, but not mentioned in any other sources. A fourth burial is not identified.
55. Turner and Turner, *Image and Pilgrimage*, 1–38.
56. Barry, "Walking on Water"; Pentcheva, *Hagia Sophia*, 122–31.
57. Milwright, "Waves of the Sea."
58. Kafescioğlu, *Constantinopolis/Istanbul*, 18–22.
59. Goodwin, "Gardens of the Dead," 66.
60. Gardet, "Djanna"; Hillenbrand, "Gardens beneath which Rivers Flow," 28–31; Smith and Haddad, *Islamic Understanding*, 87–90; Grabar, *Mediation of Ornament*, 212–13. More broadly on the role of water in Islamic aesthetics, see Puerta Vílchez, *La poética del agua en el Islam*.
61. Hillenbrand, "Gardens beneath which Rivers Flow," 32; Arabic in al-Suyuti, *al-Habāʾik fī akhbār al-malāʾik*, 14, no. 17; alternate English translation in Burge, *Angels in Islam*, 116.
62. Blessing, "Commemoration," 245–46.
63. Redford, "Intercession and Succession," 153.
64. Öcalan, Sevim, and Yavaş, *Bursa Vakfiyeleri*, 415, with reference to VGMA defter 741, sayfa 225–28, sıra 126, facsimile in ibid., 430–36.
65. Hay, "Seeing through Dead Eyes," 17–19.
66. Ibid., 27–51.
67. Hay also notes that different modes of representation applied for the parts of the tombs visible above ground: ibid., 18–20.
68. On visiting the graves of relatives, see Smith and Haddad, *Islamic Understanding*, 186. On the religious permissibility of building monumental structures on tombs, see Leisten, *Architektur für Tote*, 5–23. On the development of mausolea, see Grabar, "The Earliest Islamic Commemorative Structures"; and Michailidis, "Landmarks of the Persian Renaissance."
69. Goodwin, "Gardens of the Dead," 62.
70. O'Kane, "Arboreal Aesthetic"; Golombek, "Paysage."
71. Kalfazade, "Yeşilimaret Camii."
72. O'Kane, "The Arboreal Aesthetic," 227–31. These Timurid elements in the Üç Şerefeli Mosque are also noted in Necipoğlu, *The Age of Sinan*, 79, where they are described as "a regional variant of the international Timurid vocabulary."
73. O'Kane, "The Arboreal Aesthetic," 227 and 229. The difference between the color plates (pl. 26 and 27) and the current state of the paintings as I observed them on site in 2016 and 2019 is striking.
74. Golombek, "Paysage," 245–46; O'Kane, "The Bihbihani Anthology"; Aga-Oglu and Hall, "Landscape Miniatures," 79–85 and 91–94.
75. Aga-Oglu and Hall, "Landscape Miniatures," 78 and 86.
76. O'Kane, "The Bihbihani Anthology," 13–16.
77. Golombek, "Paysage,"
78. Grabar, *Mediation of Ornament*, 223.
79. Painted decoration is visible in Gabriel's photographs of the Cem Sultan Mausoleum (Gabriel, *Une capitale turque*, vol. 2: plate LXIV.4); the Prince Ahmed Mausoleum, although here labeled as Mustafa, son of Fatih [Mehmed II] (Gabriel, *Une capitale turque*, vol. 2: plate LXIV.1–2); and the Prince Mustafa Mausoleum (Gabriel, *Une capitale turque*, vol. 2, Plate LXV.1–2). For color photographs, see Necipoğlu, *The Age of Sinan*, 105.

80. Photographs of state before the restoration on site. For the Prince Mahmud Mausoleum, see Gabriel, *Une capitale turque*, vol. 2: plate LXVI.3.

81. Necipoğlu, "International Timurid."

82. On the connection between gardens and water, see Puerta Vílchez, *La poetica del agua en el Islam*, 54–76; Ruggles, *Islamic Gardens*, 13–27.

83. Riefstahl, "Early Turkish Tile Revetments." On the use of black-line tile in fifteenth-century Ottoman architecture, see Meinecke, *Fayencedekorationen seldschukischer Sakralbauten*, 1:102–20.

84. Necipoğlu, "International Timurid," 138–89.

85. *Sulṭān Selīm Hān bin Süleymān Hān emreden oldu hoş bu ravzegāh-i cennet. Dedi tārihin Edāyi bendesi marqad-e gülzār-e Sulṭān Muṣṭafā*, see Turnbull, "The Muradiye," 264–65.

86. Ruggles, *Islamic Gardens*, 103 and 109–16.

87. Ibid., 189–90.

88. Ibid., 110–16, 200–201, 203–04.

89. Ibid., 106–07.

90. Kafescioğlu, *Constantinopolis/Istanbul*, 45–51; Lecker, "Abū Ayyūb al-Anṣārī."

91. The sultan's wish is recorded in the *waqfiya* of his Istanbul mosque complex: Kafescioğlu, *Constantinopolis/Istanbul*, 217.

92. The pertinent law codes issued in 1925, explicitly to curb practices of *ziyārat*, are cited in Ayaşlıoğlu, "Istanbul'da Mahmut Paşa Türbesi," 148–50, n. 1.

93. See Appendix II for a list of mausolea with identified burials.

94. *BK*. I thank Selim S. Kuru for providing me with a typescript of the full text.

95. Gabriel, *Une capitale turque*.

96. Evliya Çelebi, *Seyahatnâme*, 2:13 and 29–31; Gazzizâde, *Hulāṣatü'l-vefāyāt*. Sır, "Gazzizâde Abdullatif"; Taşköprüzâde and Fındıklılı İsmet Efendi, *Şakaik-i Nu'maniye ve Zeylleri*, ed. Özcan, 329–30.

97. BOA, TSMA.d 7009, dated 909 AH 1503–04 CE. The three princes are named on fols. 18a–b, after a long introduction praising the patron and his piety.

98. BOA, TSMA.d 7009, fol. 18b, line 8, to fol. 19b, line 4.

99. Ibid., fol. 20a, lines 3–5.

100. Ibid., fols. 22b–23b.

101. Ibid., fol. 23b, lines 3–6.

102. Uluçay, *Padişahların Kadınları*; Uluçay, "Bayazid II.'in Âilesi."

103. "kim niçe yüz aded şehzâdegân bintân nisvân vâlide-i sultânlar medfûndur." Evliya Çelebi, *Seyahatnâme*, 2:31.

104. Gabriel, *Une capitale turque*, 1:119–21.

105. On the latter structure, see Gabriel, *Une capitale turque*, 1:122–25. Turan, "Mustafa Çelebi," notes that Mustafa, who had been killed near Ereğli in the Konya region, was taken to Bursa for burial near the mausoleum of Murad II soon after his execution in 1553.

106. Gabriel, *Une capitale turque*, 1:121.

107. Ibid., 1:120.

108. Turnbull, "The Muradiye," 129–31.

109. The original text: "şehzâde Alaeddîn ḳarîbine defn olundu, fâtih sulṭān Meḥemmed evlādıdır." Gazzizâde, *Hulāṣatü'l-vefāyāt*, fol. 4r, l. 11–13.

110. Gazzizâde, *Hulāṣatü'l-vefāyāt*, fol. 5v, l. 3–10; *BK*, 1:65. For Ahmed and Korkud, see İnalcık, "Selîm I," *EI2*.

111. Label on Prince Ahmed Mausoleum; Önkal, *Osmanlı Hanedan Türbeleri*, 117–21; Turnbull, "The Muradiye," 169–84.

112. Uluçay "Bayazid II.'in Âilesi."

113. *BK*, 3:386; Önkal, *Osmanlı Hanedan Türbeleri*, 159.

114. *BK*, 3:165.

115. Ibid., 4:38.

116. Necipoğlu, "Dynastic Imprints," 27.

117. "sene 909 târîhinde katl olunup cesed-i pâkın Bursa'da Murâd-ı Sânî cenbinde bir kubbe-i âlî içinde âsûde kılındı." Evliya Çelebi, *Seyahatnâme*, 2:30. See also *BK*, BS.25/90.

118. Gazzizâde, *Hulāṣatü'l-vefāyāt*, fol. 5v, l. 2; Önkal, *Osmanlı Hanedan Türbeleri*, 95.

119. Gazzizâde, *Hulāṣatü'l-vefāyāt*, fol. 5r, l. 6–14. On the accession of Selim I and the elimination of his rivals, including Korkud and Ahmed, see Çıpa, *The Making of Selim*, 58–61.

120. Evliya Çelebi, *Seyahatnâme*, 2:29; Gazzizâde, *Hulāṣatü'l-vefāyāt*, fol. 5r, l. 6–14.

121. *BK*, 3:376 and 4:33.

122. On the practice of fratricide (often extending to both brothers and nephews of the new sultan), see Akman, *Osmanlı Devletinde Kardeş Katlı*.

123. Gabriel, *Une capitale turque*, 1:148; Önkal, *Osmanlı Hanedan Türbeleri*, 75–78. For the inscription, see Önkal, *Osmanlı Hanedan Türbeleri*, 76; and Mantran, "Les inscriptions arabes de Brousse," 110, no. 40.

124. Gabriel, *Une capitale turque*, 1:148; Önkal, *Osmanlı Hanedan Türbeleri*, 75.

125. Gülbahar Hatun Türbesi, label on site. On Gülbahar Hatun: Uluçay "Bayazid II.'in Âilesi," 107–08.

126. On Cem's burial, see Evliya Çelebi, *Seyahatnâme*, 2:30; Gazzizâde, *Hulāṣatü'l-vefāyāt*, fol. 4r, l. 17 to fol. 4v, l. 6.

127. Cem Sultan Mausoleum, label on site; Önkal, *Osmanlı Hanedan Türbeleri*, 85–89; Turnbull, "The Muradiye," 129–31. On Abdullah, see Uluçay, "Bayazid II.'in Âilesi," 109. On ʿAlemşah, see ibid., 111–12.

128. Prince Ahmed Mausoleum, label on site; Önkal, *Osmanlı Hanedan Türbeleri*, 117–21; Turnbull, "The Muradiye," 169–84. On Bülbül Hatun, see Uluçay "Bayazid II.'in Âilesi," 106–07; on Ahmed, see ibid., 109–11; on Korkud, see ibid., 113–14, on Şehinşah, see ibid., 116–17.

129. Prince Mahmud Mausoleum, label on site; Turnbull, "The Muradiye," 156–69; *BK*, 3:182. On Mahmud, see Uluçay "Bayazid II.'in Âilesi," 114–16.

130. Gazzizâde, *Hulāṣatü'l-vefāyāt*, fol. 5r, l. 6–14; Uluçay, "Bayazid II.'in Âilesi," 115. All three princes are buried in the Muradiye, according to *Bursa Kütüğü*: *BK*, 3:376, 4:33.

131. Mükrime Hatun Mausoleum, label on site; Önkal, *Osmanlı Hanedan Türbeleri*, 94–98; Turnbull, "The Muradiye," 205–13.

132. Gülruh Hatun Mausoleum, label on site; *BK*, 2:148; Önkal, *Osmanlı Hanedan Türbeleri*, 131–34; Turnbull, "The Muradiye," 194–205. On Gülruh Hatun, see Uluçay, "Bayazid II.'in Âilesi," 108. On Kamer Sultan, see Uluçay, *Padişahların Kadınları*, 51.

133. Gülşah Hatun Mausoleum label on site; *BK*, 2:148; Önkal, *Osmanlı Hanedan Türbeleri*, 92–93. Turnbull, "The

Muradiye," 146, indicates several possible dates for the death of Gülşah Hatun: 1474, 1478–79, 1486, or 1487.

134. Gabriel, *Une capital turque*, 1:127–28; Önkal, *Osmanlı Hanedan Türbeleri*, 108–09; Turnbull, "The Muradiye," 184–94. On Şirin Hatun: Uluçay "Bayazid II.'in Âilesi," 109. On ʿAyn-ı Şah, see ibid., 119.

135. On the execution, see Turan, "Mustafa Çelebi," 291; Evliya Çelebi, *Seyahatnâme*, 2:31.

136. Prince Mustafa Türbesi, label on site; Önkal, *Osmanlı Hanedan Türbeleri*, 85–89; Turnbull, "The Muradiye," 214–33.

137. On the execution, see Turan, "Bayezid, Şehzade," although according to this source, Prince Bayezid and his sons were buried in Sivas.

138. Turnbull, "The Muradiye," 89–94.

5   AN OTTOMAN AESTHETIC

1. Çağman, "Baba Nakkaş"; Ünver, "Baba Nakkaş," 169–71. Before the *waqfiya* was discovered, Baba Nakkaş was thought to have been attached to the court of Bayezid II, as mentioned in Evliya Çelebi's seventeenth-century account: discussion in Ünver, "Baba Nakkaş," 169.

2. Ünver, "Baba Nakkaş," 171; Çağman, "Baba Nakkaş." His son and grandson are documented in the period of Süleyman and Selim II: Ünver, "Baba Nakkaş," 171–73.

3. Ünver, *Fatih Devri Saray Nakışhanesi*.

4. Necipoğlu, *The Age of Sinan*. On the office of imperial architects from the sixteenth to the late eighteenth centuries, see Şerafettin Turan, "Osmanlı Teşkilâtında Hassa Mimarları," where it is noted that in 1526, members of the *hassa mimarları* numbered eighteen, while in the following years, there were only fourteen, suggesting that the number was flexible.

5. Kafadar, "A Rome of One's Own," 11–16.

6. Around 1467, Bayezid was married to Ayşe Hatun, daughter of deposed Dulkadir ʿAla al-Dawla, whose brother Şehsuvar had been supported by Mehmed II in a succession conflict: Venzke, "Dulkadir."

7. Babinger, "Reliquienschacher," 11–27; Vatin, *L'ordre de Saint-Jean-de-Jérusalem*, 178, 194.

8. Vatin, *L'ordre de Saint-Jean-de-Jérusalem*, 188–93, 209–39.

9. İnalcık, "A Case Study in Renaissance Diplomacy," 67–68, 70–78.

10. Şakiroğlu, "Cem Sultan"; *An Early Ottoman History*, ed. Kastritsis, 214.

11. On Bayezid II's circle, see Reindl, *Männer um Bāyezīd*; Kappert, *Die osmanischen Prinzen*, 19–68; Karataş, "Karamânî Ulemâ"; Karataş, "The City as Historical Actor," 81–83, 103–11, 117.

12. Ayverdi and Yüksel, *Osmanlı Mimârisi*, 1:218–51. Kafescioğlu suggests that Bayezid II initially prioritized construction in other cities because of the extensive patronage Mehmed II had devoted to Istanbul: Kafescioğlu, *Constantinopolis/Istanbul*, 214.

13. BOA EV.VKF.4–10–2, a folder containing two identical, later copies of the document. Both show the original date of 890 AH / 1485–86 CE. (I was able to study the original documents in 2014 before they were digitized.)

14. Curry, *The Rise of the Halveti Order*, 52; Karataş, "The City as Historical Actor," 50, 60–62, 67–68; Karataş, "A Shaykh, a Prince, and a Sack of Corn," 83–84.

15. Karataş, "Karamânî Ulemâ," 285–88; Curry, *The Rise of the Halveti Order*, 50–68; Kafescioğlu, *Constantinopolis/Istanbul*, 220–21.

16. Kafescioğlu, *Constantinopolis/Istanbul*, 220–21 and plan on 223: fig. 150. Karataş, "Karamânî Ulemâ," 286–87.

17. Uzunçarşılı, *Kitâbeler*, 121. Uzunçarşılı does not name a source for the piece of information that Bayezid II added an endowment, but what he recounts corresponds to the content of BOA EV.VKF.4–10–2.

18. Har-El, *Struggle for Domination in the Middle East*; Venzke, "Dulkadir."

19. Yıldırım, "The Safavid-Qilzilbash Ecumene," 452–56; Karakaya-Stump, *The Kizilbash/Alevis in Ottoman Anatolia*, 220–29.

20. Yılmaz, *Caliphate Redefined*, 31–64, 241–51.

21. Balafrej, *The Making of the Artist*, 1–24, 184–213.

22. Shahin, "Qaytbay's Decoration"; Kessler, *Carved Masonry Domes*; Meinecke, *Die mamlukische Architektur*, 1:173–79.

23. Necipoğlu, "Early Modern Floral," 133.

24. A matching pair originally commissioned for Bayezid II's mosque complex in Edirne (1484–88) has survived: TİEM, inv. no. 139 A–B, published in Roxburgh, ed., *Turks*, cat. no. 256, pp. 441–42 and image on p. 299, where it is stated (442) that the candlesticks were used in the Selimiye Mosque in Edirne before entering the museum. A similar candlestick from Bayezid II's Amasya complex is preserved in the Amasya Archaeological Museum, author's observation, August 2018.

25. See Chapter 3, n. 196.

26. Çağman and Tanındı, *The Topkapı Saray Museum: The Albums*, 87. Raby, "Mehmed the Conqueror's Greek Scriptorium."

27. Necipoğlu, *Architecture, Ceremonial, and Power*, 46.

28. Ünver, *Fatih Devri Saray Nakışhanesi*, 5; Uluç, "The Perusal of the Topkapı Albums," 125.

29. Bağcı and Tanındı, "Art of the Ottoman Court," 265.

30. Ibid., 265–66; Atasoy and Raby, *Iznik*, 79–81; Roxburgh, ed. *Turks*, cat. nos. 236, 277, 278.

31. Necipoğlu, "From Byzantine Constantinople to Ottoman Kostantiniyye," 264.

32. Ibid., 262–65; Necipoğlu, "Visual Cosmopolitanism."

33. On the use of stencils, see Atasoy, Raby, and Petsopoulos, *Iznik*, 59–60.

34. Necipoğlu, "Diez Albums," 534. See also Swietochowski, "Drawing," 538–39.

35. Raby, "Mehmed II Fatih and the Fatih Albums," 47–48, unfortunately without indication of the folios in question.

36. Necipoğlu, "Diez Albums," 532–53.

37. Raby, "Mehmed II Fatih and the Fatih Albums," 48. Necipoğlu, "Diez Albums," 532, favors a date soon after Selim I's conquest of Tabriz in 1514.

38. Raby, "Mehmed II Fatih and the Fatih Albums," 48; Necipoğlu, "Diez Albums," 533.

39. The catalog is now preserved in the Library of the Hungarian Academy of Sciences in Budapest. For a detailed study and facsimile, see Necipoğlu, Kafadar, and Fleischer, eds., *Treasures of Knowledge*.

40. Kafadar, "Between Amasya and Istanbul," 91–92.

NOTES TO PAGES 183–89

41. Necipoğlu, "Spatial Organization," 1.

42. Fleischer, "Learning and Sovereignty," 155.

43. Kafadar, "Between Amasya and Istanbul," 99–100.

44. Ibid., 80.

45. Necipoğlu, "Spatial Organization," 42. For an example of a manuscript with drawings of pulleys and similar devices that show familiarity with Renaissance drawings, see ibid., 56–57; Kafadar, "Between Amasya and Istanbul," 90–91.

46. Fleischer, "Learning and Sovereignty," 159.

47. The pages measure 385 x 280 mm, according to the catalog on site at the Rare Books Library of Istanbul University Library. Since I was only able to view digital reproductions of the album, the measurements provided are calculated based on the overall measurements of the page. Since the album was rebound for the Yıldız Palace Library, it is possible that pages may have been slightly larger originally. Some designs are cut straight along the edges of the existing folios.

48. Markiewicz, Crisis of Kingship, 279.

49. Crane and Akın, Sinan's Autobiographies.

50. Roxburgh, The Persian Album, 9–11.

51. Ibid., chapter 1, section Perspectives on the Persian Album as Collection, Yale AAE e-book without page numbers.

52. Ibid.

53. The album is now in the Topkapı Palace Library, H.2154; the preface is translated in Thackston, A Century of Princes, 335–50. Roxburgh, Prefacing the Image, Roxburgh, Prefacing the Image, 160–208; Roxburgh, The Persian Album, chapter 1, section Perspectives on the Persian Album as Collection, Yale AAE e-book without page numbers.

54. Roxburgh, The Persian Album, chapter 1, section Perspectives on the Persian Album as Collection, Yale AAE e-book without page numbers.

55. Such rebinding happened in the case of a number of albums selected for that library by Sultan Abdülhamid II (r. 1876–1909): Roxburgh, The Persian Album, chapter 1, section Perspectives on the Persian Album as Collection, Yale AAE e-book without page numbers.

56. Atasoy, Raby, and Petsopoulos, Iznik, 82–83. For the attribution of production to Miletus based on the large numbers of fragments excavated there, see Wulzinger, Wittek, and Sarre, Das islamische Milet, 72–74.

57. Aslanapa, "Pottery and Kilns from the Iznik Excavations," 142 and fig. 5; Atasoy, Raby, and Petsopoulos, Iznik, 82. On new finds of such wares in Iznik, see Demirsar Arlı, "İznik Çini Fırınları Kazısı 2017 Yılı Çalışmaları," 351–52 and figs. 8–9. Further wasters were found in Kütahya and Akçaalan near Ezine: Atasoy, Raby, and Petsopoulos, Iznik, 82. Further on the Miletus and Iznik excavations, see Yenişehirlioğlu, "Ottoman Anatolia," 176–79.

58. Raby and Henderson, "The Technology of Fifteenth-Century Turkish Tile," 115. For a comparative analysis of glazes using many of the same examples, see Simseka, Demirsar Arlı, Kayac and Philippe, "On-site pXRF Analysis."

59. Raby and Henderson, "The Technology of Fifteenth-Century Turkish Tile," 116.

60. Ibid., 117–18. The authors do not problematize the notion of a unified, continuous workshop, but of course this approach also provides a convenient explanation for the lack of large-scale tile programs dating from the 1480s to the 1510s.

61. Ibid., 118.

62. Blessing, "Blue-and-White Tiles, 116; Yenişehirlioğlu, "Les grandes lignes," 457.

63. British Museum, London, inv. no, G1, object record at www.britishmuseum.org/research/collection_online/collection_object_details.aspx?objectId=236618&partId=1 (accessed May 23, 2019).

64. Atasoy, Raby, and Petsopoulos, Iznik, 77. Excavations in Iznik were first conducted by Oktay Aslanapa in the 1960s: Aslanapa, "Pottery and Kilns from the Iznik Excavations." For the most recent excavation work on the İznik kilns, under the direction of Belgin Demirsar Arlı, see Demirsar Arlı, "İznik Çini Fırınları Kazısı 2017 Yılı Çalışmaları"; and Demirsar Arlı, "İznik Çini Fırınları Kazı Buluntularından Çini Örneklerin Değerlendirilmesi."

65. Atasoy, Raby, and Petsopoulos, Iznik, 77.

66. Examples in Atasoy, Raby, and Petsopoulos, Iznik, 78, figs. 55–58; Roxburgh, ed., Turks, cats. 277 and 278.

67. Louvre, Paris, inv. no. OA6321: Roxburgh, ed., Turks, cat. 277, notice on p. 447, image on p. 314.

68. British Museum, London, OA.1897.0618.1; see Roxburgh, ed., Turks, cat. 275, notice on p. 446–47, image on p. 312.

69. Metropolitan Museum of Art, New York, Rogers Fund, 1932, Accession Number 32.34, object record at www.metmuseum.org/art/collection/search/448664 (accessed July 4, 2020).

70. Yenişehirlioğlu, "Les grandes lignes," 457–60.

71. For examples of metalwork, see Atasoy, Raby, and Petsopoulos, Iznik, 78, figs. 66a, c, d.

72. Denny, "Dating Ottoman Works in the Saz Style"; Mackie, Symbols of Power, 286 and 305–06.

73. Atıl, ed. The Age of Sultan Süleyman, 38 and 255–57.

74. Metropolitan Museum of Art, New York, Harris Brisbane Dick Fund, 1959, Accession Number: 59.69.3, object record at: www.metmuseum.org/art/collection/search/451492, accessed 18 February 2021.

75. Atıl, ed. The Age of Sultan Süleyman, 38–42, figs. 1–5.

76. Ayverdi and Yüksel, Osmanlı Mimârisi, 1:191–302. This volume also includes monuments that have not survived, among them ones only recorded in Hüseyin Hüsameddin's Amasya Tarihi (see Chapter 3), so there is a certain margin for error.

77. Özcan, "Amasya'da Sancak Beyliği," 76–77; Karataş, "The City as Historical Actor," 93.

78. Özcan, "Amasya'da Sancak Beyliği," 72; Kafadar, "Between Amasya and Istanbul," 86.

79. Karataş, "The City as Historical Actor," 117; Kafescioğlu, Constantinopolis/Istanbul, 220–21. On the calligrapher, see Serin, "Hamdullah, Şeyh Efendi" and Kappert, Die osmanischen Prinzen, 50–53.

80. Karataş, "The City as Historical Actor," 49–53. Karataş argues that Amasya was neglected because Bayezid would not have had the financial resources for architectural patronage before becoming sultan, largely because Mehmed II favored Cem.

81. For a full catalog of extant or otherwise documented buildings in Amasya, see Ayverdi and Yüksel, Osmanlı Mimârisi, vol. 1 (letter A).

82. Ayverdi and Yüksel, Osmanlı Mimârisi, vol. 1 (letter A): 218–19, 223–52. The buildings are described in a document

83. Uluçay, "Bayazid II'in Âilesi," 109–10.

84. Ayverdi and Yüksel, *Osmanlı Mimârisi*, vol. 1 (letter A): 250, figs. 287 and 288; Dündar, "Bir Belgeye Göre Amasya II. Bayezid Külliyesi," 149. An undated photograph in the SALT Research archive in Istanbul shows the mosque with a collapsed porch, sometime before 1950: https://archives.salt research.org/handle/123456789/78828 (accessed May 22, 2020). According to Dündar, the porch collapsed in the 1939 earthquake: Dündar, "Bir Belgeye Göre Amasya II. Bayezid Külliyesi," 141.

85. Ayverdi and Yüksel, *Osmanlı Mimârisi*, vol. 1 (letter A): 225–26 and 240–41, figs. 266–68.

86. Ayverdi and Yüksel, *Osmanlı Mimârisi*, vol. 1 (letter A): 225.

87. The last examples are the Piri Pasha İmaret in Silivri (1530), the Gazi Hüsrev Beg Mosque in Sarajevo (1530), and the Hüsrev Pasha Mosque in Aleppo (1535): Eyice, "İlk Osmanlı Devrinin Dini İçtimai Bir Müessesesi," 47–48.

88. Dündar, "Bir Belgeye Göre Amasya II. Bayezid Külliyesi," 136, and 149–51. The interior decoration was once more redone in a new restoration campaign, limited to the mosque, begun in 2016 (author's observation, Amasya, August 2018).

89. Kuran, *Mosque in Early Ottoman Architecture*, 54; Kappert, *Die osmanischen Prinzen*, 71–72, 74. On the variants in accounts about Mehmed Pasha's career, see Keskin "II. Bayezid Dönemi Amasya Çevresinde Yerel Bir Bani," 64–65. On Mehmed Pasha's endowments, see ibid., 65–66.

90. Ayverdi and Yüksel, *Osmanlı Mimârisi*, 1:260; Uzunçarşılı, *Kitâbeler*, 126; Keskin "II. Bayezid Dönemi Amasya Çevresinde Yerel Bir Bani," 67.

91. Ayverdi and Yüksel, *Osmanlı Mimârisi*, 1:260.

92. Ibid., 1:263–64. On the mausoleum, see also Keskin "II. Bayezid Dönemi Amasya Çevresinde Yerel Bir Bani," 67.

93. Gabriel, *Monuments turcs*, 2:42; Keskin "II. Bayezid Dönemi Amasya Çevresinde Yerel Bir Bani," 66 and 68; Ayverdi and Yüksel, *Osmanlı Mimârisi*, 1:262. Ayverdi (263) lists further subsidiary structures that are mentioned in Hüseyin Hüsameddin's *Amasya Tarihi* but have vanished without a trace.

94. Ayverdi and Yüksel, *Osmanlı Mimârisi*, 1:267, for the plan drawing and cross-section.

95. Necipoğlu, *The Age of Sinan*, 52; Kafescioğlu, "Lives and Afterlives of an Urban Institution," 284.

96. On carpets, see İnalcık, *Studies in the History of Textiles in Turkey*, 31–57; Denny, *Anatolian Carpet*, 33–45.

97. TKSM, inv. no. 13/1515, 81.5 x 727 cm, published in Roxburgh, ed., *Turks*, cat. no. 292, pp. 321–23 and 451.

98. TİEM, inv. no. 67, 670 x 350 cm, published in Roxburgh, ed., *Turks*, cat. no. 248, pp. 292–93 and 440.

99. Ayverdi and Yüksel, *Osmanlı Mimârisi*, 1:259, under the name Kilari Selim Ağa Mosque, since "Selim" is the founder's name that appears in the foundation inscription.

100. Founded as a Friday mosque (*jāmiʿ*): inscription in ibid., 1:192.

101. In Istanbul, he was responsible for adding an endowment for convent rooms, a mausoleum, and a hammam connected to the Küyük Aya Sofya Mosque, the converted sixth-century church of Saints Sergius and Bacchus, which became an important Halveti center in the capital: Kafescioğlu, *Constantinopolis/Istanbul*, 223–24.

102. Ayverdi and Yüksel, *Osmanlı Mimârisi*, 1:257. Plan reconstruction in ibid., 1:278.

103. Ibid., 1:258.

104. Atasoy, Denny, and Mackie, *İpek*, 155; Kafadar, "Between Amasya and Istanbul," 86; Phillips, *Sea Change*, 77–81.

105. Atasoy, Denny, and Mackie, *İpek*, 155. On Tokat as a site of textile production in the late fifteenth century, see Phillips, *Sea Change*, 71–73.

106. Atasoy, Denny, and Mackie, *İpek*, 156; Çizakça, "A Short History of the Bursa Silk Industry," 143–44; Kafadar, "Between Amasya and Istanbul," 88.

107. Atasoy, Denny, and Mackie, *İpek*, 156–58.

108. Ćurčić, *Architecture in the Balkans*, 754.

109. Kuran, *Mosque in Early Ottoman Architecture*, 5.

110. On Ottoman Serres before the construction of this mosque, see Salgırlı, "Anatomy of an Ottoman Execution," 305–10; on the building, see Yüksel, *II. Bayezid*, 366–68; Ćurčić, *Architecture in the Balkans*, 752–53, Lowry, *In the Footsteps of the Ottomans*, 156–57. On Serres in the Ottoman period, see also Lowry, *The Shaping of the Ottoman Balkans*, 139–208, and Androudis, *Hē prōimē Othōmanikē technē kai architektonikē*, 519–29.

111. While the nearby Zincirli Camii – undated and without a foundation inscription – has been attributed to Selçuk Sultan and Heath Lowry has suggested a late fifteenth-century date, Maximilian Hartmuth has convincingly argued that the building must have been constructed in the late sixteenth century, quite possibly with funds from Selçuk Sultan's *waqf*: Hartmuth, "The Princess and the Mosque."

112. For a plan, see Osmanlı İzleri, http://ottoman.mfa.gov.tr/es er.aspx?g=88ad6ac6-6461-4d60-ab14-de1c59cf735a (accessed May 26, 2020). The building measures roughly 30.5 m x 30.5 m, and the dome has a span of 14.58 m: Ćurčić, *Architecture in the Balkans*, 753. Also see Androudis, *Hē prōimē Othōmanikē technē,* 527 and figures 859–74.

113. Plan in Ayverdi, *Avrupaʾda Osmanlı Mimârî Eserleri*, vol. 3 (Yugoslavya): 263, fig. 1363. Measurements in Ćurčić, *Architecture in the Balkans*, 756.

114. Ayverdi, *Avrupaʾda Osmanlı Mimârî Eserleri*, vol. 3 (Yugoslavya): 262. Ćurčić, *Architecture in the Balkans*, 756, maintains the erroneous identification of the patron as Koca Mustafa Pasha.

115. Ayverdi, *Avrupaʾda Osmanlı Mimârî Eserleri*, vol. 3 (Yugoslavya): 265–68; Hartmuth, "Ottoman Architecture in the Republic of Macedonia," 2.

116. Hartmuth, "Ottoman Architecture in the Republic of Macedonia," 5.

117. Late fifteenth- to sixteenth-century examples and plan types in Ćurčić, *Architecture in the Balkans*, 775–82.

118. Hartmuth, "Ottoman Architecture in the Republic of Macedonia," 4–5; Pelidija and Emecen, "İsa Beğ."

119. Boykov, "Reshaping Urban Space," 45–49.

120. Eyice, "Dâvud Paşa Hamamı"; Ćurčić, *Architecture in the Balkans*, 758–59.

121. Kafescioğlu, *Constantinopolis/Istanbul*, 215–17.

122. Plan in Hartmuth, "Ottoman Architecture in the Republic of Macedonia," fig. 6.

123. Ayverdi, *Avrupa'da Osmanlı Mimârî Eserleri*, vol. 3 (Yugoslavya): 264.

124. Author's observation on site, June 2016.

125. Examples attributed to Italy or Ottoman Anatolia are Metropolitan Museum of Art, New York, Rogers Fund, 1953, Accession Number: 53.157, object record at www.metmuseum.org/art/collection/search/201587 (accessed June 24, 2019), and Metropolitan Museum of Art, New York, Rogers Fund, 1912, Accession Number: 12.49.5, object record at www.metmuseum.org/art/collection/search/219393 (accessed June 24, 2019).

126. Yüksel, *Osmanlı Mimârîsinde II. Bâyezid, Yavuz Selim Devri*, 336–39 and 380–89.

127. Ibid., 103; Gökbilgin, *Edirne ve Paşa Livâsı*, 357–58. For the *waqfiya*, which survives in several versions in Arabic and Ottoman Turkish, see Gökbilgin, *Edirne ve Paşa Livâsı*, 358–61. See ibid., appendix, 3–172, for a full transliteration and black-and-white facsimile (without the margins) of the Ottoman Turkish *waqfiya*, dated 895 AH / 1489–90 CE, preserved as İ.B.B.A.K., MC O.61, accessible in color at http://ataturkkitapligi.ibb.gov.tr/kutuphane3/yazmalar/MC_Yz_O0061.pdf (accessed May 31, 2020).

128. Goodwin, *Ottoman Architecture*, 142.

129. Kafadar, "Between Amasya and Istanbul," 81.

130. Kafescioğlu, *Constantinopolis/Istanbul*, 213.

131. Yüksel, *Osmanlı Mimârîsinde II. Bâyezid, Yavuz Selim Devri*, 106–27, site plan on p. 109.

132. For the museum, see Tunca, *Edirne Sultan II. Bayezit Külliyesi ve Sağlık Müzesi*.

133. The attribution is, for instance, used in Mayer, *Islamic Architects*, 81–82. For critical analysis of this individual's role, see Eyice, "Hayreddin, Mimar"; Keskin, "Mehmed Paşa," 72; Necipoğlu, *The Age of Sinan*, 154–55. For sources about Hayrüddin, see Necipoğlu, *The Age of Sinan*, 154–55; Meriç, "Beyazıd Câmii Mimârî," 27–28.

134. See Kafescioğlu, *Constantinopolis/Istanbul*, 218, for a site plan.

135. Necipoğlu, "Architectural Dialogues," 601.

136. Kafescioğlu, *Constantinopolis/Istanbul*, 218–19.

137. Ibid., 222.

138. Ibid., 213–14, 222.

139. Ibid., 291–92; Kafadar, "Between Amasya and Istanbul," 81; İnalcık, "A Case Study in Renaissance Diplomacy," 69.

140. Necipoğlu, *The Age of Sinan*, 50, 52–53, 63; Kafescioğlu, *Constantinopolis/Istanbul*, 213.

141. Necipoğlu, *The Age of Sinan*, 153 and 155.

142. Şerafettin Turan, "Osmanlı Teşkilâtında Hassa Mimarları," 157–60; Necipoğlu, *The Age of Sinan*, 153.

143. Şerafettin Turan, "Osmanlı Teşkilâtında Hassa Mimarları," 159–60; Necipoğlu, *The Age of Sinan*, 153–57.

144. İ.B.B.A.K., MC O.71, accessible online at http://ataturkkitapligi.ibb.gov.tr/kutuphane3/yazmalar/MC_Yz_O0071.pdf (accessed May 22, 2020); full transcription and analysis in Gök, "Atatürk Kitaplığı M.C. O.71 Numaralı 909–933/1503–1527 Tarihli In'âmât Defteri." A transcription of the year 909 AH by Ömer Lütfi Barkan was published posthumously in 1979, without a foreword the author had intended to write before his death: Barkan, "İstanbul Saraylarına Ait Muhasebe Defterleri," 296–380. Contents relating to architecture are discussed in Meriç, "Beyazıd Câmii Mimârî."

145. İ.B.B.A.K., MC O.71, p. 24 (numbers in Arabic penciled in); Barkan, "İstanbul Saraylarına Ait Muhasebe Defterleri," 327; Gök, "Atatürk Kitaplığı M.C. O.71 Numaralı 909–933/1503–1527 Tarihli In'âmât Defteri," 155.

146. İ.B.B.A.K, MC O.71, p. 24 (numbers in Arabic penciled in); Barkan, "İstanbul Saraylarına Ait Muhasebe Defterleri," 327; Gök, "Atatürk Kitaplığı M.C. O.71 Numaralı 909–933/1503–1527 Tarihli In'âmât Defteri," 155; Necipoğlu, "Spatial Organization," 61n27.

147. Meriç, "Beyazıd Câmii Mimârî," 28–30. Notices in the Bursa court records relating to the construction of the Pirinç Han relate that *mi'mar* Ya'qubshah participated in the construction and give the name of his father, Sultanshah: Meriç, "Beyazıd Câmii Mimârî," 29.

148. Necipoğlu, *The Age of Sinan*, 130 and 155.

149. İ.B.B.A.K, MC O.71, p. 35 (numbers in Arabic penciled in); Gök, "Atatürk Kitaplığı M.C. O.71 Numaralı 909–933/1503–1527 Tarihli In'âmât Defteri," 179; Barkan, "İstanbul Saraylarına Ait Muhasebe Defterleri," 344–45.

150. İ.B.B. Atatürk Kitaplığı, MC O.71, p. 60; Gök, "Atatürk Kitaplığı M.C. O.71 Numaralı 909–933/1503–1527 Tarihli In'âmât Defteri," 237; Barkan, "İstanbul Saraylarına Ait Muhasebe Defterleri," 378.

151. Necipoğlu, *The Age of Sinan*, 155.

152. Ibid., 137. For the historical figure, see Sönmez, "Sinân-ı Atik."

153. Yerasimos, *La fondation de Constantinople*, 34; Evliya Çelebi, *Seyahatnâme*, 1:73, where the architect remains anonymous.

154. Yerasimos, *La fondation de Constantinople*, 34; Evliya Çelebi, *Seyahatnâme*, 1:73–74.

155. Barkan, *Süleymaniye Cami*, 1:107; French translation in Yerasimos, *La foundation de Constantinople*, 34; English translation in Necipoğlu, *The Age of Sinan*, 137.

156. İ.B.B.A.K., MC O.71, p. 24 (numbers in Arabic penciled in); Barkan, "İstanbul Saraylarına Ait Muhasebe Defterleri," 327; Gök, "Atatürk Kitaplığı M.C. O.71 Numaralı 909–933/1503–1527 Tarihli In'âmât Defteri," 155.

157. İ.B.B.A.K., MC O.71, p. 35; Gök, "Atatürk Kitaplığı M.C. O.71 Numaralı 909–933/1503–1527 Tarihli In'âmât Defteri," 172.

158. İ.B.B. Atatürk Kitaplığı, MC O.71, p. 60; Gök, "Atatürk Kitaplığı M.C. O.71 Numaralı 909–933/1503–1527 Tarihli In'âmât Defteri," 237.

159. Meriç, "Beyazıd Câmii Mimârî," 23.

160. Necipoğlu, *The Age of Sinan*, 177.

161. Ibid., 176.

162. Ibid., 178.

163. Barkan, *Süleymaniye Cami*, 1:341.

164. While we do not know where materials for Bayezid II's mosque came from, for the Süleymaniye, stone (both newly cut and spolia), timber, iron, and lead were sourced from across the Ottoman Empire: Barkan, *Süleymaniye Cami*, 1:331–93.

165. Taddei, "The Conversion of Byzantine Buildings"; Kiel, "Notes on the History of Some Turkish Monuments in Thessaloniki"; Ćurčić, *Architecture in the Balkans*, 748–54; Androudis, *Hē prōimē Othōmanikē technē kai architektonikē*, 283–408.

166. İpşirli, "Kayseri"; Çayırdağ, "Kayseri'de Kitabelerinden XV. Yüzyılda Yapıldığı Anlaşılan İlk Osmanlı Yapıları," 545–49.

167. Yıldız, "Post-Mongol Pastoral Polities," 37–39.

168. Yürekli, *Architecture and Hagiography*, 9. On Seyyitgazi, see also Yüksel, *Osmanlı Mimârîsinde II. Bâyezid, Yavuz Selim Devri*, 369–72.

169. Karataş, "Karamânî Ulemâ," 285–86, 289–90.

170. Blessing, *Rebuilding Anatolia*, 62–66.

171. Meinecke, *Fayencedekorationen*, 2:345; Karpuz, "Mevlânâ Külliyesi"; Önge, "Mevlana Türbesinin Çini Tezyinatı," 402–03.

172. Meinecke, *Fayencedekorationen*, 2:345; Karpuz, "Mevlânâ Külliyesi"; Önge, "Mevlana Türbesinin Çini Tezyinatı," 403.

173. Yürekli, *Architecture and Hagiography*, 17–18; Necipoğlu, *The Age of Sinan*, 63 and 65, fig. 36.

174. For the thirteenth-century shrine and changes made to it in the fifteenth and sixteenth centuries, see Yürekli, *Architecture and Hagiography*, 83–101. For the sixteenth-century interventions, see also Yüksel, *Osmanlı Mimârîsinde II. Bâyezid, Yavuz Selim Devri*, 369–72.

175. Yürekli, *Architecture and Hagiography*, 87–88.

176. For the early phases, see Yürekli, *Architecture and Hagiography*, 101–10. Discussion of a possible attribution of the first Ottoman phase to patronage of the Evrenosoğlu family: Yürekli, *Architecture and Hagiography*, 110–12. On Bayezid II's invitation to Balım Sultan, see Kafadar, "Between Amasya and Istanbul," 89. On the introduction of the term *kızılbaş* in the Ottoman Empire, see Baltacıoğlu-Brammer, "One Word, Many Implications," 47–48, 52–54.

177. Yürekli, *Architecture and Hagiography*, 112–13.

178. Kafadar, *Between Two Worlds*, 97.

179. Yüksel, "Hatuniye Külliyesi"; Yüksel, *Osmanlı Mimârîsinde II. Bâyezid, Yavuz Selim Devri*, 336–39; Riefstahl, *Turkish Architecture in Southwestern Anatolia*, 22–24.

180. Yüksel, *Osmanlı Mimârîsinde II. Bâyezid, Yavuz Selim Devri*, 380–89; Gabriel, *Monuments turcs*, 2:89–90.

181. Uzunçarşılı, *Anadolu Beylikleri*, 169–79.

182. Meinecke, *Die mamlukische Architektur*, vol. 2: 368, cat. 35/46; *Vakıf Abideler*, 1:35–37; *Thésaurus d'épigraphie islamique*, no. 30482. It is not clear why the mosque's current name in Turkish seems to evoke the name of Mamluk sultan Khushqadam (r. 1460–67), except perhaps for a mix-up based on the fact that both he and Chaqmaq used the title al-Malik al-Zahir and the *laqab* Sayf al-Din. The explicatory panel in Turkish on site has "Abudullah Hoşkadem, one of the *amīr*s of al-Malik al-Zahir Chaqmaq" as the patron (author's observation on site, December 2018).

183. It is possible that the inscription was recreated during a restoration. The minaret, for instance, may date to the nineteenth century, and the same is true for a portal on the west side of the building.

184. Photographs taken before a restoration in 2011 show the mihrab inscription highlighted with dark paint. This paint was removed in the restoration, unfortunately leaving the inscription largely illegible (author's observation on site, December 2018). On the restoration, see www.haberler.co m/563-yillik-tarihi-hoskadem-camii-restore-ediliyor-304167 4-haberi/ (accessed June 16, 2019). For the photographs, see www.adanadan.biz/icerik.asp?ICID=188 (accessed June 16, 2019).

185. The name Ramazanoğlu Mosque is also used in English-language scholarship about this building. Here I prefer to refer to it as Adana's Great Mosque (Ulu Cami), based on local present-day names, and to avoid confusion with the neo-Ottoman Ramazanoğlu Cami built in Adana in 2006. For the plan, see Erdmann, "Zur türkischen Baukunst," 24, fig. 7; and Aslanapa, *Türk Sanatı*, 2:244–45, line drawings 112 and 113.

186. Max von Oppenheim has the beginning of the inscription as the *basmala*, with the patron's name appearing later on: Oppenheim, *Inschriften*, 109–10, no. 144. In its present state, the sequence of the inscription starting on the right side of the portal recess, following the normal direction of Arabic, begins with the phrase "*al-ʿālī al-gharsī Khalīl ibn Ramaḍān ʿazza allāhu anṣārahu bi-taʾrīkh ṣaḥḥa khayrahu*" – that is, the patron's name and the chronogram. The *basmala* appears at the beginning of the panel over the doorway, followed by a Qurʾan passage. The inscription on the left side of the recess again begins with a *basmala*, followed by "*anshāʾ hadhā l-masjid l-mubārak l-muqarrar al-karīm.*" It is unclear whether this is the original arrangement or the result of a restoration that could have taken place anytime between Oppenheim's visit in 1899 and my own in 2018. The Arabic inscriptions published by Oppenheim as part of a larger project covering several languages were read by Max van Berchem based on Oppenheim's notes, photographs, and squeezes (see Van Berchem's introductory note in Oppenheim, *Inschriften*, 2–3). It is possible that Van Berchem, without having seen the building, arranged Oppenheim's materials in a sequence that would be more common – that is, with the *basmala* at the beginning and the date at the end of the text.

187. Oppenheim, *Inschriften*, 111, no. 149.

188. The second copy had "*anshā ʾhu*" instead of "Mustafa bin": Oppenheimer, *Inschriften*, 111n4. Mustafa died in 1552, as noted in the inscription on his cenotaph in the mausoleum at the Great Mosque in Adana (see later in this chapter). Piri Mehmed Pasha's surviving sons are named as Derviş Mehmed (d. 1569) and Ibrahim (d. 1586) in Uzunçarşılı, *Anadolu Beylikleri*, 178–79. Aslanapa, *Türk Sanatı*, 2:241, mentions Piri Mehmed Pasha as the patron of the 1541 project but does not comment on the inscriptions. Otto-Dorn, "Islamische Denkmäler Kilikiens," 119, cites the reading in Oppenheim's publication.

189. My reading. It is not clear if the title is spelled with the Ottoman Turkish "p" or with "b" in Arabic (*bāshā*). The start and end of the line are correctly read in Van Berchem's version: Oppenheimer, *Inschriften*, 111, no. 149.

190. Babinger, "Ramaḍan Oghullarī"; Sümer, "Ramazanoğulları"; Kurt, "Pîrî Mehmed Paşa, Ramazanoğlu". Not to be confused with grand vizier Piri Mehmed Pasha (d. 1532), in office from 1518 to 1523: Küçükdağ, "Pîrî Mehmed Paşa."

191. Oppenheim, *Inschriften*, 110–11, nos. 146 and 148.

192. Denny, "Ceramic Revetments," 58; Erdmann, "Zur türkischen Baukunst," 24–25, suggests that the *terminus post*

quem may also be valid for the tile decoration in the mosque and notes that, stylistically, a date around 1560 might be possible (25n100). Otto-Dorn, "Islamische Denkmäler Kilikiens," 121, suggests a date circa 1541. I follow Denny's detailed chronology, which results from his expertise on the tiles of the Rüstem Pasha Mosque in Istanbul.

193. Denny, "Ceramic Revetments," 61 and 64.

194. Ibid., 62–64.

195. Ibid., 59 and 64. Oktay Aslanapa suggests the wall tiles in the mausoleum were produced in Istanbul in the late eighteenth or early nineteenth century, but does not elaborate on his reasons for this date: Aslanapa, *Türk Sanatı*, 2:243. Otto-Dorn, "Islamische Denkmäler Kilikiens," 122, suggests these tiles are eighteenth-century Kütahya wares.

196. Denny, "Ceramic Revetments," 64.

197. Ibid., 64.

198. Ibid., 65.

199. Meinecke, *Die mamlukische Architektur*, vol. 2: 323, cat. no. 29/32, and vol. 1: 187.

200. Ibid., 1:187.

201. Ibid., 1:184n345, 187n355; vol. 2: 276, cat. no. 25A/53.

202. Uzunçarşılı, *Anadolu Beylikleri*, 178. For the Ottomans' unsuccessful attempts at gaining control over Cilicia in 1485–87 and 1488, see Har-El, *Struggle for Domination*, 133–51 and 163–91.

203. Uzunçarşılı, *Anadolu Beylikleri*, 178; Kurt, "Pîrî Mehmed Paşa, Ramazanoğlu."

204. Kurt, "Pîrî Mehmed Paşa, Ramazanoğlu."

205. Oppenheim, *Inschriften*, 111, no. 149.

206. Gündüz Küskü, *Osmanlı Beyliği*, 196–205; Uysal, "Adana Ulu Camii," 279–81.

207. Kurt, "Pîrî Mehmed Paşa, Ramazanoğlu."

208. Similar developments took place at a larger scale in Cairo after the Ottoman conquest: see Behrens-Abouseif, *Egypt's Adjustment to Ottoman Rule*.

BIBLIOGRAPHY

ABBREVIATIONS

Dates

AH = *anno hegirae*, Islamic lunar *hijrī* calendar
CE = Common Era
RH = *rūmī hijrī*, Ottoman solar *hijrī* calendar

Books, Journals, Archives

AÜİFD = *Ankara Üniversitesi İlahiyat Fakültesi Dergisi*
BK = Kâmil Kepecioğlu, Hüseyin Algül, and Enes Keskin, eds. *Bursa Kütüğü*. 4 vols. Bursa: Bursa Büyükşehir Belediyesi, 2009.
BOA = Türkiye Cumhuriyeti Cumhurbaşkanlığı Devlet Arşivleri Başkanlığı Osmanlı Arşivi Külliyesi, Istanbul (formerly Başbakanlık Osmanlı Arşivi)
    AE = Ali Emiri
    EV.VKF. = Evrak Vakfiyeler
BSOAS = *Bulletin of the School of Oriental and African Studies*
DOP = *Dumbarton Oaks Papers*
EI2 = *Encyclopaedia of Islam*, second edition, ed. Peri Bearman, Thierry Bianquis, Clifford E. Bosworth, Emeri van Donzel, and Wolfhart P. Heinrichs. Leiden: Brill, 2012. Brill Online Reference. https://reference works-brillonline-com/browse/encyclopaedia-of-islam-2
EI3 = *Encyclopaedia of Islam, THREE*, ed. Kate Fleet, Gudrun Krämer, Denis Matringe, John Nawas, and Everett Rowson. Leiden: Brill, 2012. Brill Online Reference. https://referenceworks-brillonline-com/browse/encyclopaedia-of-islam-3
EIr = *Encyclopaedia Iranica*, ed. Elton L. Daniel. New York: Iranica Foundation and Columbia University, 1990–2021. https://iranicaonline.org
İ.B.B.A.K. = İstanbul Büyükşehir Belediyesi Atatürk Kitaplığı, Istanbul
    MC_Fr Muallim Cevdet Fermanları
IJIA = *International Journal of Islamic Architecture*
JESHO = *Journal of the Economic and Social History of the Orient*
JSAH = *Journal of the Society of Architectural Historians*
JOTSA = *Journal of the Ottoman and Turkish Studies Association*

TDVİA = *Türkiye Diyanet Vakfı İslam Ansiklopedisi*. Istanbul: Türkiye Diyanet Vakfı, 1988–2022. https://islamansiklopedisi.org.tr
TİEM = Türk ve İslam Eserleri Müzesi, Istanbul
TOEM = *Tarih-i Osmani Encümeni Mecmuası*
TSMA = Topkapı Sarayı Müzesi Arşivi, Istanbul
TSMK = Topkapı Sarayı Müzesi Kütüphanesi, Istanbul
VD = *Vakıflar Dergisi*
VGMA = Vakıflar Genel Müdürlüğü Arşivi, Ankara

PRIMARY SOURCES

Ahmed Paşa Divanı, ed. Ali Nihad Tarlan. Istanbul: Milli Eğitim Basımevi, 1966.

Aköz, Alaaddin. "Karamanoğlu II. İbrahim Beyin Osmanlı Sultanı II. Murad'a Vermiş Olduğu Ahidnâme," *Türkiyat Araştırmaları* 18 (2005): 159–78.

ʿAşıkpaşazâde. *Âşıkpaşazâde Tarihi [Osmanlı Tarihi (1285–1502)]*, ed. Necdet Öztürk. Istanbul: Bilge, Kültür, Sanat, 2013.

ʿAşıkpaşazâde. *Vom Hirtenzelt zur Hohen Pforte: Frühzeit und Aufstieg des Osmanenreiches nach der Chronik "Denkwürdigkeiten und Zeitläufte des Hauses 'Osman" vom Derwisch Ahmed, genannt 'Asik-Paşa-Sohn*. Graz: Styria, 1959.

Barkan, Ömer Lütfi. "İstanbul Saraylarına Ait Muhasebe Defterleri," *Belgeler* 9, no. 13 (1979): 3–380.

Barkan, Ömer Lütfi. *Süleymaniye Cami ve İmareti İnşaatı (1550–1557)*. 2 vols. Ankara: Türk Tarih Kurumu], 1972.

Burge, S. R. *Angels in Islam: Jalāl al-Dīn al-Suyūtī's al-Ḥabāʾik fi akhbār al-malāʾik*. London: Routledge, 2012.

Crane, Howard, and Esra Akın, eds. and trans. *Sinan's Autobiographies: Five Sixteenth-Century Texts*. Leiden: Brill, 2006.

Dijkema, Fokke Theodoor, ed. *The Ottoman Historical Monumental Inscriptions in Edirne*. Leiden: Brill, 1977.

Dündar, Abdulkadir. "Bir Belgeye Göre Amasya II. Bayezid Külliyesi," *AÜİFD* 44, no. 2 (2003): 131–72.

Eren, Halit, Önder Bayır, Mustafa Oğuz, and Zekai Mete, eds. *Balkanlar'da Osmanlı Vakıfları: Vakfiyeler, Bulgaristan*. 3 vols. Istanbul: IRCICA, 2012.

Eren, Halit, Mustafa Oğuz, and Zekai Mete, eds. *Balkanlar'da Osmanlı Vakıfları: Vakfiyeler, Yunanistan.* 5 vols. Istanbul: IRCICA, 2017.

Evliya Çelebi. *Evliya Çelebi Seyahatnâmesi: Topkapı Sarayı Bağdat 304 Yazmasının transkripsiyonu*, ed. Orhan Şaik Gökyay, Seyit Ali Kahraman, Yücel Dağlı, Robert Dankoff, and Zekeriya Kurşun. 10 vols. Istanbul: Yapı Kredi Yayınları, 1996–2007.

Fatih Mehmet II vakfiyeleri, second edition. 3 vols. Istanbul: Çamlıca Kültür ve Yardım Vakfı, 2003.

Fatih Mehmet II vakfiyeleri, first edition. Ankara: Vakıflar Umum Müdürlüğü Neşriyat, 1938.

Gazzizāde ʿAbdüllatif Efendi. *Hulāṣatü'l-vefāyāt.* Süleymaniye Kütüphanesi. Istanbul, Esad Efendi, 2392.

Gök, İlhan. "Atatürk Kitaplığı M.C. O.71 Numaralı 909–933/1503–1527 Tarihli In'âmât Defteri (Transkripsiyon-Değerlendirme)," PhD dissertation, Marmara University, 2014.

Gökbilgin, M. Tayyib. "Murad I Tesisleri ve Bursa İmareti Vakfiyesi," *Türkiyat Mecmuası* 10 (1953): 217–34.

Halil Edhem [Eldem]. "Karamanoğulları Hakkında Vesâik-i Mahkuke," *TOEM* 3, no. 11 (1 Kanunuevvel 1327 RH [December 14, 1911 CE/ 22 Dhū 'l-hijja 1329 AH]): 697–712; vol. 3, no. 12 (1 Şubat 1327 RH [February 14, 1912 CE/ 25 Safar 1330 AH]): 741–60; vol. 3, no. 13 (1 Nisan 1328 RH [April 14, 1912 CE/ 26 Rabī ʿ 'l-Ākhar 1330 AH]: 821–36; vol. 3, no. 14 (1 Haziran 1328 RH [June 14, 1912 CE/ 28 Jumādha 'l-Ākhar 1330 AH]): 873–81.

Halil Edhem [Eldem]. "Yörgüç Paşa ve Evlâdına Âit Birkaç Kitâbe," *TOEM* 2, no. 9 (1 Ağustos 1327 RH [August 14, 1911 CE/ 18 Shaʿbān 1329 AH]): 530–41.

Hüseyin Hüsameddin, [Yaşar]. *Amasya Tarihi*, ed. Ali Yılmaz and Mehmet Akkuş, Ankara: Amasya Belediyesi Kültür Yayınları, 1986.

Hüseyin Hüsameddin, [Yaşar]. *Amasya Tarihi*, vol. 1, Istanbul: Hikmet Matbaası, 1327 RH/1911 CE, vols. 2–3. Istanbul: Necm-i İstikbal Matbaası, 1330 RH/ 1915 CE.

Ibn Baṭṭūta, *Riḥlat*, ed. ʿAbd al-Khaliq al-Mahidi. Cairo: al-Maṭbaʿat al-Azhariyya, 1928.

Ikhwān al-Ṣafāʾ. *Epistles of the Brethren of Purity: On Composition and the Arts. An Arabic Critical Edition and English Translation of Epistles 6–8*, ed. and trans. Nader el-Bizri and Godefroid de Callataÿ. Oxford: Oxford University Press, 2018.

İnalcık, Halil. *Fatih Devri Üzerinde Tetkikler ve Vesikalar.* Ankara: Türk Tarih Kurumu Basımevi, 1954.

Kastritsis, Dimitris J. *An Early Ottoman History: The Oxford Anonymous Chronicle, Bodleian Library, Ms Marsh 313.* Liverpool: Liverpool University Press, 2017.

Kastritsis, Dimitris J. "The Historical Epic Ahvāl-i Sultān Mehemmed (The Tales of Sultan Mehmed) in the Context of Early Ottoman Historiography," in *Writing History at the Ottoman Court: Editing the Past, Fashioning the Future*, ed. Emine Fetvacı and H. Erdem Çıpa. Bloomington: Indiana University Press, 2013, 1–22.

Kastritsis, Dimitris J., ed. and trans. *The Tales of Sultan Mehmed, Son of Bayezid Khan, Annotated English Translation, Turkish Edition, and Facsimiles.* Sources of Oriental Languages and Literatures 78. Cambridge, MA: Harvard Near Eastern Languages and Civilizations, 2007.

Kemal. *Selâtînnâme [Manzum Osmanı Tarihi (684–895/1296–1490)]*, ed. Necdet Öztürk. Istanbul: Bilge Kültür Sanat, 2018.

Kepecioğlu, Kâmil, Hüseyin Algül, and Enes Keskin, eds. *Bursa Kütüğü.* 4 vols. Bursa: Bursa Büyükşehir Belediyesi, 2009.

Kritovoulos. *History of Mehmed the Conqueror*, trans. Charles T. Riggs. Princeton, NJ: Princeton University Press, 1954.

Mantran, Robert. "Les inscriptions turques de Brousse," *Oriens* 11 (1959): 115–70.

Mantran, Robert. "Les inscriptions arabes de Brousse," *Bulletin d'Etudes Orientales* 14 (1954): 87–114.

Mayer, Leo Ary. *Islamic Architects and Their Works.* Geneva: A. Kundig, 1956.

Mecmaʿuʾl-ʿacâʾib, Nadir Eserleri Kütüphanesi, İstanbul Üniversitesi Kütüphanesi, Istanbul, F.1423.

Necipoğlu, Gülru, ed. *The Arts of Ornamental Geometry: A Persian Compendium on Similar and Complementary Interlocking Figures.* Fī tadākhul al-ashkāl al-mutashābiha aw al-mutawāfiqa (Bibliothèque nationale de France, Ms. Persan 169, fols. 180r–199r), a volume commemorating Alpay Özdural. Leiden: Brill, 2017.

Necipoğlu, Gülru, Cemal Kafadar, and Cornell H. Fleischer, eds. *Treasures of Knowledge: An Inventory of the Ottoman Palace Library (1502/3–1503/4).* 2 vols. Leiden: Brill, 2019.

Neşri, Mevlana Mehmed. *Cihânnümâ: 6. Kısım: Osmanlı Tarihi (687–890/1288–1485), Giriş, Çevri Metin, Kronoloji, Dizin, Tıpkıbasım*, ed. Necdet Öztürk. Istanbul: Bilge, Kültür, Sanat, 2013.

Neşri, Mevlana Mehmed. *Ǧihānnümā: Die altosmanische Chronik des Mevlānā Meḥemmed Neschñ*, ed. Franz Taeschner. 2 vols. Leipzig: O. Harrassowitz, 1951–55.

Öcalan, Hasan Basri, Sezai Sevim, and Doğan Yavaş. *Bursa Vakfiyeleri I.* Bursa: Bursa Büyükşehir Belediyesi, 2013.

Oppenheim, Max von. *Inschriften aus Syrien, Mesopotamien und Kleinasien, gesammelt im Jahre 1899.* Leipzig: J. C. Hinrichs'sche Buchhandlung and Baltimore: Johns Hopkins University Press, 1913.

Oruç Beğ. *Oruç Beğ Tarihi: Giriş, Metin, Kronoloji, Dizin, Tıpkıbasım*, ed. Necdet Öztürk. Istanbul: Çamlıca, 2007.

Sadeddin, Hoca. *Tacü't-tevarih*, ed. İsmet Parmaksızoğlu. Ankara: Kültür Bakanlığı, 1992.

Sadeddin, Hoca. *Tâcü't-Tevârih*. 2 vols. Istanbul: Tabhane-yi Âmire, 1279–80 RH/1862–63 CE.

Sakhawi, Muhammad ibn ʿAbd al-Rahman. *al-Ḍawʾ al-lāmiʿ li-ahl al-qarn al-tāsiʿ*. 12 vols. Cairo: Maktaba al-Quds, 1353–55 AH/1934–36 CE.

Samsakçı, Mehmet, ed. *Kosova Kitâberleri*. Istanbul: Istanbul Fetih Cemiyeti, 2014.

Sertoğlu, Mithat. "İkinci Murad'ın Vasiyetnamesi," *Vakıflar Dergisi* 8 (1969): 67–69 plus unpaginated plates.

Sevim, Sezai, and Hasan Basri Öcalan. *Osmanlı Kuruluş Dönemi Bursa Vakfiyeleri*. Bursa: Bursa Osmangazi Belediyesi Yayınları, 2010.

Şikari, Ahmet. *Şikâri'nin Karaman Oğulları Tarihi*, trans. Mesud Koman. Konya: Yeni Kitab Basımevi, 1946.

Sılay, Kemal. "Aḥmedī's History of the Ottoman Dynasty," *Journal of Turkish Studies – Türklük Bilgisi Araştırmaları* 16 (1992): 129–200.

al-Suyuti, Jalal al-Din ʿAbd al-Rahman. *al-Ḥabāʾik fi akhbār al-malāʾik*, ed. Abū Hājir Muḥammad al-Saʿīd ibn Basyūnī Zaghlūl. Beirut: Dār al-Kutub al-ʿIlmīya, 1985.

Taci-zāde, Cafer Çelebi. *Heves-nâme (İnceleme – Tenkitli Metin)*, ed. Necati Sungur. Ankara: Türk Dil Kurumu, 2006.

Tamer, Vehbi. "Fatih Devri Ricalinden İshak Paşa'nın Vakfiyeleri ve Vakıfları," *VD* 4 (1958): 107–24 plus plates.

Taşköprüzāde, Ahmed b. Mustafa. *al-Shaqāʾiq al-Nuʿmānīyah fi ʿulāmāʾ al-Dawlah al-ʿUthmānīyah*. Beyrut: Dār al-Kitāb al-ʿArabī, 1975.

Taşköprüzāde, Ahmed b. Mustafa. *Eš-Šaqāʾiq en-Noʿmânijje: enthaltend die Biographien der türkischen und im osmanischen Reiche wirkenden Gelehrten, Derwisch-Scheih's und Ärzte von der Regierung Sultân Otmân's bis zu der Sülaimân's des Grossen*, ed. and trans. O. Rescher. Constantinople-Galata: Buch- und Steindruckerei Phoenix, 1927.

Taşköprüzāde, Ahmed b. Mustafa, and Fındıklılı İsmet Efendi, *Şakaik-i Nuʾmaniye ve Zeyller*, vol. 5, *Tekmiletüʾş-Şakaik fî Hakk-ı Ehliʾl-Hakaik*, ed. Abdülkadir Özcan. Istanbul: Çağrı Yayınları, 1989.

Thackston, Wheeler M. *Album Prefaces and Other Documents on the History of Calligraphers and Painters*. Leiden: Brill, 2001.

Thackston, Wheeler M. *A Century of Princes: Sources on Timurid History and Art*. Cambridge, MA: Aga Khan Program for Islamic Architecture, 1989.

Thesaurus d'épigraphie islamique, www.epigraphie-islamique.org.

Toruk, Ferruh. "Yörgüç Paşa Vakfiyesi," *Bilge* 12, no. 48 (2006): 16–26.

Tursun Beğ. *The History of Mehmed the Conqueror*, ed. and trans. Halil İnalcık and Rhoads Murphey. Minneapolis and Chicago, 1978.

Tursun Beğ. *Târîh-i Ebüʾl-Feth*, ed. Mertol Tulum. Istanbul: Baha Matbaası, 1977.

Ünver, Süheyl. "Mahmud Paşa Vakıfları ve Ekleri," *VD* 4 (1958): 65–76 plus unpaginated plates.

Uzunçarşılı, İsmail Hakkı. "Niğde'de Karamanoğlu Ali Bey Vakfiyesi," *VD* 2 (1942): 45–69.

Uzunçarşılı, İsmail Hakkı. *Afyon Karahisar, Sandıklı, Bolvadin, Çay, İsaklı, Manisa, Birgi, Muğla, Milas, Peçin, Denizli, Isparta, Atabey ve Eğirdir Deki Kitabeler ve Sahip, Saruhan, Aydın, Menteşe, İnanç, Hamit Oğulları Hakkında Malûmat*. Istanbul: Devlet Matbaası, 1929.

Uzunçarşılı, İsmail Hakkı. *Kitâbeler: Tokat, Niksar, Zile, Turhal, Pazar, Amasya Vilâyeti, Kaza ve Nahiye Merkezlerindeli Kitabeler*. Istanbul: Millî Matbaası, 1927.

Yardım, Ali. *Amasya Kaya Kitâbesi: Bâyezid Paşa İmâreti Vakfiyesi*. Ankara: T. C. Amasya Valiliği, 2004.

Yerasimos, Stefanos. *La fondation de Constantinople et de Sainte-Sophie dans les traditions turques: Légendes d'empire*. Istanbul: Institut français d'études anatoliennes, 1990.

SECONDARY SOURCES

Aga-Oglu, Mehmet and Helen B. Hall. "The Landscape Miniatures of an Anthology Manuscript of the Year 1398 A.D." Ars Islamica 3, no. 1 (1936): 76–98.

Ahmed, Shahab. *What Is Islam? The Importance of Being Islamic*. Princeton, NJ: Princeton University Press, 2016.

Ahmed Tevhid. "İlk Altı Padişahımızın Bursa'da Kāʾin Türbelerinden Hüdavendigar Murad Han Türbesi ve Sultan Murad Han Sani Türbesi," *TOEM* 3, no. 17 (1 Kanunuevvel 1328 RH [December 14, 1912 CE/ 4 Muharram 1331 AH): 1047–60.

Ahmed Tevhid, "İlk Altı Padişahımızın Bursa'da Kāʾin Türbeleri," *TOEM* 3, no. 16 (1 Tişrinievvel 1328 RH [14 October 1912 CE/ 3 Dhūʾl-Qaʿda 1330 AH]): 977–81.

Akbarnia, Ladan. "Khitāʾī: Cultural Memory and the Creation of a Mongol Visual Idiom in Iran and Central Asia," PhD diss., Harvard University, 2007.

Akçil, N. Çiçek, and Cebe Özer, "Murâdiye Külliyesi," *TDVİA* 31 (2006): 199–201.

Akman, Mehmet. *Osmanlı Devletinde Kardeş Katlı*. Istanbul: Eren, 1997.

Akok, Mahmut. "Merzifonda Çelebi Mehmet Medresesi," *Mimarlık* 9, no. 1–2 (1952): 29–37.

Ali, Samer M. *Arabic Literary Salons in the Islamic Middle Ages: Poetry, Performance, and the Presentation of the Past*. Notre Dame, IN: Notre Dame University Press, 2010.

Alpers, Svetlana. "No Telling, with Tiepolo," in *Sight and Insight: Essays on Art and Culture in Honour of E. H. Gombrich at 85*, ed. John Onians. London: Phaidon, 1994, 327–40.

Amitai-Preiss, Reuven. *Mongols and Mamluks: The Mamluk–Īlkhānid War, 1260–1281*. Cambridge: Cambridge University Press, 1995.

Anderson, Benjamin. "The Complex of Elvan Çelebi: Problems in Fourteenth-Century Architecture," *Muqarnas* 31 (2014): 73–97.

Androudis, Paschalis. *Hē prōimē Othōmanikē technē kai architektonikē stēn Hellada (14os-16os aiōnas)*. Thessaloniki: Barmpounakes, 2016.

Anhegger, Robert. "Beiträge zur osmanischen Baugeschichte II," *Istanbuler Mitteilungen* 8 (1958): 40–56.

Arel, Ayda. "The Architecture of the Menteşe Emirate and the İlyas Bey İmaret in Balat: A Question of Belonging," in *Balat İlyas Bey Külliyesi: Tarih, Mimari, Restorasyon*, ed. M. Baha Tanman and Leyla Kayhan Elbirlik, Istanbul: Söktaş, 2011, 55–86.

Arık, Rüçhan. *Tiles: Treasures of Anatolian Soil: Tiles of the Seljuk and Beylik Periods*. Istanbul: Kale Group, 2008.

Aşkar, Mustafa. "Osmanlı Devletinde Alim-Mutasavvıf Prototipi Olarak; İlk Şeyhülislam Molla Fenarî ve Tasavvuf Anlayışı," *AÜİFD* 37 (1997): 385–401.

Aslanapa, Oktay. *Türk Sanatı*. 2 vols. Istanbul: Milli Eğitim Basımevi, 1972–73.

Aslanapa, Oktay. "Pottery and Kilns from the Iznik Excavations," in *Forschungen zur Kunst Asiens in memoriam Kurt Erdmann*, ed. Ostay Aslanapa and Rudolf Naumann. Istanbul: Istanbul Üniversitesi Edebiyat Fakültesi, Türk ve Islâm Sanati Kürsüsü, 1969, 140–46.

Aslanapa, Oktay. *Anadoluda Türk Çini ve Keramik Sanatı*. Istanbul: Baha Matbaası, 1965.

Aslanapa, Oktay. *Edirnede Osmanlı Devri Âbideleri*. Istanbul: Üçler Basımevi, 1949.

Atasoy, Nurhan, Walter Denny, Louise Mackie, Julian Raby, and Alison Effeny. *İpek: Imperial Ottoman Silks and Velvets*. London: Azimuth Editions Limited on behalf of TEB İletişim ve Yaypıncılık, 2001.

Atasoy, Nurhan, Julian Raby, and Yanni Petsopoulos. *Iznik: The Pottery of Ottoman Turkey*. London: Alexandria Press in association with Laurence King, 1994.

Atbaş, Zeynep. "Artistic Aspects of Sultan Bayezid II's Book Treasury Collection: Extant Volumes Preserved at the Topkapı Palace Museum Library," in *Treasures of Knowledge: An Inventory of the Ottoman Palace Library (1502/3–1503/4)*, vol. 1, ed. Gülru Necipoğlu, Cemal Kafadar, and Cornell H. Fleischer. Leiden: Brill, 2019, 161–211.

Atçıl, Abdurrahman. *Scholars and Sultans in the Early Modern Ottoman Empire*. Cambridge: Cambridge University Press, 2017.

Atçıl, Abdurrahman. "Mobility of Scholars and Formation of a Self-sustaining Scholarly System in the Lands of Rūm in the Fifteenth Century," in *Islamic Literature and Intellectual Life in Fourteenth- and Fifteenth-Century Anatolia*, ed. Andrew C. S. Peacock and Sara Nur Yıldız. Würzburg: Ergon, 2016, 315–32.

Ateş, Sabri. "Bones of Contention: Corpse Traffic and Ottoman–Iranian Rivalry in Nineteenth-Century Iraq," *Comparative Studies of South Asia, Africa and the Middle East* 30, no. 3 (2010): 512–32.

Aube, Sandra. *La céramique dans l'architecture en Iran au XVe siècle: Les arts qarâ quyûnlûs et âq quyûnlûs*. Paris: Presses de l'Université Paris-Sorbonne, 2017.

Aube, Sandra. "Skills and Style in Heritage: The Woodworker Faḫr al-Dīn and His Son ʿAlī in the Mazandaran (Iran, ca. 1440–1500)," *Eurasian Studies* 15 (2017): 283–303.

Aube, Sandra. "The Uzun Hasan Mosque in Tabriz: New Perspectives on a Tabrizi Ceramic Tile Workshop," *Muqarnas* 33 (2016): 33–64.

Aube, Sandra. "Tabriz x. monuments x(1). The Blue Mosque," *EIr* (accessed November 27, 2014).

Aube, Sandra. "La mosquée bleue de Tabriz (1465): Remarques sur la céramique architecturale Qarā Qoyulu," *Studia Iranica* 37 (2008): 241–77.

Aube, Sandra, Thomas Lorain, and Julio Bendezu-Sarmiento. "The Complex of Gawhar Shad in Herat: New Findings about Its Architecture and Ceramic Tile Decorations," *Iran* 58, no. 1 (2020): 62–83.

Avcıoğlu, Nebahat. "Istanbul: The Palimpsest City in Search of Its Architext," *RES: Anthropology and Aesthetics* 53/54 (2008): 190–210.

Ayaşlıoğlu, Mustafa. "Istanbul'da Mahmut Paşa Türbesi," *Güzel Sanatlar* 6 (1949): 148–58.

Aydın, Hakkı. "Molla Fenârî," *TDVİA* 30 (2005): 247–48.

Ayverdi, Ekrem Hakkı. *Avrupa'da Osmanlı Mimârî Eserleri*. 4 vols. Istanbul: İstanbul Fetih Cemiyeti, 1977.

Ayverdi, Ekrem Hakkı. *Osmanlı Mimârîsinde Çelebi ve II. Sultan Murad Devri, 806–855 (1403–1451)*. Istanbul: Baha Matbaası, 1972.

Ayverdi, Ekrem Hakkı. *Osmanlı Mimârîsinin İlk Devri, 630–805 (1230–1402)*. Istanbul: Baha Matbaası, 1966.

Ayverdi, Ekrem Hakkı. "Dimetoka'da Çelebi Sultan Mehmed Cami'i," *VD* 3 (1956): 13–18.

Ayverdi, Ekrem Hakkı. *Fatih Devri Mimarî Eserleri*. Istanbul: Istanbul Matbaası, 1953.

Ayverdi, Ekrem Hakkı, and İ. Aydın Yüksel. *Osmanlı Mimârisi*, vol. 1 (letter A). Istanbul: Fetih Cemiyeti, 2016.

Babaie, Sussan. "Chasing after the Muhandis: Visual Articulations of the Architect and Architectural Historiography," in *Affect, Emotion, and Subjectivity in Early Modern Muslim Empires: New Studies in Ottoman, Safavid, and Mughal Art and Culture*, ed. Kishwar Rizvi. Leiden and Boston: Brill, 2018, 21–44.

Babaie, Sussan. "Qavam al-Din Shirazi, Architect to the House of Tamerlane," in *The Great Builders*, ed. Kenneth Powell. London: Thames & Hudson, 2011, 29–33.

Babaie, Sussan. *Isfahan and Its Palaces: Statecraft, Shi'ism and the Architecture of Conviviality in Early Modern Iran*. Edinburgh: Edinburgh University Press, 2008.

Babinger, Franz. "Reliquienschacher am Osmanenhof im XV. Jahrhundert," *Sitzungsberichte der bayerischen Akademie der Wissenschaften*, philosophisch-historische Klasse, Jahrgang 1956, Heft 2, 3–47.

Babinger, Franz. "Ramaḍān Oghullari," *EI2*, http://dx .doi.org/10.1163/1573-3912_islam_SIM_6209, accessed June 16, 2019.

Babinger, Franz. "Mehmed's II. Heirat mit Sitt-Chatun (1449)," *Der Islam* 29 (1950): 215–35.

Bağcı, Serpil, and Zeren Tanındı. "Art of the Ottoman Court," in *Turks: A Journey of a Thousand Years, 600–1600*, ed. David J. Roxburgh. London: Royal Academy of Arts, 2005, 262–71.

Balafrej, Lamia, *The Making of the Artist in Late Timurid Painting*. Edinburgh: Edinburgh University Press, 2019.

Balivet, Michel. *Islam mystique et révolution armée dans les Balkans ottomans: Vie du Cheikh Bedreddîn le "hallâj des Turcs" (1358/59–1416)*. Istanbul: Editions Isis, 1995.

Baltacı, Cahid. *XV–XVI: Yüzyıllarda Osmanlı Medreseleri*. 2 vols. Istanbul: Marmara Üniversitesi İlâhiyat Fakültesi Vakfi Yayınları, 2005.

Baltacıoğlu-Brammer, Ayşe. "One Word, Many Implications: The Term 'Kızılbaş' in the Early Moden Ottoman Context," in *Ottoman Sunnism: New Perspectives*, ed. Vefa Erginbaş. Edinburgh: Edinburgh University Press, 2019, 47–70.

Barkan, Ömer Lütfi. "Osmanlı İmperatorluğunda Bir İskân ve Kolonizasyon Metodu Olarak Vakıflar ve Temlikler I: İstilâ Devirlerinin Kolonizatör Türk Dervişleri ve Zâviyeler," *VD* 2 (1942): 279–386.

Barry, Fabio. "Walking on Water: Cosmic Floors in Antiquity and the Middle Ages," *The Art Bulletin* 89, no. 4 (2007): 627–56.

Bartol'd, Vasilyi V. *Ulugh Beg*, vol. 2 of *Four Studies on the History of Central Asia*, trans. Vladimir Minorsky and Tatiana Minorsky. Leiden: Brill, 1956.

Başar, Fahameddin. "Yörgüç Paşa," *TDVİA* 43 (2013): 566–67.

Başpınar, Fatih. "Sultan II. Bayezid'in Farsça Şiirleri Üzerine," *Divan Edebiyatı Araştırmaları Dergisi* 8 (2012): 37–66.

Baykara, Tuncer. "Balat during the Period of the Anatolian Emirates," in *Balat İlyas Bey Külliyesi: Tarih, Mimari, Restorasyon*, ed. M. Baha Tanman and Leyla Kayhan Elbirlik. Istanbul: Söktaş, 2011, 39–48.

Behrens-Abouseif, Doris. *Practising Diplomacy in the Mamluk Sultanate: Gifts and Material Culture in the Medieval Islamic World*. London: I. B. Tauris, 2014.

Behrens-Abouseif, Doris. "Craftsmen, Upstarts and Sufis in the Late Mamluk Period," *BSOAS* 74, no. 3 (2011): 375–95.

Behrens-Abouseif, Doris. "*Muhandis, Shād, Mu'allim*: Note on the Building Craft in the Mamluk Period," *Der Islam* 72, no. 2 (1995): 293–309.

Behrens-Abouseif, Doris. *Egypt's Adjustment to Ottoman Rule: Institutions, Waqf and Architecture in Cairo, 16th and 17th Centuries*. Leiden: Brill, 1994.

Ben Cheneb, Mohammed. , "Ibn al-Djazarī," *EI2*, http:// dx.doi.org/10.1163/1573-3912_islam_SIM_3141, accessed May 22, 2019.

Beránek, Ondřej, and Pavel Ťupek. *The Temptation of Graves in Salafi Islam: Iconoclasm, Destruction and Idolatry*. Edinburgh: Edinburgh University Press, 2018.

Bernardini, Michele. "Lo *Şehrengīz-i Borūsā* di Lāmi'ī Çelebī come fonte storica," in *Turcica et Islamica: Studi in memoria di Aldo Gallotta*, vol. 1, ed. Ugo Marazzi. Naples: Università degli Studi di Napoli "L'Orientale, 2003, 37–70.

Bernardini, Michele. "The *masnavī-shahrāshūb*s as Town Panegyrics: An International Genre in Islamic Mashriq," in *Erzählter Raum in Literaturen der islamischen Welt*, ed. Roxane Haag-Higuchi and Christian Szyska. Wiesbaden: Harrasowitz, 2001, 81–94.

Bernus-Taylor, Marthe. "Le décor du 'Complexe Vert' à Bursa, reflet de l'art timouride," in *L'Héritage timouride, Iran – Asie centrale – Inde, XVe–XVIIIe siècles*, ed. Maria Szuppe. Cahiers d'Asie centrale 3–4. Tashkent and Aix-en-Provence: Institut Français d'Etudes sur l'Asie centrale, 1997, 251–66.

Beyazit, Deniz, ed. *At the Crossroads of Empires: 14th–15th-century Eastern Anatolia: Proceedings of the International Symposium Held in Istanbul, 4th–6th May 2007*, Varia Anatolica, 25. Paris: De Boccard, 2012.

Beyazıt, Mustafa. "Erken Osmanlı Devri'nde Tebrizli Usta Gruplarının İzi Nasıl Sürülmeli?" *History Studies*, special issue: *A Tribute to Prof. Dr. Şerafettin Turan*, 6, no. 3 (2014): 45–70.

Bilge, Mustafa. *İlk Osmanlı Medreseleri*. İstanbul: İstanbul Üniversitesi Edebiyat Fakültesi, 1984.

Binbaş, İlker Evrim. *Intellectual Networks in Timurid Iran: Sharaf Al-Dīn ʿAlī Yazdī and the Islamicate Republic of Letters*. Cambridge: Cambridge University Press, 2016.

Björkman, Walther. "Die frühesten türkisch-ägyptischen Beziehungen im 14. Jahrhundert," in *60. Doğum Yılı Münasebetiyle Fuad Köprülü Armağanı*, ed. Osman Turan. Ankara: Türk Tarih Kurumu, 1953; reprint, 2010, 57–64.

Blair, Sheila. "Place, Space and Style: Craftsmen's Signatures in Medieval Islamic Art," in *Viewing Inscriptions in the Late Antique and Medieval World*, ed. Antony Eastmond. Cambridge: Cambridge University Press, 2015, 230–48.

Blair, Sheila. "Tabriz: International Entrepôt under the Mongols," in *Politics, Patronage and the Transmission of Knowledge in 13th–15th Century Tabriz*, ed. Judith Pfeiffer. Leiden: Brill, 2014, 321–56.

Blair, Sheila. "The Mongol Capital of Sulṭāniyya, 'the Imperial,'" *Iran: Journal of the British Institute of Persian Studies* 24 (1986): 139–51.

Blair, Sheila, and Jonathan Bloom, "From Iran to the Deccan: Architectural Transmission and the Madrasa of Mahmud Gavan at Bidar," in *Iran and the Deccan: Persianate Art, Culture, and Talent in Circulation, 1400–1700*, ed. Keelan Overton. Bloomington: Indiana University Press, 2020, 175–202.

Blessing, Patricia. "Blue-and-White Tiles of the Muradiye in Edirne: Architectural Decoration between Tabriz, Damascus, and Cairo," *Muqarnas* 36 (2019): 101–29.

Blessing, Patricia. "The Vessel as Garden: The 'Alhambra Vases' and Sensory Perception in Nasrid Architecture," in *Sensory Reflections: Traces of Experience in Medieval Artifacts*, ed. Fiona Griffiths and Kathryn Starkey. Berlin: De Gruyter, 2018, 116–41.

Blessing, Patricia. "All Quiet on the Eastern Frontier? Early Ottoman Architecture and Its Contemporaries in Eastern Anatolia," in *Architecture and Landscape in Medieval Anatolia, 1100–1500*, ed. Patricia Blessing and Rachel Goshgarian. Edinburgh: Edinburgh University Press, 2017, 200–223.

Blessing, Patricia. "Seljuk Past and Timurid Present: Tile Decoration of the Yeşil Complex in Bursa, Turkey," *Gesta* 56, no. 2 (Fall 2017): 225–50.

Blessing, Patricia. "'Medieval Monuments from Empire to Nation-State: Beyond Armenian and Islamic Architecture in the South Caucasus (1180–1300),' in *The Medieval South Caucasus: Artistic Cultures of Albania, Armenia, and Georgia*, ed. Ivan Foletti and Erik Thunø," *Convivium: Exchanges and Interactions in the Arts of Medieval Europe, Byzantium, and the Mediterranean, Seminarium Kondakovianum* (Supplementum 2016): 52–69.

Blessing, Patricia. "Buildings of Commemoration in Medieval Anatolia: The Funerary Complexes Ṣāḥib ʿAṭā Fakhr al-Dīn Alī and Māhperī Khātūn," *al-Masāq: Journal of the Medieval Mediterranean* 27, no. 3 (December 2015): 225–52.

Blessing, Patricia. "Allegiance, Praise, and Space: Monumental Inscriptions in Thirteenth-Century Anatolia as Architectural Guides," in *Calligraphy and Architecture in the Muslim World*, ed. Mohammad Gharipour and İrvin Cemil Schick. Edinburgh: Edinburgh University Press, 2013, 431–46.

Blessing, Patricia. *Rebuilding Anatolia after the Mongol Conquest: Islamic Architecture in the Lands of Rūm, 1240–1330*, Birmingham Byzantine and Ottoman Studies 17. Farnham: Ashgate, 2014.

Blessing, Patricia, and Rachel Goshgarian, "Introduction: Space and Place: Applications to Medieval Anatolia," in *Architecture and Landscape in Medieval Anatolia, 1100–1500*, ed. Patricia Blessing and Rachel Goshgarian. Edinburgh: Edinburgh University Press, 2017, 1–24.

Bloom, Jonathan M. *Paper before Print: The History and Impact of Paper in the Islamic World*. New Haven, CT: Yale University Press, 2001.

Bloom, Jonathan M. "The 'Qubbat al-Khaḍrā' and the Iconography of Height in Early Islamic Architecture," *Ars Orientalis*, special issue: Pre-modern Islamic Palaces 23 (1993): 135–41.

Boyar, Ebru. "Ottoman Expansion in the East," in *Cambridge History of Turkey: Volume 2, The Ottoman Empire as World Power, 1453–1603*, ed. Kate Fleet and Suraiya Faroqhi. Cambridge: Cambridge University Press, 2013, 74–140.

Boykov, Grigor. "The T-shaped Zaviye/İmarets of Edirne: A Key Mechanism for Ottoman Urban Morphological Transformation," *JOTSA* 3, no. 1 (May 2016): 29–48.

Boykov, Grigor. "The Borders of the Cities: Revisiting Early Ottoman Urban Morphology in Southeastern Europe," in *Bordering Early Modern Europe*, ed. Maria Baramova, Grigor Boykov, and Ivan Parvev. Wiesbaden: Harrassowitz, 2015, 243–56.

Boykov, Grigor. "Anatolian Emir in Rumelia: İsfendiyaroğlu İsmail Bey's Architectural Patronage and Governorship of Filibe (1460s–1470s)," *Bulgarian Historical Review* 1–2 (2013): 137–47.

Boykov, Grigor. "Reshaping Urban Space in the Ottoman Balkans: A Study on the Architectural Development of Edirne, Plovdiv, and Skopje (14th–15th Centuries)," in *Centres and Peripheries in Ottoman Architecture: Rediscovering a Balkan Heritage*, ed. Maximilian Hartmuth. Sarajevo: Cultural Heritage without Borders, 2011, 32–45.

Bozdoğan, Sibel, and Gülru Necipoğlu. "Entangled Discourses: Scrutinizing Orientalist and Nationalist

Legacies in the Architectural Historiography of the 'Lands of Rum,'" *Muqarnas* 24 (2007): 1–6.

Brend, Barbara. "The Patronage of Faḫr al-Din 'Ali ibn al-Husain and the Work of Kaluk ibn 'Abd Allah in the Development of the Decoration of Portals in Thirteenth Century Anatolia," *Kunst des Orients* 11, no. 2 (1975): 160–85.

Bryer, Anthony. "Greek Historians on the Turks: The Case of the First Byzantine-Ottoman Marriage," in *The Writing of History in the Middle Ages: Essays Presented to Richard William Southern*, ed. Ralph Henry Carless Davis and John Michael Wallace-Hadrill. Oxford: Clarendon Press, 1981, 471–93.

Büchner, Victor F., "Sīs," *EI2*, http://dx.doi.org/10.1163/1573-3912_islam_SIM_7070, accessed January 6, 2019.

Çağaptay, Suna. *The First Capital of the Ottoman Empire: The Religious, Architectural, and Social History of Bursa*. London: I. B. Tauris, 2021.

Çağaptay, Suna. "Results of the Tophane Area GPR Survey, Bursa, Turkey," *DOP* 68 (2014): 387–404.

Çağaptay, Suna. "Depremler, Arkeoloji ve Bursa'nın Erken Osmanlı Dönemin Arkeolojisi," in *Uluslararası Katılımlı XV: Ortaçağ ve Türk Dönemi Kazıları ve Sanat Tarihi Araştırmaları Sempozyumu: Anadolu Üniversitesi Eskişehir 19–20 Ekim 2011*, vol. 1, ed. Zeliha Demirel Gökalp. Eskişehir: Anadolu Üniversitesi, 2012, 179–90.

Çağaptay, Suna. "Frontierscape: Reconsidering Bithynian Structures and Their Builders on the Byzantine–Ottoman Cusp," *Muqarnas* 28 (2011): 156–91.

Çağaptay, Suna. "Prousa/Bursa, a City within the City: Chorography, Conversion and Choreography," *Byzantine and Modern Greek Studies* 35, no. 1 (2011): 45–69.

Çağaptay, Suna. "The Road from Bithynia to Thrace: Gazi Evrenos' Imaret in Komotini and Its Architectural Framework," *Byzantinische Zeitschrift* 30 (2011): 429–42 and 822–24.

Çağman, Filiz. "Baba Nakkaş," *TDVİA* 4 (1991): 369–70.

Çağman, Filiz, and Zeren Tanındı. *The Topkapı Saray Museum: The Albums and Illustrated Manuscripts*, trans. J. Michael Rogers. Boston: Little, Brown, 1986.

Cahen, Claude. *The Formation of Turkey: The Seljukid Sultanate of Rūm: Eleventh to Fourteenth Century*, trans. Peter M Holt. Harlow: Longman, 2001.

Campbell, Aurelia. *What the Emperor Built: Architecture and Empire in the Early Ming*. Seattle: University of Washington Press, 2020.

Campbell, Stephen J. "Artistic Geographies," in *The Cambridge Companion to the Italian Renaissance*, ed. Michael Wyatt. Cambridge: Cambridge University Press, 2014, 17–39.

Caner Yüksel, Çağla. "A Tale of Two Port Cities: Ayasuluk (Ephesus) and Balat (Miletus) during the Beyliks Period," *Al-Masāq* 31, no. 3 (2019): 338–65.

Cantay, Gönül. "Türklerde Vakıf ve Taş Vakfiyeler," *Vakıf Haftası Dergisi* 11 (1994): 147–62.

Cantay, Tanju. "Amasya Sultan Mesud Türbesi'nin İnşa Yılı," *VD* 25 (1995): 35–38.

Carboni, Stefano, ed. *Venice and the Islamic World, 828–1797*. New Haven, CT: Yale University Press, 2007.

Carra de Vaux, Bernard. , "Barzakh," *EI2*. Brill Online, 2014, http://jdx.doi.org/10.1163/1573-3912_islam_SIM_1249, accessed May 5, 2020.

Carswell, John. "Six Tiles," in *Islamic Art in the Metropolitan Museum of Art*, ed. Richard Ettinghausen. New York: Metropolitan Museum of Art, 1972, 99–124.

Castelnuovo, Enrico, and Ginzburg, Carlo. "Symbolic Domination and Artistic Geography in Italian Art History," trans. M. Currie and intro. D. Gamboni. *Art in Translation* 1 (2009): 5–48 [first published as "Domination symbolique et géographie artistique dans l'histoire de l'art italien," *Actes de la recherche en sciences sociales*, no. 40, November 1981].

Çayırdağ, Mehmet. "Kayseri'de Kitabelerinden XV: Yüzyılda Yapıldığı Anlaşılan İlk Osmanlı Yapıları," *VD* 13 (1981): 531–82.

Çeken, Muharrem. "Anadolu'da bir Seramik Üretim Merkezi: Hasankeyf (Fırın ve Atöyeler)," in *Çanak: Late Antique and Medieval Pottery and Tiles in Mediterranean Archaeological Contexts*, ed. Beate Böhlendorf-Arslan, Ali Osman Uysal, and Johanna Witte-Orr. BYZAS 7, Veröffentlichungen des Deutschen Archäologischen Instituts Istanbul. Istanbul: Ege Yayınları, 2007, 469–88.

Çelebi, Mehmet Ali. "Konya İç Kalesi ve Anadolu Selçuklu Sarayı," in *Selçuklu Dönemi Saraylar ve Köşkler*, vol. 1, ed. Mehmet Ali Hacıgökmen. Konya: Selçuk Üniversitesi, 2021, 188–299.

Çerkez, Murat. "Merzifon'da Türk Devri Mimari Eserleri," PhD dissertation, Ankara University, 2005.

Çiftiçi, Mehdin. *1037–1038 (1628–1629) Tarihli Rumeli Kadıaskerliği Rûznâmçesine Göre Osmanlı Medreseleri*. Bursa: Emin Yayınları, 2016.

Çıpa, H. Erdem. *The Making of Selim: Succession, Legitimacy, and Memory in the Early Modern Ottoman World*. Bloomington: Indiana University Press, 2017.

Çizakça, Murat. "Price History and the Bursa Silk Industry: A Study in Ottoman Industrial Decline, 1550–1650," *Journal of Economic History* 40, no. 3 (September1980): 533–50.

Çizakça, Murat. "A Short History of the Bursa Silk Industry (1500–1900)," *JESHO* 23 (1980): 142–52.

Campo, Juan Eduardo, "Burial," *Encyclopaedia of the Qur'ān*, http://dx.doi.org/10.1163/1875-3922_q3_EQSIM_00065, accessed October 6, 2018.

Carlson, Thomas A. *Christianity in Fifteenth-Century Iraq.* Cambridge: Cambridge University Press, 2018.

Clinton, Jerome W. "Image and Metaphor: Textiles in Persian Poetry," in *Woven from the Soul, Spun from the Heart: Textile Arts of Safavid and Qajar Iran, 16th–19th Centuries*, ed. Carol Bier. Washington, DC: The Textile Museum, 1987, 7–11.

Clinton, Jerome W. "Esthetics by Implication: What Metaphors of Crafts Tell Us about the 'Unity' of the Persian Qasida," *Edebiyat* 4, no. 1 (1979): 73–96.

Colomban, Philippe, Véronique Milande, and Lionel Le Bihan. "On Site Raman Analysis of Iznik Pottery Glazes and Pigments," *Raman* 35 (2004): 527–35.

Contadini, Anna. "L'ornamento nel mondo ottoman e nell'Italia del Rinascimento: Transmissione e congiunzione," in *Incontri di civiltà nel Mediterraneo: l'Impero Ottomano e l'Italia del Rinascimento, storia, arte e architettura*, ed. Alireza Naser Eslami. Florence: Leo S. Olschki Edittore, 2014, 57–73.

Contadini, Anna. "Sharing a Taste? Material Culture and Intellectual Curiosity around the Mediterranean, from the Eleventh to the Sixteenth Century," in *The Renaissance and the Ottoman World*, ed. Anna Contadini and Claire Norton. Farnham: Ashgate, 2013, 23–61.

Contadini, Anna, and Claire Norton, ed. *The Renaissance and the Ottoman World*. Farnham: Ashgate, 2013.

Crane, Howard. "Notes on Saljūq Architectural Patronage in 13th Century Anatolia," *JESHO* 36, no. 1 (1993): 1–57.

Crane, Howard. "The Ottoman Sultan's Mosques: Icons of Imperial Legitimacy," in *The Ottoman City and Its Parts: Urban Structure and Social Order*, ed. Irene Bierman, Rifa'at A. Abou-El-Haj, and Donald Preziosi. New Rochelle, NY: Aristide D. Caratzas, 1991, 173–243.

Ćurčić, Slobodan. *Architecture in the Balkans from Diocletian to Süleyman the Magnificent*. New Haven, CT: Yale University Press, 2010.

Curry, John J. *The Transformation of Muslim Mystical Thought in the Ottoman Empire: The Rise of the Halveti Order, 1350–1650*. Edinburgh: Edinburgh University Press, 2010.

Danalı Cantarella, Merih. "Art, Science, and Neoplatonic Cosmology in Fourteenth-Century Byzantium: The Illustrations of Marcianus Graecus 516 (=904)," PhD dissertation, Harvard University, 2019.

Darling, Linda T., "Introduction: Ottoman Identity and the Development of an Imperial Culture in the Fifteenth Century," *JOTSA* 1, no. 1–2 (2014): 53–55.

Darling, Linda T., "Political Literature and the Development of an Ottoman Imperial Culture in the Fifteenth Century," *JOTSA* 1, no. 1–2 (2014): 57–69.

Darling, Linda T., "The Renaissance and the Middle East," in *A Companion to the Worlds of the Renaissance*, ed. Guido Ruggiero. Oxford: Blackwell, 2002, 55–69.

Daş, Ertan. *Erken Dönem Osmanlı Türbeleri*. Istanbul: Gökkubbe, 2007.

Degeorge, Gérard, and Yves Porter. *L'art de la céramique dans l'architecture musulmane*. Paris: Flammarion, 2001.

Deleuze, Gilles, and Félix Guattari. "The Smooth and the Striated," in *A Thousand Plateaus: Capitalism and Schizophrenia*, trans. Brian Massumi. Minneapolis: University of Minnesota Press, 1987, 474–500.

Delibaş, Nurullah, ed. *Kitabelerin Kitabı: Fatih*. Istanbul: Fatih Belediye Başkanlığı, 2016.

Deliçay, Tahsin. "Mehmed Şah Fenârî," *TDVİA* 28 (2003): 529–30.

Demiralp, Yekta. *Erken Dönem Osmanlı Medreseleri (1300–1500)*. Ankara: Kültür Bakanlığı Yayınları, 1999.

Demirsar Arlı, V. Belgin. "İznik Çini Fırınları Kazısı 2017 Yılı Çalışmaları," *Kazı Sonuçları Toplantısı* 40, no. 1 (2018): 345–60.

Demirsar Arlı, V. Belgin. "İznik Çini Fırınları Kazı Buluntularından Çini Örneklerin Değerlendirilmesi," *Tarih, Kültür ve Sanat Araştırmaları Dergisi* 7, no. 1 (March 2018): 578–94.

Denny, Walter B. *Iznik: The Artistry of Ottoman Ceramics*. London: Thames & Hudson, 2004.

Denny, Walter B. "Dating Ottoman Works in the *Saz* Style," *Muqarnas* 1 (1983): 103–21.

Denny, Walter B. "Ceramic Revetments of the Mosque of the Ramazan Oğlu in Adana," in *IVème congrès international d'art turc: Aix-en-Provence, 10–15 septembre 1971*. Aix-en-Provence: Éditions de l'Université de Provence, 1976, 57–65.

Denny, Walter B. "Blue-and-White Islamic Pottery on Chinese Themes," *Boston Museum Bulletin* 72, no. 368 (1974): 76–99.

Dietrich, Albert. "Kāfūr," *EI2*, http://dx.doi.org/10.1163/1573-3912_islam_SIM_3780, accessed September 14, 2019.

Dietrich, Albert. "Mūmiyā'." *EI2*, http://dx.doi.org/10.1163/1573-3912_islam_SIM_5495, accessed September 14, 2019.

Diez, Ernst, Oktay Aslanapa, and Mahmut Mesut Koman. *Karaman Devri Sanati*. Istanbul: Istanbul Universitesi Edebiyat Fakultesi Yayınları, 1950.

Dold-Samplonius, Yvonne, and Silvia L. Harmsen. "The Muqarnas Plate Found at Takht-i Sulayman: A New Interpretation," *Muqarnas* 22 (2005): 85–94.

Dönmez, Emine Naza. "Yörgüç Paşa Camii," *TDVİA* 43 (2013): 567–68.

Durukan, Aynur. "Köşkmedrese," *TDVİA* 26 (2002): 282–83.

Durukan, Aynur. "İlyas Bey Külliyesi," *TDVİA* 22 (2000): 164–66.

Eldem, Edhem. *İstanbul'da Ölüm: Osmanlı-İslam Kültüründe Ölüm ve Ritüelleri*, Istanbul: Osmanlı Bankası Arşiv ve Araştırma Merkezi, 2005.

Emecen, Feridun M. "Western Anatolia in the Period of the Emirates: The Menteşe Emirate and İlyas Bey," in *Balat İlyas Bey Külliyesi: Tarih, Mimari, Restorasyon*, ed. M. Baha Tanman and Leyla Kayhan Elbirlik, Istanbul: Söktaş, 2011, 31–38.

Emir, Sedat. "Reconstructing an Early Ottoman Building: The *Zawiya* of Murad II in Bursa," *Arab Historical Review for Ottoman Studies* 19–20 (1999): 269–98.

Erdmann, Kurt. "Zur türkischen Baukunst seldschukischer und osmanischer Zeit," *Istanbuler Mitteilungen* 8 (1958): 1–39.

Eren, İsmail. "Kosova'da I. Murad Hüdavendigar Türbesine Ait Tarihî Bir Belge," *Güneydoğu Avrupa Araştırmaları Dergisi* 4–5 (1976): 67–80.

Ergenç, Özer. *XVI. Yüzyılın Sonlarında Bursa: Yerleşimi, Yönetimi, Ekonomik ve Sosyal Durumu üzerine Bir Araştırma*. Ankara: Atatürk Kültür, Dil ve Tarih Yüksek Kurumu, Türk Tarih Kurumu Yayınları, 2006.

Ergin, Nina. "A Sound Status among the Ottoman Elite: Architectural Patrons of Sixteenth-Century Istanbul Mosques and Their Recitation Programs," in *Music, Sound, and Architecture in Islam*, ed. Michael Frishkopf and Federico Spinetti. Austin: University of Texas Press, 2018, 37–58.

Ergin, Nina. "The Fragrance of the Divine: Ottoman Incense Burners and Their Context," *The Art Bulletin* 96, no. 1 (2014): 70–97.

Ergin, Nina. "The Soundscape of Sixteenth-Century Istanbul Mosques: Architecture and Qur'an Recital," *JSAH* 67, no. 2 (June 2008): 204–21.

Ermiş, Ü. Melda. "The Reuse of Byzantine Spolia in the Green Mosque of Bursa," *Art/ Sanat* 6 (2016): 99–108.

Eroğlu, Süreyya, and Hayal Başaran Güleç. "Victoria & Albert Müzesi Deposunda Bulunan Yeşil Cami ve Yeşil Türbesi Çinileri ile Léon Parvillée İlişkisi," *Journal of International Social Research* 9, no. 47 (December 2016): 331–54.

Ersoy, Bozkurt. "Bergama Ulu Camii," *Arkeoloji-Sanat Tarihi Dergisi* 4 (1988): 57–66.

Ersoy, Bozkurt. "Edirne Şah Melek Camii'nin Tanıtımı ve Mimari Özellikleri Hakkında Düşünceler," *Arkeoloji-Sanat Tarihi Dergisi* 6 (1992): 47–61.

Erünsal, İsmail E. "Tâcizâde Câfer Çelebî," *TDVİA* 39 (2010): 353–56.

Erünsal, İsmail E. *The Life and Works of Tâcî-zâde Ca'fer Çelebi, with a Critical Edition of His Dîvân*. Istanbul: Edebiyat Fakültesi Basımevi, 1983.

Eyice, Semavi. "Mimar Hayreddin," *TDVİA* 17 (1998): 55–56.

Eyice, Semavi. "Dâvud Paşa Hamamı," *TDVİA* 9 (1994): 40.

Eyice, Semavi. "Bayezid Paşa Camii," *TDVİA* 5 (1992): 243–44.

Eyice, Semavi. "İlk Osmanlı Devrinin Dini İçtimai Bir Müessesesi: Zâviyeler ve Zâviyeli Camiler," *İstanbul Üniversitesi İktisat Fakültesi Mecmuası* 23 (1963): 3–80.

Eyice, Semavi. "Bursa'da Osman ve Orhan Gazi Türbeleri," *VD* 5 (1962): 131–47.

Eyice, Semavi. "Yunanistan'da Türk Mimarî Eserleri," *Türkiyat Mecmuası* 12 (1955): 205–30.

Faroqhi, Suraiya. "Ottoman Textiles in European Markets," in *The Renaissance and the Ottoman World*, ed. Anna Contadini and Claire Norton. Farnham: Ashgate, 2013, 231–44.

Fazlıoğlu, İhsan. "İlk Dönem Osmanlı İlim ve Kültür Hayatında İhvânu's-safâ ve Abdurrahmân Bistâmî," *Dîvân: İlmi Araştırmalar* 1, no. 2 (1996): 229–40.

Feldman, Marian. *Diplomacy by Design: Luxury Arts and an "International Style" in the Ancient Near East, 1400–1200 BCE*. Chicago: University of Chicago Press, 2006.

Fleet, Kate. "The Rise of the Ottomans," in *The New Cambridge History of Islam*, ed. Maribel Fierro. Cambridge: Cambridge University Press, 2010, 313–31. DOI: http://dx.doi.org/10.1017/CHOL97805 21839570.013

Fleet, Kate. *European and Islamic Trade in the Early Ottoman State: The Merchants of Genoa and Turkey*. Cambridge: Cambridge University Press, 1999.

Fleischer, Cornell H. "Learning and Sovereignty in the Fifteenth and Sixteenth Centuries," *Treasures of Knowledge: An Inventory of the Ottoman Palace Library (1502/3–1503/4)*, vol. 1, ed. Gülru Necipoğlu, Cemal Kafadar, and Cornell H. Fleischer. Leiden: Brill, 2019, 155–60.

Foletti, Ivan, and Erik Thunø. "The Artistic Cultures of the South Caucasus: Historiography, Myths, and Objects," in *The Medieval South Caucasus: Artistic Cultures of Albania, Armenia, and Georgia*, ed. Ivan Foletti and Erik Thunø, Convivium: Exchanges and Interactions in the Arts of Medieval Europe, Byzantium, and the Mediterranean, Seminarium Kondakovianum (Supplementum 2016): 11–16.

Fouchecour, Charles-Henri de, Gerhard Doerfer, and Willem Stoetzer. "Rubā'ī (pl. Rubā'iyyāt)," *EI2*, http://dx.doi.org/10.1163/1573-3912_islam_COM_ 0933, accessed February 16, 2021.

Gabriel, Albert. *Une capitale turque: Brousse, Bursa*. 2 vols. Paris: E. de Boccard, 1958.

Gabriel, Albert. "Bursa'da Murad I. Camii ve Osmanlı Mimarisinin Menşei Meselesi," *VD* 2 (1942): 37–43 (plus unpaginated plates).

Gabriel, Albert. *Voyages archéologiques dans la Turquie orientale*. Paris: E. de Boccard, 1940.

Gabriel, Albert. *Monuments turcs d'Anatolie*. 2 vols. Paris: E. de Boccard, 1931.

Gardet, L. "Djanna," *EI3*, http://dx.doi.org/10.1163/1573-3912_islam_COM_0183, accessed September 23, 2018.

Gasparini, Elisabetta. *Le pitture murali della Muradiye di Edirne*. Quaderni del Seminario di Iranistica, Uralo-altaistica e Caucasologia dell'Università degli studi di Venezia, 18. Padova: Sargon, 1985.

Genç, Vural, "Rethinking Idris-i Bidlisi: An Iranian Intellectual and Bureaucrat between the Shah and the Sultan," *Iranian Studies* 52, no. 3–4 (2019): 425–47.

Gerelyes, Ibolya, Athanasios Vionis, Vesna Bikić, Niculina Dinu, and Svitlana Bilialeva. "Ottoman Europe," in *The Oxford Handbook of Islamic Archaeology*, ed. Bethany J. Walker, Timothy Insoll, and Corisande Fenwick. Oxford: Oxford University Press, 2020, 217–39.

Gerritsen, Anne. *The City of Blue and White: Chinese Porcelain and the Early Modern World*. Cambridge: Cambridge University Press, 2020.

Ghazarian, Armen, and Robert G. Ousterhout. "A Muqarnas Drawing from Thirteenth-Century Armenia and the Use of Architectural Drawings during the Middle Ages," *Muqarnas* 18 (2001): 141–54.

Gierlichs, Joachim. "Tabrizi Woodcarving in Timurid Iran," in *Politics, Patronage, and the Transmission of Knowledge in 13th–15th Century Tabriz*, ed. Judith Pfeiffer. Leiden: Brill, 2014, 357–69.

Göde, Kemal. *Eratnalılar, 1327–1381*. Ankara: Türk Tarih Kurumu Basımevi, 1994.

Gökbilgin, M. Tayyib. "Edirne," *EI2*, http://dx.doi.org/10.1163/1573-3912_islam_COM_0200, accessed May 7, 2019.

Gökbilgin, M. Tayyib. *XV.–XVI. Asırlarda Edirne ve Paşa Livâsı: Vakıflar, Mülkler, Mukataalar*. Istanbul: Üçler Basımevi, 1952.

Golombek, Lisa. "Timurid Potters Abroad," *Oriente Moderno* N.S. 15 (1996): 577–86.

Golombek, Lisa. "The Paysage as Funerary Imagery in the Timurid Period," *Muqarnas* 10 (1993): 241–52.

Golombek, Lisa, and Donald N. Wilber. *The Timurid Architecture of Iran and Turan*. 2 vols. Princeton, NJ: Princeton University Press, 1988.

Goodwin, Godfrey, "Gardens of the Dead in Ottoman Times," *Muqarnas* 5 (1988): 61–69.

Goodwin, Godfrey. *Ottoman Architecture*. London: Thames & Hudson, 1971.

Goshgarian, Rachel. "Social Graces and Urban Spaces: Brotherhood and the Ambiguities of Masculinity and Religious Practice in Late Medieval Anatolia," in *Architecture and Landscape in Medieval Anatolia, 1100–1500*, ed. Patricia Blessing and Rachel Goshgarian. Edinburgh: Edinburgh University Press, 2017, 114–31.

Gould, Andrew G. "Ḳōzān," *EI2*, http://dx.doi.org/10.1163/1573-3912_islam_SIM_4455, accessed May 7, 2019.

Grabar, Oleg. *The Mediation of Ornament*. Princeton, NJ: Princeton University Press, 1992.

Grabar, Oleg. "The Earliest Islamic Commemorative Structures, Notes and Documents," *Ars Orientalis* 6 (1966): 7–46.

Graves, Margaret S. *Arts of Allusion: Object, Ornament, and Architecture in Medieval Islam*. Oxford: Oxford University Press, 2018.

Green, Nile. "Introduction: The Frontiers of the Persianate World (ca. 800–1900)," in *The Persianate World: The Frontiers of a Eurasian Lingua Franca*, ed. Nile Green. Oakland: University of California Press, 2019, 1–71.

Grenier, Carlos, *The Spiritual Vernacular of the Early Ottoman Frontier: The Yazıcıoğlu Family*. Edinburgh: Edinburgh University Press, 2021.

Grigor, Talinn. *Building Iran: Modernism, Architecture, and National Heritage under the Pahlavi Monarchs*. Pittsburgh, PA: Periscope, 2009.

Güleç, İsmail. "Sürûrî, Muslihuddin Mustafa," *TDVİA* 38 (2010): 170–72.

Gündoğdu, Hamza. *Dulkadırlı Beyliği Mimarisi*. Ankara: Kültür ve Turizm Bakanlığı, 1986.

Gündüz Küskü, Sema. *Osmanlı Beyliği Mimarisinde Anadolu Selçuklu Geleneği*. Ankara: Türk Tarih Kurumu, 2014.

Gurlitt, Cornelius. *İstanbul'un Mimari Sanatı = Architecture of Constantinople = Die Baukunst Konstantinopels*, trans. Rezan Kızıltan. Ankara: Enformasyon ve Dokümantasyon Hizmetleri Vakfi, 1999.

Hagen, Gottfried. "Translations and Translators in a Multilingual Society: A Case Study of Persian–Ottoman Translations, Late Fifteenth to Early Seventeenth Century," *Eurasian Studies* 2 (2003): 95–134.

Halevi, Leor. *Muhammad's Grave: Death Rites and the Making of Islamic Society*. New York: Columbia University Press, 2007.

Har-El, Shai. *Struggle for Domination in the Middle East: The Ottoman–Mamluk War, 1485–91*. Leiden: Brill, 1995.

Harb, Lara. *Arabic Poetics: Aesthetic Experience in Classical Arabic Literature*. Cambridge: Cambridge University Press, 2020.

Harb, Lara. "Poetic Marvels: Wonder and Aesthetic Experience in Medieval Arabic Literary Theory," PhD dissertation, New York University, 2013.

Harmanşah, Ömür. "Introduction: Towards an Archaeology of Place," in *Of Rocks and Water: Towards an Archaeology of Place*, ed. Ömür Harmanşah. Oxford: Oxbow Books, 2014, 1–12.

Hartmuth, Maximilian. "Building the Ottoman City: A Linear or Cumulative Process? Lessons from Fifteenth-Century Skopje," Centre and Periphery? Islamic Architecture in Ottoman Macedonia, 1383–1520, unpublished research paper, 2017.

Hartmuth, Maximilian. "A Late Fifteenth-Century Change in the Rapport of Friday Mosque and Ottoman City? A Case Study of Macedonia," Centre and Periphery? Islamic Architecture in Ottoman Macedonia, 1383–1520, unpublished research paper, 2017.

Hartmuth, Maximilian. "Ottoman Architecture in the Republic of Macedonia: A Critical Survey of Key Monuments from the Fifteenth through Nineteenth Centuries," Centre and Periphery? Islamic Architecture in Ottoman Macedonia, 1383–1520, unpublished research paper, 2017.

Hartmuth, Maximilian. "The Princess and the Mosque: Ottoman Royal Women's Architectural Patronage in the Province and the Case of the So-Called Zincirli Câmi' at Serres," in *Bâtir au féminin? Traditions et stratégies en Europe et dans l'Empire ottoman*, ed. Juliette Dumas and Sabine Frommel. Paris: Picard, 2013, 79–88.

Hartmuth, Maximilian, ed. *Centres and Periphery in Ottoman Architecture: Rediscovering a Balkan Heritage*. Sarajevo: Cultural Heritage without Borders Regional Office, 2011.

Hay, Jonathan. "The Passage of the Other: Elements for a Redefinition of Ornament," in *Histories of Ornament: From Global to Local*, ed. Gülru Necipoğlu and Alina Payne. Princeton, NJ: Princeton University Press, 2016, 62–69.

Hay, Jonathan. "Seeing through Dead Eyes: How Early Tang Tombs Staged the Afterlife," *RES: Anthropology and Aesthetics* 57/58 (Spring/Autumn 2010): 16–54.

Hay, Jonathan. *Sensuous Surfaces: The Decorative Object in Early Modern China*. Honolulu: University of Hawaii Press, 2010.

Hayes, Kenneth. "The Wooden Hypostyle Mosques of Anatolia: Mosque- and State-Building under Mongol Suzerainty," PhD dissertation, Middle East Technical University, Ankara, 2010.

Heffening, Willi, and Joseph Schacht. "Ḥanafiyya," *EI2*, http://dx.doi.org.10.1163/1573-3912_islam_SIM_2703, accessed February 8, 2022.

Heidarzadeh, Tofigh. "Patronage, Networks, Migration: Turco-Persian Scholarly Exchanges in the 15th, 16th, 17th Centuries," *Archives Internationals d'Histoire des Sciences* 55 (2005): 419–34.

Hillenbrand, Carole. "Gardens beneath which Rivers Flow: The Significance of Water in Classical Islamic Culture," in *Rivers of Paradise: Water in Islamic Art and Culture*, ed. Sheila Blair and Jonathan Bloom. New Haven, CT: Yale University Press, 2009, 27–58.

Hinz, Walther. *Islamische Masse und Gewichte: Umgerechnet ins metrische System*. Leiden: Brill, 1955.

Hoffman, Eva R., and Scott Redford, "Transculturation in the Eastern Mediterranean," in *A Companion to Islamic Art and Architecture*, vol. 1, ed. Finbarr Barry Flood and Gülru Necipoğlu. Hoboken, NJ: Wiley, 2017, 405–30.

Hogendijk, Jan P. "A Mathematical Classification of the Contents of an Anonymous Persian Compendium on Decorative Patterns," in *The Arts of Ornamental Geometry: A Persian Compendium on Similar and Complementary Interlocking Figures. Fī tadākhul al-ashkāl al-mutashābiha aw al-mutawāfiqa* (Bibliothèque nationale de France, Ms. Persan 169, fols. 180r–199r), a volume commemorating Alpay Özdural, ed. Gülru Necipoğlu. Leiden: Brill, 2017, 145–62.

Holod, Renata. "The Monuments of Yazd: Architecture, Patronage and Setting, 1300–1450," PhD dissertation, Harvard University, 1972.

Howard, Deborah. *Venice & the East: The Impact of the Islamic World on Venetian Architecture, 1100–1500*, ed. Stefano Carboni. New Haven, CT: Yale University Press, 2000.

Huisman, August J. W. "Abū Ḳalamūn," *EI2*, http://dx.doi.org/10.1163/1573-3912_islam_SIM_0210, accessed May 7, 2019.

Huppert, Ann C. "Material Matters: Training the Renaissance Architect," in *Artistic Practice and Cultural Transfer in Early Modern Italy: Essays in Honour of Deborah Howard*, ed. Nebahat Avcıoğlu and Allison Sherman. Farnham: Ashgate, 2015, 89–106.

Hurx, Merlijn. *Architecture as Profession: The Origins of Architectural Practice in the Low Countries in the Fifteenth Century*. Turnhout: Brepols, 2018.

Ibrahim, Laila, and Bernard O'Kane, "The Madrasa of Badr al-Dīn al-ʿAynī and Its Tiled Miḥrāb," *Annales Islamologiques* 24 (1988): 253–68.

İlgürel, Murtaza. "Balıkesir," *TDVİA* 5 (1992): 12–14.

Imber, Colin H. "ʿOthmān I," *EI2* http://dx.doi.org/10.1163/1573-3912_islam_SIM_6038, accessed May 7, 2019.

İnalcık, Halil. *Studies on the History of Textiles in Turkey*. Istanbul: Türkiye İş Bankası Kültür Yayınları, 2010.

İnalcık, Halil. "Pâdişâh," *TDVİA* 34 (2007): 140–43.

İnalcık, Halil. "Murad I," *TDVİA* 31 (2006): 156–64.

İnalcık, Halil. "Murad II," *TDVİA* 31 (2006): 164–72.

İnalcık, Halil. "How to Read ʿĀshık Pasha-Zāde's History," in *Studies in Ottoman History in Honour of Professor V. L. Ménage*, ed. Colin Imber and Colin Heywood. Istanbul: Isis, 1994, 139–56.

İnalcık, Halil. "A Case Study in Renaissance Diplomacy: The Agreement between Innocent VIII and Bayezid II on Djem Sultan," *Journal of Turkish Studies* 3 (1979): 212–30, reprinted in *Ottoman Diplomacy: Conventional or Unconventional?* ed. A. Nuri Yurdusev. Basingstoke: Palgrave Macmillan, 2004, 66–88.

İnalcık, Halil. "The Conquest of Edirne (1361)," *Archivum Ottomanicum* 3 (1971): 185–210.

İnalcık, Halil. "Ottoman Methods of Conquest," *Studia Islamica* 2 (1964): 103–29.

İnalcık, Halil. "The Rise of Ottoman Historiography," in *Historians of the Middle East*, ed. Peter Holt and Bernard Lewis. London: Oxford University Press, 1962, 152–67.

İnalcık, Halil. "Bursa," *EI2*, http://dx.doi.org/10.1163/1573-3912_islam_SIM_1552, accessed May 7, 2019.

İnalcık, Halil. "Meḥemmed I," *EI2*, http://dx.doi.org/10.1163/1573-3912_islam_COM_0728, accessed May 7, 2019.

İnalcık, Halil. "Meḥemmed II," *EI2*, http://dx.doi.org/10.1163/1573-3912_islam_SIM_5111, accessed May 7, 2019.

İnalcık, Halil, "Selīm I," *EI2*, http://dx.doi.org/10.1163/1573-3912_islam_COM_1015, accessed August 2, 2017.

Inan, Murat Umut. "Imperial Ambitions, Mystical Aspirations: Persian Learning in the Ottoman World," in *The Persianate World: The Frontiers of a Eurasian Lingua Franca*, ed. Nile Green. Oakland: University of California Press, 2019, 75–92.

Ingold, Tim. *Making: Anthropology, Archaeology, Art and Architecture*. New York: Routledge, 2013.

The International Style: The Arts in Europe around 1400, October 23–December 2, 1962. Baltimore, MD: Walters Art Gallery, 1962.

İpşirli, Mehmet. "Kayseri," *TDVİA* 25 (2002): 96–101.

İskit, Server R., and Zarif Orgun. *Resemli-Haritalı Mufassal Osmanlı Tarihi*. Istanbul: İskit Yayını, 1957.

Jardine, Lisa, and Jerry Brotton. *Global Interests: Renaissance Art between East and West: Picturing History*. London: Reaktion, 2000.

Jenkins, Marilyn. "Mamluk Underglaze-Painted Pottery: Foundations for Future Study," *Muqarnas* 2 (1984): 95–114.

Jennings, Ronald C. "Ḳayṣariyya," *EI2*, http://dx.doi.org/10.1163/1573-3912_islam_COM_0477, accessed July 21, 2017.

Kadoi, Yuka. "From Acquisition to Display: The Reception of Chinese Ceramics in the Pre-modern Persian World," in *Persian Art: Image-Making in Eurasia*, ed. Yuka Kadoi. Edinburgh: Edinburgh University Press, 2018, 60–77.

Kadoi, Yuka. *Islamic Chinoiserie: The Art of Mongol Iran*. Edinburgh: Edinburgh University Press, 2009.

Kafadar, Cemal. "Between Amasya and Istanbul: Bayezid II, His Librarian, and the Textual Turn of the Late Fifteenth Century," in *Treasures of Knowledge: An Inventory of the Ottoman Palace Library (1502/3–1503/4)*, vol. 1, ed. Gülru Necipoğlu, Cemal Kafadar, and Cornell H. Fleischer. Leiden: Brill, 2019, 79–153.

Kafadar, Cemal. "A Rome of One's Own: Reflections on Cultural Geography and Identity in the Lands of Rum," *Muqarnas* 24 (2007): 7–25.

Kafadar, Cemal. *Between Two Worlds: The Construction of the Ottoman State*. Berkeley: University of California Press, 1995.

Kafescioğlu, Çiğdem. *Constantinopolis/Istanbul: Cultural Encounter, Imperial Vision, and the Construction of the Ottoman Capital*. University Park: Pennsylvania State University Press, 2009.

Kafescioğlu, Çiğdem. "Lives and Afterlives of an Urban Institution and Its Spaces: The Early Ottoman ʿİmāret as Mosque," in *Historicizing Sunni Islam in the Ottoman Empire, c. 1450–c. 1750*, ed. Tijana Krstić and Derin Terzioğlu. Leiden: Brill, 2020, 255–307.

Kafesoğlu, İbrahim. *A History of the Seljuks: İbrahim Kafesoğlu's Interpretation and the Resulting Controversy*, trans. and ed. Gary Leiser. Carbondale: Southern Illinois University Press, 1988.

Kalfazade, Selda. "Yeşilimaret Camii," *TDVİA* 43 (2013): 496–98.

Kanda, Yui. "Revisiting the So-Called Ghaybī Workshop: Toward a History of Burjī Mamluk Ceramics," *Orient* 52 (2017): 39–57.

Kappert, Petra. *Die osmanischen Prinzen und ihre Residenz Amasya im 15. und 16. Jahrhundert*. Istanbul: Nederlands Historisch-Archaeologisch Instituut Te Istanbul, 1976.

Karakaya-Stump, Ayfer. *The Kizilbash/Alevis in Ottoman Anatolia: Sufism, Politics and Community*. Edinburgh: Edinburgh University Press, 2020.

Karamustafa, Ahmet T., "Origins of Anatolian Sufism," in *Sufism and Sufis in Ottoman Society: Sources, Doctrine, Rituals, Turuq, Architecture, Literature and Fine Arts, Modernism*, ed. Ahmet Yaşar Ocak. Ankara: Turkish Historical Society, 2005, 67–95.

Karamustafa, Ahmet T., *God's Unruly Friends: Dervish Groups in the Islamic Later Middle Period, 1220–1550*. Salt Lake City: University of Utah Press, 1994.

Karataş, Hasan. "A Shaykh, a Prince, and a Sack of Corn: An Anatolian Sufi Becomes Ottoman," in *Living in the Ottoman Realm: Empire and Identity, 13th to 20th*

Centuries, ed. Christine Isom-Verhaaren and Kent F. Schull. Bloomington: Indiana University Press, 2016, 79–94.

Karataş, Hasan. "Onbeşinci Yüzyılda Karamânî Ulemâ ve Meşayıh İlişki Ağları Üzerine Tesbitler," in *Osmanlı'da İlim ve Fikir Dünyası: İstanbul'un Fethinden Süleymaniye Medreselerinin Kuruluşuna Kadar*, ed. Ömer Mahir Alper and Mustakim Arıcı. Istanbul: Klasik, 2015, 283–98.

Karataş, Hasan. "The City as Historical Actor: The Urbanization and Ottomanization of the Halvetiye Sufi Order by the City of Amasya in the Fifteenth and Sixteenth Centuries," PhD dissertation, University of California, Berkeley, 2011.

Karpuz, Haşim. "Mevlânâ Külliyesi," *TDVİA* 29 (2004): 448–52.

Kastritsis, Dimitris. "Tales of Viziers and Wine: Interpreting Early Ottoman Narratives of State Centralization," in *Trajectories of State Formation across Fifteenth-Century Islamic West Asia*, ed. Jo van Steenbergen. Leiden: Brill, 2020, 224–54.

Kastritsis, Dimitris. The Historical Epic *Aḥvāl-i Sulṭān Mehemmed* (*The Tales of Sultan Mehmed*) in the Context of Early Ottoman Historiography," in *Writing History at the Ottoman Court: Editing the Past, Fashioning the Future*, ed. H. Erdem Çıpa and Emine Fetvacı. Bloomington: Indiana University Press, 2013, 1–22.

Kastritsis, Dimitris. "The Şeyh Bedreddin Uprising in the Context of the Ottoman Civil War of 1402–13," in *Political Initiatives "From the Bottom Up" in the Ottoman Empire: Halcyon Days in Crete VII. A Symposium held in Rethymo 9–11 January 2009*, ed. Antonis Anastasopoulos. Rethymno: Crete University Press, 2012, 233–50.

Kastritsis, Dimitris. *The Sons of Bayezid: Empire Building and Representation in the Ottoman Civil War of 1402–1413*. Leiden: Brill, 2007.

Kaufmann, Thomas DaCosta. *Toward a Geography of Art*. Chicago: University of Chicago Press, 2004.

Kazan, Hilâl. "XV. ve XVI. Asırlarda Osmanlı Sarayının Sanat Himayesi," PhD Dissertation, Marmara University, 2007.

Kee, Joan, and Emanuele Lugli. "Scale to Size: An Introduction," *Art History* 38, no. 2 (April 2015): 250–67.

Kenney, Ellen. "A Mamluk Monument Reconstructed: An Architectural History of the Mosque and Mausoleum of Tankiz al-Nasiri in Damascus," in *The Arts of the Mamluks in Egypt and Syria: Evolution and Impact*, ed. Doris Behrens-Abouseif. Bonn: V&R Unipress and Bonn University Press, 2012, 141–61.

Kenney, Ellen. "A Mamluk Monument 'Restored': The Dār al-Qur'ān wa-al-Ḥadīth of Tankiz al-Nāṣirī in Damascus," *Mamluk Studies Review* 11, no.1 (2007): 85–118.

Keskin, Mustafa Çağhan. "Umur Bey Taş Vakfiyesi: Esin ve İçerik Üzerine Bir Değerlendirme," *Osmanlı Araştırmaları* 53 (2019): 121–51.

Keskin, Mustafa Çağhan. "II. Yakub Bey Türbesi Çini Dekorasyonu Üzerine," in *Uluslararası Batı Anadolu Beylikleri Tarih, Kültür ve Medeniyeti Sempozyumu-III: Germiyanoğulları Beyliği, Kütahya 8-10 Mayıs 2014*, ed. Mehmet Ersan and Mehmet Şeker. Ankara: Türk Tarih Kurum Yayınları, 2017, 155–68.

Keskin, Mustafa Çağhan. "Bayezid Paşa: Vezir, Entelektüel, Sanat Hamisi," *Osmanlı Araştırmaları* 48 (2016): 1–38.

Keskin, Mustafa Çağhan. "II. Bayezid Dönemi Amasya Çevresinde Yerel Bir Bani: Hızır Paşa Oğlu Mehmed Paşa," *Art-Sanat* 5 (2016): 63–82.

Keskin, Mustafa Çağhan. "Syrian-Origin Architects around Amasya Region in the Early 15th Century," *A | Z ITU Journal of the Faculty of Architecture* 12, no. 2 (July2015): 19–33.

Keskin, Mustafa Çağhan. "Siyasi-kültürel İlişkiler Çerçevesinde Tebrizli Çini Ustaların Anadolu Yolculuğu (1419-1433)," *Belleten* 77, no. 279 (August 2013): 445–65.

Kessler, Christel. *The Carved Masonry Domes of Cairo*. Cairo: American University in Cairo Press, 1976.

Key, Alexander. *Language between God and the Poets: Ma'nā in the Eleventh Century*. Berkeley: University of California Press, 2018.

Kheirandish, Elaheh. "An Early Tradition in Practical Geometry: The Telling Lines of Uniques Arabic and Persian Sources," in *The Arts of Ornamental Geometry: A Persian Compendium on Similar and Complementary Interlocking Figures*. Fī tadākhul al-ashkāl al-mutashābiha aw al-mutawāfiqa (Bibliothèque nationale de France, Ms. Persan 169, fols. 180r–199r), a volume commemorating Alpay Özdural, ed. Gülru Necipoğlu. Leiden: Brill, 2017, 79–144.

Kiel, Machiel. "The Incorporation of the Balkans into the Ottoman Empire, 1353–1453," *The Cambridge History of Turkye, Volume 1: Byzantium to Turkey, 1071–1453*, ed. Kate Fleet. Cambridge: Cambridge University Press, 2009, 138–91.

Kiel, Machiel. "Selânik," *TDVİA* 36 (2009): 352–57.

Kiel, Machiel. "Cross-Cultural Contacts in 14th-Century Anatolia: Gothic Influences on the Architecture of the Turcoman Principalities of Western and Central Anatolia (examples from Antalya, Bergama, İstanoz, Niğde and Peçin," *Sanat Tarihi Defterleri* 10 (2006): 67–89.

Kiel, Machiel. *Studies on the Ottoman Architecture of the Balkans*. Aldershot: Ashgate Variorum, 1990.

Kiel, Machiel. "Notes on the History of Some Turkish Monuments in Thessaloniki and Their Founders," *Balkan Studies* 11 (1970): 123–48, reprinted in Kiel, *Studies on the Ottoman Architecture of the Balkans*, I.

Kırımlı, Faik. "İstanbul Çiniciliği," *Sanat Tarihi Yıllığı* 11 (1981): 96–110.

Kolay, İlknur Artuğ. "The Influence of Byzantine and Local Western Anatolian Architecture on the 14th Century Architecture of the Turkish Principalities," *Sanat Tarihi Defterleri* 6 (2002): 199–213.

Kolay, İlknur Artuğ. *Batı Anadolu 14. Yüzyıl Beylikler Mimarisinde Yapım Teknikler.* Ankara: Atatürk Kültür Merkezi, 1999.

Kolsuk, Asuman. "Turkish Tiles and Ceramics," *Apollo* 92 (July 1971): 58–61.

Kononenko, Evgenii I. "Ulu-dzhami Aksaraia: Mezhdu Osmanami i Karamanom," *Voprosy Vseobshchei Istorii Arkhitektury/ Questions of the History of World Architecture* 8, no. 1 (2017): 150–64.

Konyalı, İbrahim Hakkı. *Âbideleri ve Kitâbeleri ile Karaman Tarihi; Ermenak ve Mut Âbideleri.* Istanbul: Faha Matbaası, 1967.

Konyalı, İbrahim Hakkı. "Türklerde Mumya ve Mumyacılık," *Tarih Konuşuyor* 3, no. 15 (April 1965): 1196–99, 1257.

Konyalı, İbrahim Hakkı. *Ankara Abidelerinden Karacabey Mamuresi, Vakfiyesi, Tarihi ve Eserleri.* Istanbul: Nümune Matbaası, 1943.

Köprülü, Mehmed Fuad. *Les origines de l'empire ottoman*, reprint, Philadelphia: Porcupine Press, 1978 [first published Paris: E. de Boccard, 1935].

Köprülü, Mehmed Fuad. "Anadolu Selçuklu Tarihinin Yerel Kaynakları," *Belleten* 7 (1943): 379-458, translated into English as *The Seljuks of Anatolia: Their History and Culture According to Local Muslim Sources*, trans. and ed. Gary Leiser. Salt Lake City: University of Utah Press, 1992.

Köprülü, Mehmed Fuad. *Bizans Müesseselerinin Osmanlı Müesseselerine Te'siri Hakkında Bazı Mülâhazalar.* Istanbul: Evkaf Matbaası, 1931.

Köprülü, Mehmed Fuad. "Anadolu'da İslâmiyet: Türk İstilâsından Sonra Anadolu Tarih-i Dinisine Bir Nazar ve Bu Tarihin Menba'ları," *Dârü'l-Fünûn Edebîyât Fakültesi Mecmû'ası* 2 (1922–23): 281–311, 385–420, 457–86. English translation: *Islam in Anatolia after the Turkish Invasion (Prolegomena)*, trans. Gary Leiser. Salt Lake City: University of Utah Press, 1993.

Köprülü, Mehmet Fuad. *Türk Edebiyatında İlk Mutasavvıflar.* Istanbul: Matbaa-yi Amire, 1919, translated into English as *Early Mystics in Turkish Literature*, trans. and ed. Gary Leiser and Robert Dankoff. London: Routledge, 2006.

Kovács, Gergő Máté, and Péter Rabb. "The Preservation of Ottoman Monuments in Hungary: Historical Overview and Present Endeavours," *IJIA* 9, no. 1 (2020): 169–90.

Kramers, Johannes H. "Murād I," *EI2*, http://dx.doi.org/10.1163/1573-3912_islam_SIM_5530, accessed May 7, 2019.

Kramers, Johannes H. "Murād II," *EI2* http://dx.doi.org/10.1163/1573-3912_islam_SIM_5531, accessed May 7, 2019.

Kramers, Johannes H. "Karamān-Oghlu," *Encyclopaedia of Islam*, first edition, vol. 2, ed. Martijn Th. Houtsma, Thomas W. Arnold, Rene Basset, and Richard Hartmann. Leiden: Brill, 1908–34, 748–53.

Kuban, Doğan. "Bursa, Art and Architecture," *EI3*, http://dx.doi.org/10.1163/1573-3912_ei3_COM_24026, accessed May 7, 2019.

Küçükdağ, Yusuf. "Pîrî Mehmed Paşa," *TDVİA* 34 (2007): 280–81.

Kuniholm, Peter Ian. "Dendrochronologically Dated Ottoman Monuments," in *A Historical Archaeology of the Ottoman Empire*, ed. Uzi Baram and Linda Carroll. New York, 2000, 93–136.

Kunter, Halim Baki. "Kitâbelerimiz," *VD* 2 (1942): 431–55.

Kural, Macit R. "Çelebi Mehmed'in Yeşil Türbesi ve 1941–1943 Restorasyonu," *Güzel Sanatlar* 5 (1944): 50–102.

Kuran, Aptullah. "A Spatial Study of Three Ottoman Capitals: Bursa, Edirne, and Istanbul," *Muqarnas* 13 (1996): 114–31.

Kuran, Aptullah. *The Mosque in Early Ottoman Architecture.* Chicago: University of Chicago Press, 1968.

Kurt, Yılmaz. "Pîrî Mehmed Paşa, Ramazanoğlu," *TDVİA* 34 (2007): 281–82.

Kuru, Selim S. "The Literature of Rum: The Making of a Literary Tradition (1450–1600)," in *The Cambridge History of Turkye, Volume 1: Byzantium to Turkey, 1071–1453*, ed. Kate Fleet. Cambridge: Cambridge University Press, 2009, 548–92.

Lasser, Ethan W. "The Maker's Share: Tools for the Study of Process in American Art," in *A Companion to American Art*, ed. John Davis, Jennifer A. Greenhill, and Jason D. LaFountain. Malden, MA: Wiley, 2015, 95–110.

Lecker, Michael. "Abū Ayyūb al-Anṣārī," in *EI3*, http://dx.doi.org/10.1163/1573-3912_ei3_COM_24717, accessed September 1, 2017.

Leisten, Thomas. *Architektur für Tote: Bestattung in architektonischem Kontext in den Kernländern der islamischen Welt zwischen dem 3./9. und 6./12. Jahrhundert.* Materialien zur iranischen Archäologie 4. Berlin: D. Reimer, 1998.

Leisten, Thomas. "Between Orthodoxy and Exegesis: Some Aspects of Attitudes in the Shari'a toward Funerary Architecture," *Muqarnas* 7 (1990): 12–22.

Lentz, Thomas W., and Glenn D. Lowry. *Timur and the Princely Vision: Persian Art and Culture in the Fifteenth*

Century. Los Angeles: Los Angeles County Museum of Art, 1989.

Lewis, Stephen. "The Ottoman Architectural Patrimony of Bulgaria Revisited: Infrastructure, Intentionality, and the Genesis and Survival of Monuments," in *Monuments, Patrons, Contexts: Papers on Ottoman Europe Presented to Machiel Kiel*, ed. Maximilian Hartmuth and Ayşe Dilsiz. Leiden: Nederlands Instituut voor het Nabije Oosten, 2010, 153–70.

Lindner, Rudi Paul. "Anatolia, 1300–1451," in *The Cambridge History of Turkye, Volume 1: Byzantium to Turkey, 1071–1453*, ed. Kate Fleet. Cambridge: Cambridge University Press, 2009, 102–37.

Losensky, Paul. "Square like a Bubble: Architecture, Power, and Poetics in Two Inscriptions by Kalim Kāshānī," *Journal of Persianate Studies* 8 (2015): 42–70.

Lowry, Heath W. *Fourteenth Century Ottoman Realities: In Search of Hâcı-Gâzi Evrenos = On Dördüncü Yüzyıl Osmanlı Gerçekleri: Hacı-Gazi Evrenos'un İzinde*. Istanbul: Bahçeşehir University Press, 2012.

Lowry, Heath W. *In the Footsteps of the Ottomans: A Search for Sacred Spaces & Architectural Monuments in Northern Greece*. Istanbul: Bahçeşehir University Publications, 2009.

Lowry, Heath W. *The Shaping of the Ottoman Balkans, 1350–1550: The Conquest, Settlement & Infrastructural Development of Northern Greece*. Istanbul: Bahçeşehir University Publications, 2008.

Lu, Peter J., and Paul J. Steinhardt. "Decagonal and Quasi-crystalline Tilings in Medieval Islamic Architecture," *Science* 315 (2007): 1106–10.

Macaraig, Nina [formerly Ergin]. *Çemberlitaş Hamami in Istanbul: The Biographical Memoir of a Turkish Bath*. Edinburgh Studies on the Ottoman Empire. Edinburgh: Edinburgh University Press, 2018.

Mack, Rosamond E. *Bazaar to Piazza: Islamic Trade and Italian Art, 1300–1600*. Berkeley: University of California Press, 2002.

Mackie, Louise W. *Symbols of Power: Luxury Textiles from Islamic Lands, 7th–21st Century*. Cleveland, OH: Cleveland Museum of Art, 2015.

MacLean, Gerald. "Introduction: Re-Orienting the Renaissance," in *Re-Orienting the Renaissance: Cultural Exchanges with the East*, ed. Gerald MacLean. Basingstoke: Palgrave Macmillan, 2005, 1–28.

Mahi, Khalida. "Les 'Maîtres de Tabriz', céramistes dans l'empire ottoman: Une mise au point sur leur identification," *Eurasian Studies* 15, no. 1 (2017): 36–79.

Mahi, Khalida. "Tile Revetments from the 15th Century in Eastern Anatolia: A Problem of Attribution," in *At the Crossroads of Empires, 14th–15th-century Eastern Anatolia: Proceedings of the International Symposium held in Istanbul, 4th–6th May 2007*, ed. Deniz Beyazit. Paris: De Boccard, 2012, 181–205.

Manz, Beatrice Forbes. *Power, Politics and Religion in Timurid Iran*. Cambridge: Cambridge University Press, 2007.

Maranci, Christina, *The Art of Armenia: An Introduction*. Oxford: Oxford University Press, 2018.

Marçais, George. *Les faïences à reflets métalliques de la Grande Mosquée de Kairouan*. Paris: P. Geuthner, 1928.

Marén, Manuela. "Odors and Smells," in *Encyclopaedia of the Qur'an*, vol. 3, ed. Jane Dammen McAuliffe. Leiden: Brill Academic, 2003, 573–74.

Markiewicz, Christopher. *The Crisis of Kingship in Late Medieval Islam: Persian Emigres and the Making of Ottoman Sovereignty*. Cambridge: Cambridge University Press, 2019.

Marks, Laura U. "The Taming of the Haptic Space, from Málaga toValencia to Florence," *Muqarnas* 32 (2015): 253–78.

Mauder, Christian. "Being Persian in Late Mamluk Egypt: The Construction and Significance of Persian Ethnic Identity in the Salons of Sultan Qāniṣawh al-Ghawrī (r. 906–922/1501–1516)," *al-ʿUṣūr al-Wusṭā* 28 (2020): 376–406.

Mazlum, Deniz. *1766 İstanbul Depremi: Belgeler Işığında Yapı Onarımları*. Istanbul: İstanbul Araştırmaları Enstitüsü, 2011.

McChesney, Robert D. "A Note on the Life and Works of Ibn 'Arabshāh," *History and Historiography of Post-Mongol Central Asia and the Middle East: Studies in Honor of John E. Woods*, ed. Judith Pfeiffer and Sholeh A. Quinn. Wiesbaden: Harrassowitz, 2006, 205–49.

Meinecke, Michael. *Patterns of Stylistic Changes in Islamic Architecture: Local Traditions versus Migrating Artists*. New York: New York University Press, 1996.

Meinecke, Michael. *Die mamlukische Architektur in Ägypten und Syrien (648/1250 bis 923/1517)*. Abhandlungen des Deutschen Archäologischen Instituts Kairo, Islamische Reihe, Bd. 5. 2 vols. Glückstadt: J. J. Augustin, 1992.

Meinecke, Michael. "The Ulu Cami and the İsa Bey Cami at Selçuk: Seljuk Revival versus Mamluk Influences," in *The 8th International Congress of Turkish Art: Cairo, 26th September–1st October 1987*. Cairo: Ministry of Culture, Egyptian Antiquities Organization, 1989, 43.

Meinecke, Michael "Syrian Blue-and-White Tiles of the 9th/15th Century," *Damaszener Mitteilungen* 3 (1988): 203–14.

Meinecke, Michael. "Die mamlukischen Fayencemosaikdekorationen: Eine Werkstätte aus Tabrīz in Kairo (1330–1350)," *Kunst des Orients* XI (1976–77): 85–144.

Meinecke, Michael. *Fayencedekorationen seldschukischer Sakralbauten in Kleinasien*. 2 vols. Istanbuler Mitteilungen 13. Tübingen: Wasmuth, 1976.

Meinecke, Michael, and Aalund Flemming. *Die Restaurierung der Madrasa des Amīrs Sābiq ad-Dīn Miṭqāl al-Ānūkī und die Sanierung des Darb Qirmiz in Kairo*. Mainz: P. von Zabern, 1980.

Meisami, Julie Scott. "Palaces and Paradises: Palace Description in Medieval Persian Poetry," in *Islamic Art and Literature*, ed. Oleg Grabar and Cynthia Robinson. Princeton, NJ: Markus Wiener, 2001, 21–54.

Melville, Charles. "Historical Monuments and Earthquakes in Tabriz," *Iran* 19 (1981): 159–77.

Melvin-Koushki, Matthew. "Toward a Neopythagorean Historiography: Kemālpaşazāde's (d. 1534) Lettrist Call for the Conquest of Cairo and the Development of Ottoman Occult-Scientific Imperialism," in *Islamicate Occult Sciences in Theory and Practice*, ed. Liana Saif, Francesca Leoni, Matthew Melvin-Koushki, and Farouk Yahya. Leiden: Brill, 2020, 380–419.

Melvin-Koushki, Matthew. "Early Modern Islamicate Empire: New Forms of Religiopolitical Legitimacy," in *The Wiley Blackwell History of Islam*, ed. Armando Salvatore, Roberto Tottoli, Babak Rahimi, M. Fariduddin Attar, and Naznin Patel. Hoboken, NJ: Wiley, 2018, 353–75.

Mengüç, Murat Cem. "Histories of Bayezid I, Historians of Bayezid II: Rethinking Late Fifteenth-Century Ottoman Historiography," *BSOAS* 76, no. 3 (2013): 373–89.

Merçil, Erdoğan. "Alâiye Beyliği," *TDVİA* 2 (1989): 332–33.

Meri, Josef W. *The Cult of Saints among Muslims and Jews in Medieval Syria*. Oxford: Oxford University Press, 2002.

Meriç, Rıfkı Melûl. "Beyazıd Câmii Mimârı: II. Sultan Bâyezîd Devri Mimarları ile Bazı Binaları," *Ankara Üniversitesi İlâhiyat Fakültesi Türk ve İslâm Sanatları Yıllık Araştırmalar Dergisi* 2 (1958): 5–76, https://dspace.ankara.edu.tr/xmlui/handle/20.500.12575/45478, accessed May 15, 2020.

Mermutlu, Bedri, and Hasan Basri Öcalan. *Bursa Hazireleri*. Bursa: Bursa Kitaplığı, 2011.

Michailidis, Melanie Dawn. "Landmarks of the Persian Renaissance: Monumental Funerary Architecture in Iran and Central Asia in the Tenth and Eleventh Centuries," PhD dissertation, Massachusetts Institute of Technology, 2007.

Mijtaev, Petâr. *Ottoman Monuments in Bulgaria*, trans. Yaşar Yücel. Ankara: Türk Tarih Kurum Basımevi, 1987.

Miller, Barnette. *Beyond the Sublime Porte: The Grand Seraglio of Stambul*. New Haven, CT: Yale University Press, 1931.

Millner, Arthur. *Damascus Tiles: Mamluk and Ottoman Architectural Ceramics from Syria*. Munich: Prestel, 2015.

Milwright, Marcus. "'Waves of the Sea': Reponses to Marble in Written Sources," in *The Iconography of Islamic Art: Studies in Honor of Robert Hillenbrand*, ed. Bernard O'Kane. Cairo: American University in Cairo Press, 2005, 211–21.

Milwright, Marcus, and Evanthia Baboula. "Bayezid's Cage: A Re-examination of a Venerable Academic Controversy," *Journal of the Royal Asiatic Society*, ser. 3, 21, no. 3 (2011): 239–60.

Minorsky, Vladimir. "Tabrīz," in *Encyclopaedia of Islam*, first edition, vol. 7. Repr. Leiden: Brill, 1987, 583–95.

Mondini, Sara. "Vague Traits: Strategy and Ambiguities in the Decorative Programme of the Aḥmad Šāh I Bahmanī Mausoleum," *Eurasiatica* 5 (2016): 155–80.

Morabia, Alfred. "Lawn," *EI2*, http://dx.doi.org.ccl.idm.oclc.org/10.1163/1573-3912_islam_COM_0577, accessed May 7, 2019.

Mottahedeh, Roy. "ʿAjāʾib in *The Thousand and One Nights*," in *The Thousand and One Nights in Arabic Literature and Society*, ed. Richard G. Hovannisian and Georges Sabagh. Cambridge: Cambridge University Press, 1997, 29–39.

Muhanna, Elias. "The Sultan's New Clothes: Ottoman–Mamluk Gift Exchange in the Fifteenth Century," *Muqarnas* 27 (2010): 189–207.

Munroe, Nazanin Hedayat. "Silks from Ottoman Turkey," *Heilbrunn Timeline of Art History*, www.metmuseum.org/toah/hd/tott/hd_tott.htm (November 2012), accessed May 21, 2020.

Nakash, Yitzhak. *The Shi'is of Iraq*. Princeton, NJ: Princeton University Press, 1994.

Naser Eslami, Alireza. "Emulazione, appropriazione, interazione culturale: Architettura tra il Rinascimento italiano e l'Impero Ottomano," in *Incontri di civiltà nel Mediterraneo: l'Impero Ottomano e l'Italia del Rinascimento, storia, arte e architettura*, ed. Alireza Naser Eslami. Florence: Leo S. Olschki Edittore, 2014, 133–78.

Naser Eslami, Alireza. "Introcontri di culture tra Rinascimento italiano e la 'Sublime Porta,'" in *Incontri di civiltà nel Mediterraneo: l'Impero Ottomano e l'Italia del Rinascimento, storia, arte e architettura*, ed. Alireza Naser Eslami. Florence: Leo S. Olschki Edittore, 2014, 1–10.

Necipoğlu, Gülru. "The Spatial Organization of Knowledge in the Ottoman Palace Library: An Encyclopedic Collection and its Inventory," in *Treasures of Knowledge: An Inventory of the Ottoman Palace Library (1502/3–1503/4)*, ed. Gülru Necipoğlu, Cemal Kafadar, and Cornell H. Fleischer, vol. 1. Leiden: Brill, 2019, 1–77.

Necipoğlu, Gülru. "Architectural Dialogues across the Eastern Mediterranean: Monumental Domed Sanctuaries in the Ottoman Empire and Renaissance Italy," in *The Companion to the History of Architecture, Volume I, Renaissance and Baroque Architecture*, ed. Alina Payne. Malden, MA: Wiley, 2017, 594–623.

Necipoğlu, Gülru. "Ornamental Geometries: A Persian Compendium at the Intersection of the Visual Arts and Mathematical Sciences," in *The Arts of Ornamental Geometry: A Persian Compendium on Similar and Complementary Interlocking Figures*. Fī tadākhul al-ashkāl al-mutashābiha aw al-mutawāfiqa (Bibliothèque nationale de France, Ms. Persan 169, fols. 180r–199r), a volume commemorating Alpay Özdural, ed. Gülru Necipoğlu. Leiden: Brill, 2017, 11–78.

Necipoğlu, Gülru. "Persianate Images between Europe and China: The 'Frankish Manner' in the Diez and Topkapı Albums, c. 1350–1450," in *The Diez Albums: Contexts and Contents*, ed. Julie Gonnella, Friederike Weis, and Christoph Rauch. Leiden: Brill, 2017, 531–91.

Necipoğlu, Gülru. "Early Modern Floral: The Agency of Ornament in Ottoman and Safavid Visual Cultures," in *Histories of Ornament: From Global to Local*, ed. Gülru Necipoğlu and Alina Payne. Princeton, NJ: Princeton University Press, 2016, 132–55.

Necipoğlu, Gülru. "'Virtual Archaeology' in Light of a New Document on the Topkapı Palace's Waterworks and Earliest Buildings, ca. 1509," *Muqarnas* 30 (2013): 315–50.

Necipoğlu, Gülru. "Visual Cosmopolitanism and Creative Translation: Artistic Conversations with Renaissance Italy in Mehmed II's Constantinople," *Muqarnas* 29 (2012): 1–81.

Necipoğlu, Gülru. "From Byzantine Constantinople to Ottoman Kostantiniyye: Creation of a Cosmopolitan Capital and Visual Culture under Sultan Mehmed II," in *From Byzantion to Istanbul: 8000 Years of a Capital*. Istanbul: Sakıp Sabancı Museum, 2010, 262–77.

Necipoğlu, Gülru. "Creation of a National Genius: Sinan and the Historiography of 'Classical' Ottoman Architecture," *Muqarnas* 24 (2007): 141–83.

Necipoğlu, Gülru. *The Age of Sinan: Architectural Culture in the Ottoman Empire*. Princeton, NJ: Princeton University Press, 2005.

Necipoğlu, Gülru. "Dynastic Imprint on the Cityscape: The Collective Message of Imperial Funerary Mosque Complexes in Istanbul," in *Cimetières et traditions funéraires dans le monde islamique: Acte du Colloque International, Istanbul 28–30 Septembre 1991*, vol. 2, ed. Jean-Louis Bacqué-Grammont and Aksel Tibet. Ankara: Türk Tarih Kurumu 1996, 23–36.

Necipoğlu, Gülru. *The Topkapı Scroll: Geometry and Ornament in Islamic Architecture*. Los Angeles: Getty Center for the History of Art and the Humanities, 1995.

Necipoğlu, Gülru. *Architecture, Ceremonial, and Power: The Topkapi Palace in the Fifteenth and Sixteenth centuries*. Cambridge, MA: MIT Press, 1991.

Necipoğlu, Gülru. "From International Timurid to Ottoman: A Change of Taste in Sixteenth-Century Ceramic Tiles," *Muqarnas* 7 (1990): 136–70.

Necipoğlu, Gülru. "The Account Book of a Fifteenth-Century Royal Kiosk," in *Raiyyet Rusumu: Essays Presented to Halil İnalcık on His Seventieth Birthday*, ed. Şinasi Tekin and Gönül Alpay-Tekin. Cambridge, MA: Harvard University Press, 1987, 31–45.

Necipoğlu, Gülru. "Plans and Models in 15th- and 16th-Century Ottoman Architectural Practice," *JSAH* 45.3 (September 1986): 224–43.

Necipoğlu, Gülru and Alina Payne. "Introduction," in *Histories of Ornament: From Global to Local*, ed. Gülru Necipoğlu and Alina Payne. Princeton, NJ: Princeton University Press, 2016, 1–6.

Necipoğlu, Gülru, and Alina Payne, eds. *Histories of Ornament: From Global to Local*. Princeton, NJ: Princeton University Press, 2016.

Nethersole, Scott. "Review of Exhibition: Bagliori dorati: Il Gotico Internazionale a Firenze, 1375–1440 (Galleria degli Uffizi, Florence, 19 June–4 November 2012)," *Renaissance Studies* 27, no. 5 (2013): 754–64.

Nora, Pierre. "Between Memory and History: *Les Lieux de Mémoire*," in "Memory and Counter-Memory," *Representations* 26 (1989): 7–24.

Norton, Claire. "Blurring the Boundaries: Intellectual and Cultural Interaction between the Eastern and Western, Christian and Muslim Worlds," in *The Renaissance and the Ottoman World*, ed. Anna Contadini and Claire Norton. Farnham: Ashgate, 2013, 3–21.

Ogan, Aziz. "Aydın Oğullarından İsa Bey Cami'i," *VD* 3 (1956): 73–80, plus plates.

Oğuz Kursar, Zeynep. "Sultans as Saintly Figures in Early Ottoman Mausolea," in *Sacred Spaces and Urban Networks*, ed. Suzan Yalman and A. Hilâl Uğurlu. Istanbul: Koç University Research Center for Anatolian Civilizations, 2019, 67–88.

O'Kane, Bernard. "Architecture of the Interregnum: The Mozafferid, Jalayerid, and Kartid Contributions," in *Iran after the Mongols*, ed. Sussan Babaie. London: I. B. Tauris, 2019, 211–33.

O'Kane, Bernard. "Tiles of Many Hues: The Development of Iranian *Cuerda Seca* Tiles and the Transfer of Tilework Technology," in *And Diverse Are Their Hues: Color in Islamic Art and Culture*, ed.

Jonathan Bloom and Sheila Blair. New Haven, CT: Yale University Press, 2011, 174–203.

O'Kane, Bernard. *The Appearance of Persian on Islamic Art.* New York: Persian Heritage Foundation, 2009.

O'Kane, Bernard. "The Arboreal Aesthetic: Landscape, Painting and Architecture from Mongol Iran to Mamluk Egypt," in *The Iconography of Islamic Art: Studies in Honor of Robert Hillenbrand*, ed. Bernard O'Kane. Cairo: American University in Cairo Press, 2005, 223–51.

O'Kane, Bernard. "The Bihbihani Anthology and Its Antecedents," *Oriental Art* 45(1999): 9–18.

O'Kane, Bernard. "From Tents to Pavilions: Royal Mobility and Persian Palace Design," *Ars Orientalis* 23 (1993): 249–68.

O'Kane, Bernard. "Poetry, Geometry and the Arabesque: Notes on Timurid Aesthetics," *Annales islamologiques* 26 (1992): 63–78.

O'Kane, Bernard. *Timurid Architecture in Khurasan.* Costa Mesa, CA: Mazdâ in association with Undena, 1987.

Ökten, Ertuğrul. "Imperial Aqquyunlu Construction of Religious Establishments in the Late Fifteenth Century," in *Politics, Patronage, and the Transmission of Knowledge in 13th–15th Century Tabriz*, ed. Judith Pfeiffer. Leiden: Brill, 2014, 371–85.

Öney, Gönül. *Beylikler Devri Sanatı XIV.–XV. Yüzyıl, 1300–1453.* Ankara: Türk Tarih Kurumu Basımevi, 1989.

Önge, Yılmaz. "Mevlana Türbesinin Çini Tezyinatı," in *1. Millî Mevlânâ Kongresi, 3–5 May 1985 – Tebliğler.* Konya: Selçuk Üniversitesi Yayınları, 1986, 401–08.

Önkal, Hakkı. *Osmanlı Hanedan Türbeleri*, second edition. Ankara: Atatürk Kültür Merkezi Başkanlığı, 2017.

Önkal, Hakkı. "Türk Türbe Mimarisinde Cenaze Katının Gelişimi," *Türk Kültürü* 307 (1988): 732–38.

Otto-Dorn, Katharina. "Nachleben byzantinischer Traditionen in der Moschee Murads II. in Edirne," in *Aspects of the Balkans: Continuity and Change: Contributions to the International Balkan Conference Held at UCLA, October 23–28,1969*, ed. Henrik Birnbaum and Speros Vryonis Jr. The Hague: Mouton, 1972, 198–210.

Otto-Dorn, Katharina. "Seldschukische Holzsäulen moscheen in Kleinasien," in *Aus der Welt der islamischen Kunst: Festschrift für Ernst Kühnel zum 75. Geburtstag am 26. 10. 1957*, ed. Richard Ettinghausen. Berlin: Gebrüder Mann, 1959, 59–88.

Otto-Dorn, Katharina. "Islamische Denkmäler Kilikiens," *Jahrbuch für kleinasiatische Forschung* 2, no. 2 (1952): 113–26.

Otto-Dorn, Katharina. "Die İsa Bey Moschee in Ephesus," *Istanbuler Forschungen* 17 (1950): 115–31.

Ousterhout, Robert G. "The East, the West, and the Appropriation of the Past in Early Ottoman Architecture," *Gesta* 43, no. 2 (2004): 165–76.

Ousterhout, Robert G. "Ethnic Identity and Cultural Appropriation in Early Ottoman Architecture," *Muqarnas* 12 (1995): 48–62.

Overton, Keelan. "Introduction to Iranian Mobilites and Persianate Mediations in the Deccan," in *Iran and the Deccan: Persianate Art, Culture, and Talent in Circulation, 1400–1700*, ed. Keelan Overton. Bloomington: Indiana University Press, 2020, 3–76.

Özcan, Selim. "Amasya'da Sancak Beyliği Yapan Şehzadeler Döneminde Amasya Şehri," *Amasya Üniversitesi İlahiyat Fakültesi Dergisi* 5 (2015): 69–95.

Özcan, Tahsin. "Osmanlı Şehiriciliği ve Vakıflar," in *Selçukludan Cumhuriyete Şehir Yönetimi*, ed. Erol Özvar. Istanbul: Türk Dünyası Belediyeler Birliği, 2008, 113–28.

Özer, Mustafa. *The Ottoman Imperial Palace in Edirne (Saray-ı Cedîd-i Âmire): A Brief Introduction.* Istanbul: Bahçeşehir University Press, 2014.

Özer, Mustafa. "Edirne-Karaağaç-Timurtaş Köyü Timurtaş Paşa Camisi," *Belleten* 69, no. 254 (April 2005): 145–59.

Pächt, Otto. "Die Gotik der Zeit um 1400 als gesamteuropäische Kunstsprache," in *Europäische Kunst um 1400: Achte Ausstellung unter den Auspizien des Europarates.* Vienna: Kunsthistorisches Museum, 1962, 52–65.

Pallasmaa, Juhani. *The Eyes of the Skin: Architecture and the Senses.* Chichester: Wiley-Academy, 2005.

Pancaroğlu, Oya. "Bursa Yeşil Cami İnşa Kitabesinde Hiyerarşik İmgeleme," *Arkeoloji ve Göstergebilim, TAS* 3 (2019): 177–88.

Pancaroğlu, Oya. "The Mosque-Hospital Complex at Divriği: A History of Relations and Transitions," *Anadolu ve Çevresinde Ortaçağ* 3 (2009): 169–98.

Pancaroğlu, Oya. "Formalism and the Academic Foundation of Turkish Art in the Early Twentieth Century," *Muqarnas* 24 (2007): 67–78.

Pancaroğlu, Oya. "Architecture, Landscape, and Patronage in Bursa: The Making of an Ottoman Capital City," *Turkish Studies Association Bulletin* 20, no. 1 (1995): 40–55.

Parvillée, Léon. *Architecture et décoration turques au XVe siècle.* Paris: Morel, 1874.

Paterson, Mark. *The Senses of Touch: Haptics, Affects and Technologies.* Oxford: Berg, 2007.

Paul, Jürgen, "Mongol Aristocrats and Beyliks in Anatolia: A Study of Astarābādī's *Bazm va Razm*," *Eurasian Studies* 9, no. 1–2 (2011): 105–58.

Pay, Salih. *Bursa İvaz Paşa Külliyesi.* Bursa: Eğit-San, 1996.

Peacock, Andrew C. S. "Waqf Inscriptions from Medieval Anatolia," in *Philanthropy in Anatolia through the Ages: The First Sunan & İnan Kıraç Symposium on Mediterranean Civilizations, March 26–29, 2019, Antalya, Proceedings*, ed. Oğuz Tekin, Christopher H. Roosevelt, and Engin Akyürek. Antalya: Suna & İnan Kıraç Akdeniz Medeniyetleri Araştırma Merkezi, 2020, 183–93.

Peacock, Andrew C. S. "Seljuq Legitimacy in Islamic History," in *The Seljuqs: Politics, Society, and Culture*, ed. Christian Lange and Songül Mecit. Edinburgh: Edinburgh University Press, 2011, 79–96.

Peacock, Andrew C. S. "Introduction: The Ottoman Empire and its Frontiers," in *The Frontiers of the Ottoman World*, ed. Andrew C. S. Peacock. Oxford: Oxford University Press, 2009, 1–27.

Peacock, Andrew C. S. "Aḥmad of Niğde's *al-Walad al-Shafīq* and the Seljuk Past," *Anatolian Studies* 54 (2004): 95–107.

Peacock, Andrew C. S., and Sara Nur Yıldız, eds. *Islamic Literature and Intellectual Life in Fourteenth- and Fifteenth-Century Anatolia*. Würzburg: Ergon, 2016.

Pedersen, Johannes. "Ibn ʿArabshāh," *EI2*, http://dx.doi.org/10.1163/1573-3912_islam_SIM_3081, accessed May 22, 2019.

Peirce, Leslie. *The Imperial Harem: Women and Sovereignty in the Ottoman Empire*. New York: Oxford University Press, 1993.

Pelidija, Enes, and Feridun Emecen. "İsa Beğ," *TDVİA* 22(2000): 475–76.

Pellat, Charles. "Ḥirbāʾ," *EI2*, http://dx.doi.org/10.1163/1573-3912_islam_SIM_2892, accessed May 7, 2019.

Pentcheva, Bissera V. *Hagia Sophia: Sound, Space, and Spirit in Byzantium*. University Park: Pennsylvania State University Press, 2017.

Petersen, Andrew. "'Under the Yoke': The Archaeology of the Ottoman Period in Bulgaria," *Journal of Islamic Archaeology* 4, no. 1 (2017): 23–48.

Pevsner, Nikolaus. "The Term 'Architect' in the Middle Ages," *Speculum* 17, no. 4 (October 1942): 549–62.

Pfeiffer, Judith. "Introduction: From Baghdad to Marāgha, Tabriz, and Beyond: Tabriz and the Multi-cephalous Cultural, Religious, and Intellectual Landscape of the 13th to 15th Century Nile-to-Oxus Region," in *Politics, Patronage, and the Transmission of Knowledge in 13th–15th Century Tabriz*, ed. Judith Pfeiffer. Leiden: Brill, 2014, 1–11.

Pfeiffer, Judith, ed. *Politics, Patronage, and the Transmission of Knowledge in 13th–15th Century Tabriz*. Leiden: Brill. 2014.

Phillips, Amanda. *Sea Change: Ottoman Textiles between the Mediterranean and the Indian Ocean*. Berkeley: University of California Press, 2021.

Phillips, Barty. *Tapestry*. London: Phaidon, 1994.

Piemontese, Angelo M. "Angiolello, Giovanni Maria," *EIr*, www.iranicaonline.org/articles/angiolello-giovanni-maria-1451-ca-1525 accessed February 16, 2021.

Puerta Vílchez, José Miguel. *La poética del agua en el Islam = The Poetics of Water in Islam*. Sabarís, Baiona (Pontevedra): Trea, 2011.

Puerta Vílchez, José Miguel. *Historia del pensamiento estético árabe: Al-Andalus y la estética árabe clásica*. Madrid: Akal, 1997, translated as: José Miguel Puerta Vílchez, *Aesthetics in Arabic Thought: From Pre-Islamic Arabia through al-Andalus*, trans. Consuelo López Morillas. Leiden: Brill, 2017.

Pyle, Nancy Stephenson. "Seljuk Portals of Anatolia." 2 vols. PhD dissertation, Harvard University, 1980.

Quiring Zoche, Rosemarie. "Āq Qoyunlū," *EIr*, www.iranicaonline.org/articles/aq-qoyunlu-confederation, accessed June 8, 2018.

Rabbat, Nasser. "Design without Representation in Islamic Egypt," *Muqarnas* 25 (2008): 147–53.

Rabbat, Nasser. "ʿAjīb and Gharīb: Artistic Perception in Medieval Arabic Sources," *TMedieval History Journal* 9.1 (2006): 99–113.

Rabbat, Nasser. *The Citadel of Cairo: A New Interpretation of Royal Mamluk Architecture*. Leiden: Brill, 1995.

Raby, Julian. "Mehmed the Conqueror's Greek Scriptorium," *DOP* 37 (1983): 15–34.

Raby, Julian. "A Sultan of Paradox: Mehmed the Conqueror as a Patron of the Arts," *Oxford Art Journal* 5, no. 1 (1982): 3–8.

Raby, Julian. "Mehmed II Fatih and the Fatih Albums," *Islamic Art* 1 (1981): 42–50.

Raby, Julian. "Cyriacus of Ancona and the Ottoman Sultan Mehmed II," *Journal of the Warburg and Courtauld Institutes* 43 (1980): 242–46.

Raby, Julian, and J. Henderson. "The Technology of Fifteenth-century Turkish Tile: An Interim Statement of the Origins of Iznik Tile," *World Archaeology* 21 (June 1989): 115–32.

Ramírez-Weaver, Eric. "Reading the Heavens: Revelation and Reification in the Astronomical Anthology for Wenceslas IV," *Gesta* 53, no. 1 (2014): 73–94.

Redford, Scott, "Intercession and Succession, Enlightenment and Reflection: The Inscriptional Program of the Karatay Madrasa, Konya," in *Viewing Inscriptions in the Late Antique and Medieval World*, ed. Antony Eastmond. Cambridge: Cambridge University Press, 2015, 148–69.

Redford, Scott, "Paper, Stone, Scissors: ʿAlā al-Dīn Kayqubād, ʿIṣmat al-Dunyā wa ʾl-Dīn, and the writing of Seljuk History," in *The Seljuks of Anatolia: Court and Society in the Medieval Middle*

East, ed. Andrew C. S. Peacock and Sara Nur Yıldız. London: I. B. Tauris, 2013, 151–70.

Redford, Scott. "Portable Palaces: On the Circulation of Objects and Ideas about Architecture in Medieval Anatolia and Mesopotamia," *Medieval Encounters* 18 (2012): 382–412.

Redford, Scott. "'What Have You Done for Anatolia Today?': Islamic Archaeology in the Early Years of the Turkish Republic," *Muqarnas* 24 (2007): 243–52.

Redford, Scott. "Byzantium and the Islamic World, 1261–1557," in *Byzantium: Faith and Power (1261–1557)*, ed. Helen C. Evans. New York: Metropolitan Museum of Art, 2004, 388–96.

Redford, Scott. *Landscape and the State In Medieval Anatolia: Seljuk Gardens and Pavilions of Alanya, Turkey*. Oxford: Archaeopress, 2000.

Redford, Scott. "The Alaeddin Mosque in Konya Reconsidered," *Artibus Asiae* 51, no. 1/2 (1991): 54–74.

Reindl, Hedda. *Männer um Bāyezīd: Eine prosopographische Studie über die Epoche Sultan Bāyezīds II (1481–1512)*. Berlin: K. Schwarz, 1983.

Reindl-Kiel, Hedda. "Rum Mehmed Paşa," *TDVİA* 35 (2008): 335–37.

Riedlmayr, András. "Foundations of the Ottoman Period in the Balkan Wars of the 1990s," in *Balkan'larda Osmanlı Vakıfları ve Eserleri Uluslararası Sempozyumu, İstanbul-Edirne 9-10-11 Mayıs 2012*, ed. Mehmet Kurtoğlu. Ankara: T. C. Başbakanlık Vakıflar Genel Müdürlüğü, 2012: 89–110.

Riefstahl, Rudolf M. "Early Turkish Tile Revetments in Edirne," *Art Islamica* 4 (1937): 251–81.

Riefstahl, Rudolf M. *Turkish Architecture in Southwestern Anatolia*. Cambridge, MA: Harvard University Press, 1931.

Rizvi, Kishwar, ed. *Affect, Emotion, and Subjectivity in Early Modern Muslim Empires: New Studies in Ottoman, Safavid, and Mughal Art and Culture*. Leiden: Brill, 2018.

Rizvi, Kishwar. "Art History and the Nation: Arthur Upham Pope and the Discourse on 'Persian Art' in the Early Twentieth Century," *Muqarnas* 24 (2007): 45–65.

Rodini, Elizabeth. *Gentile Bellini's Portrait of Sultan Mehmed II: Lives and Afterlives of an Iconic Image*. London: I. B. Tauris, 2020.

Rogers, J. Michael. "Evidence for Mamluk–Mongol Relations." *Colloque international sur l'histoire du Caire (1969)*. Cairo: General Egyptian Book Organisation, 1972, 385–403.

Rogers, J. Michael. "Patronage in Seljuk Anatolia, 1200–1300," PhD dissertation, Oxford University, 1971.

Roxburgh, David J. "Persianate Arts of the Book in Iran and Central Asia," in *A Companion to Islamic Art and Architecture*, vol. 2, ed. Finbarr Barry Flood and Gülru Necipoğlu. Hoboken, NJ: Wiley, 2017, 668–90.

Roxburgh, David J. "Timurid Architectural Revetment in Central Asia, 1370–1430: The Mimeticism of Mosaic Faience," in *Histories of Ornament: From Global to Local*, ed. Gülru Necipoğlu and Alina Payne. Princeton, NJ: Princeton University Press, 2016, 116–29.

Roxburgh, David J. *The Persian Album, 1400–1600: From Dispersal to Collection*. New Haven, CT: Yale University Press, 2005.

Roxburgh, David J., ed. *Turks: A Journey of a Thousand Years, 600-1600*. London: Royal Academy of Arts, 2005.

Roxburgh, David J. *Prefacing the Image: The Writing of Art History in Sixteenth-Century Iran*. Leiden: Brill, 2001.

Roxburgh, David J. "Kamal al-Din Bihzad and Authorship in Persianate Painting," *Muqarnas* 17 (2000): 119–46.

Ruggles, D. Fairchild. "Listening to Islamic Gardens and Landscapes," in *Music, Sound, and Architecture in Islam*, ed. Michael Frishkopf and Federico Spinetti. Austin: University of Texas Press, 2018, 19–34.

Ruggles, D. Fairchild. *Islamic Gardens and Landscapes*. Philadelphia: University of Pennsylvania Press, 2008.

Saba, Matthew D. "Abbasid Lusterwares and the Aesthetics of 'Ajab," *Muqarnas* 29 (2012): 187–212.

Sachedina, Abdulaziz, "Ziyārah," *The Oxford Encyclopedia of the Islamic World*, vol. 6. Oxford: Oxford University Press, 2009, 50–51.

Şahin, İlhan, and Feridun Emecen, "Amasya," *TDVİA* 3 (1991): 1–3.

Saʿīdī Sīrjānī, ʿAli-Akbar. "Bāġ-e Fīn," *EIr*, www .iranicaonline.org/articles/bag-e-fin, accessed May 18, 2019.

Şakiroğlu, Mahmut H. "Cem Sultan," *TDVİA* 7 (1993): 284–86.

Salgırlı, Saygın. "Radicalizing Premodern Space: A Perspective from the Late Medieval Ottoman World," *Radical History Review* 130 (January 2018): 45–61.

Salgırlı, Saygın. "Architectural Anatomy of an Ottoman Execution," *JSAH* 72, no. 3 (September 2013): 301–21.

Salgırlı, Saygın. "The Rebellion of 1416: Recontextualizing an Ottoman Social Movement," *JESHO* 55, no. 1 (2012): 32–73.

Şaman Doğan, Nermin. "Kültürel Etkileşim Üzerine: Karamanoğulları - Memluklu Sanatı," *Hacettepe Üniversitesi Edebiyat Fakültesi Dergisi* 23/I: (2006) 131–49.

Samkoff, Aneta. "From Central Asia to Anatolia: The Transmission of the Black-Line Technique and the Development of Pre-Ottoman Tilework," *Anatolian Studies* 64 (2014): 199–215.

Sardjono, Sandra. "Ottoman or Italian Velvets? A Technical Investigation," in *Venice & the East: The*

Impact of the Islamic World on Venetian Architecture, 1100–1500, ed. Stefano Carboni. New Haven, CT: Yale University Press, 2000, 192–203.

Schimmel, Annemarie. *A Two-Colored Brocade: The Imagery of Persian Poetry*. Columbia Lectures on Iranian Studies. Chapel Hill: University of North Carolina Press, 1992.

Schmidt, Gerhard. "The Beautiful Style," in *Prague: The Crown of Bohemia, 1347–1437*, ed. Barbara Drake Boehm and Jiří Fajt. New York: Metropolitan Museum of Art, 2005, 104–11.

Schneider, Peter. "Research on the Rizk Mosque of Hasankeyf: al-'Adil Sulayman and the Building Activities during His Reign," in *At the Crossroads of Empires: 14th–15th Century Eastern Anatolia: Proceedings of the International Symposium Held in Istanbul, 4th–6th May 2007*, ed. Deniz Beyazit. Istanbul: Institut Français d'Études Anatoliennes Georges-Dumézil, 2012, 128–46.

Schönig, Hanne. "Camphor," *Encyclopaedia of the Qur'an*, http://dx.doi.org/10.1163/1875-3922_q3_EQSIM_00071, accessed May 7, 2019.

Sears, Tamara. "Following River Routes and Artistic Transmissions in Medieval Central India," *Ars Orientalis* 45 (2015): 43–77.

Şen, A. Tunç. "Reading the Stars at the Ottoman Court: Bāyezīd II (r. 886/1481–918/1512) and His Celestial Interests," *Arabica* 64 (2017): 557–608.

Serin, Muhittin. "Hamdullah, Şeyh Efendi," *TDVİA* 15 (1997): 449–52.

Shahin, Alaa al-Din. "Qaytbay's Decoration: An Analysis of the Decoration of Various Cairene Façades from the Period of Qaytbay," MA thesis, American University in Cairo, 1987.

Shaw, Wendy M. K. *What Is "Islamic" Art? Between Religion and Perception*. Cambridge: Cambridge University Press, 2019.

Şimşek, Gülsu, Belgin Demirsar Arlı, Sennur Kayac and Philippe Colomband. "On-site pXRF Analysis of Body, Glaze and Colouring Agents of the Tiles at the T excavation Site of Iznik Kilns," *Journal of the European Ceramics Society* 39 (2019): 2199–2209.

Şimşirgil, Ahmet. "Rum Beylerbeyi Yörgüç Paşa'nın Hayatı ve Vakıf Eserleri," in *Prof. Dr. Hakkı Dursun Yıldız Armağanı*. Istanbul: Marmara Üniversitesi, 1995, 457–71.

Sinclair, Tom. "The Venetian Merchants in the Il-Khanid Empire and Its Vassal States," in *Orta Çağ'da Anadolu'da Kültürel Karşılaşmalar: 12–15. Yüzyıllarda Anadolu'da İtalyanlar, Sempozyum Bildiriler*, ed. Filiz Yenişehirlioğlu. Ankara: VEKAM, 2019, 37–46.

Singer, Amy. "Enter, Riding on an Elephant: How to Approach Early Ottoman Edirne," *JOTSA* 3, no. 1 (Spring 2016): 89–109.

Singer, Amy. *Charity in Islamic Societies*. Cambridge: Cambridge University Press, 2008.

Sır, Ayşe Nur. "Gazzizâde Abüllatîf Efendi'nin Hulâsatü'l-vefâyât'ında Bursa Yer Adları," *Turkish Studies* 10–12 (2015): 953–80.

Smith, Jane Idleman, and Yvonne Yazbeck Haddad. *The Islamic Understanding of Death and Resurrection*. Oxford: Oxford University Press, 2002 (first published: Albany: State University of New York Press, 1981).

Smith, Pamela H. *The Body of the Artisan: Art and Experience in the Scientific Revolution*. Chicago: University of Chicago Press, 2004.

Sohrweide, Hanna. "Dichter und Gelehrte aus dem Osten im osmanischen Reich (1453–1600): Ein Beitrag zur türkisch-persischen Kulturgeschichte," *Der Islam* 46 (1970): 263–302.

Sohrweide, Hanna. "Der Sieg der Safaviden in Persien und seine Rückwirkungen auf die Schiiten Anatoliens im 16. Jahrhundert," *Der Islam* 41 (1965): 95–223.

Sönmez, Zeki. "Sinân-ı Atik," *TDVİA* 37 (2009): 228.

Sönmez, Zeki. "Acem Ali," *TDVİA* 1 (1988): 322.

Sourdel-Thomine, Janine. "Diwrīgī," *EI2*, http://dx.doi.org/10.1163/1573-3912_islam_SIM_1881, accessed July 21, 2017.

Sourdel-Thomine, Janine, and Yvon Linant de Bellefonds. "Ḳabr," *EI2*, http://dx.doi.org/10.1163/1573-3912_islam_SIM_3744, accessed September 14, 2019.

Sözen, Metin. *Anadolu Medreseleri: Selçuklu ve Beylikler Devri*. 2 vols. Istanbul: İstanbul Teknik Üniversitesi - Mimarlık Tarihi ve Rölöve Kürsüsü, 1970.

Sperl, Stefan. "Crossing Enemy Boundaries: al-Buḥturī's Ode on the Ruins of Ctesiphon Re-read in the Light of Virgil and Wilfred Owen," *BSOAS* 69 (2006): 365–79.

Stanley, Tim. "The Books of Umur Bey," *Muqarnas* 21, Essays in Honor of J. M. Rogers (2004): 323–31.

Stavrides, Theoharis. *The Sultan of Vezirs: The Life and Times of the Ottoman Grand Vezir Mahmud Pasha Angelović (1453–1474)*. Leiden: Brill, 2001.

St. Laurent, Beatrice. "Ottomanization and Modernization: The Architectural and Urban Development of Bursa and the Genesis of Tradition, 1839–1914," PhD dissertation, Harvard University, 1989.

St. Laurent, Beatrice. "Léon Parvillée: His Role as Restorer of Bursa's Monuments after the 1855 Earthquake and His Contribution to the Exposition Universelle of 1867," in *L'Empire ottoman, la République de Turquie et la France*, ed. Hâmit Batu and Jean-Louis Bacqué-Grammont. Istanbul: Isis, 1986, 247–82.

Strohmeier, Martin. *Seldschukische Geschichte und türkische Geschichtswissenschaft – Die Seldschuken im Urteil moderner türkischer Historiker.* Islamkundliche Untersuchungen Band 97. Berlin: Klaus Schwarz, 1984.

Subtelny, Maria Eva. "Agriculture and the Timurid Chahārbāgh: The Evidence from a Medieval Persian Agricultural Manual," *Gardens in the Time of the Great Muslim Empires: Theory and Design,* ed. Attilio Petruccioli. Leiden: Brill, 1997, 110–28.

Sümer, Faruk. "Ramazanoğulları," *TDVİA* 34 (2007): 445–47.

Sümer, Faruk. "The Seljuk Turbehs and the Tradition of Embalming," in *Atti del Secondo Congresso Internazionale di Arte Turca, Venezia 26–29 settembre 1963.* Naples: Istituto Universitario Orientale – Seminario di Turcologia, 1965, 245–48.

Swietochowski, Marie Lukens. "Drawing," *EIr,* https://iranicaonline.org/articles/drawing, accessed February 16, 2021).

Tabbaa, Yasser. *The Transformation of Islamic Art during the Sunni Revival.* Seattle: University of Washington Press, 2001.

Tabbaa, Yasser "Ḍayfa Khātūn, Regent Queen and Architectural Patron," in *Women, Patronage, and Self-representation in Islamic Societies,* ed. D. Fairchild Ruggles. Albany: State University of New York Press, 2000, 17–34.

Taddei, Alessandro. "The Conversion of Byzantine Buildings in Early Ottoman Thessaloniki: The Prodromos Monastery and the Acheiropoietos Church," *Eurasian Studies* 8 (2010): 201–14.

Taeschner, Franz. "Die Bauinschrift Emir Süleiman's an der Türbe Bayezid's I. in Brussa," *Der Islam* 20 (1932): 138–39.

Taeschner, Franz. "Die Ješil Ǧami in Brussa, ihre historischen Inschriften und ihre Künstler," *Der Islam* 20 (1932): 139–68.

Taeschner, Franz. "Die Werke der Familie Dai Qarağa Beg in Brussa und Mihalitsch und deren Inschriften," *Der Islam* 20 (1932): 168–82.

Taeschner, Franz. "Die Vezierfamilie der Ǧandarlyzāde (14./15. Jhd.) und ihre Denkmäler," *Der Islam* 18 (1929): 60–115.

Taneri, Aydın. "Bayezid Paşa," *TDVİA* 5 (1992): 242–43.

Tanındı, Zeren. "15th-century Ottoman Manuscripts and Bindings from Bursa Libraries," *Islamic Art* 4 (1990–91): 143–73.

Tanman, M. Baha, ed. *Ekrem Hakkı Ayverdi, 1899–1984: Mimarlık Tarihçisi, Restoratör, Koleksiyoner.* Istanbul: İstanbul Araştırmaları Enstitüsü, 2014.

Tanman, M. Baha. "Some Reflections on the İlyas Bey Mosque," in *Balat İlyas Bey Külliyesi: Tarih, Mimari, Restorasyon,* ed. M. Baha Tanman and Leyla Kayhan Elbirlik. Istanbul: Söktaş, 2011, 87–96.

Tanman, M. Baha. "Mehmed I Medresesi," *TDVİA* 28 (2003): 394–95.

Tanman, M. Baha. "Mamluk Influences on Early Ottoman Architecture," in *7 Centuries of Ottoman Architecture: A Supra-national Heritage,* ed. Nur Akın, Afife Batur and Selçuk Batur. Istanbul: YEM Yayınları, 2001, 86–94.

Tanman, M. Baha. "Edirne'de Erken Dönem Osmanlı Camileri ve Özellikle Üç Şerefeli Cami Hakkında," in *Edirne: Serhattaki Payıtaht,* ed. Emin Nedret İşli and M. Sabri Koz. Istanbul: Yapı Kredi Yayınları, 1998, 324–52.

Tanman, M. Baha. "Galata Mevlevîhânesi," *TDVİA* 13 (1996): 317–21.

Tanman, M. Baha, and Leyla Kayhan Elbirlik, eds. *Balat İlyas Bey Külliyesi: Tarih, Mimari, Restorasyon.* Istanbul: Söktaş, 2011.

Tezcan, Baki. "The Memory of the Mongols in Early Ottoman Historiography," in *Writing History at the Ottoman Court: Editing the Past, Fashioning the Future,* ed. H. Erdem Çıpa and Emine Fetvacı. Bloomington: Indiana University Press, 2013, 23–38.

Thys-Şenocak, Lucienne. *Ottoman Women Builders: The Architectural Patronage of Hadice Turhan Sultan.* Aldershot: Ashgate, 2006.

Toruk, Ferruh. "Bani Yörgüç Paşa ve İmar Faaliyetleri," *VD* 29 (2005): 105–33.

Tritton, Arthur S. "Ḥināṭa," *EI2,* http://dx.doi.org/10.1163/1573-3912_islam_SIM_2879, accessed May 7, 2019.

Tritton, A. S. "Djanāza," *EI2,* http://dx.doi.org/10.1163/1573-3912_islam_SIM_1985, accessed May 7, 2019.

Trivellato, Francesca. "Renaissance Italy and the Muslim Mediterranean," *Journal of Modern History* 82, no. 1 (March 2010): 127–55.

Tunca, Ayhan. *Edirne Sultan II. Bayezit Külliyesi ve Sağlık Müzesi.* Edirne: Yöre, 2010.

Turan, Osman. "Moğol Dönemi, Dağılış ve Beyliklerin Ortaya Çıkışı," in *Anadolu Selçukluları ve Beylikler Dönemi,* vol 1, ed. Ahmet Yaşar Ocak. Ankara: T. C. Kültür ve Turizm Bakanlığı, 2006, 309–19.

Turan, Osman. *Selçuklular Zamanında Türkiye: Siyâsi Tarih Alp Arslan'dan Osman Gazi'ye (1071–1318).* Istanbul: Turan Nesriyat Yurdu, 1971.

Turan, Şerafettin. "Mustafa Çelebi," *TDVİA* 31 (2006): 290–92.

Turan, Şerafettin. "Mimarbaşı," *TDVİA* 30 (2005): 90–91.

Turan, Şerafettin. "Bayezid, Şehzade," *TDVİA* 5 (1992): 230–31.

Turan, Şerafettin. "Osmanlı Teşkilâtında Hassa Mimarları," *Tarih Araştırmaları Dergisi* 1, no. 1 (1963): 157–202.

Türer, Osman. "Gazzizâde Abdüllatîf Efendi," *TDVİA* 13 (1996): 540.

Türkantoz, Kayahan. "The Urban Fabric and Distribution of Structures in Balat during the Menteşe Period," in *Balat İlyas Bey Külliyesi: Tarih, Mimari, Restorasyon*, ed. M. Baha Tanman and Leyla Kayhan Elbirlik. Istanbul: Söktaş, 2011, 49–54.

Türkiye'de Vakıf Abideler ve Eski Eserler, vol. 1. Ankara: Vakıflar Genel Müdürlüğü, 1972.

Turnbull, Richard H. "The Muradiye Complex in Bursa and the Development of the Ottoman Funerary Tradition," PhD dissertation, Institute of Fine Arts, New York University, 2004.

Turner, Vitor, and Edith Turner. *Image and Pilgrimage in Christian Culture: Anthropological Perspectives.* New York: Columbia University Press, 1978.

Ülgen, Ali Saim. "İneğöl'de İshak Paşa Mimarî Manzumesi," *VD* 4 (1958): 192a–192d (plus unpaginated plates).

Uluç, Lâle. "The Perusal of the Topkapı Albums: A Story of Connoisseurship," in *The Diez Albums: Contexts and Aontents*, ed. Julia Gonnella, Friederike Weis, and Christoph Rauch. Leiden: Brill, 2017, 121–62.

Uluç, Lâle. "On Altıncı Yüzyılda Osmanlı-Safevî Kültürel İliskilerin Çerçevesinde Nakkaşhânenin Önemi," *Doğubatı* 54 (October 2010): 23–60.

Uluçay, M. Çağatay, *Padişahların Kadınları ve Kızları*. Istanbul, Ötüken, 2011.

Uluçay, M. Çağatay, "Bayazid II.'in Âilesi," *Tarih Dergisi* 10 (1959): 105–24.

Ünver, A. Süheyl. *Fatih Devri Saray Nakışhanesi ve Baba Nakkaş Çalışmaları*. Istanbul: İstanbul Üniversitesi, 1958.

Ünver, A. Süheyl. "Edirne Şah Melek Paşa Cami'i Nakışları Hakkında," *VD* 3 (1956): 27–30, plus plates.

Ünver, A. Süheyl. "Baba Nakkaş," *Fatih ve İstanbul* 2 (1954): 169–89.

Uysal, A. Osman. *Germiyanoğulları Beyliğinin Mimarî Eserleri*. Ankara: Atatürk Yüksek Kurumu, Atatürk Kültür Merkezi Başkanlığı, 2006.

Uysal, A. Osman. "Adana Ulu Camii," *VD* 19 (1985): 277–83.

Uzunçarşılı, İsmail Hakki. *Çandarlı Vezir Ailesi*. Ankara: Türk Tarih Kurumu Basımevi, 1974.

Uzunçarşılı, İsmail Hakkı. *Osmanlı Tarihi*. 8 vols. Ankara: Türk Tarih Kurumu Basımevi, 1947–62 [vols. 5 to 8 by Enver Ziya Karal].

Uzunçarşılı, İsmail Hakki. "Hacı İvaz Paşa'ya Dâir," *Tarih Dergisi* 10, no. 14 (1959): 25–58.

Uzunçarşılı, İsmail Hakkı. *Anadolu Beylikleri ve Akkoyunlu, Karakoyunlu Devletleri Siyasî, İdarî, Fıkrî, İktisadî Hayat; İlmî ve İctimaî Muesseseler; Halk ve Toprak*. Ankara: Türk Tarih Kurumu, 1937.

Vakıf Abideler, vol. I: 1. *Adana. Adıyaman. Afyon. Ağri. Amasya. Ankara. Antalya. Aydın*. Ankara: Vakıflar Genel Müdürlüğü, 1972.

Vámbéry, Ármin. *Arminius Vámbéry, His Life and Adventures*, third edition. London: F. Unwin, 1884.

Vatin, Nicolas. "Aux origines du pèlerinage à Eyüp des sultans ottomans," *Turcica* 27 (1995): 91–99.

Vatin, Nicolas. *L'ordre de Saint-Jean-de-Jérusalem, l'Empire ottoman et la Méditerranée orientale entre les deux sièges de Rhodes 1480–1522*. Leuven: Editions Peeters, 1994.

Vatin, Nicolas, and Gilles Veinstein. *Le sérail ébranlé: Essai sur les morts, dépositions et avènements des sultans ottomans (XIVᵉ–XIXᵉ siècle)*. Paris: Fayard, 2003.

Venzke, Margaret L. "Dulkadir," *EI3*, http://dx.doi.org/10.1163/1573-3912_ei3_COM_27743, accessed July 21, 2017.

Veselý, Rudolf. "Ein Kapitel aus den osmanisch-mamlukischen Beziehungen: Meḥemmed Çelebi und al-Mu'ayyad Shaykh," in *Armağan: Festschrift für Andreas Tietze*, ed. Ingeborg Baldauf, Suraiya Faroqhi, and Rudolf Veselý. Prague: Enigma Corporation, 1994, 241–59.

Waardenburg, Jacques. "Death and the Dead," *Encyclopaedia of the Qur'an*, vol. 1, ed. Jane Dammen McAuliffe. Leiden: Brill Academic, 2001, 505–11.

Walsh, J. R. "Gūrānī," *EI2*, http://dx.doi.org.ccl.idm.oclc.org/10.1163/1573-3912_islam_SIM_2564, accessed May 22, 2019.

Watson, Oliver. *Persian Lustre Ware*. London: Faber and Faber, 1985.

Whitehouse, David. "Siraf: A Medieval Port on the Persian Gulf," *World Archaeology* 2, no. 2 (October 1970): 141–58.

Wilber, Donald N. "Qavam al-Din ibn Zayn al-Din Shirazi: A Fifteenth-century Timurid Architect," *Architectural History* 30 (1987): 31–45.

Wilber, Donald N. "The Timurid Court: Life in Gardens and Tents," *Iran* 17 (1979): 127–33.

Wilber, Donald N. *The Architecture of Islamic Iran: The Il Khānid Period*. Princeton, NJ: Princeton University Press, 1955.

Wing, Patrick. "Submission, Defiance, and the Rules of Politics on the Mamluk Sultanate's Anatolian Frontier," *Journal of the Royal Asiatic Society* 25, no. 3 (July 2015): 377–88.

Wittek, Paul. *The Rise of the Ottoman Empire: Studies in the History of Turkey, Thirteenth-Fifteenth Centuries*, reprint, New York: Routlege, 2012.

Wolper, Ethel Sara. "Portal Patterns in Seljuk and Beylik Anatolia," in *Aptullah Kuran İçin Yazılar*, ed. Çiğdem Kafescioğlu and Lucienne Thys-Şenocak. Istanbul: Yapı Kredi Yayınları, 1999, 65–80.

Woodhead, Christine. "Cafer Çelebi, Tacizade," *EI3*, http://dx.doi.org/10.1163/1573-3912_ei3_COM_27579, accessed May 20, 2018.

Woods, John. *The Aqquyunlu: Clan, Confederation, Empire*, revised edition. Salt Lake City: University of Utah Press, 1999.

Woods, John. "The Rise of Tīmūrid Historiography," *Journal of Near Eastern Studies* 46, no. 2 (April 1987): 81–108.

Wulzinger, Karl, Paul Wittek, and Friedrich Sarre. *Das islamische Milet*. Milet: Ergebnisse der Ausgrabungen und Untersuchungen seit dem Jahre 1899, Band III, Heft 4. Berlin and Leipzig: Walter de Gruyter, 1935.

Yalman, Suzan. "The 'Dual Identity' of Mahperi Khatun: Piety, Patronage and Marriage across Frontiers in Seljuk Anatolia," in *Architecture and Landscape in Medieval Anatolia, 1100–1500*, ed. Patricia Blessing and Rachel Goshgarian. Edinburgh: Edinburgh University Press, 2017, 224–52.

Yalman, Suzan. "'Ala al-Din Kayqubad Illuminated: A Rum Seljuq Sultan as Cosmic Ruler," *Muqarnas* 29 (2012): 151–86.

Yalman, Suzan, "Building the Sultanate of Rum: Religion, Urbanism and Mysticism in the Architectural Patronage of 'Ala al-Din Kayqubad (r. 1220–1237)," PhD dissertation, Harvard University, 2011.

Yavaş, Doğan, "Yeşilcami Külliyesi," *TDVİA* 43 (2013): 492–95.

Yavaş, Doğan, "Murâdiye Külliyesi," *TDVİA* 31 (2006): 196–98.

Yavuz, Yusuf Şevki. "Taşköprizâde Ahmed Efendi," *TDVİA* 40 (2011): 412–13.

Yazıcı, Tahsin. "Dāʿī, Aḥmad" *EIr*, www.iranicaonline.org/articles/dai-ahmad, accessed January 12, 2020.

Yenişehirlioğlu, Filiz. "Ottoman Anatolia," in *The Oxford Handbook of Islamic Archaeology*, ed. Bethany J. Walker, Timothy Insoll, and Corisande Fenwick. Oxford: Oxford University Press, 2020, 173–92.

Yenişehirlioğlu, Filiz, ed. *Orta Çağ'da Anadolu'da Kültürel Karşılaşmalar: 12–15. Yüzyıllarda Anadolu'da İtalyanlar, Sempozyum Bildiriler*. Ankara: VEKAM, 2019.

Yenişehirlioğlu, Filiz. "Les grandes lignes de l'évolution du programme décoratif en céramique des monuments ottomans au cours du XVIe siècle," *Erdem* 1 (1985): 456–65.

Yerasimos, Stefanos. "Fatih, une région d'Istanbul aux XVe et XVIe siècles," in *Studies in Ottoman History in Honour of Professor V.L. Ménage*, ed. Colin Heywood and Colin Imber. Istanbul: Isis, 1994, 369–81.

Yıldırım, Rıza. "The Safavid-Qizilbash Ecumene and the Formation of the Qizilbash-Alevi Community in the Ottoman Empire, c. 1500–c. 1700," *Iranian Studies*, 52, no. 3–4 (2019): 449–83. DOI: http://dx.doi.org/10.1080/00210862.2019.1646120

Yıldız, Sara Nur. "From Cairo to Ayasuluk: Hacı Paşa and the Transmission of Islamic Learning to Western Anatolia in the Late Fourteenth Century," *Journal of Islamic Studies* 25, no. 3 (2014): 263–97.

Yıldız, Sara Nur. "Ottoman Historical Writing in Persian, 1400–1600," in *Persian Historiography*, ed. Charles Melville. London: I. B. Tauris, 2012, 436–502.

Yıldız, Sara Nur. "Post-Mongol Pastoral Polities in Eastern Anatolia during the Late Middle Ages," in *At the Crossroads of Empires: 14th–15th Century Eastern Anatolia*, ed. Deniz Beyazit. Paris: De Boccard, 2012, 27–48.

Yıldız, Sara Nur. "Razing Gevele and Fortifying Konya: The Begin of the Ottoman Conquest of the Karamanid Principality in South-Central Anatolia, 1468," in *The Frontiers of the Ottoman World*, ed. Andrew C. S. Peacock. Oxford: Oxford University Press, 2009, 307–29.

Yıldız, Sara Nur. *Mongol Rule in Thirteenth-Century Seljuk Anatolia*. Leiden: Brill Academic, 2006.

Yılmaz, Gülgün. "Kazı Buluntuları Işığında İtalyanların Ayasuluk'taki Ticari Faaliyetleri," in *Orta Çağ'da Anadolu'da Kültürel Karşılaşmalar: 12–15. Yüzyıllarda Anadolu'da İtalyanlar, Sempozyum Bildiriler. Ankara, May 13, 2016*, ed. Filiz Yenişehirlioğlu. Ankara: VEKAM, 2019, 195–206.

Yılmaz, Gülgün. "Edirne'nin Erken Osmanlı Devri Yapılarında Çini Süsleme," *Trakya Üniversitesi Edebiyat Fakültesi Dergisi* 5, no. 10 (July 2015): 59–80.

Yılmaz, Hüseyin. *Caliphate Redefined: The Mystical Turn in Ottoman Political Thought*. Princeton, NJ: Princeton University Press, 2018.

Yinanç, Refet "Selçuklu Medreselerinden Amasya Halifet Gazi Medresesi ve Vakıfları," *VD* 15 (1982): 5–22.

Yüksel, İ. Aydın. *Osmanlı Mimârîsinde II. Bâyezid ve Yavuz Selim Devri (886–926/1481–1520)*, second edition. Istanbul: İstanbul Fetih Cemiyeti, 2006 [first published 1982].

Yüksel, İ. Aydın. "Hatuniye Külliyesi," *TDVİA* 16 (1997): 501–03.

Yüksel, Murat. "Kara Timurtaş-Oğlu Umur Bey'in Bursa'da Vakfettiği Kitaplar ve Vakıf Kayıtları," *Türk Dünyası Araştırmaları* 31(1984): 134–47.

Yüksel Muslu, Cihan. *The Ottomans and the Mamluks: Imperial Diplomacy and Warfare in the Islamic World*. London: I. B. Tauris, 2014.

Yüksel Muslu, Cihan. "Ottoman–Mamluk Relations and the Complex Image of Bayezid II," in *Conquête ottomane de l'Egypte (1517): arrière-plan, impact, échos*, ed.

Benjamin Lellouche and Nicholas Michel. Leiden: Brill, 2013, 51–76.

Yürekli, Zeynep. "Architectural Patronage and the Rise of the Ottomans," in *A Companion to Islamic Art and Architecture*, vol. 1, ed. Finbarr Barry Flood and Gülru Necipoğlu. Hoboken, NJ: Wiley, 2017, 733–54.

Yürekli, Zeynep. *Architecture and Hagiography in the Ottoman Empire: The Politics of Bektashi Shrines in the Classical Age.* Farnham: Ashgate, 2012.

Zachariadou, Elizabeth A. "Histoires et légendes des premiers ottomans," *Turcica* 27 (1995): 45–89.

Zachariadou, Elizabeth A. "Manuel II Palaeologos on the Strife between Bāyezīd I and Ḳāḍī Burhān al-Dīn Aḥmad," *BSOAS* 43, no. 3 (1980): 471–81.

Zaki, Mona M. "Barzakh," in *Encyclopaedia of the Qurʾān*, ed. Jane Dammen McAuliffe, Georgetown University, Washington DC, http://dx.doi.org/10.1163/1875-3922_q3_EQCOM_00023, accessed February 8, 2022.

INDEX

Abbasid caliph, 96
'Abd al-Latif al-Baghdadi, 105
'Abd al-Rahim b. Muhammad al-Muslih (kadi), 113
'Abdullah (son of Bayezid II), 169, 171, 172
ablaq, 108, 109, 126, 132, 134, 210
Abraham of Kütahya Ewer, *185*
Abu Ayyub al-Ansari, 168
Abu Bakr, 51
Abu Bakr b. Muhammad, 97, 99, 104, 105, 106, 109, 121, 123
Abu Muzaffar Jahanshah, 92
Abu Sa'id, 67
afterlife
    and the fate of the deceased, 174
    conceptions of, 162
    imaginaries of, 160
    narratives of, 173
    references to, 145, 156, 160
    representations of, 162
Ahmad b. Abdallah al-Hijazi, 142
Ahmad b. Mustafa Taşköprüzäde, *77*
Ahmed (Prince), 85, 172, *185*
Ahmed (son of Bayezid II), 170, 171, *190*
Ahmed (son of Mehmed I), 169, 170
Ahmed (son of Murad II), 154, 159, 169
Ahmed (son of Selim II), *189*
Ahmed, Shahab, 92
Ahmed-i Da'i, 119
'Ala al-Din, 20, 67, 105
'Ala al-Din 'Ali Tusi, 64
'Ala al-Din I, 22
'Ala al-Din Kayqubad I, 55, 67, 123
'Ala al-Din Kayqubad III b. Faramarz, 67
Alaca Türbe, 12, 41, 48–51, 52, *195*
'Alaeddin 'Ali (son of Murad II), 154, 159, 169, 173
Alaeddin Mosque, 123
'Alemşah (son of Bayezid II), 169, 171
'Ali al-Naqqash, *77*, 141
'Ali b. Şehsuvar, 56, 206
'Ali Beğ, 60
'Ali Beğ b. Timurtaş, 5
'Ali ibn al-Mushaymish al-Dimashqi, 97
'Ali ibn Ilyas 'Ali, *77*
'Ali ibn Mushaymish al-Dimashqi, 121, 123
'Ali, son of Bayezid II, 172
Alibey Camii, 5
Alpers, Svetlana, 3
Amasya
    architectural design in, 188–93
    architecture in, 179
    landed properties in, 113
    location on trade route, *192*

Mamluk architecture in, 13, 99–104
monuments in, 178
Ottoman architecture in, 98
Ottoman conquest of, 98
Ottoman monuments in, 13, 132
Ottomans in, 97
topography of, *189*
under Bayezid II, 98
Amir Aqbay, 207
Amir Husayn ibn Tughluq Tekin, 90
Anadoluculuk, 2
Anatolia
    and the Republic of Turkey, 2
    architectural ties with Bilad al-Sham and Egypt, 123
    as coherent political and cultural space, 2
    beyond Ottoman control, 207
    caravan routes in, 10
    Christian communities in, 121
    conquest of, 98
    garden pavilions in, 23
    Islamic architecture in, 54, 94, 98
    Islamic monuments in, 89
    madrasas in, 61
    Mamluk architecture in, 98, 121
    Mamluk workers in, 95
    Mamluks in, 97
    medieval and early modern, 2
    Mongol conquest of, 33, 55, 66
    Mongols in, 67
    monuments in, 6, 129
    mosques in, 23
    nature and landscape in, 148
    Ottoman architecture in, 56
    Ottoman builders in, 7
    Ottoman conquest of, 12, 16, 205
    Ottoman monuments in, 13
    Ottomans in, 7, 35
    political fragmentation of, 206
    pre-Ottoman, 55
    Saljuq history in, 67
    Saljuq monuments in, 48
    Saljuqs in, 2, 17, 31, 51, 52, 54, 55, 90, 93, 94
    Sufi shrines in, 179
    tile decorations in, 76
    tile mosaics in, 32, 70
    tilework in, 76
    Timur's campaigns in, 4, 20, 77
    under the Mamluks, 97
Anatolian architecture, 13
Anatolianism, 2
Angiolello, Giovanni Maria, 22

270

INDEX 271

Aqqoyunlu, 7, 11, 16, 20, 32, 52, 140, 206, 207
Aqqoyunlu architecture, 16, 22, 144
Aqqoyunlu dynasty, 92, 97
arabesques, 17, 94
Arabic language, 120, 121, 157, 180
Araq al-Silahdar
  mausoleum of, 123
architects, 3, 18, 32, 35, 47, 55, 104, 106, 142, 177, 199–205
  Armenian, 204
  Iranian, 204
  Mamluk, 121, 123
  of the Yörgüç Pasha mosque, 119
  Ottoman, 16, 177
  participating in imperial commissions, 3
  role of, 104, 107
  training of, 3
  transmittal of forms by, 123
  visibility of, 3
architectural decoration
  Ottoman, 117
architectural design, 109
architectural drawings, 107
architectural models, 107
architectural training, 203
Arel, Ayda, 125
Armenia, 47, 97. *See also* Cilicia
  decorative motifs in, 117
Arras tapestries, 144
art history, 184
artifice, 13, 15, 26, 34, 52, 160
  poetic, 30
artistic exchange, 119
Ashmolean Museum, 139
al-Ashraf Shaʿban, 97
ʿAşıkpaşazāde, 4, 5, 67
Aslanapa, Oktay, 184
Aslanhane Mosque, 23
Atasoy, Nurhan, 186
Aube, Sandra, 36, 140
Aubusson, Pierre d', 178
Ayasuluk, 97, 121, 123, 130
Aydın Beğ, 203
ʿAyn-ı Şah, 172
Ayşe Hatun, 70
Ayverdi, Ekrem Hakkı, 107
Ayyubids, 96, 123

Baba Nakkaş, 52, 175, 180, 184, *187*, 218
  designs associated with, 180, 183, 184, *185*, *186*, *187*, 218
Baba Nakkaş album, 13, 175, 179, 184, *195*, 214
Babaie, Sussan, 3, 105
Badr al-Din al-ʿAyni, 120
Baghdad, 96
Bagh-e Fin in Kashan, 167
Balım Sultan, 206
Balkans
  monuments in, 6, 194–99
  Ottoman architecture in, 205
  Ottoman conquests in, 98
Balkans-to-Bengal complex, 92
bannāʾī, 32, 69, 91
Barkan, Ömer Lütfi, 60
Barquq, 97
Barsbay, 97, 142

Bartolʾd, Vasiliy V. (Wilhelm Barthold), 11
bathhouses, 113, 148, *195*
Baybars I, 22, 66
Bayezid I, 144
  architecture under, 6
  attacking Mamluks, 119
  capture of Amasya by, 97
  conquest of Malatya, 97
  defeat by Timur, 22, 53, 55, 56, 97
  in Anatolia, 7
  marriage of, *76*, 121
  mausoleum of, 57, 65
  mosque ensemble of, 65
  patronage of, 56, 123, 129
  reign of, 19, 20, 35, 123
  Timur's defeat of, 4, 67
Bayezid I mosque, 80, 213
  muqarnas window frames, 123
Bayezid I mosque-*zāviye*, 57, 80, 123
Bayezid II, 1
  and Ottoman culture, 9
  architecture during the reign of, *188*, 188–93
  aspirations of, 183
  burial of, 168
  conflict with Cem, 177, 178, 179
  court of, 181, 183
  family of, 171, 172
  lands returned by, 7, 60, 206
  patronage of, 98, 169, 178, 179, *189*, 199, 206, 207, 215
  poems praising, 181
  reign of, 4, 5, 16, 52, 144, 171, 175, 177, *192*, *194*, 206, 207
  relatives of, 170
Bayezid II mosque, 177
  decorations on, *190*
  in Amasya, 188–93, *199*
  in Edirne, 179, *199*, *201*
  in Istanbul, 179, *191*, *199*, *200*, 203, 204, 214
  minbar, *191*
Bayezid II mosque complex, 119
Bayezid II mosque-*zāviye*
  muqarnas capitals, *194*
Bayezid Pasha, 7, 13, 60, 97
  agents of, 107
  patronage of, 99
Bayezid Pasha Mosque, 143, *189*
Bayezid Pasha mosque-*zāviye*, 95, 99–104, 121
  craftsmen associated with, 107
  design elements, 108
  geometric decorations, 118
  inscriptions, 99, 102, 105, 123
  interior decoration, 108
  interior/exterior decorations, 109
  Mamluk influences on, 109, 119
  mihrab, 111
  plan of, 99
  portal of, 121
  roles of workers, 106
beautiful style, 11
bedesten (Amasya), *190*, *192*
Behrens-Abouseif, Doris, 105
Bektashis, 214
Bellini, Gentile, 9, 19
Bernardini, Michele, 77
Bernus-Taylor, Marthe, *77*, 90
beylik architecture, 90, *202*

272   INDEX

beyliks, 32, 55, 97, 123, 129, 130, 144, 184
  Anatolian, 129, 134
  patronage of, 124
Bibi Khanum Mosque, 91
Bihbihani anthology, 163
Bihzad, 75, 179
Bilad al-Sham, 121, 123. *See also* Greater Syria
Bimarhane, 116, 117, *190*
Binbaş, Evrim, 7, 11
Bistami, ʿAbd al-Rahman al-Hanafi al-, 7
Bithynia, 13, 53, 55, 65, 68
  architecture of, 67, 90, 93
  Ottomans in, 88
Blair, Sheila, 8, *76*
Bloom, Jonathan, 29, 143
Blue Mosque, 92
Bolu, 105
book paintings, 137, 179
Börklüce Mustafa, 65
Brotton, Jerry, 9
Bukhara, 23
Bülbül Hatun, 171, 172
Burhaneddin Ahmad, 7, 32, 97
burial practices, 157, 158
  discussion of, 157
  for women and children, 169, 172
  in China, 162
Burmalı Minare Mosque, 111, 113, *192*
Bursa, 59
  architectural patronage in, 4
  architecture in, 6
  as cultural center, 55, 56, 93, 94
  as model for Yadz, 92
  as necropolis of sultans, 64, 65, 66, 147, 168
  as Ottoman capital, 66, 67, 147
  as Ottoman dynastic city, 158, 172, 173, 216
  as Ottoman funerary site, 173
  as Ottoman *lieu de mémoire*, 13
  Byzantine architecture in, 56, 98
  craftsmen in, 92
  dynastic memory in, 65–68
  funerary complexes in, 145
  Mehmed I's mosque complex in, 53
  Mehmed I's buildings in, 93
  Mehmed I's mosque-*zāviye* complex, 57–64
  Mehmed I's patronage in, 54
  monuments in, 6, 61
  Ottoman architecture in, 31
  Ottoman conquest of, 98
  Ottoman dynastic landscape in, 146
  Ottoman monuments in, 92
  Ottoman patronage in, 32, 57
  Ottomans in, 56
  restoration work in, 75
  sericulture in, *193*
  textiles from, 10
  tile decoration in, 6
  tile production in, *76*
  Timurid culture in, 57
  workshops in, 142, 219
Bursa arches, 23, 85
Bursa Kütüğü, 169
Buruciye Madrasa, 123
Büyük Ağa Madrasa, *189*, *192*
Byzantine architecture, 34, 35, 40, 56, 63, 88, 90

  in Anatolia, 6
  in Bursa, 4, 13, 98
Byzantine art, 180
Byzantine Empire, 20, 51, 55
  end of, 16, 19

Cafer Çelebi. *See* Tacizāde Cafer Çelebi
Çağaptay, Suna, 54, 60
Cairo
  ceramic production in, 144
  citadel of, 130
  Fatimid architecture in, 123
  funerary madrasa, 120
  madrasa of Mithqal al-Anuki, 99
  Selim I's conquest of, 96
  tiles imported from, *185*
  underglaze-painted tiles in, 98
  workers from, 95
calligraphers, 3, 8, 18, 35, 52, 105, 142, 184, *188*, 218
calligraphy, 8, 26, 30, 47, 88, 108, 134, 180, 183, 217
  and tile mosaic, 142
  cursive script, *191*
  imperial monograms, *187*
  in the Üç Şerefeli Mosque, 134
  kufic script, *191*
  models for, 30
  overlapping styles in, 134
  transmission of, 143
cami, 5
Çandarlı family, 7
Çandarlı Halil Pasha, 60
Çandarlı Ibrahim Pasha, 183
Cariyeler Mausoleum, 172
Carswell, John, 137
Castelnuovo, Enrico, 56
Çekirge, 148
Çelebi Halife, 178
Cem (Prince), 164, 169, 170, 171, 172, 173, 206
  burial of, 178
  conflict with Bayezid II, 177, 178, 179
  in exile, 177
Cem Sultan Mausoleum, 135, 161, 164, 169
  construction of, 171
cenotaphs, 207
  draped with textiles, *197*
  in Anatolia, 158
  in the Mustafa Pasha Mosque, *197*
  lacking inscriptions, 168, 171
  marble, 13
  of Mehmed I, 70, 153, *197*
  of Murad II, 152, 159
  of Sahib ʿAta Fakhr al-Din ʿAli, 155
  of Yakub II, 76
  open, 159
  Saljuq, 162
Central Asia, 1
  architecture of, 93
  garden pavilions in, 24
  Ottoman exchange with, 95
  tile mosaics in, 32
  tile work in, 70
ceramics, 8, 10, 13, 14, 17, 52, 137, 142, 175, 179, 184, 214
  color schemes, *186*
  designs on, *187*, 218
  fritware, *184*, *185*, *187*

from Iznik, *184, 185, 187*
Golden Horn wares, *187*
in Iznik, 184
locations for production, 184, *185*
luster, 29, 75
Miletus ware, 184
ornamentation on, 179, 180
production of, 144, 177
chahār bāgh, 166, 167
Chehel Sotun, 23
China
artistic influence of, 17
funerary practices in, 162
porcelain from, 135, 137, 141, *184, 185*
trade with, 10
Çifte Hamam, *195, 197*
Çifte Minareli Madrasa, 32
Cilicia, 55, 56, 97, 207
Çinili Köşk, 12, 17, 21–23, 160, 217
architectural influences on, 34, 35
architectural precedents for, 52
as garden pavilion, 23
commissioning of, 22
entrance façade, 23
ideological intent of, 51
inscriptions, 26–30, 51, 75
interior decoration, 30
marble facing, 24
marble porch, 23
paper models for, 30
Persian poem on, 59
poetic mention of, 29, 39
tile decoration, 30–35, 47, 164
tile mosaics, 30, 32, 35, 51
cloisonné masonry, *195*
Çoban Mustafa Pasha Mosque, *187*
columns
Byzantine, 89
from Egypt, 204
made of tiles, 30
marble, 148, 154
octagonal, 23
porphyry, 154
praised for their beauty, 15
selection of, 204
spolia used for, 88
with muqarnas capitals, 80, 126, 194
with muqarnas cells, 134
wood, 23
Constantinople. *See also* Istanbul
as Ottoman capital, 1, 35, 41
Byzantine architecture in, 40
Mehmed II's conquest of, 4
Murad II's conquest of, 120
Ottoman conquest of, 16, 19–21, 55, 217
construction sites, 104–7
craftsmen, 55, 75, *77*
foreign, *79*
from Khurasan, 17
from Tabriz, 92, 94
movement of, 57, 95
Crusaders, 96

Damascus
tiles attributed to, 139, 140, 141

underglaze-painted tiles in, 98
Danalı, Merih, 20
Danishmendids, 98
Darling, Linda, 54
Davud Pasha, *197*
Davud Pasha Hamam, *197*
Dayfa Khatun, 123
Deleuze, Gilles, 117
Denny, Walter B., 141, 209, 210
dervishes, 5, 40, 60, 61, 64, 174, *201*
design templates, 143, 217
Didymoteichon, 107
Dimetoka, 107
dome construction, 202
Dost-Muhammad, 184
drawings
architectural, 143
calligraphic designs, 108
design templates, 143
ground plans, 107, 143
pricked, 143
Dulkadir, 56, 97, 178, 205, 206, 207
Dulkadir tribes, 20
dynastic memory, 4, 31, 56, 64, 65–68, 145, 158, 168, 173, 216
funerary space and, 145–50, 168
dynastic space, 146, 172, 173, 174

Edirne
architectural patronage in, 4
as royal residence, 55
monuments in, 6
Ottoman conquest of, 98
palace in, 137
tile decoration in, 6
Timurid style in, 92
underglaze-painted tiles in, 98
Egypt, 94
architectural ties with Anatolia and Bilad al-Sham, 123
connections to, 125
Mamluks in, 95
Ottoman conquest of, 178
ekphrastic poetry, 10, 28
Elvan Çelebi, 4
embalming techniques, 158
Emine Hatun, 56
Emir (son of Prince Mahmud), 171
Emir Süleyman, 56, 65, 66, 132
Eretna, 32
Eretnids, 98
Eski Cami, *80*
prayer hall of, 132
Eşrefoğlu Mosque, 23
Evliya Çelebi, 10, 75, 169, 171, 204
Evrenosoğlu family, 7
Eyice, Semavi, 60
Eyüp Sultan Mosque, 168

Fatimid architecture, 123
Fatimids, 96
Fatma Sultan, 172
Feldman, Marian, 11, 12
Ferahşah, 172
Ferhad Pasha, 56
Fidan Han, 39
Firuz Bey Mosque, 129

274 INDEX

Fleischer, Cornell, 183
fountains, 40, 74, 106, 148, 162, 167
Friday mosques, 5, 40, 58, 61, 74, *191*, 219
    commissioned by Mehmed II, 146
    creation of, 98
    identifying elements, 5
    in Muslim cities, 98
    in the Muradiye, 148
    in Yadz, 92
    mosque-*zāviyes* converted to, 178
    Mustafa Pasha Mosque, *199*
    of Murad II, *196*
fritware, *47*, *52*, *185*, *187*
funerary space
    and dynastic memory, 145–50

Gabriel, Albert, 163, 169
garden landscapes, 35
    Saljuq, 23
garden motifs, 163
garden pavilions, 23
gardens
    and funerary landscapes, 166
    around Selim II's mausoleum, 170
    at the Muradiye, 167
    funerary, 167
    in Islamic al-Andalus, 21
    in Islamic contexts, 166
    in Mughal India, 166
    in the Muradiye complex, 166, 171
    in the Ottoman Empire, 167
    of Topkapı Palace, 167
Gawhar Shad, 105
Gawhar Shad's Great Mosque in Mashhad, 105
gazi families, 206
Gedik Ahmed Pasha, 39, *194*
Germiyan, *76*
Ghars al-Din Khalil al-Tawrizi
    mosque of, 137
Ghaybī al-Tawrīzī, 140. *See* Ghaybi Tawrizi
Ghaybi Tawrizi, 137, 140
Ghiyath al-Din Kaykhusraw II, 111
gift exchange, 95, 97, 98, 120, 143
gift register, 203, 204, 205
Ginzburg, Carlo, 56
glass, 153
    colored, 39
    production of, 10
    trade in, 10
    window, 39
Gök Madrasa, 32, 33, 48, 61, 69, 113
gold leaf, 89, 90, 164
Golden Horn wares, *187*
goldsmith, 59
Golombek, Lisa, *77*, 92, 137, 163
Goodwin, George, 161
Gothic arches, 125
Gothic art, 11
Gothic style
    international, 11, 92
Grabar, Oleg, 163
Graves, Margaret, 59
Great Mosque and Hospital of Divriği, 117
Great Mosque in Bursa, 56, *80*, 123, 148
Great Mosque in Manisa, 129, 130

Great Mosque in Sivas, 32
Great Mosque of Adana, 207, 210, 213, 214
    additions to, 213
Great Mosque of Aksaray, 120
Great Mosque of Bergama, 56
Great Mosque of Damascus
    Umayyad, 130
Great Mosque of Kairouan, 141
Great Mosque of Man, 129
Greater Syria, 52, 95, 96. *See also* Syria
ground plans, 107, 143
Guattari, Félix, 117
Güdük Minare, 32
Gülbahar Hatun, 207
Gülbahar Hatun Mausoleum, 171
Gülruh Hatun Mausoleum, 163, 164, 171, 172
Gülşah Hatun Mausoleum, 172
Gümüşlüzade Ahmed Pasha, 178

Hacı Bektaş
    shrine of, 206
Hafsa Sultan, 70
Hagia Sophia, 24, 38, 39, 147, 170, 177, *202*, 218
Hajji 'Ivaz Pasha, 7, 60, 78, *79*, 92, 94, 105, 106, 107, 129, 143, 205, 216
Hajji 'Ivaz Pasha', 124
Hājjī Iwāḍ bin Akhī Bāyazīd. *See* Hajji 'Ivaz Pasha
Halil, 209
Halil Beğ, 207
Halil Edhem, 111, 114
Halvetis, 178, 201, 206, 214
Hamam Bishtak, 123
hammams, 63. *See also* Mahmud Pasha hammam
    at the İlyas Bey mosque, 125
    double, 40, 41
    in Edirne, 39
    in Muslim cities, 98
    in Skopje, *195*
    in the Muradiye, 146, 148
    in the palace of Mehmed II, 39
    of Yalbugha al-Nasiri, 210
Hanefi Islam, 61
haptic sense, 71, 74
Harmanşah, Ömür, 148
Hartmuth, Maximilian, 48, *195*
Has Murad Pasha, 41
Hasan Kethüda Mosque, 214
Hasbey Darülhuffaz, 70
hassa mimarları, 106, 177, *188*, 203, 205, 214, 218
Hatuniye Madrasa, 32
Hatuniye Mausoleum, 171
Hatuniye Mosque (Amasya), *189*
Hatuniye Mosque (Manisa), 207
Hay, Jonathan, 8, 48
Haydar Çelebi, 5
Hayrüddin, *200*
Hayrüddin Hızır 'Atufi, 183
Henderson, J., *185*
Herat
    as cultural center, 92
    conquest of by Safavids, 179
    Timurid courts in, 17
Hesht Behesht, 23
Hillenbrand, Carole, 161
Hızır Ağa, 20

INDEX   275

Hogendijk, Jan P., 51
Holod, Renata, 92
Hoşkadem Camii, 207
Howard, Deborah, 9
Hürrem Sultan, 147
Husam Beğ, 203
Husayn Bayqara, 11, 12, 179
Hüseyin Ağa, *192*
Hüseyin Hüsameddin, 178
Husn-i Shah, 207

Ibn ʿArabshah, 119
Ibn Battuta, 159
Ibn Ghaybī, 140
Ibn Ghaybī al-Tawrīzī, 140
Ibn Mushaymish al-Dimashqi, 97, 99, 104, 105, 106, 121, 123
İbrahim Bey İmaret, *76*
    chronology of, 141
    mihrab, 32
Ibrahim, Leila Ali, 120
Idris-i Bidlisi, 184
Ilkhanid architecture, 13, 98
Ilkhanid art, 17
Ilkhanid empire, 33
Ilkhanid stone slab, 47
Ilkhanids, 10, 13, 66, 91, 206
    fall of, 67
    in Amasya, 98
    in Anatolia, 32
    Mamluk rivalry with, 22
İlyas, 125
İlyas Bey Mosque, 88, 121, 125, 129
    architectural influences on, 125
    Mamluk influence on, 126
immersive space, 55, 71
Ingold, Tim, 47
Innocent VIII (pope), 178
inscriptions, 6
    as signatures, 104
    at Çinili Köşk, 24, 26
    Ayyubid, 58
    exterior, 99
    foundation, 5, 6, 13, 24, 56, 57, 58, 59, 65, 75, 99, 104, 105, 111, 126, 132, 150, 155, 160, 166, 171, 178, *189, 190, 192, 200, 202,* 207, 210
    in black-line tile, 71
    in Çinili Köşk, 30
    in cursive script, 143
    in floral kufic script, *80*
    in interior painting, 134
    in kufic script, 88, 132, 143, *187*
    in Persian verse, *197*
    in the Gülruh Hatun Mausoleum, 163
    in the Karatay Madrasa, 89
    in the Muradiye mosque, 137
    in *thuluth* script, *80*, 88
    in tile mosaics, 30
    of the Masters of Tabriz, *76*
    on Çinili Köşk, 26–30, 51
    on mausolea, 57
    on Mehmed I's mosque-*zāviye*, 58, *78*
    on mihrabs, 126
    on monuments, 5
    on mosques, 5
    on the Bayezid Pasha mosque-*zāviye*, 99, 102, 103

    on the Great Mosque of Mashhad, 105
    on the İlyas Bey Mosque, 126
    on the Isa Bey Mosque, 123
    on the Mahmud Pasha hammam, 41
    on the sultan's lodge, *77*
    on Yörgüç Pasha's tombstone, 111
    placement of, 106
    poetic, 10
    Qur'anic, 111, 162, 166
    signatures as, 3, 8, 76, 77, 79, 97, 121, 137, 140, 143, *186*, 218
    thuluth, 207
    tile, 166
    tile mosaic, 24
    Üç Şerefeli Mosque, 38
    waqf, 99, 102, 103
    wrap-around, 123
international style, 11
Iran, 16, 67. *See also* Ilkhanids
    architecture of, 93
    garden pavilions in, 23
    Ilkhanid centers in, 33
    luster tiles from, 141
    migrating workers from, 175
    Mongol architecture in, 7
    Ottoman exchange with, 95
    regional dynasties in, 67
    Safavid, 184
    Safavids in, 219
    Shiʿi Safavids in, 178
    tile mosaics in, 32
    tile-cutters from, 12
    Timur's campaigns in, *77*
Iraq
    luster tiles from, 141
    regional dynasties in, 67
İsa (son of Bayezid I), 65
İsa Beğ, 121, 124, *195, 196*
İsa Bey Mosque, 97, 121, 123, 125
    architectural connections in, 125
    portal of, 123
Isfahan, 163
    Safavid, 23
    Shaykh Lotfollah Mosque, 29
İshak (ruler of Saruhan), 129
İshak Beğ, 48, *195, 196*
İshak Pasha, 39, 41
Iskandar Mirza, 111
Islamic architecture
    in Anatolia, 54, 98
Islamic art, *196*
    and style, 10
    Chinese elements in, 17
    girih designs in, 47
    in Venice, 9
Islamic culture
    Turkish, 2
Istanbul. *See also* Constantinople
    as Ottoman capital, 4, 20, 35, 39, 175, 205
    as Ottoman funerary site, 173
    burial of Sultans in, 173
    Byzantine monuments in, 24
    imperial projects in, 20
    monuments in, 6, 12, 15, 41
    Old Palace, 137
    Ottoman conquest of, 98

276 INDEX

Istanbul (cont.)
  textiles from, 10
  workshops in, 219
Istanbul Archaeological Museum, 21, 32
Italian Renaissance, 9, 180
Italy
  connections to, 125
Iʿtimad al-Dawlat
  mausoleum of, 167
ʿIzz al-Din Kayqawus, 123

Jalal al-Din Qaratay, 89, 162
Jalal al-Din Rumi, 64, 206
  mausoleum of, 141
janissaries, 204
Jardine, Lisa, 9
Jenkins-Madina, Marilyn, 140

Kaʿba in Mecca, 178
Kafadar, Cemal, 2, 4, 5, 177, 206
Kafescioğlu, Çiğdem, 16, 60
Kafesoğlu, İbrahim, 2
Kamer Sultan, 172
Kanda, Yui, 137, 140
Kara Devletşah, 97
Karaca Bey Mosque, 98
Karaman, 12, 20, 22, 24, 32, 51, 141, 205, 206
  Ottoman conquest of, 16, 22, 35, 41, 67,
    98, 141
  tilework in, 32, 76, 141
Karamanid architecture, 22, 34, 51
Karamanids, 7, 12, 20, 22, 51, 56, 97, 120, 207
  in Anatolia, 22
  patronage of, 206
  relationship with Ottomans, 22
Karataş, Hasan, *188*
Karatay Madrasa, 30, 33, 61, 89
Kastritsis, Dimitris, 4
Kenney, Ellen, 95
Keskin, Mustafa Çağhan, *76*
Khan Khayrbek, 210
Khatun Jan Begum, 92
khiṭāyī, 17, 38, 47, 82, 90, 114, 123, 164, 177, 180, 183, *186*, *191*, *195*,
  197, 214
Khundi Khatun, 114
Khurasan, 17
Kilari Süleyman Ağa *masjid*, *190*, *192*
Kırımlı, Faik, 35
kitabkhāna, 9, 11, 12, 30, 51, 217
  virtual, 142–44
kızılbaş, 206, 227
Knights Hospitallers, 178
Koca Mustafa Pasha, 178, *195*
Kononenko, Evgenii, 120
Konya
  architectural style, 55
  architecture of, 56
  history of, 90
Köprülü, M. Fuad, 2
Korkud (Prince), 171
Köşk Madrasa, 32
Kritoboulos of Imbros, 15
Kuran, Aptullah, 61, *194*
Küskü, Sema Gündüz, 123
Kütahya, 76

Lamiʿi Çelebi, 77
landscape. *See also* gardens
  natural, 167
Larende, *76*
Lasser, Ethan, 3
Leonardo da Vinci, 9, *200*
liminal space, 160
Losensky, Paul, 30
lunettes, 128, 36, 38, 52, 68, *80*, *85*, 88
  calligraphic, 68

Madrasa Firdaws, 121
Madrasa of Qadi Ahmad b. al-Saffah, 210
madrasa system, 5
madrasas, 57, 59, 60
  at the İlyas Bey mosque, 125
  in Amasya, *189*
  in Karaman, 20
  in Merzifon, 97
  in Muslim cities, 98
  in the Muradiye, 146, 148
  of Mehmed I, 68, 94
  of Mithqal al-Anuki, 99
  of the mosque complex of Mehmed II, 38
  Ottoman, 98
  Saljuq, 61
Mahidevran (mother of Mustafa), 170, 172
Mahmud (Prince), 85, *185*
  family of, 171
Mahmud (son of Mehmed I), 70
Mahmud Pasha, 20, 60
  patronage of, 39
Mahmud Pasha Angelović. *See* Mahmud Pasha
Mahmud Pasha hammam, 41
Mahmud Pasha Mausoleum, 12, 21, 35, 39–48, 111
  architectural precedents for, 52
  geometric decorations, 118
  tile decoration on, 41
  tile decorations, 52
  tile work on, 47
Mahmud Pasha Mosque, 15, 16, 39–48, 217
Mahperi Hatun Complex, 61
Mahperi Hatun Mausoleum, 32
maker's share, 3, 218
Malatya, 97
Mamluk architecture, 56, *202*
  chain of transmission, 130
  elements associated with, 129
  in Aleppo, 210
  in Amasya, 99–104
  in Anatolia, 121
  in Ottoman building sites, 121
  in Syria, 210
  in Syria and Egypt, 94, 95
  influence of, 13, 97, 98, 109, 123, 123, 130
  terminology, 105
Mamluk culture, 123
Mamluk style
  in Ottoman contexts, 98
  in the Üç Şerefeli Mosque, 134
Mamluks, 57
  conflicts with Ottomans, 16
  emergence of, 96
  in Anatolia, 22, 97, 207
  in Egypt and Syria, 95, 210

INDEX   277

influence of, 20
influence on Ottomans, 18
interaction with Ottomans, 98
patronage of, 97
relationship with Ottomans, 97, 119, 143
Manisa, 5, 120, 129, 130, 148, 159, 199, 207, 214
manuscripts, 183
Mara Branković, 20
marble cladding, 24, 80, 88, 160
Maristan Nuri, 214
Markiewicz, Christopher, 184
Marks, Laura, 74
Mashhad
    Great Mosque in, 105
Masjid-i Kabud, 92
Masjid-i Muzaffariya, 92
Masjid-i Shah, 92
*masjid*s, 5, 58, 60, 98, 192, 200, 201, 206
masonry, 148, 190, 216
    ashlar, 32, 195, 201
    cloisonné, *195*
    pillars and domes, 99
    stone, 202
masons, 218
Masters of Tabriz, 8, 13, 33, 76–79, 106, 107, 109, 134, 137, 149, 150,
    185, 217
    and black-line tiles, 142
    beyond Bursa, 140–42
    in Karaman, 141
    in Khurasan, 77
    inscriptions by, 76, 77
    narrative of, 141, 217
material culture
    in the Ottoman Empire, 54
material politics, 2, 3, 4, 15, 16, 17, 21, 32, 75, 143, 219
mausolea, 32. *See also* tombs
    connected to madrasas, 61
    construction of, 157
    in Anatolia, 158
    in Bursa, 57, 85
    in the Muradiye, 137, 146, 148, 158, 159, 168, 173
    in the shrine complex of Shah-i Zinda, 90
    medieval Islamic, 162
    of Araq al Silahdar, 123
    of Mahmud Pasha, 111
    of Tankiz al Nasiri, 95
    Ottoman, 145
    Saljuq, 162
    Sufi, 107
mausoleums. *See also* Yeşil İmaret
Mehmed (son of Şehinşah), 171
Mehmed b. Shaykh Bayezid, 175
Mehmed Beğ Mosque, *194*, 205
Mehmed Çelebi. *See* Mehmed I
Mehmed I, 65
    and Ottoman culture, 56
    architecture of, 98
    burial of father by, 66
    death of, 57, 147
    Eski Cami completed by, 132
    funerary complex, 41
    in Amasya, 97
    in Bursa, 67
    marriage of, 56
    patronage of, 22, 54, 65, 66, *79*, 93, 94, 98

reign of, 4, 12, 16, 53, 55, 56, 65, 67, 93, 97
titles used for, 59
Mehmed I funerary complex. *See* Yeşil İmaret
Mehmed I madrasa, 88
Mehmed I mausoleum, 30, 41, 61, 64, 68, 75, 76, 88, 106
    architectural influences on, 55
    chronology of, 92
    crypt in, 159
    influences on, 93, 94
    interior wall decoration, 92
    painting of, *197*
    subsequent burials in, 159
    tile and stone decorations, 54
    tile mosaics in, 70
    tilework on, 69, 76, 91, 140, 148
Mehmed I mosque
    in Didymoteichon (Dimetoka), 107, 112
Mehmed I mosque-*zāviye*
    tile decorations in, 33
Mehmed I mosque-*zāviye*, 52, 57–64, 68, 75, 76, 77, 123, 134, 148,
    201, 217, 219
    architectural decoration, 109
    architectural influences on, 55, 125, 216
    as example, 92
    chronology of, 92
    construction of, 57, 60, 93, 141, 143
    craftsmen associated with, 77
    exterior of, 85
    façade, 80
    frames, 80
    immersive space in, 13
    influences on, 93, 94
    inscriptions on, 58, 78, 106
    interior of, 94
    Mamluk influence on, 126
    mihrab in, 33, 150
    muqarnas portals, 79, 80, 80, 90
    plan of, 61, 64
    portal, 118, 127, 213
    rūmī motifs, 117
    sensory experience of, 74
    spolia in, 88
    tile and stone decorations, 54
    tile decorations in, 13, 68, 70, 75, 76, 89, 90, 91, 135, 148, 214
    tiles in, 140
    waqfiya of, 120
    window grilles, 82
Mehmed II, 59
    and Ottoman imperial identity, 9
    art in the court of, 175
    aspirations of, 183
    burial of, 173
    conquest of Istanbul, 24, 120
    conquest of Karaman, 35
    conquest of Trebizond by, 7
    conquests in Anatolia, 205, 207
    court of, 181, 183
    criticism of, 5
    eastward expansion under, 7
    family of, 20, 172
    marriage of, 20
    mother of, 171
    patronage of, 1, 15, 17, 19, 20, 24, 32, 35, 75, 180,
    206, 216
    poetry praising, 180

Mehmed II (cont.)
  policies of, 204, 206
  reign of, 4, 7, 20, 21, 22, 29, 52, 56, 67, 97, 152, 158, 175, 177, 178, 179, *194*, 215
  workshops in the court of, 180
Mehmed II mausoleum, 146
Mehmed II mosque, 39, 61, 76, 177
  architectural decoration in, 35
  architectural influences on, 39
  competition with Hagia Sophia, 39
  construction of, 204
  Italian influence on, 9
  plan of, *201*
  praised in poetry, 17, 39
  rejected designs for, 107
  tiles in, 52, 135
  windows in, 38
Mehmed II mosque complex, 5, 38, 64
Mehmed II mosque ensemble, 64
Mehmed Pasha, *190*
Mehmed Pasha Mosque, *189*, *190*, *192*
  plan of, *190*
Mehmed Pasha mosque-*zāviye*, *192*
Mehmed Şah Fenari, 64
Mehmed Shah, 209
Meinecke, Michael, 8, 51, 95
Mengüç, Murat Cem, 4
Menteşe, 125
Merzifon, 107
metal candlesticks, 179
metalwork, 10, 11, 17, 52, 179, 183, 214, 218
  designs on, 180, *187*, *196*
Metropolitan Museum of Art, 141
Mevlevi shrine, 206
Mevlevis, 206, 214
Michelangelo, 9, *200*
migrating workers, 94, 98, 129, 144, 175
Mihailoğlu family, 7
mihrabs, 32, 33
  at the Great Mosque of Damascus, 130
  at the İsa Bey Mosque, 121
  in Cairo, 120
  in Mehmed I's mosque, 71, 75, 76
  in the Muradiye Mosque, 135, 137, 140, 150, 164
  in the Üç Şerefeli Mosque, 129
  of Bayezid II's mosque, *190*
  of the Bayezid Pasha mosque-*zāviye*, 118
  of the İbrahim Bey İmaret, 141
  of the İlyas Bey Mosque, 126, 127
  of the İsa Bey Mosque, 123
  of the Madrasa Firdaws, 121
  tiled, 150
Milwright, Marcus, 160
minarets, 5, 132, 134, 207, 210, 214
  of the Great Mosque, 32
minbars, 5, 6, 190, 191, 195, 207, 209
Mithqal al-Anuki
  madrasa of, 99
modernist architecture, 11
Molla Fenari, 7, 64
Molla Gürani, 120
Mongol Empire, 17, 54
Mongols
  imperial architecture of, 7
  in Anatolia, 67

monuments. *See also* mosques
  beylik, 95
  built by Mehmed II, 15
  Byzantine, 6, 24, 88
  commissioned by Murad II, 13
  commissioning of, 7
  descriptions of, 15
  from previous centuries, 14
  funerary, 32
  Ilkhanid, 13, 98
  in Adana, 14
  in Amasya, 97, 98, *188*
  in Anatolia, 7, 48, 61, 67, 90, 121, 129
  in Bursa, 4
  in Cairo, 120
  in Central Asia, 4
  in Greece and the Balkans, 6
  in Iran, 4
  in Istanbul, 12, 15, 20, 24, 41
  in the Balkans, 194–99
  Islamic, 56, 90
  links to sensory perception, 10
  Mamluk, 52, 121
  multifunctional, 61
  Ottoman, 2, 6, 13, 51, 54, 94, 95, 119, 132
  paper plans for, 108
  poems praising, 10
  preservation of, 92
  religious, 51
  Roman, 88
  Saljuq, 13, 30, 48, *80*, 98, 109
  selected for discussion, 6
  Timurid, 91
mosques
  design plans, 205
  for Sufis, 60
  ground plans, *192*, *195*
  in Anatolia, 23
  in Didymoteichon (Dimetoka), *79*
  in Hasköy, 39
  in Sofia, 39
  landscape paintings in, 163
  of Tankiz al Nasiri, 95
  Ottoman, 9
  single-dome, 205
  transformation of churches into, 6
  various types of, 60, 61
mosque-*zāviyes*, 40, 53, 58
  converted to Friday mosques, 61, 178, *191*
  in Amasya, *189*
  in Skopje, *196*
  in the Muradiye, 146, 148, 150
  inscriptions on, *190*
  of Bayezid Pasha, 97
  role of, 40
mu'allim, 105
al-Mu'ayyad Shaykh, 120
Mudurnu, 105
Mughal Empire, 215
Mughals, 11
Muhammad al-Majnun, 106
Muhammad al-Tusi, 30
muhandis, 105
Mükrime Hatun Mausoleum, 171
mummification, 158

muqarnas, 71, *82*, 116, 213
  in the Bayezid II mosque, *191*
  monumental, *79*
muqarnas balcony, 214
muqarnas base, 32
muqarnas capitals, 126, *202*
muqarnas cells, 132, 134
muqarnas cornice, 210
muqarnas corniches, 108, 129
muqarnas decoration, *197*
muqarnas designs, 47
muqarnas dome, 214
muqarnas frames, 88, 126
muqarnas frieze, 150
muqarnas niche, 32, 80, *80*, 82, 90, 126, 210, 213
  in Mehmed I's mosque-*zāviye*, *80*
muqarnas portals, 61, *79*, 80
  in Mehmed I's mosque-*zāviye*, *80*, 90
  in the Great Mosque in Bursa, *80*
  monumental, 55, 56, 123
  Saljuq-style, 129
muqarnas squinches, 203
muqarnas window frames, 123
Murad I, 22
  architecture under, 6
  burial of, 66, 158
  mosque ensemble of, 65
  reign of, 123
Murad I mosque-madrasa, 80
  façade, 80
Murad II. *See also vasiyetnāme of Murad II*
  burial of, 158
  death of, 155
  eastward expansion under, 7
  funerary complex, 13
  gifts from, 97
  mentioned in inscriptions, 113
  Mustafa's rebellion against, 65
  patronage of, 13, 36, 53, 75, 98, 111, 148
  reign of, 4, 16, 20, 56, 142, 147, 158
  study of Persian language, 119
Murad II mausoleum, 145, 146, 171
  burials in, 169
  construction of, 152, 158
  dome of, 154
  inscriptions, 155
  interior/exterior elements, 153
  marble floor, 163
  open dome, 153, 157, 159, 160, 162, 217
Murad II mosque, *195*
Murad II mosque-*zāviye*, 76, 148
  construction of, 150
  tile decorations, 13, 141
Muradiye, 13
  as dynastic cemetery, 170
  construction of, 145
  foundation inscription, 150
  gardens of, 167, 171
  landscape of, 167
  location of, 172
  mausolea in, 137, 158, 159, 173, 216, 217
Muradiye cemetery, 85, 145, 146, 148, 162, 168, 169, 171, 172, 178, *185*
  dynastic burials in, 173
Muradiye complex, 135, 145

wall paintings, 163
Muradiye Mosque, 13, 30, 76, 135, 150, 217
  blue-and-white tiles on, 135
  construction of, 141
  mihrab of, 140, 164
  tiles on, 139, 140, 143, *184, 187*
  wall paintings, 163
Musa (son of Bayezid I), 53, 56, 65
Musa (son of Prince Mahmud), 171
Museum of Islamic Art (Cairo), 140
Mushaymish al-Dimashqi, 121, 140
Muslih al-Din Mustafa Sururi, 59
Muslu, Cihan Yüksel, 119
Mustafa, 169, 172, 209
Mustafa (brother of Bayezid II), 170
Mustafa (brother of Selim II), 169, 170
Mustafa (false prince), 99, 111
Mustafa (son of Bayezid I), 53, 65
Mustafa (son of Mehmed I), 70
Mustafa (son of Mehmed II), 164, 169, 171
Mustafa (son of Piri Mehmed), 213
Mustafa (son of Süleyman), 154, 172, 173
Mustafa b. Piri, 207
Mustafa Beğ, 203, 204, 205
Mustafa Pasha Mosque, *195, 197*, 205
  interior, *195*
  plan of, *195*
Mustafa-yi Cedid (Mustafa the Younger) Mausoleum, 169

nakkaşhane, 179, 180, 183, *187*, 214, 217, 218
Naṣīr al-dīn Altana, 126
Nasir Muhammad
  mosque of, 130
Nasireddin Mehmed, 56
Necipoğlu, Gülru, 6, 9, 12, 17, 18, 19, 20, 22, 23, 24, 28, 35, 47, 50, 51, 59, 107, 130, 147, 152, 164, 177, 179, 180, 200, 204, 205
necropolis, 13, 147
  Muradiye as, 146
  of Eyüp, 147
Neşri, 5
Nethersole, Scott, 11
Nuruosmaniye Mosque, 43

O'Kane, Bernard, 17, 120, 163
Old Palace (Istanbul), 137
Orhan (son of Prince Mahmud), 171
Orhan (Sultan), 65, 66, 171
Osman, 4, 65, 66, 67, 170, 172, *189*
Osman (son of Kamer Sultan), 172
Ottoman architecture, 98
  aesthetics in, *188*
  by Sinan, 1
  classic, 1
  connections with Saljuq architecture, 123
  cosmopolitan scope of, *199*
  dynastic, 16
  early, 53
  effect of worker migration on, 129
  formation of, 6
  in Amasya, 98
  in Anatolia, 56, 129
  in Bursa, 31
  in Istanbul, 16
  influences on, 14, 34, 56, 126, 144
  Mamluk influence on, 130

280 INDEX

Ottoman architecture (cont.)
material politics of, 15, 17
muqarnas window frames in, 123
Timurid style in, 94
use of tile in, 33
Ottoman art, 183
imperial style, 4, 183
Ottoman culture
Turkish-Islamic aspects of, 7
Ottoman Empire
and the Renaissance, 9–10
artistic landscape of, 7
conflicts with Mamluks, 16
power structures, 2
trade with Europe, 9
Ottoman history, 3, 4, 5, 6
Ottoman Pavilion, 22
Ottoman style
classical, *194*
in the Üç Şerefeli Mosque, 134
Ottoman Turkish, 2, 121, 157, 166, 177
Ottoman-Mamluk war, 119, 178
Ottomans
in Amasya, 97
interaction with Mamluks, 98
patronage of, 97
relationship with Mamluks, 97, 119, 142
Ottoman-Safavid wars, *193*
Ousterhout, Robert, 53

painters, 18, 142, 179, 184
painting, 75
palaces
in Istanbul, 44
in Skopje, 39
Karamanid, 22, 51
of Mehmed II, 39
Pallasmaa, Juhani, 74
Pancaroğlu, Oya, 2, 53, 117
panegyric poetry, 28, 38
paper. *See also* drawings
designs on, 179–84, 217, 218
relationship to design, 117
role of, 108, 179
use in tile production, 143
used for transmission of designs, 143, 144
paper models
for tile mosaics, 30
used for transfer of drawings, 95
paper patterns, 108
paper templates, 8, 47, 142, 175, 217
paradise
allusions to, 163
architectural representation of, 13, 162
evocation of, 137, 145, 162, 163, 167, *197*
garden, 22, 59, 167
imaginaries of, 160
Islamic concept of, 161
mythical spring of, 39
references to, 41, 155, 156, 160, 161, 163, 166
representation of, 145
Parvillée, Léon, 75, 150
Paşa Beğ, 48, *195*
Paterson, Mark, 71
Persian language, 76, 119, 121, *197*

pilgrimage, 160
Pir Ahmed, 22
Pir Hüseyin Bey Mosque, 70
Pir İlyas mausoleum, 178, *190*
Pir Muhammad b. ʿUmar-Shaykh, 119
Pir-i Bakran
shrine of, 163
Piri Mehmed Pasha, 207, 209, 213, 214
poets, 35
pottery, 52. *See also* ceramics
blue-and-white, 140
pottery fragments, 140
Prague, 92
Prince Ahmed Mausoleum, 170, 171, 172
Prince Mahmud Mausoleum, 163, 164, 171
Prince Mustafa Mausoleum, 164, 172
Prince Mustafa-yi ʿAtik Mausoleum, 169

Qadi Ahmad b. al-Saffah, 210
Qadi Burhaneddin Ahmad. *See* Burhaneddin Ahmad
qalamsiyāhī technique, 180
Qaraqoyunlu, 16, 57, 111, 140
Qaraqoyunlu dynasty, 91, 92, 97
Qaraqoyunlu style, 52
Qavam al-Din Shirazi, 105
Qaytbay, 179
Qilij Arslan, 20
kiosk of, 23
Qutluq Aqa, 90

Rabbat, Nasser, 105
Raby, Julian, 9, 19, 181, 185, 186
Ramazanoğlu, 56, 207, 210
patronage of, 179
Ramazanoğlu Mosque and Mausoleum, 141
Redford, Scott, 2, 123
reflecting pools, 22, 35
Renaissance
and the Ottoman Empire, 9–10
Renaissance architecture, 39
Renaissance Italy, 1, 19, 51, 107, *199*
Roxburgh, David, 184
Ruggles, D. Fairchild, 21, 166
Ruhi, 5
Rūm, 2, 3, 4, 55
Saljuq rulers of, 66
Rum Mehmed Pasha, 20, 41
Rum Mehmed Pasha Mosque, 35
rūmī motifs, 128, 17, 35, 38, 80, 88, 114, 116, 117, 126, 137, 164, 177, 180, *186, 191, 195, 196, 197*, 209, 214
Rūmī-ness, 2, 7, 121, 177
Rüstem Pasha, 1

Saba, Matthew, 29
sacred landscapes, 145
Safavids, 11, 12, 215
as threat, 206
conquest of Herat by, 179
defeat by Selim I, 18
in Anatolia, 207
in Iran, 219
influence of, 16, 20
Shiʿi, 178
Safaviyya Sufi order, 205
Şah Melek Pasha Mosque, 76, 141

INDEX 281

Sahib Ata Complex, 61
Sahib ʿAta Fakhr al-Din ʿAli, 162
  cenotaph of, 155
Sahn-Madrasas, 60
Saladin, 96
Salah al-Din Ayyub, 96
Salgırlı, Saygın, 60
Saljuq architecture, 13, 16, 23, 35, 52, 55, 79, *82*, 90, 144, 214
  connections with Ottoman architecture, 123
  in Amasya, 98
  influence of, 94, 126
Saljuq style
  in tiles, 68
Saljuqs, 4, 13
  caravanserais, 10
  in Amasya, 98
  in Anatolia, 2, 17, 32, 51, 52, 54, 55, 67, 90, 93, 94
  patronage of, 206
  relationship with Ayyubids, 123
  royal patronage of, 7
Samarqand
  Timurid courts in, 17
  Timurid style in, 92
Samkoff, Aneta, 141
Sayyid ʿAli (kadi), *79*, 107
Sayyida Nafisa
  mosque of, 140
saz-leaf decoration, 18
saz-style, *187*, 209
Şehinşah (son of Bayezid II), 171
Şehzadeler Mausoleum, *187*
Selçuk. *See* Ayasuluk
Selçuk Hatun, 70
Selçuk Sultan, *194*
Selim I, 168
  conquest of Cairo by, 96
  construction of mausoleum by, 170
  court of, 181, 183
  family of, 171, 172
  patronage of, 206
  reign of, 16, 17, 56, 178, 215
  relatives of, 147
Selim I mausoleum, *187*
Selim II
  architecture during the reign of, 177
  construction of mausoleum for his brother, 169
  family of, 173
Selim II mausoleum
  garden around, 170
Selim II mosque complex, 147
Selimiye Mosque, *201*
semahane, 206
Şemseddin Muhammad b. Hamza al-Fenari al-Rumi, 7
sericulture, *193*
Serres
  monuments in, *194*, *199*
Şeyh Bedreddin, 7, 8, 65
Şeyh Hamdullah, *188*
Seyyid Battal Gazi Shrine, 206
Seyyid Loqman, 22
Seyyitgazi, 206
shād, 105
Shad-e Mulk Aqa, 90
Shah Ismaʿil, 178
Shah Rukh, 92, 105

Shah-i Zinda shrine complex, *77*, 90, 91
Shahinshah (Prince), 207
Shams al-Din Muhammad ibn al-Jazari, 119
Sharaf al-Din ʿAli Yazdi, 7, 119
Shaw, Wendy M. K., 118
Shaybanid Uzbeks, 12
Shaykh Abu al-Khayr, 119, 120
Shaykh Lotfollah Mosque, 29
Shirin Bika Aqa, 90
shrines
  in Muslim cities, 98
  Sufi, 179
Şifaiye Madrasa, 32
Şikari, 22
silk trade, *192*
silver inlay, *82*
Sinan, 1, 177, 184, 203, 204, 219
Sinan al-Din Ahmad b. Abi Bakr al-Mushaymish, 97
Singer, Amy, 147
Sırçalı Madrasa, 30, 32, 33, 69
Şirin Hatun Mausoleum, 172
Sitti Hatun, 70
  cenotaph of, 30
Sitti Shah Sultan, 20
Sivas
  construction projects in, 117
Skopje, 15
  hammams in, *195*
  monuments in, *194*, *195*, *199*
skylights, 13
Sofular Mosque, *190*, *192*
spolia, 24, 88, 125, 154
squinches, 188, 203
stencils, 19, 139, 143
stone carvers, 35, 47, 50, 52, 77, *79*, 142, 175, 216
  transmittal of forms by, 123
stone carving, 13, 41, 52, 75, 79, *79*, *80*, 80, 82, 94, 108, 111, 117, 123,
    126, *126*, 134, *194*, 197, *202*, 203. *See also* stonework
  decorative styles, 17
  designs in, 218
  inscriptions, 102, 103
  of the Yörgüç Pasha mosque, 119
  railings, 85
  strapwork, 48, 52
  templates for, 143
stonemasons, 3, 77, 109, 126, 205
stonework, 32, 97, 99, 106, 107, 109, 117, 119, 121, 126, 132, 217. *See*
    also stone carving
  ablaq, 134
  Ayyubid, 123
  calligraphy in, 134
  commissioned by Bayezid I, 129
  designs in, *196*
  in Mamluk monuments, 52
  in the Üç Şerefeli Mosque, 134
  influences on, 132
  Mamluk, 123
  on the Üç Şerefeli Mosque, 132
  Syrian-style, 121
  virtuoso, 179
strapwork, 44, 48, 52, 148
stucco, 23, 75, 117
stucco decorations, *79*, *195*, *196*
Sufi communities, 214
Sufi sheikhs, 154

282   INDEX

Sufi shrines
  in Anatolia, 179
Sufism, 64, 178
Sulayman b. Dulkadir, 20
Süleyman the Magnificent, 1, 12, 56, 169, 187, 206, 207, 215
  architecture during the reign of, 177
    burial of, 147, 158
    family of, 172
Süleymaniye Mosque, 177, *202*, *204*
Sultan Han, 48
Sultan Hasan Madrasa, 123
sultan's lodge, 71, 74, 106
Sultaniye Madrasa, 64
Sulu Han, 49
Sunni Revival, 47
al-Suyuti, 161
Syria, 94. *See also* Greater Syria
  Ottoman conquest of, 178
  tiles attributed to, 139
  Timur's campaigns in, 77

Tabriz, *79*
  as cultural center, 92, 94
  ceramic production in, 144
  craftsmen from, 92, 94
  origin storied based on, 77
  tile production in, *77*, 91
  tiles imported from, *185*
  trade with, 10
  workshops in, 92, 179
Tacizāde Cafer Çelebi, 5, 17, 38
Taeschner, Franz, 58, *77*
Taj al-Din Ibrahim, 20, 22
Taj Mahal, 167
Takht-i Sulayman, 47
Tankiz al-Nasiri, 95
Taşköprüzāde, Ahmed b. Mustafa, 5
Taşluk Camii, 39
templates, 181. *See also* paper templates
  calligraphic, 175
  pricked-paper, 180
terracotta relief, 70
textiles, 39, 52, 117
  attribution of, *199*
  designs on, *187*, *196*
  motifs in, *80*
  ornamentation on, 179
  Ottoman production of, 177
  trade in, 10, 215
  used to cover cenotaphs, 153, 154, *197*
  workshops for, 219
Tezcan, Baki, 4, 67
Thessaloniki, 6, 20, 65, 98, 205, 214
tile decoration, 52
  and Ottoman visual culture, 54
  at the Muradiye, 150
  in Anatolia, 69
  in Bursa and Edirne, 6
  in Istanbul, 20
  in Mehmed I's mosque-*zāviye*, 94
  in Mehmed I's complex, 68
  in Mehmed I's mosque-*zāviye*, 13
  on Alaca Türbe, 48–51
  on Mahmud Pasha mosque, 44
  on Mahmud Pasha's mausoleum, 41

  on Mehmed I's funerary complex, 55
  on Mehmed I's mosque-*zāviye*, 76
  on Sulu Han, 50
  on the Çinili Köşk, 30–35, 47
tile makers, 3, 18, 33, 35, 47, 218
  and Timurid style, 17
tile mosaics, 12, 48, 91, 140. *See also* tile decorations
  advantages of, 30
  at Çinili Köşk, 24, 26, 30, 35, 51
  decorative styles, 17
  in Cairo, 120
  in Central Asia, 69
  in Iran, 69
  in Konya, 32
  in Mehmed I's mausoleum, 70, 140
  in Mehmed's madrasa, 68
  in Ottoman architecture, 32
  in the Karatay Madrasa, 89
  in the Muradiye mihrab, 150
  inscriptions in, 30
  paper models for, 30
  templates for, 143
  Timurid style, 35
tile work
  in Mehmed I's mosque complex, 68
  Karamanid, 32
  templates for, 47
  Timurid, 30
tile workers, 50, 121, 142
tile cutters
  from Iran, 12
  from Khurasan, 35, 51
tiles, 217. *See also* lunettes
  and the Masters of Tabriz, 76–79
  bannā'ī, 91
  black-line, 18, 32, 68, 70, 75, *76*, 77, 90, 135, 137, 140, 141, 142, 149, 150, 164, *185*, 187
  blue, 139, 150, 164
  blue and turquoise, 47, 49, 70
  blue-and-white, 13, 30, 92, 98, 134, 135–40, 143, 164, *185*, 217
  border, *85*
  by the Masters of Tabriz, 140–42
  calligraphy in, 134
  carved terracotta, 75, 140
  combined techniques, 91, 140
  cuerda seca, 70
  cut terracotta, 90
  dark blue, 71
  designs on, *187*, *196*
  exterior, 132
  fritware, 47, 52, *184*, *185*
  from Iznik, 143, *185*
  gilded, 71, 140
  glazed terra-cotta, 69
  gold overlay, 75
  green, 150
  hexagonal, 164, 209
  imported, *185*
  in Anatolia, 8
  in Mehmed I's mosque-*zāviye*, 75, 89, 90
  in museum collections, 137, 139, 141
  in relief, 90
  in the Karatay Madrasa, 89
  in the Muradiye Mosque, *184*
  in the sultan's lodge, 71

Iznik-style, 141, 166, 209, 214
luster, 92, 141
minā'ī, 23
misfired, 30
monochrome, 30, 32, 70, 75, 89, 150, *185*
Ottoman, 8
Persianate, 129
places of production for, 137
production of, 140
purple, 76, *185*
red clay, 47
reuse of, 141
saz style, *187*
set in carved stone, 44, 47, 52, 75
sharing designs among workshops, 183
shipping of, *76*, 209, 217
transportation of, 141, 143
triangular, 137
turquoise, 29, 30, 68, 70, 76, 89, 90, 126, 135, 148, 150, 164, *185*
underglaze, 70
underglaze-painted, 13, 52, 92, 98, 135, 137, 140, 164, *185*, 217
with gold leaf, 90
with gold overlay, 31, 164
workshops for, 219
Timur, 65
  craftsmen captured by, 77
  defeat of Bayezid I by, 4, 22, 53, 67
  invasion by, 55
  invasion of Anatolia, 20
  lands restored by, 13, 90, 123, 129
  Ottomans' defeat by, 7
  reign of, 17
  victory over Bayezid I, 97
Timurid architecture, 16, 22, 48, 144
Timurid art, 30, 54, 98
Timurid culture, 6, 17, 18, 57
Timurid style, 18, 32, 34, 39, 52, 54, 55, 75, *79*, 90
  exhibitions on, 11
  geometric patterns, 44
  in Ottoman architecture, 94
  in the Üç Şerefeli Mosque, 134
  in tile mosaics, 30, 35
  in tiles, 68
  international, 6, 11, 12, 20, 22, 90–93, 109, 144, 163, 164
Timurid–Turkmen style
  international, 180
Timurid visual culture, 47, 90
Timurids, 57
  cosmology of rulership, 11
  influence of, 20
  waning of influence, 16
Timurtaş *zāviye*, *80*
Toghan b. ʿAbdallah, *79*, 104, 106, 107
Tokat, 33, 48, 69, 79, 99, 113, 193, 199, 207
tomb of the Prophet Muhammad, 153, 178
tombs. *See also* mausolea
  as memento mori, 145
  elevated placement of, 119
  in China, 162
  lighting candles at, 174
  open, 154
  Ottoman, 13
  visiting of, 157, 160
tombstones, 111, 114, 148, 153, 162, 168
Topkapı Palace, 12, 17, 21, 22, 35, 39, 143, 179

gardens of, 167
Topkapı Palace Archive, 107
Topkapı Palace Library, 181
Topkapı Scroll, 47, 50, 95
Torumtay Madrasa, 113
Torumtay Mausoleum, 113, 116, 117
Trabzon. *See* Trebizond
trade networks, 10
Trebizond, 7, 16, 67, 178, 205
tuğrakeş style, *187*
Turan, Osman, 2
Turkey
  tile production in, *185*
  Turkish identity in, 2
Turkic languages, 120, 126
Turkmen tribes, 97, 111, 144
  Kızılbaş, 178
  patronage of, 91
Turner, Edith, 160
Turner, Victor, 160
Tursun Beğ, 21, 29

Üç Şerefeli Mosque, 13, 36, 129, 130, 135, 175, 177, *201, 202*, 217
  collaboration in, 142
  inscriptions, 132
  model for, 129
  overlapping styles in, 134
  stonework, 132
  tiles on, *187*
  wall paintings, 163
ulema, 64, 154, 174
Ulu Cami, 132
Uluçay, Çağatay, 169
Ulugh Beğ, 11, *77*
ʿUmar b. Ibrahim, 105
Umur Beğ b. Timurtaş, 111
underglaze, 18, 30, 52, 70, 92, 98, 134, 135, 137, 140, 164, 184, *185*, 217
Ünver, A. Süheyl, 175
Uyghur script, 180
Uzbek Empire, 215
Uzun Hasan, 7, 32
Uzun Hasan Mosque, 140
Uzunçarşılı, 178

Vambery, Armin, 158
vasiyetnāme of Murad II, 157, 158, 159, 160, 161, 172
velvet
  Ottoman, *80*
Venice, 9
  trade with, 19
Victoria and Albert Museum, 140, *197*

wall decoration, 117
wall paintings, 6, 13, 137, 143, 217
  garden motifs in, 163
  garden motifs, 163
  in the Muradiye complex, 145
  in the Muradiye mausolea, 164
  templates for, 143
waqfīya, 5, 6, 57, 58, 59, 102, 103, 106, 113, 120, 146, 162, 167, 175
  Ottoman, 5
waqfs, 60
water, 21, 41, 59, 117, 155, 223, 237, 238
  connection of marble with, 13, 22, 160, 162

284 INDEX

water (cont.)
  damage from, 69
  evocation of, 160
  in gardens, 167
  in paradise, 161
  rainwater, 13, 153, 157, 159, 160, 161
  reflections in, 22
  sounds of, 11, 21, 41, 74
water elements, 6, 164
  and the spring of paradise, 39, 160
  flowing water, 41
  fountains, 40, 74, 106, 148, 162, 167
  in Bursa, 148
  in the Muradiye complex, 162
  in Topkapı Palace, 21
  maintenance of, 167
  pools, 39, 167
  real and symbolic, 145
  reflecting pools, 22, 35
  thermal springs, 148
  water basin, 162
Wilber, Donald, 92, 105
wood carvers, 77, 79, 106
wood carvings, 71, 75, 117, 218
  designs on, 187
woodwork, 11, 39, 117, 216
  templates for, 143
workshops, 9, 150
  at Sultan Hasan Madrasa, 123
  book, 143
  building sites as, 143
  centralized, 4, 13, 52
  ceramic, 8
  changes within, 51
  claims of origin, 13
  collaborative, 179
  court, 12
  imperial, 219
  in Bursa, 142
  in Herat, 179
  in Istanbul, 214
  in Tabriz, 76, 92
  in the court of Mehmed II, 180
  in the Timurid court, 17
  locations of, 219
  Mamluk, 144
  mobile, 95, 144
  movement of, 57
  moving, 137
  producing books, 9
  role of, 3

  sharing of designs among, 183
  shifts in practices of, 16
  tile production at, 139, 143
  traveling, 8, 76, 141, 142, 150
  unified, 13, 129, 185

Yahşi Beğ, 60
Yahşi Beğ Mosque, 163
Yakub II, 66, 76
Yakub II mausoleum, 76
Yakutiye Madrasa, 102
Yalbugha al-Nasiri
  hammam of, 210
Yalbugha al-Yahyawi
  mosque of, 130
Yalman, Suzan, 123
Yaʿqub b. ʿAbdallah, 104, 105, 106
Yaʿqub Shah, 204
Yaʿqub Shah b. Sultan Shah, 204
Yardım, Ali, 99, 102, 104, 106
Yazd, 92
Yeşil Cami (in Iznik), 41, 123, 129
Yeşil İmaret, 53. *See also* Mehmed I mosque-*zāviye*
Yıldız Palace library, 184
Yıldız, Sara Nur, 22, 124
Yörgüç Pasha, 7, 13, 60, 111, 114
  patronage of, 111, 113
  tombstone inscription, 111
Yörgüç Pasha mosque
  architects of, 119
Yörgüç Pasha mosque-*zāviye*, 109–14, 162,
    189
  carvings, 117
  funerary section, 114
  geometric decorations, 118
  inscriptions, 111, 112
  rūmī motifs, 116, 117
  tile work on, 111
  unusual features, 113
Yüksel, Çağla Caner, 125
Yunus Beğ, 114
Yürekli, Zeynep, 107, 206
Yusuf (son of Mehmed I), 70

Zaganos Pasha, 39
al-Zahir Chaqmaq, 207
zāviye, 226, 229, 232, 233, 235
Zayn al-Din b. Zakariya, 104, 105
Zeynel Bey Türbe, 32
Zeyniyye Sufi order, 206
ziyārat, 157, 160